CRAFTING & IMPLEMENTING STRATEGY

TEXT AND READINGS

Sixth Edition

ARTHUR A. THOMPSON, JR.

&

A. J. STRICKLAND III

Both of The University of Alabama

IRWIN

Chicago • Bogotá • Boston • Buenos Aires • Caracas
London • Madrid • Mexico City • Sydney • Toronto

Cover: Bernard von Eichman
China Street Scene #2, 1923
Oil on cardboard
21 × 14 inches
Collection of the Oakland Museum, Gift of Louis Siegriest.

Senior sponsoring editor:	Kurt L. Strand
Senior developmental editor:	Libby Rubenstein
Senior marketing manager:	Kurt Messersmith
Project editor:	Mary Conzachi
Production manager:	Laurie Kersch
Designer:	Heidi J. Baughman
Interior Designer:	David Lansoon
Cover Designer:	Jeanne M. Rivera
Art coordinator:	Mark Malloy
Compositor:	The Clarinda Company
Typeface:	10.5/12 Times Roman
Printer:	Von Hoffman Press, Inc.

Library of Congress Cataloging-in-Publication Data

Thompson, Arthur A.
    Crafting and implementing strategy: text and readings / Arthur A.
Thompson, Jr. & A.J. Strickland III.— 6th ed.
        p. cm.
    Rev. ed. of: Strategy formulation and implementation. 5th ed.
c 1992.
    Includes index.
    ISBN 0-256-15027-3
    1. Strategic planning,   2. Corporate planning.   I. Strickland, A.
J. (Alonzo J.)   II. Thompson, Arthur A., Strategy
formulation and implementation.   III. Title.
HD30.28.T525   1995
658.4'012—dc20   94–31938

Printed in the United States of America
1 2 3 4 5 6 7 8 9 0 VH 1 0 9 8 7 6 5 4

Our intent in preparing this sixth edition has been to effectively and interestingly cover what every senior-level or MBA student needs to know about crafting, implementing, and executing business strategies—an objective reflected in the new title. The revisions and enhancements extend from cover to cover. You'll find a fresh and greatly expanded treatment of strategy implementation grounded in contemporary academic research and practitioner experience, new sections covering the latest advances in strategic analysis and strategy formation, and a readings collection that has been expanded from 9 to 15 articles, 14 of which are new. Throughout, the presentation reflects a mainstream conceptual framework, a sharp focus on analytical techniques, and cutting-edge contributions to strategic thinking.

CONTENT FEATURES OF THE SIXTH EDITION

New concepts, analytical tools, and methods of managing continue to surface at rates that mandate important edition-to-edition changes in content. While the topical additions and new treatments in prior editions were chiefly in the chapters relating to strategic analysis and strategy formation (because advances in the discipline have for many years come faster in strategy formulation than in implementation), in this edition the changes are predominantly in the chapters pertaining to strategy implementation. Since the last revision, clear signs have emerged that some fundamental changes in the theory and practice of management are underway. Books, journals, and the business press are full of research studies and reports about how companies are using new tools and techniques to revamp how they do business, streamline operations, restore competitiveness, and reach new heights of performance. Across the world, companies are reorganizing their work effort around teams, totally reengineering core business processes, instituting total quality management programs, competing on organizational capabilities (as much as on differentiated product attributes), and installing leaner, flatter organization structures.

These new approaches to internal organization are more than just strategy-blind additions to the conventional wisdom about how to manage better. Each, in its own way, represents a valuable strategy-implementing tool—one whose power is magnified when seen and used as part of a larger effort to execute company strategies more competently. Incorporating these new strategy-implementing tools into the sixth edition has prompted a comprehensive overhaul of our coverage of strategy implementation and execution. We've expanded the presentation to three solid chapters, introduced a more compelling conceptual framework for thinking strategically about the tasks of implementation, and woven in new material on employee empowerment, team and process organization, delayering and flattening organizational structure, ways to build core competencies and hard-to-match organizational capabilities, reengineering, best practice programs, total quality management, and healthy versus unhealthy corporate cultures. The outcome is a common-sense approach to implementing and executing strategy that is in sync with both recent contributions to the literature and contemporary management practice.

In the other text chapters, you'll find new sections dealing with benchmarking techniques, value-chain analysis, competence-based competitive advantage, activity-based costing (which dovetails perfectly with value-chain concepts and strategic cost analysis), outsourcing of noncritical activities, vertical integration, and why strategy is partly planned and partly reactive. Once again, there's front-to-back coverage of global issues in strategic management, prominent treatment of ethical and social responsibility issues, and margin notes in every chapter that highlight basic concepts, strategic management principles, and kernels of wisdom. Extensive rewriting to sharpen the presentations in every chapter has allowed us to include the new material and still cover everything in less than 320 pages—something that readers and adopters ought to welcome, given the jam-packed content of the course.

SPECIFIC CONTENT CHANGES

The overall organizational arrangement of chapters and topical sequences in this edition parallels the sequencing in the last three editions, but you'll find several noteworthy refinements in content and emphasis:

- Chapters 1 and 2 contain better explanations of how and why a company's strategy emerges from (a) the deliberate and purposeful actions of management and (b) as-needed reactions to unanticipated developments and fresh competitive pressures. We've also introduced the concept of a strategy-making pyramid to underscore that a company's strategic plan is a collection of strategies devised by different managers at different levels in the organizational hierarchy; the effect is to build a stronger case for why all managers are on a company's strategy-making, strategy-implementing team and thus need to know about and be skilled in using the concepts and tools of strategic management.

- The roles of *core competencies* and organizational capabilities in creating customer value and building competitive advantage have been given added prominence in the discussions of company strengths, crafting strategy around what a company does best, and building a capable organization (Chapters 2, 4, and 9).

- The treatment of value-chain analysis has been recast and expanded, new graphics added, and emphasis placed on benchmarking costs and the performance of key value-chain activities to help determine a company's cost competitiveness and overall competitive strength (Chapter 4). There are new sections describing benchmarking techniques and activity-based costing that take value-chain analysis to a new plateau of understanding and application.

- We've built the discussion of competitive strategy around five generic approaches rather than three—overall low-cost leadership, focused low-cost, broad differentiation, focused differentiation, and being the best-cost producer—see Figure 5–1 on page 517.

- We continue to believe that global competition and global strategy issues are best dealt with by integrating the relevant discussions into each chapter rather than partitioning the treatment into a separate chapter. The globalization of each chapter, a prominent feature of the previous edition, is carried over and strengthened in this edition, and we've added more illustration capsules to highlight the strategies of non-U.S. companies.

- The new three-chapter module (Chapters 9–11) on strategy implementation is structured around eight tasks: (1) building an organization capable of carrying out the strategy successfully; (2) developing budgets to steer ample resources into those value-chain activities critical to strategic success; (3) establishing strategically appropriate policies and procedures; (4) instituting best practices and mechanisms for continuous improvement; (5) installing support systems that enable company personnel to carry out their strategic roles successfully day in and day out; (6) tying rewards and incentives tightly to the achievement of performance objectives and good strategy execution; (7) creating a strategy-supportive work environment and corporate culture; and (8) exerting the internal leadership needed to drive implementation forward and to keep improving strategy execution.

- The eight-task framework for understanding the managerial components of strategy implementation and execution is explained in the first section of Chapter 9. The remainder of Chapter 9 is devoted exclusively to the management tasks of building a capable organization and features new coverage of building core competencies and unique organizational capabilities, developing the dominating depth in competence-related activities needed for competitive advantage, making strategy-critical value-chain activities the main building blocks in the organization structure, the pros and cons of outsourcing noncritical activities, downsizing and delayering hierarchical structures, employee empowerment, reengineering of core business processes, and the use of cross-functional and self-contained work teams. The result is a much revised treatment of organization building that ties together and makes strategic sense out of all the revolutionary organizational changes sweeping through today's corporations.

- Chapter 10 surveys the role of strategy-supportive budgets, policies, reward structures, and internal support systems. We explain why the benchmarking of best practices, total quality management, reengineering, and continuous improvement programs are important managerial tools for enhancing strategy execution.

- Chapter 11 deals with creating a strategy-supportive corporate culture and exercising the internal leadership needed to drive implementation forward. There's new coverage of strong versus weak cultures, low-performance and unhealthy cultures, adaptive cultures, and the sustained leadership commitment it takes to change a company with a problem culture, plus sections on ethics management and what managers can do to improve the caliber of strategy execution.

As in prior editions, we've kept the spotlight trained squarely on the strategy-related tasks of managers, the methods of strategic analysis, and sound strategic decision-making. Managers at all levels are viewed as being on a company's strategy-making, strategy-implementing team, responsible for thinking strategically, conducting strategic analysis as needed, crafting strategy, and leading the process of strategy implementation and execution in their areas of authority. Every key aspect of strategic management is examined—defining the business and developing a strategic vision, setting strategic and financial objectives, conducting industry and competitive analysis, doing company situation analysis, evaluating a diversified company's strategy and business portfolio, deciding which strategic options make the most sense, probing for sustainable competitive advantage, building a capable organization, fitting how the organization performs its work to the requirements for successful strategy execution, shaping the corporate culture, and exerting strategic leadership.

Diligent attention has been paid to improving content, clarity, and writing style. We've tried to take dead aim on creating a text presentation that is crisply written, clear and convincing, interesting to read, and comfortably mainstream, and as close to the frontiers of theory and practice as a basic textbook should be.

THE READINGS SELECTIONS

As in the two prior editions, we have included a collection of readings to complement the chapter discussions. The readings serve three purposes: to add detailed coverage of important, newly published topics; to provide readers with modest exposure to the strategic management literature; and to respond to the requests of users who, as a regular practice, include articles from current journals in their course syllabus. We have chosen 15 readings for this edition, only one of which is a carryover from the last edition.

The first reading, by C. K. Prahalad and Gary Hamel on "Strategic Intent," won a best article award in the *Harvard Business Review* for its innovative discussion of how global competitors approach strategic thinking, strategic objectives, and crafting long-range strategies; it's one of those landmark articles that every student of strategic management needs to read. The second article is by Ken Peattie of the Cardiff Business School on "Strategic Planning: Its Role in Organizational Politics;" the article examines the assumptions about why companies engage in strategic planning, the gaps between the rhetoric and the reality of strategic plans, the emergence of "invisible plans," and why managers sometimes approach the planning process with a hidden agenda. We suggest assigning these first two readings following coverage of Chapters 1 and 2.

We've selected five readings to accompany our four-chapter coverage of strategic analysis in single-business enterprises. The article by Shaker Zahra and Sherry Chaples on "Blind Spots in Competitive Analysis" describes the importance of gathering competitive intelligence, identifies the nature and causes of faulty competitive analysis, and offers recommendations to avoid them. The next article by Stalk, Evans, and Shulman on "Competing on Capabilities: The New Rules of Corporate Strategy" is another one of the landmark articles that illuminates key pieces of the nature and logic of competition; capabilities-based competition is one of the new paradigms of competing in the 1990s. The article describes how and why competition in many industries has become a "war of movement" in which success depends on quick response to market change and developing hard-to-imitate organizational capabilities that distinguish a company from its competitors in the eyes of customers. Chris Benjamin's article on "Honda and the Art of Competitive Maneuver" provides a rare insight into Honda's special competitive style and strategy-making, strategy-implementing skills—its technological creativity and verve, production and marketing disciplines, judgment of opportunities, courage to act, and suppleness in doing so. The Lorange and Roos article on "Why Some Strategic Alliances Succeed and Others Fail" is valuable because alliances have become important tools for increasing a company's speed and flexibility in carrying out multinational strategies and coping with globally competitive pressures. The last article in the business strategy grouping by John Stuckey and David White presents an analytical framework for deciding when and when not to vertically integrate; they also consider when to use quasi-integration strategies. You'll find that all five of these readings tie in nicely to the topics covered in Chapters 3, 4, 5, and 6.

We've included two articles to complement our discussion of strategic analysis of diversified companies in Chapters 7 and 8. The first article by Michael Goold and Kathleen Luchs, titled "Why Diversify? Four Decades of Management Thinking," explores all the rationales for diversifying, the causes of diversification success and failure, and the management challenges that diversification poses. It's the finest article we've seen for gaining a good perspective on what sort of diversification strategies make the most business sense. The second article, "Success in Diversification: Building on Core Competencies" by Phillippe Very, describes a study of companies pursuing diversification to test whether creating value through diversification is more dependent on strategic fit relationships between the value chains of different business units or on a common "dominant logic of general management" (defined as the way in which managers conceptualize the business and make critical resource allocation decisions).

We chose six readings to complement our much-revised approach to strategy implementation. All concern high profile topics that are receiving much attention among both researchers and practitioners. The first article on "The Horizontal Corporation" is the cover story from a recent issue of *Business Week*. It provides an excellent overview of the trend toward flatter organizations, cross-functional and process organization, self-managing teams, and the trend to drive unnecessary work out of the business; the article captures the revolutionary changes in work design and internal organization sweeping through companies and provides a wealth of company examples and experiences. The second article, taken from *Fortune,* describes business process reengineering, explains why it is the hottest trend in management, and gives numerous examples of dramatic benefits it can produce. The third article, by Judy Olion and Sara Rynes on "Making Total Quality Work: Aligning Organizational Processes, Performance Measures, and Stakeholders," provides an academic perspective on why total quality improvement programs are becoming part of the fabric of modern enterprises, the impact they have on corporate culture and organizational processes, and how total quality management (TQM) efforts contribute to effective strategy implementation and execution; it's a fine piece of field research and is filled with powerful evidence from actual company experiences. These three articles drive home the importance and relevance of the new material we've included in Chapters 9 and 10. A well-designed incentive compensation system nearly always plays a major role in effective strategy implementation; the fourth article in the strategy implementation grouping provides an excellent description of Lincoln Electric's much-heralded incentive plan. The article allows readers to see how a company can tightly link the design of its compensation system to the requirements for successful strategy execution. The fifth reading concerns how to transplant corporate cultures from one setting to another when the company operates in many different countries; we suggest assigning this reading in conjunction with your coverage of Chapter 11. The last reading concerns the ethical aspects of managing and, in particular, looks at the issue of whether ethical standards are lower in many foreign countries than in the United States; this article should prove to be a worthwhile addition to your course module on ethics and can be assigned anytime during the course.

All 15 selections are well-written and quite readable. We believe you'll find them well worth covering and that they put readers at the cutting-edge of strategic thinking—10 of the readings appeared in 1993, and only one, the classic on "Strategic Intent," was published prior to 1991.

ADDITIONAL PEDAGOGICAL FEATURES

As in previous editions, all the chapters incorporate the liberal use of examples and references to the strategic successes and failures of companies—what has worked, what hasn't, and why. The use of boxed Illustration Capsules to future highlight "strategy in action" was well received in earlier editions and has been continued. Eighteen of the 34 capsules are new to this edition. Together, the examples and the capsules keep the bridge between concept and actual practice always open, giving the reader a stronger feel for how strategic analysis concepts and techniques are utilized in real-world management circumstances.

We've also included an appendix giving students positive direction in case methods pedagogy and offering suggestions for approaching case analysis. In our experience, many students are unsure about what they are to do in preparing a case, and they are certainly inexperienced in analyzing a company from a "big picture" or strategic point of view. The appendix discussion is intended to provide explicit guidance and to focus student attention on the traditional analytical sequence of (1) identify, (2) evaluate, and (3) recommend. There is also a table on how to calculate and interpret key financial ratios, a discussion of how to prepare a case for oral class discussion, and guidelines for doing a written case analysis.

THE BUSINESS STRATEGY GAME OPTION

Version three of *The Business Strategy Game,* created as an optional accompaniment to this sixth edition, represents a major step-up in capability and performance over versions one and two. It incorporates an array of new and better features, cuts instructor processing times, and greatly reduces the potential for operator error. Our objective in preparing the new version was to make the use of a simulation as attractive and as convenient as possible. Instructor gear-up time is minimal, processing of decisions is straightforward, and the administrative requirements are modest. Version three is definitely more streamlined and user-friendly than versions one and two—thanks to some excellent feedback and suggestions from users, faster and more versatile computers, and expedited programming on our end.

The Business Strategy Game has five features that make it an uncommonly effective teaching/learning aid for strategic management courses: (1) *the product and the industry*—producing and marketing athletic footwear is a business that students can readily identify with and understand; (2) *the global industry environment*—students are provided with up-close exposure to what global competition is like and the kinds of strategic issues that managers in global industries have to address; (3) *the realistic quality of the simulation exercise*—we've designed the simulation to be as faithful as possible to real world markets, competitive conditions, and revenue-cost-profit relationships; (4) *the wide degree of strategic freedom students have in managing their companies*—we've gone to great lengths to make the game free of bias as concerns one strategy versus another; and (5) *the five-year planning and decision-making capability*—the game incorporates long-range thinking as an integral part of the exercise of running a company. These features, wrapped together as a package, provide an exciting and valuable bridge between concept and practice, the classroom and real-life management, and textbook wisdoms about how to manage and learning-by-doing.

THE VALUE A SIMULATION ADDS

Our own experiences with simulation games, along with hours of discussions with users, have convinced us that simulation games are the single best exercise available for helping students understand how the functional pieces of a business fit together and for giving students an integrated, capstone experience.

First and foremost, the exercise of running a simulated company over a number of decision periods helps develop students' business judgment. Simulation games provide a live case situation where events unfold and circumstances change as the game progresses. Their special hook is an ability to get students personally involved in the subject matter. *The Business Strategy Game* is very typical in this respect. In plotting their competitive strategies each decision period, students learn about risk-taking. They have to respond to changing market conditions, react to the competitors' moves and choose among alternative courses of action. They get valuable practice in reading the signs of industry change, spotting market opportunities, evaluating threats to their company's competitive position, weighing the trade-offs between profits now and profits later, and assessing the long-term consequences of short-term decisions. They chart a long-term direction, set strategic and financial objectives, and try out different strategies in pursuit of competitive advantage. They become active strategic thinkers, planners, analysts, and decision-makers. And by having to live with the decisions they make, they experience what it means to be accountable for decisions and responsible for achieving satisfactory results. All this serves to drill students in responsible decision-making and improve their business acumen and managerial judgment.

Second, students learn an enormous amount from working with the numbers, exploring options, and trying to unite production, marketing, finance, and human resource decisions into a coherent strategy. They begin to see ways to apply knowledge from prior courses and figure out what really makes a business tick. The effect is to help students integrate a lot of material, look at decisions from the standpoint of the company as a whole, and see the importance of thinking strategically about a company's competitive position and future prospects. Since a simulation game is by its very nature a hands-on exercise, the lessons learned are forcefully planted in students' minds—the impact may be far more lasting than what is remembered from lectures. Third, students' entrepreneurial instincts blossom as they get caught up in the competitive spirit of the game. The resulting entertainment value helps maintain an unusually high level of student motivation and emotional involvement in the course throughout the term.

ABOUT THE SIMULATION

We designed *The Business Strategy Game* around athletic footwear because it is a product students can understand and because the athletic footwear market displays the characteristics of globally competitive industries in the 1990s—fast growth, worldwide use of the product, competition among companies from several continents, production located in low-wage locations, and ample room for a variety of competitive approaches and business strategies. The simulation allows companies to manufacture and sell their brands in North America, Europe, and Asia, and there's the option to compete for supplying private-label sales to chain discounters. Competition is head-to-head. Each team of students must match its strategic wits against the other company teams. Companies can focus their branded marketing efforts on one geographic market or two or all three, or they can deemphasize branded sales and specialize in private-label production (an attractive strategy for low-cost producers). They can establish a one-country production base or they can manufacture in all three of the geographic markets. Low-cost leadership, differentiation strategies, best-cost producer strategies, and focus strategies are all viable competitive options. Companies can position their products in the low end of the market, the high end, or stick close to the middle on price, quality, and service; they can have a wide or narrow product line, small or big dealer networks, extensive or limited advertising. Company market shares are based on how each company's competitive effort stacks up against the efforts of rivals. Demand conditions, tariffs, and wage rates vary from geographic area to geographic area. Raw materials used in footwear production are purchased in a worldwide commodity market at prices that move up or down in response to supply-demand conditions.

The company that students manage has plants to operate, a workforce to compensate, distribution expenses and inventories to control, capital expenditure decisions to make, marketing and sales campaigns to wage, sales forecasts to consider, and ups and downs in exchange rates, interest rates, and the stock market to take into account. Students must weave functional decisions in production, distribution, marketing, finance, and human resources into a cohesive action plan. They have to react to changing market and competitive conditions, move to build competitive advantage, and defend against aggressive actions of competitors. And they must endeavor to maximize shareholder wealth via increased dividend payments and stock price appreciation. Each team of students is challenged to use their entrepreneurial and strategic skills to become the next Nike or Reebok and ride the wave of growth to the top of the worldwide athletic footwear industry. The exercise is as realistic and true to actual business practice in a real-world competitive market as we could make it.

There are built-in planning and analysis features that allow students to (1) craft a five-year strategic plan, (2) gauge the long-range financial impact of current decisions, (3) do the number-crunching to make informed short-run versus long-run trade-offs, (4) assess the revenue-cost-profit consequences of alternative strategic actions, and (5) build different strategy scenarios. Calculations at the bottom of each decision screen provide instantly updated projections of sales revenues, profits, return on equity, cash flow, and other key outcomes as each decision entry is made. The sensitivity of financial and operating outcomes to different decision entries is easily observed on the screen and on detailed printouts of projections. With the speed of today's personal computers, the relevant number-crunching is done in a split second. The game is designed to lead students to decisions based on "My analysis shows . . ." and away from the quicksand of seat-of-the-pants approaches based on "I think," "It sounds good," and "Maybe, it will work out."

The Business Strategy Game can be used with any IBM or compatible PC with 640K memory and it is suitable for both senior-level and MBA courses. The game is programmed to accommodate a wide variety of computer setups as concerns disk drives, monitors, and printers.

FEATURES OF THE THIRD EDITION

This much upgraded version of *The Business Strategy Game* makes things easier and better for both the players and the game administrator:

- **New Decision Variables.** Four new decision variables have been added to enhance the game's realism and provide greater strategic latitude. Each plant can now produce different quality shoes and different numbers of models, allowing both product quality and product line breadth to vary by market segment. Portions of plants can now be sold or closed. There are more options for revamping less efficient plants to make them more cost competitive. And we've changed some decision entries to give companies more flexibility in competing simultaneously in the private-label and branded segments.

- **Expanded Decision Support.**   We've greatly expanded the number of on-screen calculations at the bottom of each decision entry screen, achieving a quantum improvement in players' ability to do what-iffing and immediately see the sensitivity of key outcomes without having to move to a new file and consult the projected company reports.

- **The Competitor Analysis Report.**   A new set of Competitor Analysis Reports has been added that reorganizes the competitive effort information appearing in the Footwear Industry Reports into formats suitable for easy diagnosis of competitors' actions and strategies, market segment by market segment and year by year. Printouts for any year and any competitor of interest are easily obtained and easily used as a diagnostic tool.

- **Other Information Enhancements.**   In addition to the Competitor Analysis Reports, we've improved the information in the Footwear Industry Report by including a whole page of cross-company comparisons of income statement and balance sheet statistics, additional plant construction data, and more information on the private-label segment. Plus we've beefed up the Administrator's Report with more diagnostic information and cross-company comparisons.

- **A New Look.**   We've given the screens a new look. The redesigned decision entry and report screens are easier to read, simpler to use, and more pleasing to the eye. There's a new menu bar that speeds access to all decision screens. It is also quicker to move from file to file.

- **The Mouse.**   All programs and disks used by both players and the game administrator are now "mouse aware." The mouse may be used to make menu selections and to invoke the [Enter] and [Esc] keys when necessary.

- **Error Trapping and Entry Validation.**   There's expanded error trapping capability that rejects any decision entry that falls outside the valid range or that is the wrong type (a letter versus a number).

- **Programming Refinements.**   We've refined the interaction among some key variables, adjusted several algorithms, improved the methodology of calculating the strategy rating, eliminated the need for students to manually update announced changes in costs and rates (it's now done automatically on the company disk during processing), relocated the what-if entries to boxes just below the relevant decision entries, and reformatted the decision screens so that all current-year decisions can be made on 6 decision screens instead of 14. There's also a more sophisticated and user friendly printer setup program.

- **Streamlined Processing.**   Just as in the last version, we've implemented another round of streamlining in processing decisions. Instructors/game administrators have more processing flexibility and options.

- **Improved Manuals.**   The *Player's Manual* has been reworked to provide better explanations of cause-effect relationships and more information on the conditions surrounding decision entries. The *Instructor's Manual* has been expanded by 20 percent to provide more details on administering a successful simulation.

At the same time, though, we've kept intact the features that users told us made them enthusiastic about the last two versions:

- There's no paperwork associated with student decisions or with returning the results. Students turn in disks with their decisions already entered. When you process the results, everything the students need is automatically written onto their company disks, and they make their own printouts. It takes only a few minutes to collect the disks and return them. A printout of the industry scoreboard and a printout of the administrator's report are automatically generated during processing.
- Decisions can be processed in 40 minutes (less than 25 minutes on a fast PC); simple procedures allow most or all of the processing to be delegated to a student assistant.
- Students will find it convenient and uncomplicated to use the PC to play *The Business Strategy Game* even if they have had no prior exposure to PCs; *no programming of any kind is involved* and full instructions are presented in the *Player's Manual* and on the screens themselves.
- A scoreboard of company performance is automatically calculated each decision period. Instructors determine the weights to be given to each of six performance measures—revenues, after-tax profits, return on stockholders' investment, stock value, bond rating, and strategy rating. Students always know where their company stands and how well they are doing; the overall performance score can be used to grade team performance.
- An *Instructor's Manual* describes how to integrate the game into your course, provides pointers on how to administer the game, and contains step-by-step processing instructions.

THE INSTRUCTOR'S PACKAGE

A full complement of instructional aids is available to assist adopters in using the sixth edition successfully. The *Instructor's Manual* contains suggestions for using the text materials, various approaches to course design and course organization, a sample syllabus, alternative course outlines, a thoroughly revised and expanded set of 940 multiple-choice and essay questions. There is also a computerized test bank for generating examinations, a set of color transparencies depicting the figures and tables in the eleven text chapters, and a package of over 400 transparency masters that thoroughly cover the text presentation and can be used to support the instructor's classroom lectures.

ACKNOWLEDGMENTS

We have benefited from the help of many people during the evolution of this book. Students, adopters, and reviewers have generously supplied an untold number of insightful comments and helpful suggestions. Our intellectual debt to those academics, writers, and practicing managers who have blazed new trails in the strategy field will be obvious to any reader familiar with the literature of strategic management; we have endeavored to acknowledge their specific contributions in footnote references and in the list of suggested readings at the end of each chapter.

Naturally, as custom properly dictates, we are responsible for whatever errors of fact, deficiencies in coverage or in exposition, and oversights that remain. As always we value your recommendations and thoughts about the book. Your comments regarding coverage and contents will be most welcome, as will calling our attention to specific errors. Please fax us at (205) 348-6695 or write us at P.O. Box 870225, Department of Management and Marketing, The University of Alabama, Tuscaloosa, Alabama 35487-0225.

Arthur A. Thompson
A. J. Strickland

CONTENTS

xiv

PART ONE

THE CONCEPTS AND TECHNIQUES OF STRATEGIC MANAGEMENT

CHAPTER ONE

THE STRATEGIC MANAGEMENT PROCESS
AN OVERVIEW

"Cheshire Puss," she [Alice] began . . . "would you please tell me which way I ought to go from here?"
"That depends on where you want to get to," said the cat.

Lewis Carroll

My job is to make sure the company has a strategy and that everybody follows it.

Kenneth H. Olsen
Former CEO, Digital Equipment Corporation

A strategy is a commitment to undertake one set of actions rather than another.

Sharon M. Oster
Professor, Yale University

This book is about the managerial tasks of crafting, implementing, and executing company strategies. Strategy is grounded in the array of competitive moves and business approaches management depends on to produce successful performance. Strategy, in effect, is management's game plan for strengthening the organization's position, pleasing customers, and achieving performance targets. Managers devise strategies to guide *how* the company's business will be conducted and to help them make reasoned, cohesive choices among alternative courses of action. The strategy managers decide on indicates that "among all the paths and actions we could have chosen, we decided to follow this route and conduct our business in this manner." Without a strategy, a manager has no thought-out course to follow, no roadmap to manage by, no unified action program to produce the intended results.

Management's game plan involves every major function and department—purchasing, production, finance, marketing, human resources, R&D. Each has a role in the strategy. The strategy-making challenge is to mold business decisions and competitive actions taken across the company into a cohesive *pattern*. The prevailing pattern of moves and approaches indicates what the current strategy is; new moves and approaches under consideration signal how the current strategy may be embellished or recast.

Crafting and implementing strategy are core management functions. Among all the things managers do, few affect company performance more fundamentally than how well its management team charts the company's long-term direction, develops competitively effective strategic moves and business approaches, and executes the strategy in ways that produce the targeted results. Indeed, *good strategy and good strategy execution are the most trustworthy signs of good management.*

There's a strong case for linking "good management" to how well managers craft and execute strategy. Some managers design shrewd strategies but fail to carry them out well. Others design mediocre strategies but execute them competently. Both situations open the door to shortfalls in performance. Managers must combine good strategy-making with good strategy execution for company performance to approach maximum potential. The better conceived a company's strategy and the more proficient its execution, the greater the chance the company will be a solid performer. Powerful execution of a powerful strategy is not only a proven recipe for business success but also the best test of excellent management.

Granted, good strategy combined with good strategy execution doesn't *guarantee* that a company will avoid periods of weak or ho-hum performance. On occasion it takes time for management's efforts to show good results. And even well-managed organizations can face adverse and unforeseen conditions. But neither the "we need more time" reason nor the bad luck of adverse events excuses mediocre performance year after year. It is management's responsibility to adjust to unexpectedly tough conditions by undertaking strategic defenses and business approaches that can overcome adversity. Indeed, the essence of good strategy-making is to build a market position strong enough and an organization capable enough to produce successful performance despite unforeseeable events, potent competition, and internal problems.

> To qualify as excellently managed, an organization must exhibit excellent execution of an excellent strategy.

THE FIVE TASKS OF STRATEGIC MANAGEMENT

The strategy-making, strategy-implementing process consists of five interrelated managerial tasks:

1. Deciding what business the company will be in and forming a strategic vision of where the organization needs to be headed—in effect, infusing the organization with a sense of purpose, providing long-term direction, and establishing a clear mission to be accomplished.
2. Converting the strategic vision and mission into measurable objectives and performance targets.
3. Crafting a strategy to achieve the desired results.
4. Implementing and executing the chosen strategy efficiently and effectively.
5. Evaluating performance, reviewing new developments, and initiating corrective adjustments in long-term direction, objectives, strategy, or implementation in light of actual experience, changing conditions, new ideas, and new opportunities.

Figure 1–1 illustrates this process. Together, these five components define what we

F I G U R E 1-1 | **The Five Tasks of Strategic Management**

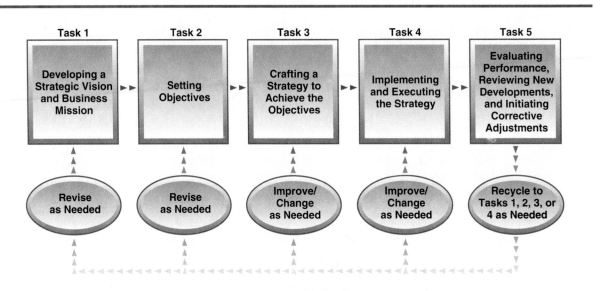

mean by the term strategic management. Let's explore this framework in more detail to set the stage for all that follows.

DEVELOPING A STRATEGIC VISION AND BUSINESS MISSION

The foremost direction-setting question senior managers need to ask is "What is our vision for the company—what are we trying to do and to become?" Developing a carefully reasoned answer to this question pushes managers to consider what the company's business character is and should be and to develop a clear picture of where the company needs to be headed over the next 5 to 10 years. Management's answer to "who we are, what we do, and where we're headed" charts a course for the organization to take and helps establish a strong organizational identity. What a company seeks to do and to become is commonly termed the company's mission. A mission statement defines a company's business and provides a clear view of what the company is trying to accomplish for its customers. But managers also have to think strategically about where they are trying to take the company. Management's concept of the business needs to be supplemented with a concept of the company's future business makeup and long-term direction. Management's view of the kind of company it is trying to create and its intent to stake out a particular business position represent a *strategic vision* for the company. By developing and communicating a business mission and strategic vision, management infuses the workforce with a sense of purpose and a persuasive rationale for the company's future direction. Some examples of company mission and vision statements are presented in Illustration Capsule 1.

A well-conceived strategic vision prepares a company for the future, establishes long-term direction, and indicates the company's intent to stake out a particular business position.

SETTING OBJECTIVES

The purpose of setting objectives is to convert managerial statements of business mission and company direction into specific performance targets, something the organization's progress can be measured by. Objective-setting implies challenge, establishing performance targets that require stretch and disciplined effort. The chal-

EXAMPLES OF COMPANY MISSION AND VISION STATEMENTS

Otis Elevator

Our mission is to provide any customer a means of moving people and things up, down, and sideways over short distances with higher reliability than any similar enterprise in the world.

Avis Rent-a-Car

Our business is renting cars. Our mission is total customer satisfaction.

McCormick & Company

The primary mission of McCormick & Company is to expand our worldwide leadership position in the spice, seasoning, and flavoring markets.

The Saturn Division of General Motors

To market vehicles developed and manufactured in the United States that are world leaders in quality, cost, and customer satisfaction through the integration of people, technology, and business systems and to transfer knowledge, technology, and experience throughout General Motors.

Public Service Company of New Mexico

Our mission is to work for the success of people we serve by providing our customers reliable electric service, energy information, and energy options that best satisfy their needs.

American Red Cross

The mission of the American Red Cross is to improve the quality of human life; to enhance self-reliance and concern for others; and to help people avoid, prepare for, and cope with emergencies.

Eastman Kodak

To be the world's best in chemical and electronic imaging.

McCaw Cellular Communications

Develop a reliable wireless network that empowers people with the freedom to travel anywhere—across the hall or across the continent—and communicate effortlessly.

Compaq Computer

To be the leading supplier of PCs and PC servers in all customer segments.

Long John Silver's

To be America's best quick service restaurant chain. We will provide each guest great tasting, healthful, reasonably priced fish, seafood, and chicken in a fast, friendly manner on every visit.

Source: Company annual reports.

lenge of trying to close the gap between actual and desired performance pushes an organization to be more inventive, to exhibit some urgency in improving both its financial performance and its business position, and to be more intentional and focused in its actions. Setting challenging but achievable objectives thus helps guard against complacency, drift, internal confusion over what to accomplish, and status quo organizational performance. As Mitchell Leibovitz, CEO of Pep Boys—Manny, Moe, and Jack, puts it, "If you want to have ho-hum results, have ho-hum objectives."

Objectives are yardsticks for tracking an organization's performance and progress.

The objectives managers establish should ideally include both short-range and long-range performance targets. Short-range objectives spell out the immediate improvements and outcomes management desires. Long-range objectives prompt managers to consider what to do *now* to position the company to perform well over the longer term. As a rule, when tradeoffs have to be made between achieving long-run objectives and achieving short-run objectives, long-run objectives should take precedence. Rarely does a company prosper from repeated management actions that sacrifice better long-run performance for better short-term performance.

Objective-setting is required of *all* managers. Every unit in a company needs concrete, measurable performance targets that contribute meaningfully toward achieving company objectives. When companywide objectives are broken down into specific targets for each organizational unit and lower-level managers are held accountable for achieving them, a results-oriented climate builds throughout the enterprise. The ideal situation is a team effort where each organizational unit is striving hard to produce results in its area of responsibility that will help the company reach its performance targets and achieve its strategic vision.

From a companywide perspective, two types of performance yardsticks are called for: financial objectives and strategic objectives. *Financial objectives* are important because without acceptable financial performance an organization risks being denied the resources it needs to grow and prosper. *Strategic objectives* are needed to prompt managerial efforts to strengthen a company's overall business and competitive position. Financial objectives typically relate to such measures as earnings growth, return on investment, borrowing power, cash flow, and shareholder returns. Strategic objectives, however, concern a company's competitiveness and long-term business position in its markets: growing faster than the industry average, overtaking key competitors on product quality or customer service or market share, achieving lower overall costs than rivals, boosting the company's reputation with customers, winning a stronger foothold in international markets, exercising technological leadership, gaining a sustainable competitive advantage, and capturing attractive growth opportunities. Strategic objectives serve notice that management not only intends to deliver good financial performance but also to improve the organization's competitive strength and long-range business prospects.

Examples of the kinds of strategic and financial objectives companies set are shown in Illustration Capsule 2.

CRAFTING A STRATEGY

Strategy-making brings into play the critical managerial issue of *how* to achieve the targeted results in light of the organization's situation and prospects. Objectives are the "ends," and strategy is the "means" of achieving them. In effect, strategy is the pattern of actions managers employ to achieve strategic and financial performance targets. The task of crafting a strategy starts with solid diagnosis of the company's internal and external situation. Only when armed with hard analysis of the big picture are managers prepared to devise a sound strategy to achieve targeted strategic and financial results. Why? Because misdiagnosis of the situation greatly raises the risk of pursuing ill-conceived strategic actions.

A company's strategy is typically a blend of (1) deliberate and purposeful actions and (2) as-needed reactions to unanticipated developments and fresh competitive pressures. As illustrated in Figure 1–2, strategy is more than what managers have carefully plotted out in advance and *intend* to do as part of some grand strategic plan. New circumstances always emerge, whether important technological developments, rivals' successful new product introductions, newly enacted government regulations and policies, widening consumer interest in different kinds of performance features, or whatever. There's always enough uncertainty about the future that managers cannot plan every strategic action in advance and pursue their *intended strategy* without alteration. Company strategies end up, therefore, being a composite of planned actions (intended strategy) and as-needed reactions to unforeseen conditions ("unplanned" strategy responses). Consequently, *strategy is best conceived as a combination of planned actions and on-the-spot adaptive reactions to fresh develop-*

Companies need both financial objectives and strategic objectives.

An organization's strategy consists of the actions and business approaches management employs to achieve the targeted organizational performance.

Strategy is both proactive (intended) and reactive (adaptive).

STRATEGIC AND FINANCIAL OBJECTIVES OF WELL-KNOWN CORPORATIONS

NationsBank

To build the premier financial services company in the U.S.

Ford Motor Company

To satisfy our customers by providing quality cars and trucks, developing new products, reducing the time it takes to bring new vehicles to market, improving the efficiency of all our plants and processes, and building on our teamwork with employees, unions, dealers, and suppliers.

Exxon

To provide shareholders a secure investment with a superior return.

Alcan Aluminum

To be the lowest-cost producer of aluminum and to out-perform the average return on equity of the Standard and Poor's industrial stock index.

General Electric

To become the most competitive enterprise in the world by being number one or number two in market share in every business the company is in.

Apple Computer

To offer the best possible personal computing technology, and to put that technology in the hands of as many people as possible.

Atlas Corporation

To become a low-cost, medium-size gold producer, producing in excess of 125,000 ounces of gold a year and building gold reserves of 1,500,000 ounces.

Quaker Oats Company

To achieve return on equity at 20% or above, "real" earnings growth averaging 5% or better over time; to be a leading marketer of strong consumer brands; and to improve the profitability of low-return businesses or divest them.

Source: Company annual reports.

---

ing industry and competitive events. The strategy-making task involves developing a game plan, or intended strategy, and then adapting it as events unfold. A company's actual strategy is something managers must craft as events transpire outside and inside the company.

Strategy and Entrepreneurship Crafting strategy is an exercise in entrepreneurship and outside-in strategic thinking. The challenge is for company managers to keep their strategies closely matched to such outside drivers as changing buyer preferences, the latest actions of rivals, market opportunities and threats, and newly appearing business conditions. Company strategies can't be responsive to changes in the business environment unless managers exhibit entrepreneurship in studying market trends, listening to customers, enhancing the company's competitiveness, and steering company activities in new directions in a timely manner. Good strategy-making is therefore inseparable from good business entrepreneurship. One cannot exist without the other.

A company encounters two dangers when its managers fail to exercise strategy-making entrepreneurship. One is a stale strategy. The faster a company's business environment is changing, the more critical it becomes for its managers to be good entrepreneurs in diagnosing shifting conditions and instituting strategic adjustments. Coasting along with a status quo strategy tends to be riskier than making modifications. Strategies that are increasingly out of touch with market realities make a company a good candidate for a performance crisis.

> Strategy-making is fundamentally a market-driven entrepreneurial activity—risk-taking, venturesomeness, business creativity, and an eye for spotting emerging market opportunities are all involved in crafting a strategic action plan.

F I G U R E 1–2 | **A Company's Actual Strategy Is Partly Planned and Partly Reactive to Changing Circumstances**

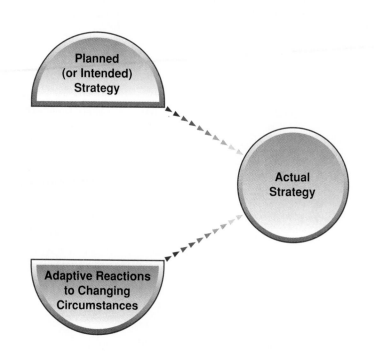

The second danger is inside-out strategic thinking. Managers with weak entrepreneurial skills are usually risk-averse and hesitant to embark on a new strategic course so long as the present strategy produces acceptable results. They pay only perfunctory attention to market trends and listen to customers infrequently. Often, they either dismiss new outside developments as unimportant ("we don't think it will really affect us") or else study them to death before taking actions. Being comfortable with the present strategy, they focus their energy and attention inward on internal problem-solving, organizational processes and procedures, reports and deadlines, company politics, and the administrative demands of their jobs. Consequently the strategic actions they initiate tend to be inside-out and governed by the company's traditional approaches, what is acceptable to various internal political coalitions, what is philosophically comfortable, and what is safe, both organizationally and careerwise. Inside-out strategies, while not disconnected from industry and competitive conditions, stop short of being market-driven and customer-driven. Rather, outside considerations end up being compromised to accommodate internal considerations. The weaker a manager's entrepreneurial instincts and capabilities, the greater a manager's propensity to engage in inside-out strategizing, an outcome that raises the potential for reduced competitiveness and weakened organizational commitment to total customer satisfaction.

How boldly managers embrace new strategic opportunities, how much they emphasize out-innovating the competition, and how often they lead actions to improve organizational performance are good barometers of their entrepreneurial spirit. Entrepreneurial strategy-makers are inclined to be first-movers, responding quickly and opportunistically to new developments. They are willing to take prudent risks and ini-

Good strategy-making is more outside-in than inside-out.

tiate trailblazing strategies. In contrast, reluctant entrepreneurs are risk-averse; they tend to be late-movers, hopeful about their chances of soon catching up and alert to how they can avoid whatever "mistakes" they believe first-movers have made. They prefer incremental strategic change over bold and sweeping strategic moves.

In strategy-making, all managers, not just senior executives, must take prudent risks and exercise entrepreneurship. Entrepreneurship is involved when a district customer service manager, as part of a company's commitment to better customer service, crafts a strategy to speed the response time on service calls by 25 percent and commits $15,000 to equip all service trucks with mobile telephones. Entrepreneurship is involved when a warehousing manager contributes to a company's strategic emphasis on total quality by figuring out how to reduce the error frequency on filling customer orders from one error every 100 orders to one error every 100,000. A sales manager exercises strategic entrepreneurship by deciding to run a special promotion and cut sales prices by 5 percent to wrest market share away from rivals. A manufacturing manager exercises strategic entrepreneurship in deciding, as part of a companywide emphasis on greater cost competitiveness, to source an important component from a lower-priced South Korean supplier instead of making it in-house. Company strategies can't be truly market- and customer-driven unless the strategy-related activities of managers all across the company have an outside-in entrepreneurial character and contribute to boosting customer satisfaction and achieving sustainable competitive advantage.

Why Company Strategies Evolve   Frequent finetuning and tweaking of a company's strategy, first in one department or functional area and then in another, are quite normal. On occasion, quantum changes in strategy are called for—when a competitor makes a dramatic move, when technological breakthroughs occur, or when crisis strikes and managers are forced to make radical strategy alterations very quickly. Because strategic moves and new action approaches are ongoing across the business, an organization's strategy forms over a period of time and then reforms as the number of changes begin to mount. Current strategy is typically a blend of holdover approaches, fresh actions and reactions, and potential moves in the planning stage. Except for crisis situations (where many strategic moves are often made quickly to produce a substantially new strategy almost overnight) and new company start-ups (where strategy exists mostly in the form of plans and intended actions), it is common for key elements of a company's strategy to emerge in bits and pieces as the business develops.

> A company's strategy is dynamic, emerging in bits and pieces as the enterprise develops, always subject to revision whenever managers see avenues for improvement or a need to adapt business approaches to changing conditions.

Rarely is a company's strategy so well-conceived and durable that it can withstand the test of time. Even the best-laid business plans must be adapted to shifting market conditions, altered customer needs and preferences, the strategic maneuvering of rival firms, the experience of what is working and what isn't, emerging opportunities and threats, unforeseen events, and fresh thinking about how to improve the strategy. This is why strategy-making is a dynamic process and why a manager must reevaluate strategy regularly, refining and recasting it as needed.

However, when strategy changes so fast and so fundamentally that the game plan undergoes major overhaul every few months, managers are almost certainly guilty of poor strategic analysis, erratic decision-making, and weak "strategizing." Quantum changes in strategy are needed occasionally, especially in crisis situations, but they cannot be made too often without creating undue organizational confusion and disrupting performance. Well-crafted strategies normally have a life of at least several years, requiring only minor tweaking to keep them in tune with changing circumstances.

What Does a Company's Strategy Consist Of?   Company strategies concern *how:* how to grow the business, how to satisfy customers, how to outcompete rivals, how to respond to changing market conditions, how to manage each functional piece of the business, how to achieve strategic and financial objectives. The hows of strategy tend to be company-specific, customized to a company's own situation and performance objectives. In the business world, companies have a wide degree of strategic freedom. They can diversify broadly or narrowly, into related or unrelated industries, via acquisition, joint venture, strategic alliances, or internal start-up. Even when a company elects to concentrate on a single business, prevailing market conditions usually offer enough strategy-making latitude that close competitors can easily avoid carbon-copy strategies—some pursue low-cost leadership, others stress various combinations of product/service attributes, and still others elect to cater to the special needs and preferences of narrow buyer segments. Hence, descriptions of the content of company strategy necessarily have to be suggestive rather than definitive.

> Company strategies are partly visible and partly hidden to outside view.

Figure 1–3 depicts the kinds of actions and approaches that reflect a company's overall strategy. Because many are visible to outside observers, most of a company's strategy can be deduced from its actions and public pronouncements. Yet, there's an unrevealed portion of strategy outsiders can only speculate about—the actions and moves company managers are considering. Managers often, for good reason, choose not to reveal certain elements of their strategy until the time is right.

To get a better understanding of the content of company strategies, see the overview of McDonald's strategy in Illustration Capsule 3 on page 12.

F I G U R E 1-3   **| Understanding a Company's Strategy—What to Look For**

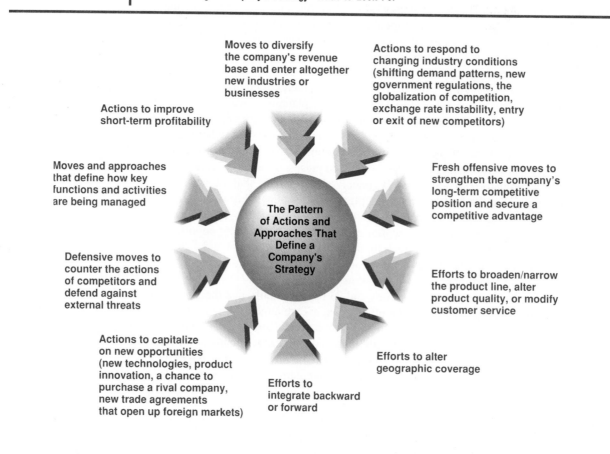

- Moves to diversify the company's revenue base and enter altogether new industries or businesses
- Actions to respond to changing industry conditions (shifting demand patterns, new government regulations, the globalization of competition, exchange rate instability, entry or exit of new competitors)
- Actions to improve short-term profitability
- Moves and approaches that define how key functions and activities are being managed
- Fresh offensive moves to strengthen the company's long-term competitive position and secure a competitive advantage
- Defensive moves to counter the actions of competitors and defend against external threats
- **The Pattern of Actions and Approaches That Define a Company's Strategy**
- Efforts to broaden/narrow the product line, alter product quality, or modify customer service
- Actions to capitalize on new opportunities (new technologies, product innovation, a chance to purchase a rival company, new trade agreements that open up foreign markets)
- Efforts to alter geographic coverage
- Efforts to integrate backward or forward

Strategy and Strategic Plans   Developing a strategic vision and mission, establishing objectives, and deciding on a strategy are basic direction-setting tasks. They map out where the organization is headed, its short-range and long-range performance targets, and the competitive moves and internal action approaches to be used in achieving the targeted results. Together, they constitute a *strategic plan*. In some companies, especially large corporations committed to regular strategy reviews and formal strategic planning, a document describing the upcoming year's strategic plan is prepared and circulated to managers and employees (although parts of the plan may be omitted or expressed in general terms if they are too sensitive to reveal before they are actually undertaken). In other companies, the strategic plan is not put in writing for widespread distribution but rather exists in the form of consensus and commitments among managers about where to head, what to accomplish, and how to proceed. Organizational objectives are the part of the strategic plan most often spelled out explicitly and communicated to managers and employees.

However, annual strategic plans seldom anticipate all the strategically relevant events that will transpire in the next 12 months. Unforeseen events, unexpected opportunities or threats, plus the constant bubbling up of new proposals encourage managers to modify planned actions and forge "unplanned" reactions. Postponing the recrafting of strategy until it's time to work on next year's strategic plan is both foolish and unnecessary. Managers who confine their strategizing to the company's regularly scheduled planning cycle (when they can't avoid turning something in) have a wrongheaded concept of what their strategy-making responsibilities are. Once-a-year strategizing under "have to" conditions is not a prescription for managerial success.

STRATEGY IMPLEMENTATION AND EXECUTION

The strategy-implementing function consists of seeing what it will take to make the strategy work and to reach the targeted performance on schedule—the skill here is being good at figuring out what must be done to put the strategy in place, execute it proficiently, and produce good results. The job of implementing strategy is primarily a hands-on, close-to-the-scene administrative task that includes the following principal aspects:

- Building an organization capable of carrying out the strategy successfully.
- Developing budgets that steer resources into those internal activities critical to strategic success.
- Establishing strategy-supportive policies.
- Motivating people in ways that induce them to pursue the target objectives energetically and, if need be, modifying their duties and job behavior to better fit the requirements of successful strategy execution.
- Tying the reward structure to the achievement of targeted results.
- Creating a company culture and work climate conducive to successful strategy implementation.
- Installing internal support systems that enable company personnel to carry out their strategic roles effectively day in and day out.
- Instituting best practices and programs for continuous improvement.
- Exerting the internal leadership needed to drive implementation forward and to keep improving on how the strategy is being executed.

The administrative aim is to create "fits" between the way things are done and what it takes for effective strategy execution. The stronger the fits, the better the execution of

A STRATEGY EXAMPLE: MCDONALD'S

In 1993 McDonald's was the leading food service retailer in the global consumer marketplace, with a strong brand name and systemwide restaurant sales exceeding $22 billion. Two-thirds of its 13,000 restaurants were franchised to 3,750 owner/operators around the world. Sales had grown an average of 8 percent in the U.S. and 20 percent outside the U.S. over the past 10 years.

The company-pioneered food quality specifications, equipment technology, marketing and training programs, operating systems, and supply systems were considered industry standards throughout the world. The Company's strategic priorities were continued growth, providing exceptional customer care, remaining an efficient and quality producer, offering high value, and effectively marketing McDonald's brand on a global scale. McDonald's strategy had the following core elements:

Growth Strategy

• Add 700 to 900 restaurants annually, some company-owned and some franchised, with about two-thirds outside the United States.

• Promote more frequent customer visits via the addition of breakfast and dinner menu items, low-price specials, and Extra Value Meals.

Franchising Strategy

• Be highly selective in granting franchises. (McDonald's approach was to recruit only highly motivated, talented entrepreneurs with integrity and business experience and train them to become active, on-premise owners of McDonald's; no franchises were granted to corporations, partnerships, or passive investors.)

Store Location and Construction Strategy

• Locate restaurants only on sites that offer convenience to customers and afford long-term sales growth potential. (The company utilized sophisticated site selection techniques to obtain premier locations. In the U.S., the company supplemented its traditional suburban and urban locations with outlets in food courts, major airports, hospitals, and universities; outside the U.S., the strategy was to establish an initial presence in center cities, then open freestanding units with drive-thrus outside center cities. Where site ownership was not practical, McDonald's secured long-term leases.)

• Reduce site costs and building costs by using standardized, cost-efficient store designs and consolidating purchases of equipment and materials via a global sourcing system. (One of the company's four approved designs was half the size of a traditional restaurant, required a smaller parcel of land, was about 25% cheaper, and could accommodate nearly the same volume.)

• Utilize store and site designs that are attractive and pleasing inside and out, and where feasible provide drive-thru service and play areas for children.

Product Line Strategy

• Offer a limited menu.

(continued)

strategy. The most important fits are between strategy and organizational capabilities, between strategy and the reward structure, between strategy and internal support systems, and between strategy and the organization's culture (the latter emerges from the values and beliefs shared by organizational members, the company's approach to people management, and ingrained behaviors, work practices, and ways of thinking). Fitting the ways the organization does things internally to what it takes for effective strategy execution helps unite the organization behind the accomplishment of strategy.

The strategy-implementing task is easily the most complicated and time-consuming part of strategic management. It cuts across virtually all facets of managing and must be initiated from many points inside the organization. The strategy-implementer's

(concluded)

- Expand product offerings into new categories of fast food (chicken, Mexican, pizza, and so on) and include more items for health-conscious customers.
- Do extensive testing to ensure consistent high quality and ample customer appeal before rolling out new menu items systemwide.

Store Operations

- Establish stringent product standards, strictly enforce restaurant operating procedures (especially as concerns food preparation, store cleanliness and friendly, courteous counter service), and build close working relationships with suppliers to assure that food is safe and of the highest quality. (Generally, McDonald's does not supply food, paper products, or equipment to restaurants; instead, it approves suppliers from whom these items can be purchased.)
- Develop new equipment and production systems that improve the ability to serve hotter, better-tasting food, faster and with greater accuracy.

Sales Promotion, Marketing, and Merchandising

- Enhance the McDonald's image of quality, service, cleanliness, and value globally via heavy media advertising and in-store merchandise promotions funded with fees tied to a percent of sales revenues at each restaurant.
- Continue to use value pricing and Extra Value Meals to build customer traffic.
- Use Ronald McDonald to create greater brand

awareness among children and the Mc prefix to reinforce the connection of menu items and McDonald's.

Human Resources and Training

- Offer wage rates that are equitable and nondiscriminatory in every location; teach job skills; reward both individual accomplishments and teamwork; offer career opportunities.
- Hire restaurant crews with good work habits and courteous attitudes and train them to act in ways that will impress customers.
- Provide proper training on delivering customer satisfaction and running a fast-food business to franchisees, restaurant managers, and assistant managers. (Instructors at four Hamburger University campuses in Illinois, Germany, England, and Japan in 1992 trained over 3,000 students in 20 languages.)

Social Responsibility

- Operate in a socially responsible manner by supporting educational programs for student employees, Ronald McDonald Houses (at year-end 1992, there were 150 houses in nine countries providing a home-away-from-home for families of seriously ill children receiving treatment at nearby hospitals), workforce diversity and voluntary affirmative action, minority-owned franchises (McDonald's franchises included the largest and most successful group of minority entrepreneurs in the U.S.), recycling (McDonald's McRecycle USA program has won national awards), and by providing nutritional information on McDonald's products to customers.

Source: Company annual reports.

agenda for action emerges from careful assessment of what the organization must do differently and better to carry out the strategic plan proficiently. Each manager has to think through the answer to "What has to be done in my area to carry out my piece of the strategic plan, and how can I best get it done?" How much internal change is needed to put the strategy into effect depends on the degree of strategic change, how much internal practices deviate from what the strategy requires, and how well strategy and organizational culture already match. As needed changes and actions are identified, management must supervise all the details of implementation and apply enough pressure on the organization to convert objectives into results. Depending on the amount of internal change involved, full implementation can take several months to several years.

Strategy implementation is fundamentally an action-oriented, make-it-happen activity—organizing, budgeting, policy-making, motivating, culture-building, and leading are all part of achieving the target results.

EVALUATING PERFORMANCE, REVIEWING NEW DEVELOPMENTS, AND INITIATING CORRECTIVE ADJUSTMENTS

None of the previous four tasks are one-time exercises. New circumstances call for corrective adjustments. Long-term direction may need to be altered, the business redefined, and management's vision of the organization's future course narrowed or broadened. Performance targets may need raising or lowering in light of past experience and future prospects. Strategy may need to be modified because of shifts in long-term direction, because new objectives have been set, or because of changing conditions in the environment.

The search for ever better strategy execution is also continuous. Sometimes an aspect of implementation does not go as well as intended and changes have to be made. Progress is typically uneven—faster in some areas and slower in others. Some tasks get done easily; others prove nettlesome. Implementation has to be thought of as a process, not an event. It occurs through the pooling effect of many managerial decisions and many incremental actions on the part of work groups and individuals across the organization. Budget revisions, policy changes, reorganization, personnel changes, reengineered activities and work processes, culture-changing actions, and revised compensation practices are typical actions managers take to make a strategy work better.

A company's mission, objectives, strategy, and approach to implementation are never final; evaluating performance, reviewing changes in the surrounding environment, and making adjustments are normal and necessary parts of the strategic management process.

WHY STRATEGIC MANAGEMENT IS AN ONGOING PROCESS

Because each one of the five tasks of strategic management requires constant evaluation and a decision whether to continue or change, a manager cannot afford distractions. Nothing about the strategic management process is final—all prior actions are subject to modification as conditions in the surrounding environment change and ideas for improvement emerge. Strategic management is a process filled with motion. Changes in the organization's situation, either from the inside or outside or both, fuel the need for strategic adjustments. This is why, in Figure 1–1, we highlight the recycling feature inherent in the strategic management process.

The task of evaluating performance and initiating corrective adjustments is both the end and the beginning of the strategic management cycle. The march of external and internal events guarantees that revisions in mission, objectives, strategy, and implementation will be needed sooner or later. It is always incumbent on management to push for better performance—to find ways to improve the existing strategy and how it is being executed. Changing external conditions add further impetus to the need for periodic revisions in a company's mission, performance objectives, strategy, and approaches to strategy execution. Adjustments usually involve fine-tuning, but occasions for major strategic reorientation do arise—sometimes prompted by significant external developments and sometimes by sharply sliding financial performance. Strategy managers must stay close enough to the situation to detect when changing conditions require a strategic response and when they don't. It is their job to sense the winds of change, recognize significant changes early, and initiate adjustments.

CHARACTERISTICS OF THE PROCESS

Although developing a mission, setting objectives, forming a strategy, implementing and executing the strategic plan, and evaluating performance portray what strategic management involves, actually performing these five tasks is not so cleanly divided into separate, neatly sequenced compartments. There is much interplay among the five tasks. For example, considering what strategic actions to take raises issues about whether and how the strategy can be satisfactorily implemented. Deciding on a company mission shades into setting objectives (both involve directional priorities). To establish challenging but achievable objectives, managers must consider both current performance and the strategy options available to improve performance. Deciding on a strategy is entangled with decisions about long-term direction and whether objectives have been set too high or too low. Clearly, the direction-setting tasks of developing a mission, setting objectives, and crafting strategy need to be integrated and done as a package, not individually.

> Strategic management is a process; the boundaries between the five tasks are conceptual, not real.

Second, the five strategic management tasks are not done in isolation from a manager's other job responsibilities—supervising day-to-day operations, dealing with crises, going to meetings, preparing reports, handling people problems, and taking on special assignments and civic duties. Thus, while the job of managing strategy is the most important managerial function insofar as organizational success or failure is concerned, it isn't all managers must do or be concerned about.

Third, crafting and implementing strategy make erratic demands on a manager's time. Change does not happen in an orderly or predictable way. Events can build quickly or gradually; they can emerge singly or in rapid-fire succession; and their implications for strategic change can be easy or hard to diagnose. Hence the task of reviewing and adjusting the strategic game plan can take up big chunks of management time in some months and little time in other months. As a practical matter, there is as much skill in knowing *when* to institute strategic changes as there is in knowing *what* to do.

Last, the big day in, day out time-consuming aspect of strategic management involves trying to get the best strategy-supportive performance out of every individual and trying to perfect the current strategy by refining its content and execution. Managers usually spend most of their efforts improving bits and pieces of the current strategy rather than developing and instituting radical changes. Excessive changes in strategy can be disruptive to employees and confusing to customers, and they are usually unnecessary. Most of the time, there's more to be gained from improving execution of the present strategy. Persistence in making a sound strategy work better is often the key to managing the strategy to success.

WHO PERFORMS THE FIVE TASKS OF STRATEGIC MANAGEMENT?

An organization's chief executive officer, as captain of the ship, is the most visible and important strategy manager. The title of CEO carries with it the mantles of chief direction-setter, chief objective-setter, chief strategy-maker, and chief strategy-implementer for the total enterprise. Ultimate responsibility for leading the tasks of formulating and implementing a strategic plan for the whole organization rests with the CEO, even though many other managers normally have a hand in the process. What the CEO views as strategically important usually is reflected in the company's strategy, and the CEO customarily puts a personal stamp of approval on big strategic decisions and actions.

Vice presidents for production, marketing, finance, human resources, and other functional departments have important strategy-making and strategy-implementing responsibilities as well. Normally, the production VP has a lead role in developing the company's production strategy; the marketing VP oversees the marketing strategy effort; the financial VP is in charge of devising an appropriate financial strategy; and so on. Usually, functional vice presidents are also involved in proposing key elements of the overall company strategy and developing major new strategic initiatives, working closely with the CEO to hammer out a consensus and coordinate various aspects of the strategy more effectively. Only in the smallest, owner-managed companies is the strategy-making, strategy-implementing task small enough for a single manager to handle.

But managerial positions with strategy-making and strategy-implementing responsibility are by no means restricted to CEOs, vice presidents, and owner-entrepreneurs. Every major organizational unit in a company—business unit, division, staff support group, plant, or district office—normally has a leading or supporting role in the company's strategic game plan. And the manager in charge of that organizational unit, with guidance from superiors, usually ends up doing some or most of the strategy-making for the unit and deciding how to implement whatever strategic choices are made. While managers farther down in the managerial hierarchy obviously have a narrower, more specific strategy-making/strategy-implementing role than managers closer to the top, every manager is a strategy-maker and strategy-implementer for the area he/she supervises.

One of the primary reasons why middle- and lower-echelon managers are part of the strategy-making/strategy-implementing team is that the more geographically scattered and diversified an organization's operations are, the more unwieldy it becomes for senior executives to craft and implement all the necessary actions and programs. Managers in the corporate office seldom know enough about the situation in every geographic area and operating unit to direct every move made in the field. It is common practice for top-level managers to grant some strategy-making responsibility to managerial subordinates who head the organizational subunits where specific strategic results must be achieved. Delegating a strategy-making role to on-the-scene managers charged with implementing whatever strategic moves are made in their areas fixes accountability for strategic success or failure. When the managers who implement the strategy are also its architects, it is hard for them to shift blame or make excuses if they don't achieve the target results. And since they have participated in developing the strategy they are trying to implement and execute, they ought to have strong buy-in and support for the strategy, an essential condition for effective strategy execution.

In diversified companies where the strategies of several different businesses have to be managed, there are usually four distinct levels of strategy managers:

- The chief executive officer and other senior corporation-level executives who have primary responsibility and personal authority for big strategic decisions affecting the total enterprise and the collection of individual businesses the enterprise has diversified into.
- Managers who have profit-and-loss responsibility for one specific business unit and who are delegated a major leadership role in formulating and implementing strategy for that unit.
- Functional area managers within a given business unit who have direct authority over a major piece of the business (manufacturing, marketing and sales, finance, R&D, personnel) and whose role it is to support the business unit's overall strategy with strategic actions in their own areas.
- Managers of major operating units (plants, sales districts, local offices) who have on-the-scene responsibility for developing the details of strategic efforts in their areas and for implementing and executing the overall strategic plan at the grassroots level.

All managers are involved in the strategy-making and strategy-implementing process.

Single-business enterprises need no more than three of these levels (a business-level strategy manager, functional area strategy managers, and operating-level strategy managers). In a large single-business company, the team of strategy managers consists of the chief executive, who functions as chief strategist with final authority over both strategy and its implementation; the vice presidents in charge of key functions (R&D, production, marketing, finance, human resources, and so on); plus as many operating-unit managers of the various plants, sales offices, distribution centers, and staff support departments as it takes to handle the company's scope of operations. Proprietorships, partnerships, and owner-managed enterprises, however, typically have only one or two strategy managers since in small-scale enterprises the whole strategy-making/strategy-implementing function can be handled by just a few key people.

Managerial jobs involving strategy formulation and implementation abound in not-for-profit organizations as well. In federal and state government, heads of local, district, and regional offices function as strategy managers in their efforts to respond to the needs and situations of the areas they serve (a district manager in Portland may need a slightly different strategy than a district manager in Orlando). In municipal government, the heads of various departments (fire, police, water and sewer, parks and recreation, health, and so on) are strategy managers because they have line authority for the operations of their departments and thus can influence departmental objectives, the formation of a strategy to achieve these objectives, and how the strategy is implemented.

Managerial jobs with strategy-making/strategy-implementing roles are thus the norm rather than the exception. The job of crafting and implementing strategy touches virtually every managerial job in one way or another, at one time or another. Strategic management is basic to the task of managing; it is not something just top-level managers deal with.

THE ROLE AND TASKS OF STRATEGIC PLANNERS

If senior and middle managers have the lead roles in strategy-making and strategy-implementing in their areas of responsibility, what should strategic planners do? Is there a legitimate place in big companies for a strategic planning department staffed with specialists in planning and strategic analysis? The answer is yes. But the planning department's role and tasks should consist chiefly of helping to gather and organize information that strategy-makers need, establishing and administering an annual strategy review cycle whereby managers reconsider and refine their strategic plans, and coordinating the process of reviewing and approving the strategic plans developed for all the various parts of the company. Strategic planners can help managers at all levels crystallize the strategic issues that ought to be addressed; in addition, they can provide data, help analyze industry and competitive conditions, and distribute information on the company's strategic performance. But strategic planners should not make strategic decisions, prepare strategic plans (for someone else to implement), or make strategic action recommendations that usurp the strategy-making responsibilities of managers in charge of major operating units.

When strategic planners are asked to go beyond providing staff assistance and actually prepare a strategic plan for management's consideration, either of two adverse consequences may occur. First, some managers will gladly toss their tough strategic problems onto the desks of strategic planners and let the planners do their strategic thinking for them. The planners, not knowing as much about the situation as managers do, are in a weaker position to design a workable action plan. And they can't be held responsible for implementing what they recommend. Giving planners responsibility for strategy-making and line managers responsibility for implementation makes it hard to fix accountability for poor results. It also deludes line managers into thinking they shouldn't be held responsible for crafting a strategy for their own organizational unit or for devising solutions to strategic problems in their area of responsibility. The hard truth is that strategy-making is not a staff function, nor is it something that can be handed off to an advisory committee of lower-ranking managers. Second, when line managers have no ownership stake in or personal commitment to the strategic agenda proposed by the planners, they give it lip service, perhaps make a few token implementation efforts, and quickly get back to business as usual, knowing that the formal written plan concocted by the planners carries little weight in shaping their own action agenda and decisions. Unless the planners' written strategic plan has visible, credible top-management support, it quickly collects dust on managers' shelves. Absent belief in and commitment to the actions recommended by the planners, few managers will take the work of the strategic planning staff seriously enough to pursue implementation—strategic planning then comes to be seen as just another bureaucratic exercise.

Either consequence renders formal strategic planning efforts ineffective and opens the door for a strategy-making vacuum conducive to organizational drift or to fragmented, uncoordinated strategic decisions. The odds are that the organization will have no strong strategic rudder and insufficient top-down direction. Having staffers or advisory committees formulate strategies for areas they do not directly manage is therefore flawed in two respects: (1) they can't be held accountable if their recommendations don't produce the desired results since they don't have authority for directing implementation, and (2) there's a strong chance that what they recommend won't be well accepted or enthusiastically implemented by those who "have to sing the song the planners have written"—lukewarm buy-in is a guaranteed plan-killer.

On the other hand, when line managers are expected to be the chief strategy-makers and strategy-implementers for the areas they head, their own strategy and implementation end up being put to the test. As a consequence, their buy-in becomes a given, and they usually commit the time and resources to make the plan work (their annual performance reviews and perhaps even their future careers with the organization are at risk if the plan fails and they fail to achieve the target results!). When those who craft strategy are also those who must implement strategy, there's no question who is accountable for results. Moreover, when authority for crafting and implementing the strategy of an organizational unit is placed on the shoulders of the unit manager, it's easy to fix accountability for results and it pushes strategic decisions down to the manager closest to the action who *should* know what to do. Unit managers who consistently prove incapable of crafting and implementing good strategies and achieving target results have to be moved to less responsible positions.

THE STRATEGIC ROLE OF THE BOARD OF DIRECTORS

Since lead responsibility for crafting and implementing strategy falls to key managers, the chief strategic role of an organization's board of directors is to see that the overall task of managing strategy is adequately done. Boards of directors normally review important strategic moves and officially approve the strategic plans submitted by senior management—a procedure that makes the board ultimately responsible for the strategic actions taken. But directors rarely can or should play a direct role in formulating strategy. The immediate task of directors is to ensure that all proposals have been adequately analyzed and considered and that the proposed strategic actions are superior to available alternatives; flawed proposals are customarily withdrawn for revision by management.

The longer-range task of directors is to evaluate the caliber of senior executives' strategy-making and strategy-implementing skills. The board must determine whether the current CEO is doing a good job of strategic management (as a basis for awarding salary increases and bonuses and deciding on retention or removal) and evaluate the strategic skills of other senior executives in line to succeed the CEO. In recent years, at General Motors, IBM, American Express, Goodyear, and Compaq Computer, company directors concluded that executives were not adapting their company's strategy fast enough and fully enough to the changes sweeping their markets. They pressured the CEOs to resign, and installed new leadership to provide the impetus for strategic renewal. Boards who fail to review the strategy-making, strategy-implementing skills of senior executives face embarrassment or even lawsuits when an out-dated strategy sours company performance and management fails to come up with a promising turnaround strategy.

THE BENEFITS OF A "STRATEGIC APPROACH" TO MANAGING

The message of this book is that doing a good job of managing inherently requires good strategic thinking and good strategic management. Today's managers have to think strategically about their company's position and about the impact of changing conditions. They have to monitor the external situation closely enough to know when to institute strategy change. They have to know the business well enough to know what kinds of strategic changes to initiate. Simply said, the fundamentals of strategic management need to drive the whole approach to managing organizations. The chief executive officer of one successful company put it well when he said:

> In the main, our competitors are acquainted with the same fundamental concepts and techniques and approaches that we follow, and they are as free to pursue them as we are. More often than not, the difference between their level of success and ours lies in the relative thoroughness and self-discipline with which we and they develop and execute our strategies for the future.

The advantages of first-rate strategic thinking and conscious strategy management (as opposed to freewheeling improvisation, gut feel, and drifting along) include (1) providing better guidance to the entire organization on the crucial point of "what it is we are trying to do and to achieve," (2) making managers more alert to the winds of change, new opportunities, and threatening developments, (3) providing managers with a rationale for evaluating competing budget requests for investment capital and new staff—a rationale that argues strongly for steering resources into strategy-supportive, results-producing areas, (4) helping to unify the numerous strategy-related decisions by managers across the organization, and (5) creating a more proactive management posture and counteracting tendencies for decisions to be reactive and defensive.

The advantage of being proactive is that trailblazing strategies can be the key to better long-term performance. Business history shows that high-performing enterprises often initiate and lead, not just react and defend. They launch strategic offensives to out-innovate and out-maneuver rivals and secure sustainable competitive advantage, then use their market edge to achieve superior financial performance. Aggressive pursuit of a creative, opportunistic strategy can propel a firm into a leadership position, paving the way for its products/services to become the industry standard.

TERMS TO REMEMBER

In the chapters to come, we'll be using some key phrases and terms again and again. You'll find the following definitional listing helpful.

Strategic vision—a view of an organization's future direction and business course; a guiding concept for what the organization is trying to do and to become.

Organization mission—management's customized answer to the question "What is our business and what are we trying to accomplish on behalf of our customers?" A mission statement broadly outlines the organization's activities and business makeup.

Financial objectives—the targets management has established for the organization's financial performance.

Strategic objectives—the targets management has established for strengthening the organization's overall business position and competitive vitality.

Long-range objectives—the results to be achieved either within the next three to five years or else on an ongoing basis year after year.

Short-range objectives—the organization's near-term performance targets; the amount of short-term improvement signals how fast management is trying to achieve the long-range objectives.

Strategy—the pattern of actions managers employ to achieve organizational objectives; a company's actual strategy is partly planned and partly reactive to changing circumstances.

Strategic plan—a statement outlining an organization's mission and future direction, near-term and long-term performance targets, and strategy.

Strategy formulation—the entire direction-setting management function of conceptualizing an organization's mission, setting performance objectives, and crafting a strategy. The end product of strategy formulation is a strategic plan.

Strategy implementation—the full range of managerial activities associated with putting the chosen strategy into place, supervising its pursuit, and achieving the targeted results.

On the following pages, we will probe the strategy-related tasks of managers and the methods of strategic analysis much more intensively. When you get to the end of the book, we think you will see that two factors separate the best-managed organizations from the rest: (1) superior strategy-making and entrepreneurship, and (2) competent implementation and execution of the chosen strategy. There's no escaping the fact that the quality of managerial strategy-making and strategy-implementing has a significant impact on organization performance. A company that lacks clear-cut direction, has vague or undemanding objectives, has a muddled or flawed strategy, or can't seem to execute plans competently is a company whose performance is probably suffering, whose business is at long-term risk, and whose management is less than capable.

SUGGESTED READINGS

Andrews, Kenneth R. *The Concept of Corporate Strategy.* 3rd ed. Homewood, Ill.: Richard D. Irwin, 1987, chap. 1.

Gluck, Frederick W. "A Fresh Look at Strategic Management." *Journal of Business Strategy* 6 no. 2 (Fall 1985), pp. 4–21.

Hax, Arnoldo C., and Nicolas S. Majluf. *The Strategy Concept and Process: A Pragmatic Approach.* Englewood Cliffs, N.J.: Prentice-Hall, 1991, chaps. 1 and 2.

Kelley, C. Aaron. "The Three Planning Questions: A Fable." *Business Horizons* 26, no. 2 (March–April 1983), pp. 46–48.

Mintzberg, Henry. "The Strategy Concept: Five Ps for Strategy." *California Management Review* 30, no. 1 (Fall 1987), pp. 11–24.

———. "The Strategy Concept: Another Look at Why Organizations Need Strategies." *California Management Review* 30, no. 1 (Fall 1987), pp. 25–32.

———. "Crafting Strategy." *Harvard Business Review* 65, no. 4 (July–August 1987), pp. 66–75.

Quinn, James B. *Strategies for Change: Logical Incrementalism.* Homewood, Ill.: Richard D. Irwin, 1980, chaps. 2 and 3.

Ramanujam, V., and N. Venkatraman. "Planning and Performance: A New Look at an Old Question." *Business Horizons* 30, no. 3 (May–June 1987), pp. 19–25.

Yip, George S. *Total Global Strategy: Managing for Worldwide Competitive Advantage.* Englewood Cliffs, N.J.: Prentice-Hall, 1992, chap. 1.

CHAPTER TWO

THE THREE STRATEGY-MAKING TASKS
DEVELOPING A STRATEGIC VISION, SETTING OBJECTIVES, AND CRAFTING A STRATEGY

How can you lead if you don't know where you are going?

George Newman
The Conference Board

Management's job is not to see the company as it is . . . but as it can become.

John W. Teets
CEO, Greyhound Corporation

Once your direction becomes clear to you and fully visible to others, all the elements of winning—attitude, performance, teamwork, and competition—begin to come together.

Dennis Conner

Without a strategy the organization is like a ship without a rudder, going around in circles. It's like a tramp; it has no place to go.

Joel Ross and Michael Kami

In this chapter, we provide a more in-depth look at each of the three strategy-making tasks: developing a strategic vision and business mission, setting performance objectives, and crafting a strategy to produce the desired results. We also examine the kinds of strategic decisions made at each management level, the major determinants of a company's strategy, and four frequently used managerial approaches to forming a strategic plan.

DEVELOPING A STRATEGIC VISION AND MISSION: THE FIRST DIRECTION-SETTING TASK

Management's views about what activities the organization intends to pursue and the long-term course it charts for the future constitute a *strategic vision*. A strategic vision provides a big picture perspective of "who *we* are, what *we* do, and where *we* are headed." It leaves no doubt about the company's long-term direction and where management intends to take the company. A well-conceived strategic vision is a prerequisite to effective strategic leadership. A manager cannot function effectively as either leader or strategy-maker without a sound concept of the business, what activities to pursue, what not to pursue, and what kind of long-term competitive position to build vis-à-vis both customers and competitors.

Although we use the following terms interchangeably, we like *strategic vision* better than the more common term *business mission* or *mission statement.* Missions tend to be more concerned with the present ("What is our business?") than with the bigger issue of long-term direction (where are we headed, what new things do we intend to pursue, what will our business makeup be in 5 to 10 years, what kind of company are we trying to become, and what sort of long-term market position do we aspire to achieve?).

Strategic visions and company mission statements are always highly personalized. Generic statements, applicable to any company or to any industry, have no managerial value. A strategic vision/mission statement sets an organization apart from others in its industry and gives it its own special identity, business emphasis, and path for development. For example, the mission of a globally active New York bank like Citicorp has little in common with that of a locally owned small-town bank even though both are in the banking industry. Compaq Computer is not on the same strategic path as IBM, even though both sell personal computers. General Electric is not on the same long-term strategic course as Whirlpool Corp., even though both are leaders in the major home appliance business; while Whirlpool's business is concentrated in appliances, GE has major business positions in aircraft engines, defense electronics, engineering plastics, electric power generation equipment, factory automation, locomotives, lighting, medical diagnostic imaging, and TV broadcasting (it owns NBC). Similarly, there are important differences between the long-term strategic direction of such fierce business rivals as Intel and Motorola, Philips and Matsushita, Eastman Kodak and Fuji Photo Film Co., Michelin and Bridgestone/Firestone, Procter & Gamble and Unilever, and British Telecom and AT&T. Illustration Capsule 4 describes Delta Airlines' strategic vision.

Sometimes companies mistakenly couch their mission in terms of making a profit. However, profit is more correctly an *objective* and a *result* of what the company does. The desire to make a profit says nothing about the business arena in which profits are to be sought. Missions based on making a profit are incapable of distinguishing one type of profit-seeking enterprise from another—the business and long-term direction of Sears are plainly different from the business and long-term direction of Toyota, even though both endeavor to earn a profit. A company that says its mission is to make a profit begs the question "What will we do to make a profit?" To know anything useful about a company's business mission, we must know management's answer to "make a profit doing what and for whom?"

There are three distinct aspects involved in forming a well-conceived strategic vision and expressing it in a company mission statement:

- Understanding what business a company is really in.
- Communicating the vision and mission in ways that are clear, exciting, and inspiring.
- Deciding when to alter the company's strategic course and change its business mission.

Effective strategy-making begins with a concept of what the organization should and should not do and a vision of where the organization needs to be headed.

Visionless companies are unsure what business position they are trying to stake out.

ILLUSTRATION CAPSULE 4

DELTA AIRLINES' STRATEGIC VISION

In late 1993, Ronald W. Allen, Delta's chief executive officer, described the company's vision and business mission in the following way:

. . . we want Delta to be the **Worldwide Airline of Choice.**

Worldwide, because we are and intend to remain an innovative, aggressive, ethical, and successful competitor that offers access to the world at the highest standards of customer service. We will continue to look for opportunities to extend our reach through new routes and creative global alliances.

Airline, because we intend to stay in the business we know best—air transportation and related services. We won't stray from our roots. We believe in the long-term prospects for profitable growth in the airline industry, and we will continue to focus time, attention, and investment on enhancing our place in that business environment.

Of Choice, because we value the loyalty of our customers, employees, and investors. For passengers and shippers, we will continue to provide the best service and value. For our personnel, we will continue to offer an ever more challenging, rewarding, and result-oriented workplace that recognizes and appreciates their contributions. For our shareholders, we will earn a consistent, superior financial return.

Source: Sky Magazine, December 1993, p. 10.

UNDERSTANDING AND DEFINING THE BUSINESS

Deciding what business an organization is in is neither obvious nor easy. Is IBM in the computer business (a product-oriented definition) or the information and data processing business (a customer service or customer needs type of definition) or the advanced electronics business (a technology-based definition)? Is Coca-Cola in the soft-drink business (in which case its strategic vision can be trained narrowly on the actions of Pepsi, 7UP, Dr Pepper, Canada Dry, and Schweppes)? Or is it in the beverage industry (in which case management must think strategically about positioning Coca-Cola products in a market that includes fruit juices, alcoholic drinks, milk, bottled water, coffee, and tea)? This is not a trivial question for Coca-Cola. Many young adults get their morning caffeine fix by drinking cola instead of coffee; with a beverage industry perspective as opposed to a soft-drink industry perspective, Coca-Cola management is more likely to perceive a long-term growth opportunity in winning youthful coffee drinkers over to its colas.

Arriving at a good business definition usually requires taking three factors into account:[1]

> A company's business is defined by what needs it is trying to satisfy, by which customer groups it is targeting, and by the technologies it will use and the functions it will perform in serving the target market.

1. Customer needs, or *what* is being satisfied.
2. Customer groups, or *who* is being satisfied.
3. The technologies used and functions performed—*how* customers' needs are satisfied.

Defining a business in terms of what to satisfy, who to satisfy, and how the organization will go about producing the satisfaction makes a complete definition. It takes all three. Just knowing what products or services a firm provides is never enough. Products or services *per se* are not important to customers; a product or service becomes a

---

[1]Derek F. Abell, *Defining the Business: The Starting Point of Strategic Planning* (Englewood Cliffs, N.J.: Prentice-Hall, 1980), p. 169.

business when it satisfies a need or want. Without the need or want there is no business. Customer groups are relevant because they indicate the market to be served—the geographic domain to be covered and the types of buyers the firm is going after.

Technology and functions performed are important because they indicate *how* the company will satisfy the customers' needs and how much of the industry's production-distribution chain its activities will span. For instance, a firm's business can be *specialized,* concentrated in just one stage of an industry's total production-distribution chain, or *fully integrated,* spanning all parts of the industry chain. Wal-Mart, Home Depot, Toys-R-Us, and The Limited are essentially one-stage firms. Their operations focus on the retail end of the consumer goods business; they don't manufacture the items they sell. Delta Airlines is a one-stage enterprise; it doesn't manufacture the airplanes it flies, and it doesn't operate the airports where it lands. Delta made a conscious decision to limit its business mission to moving travelers from one location to another via commercial jet aircraft. Major international oil companies like Exxon, Mobil, and Chevron, however, are fully integrated. They lease drilling sites, drill wells, pump oil, transport crude oil in their own ships and pipelines to their own refineries, and sell gasoline and other refined products through their own networks of branded distributors and service station outlets. Because of the disparity in functions performed and technology employed, the business of a retailer like Lands' End or Wal-Mart is much narrower and quite different than that of a fully integrated enterprise like Exxon.

Between these two extremes, firms can stake out *partially integrated* positions, participating only in selected stages of the industry. Goodyear, for instance, both manufactures tires and operates a chain of company-owned retail tire stores, but it has not integrated backward into rubber plantations and other tire-making components. General Motors, the world's most integrated manufacturer of cars and trucks, makes between 60 and 70 percent of the parts and components used in assembling GM vehicles. But GM is moving to outsource a greater fraction of its parts and systems components, and it relies totally on a network of independent, franchised dealers to handle sales and service functions.

So one way of distinguishing a firm's business, especially among firms in the same industry, is by looking at which functions it performs in the production-distribution chain and how far its scope of operation extends across all the business activities involved in getting products to end-users.

One good example of a business definition that incorporates all three components—needs served, target market, and functions performed— is Polaroid's business definition during the early 1970s: "perfecting and marketing instant photography to satisfy the needs of more affluent U.S. and West European families for affection, friendship, fond memories, and humor." McDonald's mission is focused on "serving a limited menu of hot, tasty food quickly in a clean, friendly restaurant for a good value" to a broad base of fast-food customers worldwide (McDonald's serves approximately 25 million customers daily at some 13,000 restaurants in over 65 countries). The concepts that McDonald's uses to define its business are a limited menu, good-tasting fast-food products of consistent quality, value pricing, exceptional customer care, convenient locations, and global market coverage.

Trying to identify needs served, target market, and functions performed in a single, snappy sentence is a challenge, and many firms' mission statements fail to illuminate all three bases explicitly. The mission statements of some companies are thus better than others in terms of how they cut to the chase of what the enterprise is really about.

A Broad or Narrow Business Definition?   A small Hong Kong printing company that defines its business broadly as "Asian-language communications" gains no practical guidance in making direction-setting decisions. With such a definition the company could pursue limitless courses, many well beyond its scope and capability. To have managerial value, strategic visions, business definitions, and mission statements must be narrow enough to pin down the company's real arena of business interest. Consider the following definitions based on broad-narrow scope:

Broad Definition	Narrow Definition
• Beverages	• Soft drinks
• Footwear	• Athletic footwear
• Furniture	• Wrought iron lawn furniture
• Global mail delivery	• Overnight package delivery
• Travel and tourism	• Ship cruises in the Caribbean

Broad-narrow definitions are relative, of course. Being in "the furniture business" is probably too broad a concept for a company intent on being the largest manufacturer of wrought-iron lawn furniture in North America. On the other hand, "soft drinks" has proved too narrow a scope for a growth-oriented company like Coca-Cola, which, with its beverage-industry perspective, acquired Minute-Maid and Hi-C (to capitalize on growing consumer interest in fruit-juice products) and Taylor Wine Company (using the California Cellars brand to establish a foothold in wines).[2] The U.S. Postal Service operates with a broad definition, providing global mail-delivery services to all types of senders. Federal Express, however, operates with a narrow business definition based on handling overnight package delivery for customers who have unplanned emergencies and tight deadlines.

Diversified firms have more sweeping business definitions than do single-business enterprises. Their mission statements typically are phrased narrowly enough to pinpoint their current customer-market-technology arenas but are open-ended and adaptable enough to incorporate expansion into new businesses. Alcan, Canada's leading aluminum company, used broad, inclusive words in expressing its strategic vision and mission:

> Alcan is determined to be the most innovative diversified aluminum company in the world. To achieve this position, Alcan will be one, global, customer-oriented enterprise committed to excellence and lowest cost in its chosen aluminum businesses, with significant resources devoted to building an array of new businesses with superior growth and profit potential.

Thermo Electron Corp., a substantially more diversified enterprise, used simultaneous broad-narrow terms to define its arenas of business interest:

> Thermo Electron Corporation develops, manufactures, and markets environmental, analytical, and test instruments, alternative-energy power plants, low-emission combustion systems, paper- and waste-recycling equipment, and biomedical products. The company also operates power plants and provides services in environmental sciences and

Diversified companies have broader missions and business definitions than single-business enterprises.

---

[2]Coca-Cola's foray into wines was not viewed as successful enough to warrant continuation; the division was divested about five years after initial acquisition.

analysis, thermal waste treatment, and specialty metals fabrication and processing, as well as research and product development in unconventional imaging, laser technology, and direct-energy conversion.

Times Mirror Corp., also a diversified enterprise, describes its business scope in broad but still fairly explicit terminology:

> Times Mirror is a media and information company principally engaged in newspaper publishing; book, magazine and other publishing; and cable and broadcast television.

John Hancock's mission statement communicates a shift from its long-standing base in insurance to a broader mission in insurance, banking, and diversified financial services:

> At John Hancock, we are determined not just to compete but to advance, building our market share by offering individuals and institutions the broadest possible range of products and services. Apart from insurance, John Hancock encompasses banking products, full brokerage services and institutional investment, to cite only a few of our diversified activities. We believe these new directions constitute the right moves . . . the steps that will drive our growth throughout the remainder of this century.

Mission Statements for Functional Departments   There's also a place for mission statements for key functions (R&D, marketing, finance) and support units (human resources, training, information systems). Every department can benefit from a consensus statement spelling out its contribution to the company mission, its principal role and activities, and the direction it needs to be moving. Functional and departmental managers who think through and debate with subordinates and higher-ups what their unit needs to focus on and do have a clearer view of how to lead the unit. Three examples from actual companies indicate how a functional mission statement puts the spotlight on a unit's organizational *role* and *scope:*

- The mission of the human resources department is to contribute to organizational success by developing effective leaders, creating high-performance teams, and maximizing the potential of individuals.
- The mission of the corporate claims department is to minimize the overall cost of liability, workers compensation, and property damage claims through competitive cost containment techniques and loss prevention and control programs.
- The mission of corporate security is to provide services for the protection of corporate personnel and assets through preventive measures and investigations.

COMMUNICATING THE STRATEGIC VISION

How to describe the strategic vision, word it in the form of a mission statement, and communicate it down the line to lower-level managers and employees is almost as important as the strategic soundness of the organization's business concept and long-term direction. A vision and mission couched in words that inspire and challenge help build committed effort from employees and serve as powerful motivational tools. Bland language, platitudes, and motherhood-and-apple-pie-style verbiage must be scrupulously avoided—they can be a turn-off rather than a turn-on. Managers need to communicate the vision in words that arouse a strong sense of organizational purpose, build pride, and induce employee buy-in. People are proud to be associated with a company that has a worthwhile mission and is trying to be the world's best at something competitively significant. Having an exciting mission or cause brings the workforce together, galvanizes people to act, stimulates extra effort, and causes people to live the business instead of just coming to work.[3] In organizations with freshly changed missions, executives need to provide a compelling rationale for the new direction and why things must be done differently. Unless people understand how a company's business environment is changing and why a new direction is needed, a new mission statement does little to win employees' commitment or alter work practices—outcomes that can open up a trust gap and make it harder to move the organization down the chosen path.

The best-worded mission statements are simple and concise; they speak loudly and clearly, generate enthusiasm for the firm's future course, and elicit personal effort and dedication from everyone in the organization. They have to be presented and then repeated over and over as a worthy organizational challenge, one capable of benefiting customers in a valuable and meaningful way—indeed it is crucial that the mission stress the payoff for customers and not the payoff for stockholders. It goes *without saying* that the company intends to profit shareholders from its efforts to provide real value to its customers. A crisp, clear, often-repeated, inspiring strategic vision has the power to turn heads in the intended direction and begin a new organizational march. When this occurs, the first step in organizational direction-setting is successfully completed. Illustration Capsule 5 is a good example of an inspiration-oriented company vision and mission.

WHEN TO CHANGE THE MISSION—
WHERE ENTREPRENEURSHIP COMES IN

A member of Maytag's board of directors summed it up well when commenting on why the company acquired a European appliance-maker and expanded its arena of business into international markets: "Times change, conditions change." The march of new events and altered circumstances make it incumbent on managers to continually reassess their company's position and prospects, always checking for *when* it's time to steer a new course and adjust the mission. The key strategic question here is "What new directions should we be moving in *now* to get ready for the changes we see coming in our business?"

Repositioning an enterprise in light of emerging developments and changes on the horizon lessens the chances of getting trapped in a stagnant or declining core business or letting attractive new growth opportunities slip away because of inaction. Good entrepreneurs have a sharp eye for shifting customer wants and needs, emerging technological capabilities, changing international trade conditions, and other important signs of growing or shrinking business opportunity. They attend quickly to users' problems and complaints with the industry's current products and services. They listen intently when a customer says, "If only . . ." Such clues and information tidbits stimulate them to think creatively and strategically about ways to break new ground. Appraising new customer-market-technology opportunities ultimately leads to entrepreneurial judgments about which fork in the road to take. It is the strategy-

A well-worded mission statement creates enthusiasm for the future course management has charted; the motivational goal in communicating the mission is to pose a challenge that inspires and engages everyone in the organization.

The entrepreneurial challenge in developing a mission is to recognize when emerging opportunities and threats in the surrounding environment makes it desirable to revise the organization's long-term direction.

---

[3]Tom Peters, *Thriving on Chaos* (New York: Harper & Row, Perennial Library Edition, 1988), pp. 486–487; and Andrall E. Pearson, "Corporate Redemption and The Seven Deadly Sins," *Harvard Business Review* 70, no. 3 (May–June 1992), pp. 66–68.

NOVACARE'S BUSINESS MISSION

NovaCare is a fast-growing health care company specializing in providing patient rehabilitation services on a contract basis to nursing homes. Rehabilitation therapy is a $10 billion industry, of which 35 percent is provided contractually; the contract segment is highly fragmented with over 1,000 competitors. In 1990 NovaCare was a $100 million company, with a goal of being a $300 million business in 1994. The company stated its business mission and vision as follows:

> NovaCare is people committed to making a difference . . . enhancing the future of all patients . . . breaking new ground in our professions . . . achieving excellence . . . advancing human capability . . . changing the world in which we live.
>
> We lead the way with our enthusiasm, optimism, patience, drive, and commitment.
>
> We work together to enhance the quality of our patients' lives by reshaping lost abilities and teaching new skills. We heighten expectations for the patient and family. We rebuild hope, confidence, self-respect, and a desire to continue.
>
> We apply our clinical expertise to benefit our patients through creative and progressive tech-

niques. Our ethical and performance standards require us to expend every effort to achieve the best possible results.

> Our customers are national and local health care providers who share our goal of enhancing the patients' quality of life. In each community, our customers consider us a partner in providing the best possible care. Our reputation is based on our responsiveness, high standards, and effective systems of quality assurance. Our relationship is open and proactive.
>
> We are advocates of our professions and patients through active participation in the professional, regulatory, educational, and research communities at national, state, and local levels.
>
> Our approach to health care fulfills our responsibility to provide investors with a high rate of return through consistent growth and profitability.
>
> Our people are our most valuable asset. We are committed to the personal, professional, and career development of each individual employee. We are proud of what we do and dedicated to our Company. We foster teamwork and create an environment conducive to productive communication among all disciplines.
>
> NovaCare is a company of people in pursuit of this Vision.

Source: Company annual report.

maker's job to evaluate the risks and prospects of alternative paths and make direction-setting decisions to position the enterprise for success in the years ahead. *A well-chosen mission prepares a company for the future.*

Many companies in consumer electronics and telecommunications believe their future products will incorporate microprocessors and other elements of computer technology. So they are broadening their vision about industry boundaries and establishing new business positions through acquisitions, alliances, and joint ventures to gain better access to cutting-edge technology. Cable TV companies and telephone companies are in a strategic race to install fiber optics technology and position themselves to market a whole new array of services—pay-per-view TV, home shopping, electronic mail, electronic banking, home security systems, energy management systems, information services, and high-speed data transfer—to households and businesses. Numerous companies in manufacturing, seeing the collapse of trade barriers and the swing to a world economy, are broadening their strategic vision from serving domestic markets to serving global markets. Coca-Cola, Kentucky Fried Chicken, and McDonald's are pursuing market opportunities in China, Europe, Japan, and Russia. Japanese automobile companies are working to establish a much bigger presence in the European car market. CNN, Turner Broadcasting's very successful all-news cable channel, is fast winning its way into more and more homes the world over, solidifying its position as the first global all-news channel, a major shift from 10 years ago when its mission was to build a loyal U.S. audience. A company's mission has a finite life, one subject to change whenever top management concludes that the present mission is no longer adequate.

A well-conceived, well-worded mission statement has real managerial value: (1) it crystalizes senior executives' own views about the firm's long-term direction and business makeup, (2) it reduces the risk of visionless management and rudderless decision-making, (3) it conveys an organizational purpose and identity that motivate employees to go all out and do their very best work, (4) it provides a beacon lower-level managers can use to form departmental missions, set departmental objectives, and craft functional and departmental strategies that are in sync with the company's direction and strategy, and (5) it helps an organization prepare for the future.

SETTING OBJECTIVES: THE SECOND DIRECTION-SETTING TASK

Objectives represent a managerial commitment to achieving specific performance targets by a certain time.

Setting objectives converts the strategic vision and directional course into target outcomes and performance milestones. Objectives represent a managerial commitment to producing specified results in a specified time frame. They spell out *how much* of *what kind* of performance *by when.* They direct attention and energy to what needs to be accomplished.

THE MANAGERIAL VALUE OF SETTING OBJECTIVES

Unless an organization's long-term direction and business mission are translated into *measurable* performance targets and managers are pressured to show progress in reaching these targets, statements about direction and mission will end up as nice words, window dressing, and unrealized dreams of accomplishment. The experiences of countless companies and managers teach that *companies whose managers set objectives for each key result area and then aggressively pursue actions calculated to achieve their performance targets typically outperform companies whose managers have good intentions, try hard, and hope for success.*

For performance objectives to have value as a management tool, they must be stated in *quantifiable* or measurable terms and they must contain a *deadline for achievement*. This means avoiding generalities like "maximize profits," "reduce costs," "become more efficient," or "increase sales," which specify neither how much or when. Objective-setting is a call for action—what to achieve, when to achieve it, and who is responsible. As Bill Hewlett, co-founder of Hewlett-Packard, once observed, "You cannot manage what you cannot measure . . . And what gets measured gets done."[4] Spelling out organization objectives in measurable terms and then holding managers accountable for reaching their assigned targets within a specified time frame (1) substitutes purposeful strategic decision-making for aimless actions and confusion over what to accomplish and (2) provides a set of benchmarks for judging the organization's performance.

---

[4]As quoted in Charles H. House and Raymond L. Price, "The Return Map: Tracking Product Teams," Harvard Business Review 60, no. 1 (January–February 1991), p. 93.

WHAT KINDS OF OBJECTIVES TO SET

Objectives are needed for each *key result* managers deem important to success.[5] Two types of key result areas stand out: those relating to *financial performance* and those relating to *strategic performance*. Achieving acceptable financial performance is a must; otherwise the organization's survival ends up at risk. Achieving acceptable strategic performance is essential to sustaining and improving the company's long-term market position and competitiveness. Specific kinds of financial and strategic performance objectives are shown below:

Strategic Management Principle
Every company needs both strategic objectives and financial objectives.

Financial Objectives	Strategic Objectives
• Faster revenue growth	• A bigger market share
• Faster earnings growth	• A higher, more secure industry rank
• Higher dividends	• Higher product quality
• Wider profit margins	• Lower costs relative to key competitors
• Higher returns on invested capital	• Broader or more attractive product line
• Stronger bond and credit ratings	• A stronger reputation with customers
• Bigger cash flows	• Superior customer service
• A rising stock price	• Recognition as a leader in technology and/or product innovation
• Recognition as a "blue chip" company	• Increased ability to compete in international markets
• A more diversified revenue base	• Expanded growth opportunities
• Stable earnings during recessionary periods	• Total customer satisfaction

Illustration Capsule 6 provides a sampling of the strategic and financial objectives of three well-known enterprises.

Strategic Objectives versus Financial Objectives: Which Take Precedence? Both financial and strategic objectives carry top priority. However, sometimes companies under pressure to improve near-term financial performance elect to kill or postpone strategic moves that hold promise for strengthening the enterprise's business and competi-

---

[5]The literature of management is filled with references to *goals* and *objectives*. These terms are used in a variety of ways, many of them conflicting. Some writers use the term goals to refer to the long-run results an organization seeks to achieve and the term objectives to refer to immediate, short-run performance targets. Some writers reverse the usage, referring to objectives as the desired long-run results and goals as the desired short-run results. Others use the terms interchangeably. And still others use the term goals to refer to broad organizationwide performance targets and the term objectives to designate specific targets set by subordinate managers in response to the broader, more inclusive goals of the whole organization. In our view, little is gained from semantic distinctions between goals and objectives. The important thing is to recognize that the results an enterprise seeks to attain vary both in scope and in time perspective. Nearly always, organizations need to have broad and narrow performance targets for both the near-term and long-term. It is inconsequential which targets are called goals and which objectives. To avoid a semantic jungle, we use the single term *objectives* to refer to the performance targets and results an organization seeks to attain. We use the adjectives *long-range* (or long-run) and *short-range* (or short-run) to identify the relevant time frame, and we try to describe objectives in words that indicate their intended scope and level in the organization.

ILLUSTRATION CAPSULE 6

EXAMPLES OF CORPORATE OBJECTIVES: MCDONALD'S, RUBBERMAID, AND MCCORMICK & COMPANY

McDonald's

- To achieve 100 percent total customer satisfaction . . . everyday . . . in every restaurant . . . for every customer.

Rubbermaid

- To increase annual sales from $1 billion to $2 billion in five years.
- To enter a new market every 18 to 24 months.
- To have 30 percent of sales each year come from products not in the company's product line five years earlier.
- To be the lowest cost, highest quality producer in the household products industry.

- To achieve a 15 percent average annual growth in sales, profits, and earnings per share.

McCormick & Company

- To achieve a 20 percent return on equity.
- To achieve a net sales growth rate of 10 percent per year.
- To maintain an average earnings per share growth rate of 15 percent per year.
- To maintain total debt-to-total capital at 40 percent or less.
- To pay out 25 percent to 35 percent of net income in dividends.
- To make selective acquisitions which complement our current businesses and can enhance our overall returns.
- To dispose of those parts of our business which do not or cannot generate adequate returns or do not fit our business strategy.

Source: Company annual reports.

Strategic objectives need to be competitor-focused, usually aiming at unseating a competitor considered to be the industry's best in a particular category.

Strategic Management Principle
Building a stronger long-term competitive position benefits shareholders more lastingly than improving short-term profitability.

tive position for the long haul. The pressures on managers to opt for better near-term financial performance and to sacrifice at least some strategic moves aimed at building a stronger competitive position are especially pronounced when (1) an enterprise is struggling financially, (2) the resource commitments for strategically beneficial moves will materially detract from the bottom line for several years, and (3) the proposed strategic moves are risky and have an uncertain market and competitive payoff.

Yet, there are dangers in management's succumbing time and again to the lure of immediate gains in margins and return on investment when it means paring or forgoing strategic moves that would build a stronger business position. A company that consistently passes up opportunities to strengthen its long-term competitive position in order to realize better near-term financial gains risks diluting its competitiveness, losing momentum in its markets, and impairing its ability to stave off market challenges from ambitious rivals. The business landscape is littered with ex–market leaders who put more emphasis on boosting next quarter's profit than strengthening long-term market position. The danger of trading off long-term gains in market position for near-term gains in bottom-line performance is greatest when a profit-conscious market leader has competitors who invest relentlessly in gaining market share in preparation for the time when they will be big and strong enough to outcompete the leader in a head-to-head market battle. One need look no further than Japanese companies' patient and persistent strategic efforts to gain market ground on their more profit-centered American and European rivals to appreciate the pitfall of letting short-term financial objectives dominate. The surest path to protecting and sustaining a company's profitability quarter after quarter and year after year is to pursue strategic actions that strengthen its competitiveness and business position.

The Concept of Strategic Intent   A company's strategic objectives are important for another reason—they indicate *strategic intent* to stake out a particular business position.[6] The strategic intent of a large company may be industry leadership on a national or global scale. The strategic intent of a small company may be to dominate a market niche. The strategic intent of an up-and-coming enterprise may be to overtake the market leaders. The strategic intent of a technologically innovative company may be to pioneer a promising discovery and open a whole new vista of products and market opportunities—as did Xerox, Apple Computer, Microsoft, Merck, and Sony.

> **Basic Concept**
> A company exhibits *strategic intent* when it relentlessly pursues a certain long-term strategic objective and concentrates its strategic actions on achieving that objective.

The time horizon underlying a company's strategic intent is long-term. Companies that rise to prominence in their markets almost invariably begin with strategic intents that are out of proportion to their immediate capabilities and market positions. But they set ambitious long-term strategic objectives and then pursue them relentlessly, sometimes even obsessively, over a 10 - to 20-year period. In the 1960s, Komatsu, Japan's leading earth-moving equipment company, was less than one-third the size of Caterpillar, had little market presence outside Japan, and depended on its small bulldozers for most of its revenue. Komatsu's strategic intent was to "encircle Caterpillar" with a broader product line and then compete globally against Caterpillar. By the late 1980s, Komatsu was the industry's second-ranking company, with a strong sales presence in North America, Europe, and Asia plus a product line that included industrial robots and semiconductors as well as a broad array of earth-moving equipment.

Often, a company's strategic intent takes on a heroic character, serving as a rallying cry for managers and employees alike to go all out and do their very best. Canon's strategic intent in copying equipment was to "Beat Xerox." Komatsu's motivating battle cry was "Beat Caterpillar." The strategic intent of the U.S. government's Apollo space program was to land a person on the moon ahead of the Soviet Union. Throughout the 1980s, Wal-Mart's strategic intent was to "overtake Sears" as the largest U.S. retailer (a feat accomplished in 1991). In such instances, strategic intent signals a deep-seated commitment to winning—unseating the industry leader, remaining the industry leader (and becoming more dominant in the process), or otherwise beating long odds to gain a significantly stronger business position. A capably managed enterprise whose strategic objectives exceed its present reach and resources can be a more formidable competitor than a company with modest strategic intent.

Long-Range versus Short-Range Objectives   An organization needs both long-range and short-range objectives. Long-range objectives serve two purposes. First, setting performance targets five or more years ahead pushes managers to take actions *now* in order to achieve the targeted long-range performance *later* (a company that has an objective of doubling its sales within five years can't wait until the third or fourth year of its five-year strategic plan to begin growing its sales and customer base!). Second, having explicit long-range objectives prompts managers to weigh the impact

---

[6]The concept of strategic intent is described in more detail in Gary Hamel and C. K. Pralahad, "Strategic Intent," *Harvard Business Review* 89, no. 3 (May–June 1989), pp. 63–76. This section draws upon their pioneering discussion.

of today's decisions on longer-range performance. Without the pressure to make progress in meeting long-range performance targets, it is human nature to base decisions on what is most expedient and worry about the future later. The problem with short-sighted decisions, of course, is that they put a company's long-term business position at greater risk.

Short-range objectives spell out the immediate and near-term results to be achieved. They indicate the *speed* at which management wants the organization to progress as well as the *level of performance* being aimed for over the next two or three periods. Short-range objectives can be identical to long-range objectives anytime an organization is already performing at the targeted long-term level. For instance, if a company has an ongoing objective of 15 percent profit growth every year and is currently achieving this objective, then the company's long-range and short-range profit objectives coincide. The most important situation where short-range objectives differ from long-range objectives occurs when managers are trying to elevate organizational performance and cannot reach the long-range/ongoing target in just one year. Short-range objectives then serve as stairsteps or milestones.

THE "CHALLENGING BUT ACHIEVABLE" TEST

Objectives should not represent whatever levels of achievement management decides would be "nice." Wishful thinking has no place in objective-setting. For objectives to serve as a tool for *stretching* an organization to reach its full potential, they must be *challenging but achievable.* Satisfying this criterion means setting objectives in light of several important "inside-outside" considerations:

Company performance targets should be challenging but achievable.

- What performance levels will industry and competitive conditions realistically allow?
- What results will it take for the organization to be a successful performer?
- What performance is the organization capable of *when pushed?*

To set challenging but achievable objectives, managers must judge what performance is possible in light of external conditions against what performance the organization is capable of achieving. The tasks of objective-setting and strategy-making often become intertwined at this point. Strategic choices, for example, cannot be made in a financial vacuum; the money has to be there to execute them. Consequently, decisions about strategy are contingent on setting the organization's financial performance objectives high enough to (1) execute the chosen strategy, (2) fund other needed actions, and (3) please investors and the financial community. Objectives and strategy also intertwine when it comes to matching the means (strategy) with the ends (objectives). If a company can't achieve established objectives (because the objectives are set unrealistically high or the present strategy can't deliver the desired performance), the objectives or the strategy need adjustment to produce a better fit.

THE NEED FOR OBJECTIVES AT ALL MANAGEMENT LEVELS

For strategic thinking and strategy-driven decision-making to permeate organization behavior, performance targets must be established not only for the organization as a whole but also for each of the organization's separate businesses, product lines, functional areas, and departments.[7] Only when every manager, from the CEO to the lowest-

---

[7]Peter F. Drucker, *Management: Tasks, Responsibilities, Practices* (New York: Harper & Row, 1974), p. 100. See also Charles H. Granger, "The Hierarchy of Objectives," *Harvard Business Review* 42, no. 3 (May–June 1963), pp. 63–74.

level manager, is held accountable for achieving specific results and when each unit's objectives support achievement of company objectives is the objective-setting process complete enough to ensure that the whole organization is headed down the chosen path and that each part of the organization knows what it needs to accomplish.

The objective-setting process is more top-down than bottom-up. To see why strategic objectives at one managerial level tend to drive objectives and strategies at the next level down, consider the following example. Suppose the senior executives of a diversified corporation establish a corporate profit objective of $5 million for next year. Suppose further, after discussion between corporate management and the general managers of the firm's five different businesses, each business is given the challenging but achievable profit objective of $1 million by year-end (i.e., if the five business divisions contribute $1 million each in profit, the corporation can reach its $5 million profit objective). A concrete result has thus been agreed on and translated into measurable action commitments at two levels in the managerial hierarchy. Next, suppose the general manager of business unit X, after some analysis and discussion with functional area managers, concludes that reaching the $1 million profit objective will require selling 100,000 units at an average price of $50 and producing them at an average cost of $40 (a $10 profit margin times 100,000 units equals $1 million profit). Consequently, the general manager and the manufacturing manager settle on a production objective of 100,000 units at a unit cost of $40; and the general manager and the marketing manager agree on a sales objective of 100,000 units and a target selling price of $50. In turn, the marketing manager breaks the sales objective of 100,000 units into unit sales targets for each sales territory, each item in the product line, and each salesperson.

A top-down process of establishing performance targets for strategy-critical activities, business processes, and departmental units is a logical way of breaking down companywide targets into pieces that lower-level units and managers are responsible for achieving. Such an approach also provides a valuable degree of *unity* and *cohesion* to objective-setting and strategy-making in different parts of the organization. Generally speaking, organizationwide objectives and strategy need to be established first so they can *guide* objective-setting and strategy-making at lower levels. Top-down objective-setting and strategizing steer lower-level units toward objectives and strategies that take their cues from those of the total enterprise. When objective-setting and strategy-making begin at the bottom levels of an organization and organizationwide objectives and strategies reflect the aggregate of what has bubbled up from below, the resulting strategic action plan is likely to be inconsistent, fragmented, or uncoordinated. Bottom-up objective-setting, with no guidance from above, nearly always signals an absence of strategic leadership on the part of senior executives.

Strategic Management Principle
Objective-setting needs to be more of a top-down than a bottom-up process in order to guide lower-level managers and organizational units toward outcomes that support the achievement of overall business and company objectives.

CRAFTING A STRATEGY: THE THIRD DIRECTION-SETTING TASK

Organizations need strategies to guide *how* to achieve objectives and *how* to pursue the organization's mission. Strategy-making is all about *how*—how to reach performance targets, how to outcompete rivals, how to achieve sustainable competitive advantage, how to strengthen the enterprise's long-term business position, how to make management's strategic vision for the company a reality. A strategy is needed for the company as a whole, for each business the company is in, and for each functional piece of each business—R&D, purchasing, production, sales and marketing, finance, human resources, and so on. An organization's overall strategy and

Basic Concept
An organization's *strategy* is all about *how* to get the company from where it is to where it wants to go—it is the means to achieving the desired end results.

managerial game plan emerge from the *pattern* of actions already initiated and the plans managers have for fresh moves. In forming a strategy out of the many feasible options, a manager acts as a forger of responses to market change, a seeker of new opportunities, and a synthesizer of the different moves and approaches taken at various times in various parts of the organization.[8]

The strategy-making spotlight, however, needs to be kept trained on the important facets of management's game plan for running the enterprise—those actions that determine what market position the company is trying to stake out and that underpin whether the company will succeed. Low-priority issues (whether to increase the advertising budget, raise the dividend, locate a new plant in country X or country Y) and routine managerial housekeeping (whether to own or lease company vehicles, how to reduce sales force turnover) are not basic to the strategy, even though they must be dealt with. Strategy is inherently action-oriented; it concerns what to do, when to do it, and who should be involved. Unless there is action, unless something happens, unless somebody does something, strategic thinking and planning simply go to waste and, in the end, amount to nothing.

An organization's strategy evolves over time. It's seldom possible to plan all the bits and pieces of a company's strategy in advance and then go for long periods without change. Reacting and responding to happenings either inside the company or in the surrounding environment is a normal part of the strategy-making process. The dynamic and partly unpredictable character of competition, budding trends in buyer needs and expectations, unplanned increases or decreases in costs, mergers and acquisitions among major industry players, new regulations, the raising or lowering of trade barriers, and countless other events can make parts of the strategy obsolete. There is always something new to react to and some new strategic window opening up. This is why the task of crafting strategy is never ending. And it is why a company's actual strategy turns out to be a blend of its intended or planned strategy and its unplanned reactions to fresh developments.

THE STRATEGY-MAKING PYRAMID

As we emphasized in the opening chapter, strategy-making is not just a task for senior executives. In large enterprises, decisions about what approaches to take and what new moves to initiate involve senior executives in the corporate office, heads of business units and product divisions, the heads of major functional areas within a business or division (manufacturing, marketing and sales, finance, human resources, and the like), plant managers, product managers, district and regional sales managers, and lower-level supervisors. In diversified enterprises, strategies are initiated at four distinct organization levels. There's a strategy for the company and all of its businesses as a whole *(corporate strategy)*. There's a strategy for each separate business the company has diversified into *(business strategy)*. Then there is a strategy for each specific functional unit within a business *(functional strategy)*—each business usually has a production strategy, a marketing strategy, a finance strategy, and so on. And, finally, there are still narrower strategies for basic operating units—plants, sales districts and regions, and departments within functional areas *(operating strategy)*. Figure 2–1 shows the strategy-making pyramid for a diversified company. In single-business enterprises, there are only three levels of strategy-making (business strategy, functional strategy, and operating strategy) unless diversification into other businesses becomes an active

---

[8]Henry Mintzberg, "The Strategy Concept II: Another Look at Why Organizations Need Strategies," California Management Review 30, no. 1 (Fall 1987), pp. 25–32.

F I G U R E 2-1 | **The Strategy-Making Pyramid**

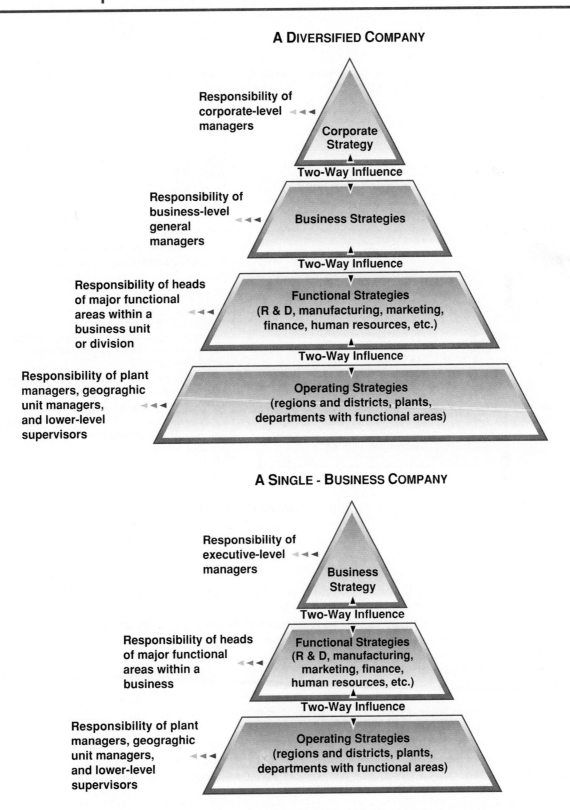

T A B L E 2–1 | **How the Strategy-Making Task Tends to Be Shared**

Strategy Level	Lead Responsibility	Primary Strategy-Making Concerns at Each Managerial Level
• Corporate strategy	• CEO, other key executives (decisions are typically reviewed/approved by boards of directors)	• Building and managing a high-performing portfolio of business units (making acquisitions, strengthening existing business positions, divesting businesses that no longer fit into management's plans) • Capturing the synergy among related business units and turning it into competitive advantage • Establishing investment priorities and steering corporate resources into businesses with the most attractive opportunities • Reviewing/revising/unifying the major strategic approaches and moves proposed by business-unit managers
• Business strategies	• General manager/head of business unit (decisions are typically reviewed/approved by a senior executive or a board of directors)	• Devising moves and approaches to compete successfully and to secure a competitive advantage • Forming responses to changing external conditions • Uniting the strategic initiatives of key functional departments • Taking action to address company-specific issues and operating problems
• Functional strategies	• Functional managers (decisions are typically reviewed/approved by business-unit head)	• Crafting moves and approaches to support business strategy and to achieve functional/departmental performance objectives • Reviewing/revising/unifying strategy-related moves and approaches proposed by lower-level managers
• Operating strategies	• Field-unit heads/lower-level managers within functional areas (decisions are reviewed/approved by functional area head/department head)	• Crafting still narrower and more specific approaches/moves aimed at supporting functional and business strategies and at achieving operating-unit objectives

consideration. Table 2–1 highlights the kinds of strategic actions that distinguish each of the four strategy-making levels.

CORPORATE STRATEGY

Corporate strategy is the overall managerial game plan for a diversified company. Corporate strategy extends companywide—an umbrella over all a diversified company's businesses. It consists of the moves made to establish business positions in different industries and the approaches used to manage the company's group of businesses. Figure 2–2 depicts the core elements that identify a diversified company's corporate strategy. Crafting corporate strategy for a diversified company involves four kinds of initiatives:

> **Basic Concept**
> *Corporate strategy* concerns how a diversified company intends to establish business positions in different industries and the actions and approaches employed to improve the performance of the group of businesses the company has diversified into.

1. *Making the moves to accomplish diversification.* The first concern in diversification is what the company's portfolio of businesses should consist of—specifically, what industries to diversify into, and whether to enter the industries by starting a new business or acquiring another company (an established leader, an up-and-coming company, or a troubled company with

FIGURE 2–2 | Identifying the Corporate Strategy of a Diversified Company

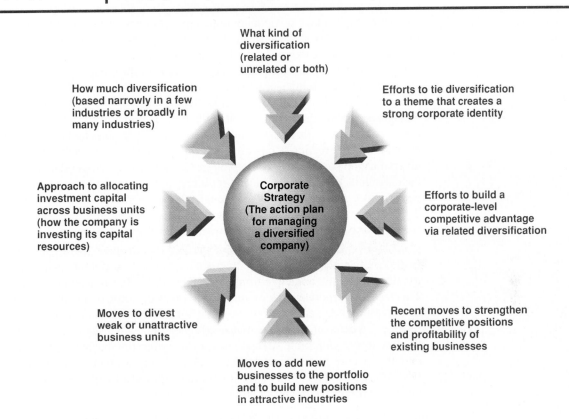

turnaround potential). This piece of corporate strategy establishes whether diversification is based narrowly in a few industries or broadly in many industries, and it shapes how the company will be positioned in each of the target industries.

2. *Initiating actions to boost the combined performance of the businesses the firm has diversified into.* As positions are created in the chosen industries, corporate strategy-making concentrates on ways to get better performance out of the business-unit portfolio. Decisions must be reached about how to strengthen the long-term competitive positions and profitabilities of the businesses the firm has invested in. Corporate parents can help their business subsidiaries be more successful by financing additional capacity and efficiency improvements, by supplying missing skills and managerial know-how, by acquiring another company in the same industry and merging the two operations into a stronger business, and/or by acquiring new businesses that strongly complement existing businesses. The overall plan for managing a group of diversified businesses usually involves pursuing rapid-growth strategies in the most promising businesses, keeping the other core businesses healthy, initiating turnaround efforts in weak-performing businesses with potential, and divesting businesses that are no longer attractive or that don't fit into management's long-range plans.

3. *Finding ways to capture the synergy among related business units and turn it into competitive advantage.* When a company diversifies into businesses with

related technologies, similar operating characteristics, the same distribution channels, common customers, or some other synergistic relationship, it gains competitive advantage potential not open to a company that diversifies into totally unrelated businesses. Related diversification presents opportunities to transfer skills, share expertise, or share facilities, thereby reducing overall costs, strengthening the competitiveness of some of the company's products, or enhancing the capabilities of particular business units—any of which can represent a significant source of competitive advantage. The greater the relatedness among the businesses of a diversified company, the greater the opportunities for skills transfer and/or sharing across businesses and the bigger the window for creating competitive advantage. Indeed, what makes related diversification so attractive is the synergistic *strategic fit* across related business units that allows company resources to be leveraged into a combined performance *greater* than the units could achieve operating independently. The $2 + 2 = 5$ aspect of strategic fit makes related diversification a very appealing strategy for boosting corporate performance and shareholder value.

4. *Establishing investment priorities and steering corporate resources into the most attractive business units.* A diversified company's different businesses are usually not equally attractive from the standpoint of investing additional funds. This facet of corporate strategy-making involves deciding on the priorities— i.e., investing more capital in some of the businesses and channeling resources into areas where earnings potentials are higher and away from areas where they are lower. Corporate strategy may include divesting business units that are chronically poor performers or those in an increasingly unattractive industry. Divestiture frees up unproductive investments for redeployment to promising business units or for financing attractive new acquisitions.

Corporate strategy is crafted at the highest levels of management. Senior corporate executives normally have lead responsibility for devising corporate strategy and for choosing among whatever recommended actions bubble up from lower-level managers. Key business-unit heads may also be influential, especially in strategic decisions affecting the businesses they head. Major strategic decisions are usually reviewed and approved by the company's board of directors.

Business Strategy

Basic Concept

Business strategy concerns the actions and the approaches crafted by management to produce successful performance in one specific line of business; the central business strategy issue is *how* to build a stronger long-term competitive position.

The term *business strategy* (or business-level strategy) refers to the managerial game plan for a single business. It is mirrored in the pattern of approaches and moves crafted by management to produce successful performance in *one specific line of business*. The core elements of business strategy are illustrated in Figure 2–3. For a stand-alone single-business company, corporate strategy and business strategy are one and the same since there is only one business to form a strategy for. The distinction between corporate strategy and business strategy is relevant only for diversified firms.

The central thrust of business strategy is how to build and strengthen the company's long-term competitive position in the marketplace. Toward this end, business strategy is concerned principally with (1) forming responses to changes under way in the industry, the economy at large, the regulatory and political arena, and other relevant areas, (2) crafting competitive moves and market approaches that can lead to sustainable competitive advantage, (3) uniting the strategic initiatives of functional departments, and (4) addressing specific strategic issues facing the company's business.

Clearly, business strategy encompasses whatever moves and new approaches managers deem prudent in light of market forces, economic trends and developments, buyer needs and demographics, new legislation and regulatory requirements, and other such broad external factors. A good strategy is well-matched to the external situation; as the external environment changes in significant ways, then adjustments in strategy are made on an as-needed basis. Whether a company's response to external change is quick or slow tends to be a function of how long events must unfold before managers can assess their implications and how much longer it then takes to form a strategic response. Some external changes, of course, require little or no response, while others call for significant strategy alterations. On occasion, external factors change in ways that pose a formidable strategic hurdle—for example, cigarette manufacturers face a tough challenge holding their own against the mounting antismoking campaign.

What separates a powerful business strategy from a weak one is the strategist's ability *to forge a series of moves and approaches capable of producing sustainable competitive advantage.* With a competitive advantage, a company has good prospects for above-average profitability and success in the industry. Without competitive advantage, a company risks being outcompeted by stronger rivals and locked into

FIGURE 2-3 | **Identifying Strategy for a Single-Business Company**

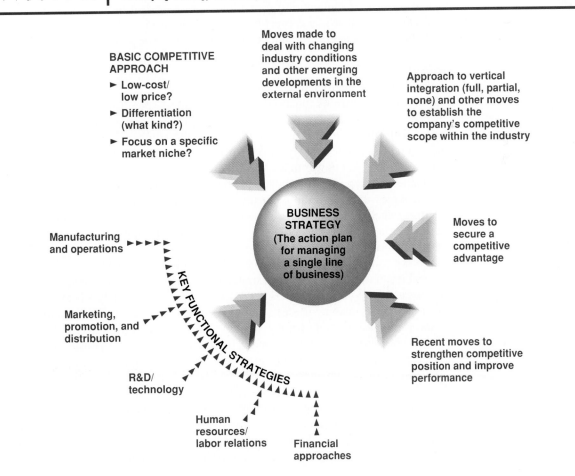

A business strategy is powerful if it produces a sizable and sustainable competitive advantage; it is weak if it results in competitive disadvantage.

mediocre performance. Crafting a business strategy that yields sustainable competitive advantage has three facets: (1) deciding where a firm has the best chance to win a competitive edge, (2) developing product/service attributes that have strong buyer appeal and set the company apart from rivals, and (3) neutralizing the competitive moves of rival companies.

A company's strategy for competing is typically both offensive and defensive—some actions are aggressive and amount to direct challenges to competitors' market positions; others counter fresh moves made by rivals. Three of the most frequently used competitive approaches are (1) striving to be the industry's low-cost producer (thereby aiming for a cost-based competitive advantage over rivals), (2) pursuing differentiation based on such advantages as quality, performance, service, styling, technological superiority, or unusually good value, and (3) focusing on a narrow market niche and winning a competitive edge by doing a better job than rivals of serving the special needs and tastes of its buyers.

Internally, business strategy involves taking actions to develop the skills and capabilities needed to achieve competitive advantage. Successful business strategies usually aim at building the company's competence in one or more core activities crucial to strategic success and then using the core competence as a basis for winning a competitive edge over rivals. A *core competence* is something a firm does especially well in comparison to rival companies. It thus represents a source of competitive strength. Core competencies can relate to R&D, mastery of a technological process, manufacturing capability, sales and distribution, customer service, or anything else that is a competitively important aspect of creating, producing, or marketing the company's product or service. *A core competence is a basis for competitive advantage because it represents specialized expertise that rivals don't have and cannot readily match.*

On a broader internal front, business strategy must also aim at uniting strategic initiatives in the various functional areas of business (purchasing, production, R&D, finance, human resources, sales and marketing, and distribution). Strategic actions are needed in each functional area to *support* the company's competitive approach and overall business strategy. Strategic unity and coordination across the various functional areas add power to the business strategy.

Business strategy also extends to action plans for addressing any special strategy-related issues unique to the company's competitive position and internal situation (such as whether to add new capacity, replace an obsolete plant, increase R&D funding for a promising technology, or reduce burdensome interest expenses). Such custom tailoring of strategy to fit a company's specific situation is one of the reasons why every company in an industry has a different business strategy.

Lead responsibility for business strategy falls in the lap of the manager in charge of the business. Even if the business head does not personally wield a heavy hand in the business strategy-making process, preferring to delegate much of the task to others, he or she is still accountable for the strategy and the results it produces. The business head, as chief strategist for the business, has at least two other responsibilities. The first is seeing that supporting strategies in each of the major functional areas of the business are well-conceived and consistent with each other. The second is getting major strategic moves approved by higher authority (the board of directors and/or corporate-level officers) if needed and keeping them informed of important new developments, deviations from plan, and potential strategy revisions. In diversified companies, business-unit heads may have the additional obligation of making sure business-level objectives and strategy conform to corporate-level objectives and strategy themes.

FUNCTIONAL STRATEGY

The term *functional strategy* refers to the managerial game plan for a particular department or key functional activity within a business. A company's marketing strategy, for example, represents the managerial game plan for running the marketing part of the business. A company needs a functional strategy for every major departmental unit and piece of the business—for R&D, production, marketing, customer service, distribution, finance, human resources, and so on. Functional strategies, while narrower in scope than business strategy, add relevant detail to the overall business game plan by setting out the actions, approaches, and practices to be employed in managing a particular department or business function. The primary role of a functional strategy is to *support* the company's overall business strategy and competitive approach. A related role is to create a managerial roadmap for achieving the functional area's objectives and mission. Thus, functional strategy in the production/manufacturing area represents the game plan for *how* manufacturing activities will be managed to support business strategy and achieve the manufacturing department's objectives and mission. Functional strategy in the finance area consists of *how* financial activities will be managed in supporting business strategy and achieving the finance department's objectives and mission.

Lead responsibility for strategy-making in the functional areas of a business is normally delegated to the respective functional department heads unless the business-unit head decides to exert a strong influence. In crafting strategy, a functional department head ideally works closely with key subordinates and touches base with the heads of other functional areas and the business head often. If functional heads plot strategy independent of each other or the business head they open the door for uncoordinated or conflicting strategies. Compatible, mutually reinforcing functional strategies are essential for the overall business strategy to have maximum impact. Plainly, a business's marketing strategy, production strategy, finance strategy, and human resources strategy should be in sync rather than serving their own narrower purposes. Coordination across functional area strategies is best accomplished during the deliberation stage. If inconsistent functional strategies are sent up the line for final approval, the business head must spot the conflicts and get them resolved.

OPERATING STRATEGY

Operating strategies concern the even narrower strategic initiatives and approaches for managing key operating units (plants, sales districts, distribution centers) and for handling daily operating tasks with strategic significance (advertising campaigns, materials purchasing, inventory control, maintenance, shipping). Operating strategies, while of lesser scope, add further detail and completeness to functional strategies and to the overall business plan. Lead responsibility for operating strategies is usually delegated to front-line managers, subject to review and approval by higher-ranking managers.

Even though operating strategy is at the bottom of the strategy-making pyramid, its importance should not be downplayed. For example, a major plant that fails in its strategy to achieve production volume, unit cost, and quality targets can undercut the achievement of company sales and profit objectives and wreak havoc with the whole company's strategic efforts to build a quality image with customers. One cannot reliably judge the importance of a given strategic move by the organizational or managerial level where it is initiated.

Basic Concept
Functional strategy concerns the managerial game plan for running a major functional activity within a business—R&D, production, marketing, customer service, distribution, finance, human resources, and so on; a business needs as many functional strategies as it has major activities.

Basic Concept
Operating strategies concern how to manage key organizational units within a business (plants, sales districts, distribution centers) and how to perform strategically significant operating tasks (materials purchasing, inventory control, maintenance, shipping, advertising campaigns).

Frontline managers are part of an organization's strategy-making team because many operating units have strategy-critical performance targets and need to have strategic action plans in place to achieve them. A regional manager needs a strategy customized to the region's particular situation and objectives. A plant manager needs a strategy for accomplishing the plant's objectives, carrying out the plant's part of the company's overall manufacturing game plan, and dealing with any strategy-related problems that exist at the plant. A company's advertising manager needs a strategy for getting maximum audience exposure and sales impact from the ad budget. The following two examples illustrate how operating strategy supports higher-level strategies:

- A company with a low-price, high-volume business strategy and a need to achieve low manufacturing costs launches a companywide effort to boost worker productivity by 10 percent. To contribute to the productivity-boosting objective: (1) the manager of employee recruiting develops a strategy for interviewing and testing job applicants that is thorough enough to weed out all but the most highly motivated, best-qualified candidates; (2) the manager of information systems devises a way to use office technology to boost the productivity of office workers; (3) the employee benefits manager devises an improved incentive-compensation plan to reward increased output by manufacturing employees; and (4) the purchasing manager launches a program to obtain new efficiency-increasing tools and equipment in quicker, less costly fashion.
- A distributor of plumbing equipment emphasizes quick delivery and accurate order-filling as keystones of its customer service approach. To support this strategy, the warehouse manager (1) develops an inventory stocking strategy that allows 99 percent of all orders to be completely filled without back ordering any item and (2) institutes a warehouse staffing strategy that allows any order to be shipped within 24 hours.

UNITING THE STRATEGY-MAKING EFFORT

Objectives and strategies that are unified from an organization's top-management levels to its bottom-management levels do not come from an undirected process where managers at each level have objective-setting and strategy-making autonomy.

The previous discussion underscores that *a company's strategic plan is a collection of strategies* devised by different managers at different levels in the organizational hierarchy. The larger the enterprise, the more points of strategic initiative it has. Management's direction-setting effort is not complete until the separate layers of strategy are unified into a coherent, supportive pattern. Ideally the pieces and layers of strategy should fit together like the pieces of a picture puzzle. Unified objectives and strategies don't emerge from an undirected process where managers at each level set objectives and craft strategies independently. Indeed, functional and operating-level managers have a duty to set performance targets and invent strategic actions that will help achieve business objectives and make business strategy more effective.

Harmonizing objectives and strategies piece by piece and level by level can be tedious and frustrating, requiring numerous consultations and meetings, annual strategy review and approval processes, the experience of trial and error, and months (sometimes years) of consensus building. The politics of gaining strategic consensus and the battle of trying to keep all managers and departments focused on what's best for the total enterprise (as opposed to what's best for their departments or careers) are often big obstacles in unifying the layers of objectives and strategies.[9] Broad consen-

---

[9] Functional managers are sometimes more interested in doing what is best for their own areas, building their own empires, and consolidating their personal power and organizational influence than they are in cooperating with other functional managers to unify behind the overall business strategy. As a result, it's easy for functional area support strategies to conflict, thereby forcing the business-level general manager to spend time and energy refereeing functional strategy conflicts and building support for a more unified approach.

sus is particularly difficult when there is ample room for opposing views and disagreement. Managerial discussions about an organization's mission, basic direction, objectives and strategies often provoke heated debate and strong differences of opinion.

Figure 2–4 portrays the networking of objectives and strategies through the managerial hierarchy. The two-way arrows indicate that there are simultaneous bottom-up and top-down influences on missions, objectives, and strategies at each level. These vertical linkages, if managed in a way that promotes coordination, can help unify the direction-setting and strategy-making activities of many managers into a mutually reinforcing pattern. The tighter that coordination is enforced, the tighter the linkages in the missions, objectives, and strategies of the various organizational units. Tight linkages safeguard against organizational units straying from the company's charted strategic course.

As a practical matter, however, corporate and business missions, objectives, and strategies need to be clearly outlined and communicated down the line before much progress can be made in direction-setting and strategy-making at the functional and operating levels. Direction and guidance need to flow from the corporate level to the business level and from the business level to the functional and operating levels. The strategic disarray that occurs in an organization when senior managers don't exercise strong top-down direction-setting and strategic leadership is akin to what would happen to a football team's offensive performance if the quarterback decided not to call a play for the team, but instead let each player pick whatever play he thought would work best at his respective position. In business, as in sports, all the strategy-makers in a company are on the same team. They are obligated to perform their strategy-making tasks in a manner that benefits the whole company, not in a manner that suits personal or departmental interests. A company's strategy is at full power only when its many pieces are united. This means that the strategizing process proceeds more from the top down than from the bottom up. Lower-level managers cannot do good strategy-making without understanding the company's long-term direction and higher-level strategies.

> Consistency between business strategy and functional/operating strategies comes from organizationwide allegiance to business objectives; functional and operating-level managers have a duty to set performance targets and invent strategic actions that will help achieve business objectives and improve the execution of business strategy.

THE FACTORS THAT SHAPE A COMPANY'S STRATEGY

Many situational considerations enter into crafting strategy. Figure 2–5 depicts the primary factors that shape a company's strategic approaches. The interplay of these factors and the influence that each has on the strategy-making process vary from company to company. No two strategic choices are made in exactly the same context; even in the same industry situational factors differ enough from company to company that each company ends up pursuing a customized strategy. This is why carefully sizing up all the various situational factors, both external and internal, is the starting point in crafting strategy.

SOCIETAL, POLITICAL, REGULATORY, AND CITIZENSHIP CONSIDERATIONS

What an enterprise can and cannot do strategywise is always constrained by what is legal, by what complies with government policies and regulatory requirements, by what is socially acceptable, and by what constitutes community citizenship. Outside pressures also come from other sources—special interest groups, the glare of investigative reporting, a fear of unwanted political action, and the stigma of negative

> Societal, political, regulatory, and citizenship factors limit the strategic actions a company can or should take.

FIGURE 2-4 | The Networking of Missions, Objectives, and Strategies in the Strategy-Making Pyramid

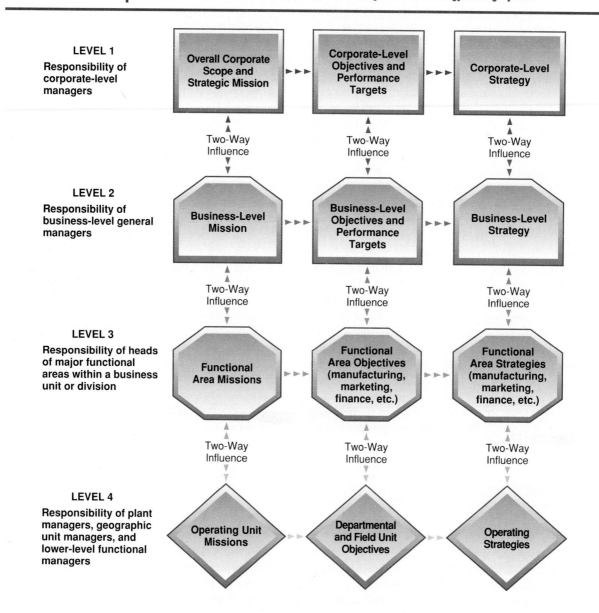

opinion. Societal concerns over health and nutrition, alcohol and drug abuse, hazardous waste disposal, sexual harassment, and the impact of plant closings on local communities affect the strategies of many companies. American concerns over the size of foreign imports and political debate over whether to impose tariffs to cure the chronic U.S. trade deficit are driving forces in the strategic decisions of Japanese and European companies to locate plants in the United States. Heightened awareness of the dangers of cholesterol have prompted most food products companies to phase out high-fat ingredients and substitute low-fat ingredients, despite the extra costs.

Factoring in societal values and priorities, community concerns, and the potential

F I G U R E 2-5 | Factors Shaping the Choice of Company Strategy

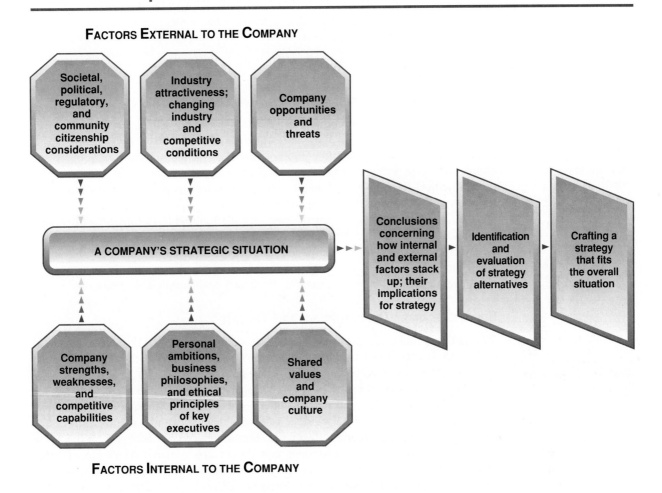

F I G U R E 2-5 | Factors Shaping the Choice of Company Strategy

for onerous legislation and regulatory requirements is a regular part of external situation analysis at more and more companies. Intense public pressure and adverse media coverage make such a practice prudent. The task of making an organization's strategy socially responsible means (1) conducting organizational activities within the bounds of what is considered ethical and in the general public interest; (2) responding positively to emerging societal priorities and expectations; (3) demonstrating a willingness to take action ahead of regulatory confrontation; (4) balancing stockholder interests against the larger interests of society as a whole; and (5) being a good citizen in the community.

Corporate social responsibility is showing up in company mission statements. John Hancock, for example, concludes its mission statement with the following sentence:

In pursuit of this mission, we will strive to exemplify the highest standards of business ethics and personal integrity; and shall recognize our corporate obligation to the social and economic well-being of our community.

At Union Electric, a St. Louis–based utility company, the following statement is official corporate policy:

> As a private enterprise entrusted with an essential public service, we recognize our civic responsibility in the communities we serve. We shall strive to advance the growth and welfare of these communities and shall participate in civic activities which fulfill that goal—for we believe this is both good citizenship and good business.

INDUSTRY ATTRACTIVENESS AND COMPETITIVE CONDITIONS

Industry attractiveness and competitive conditions are big strategy-determining factors. A company's assessment of the industry and competitive environment has a direct bearing on how it should try to position itself in the industry and on its basic competitive strategy approach. When competitive conditions intensify significantly, a company must respond with strategic actions to protect its position. Fresh moves on the part of rival companies, changes in the industry's price-cost-profit economics, and new technological developments can alter the requirements for competitive success and mandate reconsideration of strategy. When a firm concludes its industry environment has grown unattractive and it is better off investing company resources elsewhere, it may begin a strategy of disinvestment and eventual abandonment. A strategist, therefore, has to be a student of industry and competitive conditions.

SPECIFIC MARKET OPPORTUNITIES AND THREATS

The particular business opportunities open to a company and the threatening external developments that it faces are key influences on strategy. They both point to the need for strategic action. A company's strategy needs to be deliberately aimed at capturing its best growth opportunities, especially the ones that hold the most promise for building sustainable competitive advantage and enhancing profitability. Likewise, strategy should be geared to providing a defense against external threats to the company's well-being and future performance. For strategy to be successful, it has to be well-matched to market opportunities and threatening external developments; this usually means crafting offensive moves to capitalize on the company's most promising market opportunities and crafting defensive moves to protect the company's competitive position and long-term profitability.

ORGANIZATIONAL STRENGTHS, WEAKNESSES, AND COMPETITIVE CAPABILITIES

Experience shows management should build strategy around what the company does well and avoid strategies whose success depends on something the company does poorly or has never done at all. In short, *strategy must be well-matched to company strengths, weaknesses, and competitive capabilities*. Pursuing an opportunity without the organizational competencies and resources to capture it is foolish. An organization's strengths make some opportunities and strategies attractive; likewise its internal weaknesses and its present competitive market position make certain strategies risky or even out of the question.

One of the most pivotal strategy-shaping internal considerations is whether a company has or can build the core strengths or competencies needed to execute a strategy proficiently. An organization's core strengths—the things it does especially well—are an important strategy-making consideration because of (1) the skills and capabilities they provide in capitalizing on a particular opportunity, (2) the competitive edge they

---

Strategic Management Principle

A company's strategy ought to be closely matched to industry and competitive conditions.

Strategic Management Principle

A well-conceived strategy aims at capturing a company's best growth opportunities and defending against external threats to its well-being and future performance.

Strategic Management Principle

A company's strategy ought to be grounded in what it is good at doing (i.e., its organizational strengths and competitive capabilities); it is perilous for success to depend on what it is not so good at doing (i.e., its organizational and competitive weaknesses).

may give a firm in the marketplace, and (3) the potential they have for becoming a cornerstone of strategy. The best path to competitive advantage is found where a firm has core strengths in one or more of the key requirements for market success, where rivals do not have matching or offsetting competencies, and where rivals can't develop comparable strengths except at high cost and/or over an extended period of time.[10]

Even if an organization has no outstanding core competencies (and many do not), it still must shape its strategy to suit its particular skills and available resources. It never makes sense to develop a strategic plan that cannot be executed with the skills and resources a firm is able to muster.

THE PERSONAL AMBITIONS, BUSINESS PHILOSOPHIES, AND ETHICAL BELIEFS OF MANAGERS

Managers do not dispassionately assess what strategic course to steer. Their choices are often influenced by their own vision of how to compete and how to position the enterprise and by what image and standing they want the company to have. Both casual observation and formal studies indicate that managers' ambitions, values, business philosophies, attitudes toward risk, and ethical beliefs have important influences on strategy.[11] Sometimes the influence of a manager's personal values, experiences, and emotions is conscious and deliberate; at other times it may be unconscious. As one expert noted in explaining the relevance of personal factors to strategy, "People have to have their hearts in it."[12]

> The personal ambitions, business philosophies, and ethical beliefs of managers are usually stamped on the strategies they craft.

Several examples of how business philosophies and personal values enter into strategy-making are particularly noteworthy. Japanese managers are strong proponents of strategies that take a long-term view and that aim at building market share and competitive position. In contrast, some U.S. corporate executives and Wall Street financiers draw criticism for overemphasizing short-term profits at the expense of long-term competitive positioning and for being more attracted to strategies involving a financial play on assets (leveraged buyouts and stock buybacks) rather than using corporate resources to make long-term strategic investments. Japanese companies also display a quite different philosophy regarding the role of suppliers. Their preferred supplier strategy is to enter into long-term partnership arrangements with key suppliers because they believe that working closely with the same supplier year after year improves the quality and reliability of component parts, permits just-in-time delivery, and reduces inventory carrying costs. In U.S. and European companies, the traditional strategic approach has been to play suppliers off against one another, doing business on a short-term basis with whoever offers the best price and promises acceptable quality.

Attitudes toward risk also have a big influence on strategy. Risk-avoiders are inclined toward "conservative" strategies that minimize downside risk, have a quick payback, and produce sure short-term profits. Risk-takers lean more toward oppor-

---

[10]David T. Kollat, Roger D. Blackwell, and James F. Robeson, *Strategic Marketing* (New York: Holt, Rinehart & Winston, 1972), p. 24.

[11]See, for instance, William D. Guth and Renato Tagiuri, "Personal Values and Corporate Strategy," *Harvard Business Review* 43, no. 5 (September–October 1965), pp. 123–32; Kenneth R. Andrews, *The Concept of Corporate Strategy,* 3rd ed. (Homewood, Ill.: Richard D. Irwin, 1987), chap. 4; and Richard F. Vancil, "Strategy Formulation in Complex Organizations," *Sloan Management Review* 17, no. 2 (Winter 1986), pp. 4–5.

[12]Andrews, *The Concept of Corporate Strategy,* p. 63.

tunistic strategies where visionary moves can produce a big payoff over the long term. Risk-takers prefer innovation to imitation and bold strategic offensives to defensive moves to protect the status quo.

Managerial values also shape the ethical quality of a firm's strategy. Managers with strong ethical convictions take pains to see that their companies observe a strict code of ethics in all aspects of the business. They expressly forbid such practices as accepting or giving kickbacks, badmouthing rivals' products, and buying political influence with political contributions. Instances where a company's strategic actions run afoul of high ethical standards include charging excessive interest rates on credit card balances, employing bait-and-switch sales tactics, continuing to market products suspected of having safety problems, and using ingredients that are known health hazards.

THE INFLUENCE OF SHARED VALUES AND COMPANY CULTURE ON STRATEGY

An organization's policies, practices, traditions, philosophical beliefs, and ways of doing things combine to give it a distinctive culture. A company's strategic actions typically reflect its cultural traits and managerial values. In some cases a company's core beliefs and culture even dominate the choice of strategic moves. This is because culture-related values and beliefs become so embedded in management's strategic thinking and actions that they condition how the enterprise responds to external events. Such firms have a culture-driven bias about how to handle strategic issues and what kinds of strategic moves it will consider or reject. Strong cultural influences partly account for why companies gain reputations for such strategic traits as technological leadership, product innovation, dedication to superior craftsmanship, a proclivity for financial wheeling and dealing, a desire to grow rapidly by acquiring other companies, a strong people-orientation, or unusual emphasis on customer service and total customer satisfaction.

In recent years, more companies began to articulate the core beliefs and values underlying their business approaches. One company expressed its core beliefs and values like this:

> We are market-driven. We believe that functional excellence, combined with teamwork across functions and profit centers, is essential to achieving superb execution. We believe that people are central to everything we will accomplish. We believe that honesty, integrity, and fairness should be the cornerstone of our relationships with consumers, customers, suppliers, stockholders, and employees.

Wal-Mart's founder, Sam Walton, was a fervent believer in frugality, hard work, constant improvement, dedication to customers, and genuine care for employees. The company's commitment to these values is deeply ingrained in its strategy of low prices, good values, friendly service, productivity through the intelligent use of technology, and hard-nosed bargaining with suppliers.[13] At Hewlett-Packard, the company's basic values, known internally as "the HP Way," include sharing the company's success with employees, showing trust and respect for employees, providing customers with products and services of the greatest value, being genuinely interested in

A company's values and culture can dominate the kinds of strategic moves it considers or rejects.

---

[13]Sam Walton with John Huey, *Sam Walton: Made in America* (New York: Doubleday, 1992); and John P. Kotter and James L. Heskett, *Corporate Culture and Performance* (New York: Free Press, 1992), pp. 17 and 36.

providing customers with effective solutions to their problems, making profit a high stockholder priority, avoiding the use of long-term debt to finance growth, individual initiative and creativity, teamwork, and being a good corporate citizen.[14] At both Wal-Mart and Hewlett-Packard, the value systems are deeply ingrained and widely shared by managers and employees. Whenever this happens, values and beliefs are more than an expression of nice platitudes; they become a way of life within the company.[15]

LINKING STRATEGY WITH ETHICS

Strategy ought to be ethical. It should involve rightful actions, not wrongful ones; otherwise it won't pass the test of moral scrutiny. This means more than conforming to what is legal. Ethical and moral standards go beyond the prohibitions of law and the language of "thou shalt not" to the issues of *duty* and the language of "should do and should not do." Ethics concerns human duty and the principles on which this duty rests.[16]

> Every strategic action a company takes should be ethical.

Every business has an ethical duty to each of five constituencies: owners/share-holders, employees, customers, suppliers, and the community at large. Each of these constituencies affects the organization and is affected by it. Each is a stakeholder in the enterprise, with certain expectations as to what the enterprise should do and how it should do it.[17] Owners/shareholders, for instance, rightly expect a return on their investment. Even though investors may individually differ in their preferences for profits now versus profits later, their tolerances for greater risk, and their enthusiasm for exercising social responsibility, business executives have a moral duty to pursue profitable management of the owners' investment.

A company's duty to employees arises out of respect for the worth and dignity of individuals who devote their energies to the business and who depend on the business for their economic well-being. Principled strategy-making requires that employee-related decisions be made equitably and compassionately, with concern for due process and for the impact that strategic change has on employees' lives. At best, the chosen strategy should promote employee interests as concerns wage and salary levels, career opportunities, job security, and overall working conditions. At worst, the chosen strategy should not disadvantage employees. Even in crisis situations where adverse employee impact cannot be avoided, businesses have an ethical duty to minimize whatever hardships have to be imposed in the form of workforce reductions, plant closings, job transfers, relocations, retraining, and loss of income.

> A company has ethical duties to owners, employees, customers, suppliers, the communities where it operates, and the public at large.

The duty to the customer arises out of expectations that attend the purchase of a good or service. Inadequate appreciation of this duty led to product liability laws and a host of regulatory agencies to protect consumers. All kinds of strategy-related ethical issues still arise here, however. Should a seller inform consumers *fully* about the contents of its product, especially if it contains ingredients that, though officially approved for use, are suspected of having potentially harmful effects? Is it ethical for the makers of alcoholic beverages to sponsor college events, given that many college

---

[14]Kotter and Heskett, *Corporate Culture and Performance,* pp. 60–61.

[15]For another example of the impact of values and beliefs, see Richard T. Pascale, "Perspectives on Strategy: The Real Story behind Honda's Success," in Glenn Carroll and David Vogel, *Strategy and Organization: A West Coast Perspective* (Marshfield, Mass.: Pitman Publishing, 1984), p. 60.

[16]Harry Downs, "Business Ethics: The Stewardship of Power," working paper provided to the authors.

[17]Ibid.

students are under 21? Is it ethical for cigarette manufacturers to advertise at all (even though it is legal)? Is it ethical for manufacturers to produce and sell products they know have faulty parts or defective designs that may not become apparent until after the warranty expires?

A company's ethical duty to its suppliers arises out of the market relationship that exists between them. They are both partners and adversaries. They are partners in the sense that the quality of suppliers' parts affects the quality of a firm's own product. They are adversaries in the sense that the supplier wants the highest price and profit it can get while the buyer wants a cheaper price, better quality, and speedier service. A company confronts several ethical issues in its supplier relationships. Is it ethical to threaten to cease doing business with a supplier unless the supplier agrees not to do business with key competitors? Is it ethical to reveal one supplier's price quote to a rival supplier? Is it ethical to accept gifts from suppliers? Is it ethical to pay a supplier in cash?

A company's ethical duty to the community at large stems from its status as a citizen of the community and as an institution of society. Communities and society are reasonable in expecting businesses to be good citizens—to pay their fair share of taxes for fire and police protection, waste removal, streets and highways, and so on, and to exercise care in the impact their activities have on the environment and on the communities in which they operate. The community and public interest should be accorded the same recognition and attention as the other four constituencies. Whether a company is a good community citizen is ultimately demonstrated by the way it supports community activities, encourages employees to participate in community activities, handles the health and safety aspects of its operations, accepts responsibility for overcoming environmental pollution, relates to regulatory bodies and employee unions, and exhibits high ethical standards.

Carrying Out Ethical Responsibilities   Management, not constituent groups, is responsible for managing the enterprise. Thus, it is management's perceptions of its ethical duties and of constituents' claims that drive whether and how strategy is linked to ethical behavior. Ideally, managers weigh strategic decisions from each constituent's point of view and, where conflicts arise, strike a rational, objective, and equitable balance among the interests of all five constituencies. If any of the five constituencies conclude that management is not doing its duty, they have their own avenues for recourse. Concerned investors can act through the annual shareholders' meeting, by appealing to the board of directors, or by selling their stock. Concerned employees can unionize and bargain collectively, or they can seek employment elsewhere. Customers can switch to competitors. Suppliers can find other buyers or pursue other market alternatives. The community and society can do anything from staging protest marches to stimulating political and governmental action.[18]

A management that truly cares about business ethics and corporate social responsibility is proactive rather than reactive in linking strategic action and ethics. It steers away from ethically or morally questionable business opportunities. It won't do business with suppliers that engage in activities the company does not condone. It produces products that are safe for its customers to use. It operates a workplace environment that is safe for employees. It recruits and hires employees whose values and behavior match the company's principles and ethical standards. It acts to reduce any environmental pollution it causes. It cares about *how* it does business and whether its

---

[18]Ibid.

ILLUSTRATION CAPSULE 7

HARRIS CORPORATION'S COMMITMENTS TO ITS STAKEHOLDERS

Harris Corporation is a major supplier of information, communication, and semiconductor products, systems, and services to commercial and governmental customers throughout the world. The company utilizes advanced technologies to provide innovative and cost-effective solutions for processing and communicating data, voice, text, and video information. The company's sales exceed $2 billion, and it employs nearly 23,000 people. In a recent annual report, the company set forth its commitment to satisfying the expectations of its stakeholders:

Customers—For customers, our objective is to achieve ever-increasing levels of satisfaction by providing quality products and services with distinctive benefits on a timely and continuing basis worldwide. Our relationships with customers will be forthright and ethical, and will be conducted in a manner to build trust and confidence.

Shareholders—For shareholders, the owners of our company, our objective is to achieve sustained growth in earnings-per-share. The resulting stock-price appreciation combined with dividends should provide our shareholders with a total return on investment that is competitive with similar investment opportunities.

Employees—The people of Harris are our company's most valuable asset, and our objective is for every employee to be personally involved in and share the success of the business. The company is committed to providing an environment which encourages all employees to make full use of their creativity and unique talents; to providing equitable compensation, good working conditions, and the opportunity for personal development and growth which is limited only by individual ability and desire.

Suppliers—Suppliers are a vital part of our resources. Our objective is to develop and maintain mutually beneficial partnerships with suppliers who share our commitment to achieving increasing levels of customer satisfaction through continuing improvements in quality, service, timeliness, and cost. Our relationships with suppliers will be sincere, ethical, and will embrace the highest principles of purchasing practice.

Communities—Our objective is to be a responsible corporate citizen. This includes support of appropriate civic, educational, and business activities, respect for the environment, and the encouragement of Harris employees to practice good citizenship and support community programs. Our greatest contribution to our communities is to be successful so that we can maintain stable employment and create new jobs.

Source: 1988 Annual Report.

actions reflect integrity and high ethical standards. Illustration Capsule 7 describes Harris Corporation's ethical commitments to its stakeholders.

TESTS OF A WINNING STRATEGY

What are the criteria for weeding out candidate strategies? How can a manager judge which strategic option is best for the company? What are the standards for determining whether a strategy is successful or not? Three tests can be used to evaluate the merits of one strategy over another and to gauge how good a strategy is:

The Goodness of Fit Test—A good strategy is well-matched to the company's internal and external situation—without situational fit, a strategy's appropriateness is suspect.

The Competitive Advantage Test—A good strategy leads to sustainable competitive advantage. The bigger the competitive edge that a strategy helps build, the more powerful and effective it is.

The Performance Test—A good strategy boosts company performance. Two kinds of performance improvements are the most telling: gains in profitability and gains in the company's long-term business strength and competitive position.

Strategic options judged to have low potential on one or more of these criteria are candidates to be dropped from further consideration. The strategic option judged to have the highest potential on all three counts can be regarded as the best or most attractive strategic alternative. Once a strategic commitment is made and enough time elapses to see results, these same tests can be used to assess how well a company's current strategy is performing. The bigger the margins by which a strategy satisfies all three criteria when put to test in the marketplace, the more it qualifies as a winning strategy.

There are, of course, some additional criteria for judging the merits of a particular strategy: clarity, internal consistency among all the pieces of strategy, timeliness, match to the personal values and ambitions of key executives, the degree of risk involved, and flexibility. Whenever appropriate, these can be used to supplement the three tests posed above.

APPROACHES TO PERFORMING THE STRATEGY-MAKING TASK

Companies and managers perform the strategy-making task differently. In small, owner-managed companies strategy-making is developed informally. Often the strategy is never reduced to writing but exists mainly in the entrepreneur's own mind and in oral understandings with key subordinates. Large companies, however, tend to develop their plans via an annual strategic planning cycle (complete with prescribed procedures, forms, and timetables) that includes broad management participation, lots of studies, and multiple meetings to probe and question. The larger and more diverse an enterprise, the more managers feel it is better to have a structured annual process with written plans, management scrutiny, and official approval at each level.

Along with variations in the organizational process of formulating strategy are variations in how managers personally participate in analyzing the company's situation and deliberating what strategy to pursue. The four basic strategy-making styles managers use are:[19]

The Master Strategist Approach—Here the manager functions as chief strategist and chief entrepreneur, exercising *strong* influence over assessments of the situation, over the strategy alternatives that are explored, and over the details of strategy. This does not mean that the manager personally does all the work; it means that the manager personally becomes the chief architect of strategy and wields a proactive hand in shaping some or all of the major pieces of strategy. The manager acts as strategy commander and has a big ownership stake in the chosen strategy.

The Delegate-It-to-Others Approach—Here the manager in charge delegates the exercise of strategy-making to others, perhaps a strategic planning staff or a task force of trusted subordinates. The manager then personally stays off to the side,

---

[19]This discussion is based on David R. Brodwin and L. J. Bourgeois, "Five Steps to Strategic Action," in Glenn Carroll and David Vogel, *Strategy and Organization: A West Coast Perspective* (Marshfield, Mass.: Pitman Publishing, 1984), pp. 168-78.

keeps in touch with how things are progressing via reports and oral conversations, offers guidance if need be, smiles or frowns as trial balloon recommendations are informally run by him/her for reaction, then puts a stamp of approval on the strategic plan after it has been formally presented and discussed and a consensus emerges. But the manager rarely has much ownership in the recommendations and, privately, may not see much urgency in pushing *hard* to implement some or much of what has been stated in writing in the company's "official strategic plan." Also, it is generally understood that "of course, we may have to proceed a bit differently if conditions change"—which gives the manager flexibility to go slow or ignore those approaches/moves that "on further reflection may not be the thing to do at this time." This strategy-making style has the advantage of letting the manager pick and chose from the smorgasbord of strategic ideas that bubble up from below, and it allows room for broad participation and input from many managers and areas. The weakness is that a manager can end up so detached from the process of formal strategy-making that no real strategic leadership is exercised—indeed, subordinates are likely to conclude that strategic planning isn't important enough to warrant a big claim on the boss's personal time and attention. The stage is then set for rudderless direction-setting. Often the strategy-making that does occur is short-run oriented and reactive; it says more about today's problems than positioning the enterprise to capture tomorrow's opportunities.

The Collaborative Approach—This is a middle approach whereby the manager enlists the help of key subordinates in hammering out a consensus strategy that all the key players will back and do their best to implement successfully. The biggest strength of this strategy-making style is that those who are charged with crafting the strategy also are charged with implementing it. Giving subordinate managers such a clear-cut ownership stake in the strategy they must implement enhances commitment to successful execution. And when subordinates have had a hand in proposing their part of the overall strategy, they can be held accountable for making it work—the "I told you it was a bad idea" alibi won't fly.

The Champion Approach—In this style, the manager is interested neither in a big personal stake in the details of strategy nor in the time-consuming tedium of leading others through participative brainstorming or a collaborative "group wisdom" exercise. Rather, the idea is to encourage subordinate managers to develop, champion, and implement sound strategies. Here strategy moves upward from the "doers" and the "fast-trackers." Executives serve as judges, evaluating the strategy proposals reaching their desks. This approach works best in large diversified corporations where the CEO cannot personally orchestrate strategy-making in each of many business divisions. For headquarters executives to capitalize on having people in the enterprise who can see strategic opportunities that they cannot, they must delegate the initiative for strategy-making to managers at the business-unit level. Corporate executives may well articulate general strategic themes as organizationwide guidelines for strategic thinking, but the key to good strategy-making is stimulating and rewarding new strategic initiatives conceived by a champion who believes in the opportunity and badly wants the blessing to go after it. With this approach, the total strategy ends up being the sum of the championed initiatives that get approved.

These four basic managerial approaches to forming a strategy illuminate several aspects about how strategy emerges. In situations where the manager in charge per-

Of the four basic approaches managers can use in crafting strategy, none is inherently superior—each has strengths and weaknesses.

sonally functions as the chief architect of strategy, the choice of what strategic course to steer is a product of his/her own vision about how to position the enterprise and of the manager's ambitions, values, business philosophies, and sense of what moves to make next. Highly centralized strategy-making works fine when the manager in charge has a powerful, insightful vision of what needs to be done and how to do it. The primary weakness of the master strategist approach is that the caliber of the strategy depends so heavily on one person's strategy-making skills. It also breaks down in large enterprises where many strategic initiatives are needed and the strategy-making task is too complex for one person to handle alone.

On the other hand, the group approach to strategy-making has its risks too. Sometimes, the strategy that emerges is a middle-of-the-road compromise, void of bold, creative initiative. Other times, it represents political consensus, with the outcome shaped by influential subordinates, by powerful functional departments, or by majority coalitions that have a common interest in promoting their particular version of what the strategy ought to be. Politics and the exercise of power are most likely to come into play in situations where there is no strong consensus on what strategy to adopt; this opens the door for a political solution to emerge. The collaborative approach is conducive to political strategic choices as well, since powerful departments and individuals have ample opportunity to try to build a consensus for their favored strategic approach. However, the big danger of a delegate-it-to-others approach is a serious lack of top-down direction and strategic leadership.

The strength of the champion approach is also its weakness. The value of championing is that it encourages people at lower organizational levels to make suggestions and propose innovative ideas. Individuals with attractive strategic proposals are given the latitude and resources to try them out, thus helping keep strategy fresh and renewing an organization's capacity for innovation. On the other hand, the championed actions, because they come from many places in the organization, are not likely to form a coherent pattern or promote clear strategic direction. With championing, the chief executive has to work at ensuring that what is championed adds power to the overall organization strategy; otherwise, strategic initiatives may be launched in directions that have no integrating links or overarching rationale.

All four styles of handling the strategy-making task thus have strengths and weaknesses. All four can succeed or fail depending on how well the approach is managed and depending on the strategy-making skills and judgments of the individuals involved.

KEY POINTS

Management's direction-setting task involves developing a mission, setting objectives, and forming a strategy. Early on in the direction-setting process, managers need to form a vision of where to lead the organization and to answer the question, "What is our business and what will it be?" A well-conceived mission statement helps channel organizational efforts along the course management has charted and builds a strong sense of organizational identity. Effective visions are clear, challenging, and inspiring; they prepare a firm for the future, and they make sense in the marketplace. A well-conceived, well-said mission statement serves as a beacon of long-term direction and creates employee buy-in.

The second direction-setting step is to establish strategic and financial objectives for the organization to achieve. Objectives convert the mission statement into specific performance targets. The agreed-on objectives need to be challenging but achievable, and they need to spell out precisely how much by when. In other words, objectives should be measurable and should involve deadlines for achievement. Objectives are needed at all organizational levels.

The third direction-setting step entails forming strategies to achieve the objectives set in each area of the organization. A corporate strategy is needed to achieve corporate-level objectives; business strategies are needed to achieve business-unit performance objectives; functional strategies are needed to achieve the performance targets set for each functional department; and operating-level strategies are needed to achieve the objectives set in each operating and geographic unit. In effect, an organization's strategic plan is a collection of unified and interlocking strategies. As shown in Table 2–1, different strategic issues are addressed at each level of managerial strategy-making. Typically, the strategy-making task is more top-down than bottom-up. Lower-level strategy supports and complements higher-level strategy and contributes to the achievement of higher-level, companywide objectives.

Strategy is shaped by both outside and inside considerations. The major external considerations are societal, political, regulatory, and community factors; industry attractiveness; and the company's market opportunities and threats. The primary internal considerations are company strengths, weaknesses, and competitive capabilities; managers' personal ambitions, philosophies, and ethics; and the company's culture and shared values. A good strategy must be well matched to all these situational considerations. In addition, a good strategy must lead to sustainable competitive advantage and improved company performance.

There are essentially four basic ways to manage the strategy formation process in an organization: the master strategist approach where the manager in charge personally functions as the chief architect of strategy, the delegate-it-to-others approach, the collaborative approach, and the champion approach. All four have strengths and weaknesses. All four can succeed or fail depending on how well the approach is managed and depending on the strategy-making skills and judgments of the individuals involved.

SUGGESTED READINGS

Andrews, Kenneth R. *The Concept of Corporate Strategy.* 3rd ed. Homewood, Ill.: Dow Jones Irwin, 1987, chaps. 2, 3, 4, and 5.

Campbell, Andrew, and Laura Nash. *A Sense of Mission: Defining Direction for the Large Corporation.* Reading, Mass.: Addison-Wesley, 1993.

Foster, Lawrence W. "From Darwin to Now: The Evolution of Organizational Strategies." *Journal of Business Strategy* 5, no. 4 (Spring 1985), pp. 94–98.

Hamel, Gary, and C. K. Prahalad. "Strategic Intent." *Harvard Business Review* 89, no. 3 (May–June 1989), pp. 63–76.

———. "Strategy as Stretch and Leverage." *Harvard Business Review* 71, no. 2 (March–April 1993), pp. 75–84.

Hammer, Michael, and James Champy. *Reengineering the Corporation.* New York: Harper Business, 1993, chap. 9.

Hax, Arnaldo C., and Nicolas S. Majluf. *The Strategy Concept and Process: A Pragmatic Approach.* Englewood Cliffs, N.J.: Prentice-Hall, 1991, chaps. 3, 4, 8, and 9.

Ireland, R. Duane, and Michael A. Hitt. "Mission Statements: Importance, Challenge, and Recommendations for Development." *Business Horizons* (May–June 1992), pp. 34–42.

Morris, Elinor. "Vision and Strategy: A Focus for the Future." *Journal of Business Strategy* 8, no. 2 (Fall 1987), pp. 51–58.

Mintzberg, Henry. "Crafting Strategy." *Harvard Business Review* 65, no. 4 (July–August 1987), pp. 66–77.

Porter, Michael E. "Toward a Dynamic Theory of Strategy." *Strategic Management Journal* 12 (1991), pp. 95–118.

Quinn, James Brian. *Strategies for Change: Logical Incrementalism.* Homewood, Ill.: Richard D. Irwin, 1980, chaps. 2 and 4.

CHAPTER THREE

INDUSTRY AND COMPETITIVE ANALYSIS

Analysis is the critical starting point of strategic thinking.

Kenichi Ohmae

Awareness of the environment is not a special project to be undertaken only when warning of change becomes deafening . . .

Kenneth R. Andrews

Crafting strategy is an analysis-driven exercise, not an activity where managers can succeed through good intentions and creativity. Judgments about what strategy to pursue have to be grounded in a probing assessment of a company's external environment and internal situation. Unless a company's strategy is well-matched to both external and internal circumstances, its suitability is suspect. The two biggest situational considerations are (1) industry and competitive conditions (these are the heart of a single-business company's "external environment") and (2) a company's own internal situation and competitive position. This chapter examines the techniques of *industry and competitive analysis,* the term commonly used to refer to external situation analysis of a single-business company. In the next chapter, we'll cover the tools of *company situation analysis.* Industry and competitive analysis looks broadly at a company's external *macroenvironment;* company situation analysis concerns a firm's immediate *microenvironment.*

Figure 3–1 illustrates the kinds of strategic thinking managers need to do to diagnose a company's situation. Note the logical flow from scrutiny of the company's external and internal situation to evaluation of alternatives to choice of strategy. Managers must have a keen grasp of the strategic aspects of a company's macro- and microenvironments to do a good job of establishing a strategic vision, setting objectives, and crafting a winning strategy. Absent such understanding, the door is wide open for managers to be seduced into a strategic game plan that doesn't fit the situation

FIGURE 3-1 | How Strategic Thinking and Strategic Analysis Lead to Good Strategic Choices

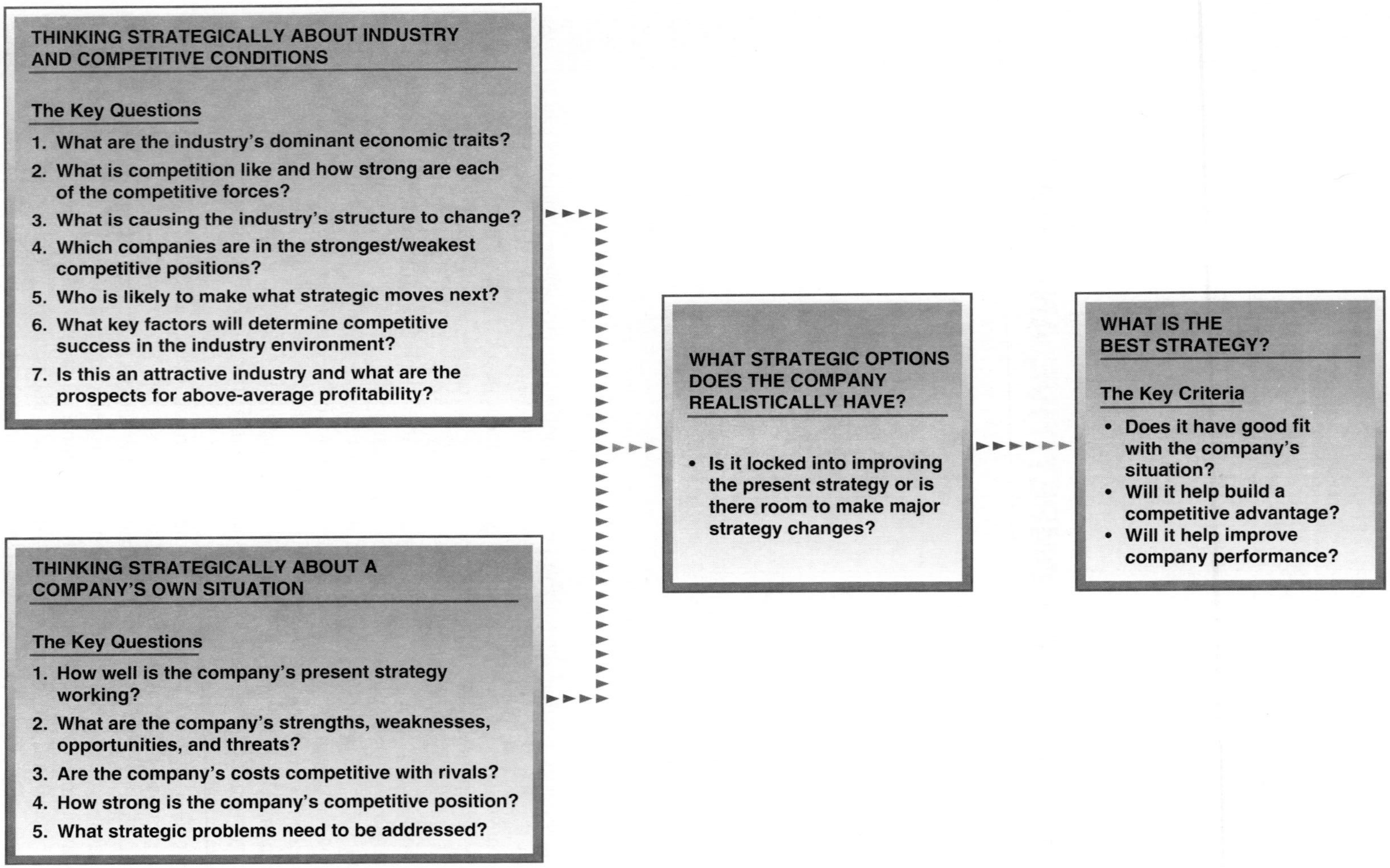

THINKING STRATEGICALLY ABOUT INDUSTRY AND COMPETITIVE CONDITIONS

The Key Questions

1. What are the industry's dominant economic traits?
2. What is competition like and how strong are each of the competitive forces?
3. What is causing the industry's structure to change?
4. Which companies are in the strongest/weakest competitive positions?
5. Who is likely to make what strategic moves next?
6. What key factors will determine competitive success in the industry environment?
7. Is this an attractive industry and what are the prospects for above-average profitability?

THINKING STRATEGICALLY ABOUT A COMPANY'S OWN SITUATION

The Key Questions

1. How well is the company's present strategy working?
2. What are the company's strengths, weaknesses, opportunities, and threats?
3. Are the company's costs competitive with rivals?
4. How strong is the company's competitive position?
5. What strategic problems need to be addressed?

WHAT STRATEGIC OPTIONS DOES THE COMPANY REALISTICALLY HAVE?

- Is it locked into improving the present strategy or is there room to make major strategy changes?

WHAT IS THE BEST STRATEGY?

The Key Criteria

- Does it have good fit with the company's situation?
- Will it help build a competitive advantage?
- Will it help improve company performance?

well, that holds little prospect for building competitive advantage, and that is unlikely to boost company performance.

THE METHODS OF INDUSTRY AND COMPETITIVE ANALYSIS

Managers are ill-prepared for the task of choosing a direction for the company to head or a strategy to get it there without first analyzing the company's present situation—what external conditions it faces and what its capabilities are.

Industries differ widely in their economic characteristics, competitive situations, and future outlooks. The pace of technological change can range from fast to slow. Capital requirements can vary from big to small. The market can extend from local to worldwide. Sellers' products can be standardized or highly differentiated. Competitive forces can be strong or weak and can reflect varying degrees of emphasis on price, product performance, service, promotion, and so on. Buyer demand can be rising briskly or declining. Industry conditions differ so much that leading companies in unattractive industries can find it hard to earn respectable profits, while even weak companies in attractive industries can turn in good performances. Moreover, industry conditions change continuously as one or more aspects grow or diminish in influence.

Industry and competitive analysis utilizes a toolkit of concepts and techniques to get a clear fix on changing industry conditions and on the nature and strength of competitive forces. This tool kit provides a way of thinking strategically about any industry's overall situation and drawing conclusions about whether the industry represents an attractive investment for company funds. Industry and competitive analysis aims at developing probing answers to seven questions:

1. What are the industry's dominant economic traits?
2. What competitive forces are at work in the industry and how strong are they?
3. What are the drivers of change in the industry and what impact will they have?
4. Which companies are in the strongest/weakest competitive positions?
5. Who's likely to make what competitive moves next?
6. What key factors will determine competitive success or failure?
7. How attractive is the industry in terms of its prospects for above-average profitability?

The answers to these questions build understanding of a firm's surrounding environment and, collectively, form the basis for matching its strategy to changing industry conditions and competitive realities.

QUESTION 1: WHAT ARE THE INDUSTRY'S DOMINANT ECONOMIC TRAITS?

Because industries differ significantly in their basic character and structure, industry and competitive analysis begins with an overview of the industry's dominant economic traits. As a working definition, we use the word *industry* to mean a group of firms whose products have so many of the same attributes that they compete for the same buyers. The factors to consider in profiling an industry's economic features are fairly standard:

- Market size.
- Scope of competitive rivalry (local, regional, national, international, or global).
- Market growth rate and where the industry is in the growth cycle (early development, rapid growth and takeoff, early maturity, late maturity and saturation, stagnant and aging, decline and decay).

- Number of rivals and their relative sizes—is the industry fragmented with many small companies or concentrated and dominated by a few large companies?
- The number of buyers and their relative sizes.
- The prevalence of backward and forward integration.
- Ease of entry and exit.
- The pace of technological change in both production process innovation and new product introductions.
- Whether the product(s)/service(s) of rival firms are highly differentiated, weakly differentiated, or essentially identical.
- Whether companies can realize scale economies in purchasing, manufacturing, transportation, marketing, or advertising.
- Whether high rates of capacity utilization are crucial to achieving low-cost production efficiency.
- Whether the industry has a strong learning and experience curve such that average unit cost declines as *cumulative* output (and thus the experience of "learning by doing") builds up.
- Capital requirements.
- Whether industry profitability is above/below par.

An industry's economic characteristics impose boundaries on the kinds of strategic approaches a company can pursue.

Table 3–1 provides a sample profile of the economic character of the sulfuric acid industry.

An industry's economic characteristics are important because of the implications they have for strategy. For example, in capital-intensive industries where investment

T A B L E 3–1 | **A Sample Profile of the Dominant Economic Characteristics of the Sulfuric Acid Industry**

Market Size: $400-$500 million annual revenues; 4 million tons total volume.

Scope of Competitive Rivalry: Primarily regional; producers rarely sell outside a 250-mile radius of plant due to high cost of shipping long distances.

Market Growth Rate: 2–3 percent annually. **Stage in Life Cycle:** Mature.

Number of Companies in Industry: About 30 companies with 110 plant locations and capacity of 4.5 million tons. Market shares range from a low of 3 percent to a high of 21 percent.

Customers: About 2,000 buyers; most are industrial chemical firms.

Degree of Vertical Integration: Mixed; 5 of the 10 largest companies are integrated backward into mining operations and also forward in that sister industrial chemical divisions buy over 50 percent of the output of their plants; all other companies are engaged solely in manufacturing.

Ease of Entry/Exit: Moderate entry barriers exist in the form of capital requirements to construct a new plant of minimum efficient size (cost equals $10 million) and ability to build a customer base inside a 250-mile radius of plant.

Technology/Innovation: Production technology is standard and changes have been slow; biggest changes are occurring in products—1–2 newly formulated specialty chemicals products are being introduced annually, accounting for nearly all of industry growth.

Product Characteristics: Highly standardized; the brands of different producers are essentially identical (buyers perceive little real difference from seller to seller).

Scale Economies: Moderate; all companies have virtually equal manufacturing costs but scale economies exist in shipping in multiple carloads to same customer and in purchasing large quantities of raw materials.

Experience Curve Effects: Not a factor in this industry.

Capacity Utilization: Manufacturing efficiency is highest between 90–100 percent of rated capacity; below 90 percent utilization, unit costs run significantly higher.

Industry Profitability: Subpar to average; the commodity nature of the industry's product results in intense price-cutting when demand slackens, but prices firm up during periods of strong demand. Profits track the strength of demand for the industry's products.

in a single plant can run several hundred million dollars, a firm can spread the burden of high fixed costs by pursuing a strategy that promotes high utilization of fixed assets and generates more revenue per dollar of fixed-asset investment. Thus commercial airlines employ strategies to boost the revenue productivity of their multimillion dollar jets by cutting ground time at airport gates (to get in more flights per day with the same plane) and by using multi-tiered price discounts to fill up otherwise empty seats on each flight. In industries characterized by one product advance after another, companies must spend enough time and money on R&D to keep their technical prowess and innovative capability abreast of competitors—a strategy of continuous product innovation becomes a condition of survival.

In industries like semiconductors, the presence of a *learning/experience* curve effect in manufacturing causes unit costs to decline about 20 percent each time *cumulative* production volume doubles. With a 20 percent experience curve effect, if the first 1 million chips cost $100 each, by a production volume of 2 million the unit cost would be $80 (80 percent of $100), by a production volume of 4 million the unit cost would be $64 (80 percent of $80), and so on. When an industry is characterized by a strong experience curve effect in its manufacturing operations, a company that moves first to initiate production of a new-style product and develops a strategy to capture the largest market share can win the competitive advantage of being the low-cost producer. The bigger the experience curve effect, the bigger the cost advantage of the company with the largest *cumulative* production volume, as shown in Figure 3–2.

Table 3–2 presents some additional examples of how an industry's economic traits are relevant to managerial strategy-making.

QUESTION 2: WHAT IS COMPETITION LIKE AND HOW STRONG ARE EACH OF THE COMPETITIVE FORCES?

One important component of industry and competitive analysis involves delving into the industry's competitive process to discover the main sources of competitive pressure and how strong each competitive force is. This analytical step is essential because managers cannot devise a successful strategy without in-depth understanding of the industry's competitive character.

FIGURE 3–2 | **Comparison of Experience Curve Effects for 10 Percent, 20 Percent, and 30 Percent Cost Reductions for Each Doubling of Cumulative Production Volume**

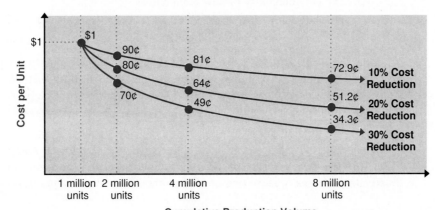

T A B L E 3–2 | **Examples of the Strategic Importance of an Industry's Key Economic Characteristics**

Factor/Characteristic	Strategic Importance
• Market size	• Small markets don't tend to attract big/new competitors; large markets often draw the interest of companies looking to acquire competitors with established positions in attractive industries.
• Market growth rate	• Fast growth breeds new entry; growth slowdowns spawn increased rivalry and a shake-out of weak competitors.
• Capacity surpluses or shortages	• Surpluses push prices and profit margins down; shortages pull them up.
• Industry profitability	• High-profit industries attract new entrants; depressed conditions encourage exit.
• Entry/exit barriers	• High barriers protect positions and profits of existing firms; low barriers make existing firms vulnerable to entry.
• Product is a big-ticket item for buyers	• More buyers will shop for lowest price.
• Standardized products	• Buyers have more power because it is easier to switch from seller to seller.
• Rapid technological change	• Raises risk factor; investments in technology facilities/equipment may become obsolete before they wear out.
• Capital requirements	• Big requirements make investment decisions critical; timing becomes important; creates a barrier to entry and exit.
• Vertical integration	• Raises capital requirements; often creates competitive differences and cost differences among fully versus partially versus nonintegrated firms.
• Economies of scale	• Increases volume and market share needed to be cost competitive.
• Rapid product innovation	• Shortens product life cycle; increases risk because of opportunities for leapfrogging.

The Five-Forces Model of Competition   Even though competitive pressures in various industries are never precisely the same, the competitive process works similarly enough to use a common analytical framework in gauging the nature and intensity of competitive forces. As Professor Michael Porter of the Harvard Business School has convincingly demonstrated, *the state of competition in an industry is a composite of five competitive forces:*[1]

1. The rivalry among competing sellers in the industry.
2. The market attempts of companies in other industries to win customers over to their own *substitute* products.
3. The potential entry of new competitors.
4. The bargaining power and leverage exercisable by suppliers of inputs.
5. The bargaining power and leverage exercisable by buyers of the product.

Porter's *five-forces model,* as depicted in Figure 3–3, is a powerful tool for systematically diagnosing the principal competitive pressures in a market and assessing how strong and important each one is. Not only is it the most widely used technique of competition analysis, but it is also relatively easy to use.

The Rivalry among Competing Sellers   The strongest of the five competitive forces is *usually* the jockeying for position and buyer favor that goes on among rival firms. Rivalry emerges because one or more competitors sees an opportunity to better meet

---

[1]For a thoroughgoing treatment of the five-forces model by its originator, see Michael E. Porter, *Competitive Strategy: Techniques for Analyzing Industries and Competitors* (New York: Free Press, 1980), chapter 1.

FIGURE 3-3 | The "Five-Forces" Model of Competition: A Key Analytical Tool

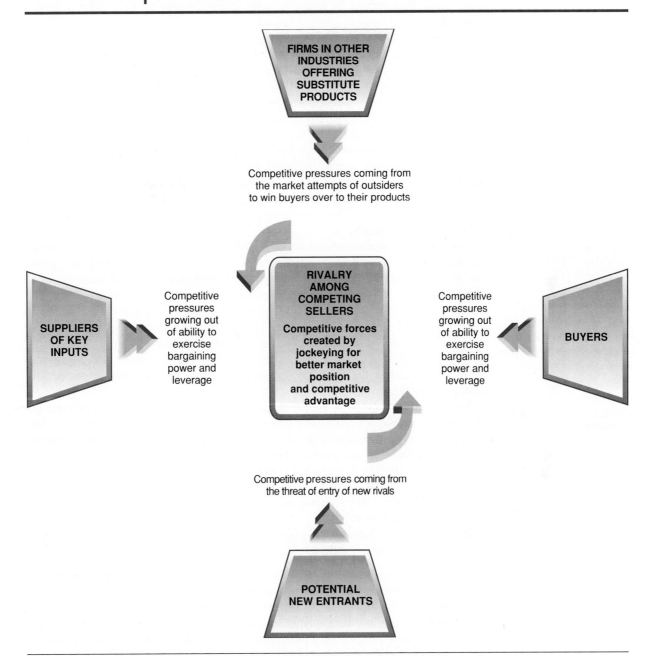

Source: Adapted from Michael E. Porter, "How Competitive Forces Shape Strategy," *Harvard Business Review 57,* no. 2 (March–April 1979), pp. 137–45.

customer needs or is under pressure to improve its performance. The intensity of rivalry among competing sellers is reflected by how vigorously they employ such competitive tactics as lower prices, snazzier features, increased customer services, longer warranties, special promotions, and new product introductions. Rivalry can range from friendly to cutthroat, depending on how frequently and how aggressively companies undertake fresh moves that threaten rivals' profitability. Ordinarily, rivals are clever at adding new wrinkles to their product offerings that enhance buyer appeal, and they persist in trying to exploit weaknesses in each other's market approaches.

Irrespective of whether rivalry is lukewarm or heated, every company is challenged to craft a successful strategy for competing—ideally, one that *produces a competitive edge over rivals* and strengthens its position with buyers. The big complication in most industries is that the success of any one firm's strategy hinges on what strategies its rivals employ and the resources rivals are willing and able to put behind their strategic efforts. The "best" strategy for one firm in its maneuvering for competitive advantage depends, in other words, on the competitive capabilities and strategies of rival companies. Such mutual interdependence means that whenever one firm makes a strategic move, its rivals often retaliate with offensive or defensive countermoves. This pattern of action and reaction makes competitive rivalry a "wargames" type of contest that is conducted in a market setting according to the rules of fair competition. Indeed, from a strategy-making perspective, *competitive markets are economic battlefields.*

Not only do competitive contests among rival sellers assume different intensities but the kinds of competitive pressures that emerge from cross-company rivalry also vary over time. The relative emphasis that rival companies put on price, quality, performance features, customer service, warranties, advertising, dealer networks, new product innovation, and so on shifts as they try different tactics to catch buyers' attention and as competitors initiate fresh offensive and defensive maneuvers. Rivalry is thus dynamic; the current competitive scene is ever-changing as companies act and react, sometimes in rapid-fire order and sometimes methodically, and as their strategic emphasis swings from one mix of competitive tactics to another.

Principle of Competitive Markets

Competitive jockeying among rival firms is a dynamic, everchanging process as firms initiate new offensive and defensive moves and emphasis swings from one mix of competitive weapons to another.

Two facets of competitive rivalry stand out: (1) the launch of a powerful competitive strategy by one company intensifies the competitive pressures on the remaining companies and (2) the manner in which rivals employ various competitive weapons to try to outmaneuver one another shapes "the rules of competition" in the industry and determines the requirements for competitive success. Once an industry's prevailing rules of competitive rivalry are understood, managers can determine whether competitive rivalry is fierce, moderate, or attractively weak and whether it is likely to increase or diminish in strength.

Regardless of the industry, several common factors seem to influence the tempo of rivalry among competing sellers:[2]

1. *Rivalry intensifies as the number of competitors increases and as competitors become more equal in size and capability.* Up to a point, the greater the number of competitors, the greater the probability of fresh, creative strategic initiatives. In addition, when rivals are more equal in size and capability, they can usually compete on a fairly even footing, making it harder for one or two firms to "win" the competitive battle and dominate the market.

2. *Rivalry is usually stronger when demand for the product is growing slowly.* In a rapidly expanding market, there tends to be enough business for everybody to grow. Indeed, it may take all of a firm's financial and managerial resources just to keep abreast of the growth in buyer demand, much less steal rivals' customers. But when growth slows or when market demand drops

---

[2]These indicators of what to look for in evaluating the intensity of intercompany rivalry are based on Porter, *Competitive Strategy,* pp. 17–21.

unexpectedly, expansion-minded firms and/or firms with excess capacity often cut prices and deploy other sales-increasing tactics, thereby igniting a battle for market share that can result in a shake-out of the weak and less efficient firms. The industry then consolidates into a smaller, but individually stronger, number of sellers.

3. *Rivalry is more intense when industry conditions tempt competitors to use price cuts or other competitive weapons to boost unit volume.* Whenever fixed costs account for a large fraction of total cost, unit costs tend to be lowest at or near full capacity since fixed costs can be spread over more units of production. Unused capacity imposes a significant cost-increasing penalty because there are fewer units carrying the fixed cost burden. In such cases, if market demand weakens and capacity utilization begins to fall off, the pressure of rising unit costs pushes rival firms into secret price concessions, special discounts, rebates, and other sales-increasing tactics, thus heightening competition. Likewise, when a product is perishable, seasonal, or costly to hold in inventory, competitive pressures build quickly anytime one or more firms decide to dump excess supplies on the market.

4. *Rivalry is stronger when customers' costs to switch brands are low.* The lower the costs of switching, the easier it is for rival sellers to raid one another's customers. On the other hand, high switching costs give a seller some protection against the efforts of rivals to raid its customers.

5. *Rivalry is stronger when one or more competitors is dissatisfied with its market position and launches moves to bolster its standing at the expense of rivals.* Firms that are losing ground or in financial trouble often react aggressively by acquiring smaller rivals, introducing new products, boosting advertising, discounting prices, and so on. Such actions can trigger a new round of competitive maneuvering and a hotly contested battle for market share.

6. *Rivalry increases in proportion to the size of the payoff from a successful strategic move.* The more rewarding an opportunity, the more likely some firm will aggressively pursue a strategy to capture it. The size of the strategic payoff varies partly with the speed of retaliation. When competitors respond slowly (or not at all), the initiator of a fresh competitive strategy can reap benefits in the intervening period and perhaps gain a first-mover advantage that is not easily surmounted. The greater the benefits of moving first, the more likely some firm will accept the risk and try it.

7. *Rivalry tends to be more vigorous when it costs more to get out of a business than to stay in and compete.* The higher the exit barriers (and thus the more costly it is to abandon a market), the stronger the incentive for firms to remain and compete as best they can, even though they may be earning low profits or even incurring losses.

8. *Rivalry becomes more volatile and unpredictable the more diverse competitors are in terms of their strategies, personalities, corporate priorities, resources, and countries of origin.* A diverse group of sellers often contains one or more mavericks willing to rock the boat with unconventional moves and market approaches, thus generating a livelier and less predictable competitive environment. Attempts by cross-border rivals to gain stronger footholds in each other's domestic markets is a surefire factor in boosting the intensity of rivalry, especially when foreign rivals have lower costs.

9. *Rivalry increases when strong companies outside the industry acquire weak firms in the industry and launch aggressive, well-funded moves to transform their newly acquired competitors into major market contenders.* A classic example of this occurred when Philip Morris, a leading cigarette firm with excellent marketing know-how, shook up the U.S. beer industry's approach to marketing by acquiring stodgy Miller Brewing Company in the late 1960s. In short order, Philip Morris revamped the marketing of Miller High Life and pushed it to the number two best-selling brand. PM also pioneered low-calorie beers with the introduction of Miller Lite—a move that made light beer the fastest-growing segment in the beer industry.

In sizing up the competitive pressures created by rivalry among existing competitors, the strategist's job is to identify what the current weapons of competitive rivalry are, to stay on top of how the game is being played, and to judge how much pressure cross-company rivalry is going to put on profitability. Competitive rivalry is considered intense when the actions of competitors are driving down industry profits, moderate when most companies can earn acceptable profits, and weak when most companies in the industry can earn above-average returns on investment. Chronic outbreaks of cutthroat competition among rival sellers make an industry brutally competitive.

The Competitive Force of Potential Entry   New entrants to a market bring new production capacity, the desire to establish a secure place in the market, and sometimes substantial resources with which to compete.[3] Just how serious the competitive threat of entry is in a particular market depends on two classes of factors: *barriers to entry* and the *expected reaction of incumbent firms to new entry.* A barrier to entry exists whenever it is hard for a newcomer to break into the market and/or economic factors put a potential entrant at a disadvantage relative to its competitors. There are several types of entry barriers:[4]

- *Economies of scale*—Scale economies deter entry because they force potential competitors either to enter on a large-scale basis (a costly and perhaps risky move) or to accept a cost disadvantage (and consequently lower profitability). Large-scale entry is a difficult barrier to hurdle because it can create chronic overcapacity problems in the industry and it can so threaten the market shares of existing firms that they retaliate aggressively (with price cuts, increased advertising and sales promotion, and similar blocking actions) to maintain their positions. Either way, a potential entrant is discouraged by the prospect of lower profits. Entrants may encounter scale-related barriers not just in production, but in advertising, marketing and distribution, financing, after-sale customer service, raw materials purchasing, and R&D as well.
- *Inability to gain access to technology and specialized know-how*—Many industries require technological capability and skills not readily available to a new entrant. Key patents can effectively bar entry as can lack of technically skilled personnel and an inability to execute complicated manufacturing techniques. Existing firms often carefully guard know-how that gives them an

[3]Michael E. Porter, "How Competitive Forces Shape Strategy," *Harvard Business Review* 57, no. 2 (March–April 1979), p. 138.
[4]Porter, *Competitive Strategy,* pp. 7–17.

edge in technology and manufacturing capability. Unless new entrants can gain access to such proprietary knowledge, they will lack the technical capability to compete on a level playing field.

- *The existence of learning and experience curve effects*—When lower unit costs are partly or mostly a result of experience in producing the product and other learning curve benefits, new entrants face a cost disadvantage competing against existing firms with more accumulated know-how.

- *Brand preferences and customer loyalty*—Buyers are often attached to established brands. European consumers, for example, are fiercely loyal to European brands of major household appliances. High brand loyalty means that a potential entrant must be prepared to spend enough money on advertising and sales promotion to overcome customer loyalties and build its own clientele. Substantial time and money can be involved. In addition, if it is difficult or costly for a customer to switch to a new brand, a new entrant must persuade buyers that its brand is worth the switching costs. To overcome the switching cost barrier, new entrants may have to offer buyers a discounted price or an extra margin of quality or service. All this can mean lower expected profit margins for new entrants—something that increases the risk to start-up companies dependent on sizable, early profits to support their new investments.

- *Capital requirements*—The larger the total dollar investment needed to enter the market successfully, the more limited the pool of potential entrants. The most obvious capital requirements are associated with manufacturing plant and equipment, working capital to finance inventories and customer credit, introductory advertising and sales promotion to establish a clientele, and cash reserves to cover start-up losses.

- *Cost disadvantages independent of size*—Existing firms may have cost advantages not available to potential entrants regardless of the entrant's size. These advantages can include access to the best and cheapest raw materials, possession of patents and proprietary technology, the benefits of learning and experience curve effects, existing plants built and equipped years earlier at lower costs, favorable locations, and lower borrowing costs.

- *Access to distribution channels*—In the case of consumer goods, a potential entrant may face the barrier of gaining adequate access to distribution channels. Wholesale distributors may be reluctant to take on a product that lacks buyer recognition. A network of retail dealers may have to be set up from scratch. Retailers have to be convinced to give a new brand ample display space and an adequate trial period. The more existing producers tie up present distribution channels, the tougher entry will be. To overcome this barrier, potential entrants may have to "buy" distribution access by offering better margins to dealers and distributors or by giving advertising allowances and other promotional incentives. As a consequence, a potential entrant's profits may be squeezed unless and until its product gains enough acceptance that distributors and retailers want to carry it.

- *Regulatory policies*—Government agencies can limit or even bar entry by requiring licenses and permits. Regulated industries like cable TV, electric and gas utilities, radio and television broadcasting, liquor retailing, and railroads feature government-controlled entry. In international markets, host governments commonly limit foreign entry and must approve all foreign investment applications. Stringent government-mandated safety regulations and environmental pollution standards are entry barriers because they raise entry costs.

- *Tariffs and international trade restrictions*—National governments commonly use tariffs and trade restrictions (antidumping rules, local content requirements, and quotas) to raise entry barriers for foreign firms. In 1988, due to tariffs imposed by the South Korean government, a Ford Taurus cost South Korean car buyers over $40,000. European governments require that certain Asian products, from electronic typewriters to copying machines, contain European-made parts and labor equal to 40 percent of selling price. And to protect European chipmakers from low-cost Asian competition, European governments instituted a rigid formula for calculating floor prices for computer memory chips.

Even if a potential entrant is willing to tackle the problems of entry barriers, it still faces the issue of how existing firms will react.[5] Will incumbent firms offer only passive resistance, or will they aggressively defend their market positions using price cuts, increased advertising, new product improvements, and whatever else is calculated to give a new entrant (as well as other rivals) a hard time? A potential entrant can have second thoughts when financially strong incumbent firms send clear signals that they will stoutly defend their market positions against entry. A potential entrant may also turn away when incumbent firms can use leverage with distributors and customers to keep their business.

The best test of whether potential entry is a strong or weak competitive force is to ask if the industry's growth and profit prospects are attractive enough to induce additional entry. When the answer is no, potential entry is not a source of competitive pressure. When the answer is yes (as in industries where lower-cost foreign competitors are exploring new markets), then potential entry is a strong force. The stronger the threat of entry, the greater the motivation of incumbent firms to fortify their positions against newcomers to make entry more costly or difficult.

One additional point: the threat of entry changes as the industry's prospects grow brighter or dimmer and as entry barriers rise or fall. For example, the expiration of a key patent can greatly increase the threat of entry. A technological discovery can create an economy of scale advantage where none existed before. New actions by incumbent firms to increase advertising, strengthen distributor-dealer relations, step up R&D, or improve product quality can raise the roadblocks to entry. In international markets, entry barriers for foreign-based firms fall as tariffs are lowered, as domestic wholesalers and dealers seek out lower-cost foreign-made goods, and as domestic buyers become more willing to purchase foreign brands.

Principle of Competitive Markets

The competitive threat that outsiders will enter the market is stronger when entry barriers are low, when incumbent firms are not inclined to fight vigorously to prevent a newcomer from gaining a market foothold, and when a newcomer can expect to earn attractive profits.

Competitive Pressures from Substitute Products   Firms in one industry are, quite often, in close competition with firms in another industry because their respective products are good substitutes. The producers of eyeglasses compete with the makers of contact lenses. The producers of wood stoves compete with such substitutes as kerosene heaters and portable electric heaters. The sugar industry competes with companies that produce artificial sweeteners. The producers of plastic containers confront strong competition from manufacturers of glass bottles and jars, paperboard cartons, and tin cans and aluminum cans. Aspirin manufacturers must consider how their product compares with other pain relievers and headache remedies.

---

[5]Porter, "How Competitive Forces Shape Strategy," p. 140, and Porter, *Competitive Strategy,* pp. 14–15.

Competitive pressures from substitute products operate in several ways. First, the presence of readily available and competitively priced substitutes places a ceiling on the prices an industry can afford to charge for its product without giving customers an incentive to switch to substitutes and risking sales erosion.[6] This price ceiling, at the same time, puts a lid on the profits that industry members can earn unless they find ways to cut costs. When substitutes are cheaper than an industry's product, industry members come under heavy competitive pressure to reduce their prices and find ways to absorb the price cuts with cost reductions. Second, the availability of substitutes inevitably invites customers to compare quality and performance as well as price. For example, firms that buy glass bottles and jars from glassware manufacturers monitor whether they can just as effectively and economically package their products in plastic containers, paper cartons, or tin cans. Competitive pressures from substitute products thus push industry participants to convince customers their product is more advantageous than substitutes. Usually this requires devising a competitive strategy to differentiate the industry's product from substitute products via some combination of lower price, better quality, better service, and more desirable performance features.

Another determinant of whether substitutes are a strong or weak competitive force is how difficult or costly it is for the industry's customers to switch to substitute products.[7] Typical switching costs include employee retraining costs, the purchase costs of any additional equipment, payments for technical help in making the changeover, the time and cost in testing the quality and reliability of the substitute, and the psychic costs of severing old supplier relationships and establishing new ones. If switching costs are high, sellers of substitutes must offer a major cost or performance benefit in order to steal the industry's customers away. When switching costs are low, it's much easier for sellers of substitutes to convince buyers to change over to their products.

As a rule, then, the lower the price of substitutes, the higher their quality and performance, and the lower the user's switching costs, the more intense the competitive pressures posed by substitute products. The best indicators of the competitive strength of substitute products are the rate at which their sales are growing, the market inroads they are making, their plans for expanding production capacity, and the size of their profits.

Principle of Competitive Markets
The competitive threat posed by substitute products is strong when prices of substitutes are attractive, buyers' switching costs are low, and buyers believe substitutes have equal or better features.

The Power of Suppliers Whether the suppliers to an industry are a weak or strong competitive force depends on market conditions in the supplier industry and the significance of the item they supply.[8] The competitive force of suppliers is greatly diminished whenever the item they provide is a standard commodity available on the open market from a large number of suppliers with ample capability to fill orders. Then it is relatively simple to obtain whatever is needed from a list of capable suppliers, dividing purchases among several to promote lively competition for orders. In such cases, suppliers have market power only when supplies become tight and users are so anxious to secure what they need that they agree to terms more favorable to suppliers. Suppliers are likewise in a weak bargaining position whenever there are good substitute inputs and switching is neither costly nor difficult. For example, soft drink bottlers can effectively check the power of aluminum can suppliers by using more plastic containers and glass bottles.

---

[6]Porter, "How Competitive Forces Shape Strategy," p. 142, and Porter, *Competitive Strategy,* pp. 23–24.
[7]Porter, *Competitive Strategy,* p. 10.
[8]Ibid., pp. 27–28.

Suppliers also have less leverage when the industry they are supplying is a *major* customer. In this case, the well-being of suppliers becomes closely tied to the well-being of their major customers. Suppliers then have a big incentive to protect the customer industry via reasonable prices, improved quality, and the development of new products and services that might enhance their customers' competitive positions, sales, and profits. When industry members form close working relationships with major suppliers, they may gain substantial benefit in the form of better quality components, just-in-time deliveries, and reduced inventory costs.

On the other hand, when the item suppliers provide accounts for a sizable fraction of the costs of an industry's product, is crucial to the industry's production process, and/or significantly affects the quality of the industry's product, suppliers have considerable influence on the competitive process. This is particularly true when a few large companies control most of the available supplies and have pricing leverage. Likewise, a supplier (or group of suppliers) possesses bargaining leverage the more difficult or costly it is for users to switch to alternate suppliers. Big suppliers with good reputations and growing demand for their output are harder to wring concessions from than struggling suppliers striving to broaden their customer base or more fully utilize their production capacity.

Suppliers are also more powerful when they can supply a component more cheaply than industry members can make it themselves. For instance, most producers of outdoor power equipment (lawnmowers, rotary tillers, snowblowers, and so on) find it cheaper to source the small engines they need from outside manufacturers rather than make their own because the quantity they need is too little to justify the investment and master the process. Specialists in small-engine manufacture, by supplying many kinds of engines to the whole power equipment industry, obtain a big enough sales volume to capture scale economies, become proficient in all the manufacturing techniques, and keep costs well below what power equipment firms could realize on their own. Small-engine suppliers then are in a position to price the item below what it would cost the user to self-manufacture but far enough above their own costs to generate an attractive profit margin. In such situations, the bargaining position of suppliers is strong *until* the volume of parts a user needs becomes large enough for the user to justify backward integration. Then the balance of power shifts from suppliers to users. The more credible the threat of backward integration into the suppliers' business becomes, the more leverage users have in negotiating favorable terms with suppliers.

A final instance in which an industry's suppliers play an important competitive role is when suppliers, for one reason or another, do not have the capability or the incentive to provide items of high or consistent quality. For example, if a manufacturer's suppliers provide components that have a relatively high defect rate or that fail prematurely, they can so increase the warranty and defective goods costs of the manufacturer that its profits, reputation, and competitive position are seriously impaired.

The Power of Buyers   Just as with suppliers, the competitive strength of buyers can range from strong to weak. Buyers have substantial bargaining leverage in a number of situations.[9] The most obvious is when buyers are large and purchase a sizable percentage of the industry's output. The bigger buyers are and the larger the quantities

---

Principle of Competitive Markets

The suppliers to a group of rival firms are a strong competitive force whenever they have sufficient bargaining power to put certain rivals at a competitive disadvantage based on the prices they can command, the quality and performance of the items they supply, or the reliability of their deliveries.

---

[9]Ibid., pp. 24–27.

they purchase, the more clout they have in negotiating with sellers. Often, purchasing in large quantities gives a buyer enough leverage to obtain price concessions and other favorable terms. Buyers also gain power when the costs of switching to competing brands or substitutes are relatively low. Any time buyers have the flexibility to fill their needs by sourcing from several sellers rather than having to use just one brand, they have added room to negotiate with sellers. When sellers' products are virtually identical, it is relatively easy for buyers to switch from seller to seller at little or no cost. However, if sellers' products are strongly differentiated, buyers are less able to switch without incurring sizable changeover costs.

One last point: all buyers are not likely to possess equal degrees of bargaining power with sellers, and some may be less sensitive than others to price, quality, or service. For example, in the apparel industry, major manufacturers confront significant customer power when selling to retail chains like Wal-Mart or Sears. But they can get much better prices selling to the small owner-managed apparel boutiques.

Principle of Competitive Markets
Buyers become a stronger competitive force the more they are able to exercise bargaining leverage over price, quality, service, or other terms of sale.

Strategic Implications of the Five Competitive Forces   The value of the five-forces model is the assist it provides in exposing the makeup of competitive forces. *To analyze the competitive environment, managers must assess the strength of each one of the five competitive forces.* The collective impact of these forces determines what competition is like in a given market. As a rule, the stronger competitive forces are, the lower is the collective profitability of participant firms. The most brutally competitive situation occurs when the five forces create market conditions tough enough to impose prolonged subpar profitability or even losses on most or all firms. The competitive structure of an industry is clearly "unattractive" from a profit-making standpoint if rivalry among sellers is very strong, entry barriers are low, competition from substitutes is strong, and both suppliers and customers are able to exercise considerable bargaining leverage. On the other hand, when competitive forces are not collectively strong, the competitive structure of the industry is "favorable" or "attractive" from the standpoint of earning superior profits. The "ideal" competitive environment from a profit-making perspective is where both suppliers and customers are in weak bargaining positions, there are no good substitutes, entry barriers are relatively high, and rivalry among present sellers is only moderate. However, even when some of the five competitive forces are strong, an industry can be competitively attractive to those firms whose market position and strategy provide a good enough defense against competitive pressures to preserve their ability to earn above-average profits.

A company's competitive strategy is increasingly effective the more it provides good defenses against the five competitive forces, influences the industry's competitive rules in the company's favor, and helps create sustainable competitive advantage.

To deal successfully with competitive forces, managers must craft strategies that (1) insulate the firm as much as possible from the five competitive forces, (2) influence the industry's competitive rules in the company's favor, and (3) provide a strong, secure position of advantage from which to "play the game" of competition as it unfolds in the industry. Managers cannot do this task well without a perceptive understanding of the industry's whole competitive picture. The five-forces model is a tool for gaining this understanding.

QUESTION 3: WHAT IS CAUSING THE INDUSTRY'S COMPETITIVE STRUCTURE AND BUSINESS ENVIRONMENT TO CHANGE?

An industry's economic features and competitive structure say a lot about the basic nature of the industry environment but very little about the ways in which the environment may be changing. All industries are characterized by trends and new developments that either gradually or speedily produce changes important enough to require a strategic response from participating firms. The popular hypothesis about industries going through evolutionary phases or life-cycle stages helps explain industry change but is still incomplete.[10] The life-cycle stages are strongly keyed to the overall industry growth rate (which is why such terms as rapid growth, early maturity, saturation, and decline are used to describe the stages). Yet there are more causes of industry change than an industry's position on the growth curve.

Industry conditions change because important forces are driving industry participants (competitors, customers, or suppliers) to alter their actions; the *driving forces* in an industry are the *major underlying causes* of changing industry and competitive conditions.

The Concept of Driving Forces   While it is important to judge what growth stage an industry is in, there's more analytical value in identifying the specific factors causing fundamental industry and competitive adjustments. Industry and competitive conditions change *because forces are in motion that create incentives or pressures for change.*[11] The most dominant forces are called *driving forces* because they have the biggest influence on what kinds of changes will take place in the industry's structure and competitive environment. Driving forces analysis has two steps: identifying what the driving forces are and assessing the impact they will have on the industry.

The Most Common Driving Forces   Many events can affect an industry powerfully enough to qualify as driving forces. Some are one of a kind, but most fall into one of several basic categories.[12]

- *Changes in the long-term industry growth rate*—Shifts in industry growth up or down are a force for industry change because they affect the balance between industry supply and buyer demand, entry and exit, and how hard it will be for a firm to capture additional sales. An upsurge in long-term demand frequently attracts new entrants to the market and encourages established firms to invest in additional capacity. A shrinking market can cause some companies to exit the industry and induce those remaining to close their least efficient plants and retrench to a smaller production base.

- *Changes in who buys the product and how they use it*—Shifts in buyer composition and new ways of using the product can force adjustments in customer service offerings (credit, technical assistance, maintenance and repair), open the way to market the industry's product through a different mix of dealers and retail outlets, prompt producers to broaden/narrow their product lines, increase/decrease capital requirements, and change sales and promotion approaches. The development of new cable-converter boxes is now allowing home computer service firms like Prodigy, CompuServe, and America Online to sign up cable companies to deliver their games, bulletin boards, data services, and electronic shopping services to home subscribers via cable television. Consumer enthusiasm for cordless and cellular telephones has opened a major new buyer segment for telephone equipment manufacturers.

- *Product innovation*—Product innovation can broaden an industry's customer base, rejuvenate industry growth, and widen the degree of product differentiation among rival sellers. Successful new product introductions strengthen the market position of the innovating companies, usually at the

---

[10]For a more extended discussion of the problems with the life-cycle hypothesis, see Porter, *Competitive Strategy,* pp. 157–62.

[11]Porter, *Competitive Strategy,* p. 162.

[12]What follows draws on the discussion in Porter, *Competitive Strategy,* pp. 164–83.

expense of companies who stick with their old products or are slow to follow with their own versions of the new product. Industries where product innovation has been a key driving force include copying equipment, cameras and photographic equipment, computers, electronic video games, toys, prescription drugs, frozen foods, and personal computer software.

- *Technological change*—Advances in technology can dramatically alter an industry's landscape, making it possible to produce new and/or better products at lower cost and opening up whole new industry frontiers. Technological developments can also produce changes in capital requirements, minimum efficient plant sizes, vertical integration benefits, and learning or experience curve effects.

- *Marketing innovation*—When firms are successful in introducing new ways to market their products, they can spark a burst of buyer interest, widen industry demand, increase product differentiation, and/or lower unit costs—any or all of which can alter the competitive positions of rival firms and force strategy revisions.

- *Entry or exit of major firms*—The entry of one or more foreign companies into a market once dominated by domestic firms nearly always shakes up competitive conditions. Likewise, when an established domestic firm from another industry attempts entry either by acquisition or by launching its own start-up venture, it usually applies its skills and resources in some innovative fashion that introduces a new element to competition. Entry by a major firm often produces a "new ballgame" not only with new key players but also with new rules for competing. Similarly, exit of a major firm changes competitive structure by reducing the number of market leaders (perhaps increasing the dominance of the leaders who remain) and causing a rush to capture the exiting firm's customers.

- *Diffusion of technical know-how*—As knowledge about how to perform a particular activity or execute a particular manufacturing technology spreads, any technically based competitive advantage held by firms originally possessing this know-how erodes. The diffusion of such know-how can occur through scientific journals, trade publications, on-site plant tours, word-of-mouth among suppliers and customers, and the hiring away of knowledgeable employees. It can also occur when the possessors of technological know-how license others to use it for a royalty fee or team up with a company interested in turning the technology into a new business venture. Quite often, technological know-how can be acquired by simply buying a company that has the wanted skills, patents, or manufacturing capabilities. In recent years technology transfer across national boundaries has emerged as one of the most important driving forces in globalizing markets and competition. As companies in more countries gain access to technical know-how, they upgrade their manufacturing capabilities in a long-term effort to compete head-on against established companies. Examples of where technology transfer has turned a largely domestic industry into an increasingly global one include automobiles, tires, consumer electronics, telecommunications, and computers.

- *Increasing globalization of the industry*—Industries move toward globalization for any of several reasons. One or more nationally prominent firms may launch aggressive long-term strategies to win a globally dominant market position. Demand for the industry's product may pop up in more and more countries.

Trade barriers may drop. Technology transfer may open the door for more companies in more countries to enter the industry arena on a major scale. Significant labor cost differences among countries may create a strong reason to locate plants for labor-intensive products in low-wage countries (wages in South Korea, Taiwan, and Singapore, for example, are about one-fourth those in the U.S.). Significant cost economies may accrue to firms with world-scale volumes as opposed to national-scale volumes. Multinational companies with the ability to transfer their production, marketing, and management know-how from country to country at very low cost can sometimes gain a significant competitive advantage over domestic-only competitors. As a consequence, global competition usually shifts the pattern of competition among an industry's key players, favoring some and disadvantaging others. Such occurrences make globalization a driving force. Globalization is most likely to be a driving force in industries *(a)* based on natural resources (supplies of crude oil, copper, and cotton, for example, are geographically scattered all over the globe), *(b)* where low-cost production is a critical consideration (making it imperative to locate plant facilities in countries where the lowest costs can be achieved), and *(c)* where one or more growth-oriented, market-seeking companies are pushing hard to gain a significant competitive position in as many attractive country markets as they can.

- *Changes in cost and efficiency*—In industries where new economies of scale are emerging or where strong learning curve effects allow firms with the most production experience to undercut rivals' prices, large market share becomes such a distinct advantage that all firms must shift to volume-building strategies—triggering a "race for growth." Likewise, sharply rising costs for a key input (either raw materials or labor) can cause a scramble to either *(a)* line up reliable supplies of the input at affordable prices or *(b)* search out lower-cost substitute inputs. Any time important changes in cost or efficiency take place in an industry, widening or shrinking cost differences among key competitors can dramatically alter the state of competition.

- *Emerging buyer preferences for differentiated products instead of a commodity product (or for a more standardized product instead of strongly differentiated products)*—Sometimes growing numbers of buyers decide that a standard "one size fits all" product with a bargain price meets their needs as effectively as premium-priced brands with snappy features and options. Such a development tends to shift patronage away from sellers of more expensive differentiated products to sellers of cheaper commodity products and create a price-competitive market environment. Pronounced shifts toward greater product standardization can so dominate a market that the strategic freedom of rival producers is limited to driving costs out of the business and competing hard on price. On the other hand, a shift away from standardized products occurs when sellers are able to win a bigger and more loyal buyer following by introducing new features, making style changes, offering options and accessories, and creating image differences via advertising and packaging. Then the driver of change is the contest among rivals to cleverly outdifferentiate one another. Industries evolve differently depending on whether the market forces in motion are acting to increase or decrease the emphasis on product differentiation.

- *Regulatory influences and government policy changes*—Regulatory and governmental actions can often force significant changes in industry practices and strategic approaches. Deregulation has been a big driving force in the airline, banking, natural gas, and telecommunications industries. President Clinton's proposal for universal health insurance recently became a driving force in the health care industry. In international markets, host governments can open up their domestic markets to foreign participation or close them off to protect domestic companies, thus shaping whether the competitive struggle occurs on a level playing field or favors domestic firms (owing to government protectionism).

- *Changing societal concerns, attitudes, and lifestyles*—Emerging social issues and changing attitudes and lifestyles can be powerful instigators of industry change. Consumer concerns about salt, sugar, chemical additives, cholesterol, and nutrition have forced food producers to reexamine food processing techniques, redirect R&D efforts into the use of healthier ingredients, and engage in contests to come up with healthier products that also taste good. Safety concerns are now altering the competitive emphasis in the automobile, toy, and outdoor power equipment industries, to mention a few. Increased interest in physical fitness has spawned whole new industries to supply exercise equipment, jogging clothes and shoes, and medically supervised diet programs. Social concerns about air and water pollution are major forces in industries that discharge waste products. Growing antismoking sentiment has emerged as the major driver of change in the tobacco industry.

- *Reductions in uncertainty and business risk*—A young, emerging industry is typically characterized by an unproven cost structure and much uncertainty over potential market size, how much time and money will be needed to surmount technological problems, and what distribution channels to emphasize in accessing potential buyers. Emerging industries tend to attract only risk-taking entrepreneurial companies. Over time, however, if pioneering firms succeed and uncertainty about the industry's viability fades, more conservative firms are usually enticed to enter the industry. Often, these later entrants are larger, financially strong firms looking to invest in attractive growth industries. In international markets, conservatism is prevalent in the early stages of globalization. Firms guard against risk by relying initially on exporting, licensing, and joint ventures to enter foreign markets. Then, as experience accumulates and perceived risk levels decline, companies move more quickly and aggressively to form wholly owned subsidiaries and to pursue full-scale, multicountry competitive strategies.

The foregoing list of *potential* driving forces in an industry indicates why it is too simplistic to view industry change only in terms of the growth stages model and why it is essential to probe for the *causes* underlying the emergence of new competitive conditions.

However, while many forces of change may be at work in a given industry, no more than three or four are likely to qualify as *driving* forces in the sense that they will act as *the major determinants* of how the industry evolves and operates. Thus, strategic analysts must resist the temptation to label everything they see changing as driving forces; the analytical task is to evaluate the forces of industry and competitive change carefully enough to separate major factors from minor ones.

Sound analysis of an industry's driving forces is a prerequisite to sound strategy-making. Without keen awareness of what external factors will have the greatest effect

The task of driving forces analysis is to separate the major causes of industry change from the minor ones; usually no more than three or four factors qualify as driving forces.

on the company's business over the next one to three years, managers are ill-prepared to craft a strategy tightly matched to changing external conditions. Similarly, if managers are uncertain about the implications of each driving force or if their views are incomplete or off-base, it's difficult for them to craft a strategy that is responsive to the driving forces and their consequences for the industry. So driving forces analysis is not something to take lightly; it has practical strategy-making value and is basic to the task of thinking strategically about the business.

Environmental Scanning Techniques   One way to get a jump on which driving forces are likely to emerge is to utilize environmental scanning techniques for early detection of new straws in the wind. *Environmental scanning* involves studying and interpreting the sweep of social, political, economic, ecological, and technological events in an effort to spot budding trends and conditions that could eventually impact the industry. Environmental scanning involves time frames well beyond the next one to three years—for example, it could involve judgments about the demand for energy in the year 2010, what kinds of household appliances will be in the "house of the future," what people will be doing with computers 20 years from now, or what will happen to our forests in the 21st century if the demand for paper continues to grow at its present rate. Environmental scanning thus attempts to spot first-of-a-kind happenings and new ideas and approaches that are catching on and to extrapolate their possible implications 5 to 20 years into the future. The purpose and value of environmental scanning is to raise the consciousness of managers about potential developments that could have an important impact on industry conditions or pose new opportunities and threats.

> Managers can use *environmental scanning* to spot budding trends and clues of change that could develop into new driving forces.

Environmental scanning can be accomplished by systematically monitoring and studying current events, constructing scenarios, and employing the Delphi method (a technique for finding consensus among a group of knowledgeable experts). Environmental scanning methods are highly qualitative and subjective. The appeal of environmental scanning, notwithstanding its speculative nature, is that it helps managers lengthen their planning horizon, translate vague inklings of future opportunities or threats into clearer strategic issues (for which they can begin to develop strategic answers), and think strategically about future developments in the surrounding environment.[13] Companies that undertake formal environmental scanning on a fairly continuous and comprehensive level include General Electric, AT&T, Coca-Cola, Ford, General Motors, Du Pont, and Shell Oil.

QUESTION 4: WHICH COMPANIES ARE IN THE STRONGEST/WEAKEST POSITIONS?

> Strategic group mapping is a technique for displaying the different competitive positions that rival firms occupy in the industry.

The next step in examining the industry's competitive structure is to study the market positions of rival companies. One technique for revealing the competitive positions of industry participants is *strategic group mapping*.[14] This analytical tool is a bridge

---

[13]For further discussion of the nature and use of environmental scanning, see Roy Amara and Andrew J. Lipinski, *Business Planning for an Uncertain Future: Scenarios and Strategies* (New York: Pergamon Press, 1983); Harold E. Klein and Robert U. Linneman, "Environmental Assessment: An International Study of Corporate Practice," *Journal of Business Strategy* 5, no. 1 (Summer 1984), pp. 55–75; and Arnoldo C. Hax and Nicolas S. Majluf, *The Strategy Concept and Process* (Englewood Cliffs, N.J.: Prentice-Hall, 1991), chapters 5 and 8.

[14]Porter, *Competitive Strategy,* chapter 7.

between looking at the industry as a whole and considering the standing of each firm separately. It is most useful when an industry has so many competitors that it is not practical to examine each one in depth.

Using Strategic Group Maps to Assess the Competitive Positions of Rival Firms A strategic group consists of those rival firms with similar competitive approaches and positions in the market.[15] Companies in the same strategic group can resemble one another in any of several ways: they may have comparable product line breadth, use the same kinds of distribution channels, be vertically integrated to much the same degree, offer buyers similar services and technical assistance, use essentially the same product attributes to appeal to similar types of buyers, emphasize the same distribution channels, depend on identical technological approaches, and/or sell in the same price/quality range. An industry contains only one strategic group when all sellers approach the market with essentially identical strategies. At the other extreme, there are as many strategic groups as there are competitors when each rival pursues a distinctively different competitive approach and occupies a substantially different competitive position in the marketplace.

The procedure for constructing a strategic group map and deciding which firms belong in which strategic group is straightforward:

- Identify the competitive characteristics that differentiate firms in the industry— typical variables are price/quality range (high, medium, low), geographic coverage (local, regional, national, global), degree of vertical integration (none, partial, full), product line breadth (wide, narrow), use of distribution channels (one, some, all), and degree of service offered (no-frills, limited, full service).
- Plot the firms on a two-variable map using pairs of these differentiating characteristics.
- Assign firms that fall in about the same strategy space to the same strategic group.
- Draw circles around each strategic group, making the circles proportional to the size of the group's respective share of total industry sales revenues.

This produces a two-dimensional *strategic group map* such as the one for the retail jewelry industry portrayed in Illustration Capsule 8.

To map the positions of strategic groups accurately in the industry's overall strategy space, several guidelines need to be observed.[16] First, the two variables selected as axes for the map should *not* be highly correlated; if they are, the circles on the map will fall along a diagonal and strategy-makers will learn nothing more about the relative positions of competitors than they would by considering just one of the variables. For instance, if companies with broad product lines use multiple distribution channels while companies with narrow lines use a single distribution channel, then one of the variables is redundant. Looking at broad versus narrow product lines reveals just as much about who is positioned where as adding single versus multiple distribution channels. Second, the variables chosen as axes for the map should expose big differences in how rivals position themselves to compete in the marketplace. This, of course, means analysts must identify the characteristics that differentiate rival firms and use these differences as variables for the axes and as

[15]Ibid., pp. 129–30.
[16]Ibid., pp. 152–54.

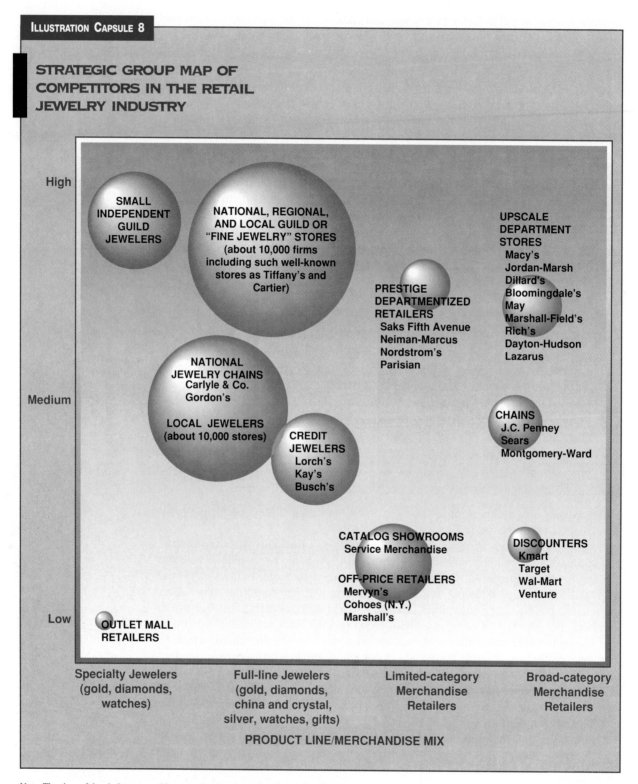

ILLUSTRATION CAPSULE 8

STRATEGIC GROUP MAP OF COMPETITORS IN THE RETAIL JEWELRY INDUSTRY

High

SMALL INDEPENDENT GUILD JEWELERS

NATIONAL, REGIONAL, AND LOCAL GUILD OR "FINE JEWELRY" STORES (about 10,000 firms including such well-known stores as Tiffany's and Cartier)

UPSCALE DEPARTMENT STORES
Macy's
Jordan-Marsh
Dillard's
Bloomingdale's
May
Marshall-Field's
Rich's
Dayton-Hudson
Lazarus

PRESTIGE DEPARTMENTIZED RETAILERS
Saks Fifth Avenue
Neiman-Marcus
Nordstrom's
Parisian

Medium

NATIONAL JEWELRY CHAINS
Carlyle & Co.
Gordon's

LOCAL JEWELERS (about 10,000 stores)

CREDIT JEWELERS
Lorch's
Kay's
Busch's

CHAINS
J.C. Penney
Sears
Montgomery-Ward

CATALOG SHOWROOMS
Service Merchandise

OFF-PRICE RETAILERS
Mervyn's
Cohoes (N.Y.)
Marshall's

DISCOUNTERS
Kmart
Target
Wal-Mart
Venture

Low

OUTLET MALL RETAILERS

Specialty Jewelers (gold, diamonds, watches)

Full-line Jewelers (gold, diamonds, china and crystal, silver, watches, gifts)

Limited-category Merchandise Retailers

Broad-category Merchandise Retailers

PRODUCT LINE/MERCHANDISE MIX

Note: The sizes of the circles are roughly proportional to the market shares of each group of competitors the basis for deciding which firm belongs in which strategic group. Third, the variables used as axes don't have to be either quantitative or continuous; rather, they can be discrete variables or defined in terms of distinct classes and combinations. Fourth, drawing the sizes of the circles on the map proportional to the combined sales of the firms in each strategic group allows the map to reflect the relative sizes of each strategic group. Fifth, if more than two good competitive variables can be used as axes for the map, several maps can be drawn to give different exposures to the competitive positioning relationships present in the industry's structure. Because there is not necessarily one best map for portraying how competing firms are positioned in the market, it is advisable to experiment with different pairs of competitive variables.

Strategic group analysis helps deepen management understanding of competitive rivalry.[17] To begin with, *driving forces and competitive pressures often favor some strategic groups and hurt others*. Firms in adversely affected strategic groups may try to shift to a more favorably situated group; how hard such a move proves to be depends on whether entry barriers into the target strategic group are high or low. Attempts by rival firms to enter a new strategic group nearly always increase competitive pressures. If certain firms are known to be trying to change their competitive positions on the map, then attaching arrows to the circles showing the targeted direction helps clarify the picture of competitive jockeying among rivals.

A second thing to look for is whether *the profit potential of different strategic groups varies due to the strengths and weaknesses in each group's market position*. Differences in profitability can occur because of differing degrees of bargaining leverage with suppliers or customers and differing degrees of exposure to competition from substitute products outside the industry.

> Some strategic groups are usually more favorably positioned than other strategic groups because driving forces and competitive pressures do not affect each group evenly and because profit prospects vary among groups based on the relative attractiveness of their market positions.

Generally speaking, *the closer strategic groups are to each other on the map, the stronger competitive rivalry among member firms tends to be*. Although firms in the same strategic group are the closest rivals, the next closest rivals are in the immediately adjacent groups. Often, firms in strategic groups that are far apart on the map hardly compete at all. For instance, Tiffany's and Wal-Mart both sell gold and silver jewelry, but the prices and perceived qualities of their products are much too different to generate any real competition between them. For the same reason, Timex is not a meaningful competitive rival of Rolex, and Subaru is not a close competitor of Lincoln or Mercedes-Benz.

QUESTION 5: WHAT STRATEGIC MOVES ARE RIVALS LIKELY TO MAKE NEXT?

Studying the actions and behavior of one's closest competitors is essential. Unless a company pays attention to what competitors are doing, it ends up flying blind into competitive battle. A company can't expect to outmaneuver its rivals without monitoring their actions and anticipating what moves they are likely to make next. As in sports, a good scouting report is invaluable. The strategies rivals are using and the actions they are likely to take next have direct bearing on a company's own best strategic moves—whether it needs to defend against specific actions taken by rivals or whether rivals' moves provide an opening for a new offensive thrust.

> Successful strategists take great pains in scouting competitors—understanding their strategies, watching their actions, sizing up their strengths and weaknesses, and trying to anticipate what moves they will make next.

---

[17]Ibid., pp. 130, 132–38, and 154–55.

Identifying Competitors' Strategies   A quick profile of key competitors can be obtained by studying where they are in the industry, their strategic objectives as revealed by actions recently taken, and their basic competitive approaches. Table 3–3 provides an easy-to-use scheme for categorizing the objectives and strategies of rival companies. Such a summary, along with a strategic group map, usually suffices to diagnose the competitive intent of rivals.

Evaluating Who the Industry's Major Players Are Going to Be   It's usually obvious who the *current* major contenders are, but these same firms are not necessarily positioned strongly for the future. Some may be losing ground or be ill-equipped to compete on the industry's future battleground. Smaller companies may be moving into contention and poised for an offensive against larger but vulnerable rivals. Long-standing market leaders sometimes slide quickly down the industry's ranks; others end up being acquired. Today's industry leaders don't automatically become tomorrow's.

In deciding whether a competitor is favorably or unfavorably positioned to gain market ground, attention needs to center on why there is potential for it to do better or worse than other rivals. Usually, how securely a company holds its present market share is a function of its vulnerability to driving forces and competitive pressures, whether it has a competitive advantage or disadvantage, and whether it is the likely target of offensive attack from other industry participants. Pinpointing which rivals are poised to gain market position and which rivals seem destined to lose market share helps a strategist anticipate what kinds of moves they are likely to make next.

Predicting Competitors' Next Moves   This is the hardest yet most useful part of competitor analysis. Good clues about what moves a specific company may make next come from studying its situation—understanding its strategic intent, monitoring how well it is faring in the marketplace, and determining how much pressure it is under to improve its financial performance. Aggressive rivals on the move are strong candidates for some type of new strategic initiative. Content rivals are likely to continue their present strategy with only minor fine-tuning. Ailing rivals can be performing so poorly that fresh strategic moves, either offensive or defensive, are virtually certain. Since managers generally operate from assumptions about the industry's future and beliefs about their own firm's situation, insights into their strategic thinking can be gleaned from their public pronouncements about where the industry is headed and what it will take to be successful, what they are saying about their firm's situation, information from the grapevine about what they are doing, and their past actions and leadership styles. Another thing to consider is whether a rival has the flexibility to make major strategic changes or whether it is locked into pursuing its same basic strategy with minor adjustments.

To succeed in predicting a competitor's next moves, one has to have a good feel for the rival's situation, how its managers think, and what its options are. Doing the necessary detective work can be tedious and time-consuming since the information comes in bits and pieces from many sources. But scouting competitors well enough to anticipate their next moves allows managers to prepare effective countermoves (perhaps even beat a rival to the punch!) and to take rivals' probable actions into account in designing the best course of action.

Managers who fail to study competitors closely risk being blindsided by "surprise" actions on the part of rivals.

T A B L E 3-3 | **Categorizing the Objectives and Strategies of Competitors**

Competitive Scope	Strategic Intent	Market Share Objective	Competitive Position/Situation	Strategic Posture	Competitive Strategy

• Local
• Regional
• National
• Multicountry
• Global
	• Be the dominant leader
	• Overtake the present industry leader
	• Be among the industry leaders (top 5)
	• Move into the top 10
	• Move up a notch or two in the industry rankings
	• Overtake a particular rival (not necessarily the leader)
	• Maintain position
	• Just survive
		• Aggressive expansion via both acquisition and internal growth
		• Expansion via internal growth (boost market share at the expense of rival firms)
		• Expansion via acquisition
		• Hold on to present share (by growing at a rate equal to the industry average)
		• Give up share if necessary to achieve short-term profit objectives (stress profitability, not volume)
			• Getting stronger; on the move
			• Well-entrenched; able to maintain its present position
			• Stuck in the middle of the pack
			• Going after a different market position (trying to move from a weaker to a stronger position)
			• Struggling; losing ground
			• Retrenching to a position that can be defended
				• Mostly offensive
				• Mostly defensive
				• A combination of offense and defense
				• Aggressive risk-taker
				• Conservative follower
					• Striving for low cost leadership
					• Mostly focusing on a market niche
					  —High end
					  —Low end
					  —Geographic
					  —Buyers with special needs
					  —Other
					• Pursuing differentiation based on
					  —Quality
					  —Service
					  —Technological superiority
					  —Breadth of product line
					  —Image and reputation
					  —More value for the money
					  —Other attributes

Note: Since a focus strategy can be aimed at any of several market niches and a differentiation strategy can be keyed to any of several attributes, it is best to be explicit about what kind of focus strategy or differentiation strategy a given firm is pursuing. All focusers do not pursue the same market niche, and all differentiators do not pursue the same differentiating attributes.

QUESTION 6: WHAT ARE THE KEY FACTORS FOR COMPETITIVE SUCCESS?

An industry's *key success factors* (KSFs) are the strategy-related action approaches, competitive capabilities, and business outcomes that every firm must be competent at doing or must concentrate on achieving in order to be competitively and financially successful. KSFs are business aspects all firms in the industry must pay close attention to—the specific outcomes crucial to market success (or failure) and the competencies and competitive capabilities with the most direct bearing on company profitability. In the beer industry, the KSFs are full utilization of brewing capacity (to keep manufacturing costs low), a strong network of wholesale distributors (to gain access to as many retail outlets as possible), and clever advertising (to induce beer drinkers to buy a particular brand and thereby pull beer sales through the established wholesale/retail channels). In apparel manufacturing, the KSFs are appealing designs and color combinations (to create buyer interest) and low-cost manufacturing efficiency (to permit attractive retail pricing and ample profit margins). In tin and aluminum cans, where the cost of shipping empty cans is substantial, one of the keys is having plants located close to end-use customers so that the plant's output can be marketed within economical shipping distances (regional market share is far more crucial than national share).

An industry's *key success factors* spell the difference between profit and loss and, ultimately, between competitive success and failure.

Determining the industry's key success factors, in light of prevailing and anticipated industry and competitive conditions, is a top-priority analytical consideration. At the very least, managers need to know the industry well enough to conclude what is more important to competitive success and what is less important. Company managers who misdiagnose what factors are truly crucial to long-term competitive success are prone to employ ill-conceived strategies or to pursue less important competitive targets. Frequently, a company with perceptive understanding of industry KSFs can gain sustainable competitive advantage by training its strategy on industry KSFs and devoting its energies to being distinctively better than rivals at succeeding on these factors. Indeed, using one or more of the industry's KSFs as *cornerstones* for the company's strategy is often a wise approach to crafting a winning managerial game plan.

Strategic Management Principle
A sound strategy incorporates industry key success factors.

Key success factors vary from industry to industry and even from time to time within the same industry as driving forces and competitive conditions change. Table 3–4 provides a shopping list of the most common types of key success factors. Only rarely does an industry have more than three or four key success factors at any one time. And even among these three or four, one or two usually outrank the others in importance. Managers, therefore, have to resist the temptation to include factors that have only minor importance on their list of key success factors—the purpose of identifying KSFs is to make judgments about what things are more important to competitive success and what things are less important. To compile a list of every factor that matters even a little bit defeats the purpose of concentrating management attention on the factors truly crucial to long-term competitive success.

QUESTION 7: IS THE INDUSTRY ATTRACTIVE AND WHAT ARE ITS PROSPECTS FOR ABOVE-AVERAGE PROFITABILITY?

The final step of industry and competitive analysis is to review the overall industry situation and develop reasoned conclusions about the relative attractiveness or unattractiveness of the industry, both near-term and long-term. An assessment that the industry is fundamentally attractive typically suggests using an aggressive grow-and-build strategy, expanding sales efforts and investing in additional facilities and equipment as needed to strengthen the firm's long-term competitive position in the

T A B L E 3-4 | **Types of Key Success Factors**

Technology-Related KSFs
- Scientific research expertise (important in such fields as pharmaceuticals, medicine, space exploration, other "high-tech" industries)
- Production process innovation capability
- Product innovation capability
- Expertise in a given technology

Manufacturing-Related KSFs
- Low-cost production efficiency (achieve scale economies, capture experience curve effects)
- Quality of manufacture (fewer defects, less need for repairs)
- High utilization of fixed assets (important in capital intensive/high fixed-cost industries)
- Low-cost plant locations
- Access to adequate supplies of skilled labor
- High labor productivity (important for items with high labor content)
- Low-cost product design and engineering (reduces manufacturing costs)
- Flexibility to manufacture a range of models and sizes/take care of custom orders

Distribution-Related KSFs
- A strong network of wholesale distributors/dealers
- Gaining ample space on retailer shelves
- Having company-owned retail outlets
- Low distribution costs
- Fast delivery

Marketing-Related KSFs
- A well-trained, effective sales force
- Available, dependable service and technical assistance
- Accurate filling of buyer orders (few back orders or mistakes)
- Breadth of product line and product selection
- Merchandising skills
- Attractive styling/packaging
- Customer guarantees and warranties (important in mail-order retailing, big ticket purchases, new product introductions)

Skills-Related KSFs
- Superior talent (important in professional services)
- Quality control know-how
- Design expertise (important in fashion and apparel industries)
- Expertise in a particular technology
- Ability to come up with clever, catchy ads
- Ability to get newly developed products out of the R&D phase and into the market very quickly

Organizational Capability
- Superior information systems (important in airline travel, car rental, credit card, and lodging industries)
- Ability to respond quickly to shifting market conditions (streamlined decision-making, short lead times to bring new products to market)
- More experience and managerial know-how

Other Types of KSFs
- Favorable image/reputation with buyers
- Overall low cost (not just in manufacturing)
- Convenient locations (important in many retailing businesses)
- Pleasant, courteous employees
- Access to financial capital (important in newly emerging industries with high degrees of business risk and in capital-intensive industries)
- Patent protection

business. If the industry and competitive situation is judged relatively unattractive, more successful industry participants may choose to invest cautiously, look for ways to protect their long-term competitiveness and profitability, and perhaps acquire smaller firms if the price is right. Weaker companies may consider leaving the industry or merging with a rival. Stronger companies may consider diversification into more attractive businesses. Outsiders considering entry may decide against investing in the business and look elsewhere for opportunities.

Important factors for company managers to consider in drawing conclusions about whether the industry is a good business to be in include

- The industry's growth potential.
- Whether the industry will be favorably or unfavorably impacted by the prevailing driving forces.
- The potential for the entry/exit of major firms (probable entry reduces attractiveness to existing firms; the exit of a major firm or several weak firms opens up market share growth opportunities for the remaining firms).
- The stability/dependability of demand (as affected by seasonality, the business cycle, the volatility of consumer preferences, inroads from substitutes, and the like).
- Whether competitive forces will become stronger or weaker.
- The severity of problems/issues confronting the industry as a whole.
- The degrees of risk and uncertainty in the industry's future.
- Whether competitive conditions and driving forces are conducive to rising or falling industry profitability.

As a general proposition, if an industry's overall profit prospects are above average, the industry can be considered attractive. If its profit prospects are below average, it is unattractive. However, it is a mistake to think of industries as being attractive or unattractive in an absolute sense. Attractiveness is relative, not absolute, and conclusions one way or the other are in the eye of the beholder. Companies on the outside may look at an industry's environment and conclude that it is an unattractive business for them to get into; they may see more profitable opportunities elsewhere. But a favorably positioned company already in the industry may survey the very same business environment and conclude that the industry is attractive because it has the resources and competitive capabilities to exploit the vulnerabilities of its weaker rivals, gain market share, build a strong leadership position, and grow its revenues and profits at a rapid clip. Hence industry attractiveness *always* has to be appraised from the standpoint of a particular company. Industries unattractive to outsiders may be attractive to insiders. Industry environments unattractive to weak competitors may be attractive to strong competitors.

A company that is uniquely well-situated in an otherwise unattractive industry can, under certain circumstances, still earn unusually good profits.

While companies contemplating entry into an industry can rely on the above list of factors, along with the answers to the first six questions, to draw conclusions about industry attractiveness, companies already in the industry need to consider the following additional aspects:

- The company's competitive position in the industry and whether its position is likely to grow stronger or weaker (being a well-entrenched leader in an otherwise lackluster industry can still produce good profitability).
- The company's potential to capitalize on the vulnerabilities of weaker rivals (thereby converting an unattractive *industry* situation into a potentially rewarding *company* opportunity).

- Whether the company is insulated from, or able to defend against, the factors that make the industry unattractive.
- Whether continued participation in this industry adds importantly to the firm's ability to be successful in other industries in which it has business interests.

ACTUALLY DOING AN INDUSTRY AND COMPETITIVE ANALYSIS

Table 3–5 provides a *format* for reporting the pertinent facts and conclusions of industry and competitive analysis. It pulls the relevant concepts and considerations together in systematic fashion and makes it easier to do a concise, understandable analysis of the industry and competitive environment.

Two things should be kept in mind in doing industry and competitive analysis. One, the task of analyzing a company's external situation cannot be reduced to a mechanical, formula-like exercise in which facts and data are plugged in and definitive conclusions come pouring out. There can be several appealing scenarios about how an industry will evolve and what future competitive conditions will be like. For this reason, strategic analysis always leaves room for differences of opinion about how all the factors add up and how industry and competitive conditions will change. However, while no strategy analysis methodology can guarantee a single conclusive diagnosis, it doesn't make sense to shortcut strategic analysis and rely on opinion and casual observation. Managers become better strategists when they know what analytical questions to pose, can use situation analysis techniques to find answers, and have the skills to read clues about which way the winds of industry and competitive change are blowing. This is why we concentrated on suggesting the right questions to ask, explaining concepts and analytical approaches, and indicating the kinds of things to look for.

Two, sweeping industry and competitive analyses need to be done every one to

T A B L E 3-5 | **Industry and Competitive Analysis Summary Profile**

1. **Dominant Economic Characteristics of the Industry Environment** (market growth, geographic scope, industry structure, scale economies, experience curve effects, capital requirements, and so on)

2. **Competition Analysis**
   - Rivalry among competing sellers (a strong, moderate, or weak force/weapons of competition)
   - Threat of potential entry (a strong, moderate, or weak force/assessment of entry barriers)
   - Competition from substitutes (a strong, moderate, or weak force/why)
   - Power of suppliers (a strong, moderate, or weak force/why)
   - Power of customers (a strong, moderate, or weak force/why)

3. **Driving Forces**

4. **Competitive Position of Major Companies/ Strategic Groups**
   - Favorably positioned/why
   - Unfavorably positioned/why

5. **Competitor Analysis**
   - Strategic approaches/predicted moves of key competitors
   - Whom to watch and why

6. **Key Success Factors**

7. **Industry Prospects and Overall Attractiveness**
   - Factors making the industry attractive
   - Factors making the industry unattractive
   - Special industry issues/problems
   - Profit outlook (favorable/unfavorable)

three years; in the interim, managers are obliged to continually update and reexamine their thinking as events unfold. There's no substitute for being a good student of industry and competitive conditions and staying on the cutting edge of what's happening in the industry. Anything else leaves a manager unprepared to initiate shrewd and timely strategic adjustments.

KEY POINTS

Thinking strategically about a company's external situation involves probing for answers to the following seven questions:

1. *What are the industry's dominant economic traits?* Industries differ significantly on such factors as market size and growth rate, the scope of competitive rivalry, the number and relative sizes of both buyers and sellers, ease of entry and exit, whether sellers are vertically integrated, how fast basic technology is changing, the extent of scale economies and experience curve effects, whether the products of rival sellers are standardized or differentiated, and overall profitability. An industry's economic characteristics are important because of the implications they have for crafting strategy.

2. *What is competition like and how strong are each of the five competitive forces?* The strength of competition is a composite of five forces: the rivalry among competing sellers, the presence of attractive substitutes, the potential for new entry, the leverage major suppliers have, and the bargaining power of customers. The task of competition analysis is to assess each force, determine whether it produces strong or weak competitive pressures, and then think strategically about what sort of competitive strategy, given the "rules" of competition in the industry, the company will need to employ to *(a)* insulate the firm as much as possible from the five competitive forces, *(b)* influence the industry's competitive rules in the company's favor, and *(c)* gain a competitive edge.

3. *What is causing the industry's competitive structure and business environment to change?* Industry and competitive conditions change because forces are in motion that create incentives or pressures for change. The most common driving forces are changes in the long-term industry growth rate, changes in buyer composition, product innovation, entry or exit of major firms, globalization, changes in cost and efficiency, changing buyer preferences for standardized versus differentiated products or services, regulatory influences and government policy changes, changing societal and lifestyle factors, and reductions in uncertainty and business risk. Sound analysis of driving forces and their implications for the industry is a prerequisite to sound strategy-making.

4. *Which companies are in the strongest/weakest competitive positions?* Strategic group mapping is a valuable, if not necessary, tool for understanding the similarities, differences, strengths, and weaknesses inherent in the market positions of rival companies. Rivals in the same or nearby strategic group(s) are close competitors whereas companies in distant strategic groups usually pose little or no immediate threat.

5. *What strategic moves are rivals likely to make next?* This analytical step involves identifying competitors' strategies, deciding which rivals are likely to be strong contenders and which weak contenders, evaluating their

competitive options, and predicting what moves they are likely to make next. Scouting competitors well enough to anticipate their actions helps prepare effective countermoves (perhaps even beat a rival to the punch) and allows managers to take rivals' probable actions into account in designing their own company's best course of action. Managers who fail to study competitors closely risk being blindsided by "surprise" actions on the part of rivals. A company can't expect to outmaneuver its rivals without monitoring their actions and anticipating what moves they may make next.

6. *What are the key factors for competitive success?* Key success factors are the strategy-related action approaches, competitive capabilities, and business outcomes which all firms in an industry must be competent at doing or must concentrate on achieving in order to be competitively and financially successful. Determining the industry's key success factors, in light of industry and competitive conditions, is a top-priority analytical consideration. Frequently, a company can gain sustainable competitive advantage by training its strategy on industry KSFs and devoting its energies to being distinctively better than rivals at succeeding on these factors. Companies that only dimly perceive what factors are truly crucial to long-term competitive success are less likely to have winning strategies.

7. *Is the industry attractive and what are its prospects for above-average profitability?* The answer to this question is a major driver of company strategy. An assessment that the industry and competitive environment is fundamentally attractive typically suggests employing an aggressive strategy to build a strong competitive position in the business, expanding sales efforts and investing in additional facilities and equipment as needed. If the industry is relatively unattractive, outsiders considering entry may decide against it and look elsewhere for opportunities, weak companies in the industry may merge with or be acquired by a rival, and strong companies may restrict further investments and employ cost-reduction strategies and/or product innovation strategies to boost long-term competitiveness and protect their profitability. On occasion, an industry that is unattractive overall is still very attractive to a favorably situated company with the skills and resources to take business away from weaker rivals.

Good industry and competitive analysis is crucial to good strategy-making. A competently done industry and competitive analysis provides the keen understanding of a company's macroenvironment managers need to craft a strategy that fits the company's external situation well.

SUGGESTED READINGS

D'Aveni, Richard A. *Hypercompetition.* New York: Free Press, 1994, chaps. 5 and 6.
Ghemawat, Pankaj. "Building Strategy on the Experience Curve." *Harvard Business Review* 64, no. 2 (March–April 1985), pp. 143–49.
Linneman, Robert E., and Harold E. Klein. "Using Scenarios in Strategic Decision Making." *Business Horizons* 28, no. 1 (January–February 1985), pp. 64–74.
Ohmae, Kenichi. *The Mind of the Strategist.* New York: Penguin Books, 1983, chaps. 3, 6, 7, and 13.
Porter, Michael E. "How Competitive Forces Shape Strategy." *Harvard Business Review* 57, no. 2 (March–April 1979), pp. 137–45.

————. *Competitive Strategy: Techniques for Analyzing Industries and Competitors.* New York: Free Press, 1980, chap. 1.

————. *Competitive Advantage.* New York: Free Press, 1985, chap. 2.

Yip, George S. *Total Global Strategy: Managing for Worldwide Competitive Advantage.* Englewood Cliffs, N.J.: Prentice-Hall, 1992, chap. 10.

Zahra, Shaker A. and Sherry S. Chaples. "Blind Spots in Competitive Analysis." *Academy of Management Executives* 7, no. 2 (May 1993), pp. 7–28.

CHAPTER FOUR

COMPANY SITUATION ANALYSIS

Understand what really makes a company "tick."

Charles R. Scott
CEO, Intermark Corporation

The secret of success is to be ready for opportunity when it comes.

Benjamin Disraeli

If a company is not "best in world" at a critical activity, it is sacrificing competitive advantage by performing that activity with its existing technique.

James Brian Quinn

In the previous chapter we described how to use the tools of industry and competitive analysis to think strategically about a company's external situation. In this chapter we discuss how to size up a company's strategic position in that environment. Company situation analysis centers on five questions:

1. How well is the present strategy working?
2. What are the company's strengths, weaknesses, opportunities, and threats?
3. Are the company's prices and costs competitive?
4. How strong is the company's competitive position?
5. What strategic issues does the company face?

To explore these questions, four new analytical techniques need to be mastered: SWOT analysis, value chain analysis, strategic cost analysis, and competitive strength assessment. These techniques are basic strategic management tools because they expose the pluses and minuses of a company's situation, the strength of its competitive position, and whether the present strategy needs to be modified.

QUESTION 1: HOW WELL IS THE PRESENT STRATEGY WORKING?

In evaluating how well a company's present strategy is working, a manager has to start with what the strategy is (see Figure 2–3 in Chapter 2 to refresh your recollection of the key components of business strategy) and what the company's strategic and financial objectives are. The first thing to pin down is the company's competitive approach—whether it is (1) striving to be a low-cost leader, (2) stressing ways to differentiate its product offering from rivals, or (3) concentrating its efforts on a narrow market niche. Another strategy-defining consideration is the firm's competitive scope within the industry—how many stages of the industry's production-distribution chain it operates in (one, several, or all), the size and diversity of its geographic market coverage, and the size and diversity of its customer base. The company's functional strategies in production, marketing, finance, human resources, and so on further characterize company strategy. In addition, the company may have initiated some recent strategic moves (for instance, a price cut, stepped-up advertising, entry into a new geographic area, or merger with a competitor) that are integral to its strategy and that aim at securing a particular competitive advantage and/or improved competitive position. Reviewing the rationale for each piece of the strategy—for each competitive move and each functional approach—clarifies what the present strategy is.

While there's merit in evaluating the strategy from a qualitative standpoint (its completeness, internal consistency, rationale, and suitability to the situation), the best evidence of how well a company's strategy is working comes from studying the company's recent strategic and financial performance and seeing what story the numbers tell about the results the strategy is producing. Obvious indicators of strategic and financial performance include (1) the firm's market share ranking in the industry, (2) whether the firm's profit margins are increasing or decreasing and how large they are relative to rival firms' margins, (3) trends in the firm's net profits and return on investment, (4) the company's credit rating, (5) whether the firm's sales are growing faster or slower than the market as a whole, (6) the firm's image and reputation with its customers, and (7) whether the company is regarded as a leader in technology, product innovation, product quality, customer service, and the like. The stronger a company's current overall performance, the less likely the need for radical changes in strategy. The weaker a company's strategic and financial performance, the more its current strategy must be questioned. Weak performance is usually a sign of weak strategy or weak execution or both.

> The stronger a company's strategic and financial performance, the more likely it has a well-conceived, well-executed strategy.

QUESTION 2: WHAT ARE THE COMPANY'S STRENGTHS, WEAKNESSES, OPPORTUNITIES, AND THREATS?

Sizing up a firm's internal strengths and weaknesses and its external opportunities and threats is commonly known as *SWOT analysis*. It is an easy-to-use technique for getting a quick *overview* of a firm's strategic situation. SWOT analysis underscores the basic principle that strategy must produce a good fit between a company's internal capability (its strengths and weaknesses) and its external situation (reflected in part by its opportunities and threats).

IDENTIFYING INTERNAL STRENGTHS AND WEAKNESSES

A *strength* is something a company is good at doing or a characteristic that gives it an important capability. A strength can be a skill, important expertise, a valuable organizational resource or competitive capability, or an achievement that puts the company in a position of market advantage (like having a better product, stronger name recognition, superior technology, or better customer service). A strength can also result from alliances or cooperative ventures with a partner having expertise or capabilities that enhance a company's competitiveness.

A *weakness* is something a company lacks or does poorly (in comparison to others) or a condition that puts it at a disadvantage. A weakness may or may not make a company competitively vulnerable, depending on how much the weakness matters in the marketplace. Table 4–1 indicates the kinds of factors managers should consider in determining a company's internal strengths and weaknesses.

Once managers identify a company's internal strengths and weaknesses, the two compilations need to be carefully evaluated from a strategy-making perspective. Some strengths are more important than others because they matter more in determining performance, in competing successfully, and in forming a powerful strategy. Likewise, some internal weaknesses can prove fatal, while others are inconsequential or easily remedied. Sizing up a company's strengths and weaknesses is akin to constructing a *strategic balance sheet* where strengths represent *competitive assets* and weaknesses represent *competitive liabilities*. The strategic issues are whether the company's strengths/assets adequately overcome its weaknesses/liabilities (50-50 balance is definitely not the desired condition!), how to meld company strengths into an effective strategy, and whether management actions are needed to tilt the company's strategic balance more toward strengths/assets and away from weaknesses/liabilities.

From a strategy-making perspective, a company's strengths are significant because they can form the cornerstones of strategy and the basis for creating competitive advantage. If a company doesn't have strong capabilities and competitive assets around which to craft an attractive strategy, managers need to take decisive remedial action to develop organizational strengths and competencies that can underpin a sound strategy. At the same time, managers have to correct competitive weaknesses that make the company vulnerable, hurt its strategic performance, or disqualify it from pursuing an attractive opportunity. The strategy-making principle here is simple: *a company's strategy should be well-suited to its strengths, weaknesses, and competitive capabilities*. It is foolhardy to pursue a strategic plan that cannot be competently executed with the skills and resources a company can marshal or that can be undermined by company weaknesses. As a rule, managers should build their strategies around what the company does best and avoid strategies that place heavy demands on areas where the company is weakest or has unproven ability.

Core Competencies   One of the "trade secrets" of first-rate strategic management is consolidating a company's technological, production, and marketing know-how into core competencies that enhance its competitiveness. *A core competence is something a company does especially well in comparison to its competitors.*[1] In practice, there

---

Basic Concept
A company's internal strengths usually represent competitive assets; its internal weaknesses usually represent competitive liabilities.

Strategic Management Principle
Successful strategists seek to capitalize on what a company does best—its expertise, strengths, core competencies, and strongest competitive capabilities.

---

[1]For a fuller discussion of the core competence concept, see C. K. Prahalad and Gary Hamel, "The Core Competence of the Corporation," *Harvard Business Review* 90, no. 3 (May–June 1990), pp. 79–93.

T A B L E 4–1 | **SWOT Analysis—What to Look for in Sizing Up a Company's Strengths, Weaknesses, Opportunities, and Threats**

Potential Internal Strengths

- Core competencies in key areas
- Adequate financial resources
- Well-thought-of by buyers
- An acknowledged market leader
- Well-conceived functional area strategies
- Access to economies of scale
- Insulated (at least somewhat) from strong competitive pressures
- Proprietary technology
- Cost advantages
- Better advertising campaigns
- Product innovation skills
- Proven management
- Ahead on experience curve
- Better manufacturing capability
- Superior technological skills
- Other?

Potential External Opportunities

- Ability to serve additional customer groups or expand into new markets or segments
- Ways to expand product line to meet broader range of customer needs
- Ability to transfer skills or technological know-how to new products or businesses
- Integrating forward or backward
- Falling trade barriers in attractive foreign markets
- Complacency among rival firms
- Ability to grow rapidly because of strong increases in market demand
- Emerging new technologies

Potential Internal Weaknesses

- No clear strategic direction
- Obsolete facilities
- Subpar profitability because . . .
- Lack of managerial depth and talent
- Missing some key skills or competencies
- Poor track record in implementing strategy
- Plagued with internal operating problems
- Falling behind in R&D
- Too narrow a product line
- Weak market image
- Weak distribution network
- Below-average marketing skills
- Unable to finance needed changes in strategy
- Higher overall unit costs relative to key competitors
- Other?

Potential External Threats

- Entry of lower-cost foreign competitors
- Rising sales of substitute products
- Slower market growth
- Adverse shifts in foreign exchange rates and trade policies of foreign governments
- Costly regulatory requirements
- Vulnerability to recession and business cycle
- Growing bargaining power of customers or suppliers
- Changing buyer needs and tastes
- Adverse demographic changes
- Other?

are many possible types of core competencies: excellent skills in manufacturing a high quality product, know-how in creating and operating a system for filling customer orders accurately and swiftly, the capability to provide better after-sale service, a unique formula for selecting good retail locations, unusual innovativeness in developing new products, better skills in merchandising and product display, superior mastery of an important technology, a carefully crafted process for researching customer needs and tastes and spotting new market trends, an unusually effective sales force, outstanding skills in working with customers on new applications and uses of the product, and expertise in integrating multiple technologies to create whole families of new products. Typically, a core competence relates to a set of skills, expertise in performing particular activities, or a company's scope and depth of technological know-how; it resides in a company's people, not in assets on the balance sheet.

The importance of a core competence to strategy-making rests with (1) the added capability it gives a company in going after a particular market opportunity, (2) the competitive edge it can yield in the marketplace, and (3) its potential for being a cornerstone of strategy. It is always easier to build competitive advantage when a firm has a core competence in performing activities important to market success, when rival companies do not have offsetting competencies, and when it is costly and time-consuming for rivals to match the competence. Core competencies are thus valuable competitive assets, capable of being the mainsprings of a company's success.

Strategic Management Principle
Core competencies empower a company to build competitive advantage.

IDENTIFYING EXTERNAL OPPORTUNITIES AND THREATS

Market opportunity is a big factor in shaping a company's strategy. Indeed, managers can't match strategy to the company's situation without first identifying each industry opportunity and appraising the growth and profit potential each one holds. Depending on industry conditions, opportunities can be plentiful or scarce and can range from wildly attractive (an absolute "must" to pursue) to marginally interesting (low on the company's list of strategic priorities).

In appraising industry opportunities and ranking their attractiveness, managers have to guard against equating industry opportunities with company opportunities. Not every company in an industry is well-positioned to pursue each opportunity that exists in the industry—some companies are more competitively situated than others and a few may be hopelessly out of contention or at least limited to a minor role. A company's strengths, weaknesses, and competitive capabilities make it better suited to pursuing some industry opportunities than others. *The industry opportunities most relevant to a particular company are those that offer important avenues for profitable growth, those where a company has the most potential for competitive advantage, and those which the company has the financial resources to pursue.* An industry opportunity that a company doesn't have the capability to capture is an illusion.

Often, certain factors in a company's external environment pose *threats* to its well-being. Threats can stem from the emergence of cheaper technologies, rivals' introduction of new or better products, the entry of low-cost foreign competitors into a company's market stronghold, new regulations that are more burdensome to a company than to its competitors, vulnerability to a rise in interest rates, the potential of a hostile takeover, unfavorable demographic shifts, adverse changes in foreign exchange rates, political upheaval in a foreign country where the company has facilities, and the like. Table 4–1 also presents a checklist of things to be alert for in identifying a company's external opportunities and threats.

Opportunities and threats not only affect the attractiveness of a company's situation but point to the need for strategic action. To be adequately matched to a company's situation, strategy must (1) be aimed at pursuing opportunities well-suited to the company's capabilities and (2) provide a defense against external threats. SWOT analysis is therefore more than an exercise in making four lists. The important part of SWOT analysis involves *evaluating* a company's strengths, weaknesses, opportunities, and threats and *drawing conclusions* about the attractiveness of the company's situation and the possible need for strategic action. Some of the pertinent strategy-making questions to consider, once the SWOT listings have been compiled, are:

Strategic Management Principle
Successful strategists aim at capturing a company's best growth opportunities and creating defenses against threats to its competitive position and future performance.

- Does the company have any internal strengths or core competencies an attractive strategy can be built around?
- Do the company's weaknesses make it competitively vulnerable and/or do they disqualify the company from pursuing certain industry opportunities? Which weaknesses does strategy need to correct?
- Which industry opportunities does the company have the skills and resources to pursue with a real chance of success? Which industry opportunities are "best" from the company's standpoint? (*Remember:* Opportunity without the means to capture it is an illusion.)
- What external threats should management be worried most about and what strategic moves should be considered in crafting a good defense?

Unless management is acutely aware of the company's internal strengths and weaknesses and its external opportunities and threats, it is ill-prepared to craft a strategy tightly matched to the company's situation. SWOT analysis is therefore an essential component of thinking strategically about a company's situation.

QUESTION 3: ARE THE COMPANY'S PRICES AND COSTS COMPETITIVE?

Company managers are often stunned when a competitor cuts price to "unbelievably low" levels or when a new market entrant comes on strong with a very low price. The competitor may not, however, be "dumping," buying market share, or waging a desperate move to gain sales; it may simply have substantially lower costs. One of the most telling signs of whether a company's market position is strong or precarious is whether its prices and costs are competitive with industry rivals. Price-cost comparisons are especially critical in a commodity-product industry where the value provided to buyers is the same from seller to seller, price competition is typically the ruling market force, and lower-cost companies have the upper hand. But even in industries where products are differentiated and competition centers around the different attributes of competing brands as much as around price, rival companies have to keep their costs *in line* and make sure that any added costs they incur and price premiums they charge create ample buyer value.

Competitors usually don't incur the same costs in supplying their products to end-users. The cost disparities can range from trivial to competitively significant and can arise from any of several factors:

- Differences in the prices paid for raw materials, components parts, energy, and other items purchased from suppliers.
- Differences in basic technology and the age of plants and equipment. (Because rival companies usually invest in plants and key pieces of equipment at different times, their facilities have somewhat different technological efficiencies and different fixed costs. Older facilities are typically less efficient, but if they were less expensive to construct or were acquired at bargain prices, they *may* still be reasonably cost competitive with modern facilities.)
- Differences in internal operating costs due to economies of scale associated with different-size plants, learning and experience curve effects, different wage rates, different productivity levels, different operating practices, different organization structures and staffing levels, different tax rates, and the like.

Assessing whether a company's costs are competitive with those of its close rivals is a necessary and crucial part of company situation analysis.

- Differences in rival firms' exposure to inflation rates and changes in foreign exchange rates (as can occur in global industries where competitors have plants located in different nations).
- Differences in marketing costs, sales and promotion expenditures, and advertising expenses.
- Differences in inbound transportation costs and outbound shipping costs.
- Differences in forward channel distribution costs (the costs and markups of distributors, wholesalers, and retailers associated with getting the product from the point of manufacture into the hands of end users).

For a company to be competitively successful, its costs must be in line with those of close rivals. While some cost disparity is justified so long as the products or services of closely competing companies are sufficiently differentiated, a high-cost firm's market position becomes increasingly vulnerable the more its costs exceed those of close rivals.

Principle of Competitive Markets
The higher a company's costs are above those of close rivals, the more competitively vulnerable it becomes.

STRATEGIC COST ANALYSIS AND VALUE CHAINS

Given the numerous opportunities for cost disparities, a company must thus be alert to how its costs compare with rivals'. This is where *strategic cost analysis* comes in. *Strategic cost analysis focuses on a firm's cost position relative to its rivals'*.

The Value Chain Concept   The primary analytical tool of strategic cost analysis is a *value chain* identifying the activities, functions, and business processes that have to be performed in designing, producing, marketing, delivering, and supporting a product or service.[2] The chain of value-creating activities starts with raw materials supply and continues on through parts and components production, manufacturing and assembly, wholesale distribution, and retailing to the ultimate end-user of the product or service.

A *company's* value chain shows the linked set of activities and functions it performs internally (see Figure 4–1). The chain includes a profit margin because a markup over the cost of performing the firm's value-creating activities is customarily part of the price (or total cost) borne by buyers—creating value that exceeds the cost of doing so is a fundamental objective of business.

By disaggregating a company's operations into strategically relevant activities and business processes, it is possible to better understand the company's cost structure and to see where the major cost elements are. Each activity in the value chain incurs costs and ties up assets; assigning the company's operating costs and assets to each individual activity in the chain provides cost estimates for each activity. The costs a company incurs in performing each activity can be driven up or down by two types of factors: *structural drivers* (scale economies, experience curve effects, technology requirements, capital intensity, and product line complexity) and *executional drivers* (how committed the work force is to continuous improvement, employee attitudes and organizational capabilities regarding product quality and process quality, cycle time in getting newly developed products to market, utilization of existing capacity,

Basic Concept
Strategic cost analysis involves comparing a company's cost position relative to key competitors activity by activity all the way from raw materials purchase to the price paid by ultimate customers.

Basic Concept
A company's value chain identifies the primary activities that create value for customers and the related support activities; value chains are a tool for thinking strategically about the relationships among activities performed inside and outside the firm—which ones are strategy-critical and how core competencies can be developed.

[2]Value chains and strategic cost analysis are described at greater length in Michael E. Porter, *Competitive Advantage* (New York: Free Press, 1985), chapters 2 and 3; Robin Cooper and Robert S. Kaplan, "Measure Costs Right: Make the Right Decisions," *Harvard Business Review* 66, no. 5 (September–October, 1988), pp. 96–103; and John K. Shank and Vijay Govindarajan, *Strategic Cost Management* (New York: Free Press, 1993), especially chapters 2–6 and 10.

FIGURE 4-1 | **Representative Company Value Chain**

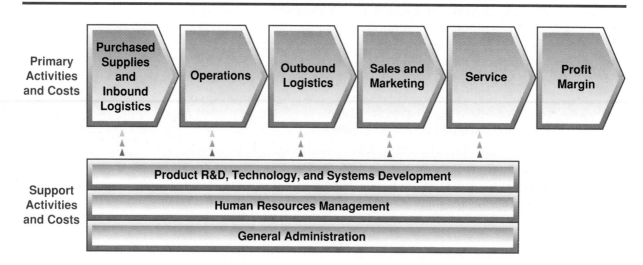

Primary Activities

- **Purchased Supplies and Inbound Logistics**—Activities, costs, and assets associated with purchasing fuel, energy, raw materials, parts components, merchandise, and consumable items from vendors; receiving, storing, and disseminating inputs from suppliers; inspection; and inventory management.
- **Operations**—Activities, costs, and assets associated with converting inputs into final product form (production, assembly, packaging, equipment maintenance, facilities, operations, quality assurance, environmental protection).
- **Outbound Logistics**—Activities, costs, and assets dealing with physically distributing the product to buyers (finished goods warehousing, order processing, order picking and packing, shipping, delivery vehicle operations).
- **Sales and Marketing**—Activities, costs, and assets related to sales force efforts, advertising and promotion, market research and planning, and dealer/distributor support.
- **Service**—Activities, costs, and assets associated with providing assistance to buyers, such as installation, spare parts delivery, maintenance and repair, technical assistance, buyer inquiries, and complaints.

Support Activities

- **Research, Technology, and Systems Development**—Activities, costs, and assets relating to product R&D, process R&D, process design improvement, equipment design, computer software development, telecommunications systems, computer-assisted design and engineering, new database capabilities, and development of computerized support systems.
- **Human Resources Management**—Activities, costs, and assets associated with the recruitment, hiring, training, development, and compensation of all types of personnel; labor relations activities; development of knowledge-based skills.
- **General Administration**—Activities, costs, and assets relating to general management, accounting and finance, legal and regulatory affairs, safety and security, management information systems, and other "overhead" functions.

Source: Adapted from Michael E. Porter, *Competitive Advantage* (New York: The Free Press, 1985), pp. 37–43.

whether internal business processes are efficiently designed and executed, and how effectively the firm works with suppliers and/or customers to reduce the costs of performing its activities). Understanding a company's cost structure means understanding

- Whether it is trying to achieve a competitive advantage based on (1) lower costs (in which case managerial efforts to lower costs along the company's value chain should be highly visible) or (2) differentiation (in which case managers may deliberately spend more performing those activities responsible for creating the differentiating attributes).

- Cost behavior in each activity in the value chain and how the costs of one activity spill over to affect the costs of others.
- Whether the linkages among activities in the company's value chain present opportunities for cost reduction (for example, Japanese VCR producers were able to reduce prices from $1,300 in 1977 to under $300 in 1984 by spotting the impact of an early step in the value chain, product design, on a later step, production, and deciding to drastically reduce the number of parts).[3]

> Value chains are also a tool for understanding the firm's cost structure and how costs are driven up or down within activities and across activities.

However, there's more to strategic cost analysis and a company's cost competitiveness than just comparing the costs of activities comprising rivals' value chains. Competing companies often differ in their degrees of vertical integration. Comparing the value chain for a partially integrated rival against a fully integrated rival requires adjusting for differences in scope of activities performed. Moreover, uncompetitive prices can have their origins in activities performed by suppliers or by forward channel allies involved in getting the product to end-users. Suppliers or forward channel allies may have excessively high cost structures or profit margins that jeopardize a company's cost competitiveness even though its costs for internally performed activities are competitive.

For example, when determining Michelin's cost competitiveness vis-à-vis Goodyear and Bridgestone in supplying replacement tires to vehicle owners, one has to look at more than whether Michelin's tire manufacturing costs are above or below Goodyear's and Bridgestone's. If a buyer has to pay $400 for a set of Michelin tires and only $350 for comparable sets of Goodyear or Bridgestone tires, Michelin's $50 price disadvantage in the replacement tire marketplace can stem not only from higher manufacturing costs (reflecting, *perhaps,* the added costs of Michelin's strategic efforts to build a better quality tire with more performance features) but also from (1) differences in what the three tiremakers pay their suppliers for materials and tire-making components and (2) differences in the operating efficiencies, costs, and markups of Michelin's wholesale-retail dealer outlets versus those of Goodyear and Bridgestone. Thus, determining whether a company's prices and costs are competitive from an end-user's standpoint requires looking at the activities and costs of competitively relevant suppliers and forward allies, as well as the costs of internally performed activities.

As the tire industry example makes clear, a company's value chain is embedded in a larger system of activities that includes the value chains of its upstream suppliers and downstream customers or allies engaged in getting its product/service to end-users.[4] Accurately assessing a company's competitiveness in end-use markets requires that company managers understand the entire value delivery system, not just the company's own value chain; at the very least, this means considering the value chains of suppliers and forward channel allies (if any)—as shown in Figure 4–2. Suppliers' value chains are relevant because suppliers perform activities and incur costs in creating and delivering the purchased inputs used in a company's own value chain; the cost

> A company's cost competitiveness depends not only on the costs of internally performed activities (its own value chain) but also on costs in the value chains of suppliers and forward channel allies.

---

[3]M. Hegert and D. Morris, "Accounting Data for Value Chain Analysis," *Strategic Management Journal* 10 (1989), p. 183.
[4]Porter, *Competitive Advantage,* p. 34.

F I G U R E 4–2 | **The Value Chain System**

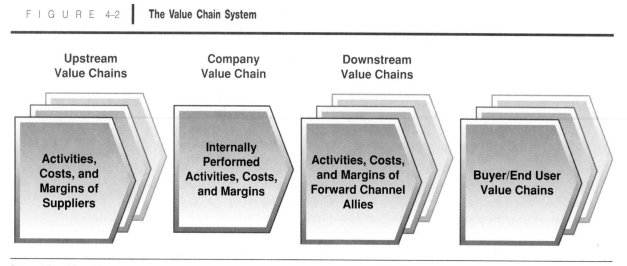

Source: Adapted from Michael E. Porter, *Competitive Advantage* (New York: The Free Press, 1985), p. 35.

quality of these inputs influence the company's cost and/or differentiation capabilities. Anything a company can do to reduce its suppliers' costs or improve suppliers' effectiveness can enhance its own competitiveness. Forward channel value chains are relevant because (1) the costs and margins of downstream companies are part of the price the ultimate end-user pays and (2) the activities forward channel allies perform affect the end-user's satisfaction. Furthermore, a company can often enhance its competitiveness by undertaking activities that have a beneficial impact on its customers' value chains. For instance, some aluminum can producers constructed plants next to beer breweries and delivered cans on overhead conveyors directly to brewers' can-filling lines. This resulted in significant savings in production scheduling, shipping, and inventory costs for both container producers and breweries.[5]

Although the value chains in Figures 4–1 and 4–2 are typical, the nature of the chains and the relative importance of the activities within them vary by industry and by company position in the value chain system. The value chain for the pulp and paper industry (timber farming, logging, pulp mills, papermaking, printing, and publishing) differs from the chain for the home appliance industry (parts and components manufacture, assembly, wholesale distribution, retail sales). The value chain for the soft drink industry (processing of basic ingredients, syrup manufacture, bottling and can filling, wholesale distribution, retailing) differs from the chain for the computer software industry (programming, disk loading, marketing, distribution). A producer of bathroom and kitchen faucets depends heavily on the activities of wholesale distributors and building supply retailers to represent its products to homebuilders and do-it-yourselfers; a producer of small gasoline engines markets directly to the makers of lawn and garden equipment. A wholesaler's most important activities and costs deal with purchased goods, inbound logistics, and outbound logistics. A hotel's most important activities and costs are in operations—check-in and check-out, maintenance and housekeeping, dining and room service, conventions and meetings, and accounting. A global public accounting firm's most important activities and costs revolve around customer service

---

[5]Hegert and Morris, "Accounting Data for Value Chain Analysis," p. 180.

and human resources management (recruiting and training a highly competent professional staff). Outbound logistics is a crucial activity at Domino's Pizza but comparatively insignificant at Blockbuster. Sales and marketing are dominant activities at Coca-Cola but only minor activities at electric and gas utilities. Consequently, generic value chains like those in Figures 4–1 and 4–2 are illustrative, not absolute, and may require adaptation to fit a particular company's circumstances.

Developing the Data for Strategic Cost Analysis   The data requirements for value chain analysis can be formidable. Typically, the analyst must break down a firm's departmental cost accounting data into the costs of performing specific activities.[6] The appropriate degree of disaggregation depends on the economics of the activities and how valuable it is to develop cross-company cost comparisons for narrowly defined activities as opposed to broadly defined activities. A good guideline is to develop separate cost estimates for activities having different economics and for activities representing a significant or growing proportion of cost.[7]

Traditional accounting identifies costs according to broad categories of expenses—wages and salaries, employee benefits, supplies, travel, depreciation, R&D, and other fixed charges. *Activity-based costing* entails assigning these broad categories of costs to the specific tasks and activities being performed, as shown in Table 4–2.[8] It also entails developing cost estimates for activities performed in the competitively relevant portions of suppliers' and downstream customers' value chains. To benchmark the firm's cost position against rivals, costs for the same activities for each rival must be estimated—an advanced art in competitive intelligence. But despite the tediousness of developing cost estimates activity by activity and the imprecision of some of the estimates, the payoff in exposing the costs of particular internal tasks and functions and the cost competitiveness of one's position vis-à-vis rivals makes activity-based costing a valuable strategic management tool. Despite the calculation problems, every company's managers should attempt to estimate the value chain for their business.[9] Illustration Capsule 9 shows a simplified value chain comparison for two prominent brewers of beer—Anheuser-Busch (the U.S. industry leader) and Adolph Coors (the third-ranking brewer).

The most important application of value chain analysis is to expose how a particular firm's cost position compares with the cost positions of its rivals. What is needed is competitor versus competitor cost estimates for supplying a product or service to a well-defined customer group or market segment. The size of a company's cost advantage/disadvantage can vary from item to item in the product line, from customer group to customer group (if different distribution channels are used), and from geographic market to geographic market (if cost factors vary across geographic regions).

BENCHMARKING THE COSTS OF KEY ACTIVITIES

Many companies today are benchmarking the costs of performing a given activity against competitors' costs (and/or against the costs of a noncompetitor in another

---

[6]For discussions of the accounting challenges in calculating the costs of value chain activities, see Shank and Govindarajan, *Strategic Cost Management,* pp. 62–72 and chapter 5, and Hegert and Morris, "Accounting Data for Value Chain Analysis," pp. 175–88.

[7]Porter, *Competitive Advantage,* p. 45.

[8]For a discussion of activity-based cost accounting, see Cooper and Kaplan, "Measure Costs Right: Make the Right Decisions," pp. 96–103; Shank and Govindarajan, *Strategic Cost Management,* Chapter 11; and Terence P. Paré, "A New Tool for Managing Costs," *Fortune,* June 14, 1993, pp. 124–29.

[9]Shank and Govindarajan, *Strategic Cost Management,* p. 62.

T A B L E 4–2 | **The Difference between Traditional Cost Accounting and Activity-Based Cost Accounting**

Traditional Cost Accounting Categories in Departmental Budget		Cost of Performing Specific Departmental Activities Using Activity-Based Cost Accounting	
Wages and salaries	$350,000	Evaluate supplier capabilities	$135,750
Employee benefits	115,000	Process purchase orders	82,100
Supplies	6,500	Expedite supplier deliveries	23,500
Travel	2,400	Expedite internal processing	15,840
Depreciation	17,000	Check quality of items purchased	94,300
Other fixed charges	124,000	Check incoming deliveries against purchase orders	48,450
Miscellaneous operating expenses	25,250	Resolve problems	110,000
		Internal administration	130,210
	$640,150		$640,150

Source: Adapted from information in Terence P. Paré, "A New Tool for Managing Costs," *Fortune,* June 14, 1993, pp. 124–29.

industry that efficiently and effectively performs much the same activity or business process). Benchmarking focuses on cross-company comparisons of how well basic functions and processes in the value chain are performed—how materials are purchased, how suppliers are paid, how inventories are managed, how employees are trained, how payrolls are processed, how fast the company can get new products to market, how the quality control function is performed, how customer orders are filled and shipped, and how maintenance is performed.[10] The ultimate objective is to understand the best practices in performing an activity, to learn how lower costs are actually achieved, and to take action to improve a company's cost competitiveness whenever benchmarking reveals that the costs of performing an activity are out of line with what other companies (competitors or noncompetitors) have been able to achieve successfully.

> Benchmarking the performance of company activities against rivals and other best-practice companies provides hard evidence of a company's cost competitiveness.

In 1979, Xerox became an early pioneer in the use of benchmarking when Japanese manufacturers began selling mid-size copiers in the U.S. for $9,600 each—less than Xerox's production costs.[11] Although Xerox management suspected its Japanese competitors were dumping, it sent a team of line managers to Japan, including the head of manufacturing, to study competitors' business processes and costs. Fortunately, Xerox's joint venture partner in Japan, Fuji-Xerox, knew the competitors well. The team found that Xerox's costs were excessive due to gross inefficiencies in its manufacturing processes and business practices; the study proved instrumental in Xerox's efforts to become cost competitive and prompted Xerox to embark on a long-term program to benchmark 67 of its key work processes against companies identified as having the "best practices" in performing these processes. Xerox quickly decided not to restrict its benchmarking efforts to its office equipment rivals but to extend them to any company regarded as "world class" in performing an activity relevant to Xerox's business. Illustration Capsule 10 describes one of Ford Motor's benchmarking experiences.

---

[10]For more details, see Gregory H. Watson, *Strategic Benchmarking: How to Rate Your Company's Performance Against the World's Best* (New York: John Wiley, 1993) and Robert C. Camp, *Benchmarking: The Search for Industry Best Practices That Lead to Superior Performance* (Milwaukee:ASQC Quality Press, 1989). See also Alexandra Biesada, "Strategic Benchmarking," *Financial World,* September 29, 1992, pp. 30–38.

[11]Jeremy Main, "How to Steal the Best Ideas Around," *Fortune,* October 19, 1992, pp. 102–3.

ILLUSTRATION CAPSULE 9

VALUE CHAINS FOR ANHEUSER-BUSCH AND ADOLPH COORS BEERS

In the table below are average cost estimates for the combined brands of beer produced by Anheuser-Busch and Coors. The example shows raw material costs, other manufacturing costs, and forward channel distribution costs. The data are for 1982.

Value Chain Activities and Costs	Estimated Average Cost Breakdown for Combined Anheuser-Busch Brands		Estimated Average Cost Breakdown for Combined Adolph Coors Brands	
	Per 6-Pack of 12-oz Cans	Per Barrel Equivalent	Per 6-Pack of 12-oz Cans	Per Barrel Equivalent
1. Manufacturing costs:				
Direct production costs:				
Raw material ingredients	$0.1384	$ 7.63	$0.1082	$ 5.96
Direct labor	0.1557	8.58	0.1257	6.93
Salaries for nonunionized personnel	0.0800	4.41	0.0568	3.13
Packaging	0.5055	27.86	0.4663	25.70
Depreciation on plant and equipment	0.0410	2.26	0.0826	4.55
Subtotal	0.9206	50.74	0.8396	46.27
Other expenses:				
Advertising	0.0477	2.63	0.0338	1.86
Other marketing costs and general administrative expenses	0.1096	6.04	0.1989	10.96
Interest	0.0147	0.81	0.0033	0.18
Research and development	0.0277	1.53	0.0195	1.07
Total manufacturing costs	$1.1203	$61.75	$1.0951	$60.34
2. Manufacturer's operating profit	0.1424	7.85	0.0709	3.91
3. Net selling price	1.2627	69.60	1.1660	64.25
4. Plus federal and state excise taxes paid by brewer	0.1873	10.32	0.1782	9.82
5. Gross manufacturer's selling price to distributor/wholesaler	1.4500	79.92	1.3442	74.07
6. Average margin over manufacturer's cost	0.5500	30.31	0.5158	28.43
7. Average wholesale price charged to retailer (inclusive of taxes in item 4 above but exclusive of other taxes)	$2.00	$110.23	$1.86	$102.50
8. Plus other assorted state and local taxes levied on wholesale and retail sales (this varies from locality to locality)	0.60		0.60	
9. Average 20% retail markup over wholesale cost	0.40		0.38	
10. Average price to consumer at retail	$3.00		$2.84	

Note: The difference in the average cost structures for Anheuser-Busch and Adolph Coors is, to a substantial extent, due to A-B's higher proportion of super-premium beer sales. A-B's super-premium brand, Michelob, was the bestseller in its category and somewhat more costly to brew than premium and popular-priced beers.

Source: Compiled by Tom McLean, Elsa Wischkaemper, and Arthur A. Thompson, Jr., from a wide variety of documents and field interviews.

FORD MOTOR COMPANY'S BENCHMARKING OF ITS ACCOUNTS PAYABLE ACTIVITY

In the 1980s Ford's North American accounts payable department employed more than 500 people. Clerks spent the majority of their time straightening out the relatively few situations where three documents—the purchase order issued by the purchasing department, the receiving document prepared by clerks at the receiving dock, and the invoice sent by the vendor/supplier to accounts payable—did not match. Sometimes resolving the discrepancies took weeks of time and the efforts of many people. Ford managers believed that by using computers to automate some functions performed manually, head count could be reduced to 400. Before proceeding, Ford managers decided to visit Mazda—a company in which Ford had recently acquired a 25 percent ownership interest. To their astonishment, Mazda handled its accounts payable function with only five people. Following Mazda's lead, Ford benchmarkers created an invoiceless system where payments to suppliers were triggered automatically when the goods were received. The reengineered system allowed Ford to reduce its accounts payable staff to under 200, a lot more than Mazda but much better than would have resulted without benchmarking the accounts payable activity.

Sources: Michael Hammer and James Champy, *Reengineering the Corporation* (New York: HarperBusiness, 1993), pp. 39–43, and Jeremy Main, "How to Steal the Best Ideas Around," *Fortune,* October 19, 1992, p. 106.

Sometimes cost benchmarking can be accomplished by collecting information from published reports, trade groups, and industry research firms and by talking to knowledgeable industry analysts, customers, and suppliers (customers, suppliers, and joint-venture partners often make willing benchmarking allies). Usually, though, benchmarking requires field trips to the facilities of competing or noncompeting companies to observe how things are done, ask questions, compare practices and processes, and perhaps exchange data on productivity, staffing levels, time requirements, and other cost components. However, benchmarking involves competitively sensitive information about how lower costs are achieved, and close rivals can't be expected to be completely open, even if they agree to host facilities tours and answer questions. But the explosive interest of companies in benchmarking costs and identifying best practices has prompted consulting organizations (for example, Andersen Consulting, A. T. Kearney, Best Practices Benchmarking & Consulting, and Towers Perrin) and several newly formed councils and associations (the International Benchmarking Clearinghouse and the Strategic Planning Institute's Council on Benchmarking) to gather benchmarking data, do benchmarking studies, and distribute information about best practices and the costs of performing activities to clients/members without identifying the sources. The ethical dimension of benchmarking is discussed in Illustration Capsule 11. Over 80 percent of *Fortune 500* companies now engage in some form of benchmarking.

Benchmarking is a manager's best tool for determining whether the company is performing particular functions and activities efficiently, whether its costs are in line with competitors, and which internal activities and business processes need to be improved. It is a way of learning which companies are best at performing certain activities and functions and then imitating—or, better still, improving on—their techniques. Toyota managers got their idea for just-in-time inventory deliveries by studying how U.S. supermarkets replenished their shelves. Southwest Airlines reduced the turnaround time of its aircraft at each scheduled stop by studying pit crews on the auto racing circuit.

ILLUSTRATION CAPSULE 11

BENCHMARKING AND ETHICAL CONDUCT

Because actions between benchmarking partners can involve competitively sensitive data and discussions, conceivably raising questions about possible restraint of trade or improper business conduct, the SPI Council on Benchmarking and The International Benchmarking Clearinghouse urge all individuals and organizations involved in benchmarking to abide by a code of conduct grounded in ethical business behavior. The code is based on the following principles and guidelines:

- In benchmarking with competitors, establish specific ground rules up front, e.g., "We don't want to talk about those things that will give either of us a competitive advantage; rather, we want to see where we both can mutually improve or gain benefit." Do not discuss costs with competitors if costs are an element of pricing.

- Do not ask competitors for sensitive data or cause the benchmarking partner to feel that sensitive data must be provided to keep the process going. Be prepared to provide the same level of information that you request. Do not share proprietary information without prior approval from the proper authorities of both parties.

- Use an ethical third party to assemble and blind competitive data, with inputs from legal counsel, for direct competitor comparisons.

- Consult with legal counsel if any information gathering procedure is in doubt, e.g., before contacting a direct competitor.

- Any information obtained from a benchmarking partner should be treated as internal, privileged information. Any external use must have the partner's permission.

- Do not:
  - Disparage a competitor's business or operations to a third party.
  - Attempt to limit competition or gain business through the benchmarking relationship.
  - Misrepresent oneself as working for another employer.

- Demonstrate commitment to the efficiency and effectiveness of the process by being adequately prepared at each step, particularly at initial contact. Be professional, honest, and courteous. Adhere to the agenda—maintain focus on benchmarking issues.

Sources: The SPI Council on Benchmarking, The International Benchmarking Clearinghouse, and conference presentation of AT&T Benchmarking Group, Des Moines, Iowa, October 1993.

STRATEGIC OPTIONS FOR ACHIEVING COST COMPETITIVENESS

Value chain analysis can reveal a great deal about a firm's cost competitiveness. One of the fundamental insights of strategic cost analysis is that a company's competitiveness depends on how well it manages its value chain relative to how well competitors manage theirs.[12] Examining the makeup of a company's own value chain and comparing it to rivals' indicates who has how much of a cost advantage/disadvantage and which cost components are responsible. Such information is vital in crafting strategies to eliminate a cost disadvantage or create a cost advantage.

Looking again at Figure 4–2, observe that there are three main areas in a company's overall value chain where important differences in the costs of competing firms can occur: in the suppliers' part of the industry value chain, in a company's own activity segments, or in the forward channel portion of the industry chain. If a firm's lack of cost competitiveness lies either in the backward (upstream) or forward (downstream) sections of the value chain, then reestablishing cost competitiveness

Strategic actions to eliminate a cost disadvantage need to be linked to the location in the value chain where the cost differences originate.

---

[12]Shank and Govindarajan, *Strategic Cost Management*, p. 50.

may have to extend beyond the firm's own in-house operations. When a firm's cost disadvantage is principally associated with the costs of items purchased from suppliers (the upstream end of the industry chain), company managers can pursue any of several strategic actions to correct the problem:[13]

- Negotiate more favorable prices with suppliers.
- Work with suppliers to help them achieve lower costs.
- Integrate backward to gain control over the costs of purchased items.
- Try to use lower-priced substitute inputs.
- Do a better job of managing the linkages between suppliers' value chains and the company's own chain; for example, close coordination between a company and its suppliers can permit just-in-time deliveries that lower a company's inventory and internal logistics costs and that may also allow its suppliers to economize on their warehousing, shipping, and production scheduling costs—a win-win outcome for both (instead of a zero-sum game where a company's gains match supplier concessions).
- Try to make up the difference by cutting costs elsewhere in the chain.

A company's strategic options for eliminating cost disadvantages in the forward end of the value chain system include[14]

- Pushing distributors and other forward channel allies to reduce their markups.
- Working closely with forward channel allies/customers to identify win-win opportunities to reduce costs. A chocolate manufacturer learned that by shipping its bulk chocolate in liquid form in tank cars instead of 10-pound molded bars, it saved its candy bar manufacturing customers the cost of unpacking and melting, and it eliminated its own costs of molding bars and packing them.
- Changing to a more economical distribution strategy, including the possibility of forward integration.
- Trying to make up the difference by cutting costs earlier in the cost chain.

When the source of a firm's cost disadvantage is internal, managers can use any of nine strategic approaches to restore cost parity:[15]

1. Initiate internal budget reductions and streamline operations.
2. Reengineer business processes and work practices (to boost employee productivity, improve the efficiency of key activities, increase the utilization of company assets, and otherwise do a better job of managing the cost drivers).
3. Try to eliminate some cost-producing activities altogether by revamping the value chain system (for example, shifting to a radically different technological approach or maybe bypassing the value chains of forward channel allies and marketing directly to end-users).

---

[13]Porter, *Competitive Advantage,* chapter 3.
[14]Ibid.
[15]Ibid.

4. Relocate high-cost activities to geographic areas where they can be performed more cheaply.

5. See if certain activities can be outsourced from vendors or performed by contractors more cheaply than they can be done internally.

6. Invest in cost-saving technological improvements (automation, robotics, flexible manufacturing techniques, computerized controls).

7. Innovate around the troublesome cost components as new investments are made in plant and equipment.

8. Simplify the product design so that it can be manufactured more economically.

9. Try to make up the internal cost disadvantage by achieving savings in the backward and forward portions of the value chain system.

Value Chain Analysis, Core Competencies, and Competitive Advantage

How well a company manages its value chain activities relative to competitors is a key to building valuable core competencies and leveraging them into sustainable competitive advantage. With rare exceptions, a firm's products or services are not a basis for sustainable competitive advantage—it is too easy for a resourceful company to clone, improve on, or find an effective substitute for them.[16] Rather, a company's competitive edge is usually grounded in its skills and capabilities relative to rivals' and, more specifically, in the scope and depth of its ability to perform competitively crucial activities along the value chain better than rivals.

Value chain analysis is a powerful managerial tool for identifying which activities in the chain have competitive advantage potential.

Core competencies emerge from a company's experience, learned skills, and focused efforts in performing one or more related value chain components. Merck and Glaxo, two of the world's most competitively capable pharmaceutical companies, built their strategic positions around expert performance of a few key activities: extensive R&D to achieve first discovery of new drugs, a carefully constructed approach to patenting, skill in gaining rapid and thorough clinical clearance through regulatory bodies, and unusually strong distribution and sales force capabilities.[17] To arrive at a sound diagnosis of a company's true competitive capabilities, managers need to do four things:

1. Construct a value chain of company activities.

2. Examine the linkages among internally performed activities and the linkages with suppliers' and customers' chains.

3. Identify the activities and competencies critical to customer satisfaction and market success.

4. Make appropriate internal and external benchmarking comparisons to determine how well the company performs activities (which activities represent core competencies and which ones are better performed by outsiders?) and how its cost structure compares with competitors.

The strategy-making lesson of value chain analysis is that increased company competitiveness hinges on managerial efforts to concentrate company resources and talent on those skills and activities where the company can gain dominating expertise to serve its target customers.

---

[16]James Brian Quinn, *Intelligent Enterprise* (New York: Free Press, 1993), p. 54.
[17]Quinn, *Intelligent Enterprise*, p. 34.

QUESTION 4: HOW STRONG IS THE COMPANY'S COMPETITIVE POSITION?

Using value chain concepts and the other tools of strategic cost analysis to determine a company's cost competitiveness is necessary but not sufficient. A more broad-ranging assessment needs to be made of a company's competitive position and competitive strength. Particular elements to single out for evaluation are (1) how strongly the firm holds its present competitive position, (2) whether the firm's position can be expected to improve or deteriorate if the present strategy is continued (allowing for fine-tuning), (3) how the firm ranks *relative to key rivals* on each important measure of competitive strength and industry key success factors, (4) whether the firm enjoys a competitive advantage or is currently at a disadvantage, and (5) the firm's ability to defend its position in light of industry driving forces, competitive pressures, and the anticipated moves of rivals.

Table 4–3 lists some indicators of whether a firm's competitive position is improving or slipping. But company managers need to do more than just identify the areas of competitive improvement or slippage. They have to judge whether the company has a net competitive advantage or disadvantage vis-à-vis key competitors and whether the company's market position and performance can be expected to improve or deteriorate under the current strategy.

Managers can begin the task of evaluating the company's competitive strength by using benchmarking techniques to compare the company against industry rivals not just on cost but also on such competitively important measures as product quality, customer service, customer satisfaction, financial strength, technological skills, and product cycle time (how quickly new products can be taken from idea to design to market). It is not enough to benchmark the costs of activities and identify best practices; a company should benchmark itself against competitors on all strategically and competitively important aspects of its business.

Systematic assessment of whether a company's competitive position is strong or weak relative to close rivals is an essential step in company situation analysis.

TABLE 4–3 | **The Signs of Strength and Weakness in a Company's Competitive Position**

Signs of Competitive Strength	Signs of Competitive Weakness
• Important core competencies	• Confronted with competitive disadvantages
• Strong market share (or a leading market share)	• Losing ground to rival firms
• A pacesetting or distinctive strategy	• Below-average growth in revenues
• Growing customer base and customer loyalty	• Short on financial resources
• Above-average market visibility	• A slipping reputation with customers
• In a favorably situated strategic group	• Trailing in product development
• Concentrating on fastest-growing market segments	• In a strategic group destined to lose ground
• Strongly differentiated products	• Weak in areas where there is the most market potential
• Cost advantages	• A higher-cost producer
• Above-average profit margins	• Too small to be a major factor in the marketplace
• Above-average technological and innovational capability	• Not in good position to deal with emerging threats
• A creative, entrepreneurially alert management	• Weak product quality
• In position to capitalize on opportunities	• Lacking skills and capabilities in key areas

COMPETITIVE STRENGTH ASSESSMENTS

The most telling way to determine how strongly a company holds its competitive position is to quantitatively assess whether the company is stronger or weaker than close rivals on each key success factor and each important indicator of competitive strength. Much of the information for competitive position assessment comes from previous analyses. Industry and competitive analysis reveals the key success factors and competitive measures that separate industry winners from losers. Competitor analysis and benchmarking data provide a basis for judging the strengths and capabilities of key rivals.

Step one is to make a list of the industry's key success factors and most telling measures of competitive strength or weakness (6 to 10 measures usually suffice). Step two is to rate the firm and its key rivals on each factor. Rating scales from 1 to 10 are best to use although ratings of stronger (+), weaker (−), and about equal (=) may be appropriate when information is scanty and assigning numerical scores conveys false precision. Step three is to sum the individual strength ratings to get an overall measure of competitive strength for each competitor. Step four is to draw conclusions about the size and extent of the company's net competitive advantage or disadvantage and to take specific note of areas where the company's competitive position is strongest and weakest.

Table 4–4 provides two examples of competitive strength assessment. The first one employs an *unweighted rating scale;* with unweighted ratings each key success factor/competitive strength measure is assumed to be equally important. Whichever company has the highest strength rating on a given measure has an implied competitive edge on that factor; the size of its edge is mirrored in the margin of difference between its rating and the ratings assigned to rivals. Summing a company's strength ratings on all the measures produces an overall strength rating. The higher a company's overall strength rating, the stronger its competitive position. The bigger the margin of deference between a company's overall rating and the scores of lower-rated rivals, the greater its implied net competitive advantage. Thus, ABC's total score of 61 (see the top half of Table 4–4) signals a greater net competitive advantage over Rival 4 (with a score of 32) than over Rival 1 (with a score of 58).

However, it is better methodology to use a weighted rating system because the different measures of competitive strength are unlikely to be equally important. In a commodity-product industry, for instance, having low unit costs relative to rivals is nearly always the most important determinant of competitive strength. In an industry with strong product differentiation the most significant measures of competitive strength may be brand awareness, amount of advertising, reputation for quality, and distribution capability. In a *weighted rating system* each measure of competitive strength is assigned a weight based on its perceived importance in shaping competitive success. The largest weight could be as high as .75 (maybe even higher) in situations where one particular competitive variable is overwhelmingly decisive or as low as .20 when two or three strength measures are more important than the rest. Lesser competitive strength indicators can carry weights of .05 or .10. No matter whether the differences between the weights are big or little, *the sum of the weights must add up to 1.0.*

Weighted strength ratings are calculated by deciding how a company stacks up on each strength measure (using the 1 to 10 rating scale) and multiplying the assigned rating by the assigned weight (a rating score of 4 times a weight of .20 gives a weighted rating of .80). Again, the company with the highest rating on a

High competitive strength ratings signal a strong competitive position and possession of competitive advantage; low ratings signal a weak position and competitive disadvantage.

A weighted competitive strength analysis is conceptually stronger than an unweighted analysis because of the inherent weakness in assuming that all the strength measures are equally important.

T A B L E 4–4 | **Illustrations of Unweighted and Weighted Competitive Strength Assessments**

A. Sample of an Unweighted Competitive Strength Assessment
Rating scale: 1 = Very weak; 10 = Very strong

Key Success Factor/Strength Measure	ABC Co.	Rival 1	Rival 2	Rival 3	Rival 4
Quality/product performance	8	5	10	1	6
Reputation/image	8	7	10	1	6
Manufacturing capability	2	10	4	5	1
Technological skills	10	1	7	3	8
Dealer network	9	4	10	5	1
Marketing/advertising	9	4	10	5	1
Financial strength	5	10	7	3	1
Relative cost position	5	10	3	1	4
Customer service	5	7	10	1	4
Unweighted overall strength rating	61	58	71	25	32

B. Sample of a Weighted Competitive Strength Assessment
Rating scale: 1 = Very weak; 10 = Very strong

Key Success Factor/Strength Measure	Weight	ABC Co.	Rival 1	Rival 2	Rival 3	Rival 4
Quality/product performance	0.10	8/0.80	5/0.50	10/1.00	1/0.10	6/0.60
Reputation/image	0.10	8/0.80	7/0.70	10/1.00	1/0.10	6/0.60
Manufacturing capability	0.10	2/0.20	10/1.00	4/0.40	5/0.50	1/0.10
Technological skills	0.05	10/0.50	1/0.05	7/0.35	3/0.15	8/0.40
Dealer network	0.05	9/0.45	4/0.20	10/0.50	5/0.25	1/0.05
Marketing/advertising	0.05	9/0.45	4/0.20	10/0.50	5/0.25	1/0.05
Financial strength	0.10	5/0.50	10/1.00	7/0.70	3/0.30	1/0.10
Relative cost position	0.35	5/1.75	10/3.50	3/1.05	1/0.35	4/1.40
Customer service	0.15	5/0.75	7/1.05	10/1.50	1/0.15	4/1.60
Sum of weights	1.00					
Weighted overall strength rating		6.20	8.20	7.00	2.10	2.90

given measure has an implied competitive edge on that measure, with the size of its edge reflected in the difference between its rating and rivals' ratings. The weight attached to the measure indicates how important the edge is. Summing a company's weighted strength ratings for all the measures yields an overall strength rating. Comparisons of the weighted overall strength scores indicate which competitors are in the strongest and weakest competitive positions and who has how big a net competitive advantage over whom.

The bottom half of Table 4–4 shows a sample competitive strength assessment for ABC Company using a weighted rating system. Note that the unweighted and weighted rating schemes produce a different ordering of the companies. In the weighted system, ABC Company dropped from second to third in strength, and Rival 1 jumped from third into first because of its high strength ratings on the two most important factors. Weighting the importance of the strength measures can thus make a significant difference in the outcome of the assessment.

Competitive strength assessments provide useful conclusions about a company's competitive situation. The ratings show how a company compares against rivals, factor by factor or measure by measure, thus revealing where it is strongest and weakest and against whom. Moreover, the overall competitive strength scores indicate whether the company is at a net competitive advantage or disadvantage against each rival. The firm with the largest overall competitive strength rating can be said to have a net competitive advantage over each rival.

Knowing where a company is competitively strong and where it is weak is essential in crafting a strategy to strengthen its long-term competitive position. As a general rule, a company should try to convert its competitive strengths into sustainable competitive advantage and take strategic actions to protect against its competitive weaknesses. At the same time, competitive strength ratings point to which rival companies may be vulnerable to competitive attack and the areas where they are weakest. When a company has important competitive strengths in areas where one or more rivals are weak, it makes sense to consider offensive moves to exploit rivals' competitive weaknesses.

Competitive strengths and competitive advantages enable a company to improve its long-term market position.

QUESTION 5: WHAT STRATEGIC ISSUES DOES THE COMPANY FACE?

The final analytical task is to home in on the strategic issues management needs to address in forming an effective strategic action plan. Here, managers need to draw upon all the prior analysis, put the company's overall situation into perspective, and get a lock on exactly where they need to focus their strategic attention. This step should not be taken lightly. Without a precise fix on what the issues are, managers are not prepared to start crafting a strategy—a good strategy must offer a plan for dealing with all the strategic issues that need to be addressed.

Effective strategy-making requires thorough understanding of the strategic issues a company faces.

To pinpoint issues for the company's strategic action agenda, managers ought to consider the following:

- Whether the present strategy is adequate in light of driving forces at work in the industry.
- How closely the present strategy matches the industry's *future* key success factors.
- How good a defense the present strategy offers against the five competitive forces—particularly those that are expected to intensify in strength.
- In what ways the present strategy may not adequately protect the company against external threats and internal weaknesses.
- Where and how the company may be vulnerable to the competitive efforts of one or more rivals.
- Whether the company has competitive advantage or must work to offset competitive disadvantage.
- Where the strong spots and weak spots are in the present strategy.
- Whether additional actions are needed to improve the company's cost position, capitalize on emerging opportunities, and strengthen the company's competitive position.

These considerations should indicate whether the company can continue the same basic strategy with minor adjustments or whether major overhaul is called for.

The better matched a company's strategy is to its external environment and internal situation, the less need there is to contemplate big shifts in strategy. On the other hand, when the present strategy is not well-suited for the road ahead, managers need to give top priority to the task of crafting a new strategy.

Table 4–5 provides a format for doing company situation analysis. It incorporates the concepts and analytical techniques discussed in this chapter and provides a way of reporting the results of company situation analysis in a systematic, concise manner.

T A B L E 4-5 | **Company Situation Analysis**

1. Strategic Performance Indicators

Performance Indicator	19—	19—	19—	19—	19—
Market share	—	—	—	—	—
Sales growth	—	—	—	—	—
Net profit margin	—	—	—	—	—
Return on equity investment	—	—	—	—	—
Other?	—	—	—	—	—

2. Internal Strengths

Internal Weaknesses

External Opportunities

External Threats

3. Competitive Strength Assessment
    Rating scale: 1 = Very weak; 10 = Very strong.

Key Success Factor/ Competitive Variable	Weight	Firm A	Firm B	Firm C	Firm D	Firm E
Quality/product performance	___	___	___	___	___	___
Reputation/image	___	___	___	___	___	___
Manufacturing capability	___	___	___	___	___	___
Technological skills	___	___	___	___	___	___
Dealer network	___	___	___	___	___	___
Marketing/advertising	___	___	___	___	___	___
Financial strength	___	___	___	___	___	___
Relative cost position	___	___	___	___	___	___
Customer service	___	___	___	___	___	___
Other?	___	___	___	___	___	___
Overall strength rating	___	___	___	___	___	___

4. Conclusions Concerning Competitive Position
    (Improving/slipping? Competitive advantages/disadvantages?)

5. Major Strategic Issues/Problems the Company Must Address

KEY POINTS

There are five key questions to consider in performing company situation analysis:

1. *How well is the present strategy working?* This involves evaluating the strategy from a qualitative standpoint (completeness, internal consistency, rationale, and suitability to the situation) and also from a quantitative standpoint (the strategic and financial results the strategy is producing). The stronger a company's current overall performance, the less likely the need for radical strategy changes. The weaker a company's performance and/or the faster the changes in its external situation (which can be gleaned from industry and competitive analysis), the more its current strategy must be questioned.

2. *What are the company's strengths, weaknesses, opportunities, and threats?* A SWOT analysis provides an overview of a firm's situation and is an essential component of crafting a strategy tightly matched to the company's situation. A company's strengths, especially its core competencies, are important because they can serve as major building blocks for strategy; company weaknesses are important because they may represent vulnerabilities that need correction. External opportunities and threats come into play because a good strategy necessarily aims at capturing attractive opportunities and at defending against threats to the company's well-being.

3. *Are the company's prices and costs competitive?* One telling sign of whether a company's situation is strong or precarious is whether its prices and costs are competitive with industry rivals. Strategic cost analysis and value chain analysis are essential tools in benchmarking a company's prices and costs against rivals, determining whether the company is performing particular functions and activities cost effectively, learning whether its costs are in line with competitors, and deciding which internal activities and business processes need to be scrutinized for improvement. Value chain analysis teaches that how competently a company manages its value chain activities relative to rivals is a key to building valuable core competencies and leveraging them into sustainable competitive advantage.

4. *How strong is the company's competitive position?* The key appraisals here involve whether the company's position is likely to improve or deteriorate if the present strategy is continued, how the company matches up against key rivals on industry KSFs and other chief determinants of competitive success, and whether and why the company has a competitive advantage or disadvantage. Quantitative competitive strength assessments, using the methodology presented in Table 4–4, indicate where a company is competitively strong and weak and provide insight into the company's ability to defend or enhance its market position. As a rule a company's competitive strategy should be built on its competitive strengths and attempt to shore up areas where it is competitively vulnerable. Also, the areas where company strengths match up against competitor weaknesses represent the best potential for new offensive initiatives.

5. *What strategic issues does the company face?* The purpose of this analytical step is to develop a complete strategy-making agenda using the results of both company situation analysis and industry and competitive analysis. The emphasis here is on drawing conclusions about the strengths and weaknesses

of a company's strategy and framing the issues that strategy-makers need to consider.

Good company situation analysis, like good industry and competitive analysis, is crucial to good strategy-making. A competently done company situation analysis exposes strong and weak points in the present strategy, company capabilities and vulnerabilities, and the company's ability to protect or improve its competitive position in light of driving forces, competitive pressures, and the competitive strength of rivals. Managers need such understanding to craft a strategy that fits the company's situation well.

SUGGESTED READINGS

Abell, Derek F. *Managing with Dual Strategies.* New York: Free Press, 1993, chaps. 9 and 10.

Andrews, Kenneth R. *The Concept of Corporate Strategy.* 3rd ed. Homewood, Ill.: Richard D. Irwin, 1987, chap. 3.

Fahey, Liam, and H. Kurt Christensen. "Building Distinctive Competencies into Competitive Advantages." Reprinted in Liam Fahey, *The Strategic Planning Management Reader,* Englewood Cliffs, N.J.: Prentice-Hall, 1989, pp. 113–18.

Hax, Arnoldo C., and Nicolas S. Majluf. *Strategic Management: An Integrative Perspective.* Englewood Cliffs, N.J.: Prentice-Hall, 1984, chap. 15.

Henry, Harold W. "Appraising a Company's Strengths and Weaknesses." *Managerial Planning,* July–August 1980, pp. 31–36.

Paine, Frank T., and Leonard J. Tischler. "Evaluating Your Costs Strategically." Reprinted in Liam Fahey, *The Strategic Planning Management Reader,* Englewood Cliffs, N.J.: Prentice-Hall, 1989, pp. 118–23.

Prahalad, C. K., and Gary Hamel. "The Core Competence of the Corporation." *Harvard Business Review* 90, no. 3 (May–June 1990), pp. 79–93.

Shank, John K., and Vijay Govindarajan. *Strategic Cost Management: The New Tool for Competitive Advantage.* New York: Free Press, 1993.

Stalk, George, Philip Evans, and Lawrence E. Shulman. "Competing on Capabilities: The New Rules of Corporate Strategy." *Harvard Business Review* 70, no. 2 (March–April 1992), pp. 57–69.

Watson, Gregory H. *Strategic Benchmarking: How to Rate Your Company's Performance Against the World's Best.* New York: John Wiley & Sons, 1993.

CHAPTER FIVE

STRATEGY AND COMPETITIVE ADVANTAGE

Competing in the marketplace is like war. You have injuries and casualties, and the best strategy wins.

John Collins

The essence of strategy lies in creating tomorrow's competitive advantages faster than competitors mimic the ones you possess today.

Gary Hamel and C. K. Prahalad

You've got to come up with a plan. You can't wish things will get better.

John F. Welch
CEO, General Electric

Winning business strategies are grounded in sustainable competitive advantage. A company has *competitive advantage* whenever it has an edge over rivals in attracting customers and defending against competitive forces. There are many sources of competitive advantage: having the best-made product on the market, delivering superior customer service, achieving lower costs than rivals, being in a more convenient geographic location, proprietary technology, features and styling with more buyer appeal, shorter lead times in developing and testing new products, a well-known brand name and reputation, and providing buyers more value for the money (a combination of good quality, good service, and acceptable price). Essentially, though, to succeed in building a competitive advantage, a company's strategy must aim at providing buyers with what they perceive as superior value—a good product at a lower price or a better product that is worth paying more for.

This chapter focuses on how a company can achieve or defend a competitive advantage.[1] We begin by describing the basic types of competitive strategies and then

---

[1]The definitive work on this subject is Michael E. Porter, *Competitive Advantage* (New York: Free Press, 1985). The treatment in this chapter draws heavily on Porter's pioneering contribution.

Investing aggressively in creating sustainable competitive advantage is a company's singlemost dependable contributor to above-average ROI.

examine how these approaches rely on offensive moves to build competitive advantage and on defensive moves to protect competitive advantage. In the concluding two sections we survey the pros and cons of a vertical integration strategy and look at the competitive importance of timing strategic moves—when it is advantageous to be a first-mover and when it is better to be a late-mover.

THE FIVE GENERIC COMPETITIVE STRATEGIES

A company's competitive strategy consists of the business approaches and initiatives it takes to attract customers, withstand competitive pressures, and strengthen its market position. The objective, quite simply, is to knock the socks off rival companies ethically and honorably, earn a competitive advantage in the marketplace, and cultivate a clientele of loyal customers. A company's strategy for competing typically contains both offensive and defensive actions, with emphasis shifting from one to the other as market conditions warrant. And it includes short-lived tactical maneuvers designed to deal with immediate conditions, as well as actions calculated to have lasting impact on the firm's long-term competitive capabilities and market position.

Competitive strategy has a narrower scope than business strategy. Business strategy not only concerns the issue of how to compete but also embraces functional area strategies, how management plans to respond to changing industry conditions of all kinds (not just those that are competition-related), and how management intends to address the full range of strategic issues confronting the business. Competitive strategy deals exclusively with management's action plan for competing successfully and providing superior value to customers.

Companies the world over try every conceivable approach to attracting customers, earning their loyalty on repeat sales, outcompeting rivals, and winning an edge in the marketplace. And since managers tailor short-run tactics and long-term maneuvers to fit their company's specific situation and market environment, there are countless strategy variations and nuances. In this sense, there are as many competitive strategies as there are competitors. However, beneath the subtleties and superficial differences are impressive similarities when one considers (1) the company's market target and (2) the type of competitive advantage the company is trying to achieve. Five categories of competitive strategy approaches stand out:[2]

1. *A low-cost leadership strategy*—Striving to be the overall low-cost provider of a product or service that appeals to a broad range of customers.

2. *A broad differentiation strategy*—Seeking to differentiate the company's product offering from rivals' in ways that will appeal to a broad range of buyers.

3. *A best-cost provider strategy*—Giving customers more value for the money by combining an emphasis on low cost with an emphasis on upscale differentiation; the target is to have the best (lowest) costs and prices relative to producers of products with comparable quality and features.

---

[2]The classification scheme is an adaptation of one presented in Michael E. Porter, *Competitive Strategy: Techniques for Analyzing Industries and Competitors* (New York: Free Press, 1980), chapter 2 and especially pp. 35–39 and 44–46.

FIGURE 5-1 | **The Five Generic Competitive Strategies**

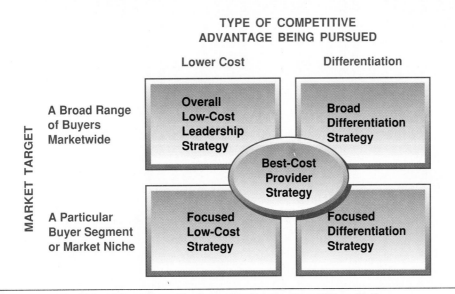

Source: Adapted from Michael E. Porter, Competitive Strategy (New York: Free Press, 1980), pp. 35–40

4. *A focused or market niche strategy based on lower cost*—Concentrating on a narrow buyer segment and outcompeting rivals on the basis of lower cost.

5. *A focused or market niche strategy based on differentiation*—Offering niche members a product or service customized to their tastes and requirements.

The five generic competitive approaches are shown in Figure 5–1; each stakes out a different market position and involves fundamentally different approaches to managing the business. Table 5–1 highlights the distinctive features of these generic competitive strategies (for simplicity, the two strains of focused strategies are combined under one heading since they differ only on one feature—the basis of competitive advantage).

LOW-COST PROVIDER STRATEGIES

Striving to be the industry's overall low-cost provider is a powerful competitive approach in markets where many buyers are price-sensitive. The aim is to open up a sustainable cost advantage over competitors and then use the company's lower-cost edge as a basis for either underpricing competitors and gaining market share at their expense or earning a higher profit margin selling at the going market price. A cost advantage generates superior profitability unless it is used up in aggressive price-cutting efforts to win sales from rivals. Achieving low-cost leadership typically means making low cost *relative to competitors* the theme of the firm's entire business strategy—though low cost cannot be pursued so zealously that a firm's offering ends up being too spartan and frills-free to generate buyer appeal. Illustration Capsule 12 describes ACX Technologies' strategy for gaining low-cost leadership in aluminum cans.

A low-cost leader's basis for competitive advantage is lower overall costs than competitors. Successful low-cost leaders are exceptionally good at finding ways to drive costs out of their businesses.

T A B L E 5-1 | **Distinctive Features of the Generic Competitive Strategies**

Type of Feature	Low-Cost Leadership	Broad Differentiation	Best-Cost Provider	Focused Low-Cost and Focused Differentiation
• Strategic target	• A broad cross-section of the market.	• A broad cross-section of the market.	• Value-conscious buyers.	• A narrow market niche where buyer needs and preferences are distinctively different from the rest of the market.
• Basis of competitive advantage	• Lower costs than competitors.	• An ability to offer buyers something different from competitors.	• Give customers more value for the money	• Lower cost in serving the niche or an ability to offer niche buyers something customized to their requirements and tastes.
• Product line	• A good basic product with few frills (acceptable quality and limited selection).	• Many product variations, wide selection, strong emphasis on the chosen differentiating features.	• Good-to-excellent attributes, several-to-many upscale features.	• Customized to fit the specialized needs of the target segment.
• Production emphasis	• A continuous search for cost reduction without sacrificing acceptable quality and essential features.	• Invent ways to create value for buyers; strive for product superiority.	• Incorporate upscale features and attributes at low cost.	• Tailor-made for the niche.
• Marketing emphasis	• Try to make a virtue out of product features that lead to low cost.	• Build in whatever features buyers are willing to pay for. • Charge a premium price to cover the extra costs of differentiating features. • Communicate the points of difference in credible ways.	• Underprice rival brands with comparable features.	• Communicate the focuser's unique ability to satisfy the buyer's specialized requirements.
• Sustaining the strategy	• Economical prices/ good value. • All elements of strategy aim at contributing to a sustainable cost advantage—the key is to manage costs down, year after year, in every area of the business.	• Stress constant improvement and use innovation to stay ahead of imitative competitors. • Concentrate on a few key differentiating features; tout them to create a reputation and brand image.	• Unique expertise in managing costs down and product/ service caliber up simultaneously.	• Remain totally dedicated to serving the niche better than other competitors; don't blunt the firm's image and efforts by entering other segments or adding other product categories to widen market appeal.

ACX TECHNOLOGIES' STRATEGY TO BECOME A LOW-COST PRODUCER OF ALUMINUM CANS

ACX Technologies began as an idea of William Coors, CEO of Adolph Coors beer company, to recycle more used aluminum cans back into new cans. Typical aluminum can–making operations involved producing thick aluminum slabs from a smelter using bauxite ore combined with as much as 50% scrap aluminum, including used aluminum beverage cans; the slabs of aluminum ingot were fed into a rolling mill to achieve the required thickness. Cans were then formed by stamping pieces of thin aluminum sheet into a seamless can with the top open for filling.

Coor's idea was to produce aluminum-can sheet from 95% recycled cans. He began by purchasing rights to technology that his company had helped develop in Europe; the technology used lower-cost electric arc furnaces to melt aluminum scrap directly, short-cutting the smelter process, which required heavy capital investment and big production volumes to be competitive. Coors then built a plant in Colorado that could grind and melt used cans and pour hot aluminum through a continuous caster to make aluminum sheet suitable for the tops and tabs of beverage cans. It took seven years to develop alloys with the desired attributes and to fine-tune the process—Coors originally believed it could be done in less than two years.

In mid-1991 Coors announced it would build a new $200 million mill in Texas to make sheet aluminum for the body of the can—the product with the most exacting specifications but also the number one end use for aluminum in the United States. Production was expected to begin by mid-1992, but problems and delays soon pushed the start-up date into fall 1993. The new plant's low-cost advantages stemmed from several factors:

- Lower capital investment.
- Use of 95% recycled aluminum cans as feedstock—reducing raw material costs in producing aluminum sheet by 10 to 15%.
- Lower electricity requirements—electric arc technology used only about one-fifth of the electricity of bauxite-smelter technology.
- Comparatively low electric rates at the Texas location.
- Reduced labor costs as compared to bauxite-smelter technology.

Overall, production costs were expected to be anywhere from 20 to 35% below the costs of aluminum can producers using traditionally produced aluminum sheet, depending on the prevailing market prices for aluminum ingot and scrap aluminum. In addition, the mill had greater flexibility than traditional producers to vary its alloy mixes to meet different customer specifications.

Meanwhile, in December 1992 during construction of the Texas plant, Coors decided to spin off all aluminum can operations (along with a paper-packaging operation making patented polyethylene cartons with high quality metallic graphics—packaging for Cascade boxes and Lever 2000 soapbars are examples; a ceramics unit making materials for high-tech applications; and several developmental businesses) into a new publicly-owned company called ACX Technologies. The new company had 1992 revenues of $570 million, about 28% of which were sales to Coors. The breakdown of revenues in 1992 was aluminum for cans 17%, graphics packaging 37%, ceramics materials 32%, and developmental businesses 14% (including corn wet milling, biotechnology, defense electronics, and biodegradable polymers).

In summer 1993, the Texas plant was in start-up and can makers began testing the quality of its aluminum sheet. Coors was the first to qualify ACX's output for use; at year-end 1993 four other can users were testing the suitability of the plant's output for their products. ACX expected the plant to ship close to 50 million pounds of aluminum by year-end 1993 and 100 million pounds or more in 1994 as new customers placed orders. Analysts believed that ACX, given its cost advantage, could grow its annual volume to 1.0 to 1.5 billion pounds in 10 years as it perfected the process and gained acceptance for the quality of its output.

The company's new shares were issued at $10.75 in December 1992 when it went public. In the first 20 days of trading the price climbed to $21.75. Later in 1993, shares traded as high as $46. In May 1994 they were trading in the mid-$30s.

Sources: Based on information published by The Robinson-Humphrey Company and on Marc Charlier, "ACX Strives to Become Aluminum's Low-Cost Producer," *The Wall Street Journal,* September 29, 1993, p. B2.

Opening Up a Cost Advantage   To achieve a cost advantage, a firm's cumulative costs across its value chain must be lower than competitors' cumulative costs. There are two ways to accomplish this:[3]

- Do a better job than rivals of performing internal value chain activities efficiently and of managing the factors that drive the costs of value chain activities.
- Revamp the firm's value chain to bypass some cost-producing activities altogether.

Let's look at each of the two avenues for gaining a cost advantage.

Controlling the Cost Drivers   A firm's cost position is the result of the behavior of costs in each activity in its total value chain. The major cost drivers which come into play in determining a company's costs in each activity segment of the chain fall into two categories: (1) structural determinants of cost that depend on the fundamental economic nature of the business; and (2) executional cost determinants that stem directly from how well internal activities are managed.[4]

Structural Cost Drivers

1. *Economies or diseconomies of scale.* Economies and diseconomies of scale can be found or created in virtually every segment of the value chain. For example, manufacturing economies can sometimes be achieved by simplifying the product line and scheduling longer production runs for fewer models. A geographically organized sales force can realize economies as regional sales volume grows because a salesperson can write larger orders at each sales call and/or because of reduced travel time between calls; on the other hand, a sales force organized by product line can encounter travel-related diseconomies if salespersons have to spend disproportionately more travel time calling on distantly spaced customers. In global industries, modifying products by country instead of selling a standard product worldwide tends to boost unit costs because of lost time in model changeover, shorter production runs, and inability to reach the most economic scale of production for each model. Boosting local or regional market share can lower sales and marketing costs per unit, whereas opting for a bigger national share by entering new regions can create scale diseconomies unless and until market penetration in the newly entered regions reaches efficient proportions.

2. *Learning and experience curve effects.* Experience-based cost savings can come from improved layout, gains in labor efficiency, debugging of technology, product design modifications that enhance manufacturing efficiency, redesign of machinery and equipment to gain increased operating speed, getting samples of a rival's products and having design engineers study how they are made, and tips from suppliers, consultants, and ex-employees of rival firms. Learning tends to vary with the amount of management attention devoted to capturing the benefits of experience of both the firm and outsiders. Learning benefits can be kept proprietary by building or modifying production equipment in-house, retaining key

---

[3]Michael E. Porter, *Competitive Advantage* (New York: Free Press, 1985), p. 97.
[4]The list and explanations are condensed from Porter, *Competitive Advantage,* pp. 70–107.

employees, limiting the dissemination of information through employee publications, and enforcing strict nondisclosure provisions in employment contracts.

3. *Linkages with other activities in the chain.* When the cost of one activity is affected by how other activities are performed, companies can lower costs of linked activities through superior coordination and/or joint optimization. Linkages with suppliers tend to center on suppliers' product-design characteristics, quality-assurance procedures, delivery and service policies, and the manner in which the supplier's product is furnished (for example, nails delivered in prepackaged 1-lb., 5-lb., and 10-lb. assortments instead of 100-lb. bulk cartons can reduce a hardware dealer's labor costs in filling individual customer orders). The easiest supplier linkages to exploit are those where both a supplier's and firm's costs fall because of coordination and/or joint optimization. Linkages with forward channels tend to center on location of warehouses, materials handling, outbound shipping, and packaging.

4. *Sharing opportunities with other business units within the enterprise.* Activities shared with a sister unit can create significant cost savings. Cost sharing can help achieve scale economies, shorten the learning curve in mastering a new technology, and/or achieve fuller capacity utilization. Sometimes the know-how gained in one division can be used to help lower costs in another; sharing know-how is significant when the activities are similar and know-how can be readily transferred from one unit to another.

5. *The benefits of vertical integration versus outsourcing.* Partially or fully integrating into the activities of either suppliers or forward channel allies can allow an enterprise to detour suppliers or buyers with considerable bargaining power. Vertical integration can also result in cost savings when it is feasible to coordinate or merge adjacent activities in the value chain. On the other hand, it is sometimes cheaper to outsource certain functions and activities to outside specialists, who by virtue of their expertise and volume can perform the activity/function more cheaply.

6. *Locational variables.* Locations differ in their prevailing wage levels, tax rates, energy costs, inbound and outbound shipping and freight costs, and so on. Opportunities may exist for reducing costs by relocating plants, field offices, warehousing, or headquarters operations. Moreover, whether sister facilities are nearby or far apart affects the costs of shipping intrafirm inventory, outbound freight on goods shipped to customers, and coordination.

Executional Cost Drivers

1. *Timing considerations associated with first-mover advantages and disadvantages.* Sometimes the first major brand in the market is able to establish and maintain its brand name at a lower cost than later brand arrivals—being a first-mover turns out to be cheaper than being a late-mover. On other occasions, such as when technology is developing fast, late-purchasers can benefit from waiting to install second- or third-generation equipment that is both cheaper and more efficient; first-generation users often incur added costs associated with debugging and learning how to use an immature and unperfected technology. Likewise, companies that follow rather

than lead new product development efforts sometimes avoid many of the costs that pioneers incur in performing pathbreaking R&D and opening up new markets.

2. *The percentage of capacity utilization.* High fixed costs as a percentage of total costs create a stiff unit-cost penalty for underutilization of existing capacity. Increased capacity utilization spreads indirect and overhead costs over a larger unit volume and enhances the efficiency of fixed assets. The more capital-intensive the business, the more important this cost driver becomes. Finding ways to minimize the ups and downs in seasonal capacity utilization can be an important source of cost advantage.[5]

3. *Strategic choices and operating decisions.* Managers at various levels affect a firm's costs through the decisions they make:

   • Increasing/decreasing the number of products offered.
   • Adding/cutting the services provided to buyers.
   • Incorporating more/fewer performance and quality features into the product.
   • Paying higher/lower wages and fringes to employees relative to rivals and firms in other industries.
   • Increasing/decreasing the number of different forward channels utilized in distributing the firm's product.
   • Raising/lowering the levels of R&D support relative to rivals.
   • Putting more/less emphasis on higher productivity and efficiency as compared to rivals.
   • Raising/lowering the specifications for purchased materials.

Managers intent on achieving low-cost leader status have to understand which structural and executional factors drive the costs of each activity in the firm's total value chain. Then they have to use their knowledge about the cost drivers to reduce costs for every activity where cost savings can be identified. The task of continuously coming up with ways to drive costs out of the business (and ways to avoid incurring some costs at all) is seldom simple or painless; rather, it is a task that managers have to attack with ingenuity and single-minded toughness.

Revamping the Makeup of the Value Chain   Dramatic cost advantages can emerge from finding innovative ways to restructure processes and tasks, cut out frills, and provide the basics more economically. The primary ways companies can achieve a cost advantage by reconfiguring their value chains include:

   • Simplifying the product design.
   • Stripping away the extras and offering only a basic, no-frills product or service, thereby cutting out activities and costs associated with multiple features and options.

---

[5]A firm can improve its capacity utilization by *(a)* serving a mix of accounts with peak volumes spread throughout the year, *(b)* finding off-season uses for its products, *(c)* serving private-label customers that can intermittently use the excess capacity, *(d)* selecting buyers with stable demands or demands that are counter to the normal peak/valley cycle, *(e)* letting competitors serve the buyer segments whose demands fluctuate the most, and *(f)* sharing capacity with sister units having a different pattern of needs.

- Reengineering core business processes to cut out needless work steps and low-value-added activities.
- Shifting to a simpler, less capital-intensive, or more streamlined technological process.
- Finding ways to bypass the use of high-cost raw materials or component parts.
- Using direct-to-end-user sales and marketing approaches that cut out the often large costs and margins of wholesalers and retailers (costs and margins in the wholesale-retail portions of the value chain often represent 50 percent of the price paid by final consumers).
- Relocating facilities closer to suppliers, customers, or both to curtail inbound and outbound logistics costs.
- Achieving a more economical degree of forward or backward vertical integration relative to competitors.
- Dropping the "something for everyone" approach and focusing on a limited product/service to meet a special, but important, need of the target buyer, thereby eliminating activities and costs associated with numerous product versions.

Successful low-cost producers usually achieve their cost advantages by exhaustively pursuing cost savings throughout the value chain. All avenues are used and no area of potential is overlooked. Normally, low-cost producers have a very cost-conscious corporate culture symbolically reinforced with spartan facilities, limited perks and frills for executives, intolerance of waste, intensive screening of budget requests, and broad employee participation in cost-control efforts. But while low-cost providers are champions of frugality, they are usually aggressive in committing funds to projects that promise to drive costs out of the business.

The Keys to Success   Managers intent on pursuing a low-cost-provider strategy have to scrutinize each cost-creating activity and identify what drives its cost. Then they have to use their knowledge about the cost drivers to manage the costs of each activity down further year after year. They have to be proactive in redesigning business processes, eliminating nonessential work steps, and reengineering the value chain. By totally revamping how activities are performed and coordinated, companies have been able to achieve savings of 30 to 70 percent, compared to the 5 to 10 percent possible with creative tinkering and adjusting. As the two examples in Illustration Capsule 13 indicate, companies can sometimes achieve dramatic cost advantages from restructuring their value chains and slicing out a number of cost-producing activities that produce little value added insofar as customers are concerned.

Companies that employ low-cost leadership strategies include Lincoln Electric in arc welding equipment, Briggs and Stratton in small gasoline engines, BIC in ballpoint pens, Black and Decker in power tools, Stride Rite in footwear, Beaird-Poulan in chain saws, Ford in heavy-duty trucks, General Electric in major home appliances, Wal-Mart in discount retailing, and Southwest Airlines in commercial airline travel.

The Competitive Defenses of Low-Cost Leadership   Being the low-cost provider in an industry provides some attractive defenses against the five competitive forces.
- In meeting the challenges of *rival competitors,* the low-cost company is in the best position to compete offensively on the basis of price, to defend against price war conditions, to use the appeal of lower price to grab sales (and market share) from rivals, and to earn above-average profits (based on bigger profit

WINNING A COST ADVANTAGE: IOWA BEEF PACKERS AND FEDERAL EXPRESS

Iowa Beef Packers and Federal Express have been able to win strong competitive positions by restructuring the traditional value chains in their industries. In beef packing, the traditional cost chain involved raising cattle on scattered farms and ranches, shipping them live to labor-intensive, unionized slaughtering plants, and then transporting whole sides of beef to grocery retailers whose butcher departments cut them into smaller pieces and package them for sale to grocery shoppers.

Iowa Beef Packers revamped the traditional chain with a radically different strategy—large automated plants employing nonunion labor were built near economically transportable supplies of cattle, and the meat was partially butchered at the processing plant into smaller high-yield cuts (sometimes sealed in plastic casing ready for purchase), boxed, and shipped to retailers. IBP's inbound cattle transportation expenses, traditionally a major cost item, were cut significantly by avoiding the weight losses that occurred when live animals were shipped long distances; major outbound shipping cost savings were achieved by not having to ship whole sides of beef with their high waste factor.

Iowa Beef's strategy was so successful that it was, in 1985, the largest U.S. meatpacker, surpassing the former industry leaders, Swift, Wilson, and Armour.

Federal Express innovatively redefined the value chain for rapid delivery of small parcels. Traditional firms like Emery and Airborne Express operated by collecting freight packages of varying sizes, shipping them to their destination points via air freight and commercial airlines, and then delivering them to the addressee. Federal Express opted to focus only on the market for overnight delivery of small packages and documents. These were collected at local drop points during the late afternoon hours and flown on company-owned planes during early evening hours to a central hub in Memphis where from 11 PM to 3 AM each night all parcels were sorted, then reloaded on company planes, and flown during the early morning hours to their destination points, where they were delivered the next morning by company personnel using company trucks. The cost structure so achieved by Federal Express was low enough to permit it to guarantee overnight delivery of a small parcel anywhere in the United States for a price as low as $11. In 1986, Federal Express had a 58 percent market share of the air-express package delivery market versus a 15 percent share for UPS, 11 percent for Airborne Express, and 10 percent for Emery/Purolator.

Source: Based on information in Michael E. Porter, *Competitive Advantage* (New York: Free Press, 1985), p. 109.

margins or greater sales volume). Low cost is a powerful defense in markets where price competition thrives.

- In defending against the power of *buyers,* low costs provide a company with partial profit-margin protection, since powerful customers are rarely able to bargain price down past the survival level of the next most cost-efficient seller.

- In countering the bargaining leverage of *suppliers,* the low-cost producer is more insulated than competitors from powerful suppliers *if* the primary source of its cost advantage is greater internal efficiency. (A low-cost provider whose cost advantage stems from being able to buy components at favorable prices from outside suppliers could be vulnerable to the actions of powerful suppliers.)

- As concerns *potential entrants,* the low-cost leader can use price-cutting to make it harder for a new rival to win customers; the pricing power of the low-cost provider acts as a barrier for new entrants.

- In competing against *substitutes,* a low-cost leader is better positioned to use low price as a defense against companies trying to gain market inroads with a substitute product or service.

A low-cost company's ability to set the industry's price floor and still earn a profit erects barriers around its market position. Anytime price competition becomes a major market force, less efficient rivals get squeezed the most. Firms in a low-cost position relative to rivals have a competitive edge in meeting the demands of buyers who want low price.

> A low-cost leader is in the strongest position to set the floor on market price.

When a Low-Cost Provider Strategy Works Best A competitive strategy predicated on low-cost leadership is particularly powerful when

1. Price competition among rival sellers is especially vigorous.
2. The industry's product is essentially standardized or a commodity readily available from a host of sellers (a condition that allows buyers to shop for the best price).
3. There are few ways to achieve product differentiation that have value to buyers (put another way, the differences between brands do not matter much to buyers), thereby making buyers very sensitive to price differences.
4. Most buyers utilize the product in the same ways—with common user requirements, a standardized product can satisfy the needs of buyers, in which case low selling price, not features or quality, becomes the dominant factor in causing buyers to choose one seller's product over another's.
5. Buyers incur low switching costs in changing from one seller to another, thus giving them the flexibility to switch readily to lower-priced sellers having equally good products.
6. Buyers are large and have significant power to bargain down prices.

As a rule, the more price sensitive buyers are and the more inclined they are to base their purchasing decisions on which seller offers the best price, the more appealing a low-cost strategy becomes. In markets where rivals compete mainly on price, low cost relative to competitors is the only competitive advantage that matters.

The Risks of a Low-Cost Provider Strategy A low-cost competitive approach has its drawbacks though. Technological breakthroughs can open up cost reductions for rivals that nullify a low-cost leader's past investments and hard-won gains in efficiency. Rival firms may find it easy and/or inexpensive to imitate the leader's low-cost methods, thus making any advantage short-lived. A company driving zealously to push its costs down can become so fixated on cost reduction that it fails to react to subtle but significant market swings—like growing buyer interest in added features or service, new developments in related products that start to alter how buyers use the product, or declining buyer sensitivity to price. The low-cost zealot risks getting left behind as buyers opt for enhanced quality, innovative performance features, faster service, and other differentiating features. Again, heavy investments in cost reduction can lock a firm into both its present technology and present strategy, leaving it vulnerable to new technologies and to growing customer interest in something other than a cheaper price.

To avoid the risks and pitfalls of a low-cost leadership strategy, managers must understand that the strategic target is *low cost relative to competitors,* not absolute low cost. In pursuing low-cost leadership, managers must take care not to strip away features and services that buyers consider essential. Furthermore, from a competitive strategy perspective, the value of a cost advantage depends on its sustainability. Sustainability, in turn, hinges on whether the company achieves its cost advantage in ways difficult for rivals to copy or match.

DIFFERENTIATION STRATEGIES

Differentiation strategies become an attractive competitive approach whenever buyers' needs and preferences are too diverse to be fully satisfied by a standardized product. To be successful with a differentiation strategy, a company has to study buyers' needs and behavior carefully to learn what buyers consider important, what they think has value, and what they are willing to pay for. Then the company has to incorporate one, or maybe several, attributes and features with buyer appeal into its product/service offering—enough to set its offering visibly and distinctively apart. Competitive advantage results once a sufficient number of buyers become strongly attached to the differentiated attributes and features. The stronger the buyer appeal of the differentiated features, the stronger the company's competitive advantage.

The essence of a differentiation strategy is to be unique in ways that are valuable to customers and that can be sustained.

Successful differentiation allows a firm to

- Command a premium price for its product, and/or
- Increase unit sales (because additional buyers are won over by the differentiating features), and/or
- Gain buyer loyalty to its brand (because some buyers are strongly attracted to the differentiating features).

Differentiation enhances profitability whenever the extra price the product commands outweighs the added costs of achieving the differentiation. Company differentiation strategies fail when buyers don't value the brand's uniqueness enough to buy it instead of rivals' brands and/or when a company's approach to differentiation is easily copied or matched by its rivals.

Types of Differentiation Themes   Companies can pursue differentiation from many angles: a different taste (Dr Pepper and Listerine), special features (Jenn Air's indoor-cooking tops with a vented built-in grill for barbecuing), superior service (Federal Express in overnight package delivery), spare parts availability (Caterpillar guarantees 48-hour spare parts delivery to any customer anywhere in the world or else the part is furnished free), more for the money (McDonald's and Wal-Mart), engineering design and performance (Mercedes in automobiles), prestige and distinctiveness (Rolex in watches), product reliability (Johnson & Johnson in baby products), quality manufacture (Karastan in carpets and Honda in automobiles), technological leadership (3M Corporation in bonding and coating products), a full range of services (Merrill Lynch), a complete line of products (Campbell's soups), and top-of-the-line image and reputation (Brooks Brothers and Ralph Lauren in menswear, Kitchen Aid in dishwashers, and Cross in writing instruments).

Activities Where Differentiation Opportunities Exist   Differentiation is not something hatched in marketing and advertising departments, nor is it limited to the catchalls of quality and service. The possibilities for successful differentiation exist in activities performed anywhere in the industry's value chain. The most common places in the chain where differentiation opportunities exist include:

1. *Purchasing and procurement activities* that ultimately spill over to affect the performance or quality of the company's end product. (McDonald's gets high ratings on its french fries partly because it has very strict specifications on the potatoes purchased from suppliers.)
2. *Product-oriented R&D activities* that hold potential for improved designs and performance features, expanded end uses and applications, wider product

variety, shorter lead times in developing new models, more frequent first-on-the-market victories, added user safety, greater recycling capability, and enhanced environmental protection.

3. *Production process–oriented R&D activities* that allow custom-order manufacture, environmentally safe production methods, and improved product quality, reliability, or appearance.

4. *Manufacturing activities* that can reduce product defects, prevent premature product failure, extend product life, allow better warranty coverages, improve economy of use, result in more end-user convenience, and enhance product appearance. (The quality edge enjoyed by Japanese automakers stems from their superior performance of manufacturing and assembly-line activities.)

5. *Outbound logistics and distribution activities* that allow for faster delivery, more accurate order filling, and fewer warehouse and on-the-shelf stockouts.

6. *Marketing, sales, and customer service activities* that can result in such differentiating attributes as superior technical assistance to buyers, faster maintenance and repair services, more and better product information provided to customers, more and better training materials for end users, better credit terms, quicker order processing, more frequent sales calls, and greater customer convenience. (IBM boosts buyer value by providing its mainframe computer customers with extensive technical support and round-the-clock operating maintenance.)

Managers need a full understanding of the sources of differentiation and the activities that drive uniqueness to devise a sound differentiation strategy and evaluate various differentiation approaches.[6]

Achieving a Differentiation-Based Competitive Advantage   One key to a successful differentiation strategy is to create buyer value in ways unmatched by rivals. There are three approaches to creating buyer value. One is to incorporate product attributes and user features that lower the buyer's overall costs of using the company's product— Illustration Capsule 14 lists options for making a company's product more economical to use. A second approach is to incorporate features that raise the performance a buyer gets out of the product—Illustration Capsule 15 contains differentiation avenues that enhance product performance and buyer value.

A differentiator's basis for competitive advantage is a product whose attributes differ significantly from the products of rivals.

A third approach is to incorporate features that enhance buyer satisfaction in noneconomic or intangible ways. Goodyear's new Aquatread tire design appeals to safety-conscious motorists wary of slick roads in rainy weather. Wal-Mart's campaign to feature products "Made in America" appeals to customers concerned about the loss of American jobs to foreign manufacturers. Rolex, Jaguar, Cartier, Ritz-Carlton, and Gucci have differentiation-based competitive advantages linked to buyer desires for status, image, prestige, upscale fashion, superior craftsmanship, and the finer things in life. L. L. Bean makes its mail-order customers feel secure in their purchases by providing an unconditional guarantee with no time limit: "All of our products are guaranteed to give 100 percent satisfaction in every way. Return anything purchased from us at anytime if it proves otherwise. We will replace it, refund your purchase price, or credit your credit card, as you wish."

---

[6]Porter, *Competitive Advantage,* p. 124.

ILLUSTRATION CAPSULE 14

DIFFERENTIATING FEATURES THAT LOWER BUYER COSTS

A company doesn't have to lower price to make it cheaper for a buyer to use its product. An alternative is to incorporate features and attributes into the company's product/service package that

- Reduce the buyer's scrap and raw materials waste. Example of differentiating feature: cut-to-size components.
- Lower the buyer's labor costs (less time, less training, lower skill requirements). Examples of differentiating features: snap-on assembly features, modular replacement of worn-out components.
- Cut the buyer's downtime or idle time. Examples of differentiating features: greater product reliability, ready spare parts availability, or less frequent maintenance requirements.
- Reduce the buyer's inventory costs. Example of differentiating feature: just-in-time delivery.
- Reduce the buyer's pollution control costs or waste disposal costs. Example of differentiating feature: scrap pickup for use in recycling.
- Reduce the buyer's procurement and order-processing costs. Example of differentiating

feature: computerized on-line ordering and billing procedures.
- Lower the buyer's maintenance and repair costs. Example of differentiating feature: superior product reliability.
- Lower the buyer's installation, delivery, or financing costs. Example of differentiating feature: 90-day payment same as cash.
- Reduce the buyer's need for other inputs (energy, safety equipment, security personnel, inspection personnel, other tools and machinery). Example of differentiating feature: fuel-efficient power equipment.
- Raise the trade-in value of used models.
- Lower the buyer's replacement or repair costs if the product unexpectedly fails later. Example of differentiating feature: longer warranty coverage.
- Lower the buyer's need for technical personnel. Example of differentiating feature: free technical support and assistance.
- Boost the efficiency of the buyer's production process. Examples of differentiating features: faster processing speeds, better interface with ancillary equipment.

Source: Adapted from Michael E. Porter, *Competitive Advantage* (New York: Free Press, 1985), pp. 135–37.

Real Value, Perceived Value, and Signals of Value   Buyers seldom pay for value they don't perceive, no matter how real the unique extras may be.[7] Thus the price premium that a differentiation strategy commands reflects *the value actually delivered* to the buyer and *the value perceived* by the buyer (even if not actually delivered). Actual and perceived value can differ whenever buyers have trouble assessing what their experience with the product will be. Incomplete knowledge on the part of buyers often causes them to judge value based on such *signals* as price (where price connotes quality), attractive packaging, extensive ad campaigns (i.e., how well-known the product is), ad content and image, the quality of brochures and sales presentations, the seller's facilities, the seller's list of customers, the firm's market share, length of time the firm has been in business, and the professionalism, appearance, and personality of the seller's employees. Such signals of value may be as important as actual value (1) when the nature of differentiation is subjective or hard to quantify, (2) when buyers are making a first-time purchase, (3) when repurchase is infrequent, and (4) when buyers are unsophisticated.

A firm whose differentiation strategy delivers only modest extra value but clearly signals that extra value may command a higher price than a firm that actually delivers higher value but signals it poorly.

---

[7]This discussion draws from Porter, *Competitive Advantage,* pp. 138–42. Porter's insights here are particularly important to formulating differentiating strategies because they highlight the relevance of "intangibles" and "signals."

ILLUSTRATION CAPSULE 15

DIFFERENTIATING FEATURES THAT RAISE THE PERFORMANCE A USER GETS

To enhance the performance a buyer gets from using its product/service, a company can incorporate features and attributes that

- Provide buyers greater reliability, durability, convenience, or ease of use.
- Make the company's product/service cleaner, safer, quieter, or more maintenance-free than rival brands.

- Exceed environmental or regulatory standards.
- Meet the buyer's needs and requirements more completely, compared to competitors' offerings.
- Give buyers the option to add on or to upgrade later as new product versions come on the market.
- Give buyers more flexibility to tailor their own products to the needs of their customers.
- Do a better job of meeting the buyer's future growth and expansion requirements.

Source: Adapted from Michael E. Porter, *Competitive Advantage,* (New York: Free Press, 1985), pp. 135–38.

Keeping the Cost of Differentiation in Line   Once company managers identify what approach to creating buyer value and establishing a differentiation-based competitive advantage makes the most sense given the nature of the company's product/service and competitive situation, they must build the value-creating attributes into the product at an acceptable cost. Attempts to achieve differentiation usually raise costs. The trick to profitable differentiation is either to keep the costs of achieving differentiation below the price premium the differentiating attributes can command in the marketplace (thus increasing the profit margin per unit sold) or offset thinner profit margins with enough added volume to increase total profits (larger volume can make up for smaller margins provided differentiation adds enough extra sales). It usually makes sense to add extra differentiating features that are not costly but add to buyer satisfaction—fine restaurants typically provide such extras as a slice of lemon in the water glass, valet parking, and complimentary after-dinner mints. The overriding condition in pursuing differentiation is that a firm must be careful not to get its unit costs so far out of line with competitors' that it has to charge a higher price than buyers are willing to pay.

What Makes a Differentiation Strategy Attractive   Differentiation offers a buffer against the strategies of rivals when it results in enhanced buyer loyalty to a company's brand or model and greater willingness to pay a little (perhaps a lot!) more for it. In addition, successful differentiation (1) erects entry barriers in the form of customer loyalty and uniqueness that newcomers find hard to hurdle, (2) mitigates buyers' bargaining power since the products of alternative sellers are less attractive to them, and (3) helps a firm fend off threats from substitutes not having comparable features or attributes. To the extent that differentiation allows a company to charge a higher price and have bigger profit margins, it is in a stronger position to withstand the efforts of powerful vendors to get a higher price for the items they supply. Thus, as with cost leadership, successful differentiation creates lines of defense for dealing with the five competitive forces.

For the most part, differentiation strategies work best in markets where (1) there are many ways to differentiate the product or service and many buyers perceive these differences as having value, (2) buyer needs and uses of the item or service are diverse, and (3) few rival firms are following a similar differentiation approach.

The most appealing approaches to differentiation are those that are hard or expensive for rivals to duplicate. Easy-to-copy differentiating features cannot produce sustainable competitive advantage. Indeed, resourceful competitors can, in time, clone almost any product. This is why sustainable differentiation usually has to be linked to unique internal skills and core competencies. When a company has skills and capabilities that competitors cannot readily match and when its expertise can be used to perform activities in the value chain where differentiation potential exists, then it has a strong basis for sustainable differentiation. As a rule, differentiation yields a longer-lasting and more profitable competitive edge when it is based on

- Technical superiority.
- Product quality.
- Comprehensive customer service.

Such differentiating attributes are widely perceived by buyers as having value; moreover, the skills and expertise required to produce them tend to be tougher for rivals to copy or overcome profitably.

The Risks of a Differentiation Strategy   There are, of course, no guarantees that differentiation will produce a meaningful competitive advantage. If buyers see little value in uniqueness (i.e., a standard item meets their needs), then a low-cost strategy can easily defeat a differentiation strategy. In addition, differentiation can be defeated if competitors can quickly copy most or all of the appealing product attributes a company comes up with. Rapid imitation means that a firm never achieves real differentiation since competing brands keep changing in like ways each time a company makes a new move to set its offering apart from rivals'. Thus, to be successful at differentiation a firm must search out lasting sources of uniqueness that are burdensome for rivals to overcome. Aside from these considerations, other common pitfalls in pursuing differentiation include[8]

- Trying to differentiate on the basis of something that does not lower a buyer's cost or enhance a buyer's well-being, as perceived by the buyer.
- Overdifferentiating so that price is too high relative to competitors, or product quality or service levels exceed buyers' needs.
- Trying to charge too high a price premium (the bigger the price differential the harder it is to keep buyers from switching to lower-priced competitors).
- Ignoring the need to signal value and depending only on intrinsic product attributes to achieve differentiation.
- Not understanding or identifying what buyers consider as value.

A low-cost producer strategy can defeat a differentiation strategy when buyers are satisfied with a basic product and don't think "extra" attributes are worth a higher price.

THE STRATEGY OF BEING A BEST-COST PROVIDER

This strategy aims at giving customers *more value for the money.* It combines a strategic emphasis on low cost with a strategic emphasis on *more than minimally acceptable* quality, service, features, and performance. The idea is to create superior

---

[8]Porter, *Competitive Advantage,* pp. 160–62.

value by meeting or exceeding buyers' expectations on quality-service-features-performance attributes and by beating their expectations on price. The strategic objective is to become the low-cost provider of a product or service with *good-to-excellent* attributes, then use the cost advantage to underprice brands with comparable attributes. Such a competitive approach is termed a *best-cost provider strategy* because the producer has the best (lowest) cost relative to producers whose brands are comparably positioned on the quality-service-features-performance scale.

The competitive advantage of a best-cost provider comes from matching close rivals on key quality-service-features-performance dimensions and beating them on cost. To become a best-cost provider, a company must match quality at a lower cost than rivals, match features at a lower cost than rivals, match product performance at a lower cost than rivals, and so on. What distinguishes a successful best-cost provider is expertise in incorporating upscale product or service attributes at a low cost, or, to put it a bit differently, an ability to contain the costs of providing customers with a better product. The most successful best-cost producers have the skills to simultaneously manage unit costs down and product calibre up—see Illustration Capsule 16.

A best-cost provider strategy has great appeal from the standpoint of competitive positioning. It produces superior customer value by balancing a strategic emphasis on low cost against a strategic emphasis on differentiation. In effect, it is a *hybrid* strategy that allows a company to combine the competitive advantage of both low cost and differentiation to arrive at superior buyer value. In markets where buyer diversity makes product differentiation the norm and many buyers are price and value sensitive, a best-cost producer strategy can be more advantageous than either a pure low-cost producer strategy or a pure differentiation strategy keyed to product superiority. This is because a best-cost provider can position itself near the middle of the market with either a medium-quality product at a below-average price or a very good product at a medium price. Often the majority of buyers prefer a mid-range product rather than the cheap, basic product of a low-cost producer or the expensive product of a top-of-the-line differentiator.

> The most powerful competitive approach a company can pursue is to strive relentlessly to become a lower-and-lower-cost producer of a higher-and-higher-caliber product, with the intention of eventually becoming the industry's absolute lowest-cost producer and, simultaneously, the producer of the industry's overall best product.

FOCUSED OR MARKET NICHE STRATEGIES

What sets focused strategies apart from low-cost or differentiation strategies is concentrated attention on a narrow piece of the total market. The target segment or niche can be defined by geographic uniqueness, by specialized requirements in using the product, or by special product attributes that appeal only to niche members. The objective is to do a better job of serving buyers in the target market niche than rival competitors. *A focuser's basis for competitive advantage is either (1) lower costs than competitors in serving the market niche or (2) an ability to offer niche members something different from other competitors.* A focused strategy based on low cost depends on there being a buyer segment whose requirements are less costly to satisfy compared to the rest of the market. A focused strategy based on differentiation depends on there being a buyer segment that demands unique product attributes.

Examples of firms employing some version of a focused strategy include Tandem Computers (a specialist in "nonstop" computers for customers who need a "fail-safe" system), Rolls Royce (in super luxury automobiles), Cannondale (in top-of-the-line mountain bikes), Fort Howard Paper (specializing in paper products for industrial and commercial enterprises only), commuter airlines like Horizon and Atlantic Southeast (specializing in low-traffic, short-haul flights linking major airports with

TOYOTA'S BEST-COST PRODUCER STRATEGY FOR ITS LEXUS LINE

Toyota Motor Co. is widely regarded as the leading low-cost producer among the world's motor vehicle manufacturers. Despite its emphasis on product quality, Toyota has achieved absolute low-cost leadership because of its considerable skills in efficient manufacturing techniques and because its models are positioned in the low-to-medium end of the price spectrum where high production volumes are conducive to low unit costs. But when Toyota decided to introduce its new Lexus models to compete in the luxury-car market, it employed a classic best-cost producer strategy. Toyota's Lexus strategy had three features:

- Transferring its expertise in making high-quality Toyota models at low cost to making premium quality luxury cars at costs below other luxury-car makers, especially Mercedes and BMW. Toyota executives reasoned that Toyota's manufacturing skills should allow it to incorporate high-tech performance features and upscale quality into Lexus models at less cost than other luxury-car manufacturers.
- Using its relatively lower manufacturing costs to underprice Mercedes and BMW, both of which had models selling in the $40,000 to $75,000 range (and some even higher). Toyota believed that with its cost advantage it could price

attractively equipped Lexus models in the $38,000 to $42,000 range, drawing price-conscious buyers away from Mercedes and BMW and perhaps inducing quality-conscious Lincoln and Cadillac owners to trade up to a Lexus.

- Establishing a new network of Lexus dealers, separate from Toyota dealers, dedicated to providing a level of personalized, attentive customer service unmatched in the industry.

In the 1993–94 model years, the Lexus 400 series models were priced in the $40,000 to $45,000 range and competed against Mercedes's 300/400E series, BMW's 525i/535i series, Nissan's Infiniti Q45, Cadillac Seville, Jaguar, and Lincoln's Continental Mark VIII series. The lower-priced Lexus 300 series, priced in the $30,000 to $38,000 range, competed against Cadillac Eldorado, Acura Legend, Infiniti J30, Buick Park Avenue, Mercedes's new C-Class series, BMW's 315 series, and Oldsmobile's new Aurora line.

Lexus's best-cost producer strategy was so successful that Mercedes, plagued by sagging sales and concerns about overpricing, reduced its prices significantly on its 1994 models and introduced a new C-Class series, priced in the $30,000 to $35,000 range, to become more competitive. The Lexus LS 400 models and the Lexus SC 300/400 models ranked first and second, respectively, in the widely watched J. D. Power & Associates quality survey for 1993 cars; the entry-level Lexus ES 300 model ranked eighth.

---

smaller cities 50 to 250 miles away), and Bandag (a specialist in truck tire recapping that promotes its recaps aggressively at over 1,000 truck stops). Illustration Capsule 17 describes Motel 6's focused low-cost strategy and Ritz-Carlton's focused differentiation strategy.

Using a focused strategy to compete on the basis of low cost is a fairly common business approach. Producers of private-label goods have lowered their marketing, distribution, and advertising costs by concentrating on direct sales to retailers and chain discounters who stock a no-frills house brand to sell at discount to name brand merchandise. Discount stock brokerage houses have lowered costs by focusing on customers who are willing to forgo the investment research, advice, and financial services offered by full-service firms like Merrill Lynch in return for 30 percent or more commission savings on their buy-sell transactions. Pursuing a cost advantage via focusing works well when a firm can find ways to lower costs significantly by limiting its customer base to a well-defined buyer segment.

At the other end of the market spectrum, companies like Ritz-Carlton, Tiffany's, Porsche, Haagen-Dazs, and W. L. Gore (the maker of Gore-tex) crafted successful differentiation-based focused strategies targeted at upscale buyers wanting

FOCUSED STRATEGIES IN THE LODGING INDUSTRY: MOTEL 6 AND RITZ-CARLTON

Motel 6 and Ritz-Carlton compete at opposite ends of the lodging industry. Motel 6 employs a focused strategy keyed to low cost; Ritz-Carlton employs a focused strategy based on differentiation.

Motel 6 caters to price-conscious travelers who want a clean, no-frills place to spend the night. To be a low-cost provider of overnight lodging, Motel 6 (1) selects relatively inexpensive sites on which to construct its units—usually near interstate exits and high traffic locations but far enough away to avoid paying prime site prices; (2) builds only basic facilities—no restaurant or bar and only rarely a swimming pool; (3) relies on standard architectural designs that incorporate inexpensive materials and low-cost construction techniques; and (4) has simple room furnishings and decorations. These approaches lower both investment costs and operating costs. Without restaurants, bars, and all kinds of guest services, a Motel 6 unit can be operated with just front desk personnel, room cleanup crews, and skeleton building-and-grounds maintenance. To promote the Motel 6 concept with travelers who have simple overnight requirements, the chain uses unique, recognizable radio ads done by nationally syndicated radio personality Tom Bodett; the ads describe Motel 6's clean rooms, no-frills facilities, friendly atmosphere, and dependably low rates (usually under $30 per night).

In contrast, the Ritz-Carlton caters to discriminating travelers and vacationers willing and able to pay for top-of-the-line accommodations and world-class personal service. Ritz-Carlton hotels feature (1) prime locations and scenic views from many rooms, (2) custom architectural designs, (3) fine dining restaurants with gourmet menus prepared by accomplished chefs, (4) elegantly appointed lobbies and bar lounges, (5) swimming pools, exercise facilities, and leisure time options, (6) upscale room accommodations, (7) an array of guest services and recreation opportunities appropriate to the location, and (8) large, well-trained professional staffs who do their utmost to make each guest's stay an enjoyable experience.

Both companies concentrate their attention on a narrow piece of the total market. Motel 6's basis for competitive advantage is lower costs than competitors in providing basic, economical overnight accommodations to price-constrained travelers. Ritz-Carlton's advantage is its capability to provide superior accommodations and unmatched personal service for a well-to-do clientele. Each is able to succeed, despite polar opposite strategies, because the market for lodging consists of diverse buyer segments with diverse preferences and abilities to pay.

products/services with world-class attributes. Indeed, most markets contain a buyer segment willing to pay a big price premium for the very finest items available, thus opening the strategic window for some competitors to employ differentiation-based focused strategies aimed at the very top of the market pyramid.

When Focusing Is Attractive   A focused strategy based either on low cost or differentiation becomes increasingly attractive as more of the following conditions are met:

- The segment is big enough to be profitable.
- The segment has good growth potential.
- The segment is not crucial to the success of major competitors.
- The focusing firm has the skills and resources to serve the segment effectively.
- The focuser can defend itself against challengers based on the customer goodwill it has built up and its superior ability to serve buyers in the segment.

A focuser's specialized skills in serving the target market niche provide a basis for defending against the five competitive forces. Multisegment rivals may not have the same competitive capability to serve the focused firm's target clientele. The focused firm's competence in serving the market niche raises entry barriers, thus making it harder for companies outside the niche to enter. A focuser's unique capabilities in serving the niche also present a hurdle that makers of substitute products must overcome. The bargaining leverage of powerful customers is blunted somewhat by their own unwillingness to shift their business to rival companies less capable of meeting their expectations.

Focusing works best (1) when it is costly or difficult for multisegment competitors to meet the specialized needs of the target market niche, (2) when no other rival is attempting to specialize in the same target segment, (3) when a firm doesn't have the resources to go after a wider part of the total market, and (4) when the industry has many different segments, thereby allowing a focuser to pick an attractive segment suited to its strengths and capabilities.

The Risks of a Focused Strategy   Focusing carries several risks. One is the chance that competitors will find effective ways to match the focused firm in serving the narrow target market. A second is the potential for the niche buyer's preferences and needs to shift toward the product attributes desired by the market as a whole. An erosion of the differences across buyer segments lowers entry barriers into a focuser's market niche and provides an open invitation for rivals in adjacent segments to begin competing for the focuser's customers. A third risk is that the segment becomes so attractive it is soon inundated with competitors, causing segment profits to be splintered.

USING OFFENSIVE STRATEGIES TO SECURE COMPETITIVE ADVANTAGE

Competitive advantage is nearly always achieved by successful offensive strategic moves; defensive strategies can protect competitive advantage but rarely are the basis for achieving competitive advantage. How long it takes for a successful offensive to create an edge is a function of the industry's competitive characteristics.[9] The *buildup period,* shown in Figure 5–2, can be short, as in service businesses that need little in the way of equipment and distribution system support to implement a new offensive move. Or the buildup can take much longer, as in capital intensive and technologically sophisticated industries where firms may need several years to debug a new technology, bring new capacity on-line, and win consumer acceptance of a new product. Ideally, an offensive move builds competitive advantage quickly; the longer it takes, the more likely rivals will spot the move, see its potential, and begin a counter-response. The size of the advantage (indicated on the vertical scale in Figure 5–2) can be large (as in pharmaceuticals where patents on an important new drug produce a substantial advantage) or small (as in apparel where popular new designs can be imitated quickly).

> Competitive advantage is usually acquired by employing a creative offensive strategy that isn't easily thwarted by rivals.

Following a successful competitive offensive is a *benefit period* during which the fruits of competitive advantage can be enjoyed. The length of the benefit period depends on how much time it takes rivals to launch counteroffensives and begin closing the competitive gap. A lengthy benefit period gives a firm valuable time to earn above-average profits and recoup the investment made in creating the advantage. The best strategic offensives produce big competitive advantages and long benefit periods.

[9]Ian C. MacMillan, "How Long Can You Sustain a Competitive Advantage?" reprinted in Liam Fahey, *The Strategic Planning Management Reader* (Englewood Cliffs, N.J.: Prentice-Hall, 1989), pp. 23–24.

F I G U R E 5-2 | **The Building and Eroding of Competitive Advantage**

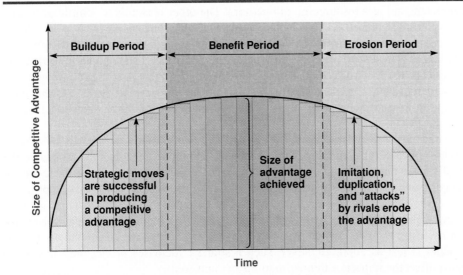

As competitors respond with serious counteroffensives to attack the advantage, the *erosion period* begins. Any competitive advantage a firm currently holds will eventually be eroded by the actions of competent, resourceful competitors.[10] Thus, to sustain an initially won advantage, a firm must devise a second strategic offensive. The groundwork for the second offensive needs to be laid during the benefit period so that everything is ready for launch when competitors mount efforts to cut into the leader's advantage. To successfully sustain a competitive advantage, a company must stay a step ahead of rivals by initiating one creative strategic offensive after another to improve its market position and retain customer favor.

There are six basic types of strategic offensives:[11]

- Initiatives to match or exceed competitor strengths.
- Initiatives to capitalize on competitor weaknesses.
- Simultaneous initiatives on many fronts.
- End-run offensives.
- Guerrilla offensives.
- Preemptive strikes.

INITIATIVES TO MATCH OR EXCEED COMPETITOR STRENGTHS

There are two good reasons to go head-to-head against rival companies, pitting one's own strengths against theirs, price for price, model for model, promotion tactic for promotion tactic, and geographic area by geographic area. The first is to try to gain market share by outcompeting weaker rivals. Challenging weaker rivals where they

---

[10]Ian C. MacMillan, "Controlling Competitive Dynamics by Taking Strategic Initiative," *The Academy of Management Executive* 2, no. 2 (May 1988), p. 111.

[11]Philip Kotler and Ravi Singh, "Marketing Warfare in the 1980s," *The Journal of Business Strategy* 1, no. 3 (Winter 1981), pp. 30–41; Philip Kotler, *Marketing Management,* 5th ed. (Englewood Cliffs, N.J.: Prentice-Hall, 1984), pp. 401–6; and Ian MacMillan, "Preemptive Strategies," *Journal of Business Strategy* 14, no. 2 (Fall 1983), pp. 16–26.

are strongest is attractive whenever a firm has a superior product offering and the organizational capabilities to win profitable sales and market share away from less competent and less resourceful competitors. The other reason is to whittle away at a strong rival's competitive advantage. Here success is measured by how much the competitive gap is narrowed. The merits of a strength-against-strength offensive challenge, of course, depend on how much the offensive costs compared to its competitive benefits. To succeed, the initiator needs enough competitive strength and resources to take at least some market share from the targeted rivals. Absent good prospects for long-term competitive gains and added profitability, such an offensive is ill-advised.

Attacking a competitor's strengths can involve initiatives on any of several fronts—price-cutting, running comparison ads, adding new features that appeal to the rival's customers, constructing major new plant capacity in the rival's backyard, or bringing out new models to match the rival model for model. In one classic ploy, the aggressor challenges the targeted rival with an equally good offering at a lower price.[12] This can produce market share gains if the competitor has strong reasons for not resorting to price cuts of its own and if the challenger convinces buyers that its product is just as good. However, such a strategy increases profits only if volume gains offset the impact of thinner margins per unit sold.

Another way to mount a price-aggressive challenge is to first achieve a cost advantage and then hit competitors with a lower price.[13] Price-cutting supported by a cost advantage is perhaps the strongest basis for launching and sustaining a price-aggressive offensive. Without a cost advantage, price-cutting works only if the aggressor has more financial resources and can outlast its rivals in a war of attrition.

One of the most powerful offensive strategies is to challenge rivals with an equally good or better product at a lower price.

Challenging larger, entrenched competitors with aggressive price-cutting is foolhardy unless the aggressor has either a cost advantage or greater financial strength.

INITIATIVES TO CAPITALIZE ON COMPETITOR WEAKNESSES

In this offensive approach, a company tries to gain market inroads by directing its competitive attention to the weaknesses of rivals. There are a number of ways to achieve competitive gains at the expense of rivals' weaknesses:

- Concentrate on geographic regions where a rival has a weak market share or is exerting less competitive effort.
- Pay special attention to buyer segments that a rival is neglecting or is weakly equipped to serve.
- Go after the customers of those rivals whose products lag on quality, features, or product performance; in such cases, a challenger with a better product can often convince the most performance-conscious customers to switch to its brand.
- Make special sales pitches to the customers of those rivals who provide subpar customer service—it may be relatively easy for a service-oriented challenger to win a rival's disenchanted customers.
- Try to move in on rivals that have weak advertising and weak brand recognition—a challenger with strong marketing skills and a recognized brand name can often win customers away from lesser-known rivals.
- Introduce new models or product versions that exploit gaps in the product lines of key rivals; sometimes "gap fillers" turn out to be a market hit and develop

---

[12]Kotler, *Marketing Management,* p. 402.
[13]Kotler, *Marketing Management,* p. 403.

into new growth segments—witness Chrysler's success in minivans. This initiative works well when new product versions satisfy certain buyer needs that heretofore have been ignored or neglected.

As a rule, initiatives that exploit competitor weaknesses stand a better chance of succeeding than do those that challenge competitor strengths, especially if the weaknesses represent important vulnerabilities and the rival is caught by surprise with no ready defense.[14]

SIMULTANEOUS INITIATIVES ON MANY FRONTS

On occasion a company may see merit in launching a grand competitive offensive involving multiple initiatives (price cuts, increased advertising, new product introductions, free samples, coupons, in-store promotions, rebates) across a wide geographic front. Such all-out campaigns can throw a rival off-balance, diverting its attention in many directions and forcing it to protect many pieces of its customer base simultaneously. Hunt's ketchup tried such an offensive several years ago in an attempt to wrest market share away from Heinz. The attack began when Hunt's introduced two new ketchup flavors (pizza and hickory) to disrupt consumers' taste preferences, create new flavor segments, and capture more shelf space in retail stores. Simultaneously, Hunt's lowered its price to 70 percent of Heinz's price, offered sizable trade allowances to retailers, and raised its advertising budget to over twice the level of Heinz's.[15] The offensive failed because not enough Heinz users tried the Hunt's brands, and many of those who did soon switched back to Heinz. Wide-scale offensives have their best chance of success when a challenger with an attractive product or service also has the financial resources to outspend rivals in courting customers; then it may be able to blitz the market with an array of promotional offers sufficient to entice large numbers of buyers to switch their brand allegiance.

END-RUN OFFENSIVES

End-run offensives seek to avoid head-on challenges tied to aggressive price-cutting, escalated advertising, or costly efforts to outdifferentiate rivals. Instead the idea is to maneuver *around* competitors and be the first to enter unoccupied market territory. Examples of end-run offensives include moving aggressively into geographic areas where close rivals have little or no market presence, trying to create new segments by introducing products with different attributes and performance features to better meet the needs of selected buyers, and leapfrogging into next-generation technologies to supplant existing products and/or production processes. With an end-run offensive, a company can gain a significant first-mover advantage in a new arena and force competitors to play catch-up. The most successful end-runs change the rules of the competitive game in the aggressor's favor.

GUERRILLA OFFENSIVES

Guerrilla offensives are particularly well-suited to small challengers who have neither the resources nor the market visibility to mount a full-fledged attack on industry leaders. A guerrilla offensive uses the hit-and-run principle, selectively attacking

---

[14]For a discussion of the use of surprise, see William E. Rothschild, "Surprise and the Competitive Advantage," *Journal of Business Strategy* 4, no. 3 (Winter 1984), pp. 10–18.

[15]As cited in Kotler, *Marketing Management,* p. 404.

where and when an underdog can temporarily exploit the situation to its own advantage. There are several ways to wage a guerrilla offensive:[16]

1. Go after buyer groups that are not important to major rivals.
2. Go after buyers whose loyalty to rival brands is weakest.
3. Focus on areas where rivals are overextended and have spread their resources most thinly (possibilities include going after selected customers located in isolated geographic areas, enhancing delivery schedules at times when competitors' deliveries are running behind, adding to quality when rivals have quality control problems, and boosting technical services when buyers are confused by competitors' proliferation of models and optional features).
4. Make small, scattered, random raids on the leaders' customers with such tactics as occasional lowballing on price (to win a big order or steal a key account).
5. Surprise key rivals with sporadic but intense bursts of promotional activity to pick off buyers who might otherwise have selected rival brands.
6. If rivals employ unfair or unethical competitive tactics and the situation merits it, file legal actions charging antitrust violations, patent infringement, or unfair advertising.

PREEMPTIVE STRIKES

Preemptive strategies involve moving first to secure an advantageous position that rivals are foreclosed or discouraged from duplicating. There are several ways to win a prime strategic position with preemptive moves:[17]

- Expand production capacity well ahead of market demand in hopes of discouraging rivals from following with expansions of their own. When rivals are "bluffed" out of adding capacity for fear of creating long-term excess supply and having to struggle with the bad profit economics of underutilized plants, the preemptor stands to win a bigger market share as market demand grows and it has the production capacity to take on new orders.
- Tie up the best (or the most) raw material sources and/or the most reliable, high-quality suppliers via long-term contracts or backward vertical integration. This move can relegate rivals to struggling for second-best supply positions.
- Secure the best geographic locations. An attractive first-mover advantage can often be locked up by moving to obtain the most favorable site along a heavily traveled thoroughfare, at a new interchange or intersection, in a new shopping mall, in a natural beauty spot, close to cheap transportation or raw material supplies or market outlets, and so on.
- Obtain the business of prestigious customers.
- Build a "psychological" image in the minds of consumers that is unique and hard to copy and that establishes a compelling appeal and rallying cry. Examples include Avis's well-known "We try harder" theme; Frito-Lay's guarantee to

---

[16]For more details, see Ian MacMillan "How Business Strategists Can Use Guerrilla Warfare Tactics," *Journal of Business Strategy* 1, no. 2 (Fall 1980), pp. 63–65; Kathryn R. Harrigan, *Strategic Flexibility* (Lexington, Mass.: Lexington Books, 1985), pp. 30–45; and Liam Fahey, "Guerrilla Strategy: The Hit-and-Run Attack," in Fahey, *The Strategic Management Planning Reader,* pp. 194–97.

[17]The use of preemptive moves is treated comprehensively in Ian MacMillan, "Preemptive Strategies," *Journal of Business Strategy,* pp. 16–26. What follows in this section is based on MacMillan's article.

retailers of "99.5% service"; Holiday Inn's assurance of "no surprises"; and Prudential's "piece of the rock" image of safety and permanence.

- Secure exclusive or dominant access to the best distributors in an area.

General Mills's Red Lobster restaurant chain succeeded in tying up access to excellent seafood suppliers. DeBeers became the dominant world distributor of diamonds by buying up the production of most of the important diamond mines. DuPont's aggressive capacity expansions in titanium dioxide, while not blocking all competitors from expanding, did discourage enough to give it a leadership position in the titanium dioxide industry. Fox's stunning $6.2 billion preemptive bid over CBS to televise NFL games is widely regarded as a strategic move to catapult Fox into the ranks of the major TV networks alongside ABC, CBS, and NBC.

To be successful, a preemptive move doesn't have to totally block rivals from following or copying; it merely needs to give a firm a "prime" position. A prime position is one that puts rivals at a competitive disadvantage and is not easily circumvented.

CHOOSING WHO TO ATTACK

Aggressor firms need to analyze which of their rivals to challenge as well as how to outcompete them. Four types of firms make good targets:[18]

1. *Market leaders.* Waging an offensive against strong leaders risks squandering valuable resources in a futile effort and perhaps even precipitating a fierce and profitless industrywide battle for market share—caution is well advised. Offensive attacks on a major competitor make the best sense when the leader in terms of size and market share is not a "true leader" in terms of serving the market well. Signs of leader vulnerability include unhappy buyers, sliding profits, strong emotional commitment to a technology the leader has pioneered, outdated plants and equipment, a preoccupation with diversification into other industries, a product line that is clearly not superior to what several rivals have, and a competitive strategy that lacks real strength based on low-cost leadership or differentiation. Attacks on leaders can also succeed when the challenger is able to revamp its value chain or innovate to gain a fresh cost-based or differentiation-based competitive advantage.[19] Attacks on leaders need not have the objective of making the aggressor the new leader, however; a challenger may "win" by simply wresting enough sales from the leader to make the aggressor a stronger runner-up.

2. *Runner-up firms.* Launching offensives against weaker runner-up firms whose positions are vulnerable entails relatively low risk. This is an especially attractive option when a challenger's competitive strengths match the runner-up's weaknesses.

3. *Struggling enterprises that are on the verge of going under.* Challenging a hard-pressed rival in ways that further sap its financial strength and competitive position can weaken its resolve and hasten its exit from the market.

4. *Small local and regional firms.* Because these firms typically have limited expertise, a challenger with broader capabilities is well-positioned to raid their biggest and best customers—particularly those who are growing rapidly, have increasingly sophisticated requirements, and may already be thinking about switching to a supplier with more full-service capability.

---

[18]Kotler, *Marketing Management,* p. 400.
[19]Porter, *Competitive Advantage,* p. 518.

As we have said, successful strategies are grounded in competitive advantage. This goes for offensive strategies too. The kinds of competitive advantages that usually offer the strongest basis for a strategic offensive include:[20]

- Having a lower-cost product design.
- Having lower-cost production capability.
- Having product features that deliver superior performance to buyers or that lower user costs.
- An ability to give buyers more responsive after-sale support.
- Having the resources to escalate the marketing effort in an undermarketed industry.
- Pioneering a new distribution channel.
- Having the capability to bypass wholesale distributors and sell direct to the end user.

Almost always, a strategic offensive should be tied to what a firm does best—its competitive strengths and capabilities. As a rule, these strengths should take the form of a *key skill* (cost reduction capabilities, customer service skills, technical expertise) a uniquely *strong functional competence* (engineering and product design, manufacturing expertise, advertising and promotion, marketing know-how) or *superior ability to perform key activities* in the value chain that lower cost or enhance differentiation.[21]

USING DEFENSIVE STRATEGIES TO PROTECT COMPETITIVE ADVANTAGE

The foremost purpose of defensive strategy is to protect competitive advantage and fortify the firm's competitive position.

In a competitive market, all firms are subject to challenges from rivals. Market offensives can come both from new entrants in the industry and from established firms seeking to improve their market positions. The purpose of defensive strategy is to lower the risk of being attacked, weaken the impact of any attack that occurs, and influence challengers to aim their efforts at other rivals. While defensive strategy usually doesn't enhance a firm's competitive advantage, it helps fortify a firm's competitive position and sustain whatever competitive advantage it does have.

There are several basic ways for a company to protect its competitive position. One approach involves trying to block the avenues challengers can take in mounting an offensive; the options include[22]

- Broadening the firm's product line to close off vacant niches and gaps to would-be challengers.
- Introducing models or brands that match the characteristics challengers' models already have or might have.
- Keeping prices low on models that most closely match competitors' offerings.
- Signing exclusive agreements with dealers and distributors to keep competitors from using the same ones.
- Granting dealers and distributors sizable volume discounts to discourage them from experimenting with other suppliers.

[20]Ibid., pp. 520–22.
[21]For more details, see MacMillan, "Controlling Competitive Dynamics," pp. 112–16.
[22]Porter, *Competitive Advantage,* pp. 489–94.

- Offering free or low-cost training to product users.
- Making it harder for competitors to get buyers to try their brands by (1) giving special price discounts to buyers who are considering trial use of rival brands, (2) resorting to high levels of couponing and sample giveaways to buyers most prone to experiment, and (3) making early announcements about impending new products or price changes to induce potential buyers to postpone switching.
- Raising the amount of financing provided to dealers and/or to buyers.
- Reducing delivery times for spare parts.
- Increasing warranty coverages.
- Patenting alternative technologies.
- Maintaining a participation in alternative technologies.
- Protecting proprietary know-how in product design, production technologies, and other strategy-critical value chain activities.
- Signing exclusive contracts with the best suppliers to block access of aggressive rivals.
- Purchasing natural resource reserves ahead of present needs to keep them from competitors.
- Avoiding suppliers that also serve competitors.
- Challenging rivals' products or practices in regulatory proceedings.

Moves such as these not only buttress a firm's present position, they also present competitors with a moving target. Protecting the status quo isn't enough. A good defense entails adjusting quickly to changing industry conditions and, on occasion, being a first-mover to block or preempt moves by would-be aggressors. A mobile defense is preferable to a stationary defense.

A second approach to defensive strategy entails signaling challengers that there is a real threat of strong retaliation if a challenger attacks. The goal is to dissuade challengers from attacking at all (by raising their expectations that the resulting battle will be more costly to the challenger than it is worth) or at least divert them to options that are less threatening to the defender. Would-be challengers can be signaled by[23]

- Publicly announcing management's commitment to maintain the firm's present market share.
- Publicly announcing plans to construct adequate production capacity to meet and possibly surpass the forecasted growth in industry volume.
- Giving out advance information about a new product, technology breakthrough, or the planned introduction of important new brands or models in hopes that challengers will be induced to delay moves of their own until they see if the announced actions actually are forthcoming.
- Publicly committing the company to a policy of matching competitors' terms or prices.
- Maintaining a war chest of cash and marketable securities.
- Making an occasional strong counter-response to the moves of weak competitors to enhance the firm's image as a tough defender.

Another way to dissuade rivals is to try to lower the profit inducement for challengers to launch an offensive. When a firm's or industry's profitability is enticingly high,

---

[23]Ibid., pp. 495–97. The listing here is selective; Porter offers a greater number of options.

challengers are more willing to tackle high defensive barriers and combat strong retaliation. A defender can deflect attacks, especially from new entrants, by deliberately forgoing some short-run profits and using accounting methods that obscure profitability.

VERTICAL INTEGRATION STRATEGIES AND COMPETITIVE ADVANTAGE

Vertical integration extends a firm's competitive scope within the same industry. It involves expanding the firm's range of activities backward into sources of supply and/or forward toward end users of the final product. Thus, if a manufacturer elects to build a new plant to make certain component parts rather than purchase them from outside suppliers, it remains in essentially the same industry as before. The only change is that it has business units in two production stages in the industry's value chain system. Similarly, if a personal computer manufacturer elects to integrate forward by opening 100 retail stores to market its brands directly to users, it remains in the personal computer business even though its competitive scope extends further forward in the industry chain.

Vertical integration strategies can aim at *full integration* (participating in all stages of the industry value chain) or *partial integration* (building positions in just some stages of the industry's total value chain). A firm can accomplish vertical integration by starting its own operations in other stages in the industry's activity chain or by acquiring a company already performing the activities it wants to bring in-house.

THE STRATEGIC ADVANTAGES OF VERTICAL INTEGRATION

The only good reason for investing company resources in vertical integration is to strengthen the firm's competitive position.[24] Unless vertical integration produces sufficient cost savings to justify the extra investment or yields a competitive advantage, it has no real payoff profitwise or strategywise.

Integrating backward generates cost savings only when the volume needed is big enough to capture the same scale economies suppliers have and when suppliers' production efficiency can be matched or exceeded. Backward integration is most advantageous when suppliers have sizable profit margins, when the item being supplied is a major cost component, and when the needed technological skills are easily mastered. Backward vertical integration can produce a differentiation-based competitive advantage when a company, by performing in-house activities that were previously outsourced, ends up with a better-quality product/service offering, improves the calibre of its customer service, or in other ways enhances the performance of its final product. On occasion, integrating into more stages along the value chain can add to a company's differentiation capabilities by allowing it to build or strengthen its core competencies, better master key skills or strategy-critical technologies, or add features that deliver greater customer value.

Backward integration can also spare a company the uncertainty of being dependent on suppliers of crucial components or support services, and it can lessen a com-

A vertical integration strategy has appeal *only* if it significantly strengthens a firm's competitive position.

---

[24]See Kathryn R. Harrigan, "Matching Vertical Integration Strategies to Competitive Conditions," *Strategic Management Journal* 7, no. 6 (November–December 1986), pp. 535–56; for a discussion of the advantages and disadvantages of vertical integration, see John Stuckey and David White, "When and When *Not* to Vertically Integrate," *Sloan Management Review* (Spring 1993), pp. 71–83.

pany's vulnerability to powerful suppliers that raise prices at every opportunity. Stockpiling, fixed-price contracts, multiple-sourcing, long-term cooperative partnerships, or the use of substitute inputs are not always attractive ways for dealing with uncertain supply conditions or with economically powerful suppliers. Companies that are low on a key supplier's customer priority list can find themselves waiting on shipments every time supplies get tight. If this occurs often and wreaks havoc in a company's own production and customer relations activities, backward integration can be an advantageous strategic solution.

The strategic impetus for forward integration has much the same roots. In many industries, independent sales agents, wholesalers, and retailers handle competing brands of the same product; they have no allegiance to any one company's brand and tend to push "what sells" and earns them the biggest profits. Undependable sales and distribution channels can give rise to costly inventory pileups and frequent underutilization of capacity, thereby undermining the economies of a steady, near-capacity production operation. In such cases, it can be advantageous for a manufacturer to integrate forward into wholesaling and/or retailing in order to build a committed group of dealers and outlets representing its products to end users. Sometimes even a small increase in the average rate of capacity utilization can boost manufacturing margins enough so a firm really profits from company-owned distributorships, franchised dealer networks, and/or a chain of retail stores. On other occasions, integrating forward into the activity of selling directly to end users can result in a relative cost advantage and lower selling prices to end users by eliminating many of the costs of using regular wholesale-retail channels.

For a raw materials producer, integrating forward into manufacturing may permit greater product differentiation and provide an avenue of escape from the price-oriented competition of a commodity business. Often, in the early phases of an industry's value chain, intermediate goods are commodities in the sense that they have essentially identical technical specifications irrespective of producer (as is the case with crude oil, poultry, sheet steel, cement, and textile fibers). Competition in the markets for commodity or commoditylike products is usually fiercely price competitive, with the shifting balance between supply and demand giving rise to volatile profits. However, the closer the activities in the chain get to the ultimate consumer, the greater the opportunities for a firm to break out of a commoditylike competitive environment and differentiate its end product via design, service, quality features, packaging, promotion, and so on. Product differentiation often reduces the importance of price compared to other value-creating activities and allows for improved profit margins.

The Strategic Disadvantages of Vertical Integration

Vertical integration has some substantial drawbacks, however. It boosts a firm's capital investment in the industry, increasing business risk (what if the industry goes sour?) and perhaps denying financial resources to more worthwhile pursuits. A vertically integrated firm has vested interests in protecting its present investments in technology and production facilities even if they are becoming obsolete. Because of the high costs of abandoning such investments before they are worn out, fully integrated firms tend to adopt new technologies slower than partially integrated or nonintegrated firms. Second, integrating forward or backward locks a firm into relying on its own in-house activities and sources of supply (that later may prove more costly than outsourcing) and potentially results in less flexibility in accommodating buyer demand for greater product variety.

The big disadvantage of vertical integration is that it locks a firm deeper into the industry; unless operating across more stages in the industry's value chain builds competitive advantage, it is a questionable strategic move.

Third, vertical integration can pose problems of balancing capacity at each stage in the value chain. The most efficient scale of operation at each activity link in the value chain can vary substantially. Exact self-sufficiency at each interface is the exception not the rule. Where internal capacity is deficient to supply the next stage, the difference has to be bought externally. Where internal capacity is excessive, customers need to be found for the surplus. And if by-products are generated, they require arrangements for disposal.

Fourth, integration forward or backward often calls for radically different skills and business capabilities. Manufacturing, wholesale distribution, and retailing are different businesses with different key success factors, even though the physical products are the same. Managers of a manufacturing company should consider carefully whether it makes good business sense to invest time and money in developing the expertise and merchandising skills to integrate forward into wholesaling or retailing. Many manufacturers learn the hard way that owning and operating wholesale-retail networks present many headaches, fit poorly with what they do best, and don't always add the kind of value to their core business they thought they would. Integrating backward into parts and components manufacture isn't as simple or profitable as it sometimes sounds either. Personal computer makers, for example, frequently have trouble getting timely deliveries of the latest semiconductor chips at favorable prices, but most don't come close to having the resources or capabilities to integrate backward into chip manufacture; the semiconductor business is technologically sophisticated and entails heavy capital requirements and ongoing R&D effort, and mastering the manufacturing process takes a long time.

Fifth, backward vertical integration into the production of parts and components can reduce a company's manufacturing flexibility, lengthening the time it takes to make design and model changes and to bring new products to market. Companies that alter designs and models frequently in response to shifting buyer preferences often find vertical integration into parts and components burdensome because of constant retooling and redesign costs and the time it takes to implement coordinated changes throughout the value chain. Outsourcing is often quicker and cheaper than vertical integration, allowing a company to be more flexible and more nimble in adapting its product offering to fast-changing buyer preferences. Most of the world's automakers, despite their expertise in automotive technology and manufacturing, have concluded that they are better off from the standpoints of quality, cost, and design flexibility purchasing many of their key parts and components from manufacturing specialists rather than integrating backward to supply their own needs.

Unbundling and Outsourcing Strategies   In recent years, some vertically integrated companies have found vertical integration to be so competitively burdensome that they have adopted vertical deintegration (or unbundling) strategies. Deintegration involves withdrawing from certain stages/activities in the value chain system and relying on outside vendors to supply the needed products, support services, or functional activities. Outsourcing pieces of the value chain formerly performed in-house makes strategic sense whenever

- An activity can be performed better or more cheaply by outside specialists.
- The activity is not crucial to the firm's ability to achieve sustainable competitive advantage and won't hollow out its core competencies, essential skills, or technical know-how.
- It reduces the company's risk exposure to changing technology and/or changing buyer preferences.

- It streamlines company operations in ways that improve organizational flexibility, cut cycle time, speed decision-making, and reduce coordination costs.
- It allows a company to concentrate on its core business and do what it does best.

Often, many of the advantages of vertical integration can be captured and many of the disadvantages avoided via long-term cooperative partnerships with key suppliers.

All in all, therefore, a strategy of vertical integration can have both important strengths and weaknesses. Which direction the scales tip on vertical integration depends on (1) whether it can enhance the performance of strategy-critical activities in ways that lower cost or increase differentiation, (2) its impact on investment costs, flexibility and response times, and administrative overheads associated with coordinating operations across more stages, and (3) whether it creates competitive advantage. Absent solid benefits, vertical integration is not likely to be an attractive competitive strategy option.

FIRST-MOVER ADVANTAGES AND DISADVANTAGES

When to make a strategic move is often as crucial as *what* move to make. Timing is especially important when *first-mover advantages* or *disadvantages* exist.[25] Being first to initiate a strategic move can have a high payoff when (1) pioneering helps build a firm's image and reputation with buyers, (2) early commitments to supplies of raw materials, new technologies, distribution channels, and so on can produce an absolute cost advantage over rivals, (3) first-time customers remain strongly loyal to pioneering firms in making repeat purchases, and (4) moving first constitutes a pre-emptive strike, making imitation extra hard or unlikely. The bigger the first-mover advantages, the more attractive that making the first move becomes.

Because of first-mover advantages and disadvantages, competitive advantage is often attached to *when* a move is made as well as to *what* move is made.

However, a wait-and-see approach doesn't always carry a competitive penalty. Being a first-mover may entail greater risks than being a late-mover. First-mover disadvantages (or late-mover advantages) arise when (1) pioneering leadership is much more costly than followership and only negligible experience curve effects accrue to the leader, (2) technological change is so rapid that early investments are soon rendered obsolete (thus allowing following firms to gain the advantages of next-generation products and more efficient processes), (3) it is easy for latecomers to crack the market because customer loyalty to pioneering firms is weak, and (4) the hard-earned skills and know-how developed by the market leaders during the early competitive phase are easily copied or even surpassed by late-movers. Good timing, therefore, is an important ingredient in deciding whether to be aggressive or cautious in pursuing a particular move.

KEY POINTS

The challenge of competitive strategy—whether it be overall low-cost, broad differentiation, best-cost, focused low-cost, or focused differentiation—is to create a competitive advantage for the firm. Competitive advantage comes from positioning a firm in the marketplace so it has an edge in coping with competitive forces and in attracting buyers.

[25]Porter, *Competitive Strategy,* pp. 232–33.

A strategy of trying to be the low-cost provider works well in situations where

- The industry's product is essentially the same from seller to seller (brand differences are minor).
- Many buyers are price-sensitive and shop for the lowest price.
- There are only a few ways to achieve product differentiation that have much value to buyers.
- Most buyers use the product in the same ways and thus have common user requirements.
- Buyers' costs in switching from one seller or brand to another are low (or even zero).
- Buyers are large and have significant power to negotiate pricing terms.

To achieve a low-cost advantage, a company must become more skilled than rivals in controlling structural and executional cost drivers and/or it must find innovative cost-saving ways to revamp its value chain. Successful low-cost providers usually achieve their cost advantages by imaginatively and persistently ferreting out cost savings throughout the value chain. They are good at finding ways to drive costs out of their businesses.

Differentiation strategies seek to produce a competitive edge by incorporating attributes and features into a company's product/service offering that rivals don't have. Anything a firm can do to create buyer value represents a potential basis for differentiation. Successful differentiation is usually keyed to lowering the buyer's cost of using the item, raising the performance the buyer gets, or boosting a buyer's psychological satisfaction. To be sustainable, differentiation usually has to be linked to unique internal skills and core competencies that give a company capabilities its rivals can't easily match. Differentiation tied just to unique physical features seldom is lasting because resourceful competitors are adept at cloning, improving on, or finding substitutes for almost any feature or trait that appeals to buyers.

Best-cost provider strategies combine a strategic emphasis on low cost with a strategic emphasis on more than minimal quality, service, features, or performance. The aim is to create competitive advantage by giving buyers more value for the money; this is done by matching close rivals on key quality-service-features-performance attributes and beating them on the costs of incorporating such attributes into the product or service. To be successful with a best-cost provider strategy, a company must have unique expertise in incorporating upscale product or service attributes at a lower cost than rivals; its core competencies must revolve around an ability to manage unit costs down and product/service calibre up simultaneously.

The competitive advantage of focusing is earned either by achieving lower costs in serving the target market niche or by developing an ability to offer niche buyers something different from rival competitors—in other words, it is either *cost-based* or *differentiation-based*. Focusing works best when

- Buyer needs or uses of the item are diverse.
- No other rival is attempting to specialize in the same target segment.
- A firm lacks the capability to go after a wider part of the total market.
- Buyer segments differ widely in size, growth rate, profitability, and intensity in the five competitive forces, making some segments more attractive than others.

A variety of offensive strategic moves can be used to secure a competitive advantage. Strategic offensives can be aimed either at competitors' strengths or at their weaknesses; they can involve end-runs or grand offensives on many fronts; they can be designed as guerrilla actions or as preemptive strikes; and the target of the offensive can be a market leader, a runner-up firm, or the smallest and/or weakest firms in the industry.

The strategic approaches to defending a company's position usually take the form of (1) making moves that fortify the company's present position, (2) presenting competitors with a moving target to avoid "out of date" vulnerability, and (3) dissuading rivals from even trying to attack.

Vertically integrating forward or backward makes strategic sense only if it strengthens a company's position via either cost reduction or creation of a differentiation-based advantage. Otherwise, the drawbacks of vertical integration (increased investment, greater business risk, increased vulnerability to technological changes, and less flexibility in making product changes) outweigh the advantages (better coordination of production flows and technological know-how from stage to stage, more specialized use of technology, greater internal control over operations, greater scale economies, and matching production with sales and marketing). There are ways to achieve the advantages of vertical integration without encountering the drawbacks.

The timing of strategic moves is important. First-movers sometimes gain strategic advantage; at other times, such as when technology is developing fast, it is cheaper and easier to be a follower than a leader.

SUGGESTED READINGS

Aaker, David A. "Managing Assets and Skills: The Key to a Sustainable Competitive Advantage." *California Management Review* 31, no. 2 (Winter 1989), pp. 91–106.

Cohen, William A. "War in the Marketplace." *Business Horizons* 29, no. 2 (March–April 1986), pp. 10–20.

Coyne, Kevin P. "Sustainable Competitive Advantage—What It Is, What It Isn't." *Business Horizons* 29, no. 1 (January–February 1986), pp. 54–61.

D'Aveni, Richard A. *Hypercompetition: The Dynamics of Strategic Maneuvering* (New York: Free Press, 1994), chaps. 1, 2, 3, and 4.

Harrigan, Kathryn R. "Guerrilla Strategies of Underdog Competitors." *Planning Review* 14, no. 16 (November 1986), pp. 4–11.

———. "Formulating Vertical Integration Strategies." *Academy of Management Review* 9, no. 4 (October 1984), pp. 638–52.

Hout, Thomas, Michael E. Porter, and Eileen Rudden. "How Global Companies Win Out." *Harvard Business Review* 60, no. 5 (September–October 1982), pp. 98–108.

MacMillan, Ian C. "Preemptive Strategies." *Journal of Business Strategy* 14, no. 2 (Fall 1983), pp. 16–26.

———. "Controlling Competitive Dynamics by Taking Strategic Initiative." *The Academy of Management Executive* 2, no. 2 (May 1988), pp. 111–18.

Porter, Michael E. *Competitive Advantage* (New York: Free Press, 1985), chaps. 3, 4, 5, 7, 14, and 15.

Rothschild, William E. "Surprise and the Competitive Advantage." *Journal of Business Strategy* 4, no. 3 (Winter 1984), pp. 10–18.

Stuckey, John and David White, "When and When *Not* to Vertically Integrate," *Sloan Management Review* (Spring 1993), pp. 71–83.

Venkatesan, Ravi. "Strategic Outsourcing: To Make or Not to Make." *Harvard Business Review* 7, no. 6 (November–December 1992), pp. 98–107.

CHAPTER SIX

MATCHING STRATEGY TO A COMPANY'S SITUATION

Strategy isn't something you can nail together in slapdash fashion by sitting around a conference table . . .

Terry Haller

The essence of formulating competitive strategy is relating a company to its environment . . . the best strategy for a given firm is ultimately a unique construction reflecting its particular circumstances.

Michael E. Porter

You do not choose to become global. The market chooses for you; it forces your hand.

Alain Gomez
CEO, Thomson, S.A.

The task of matching strategy to a company's situation is complicated because of the many external and internal factors managers have to weigh. However, while the number and variety of considerations is necessarily lengthy, the most important drivers shaping a company's strategic options fall into two broad categories:

- The nature of industry and competitive conditions.
- The firm's own competitive capabilities, market position, and best opportunities.

The dominant strategy-shaping industry and competitive conditions revolve around what stage in the life-cycle the industry is in (emerging, rapid growth, mature, declining), the industry's structure (fragmented versus concentrated), the nature and relative strength of the five competitive forces, and the scope of competitive rivalry (particularly whether the company's market is globally competitive). The pivotal company-specific considerations hinge on (1) whether the company is an industry leader, an up-and-coming challenger, a content runner-up, or an also-ran struggling to survive, and (2) the company's particular set of strengths, weaknesses, opportunities, and threats. But even these few categories occur in too many combinations to cover here. However, we can demonstrate what the task of matching strategy to the situation involves by considering five classic types of industry environments:

1. Competing in emerging and rapidly growing industries.
2. Competing in maturing industries.
3. Competing in stagnant or declining industries.
4. Competing in fragmented industries.
5. Competing in international markets.

and three classic types of company situations:

1. Firms in industry leadership positions.
2. Firms in runner-up positions.
3. Firms that are competitively weak or crisis-ridden.

STRATEGIES FOR COMPETING IN EMERGING INDUSTRIES

An emerging industry is one in the early, formative stage. Most companies in an emerging industry are in a start-up mode, adding people, acquiring or constructing facilities, gearing up production, trying to broaden distribution and gain buyer acceptance. Often, there are important product design problems and technological problems to be worked out as well. Emerging industries present managers with some unique strategy-making challenges:[1]

- Because the market is new and unproven, there are many uncertainties about how it will function, how fast it will grow, and how big it will get; the little historical data available is virtually useless in projecting future trends.
- Much of the technological know-how tends to be proprietary and closely guarded, having been developed in-house by pioneering firms; some firms may file patents in an effort to secure competitive advantage.
- Often, there is no consensus regarding which of several competing production technologies will win out or which product attributes will gain the most buyer favor. Until market forces sort these things out, wide differences in product quality and performance are typical and rivalry centers around each firm's efforts to get the market to ratify its own strategic approach to technology, product design, marketing, and distribution.
- Entry barriers tend to be relatively low, even for entrepreneurial start-up companies; well-financed, opportunity-seeking outsiders are likely to enter if the industry has promise for explosive growth.
- Experience curve effects often permit significant cost reductions as volume builds.
- Firms have little hard information about competitors, how fast products are gaining buyer acceptance, and users' experiences with the product; there are no trade associations gathering and distributing information.

---

[1]Michael E. Porter, *Competitive Strategy* (New York: Free Press, 1980), pp. 216–23.

- Since all buyers are first-time users, the marketing task is to induce initial purchase and to overcome customer concerns about product features, performance reliability, and conflicting claims of rival firms.
- Many potential buyers expect first-generation products to be rapidly improved, so they delay purchase until technology and product design mature.
- Often, firms have trouble securing ample supplies of raw materials and components (until suppliers gear up to meet the industry's needs).
- Many companies, finding themselves short of funds to support needed R&D and get through several lean years until the product catches on, end up merging with competitors or being acquired by outsiders looking to invest in a growth market.

The two critical strategic issues confronting firms in an emerging industry are (1) how to finance the start-up phase and (2) what market segments and competitive advantages to go after in trying to secure a leading industry position.[2] Competitive strategies keyed either to low cost or differentiation are usually viable. Focusing should be considered when financial resources are limited and the industry has too many technological frontiers to pursue at once; one option for financially constrained enterprises is to form a strategic alliance or joint venture with another company to gain access to needed skills and resources. Because an emerging industry has no established "rules of the game" and industry participants employ widely varying strategic approaches, a well-financed firm with a powerful strategy can shape the rules and become a recognized industry leader.

Dealing with all the risks and opportunities of an emerging industry is one of the most challenging business strategy problems. To be successful in an emerging industry, companies usually have to pursue one or more of the following strategic avenues:[3]

1. Try to win the early race for industry leadership with risk-taking entrepreneurship and a bold, creative strategy. Broad or focused differentiation strategies keyed to product superiority typically offer the best chance for early competitive advantage.
2. Push to perfect the technology, to improve product quality, and to develop attractive performance features.
3. Try to capture any first-mover advantages associated with more models, better styling, early commitments to technologies and raw materials suppliers, experience curve effects, and new distribution channels.
4. Search out new customer groups, new geographical areas to enter, and new user applications. Make it easier and cheaper for first-time buyers to try the industry's first-generation product.
5. Gradually shift the advertising emphasis from building product awareness to increasing frequency of use and creating brand loyalty.
6. As technological uncertainty clears and a dominant technology emerges, adopt it quickly. While there's merit in trying to pioneer the "dominant design" approach, such a strategy carries high risk when there are many competing

> Strategic success in an emerging industry calls for bold entrepreneurship, a willingness to pioneer and take risks, an intuitive feel for what buyers will like, quick response to new developments, and opportunistic strategy-making.

---

[2]Charles W. Hofer and Dan Schendel, *Strategy Formulation: Analytical Concepts* (St. Paul, Minn.: West Publishing, 1978), pp. 164–65.

[3]Phillip Kotler, *Marketing Management,* 5th ed. (Englewood Cliffs, N.J.: Prentice-Hall, 1984), p. 366, and Porter, *Competitive Strategy,* chapter 10.

technologies, R&D is costly, and rapidly moving technological developments quickly make early investments obsolete.

7. Use price cuts to attract the next layer of price-sensitive buyers into the market.

8. Expect well-financed outsiders to move in with aggressive strategies as industry sales start to take off and the perceived risk of investing in the industry lessens. Try to prepare for the entry of powerful competitors by forecasting *(a)* who the probable entrants will be (based on present and future entry barriers) and *(b)* the types of strategies they are likely to employ.

The short-term value of winning the early race for growth and market share leadership has to be balanced against the longer-range need to build a durable competitive edge and a defendable market position.[4] New entrants, attracted by the growth and profit potential, may crowd the market. Aggressive newcomers, aspiring to industry leadership, can quickly become major players by acquiring and merging the operations of weaker competitors. Young companies in fast-growing markets face three strategic hurdles: (1) managing their own rapid expansion, (2) defending against competitors trying to horn in on their success, and (3) building a competitive position extending beyond their initial product or market. Such companies can help their cause by selecting knowledgeable members for their boards of directors, by hiring entrepreneurial managers with experience in guiding young businesses through the start-up and takeoff stages, by concentrating on out-innovating the competition, and perhaps by merging with or acquiring another firm to gain added expertise and a stronger resource base.

STRATEGIES FOR COMPETING IN MATURING INDUSTRIES

The rapid-growth environment of a young industry cannot go on forever. However, the transition to a slower-growth, maturing industry environment does not begin on an easily predicted schedule, and the transition can be forestalled by a steady stream of technological advances, product innovations, or other driving forces that keep rejuvenating market demand. Nonetheless, when growth rates do slacken, the transition to market maturity usually produces fundamental changes in the industry's competitive environment:[5]

1. *Slowing growth in buyer demand generates more head-to-head competition for market share.* Firms that want to continue on a rapid-growth track start looking for ways to take customers away from competitors. Outbreaks of price-cutting, increased advertising, and other aggressive tactics are common.

2. *Buyers become more sophisticated, often driving a harder bargain on repeat purchases.* Since buyers have experience with the product and are familiar with competing brands, they are better able to evaluate different brands and can use their knowledge to negotiate a better deal with sellers.

3. *Competition often produces a greater emphasis on cost and service.* As sellers all begin to offer the product attributes buyers prefer, buyer choices increasingly depend on which seller offers the best combination of price and service.

---

[4]Hofer and Schendel, *Strategy Formulation,* pp. 164–65.
[5]Porter, *Competitive Strategy,* pp. 238–40.

4. *Firms have a "topping out" problem in adding production capacity.* Slower rates of industry growth mean slowdowns in capacity expansion. Each firm has to monitor rivals' expansion plans and time its own capacity additions to minimize oversupply conditions in the industry. With slower industry growth, the mistake of adding too much capacity too soon can adversely affect company profits well into the future.

5. *Product innovation and new end-use applications are harder to come by.* Producers find it increasingly difficult to create new product features, find further uses for the product, and sustain buyer excitement.

6. *International competition increases.* Growth-minded domestic firms start to seek out sales opportunities in foreign markets. Some companies, looking for ways to cut costs, relocate plants to countries with lower wage rates. Greater product standardization and diffusion of technological know-how reduce entry barriers and make it possible for enterprising foreign companies to become serious market contenders in more countries. Industry leadership passes to companies that succeed in building strong competitive positions in most of the world's major geographic markets and in winning the biggest global market shares.

7. *Industry profitability falls temporarily or permanently.* Slower growth, increased competition, more sophisticated buyers, and occasional periods of overcapacity put pressure on industry profit margins. Weaker, less-efficient firms are usually the hardest hit.

8. *Stiffening competition induces a number of mergers and acquisitions among former competitors, drives the weakest firms out of the industry, and, in general, produces industry consolidation.* Inefficient firms and firms with weak competitive strategies can survive in a fast-growing industry with booming sales. But the intensifying competition that accompanies industry maturity exposes competitive weakness and throws second- and third-tier competitors into a survival-of-the-fittest contest.

As industry maturity begins to hit full force, and changes in the competitive environment set in, several strategic moves can strengthen firms' competitive positions.[6]

In a maturing industry, strategic emphasis needs to be on efficiency-increasing, profit-preserving measures: pruning the product line, improving production methods, reducing costs, accelerating sales promotion efforts, expanding internationally, and acquiring distressed competitors.

Pruning the Product Line   A wide selection of models, features, and product options has competitive value during the growth stage when buyers' needs are still evolving. But such variety can become too costly as price competition stiffens and profit margins are squeezed. Maintaining too many product versions prevents firms from achieving the economies of long production runs. In addition, the prices of slow-selling versions may not cover their true costs. Pruning marginal products from the line lowers costs and permits more concentration on items whose margins are highest and/or where the firm has a competitive advantage.

More Emphasis on Process Innovations   Efforts to "reinvent" the manufacturing process can have a fourfold payoff: lower costs, better production quality, greater capability to turn out multiple product versions, and shorter design-to-market cycles. Process innovation can involve mechanizing high-cost activities, revamping production lines

---

[6]The following discussion draws on Porter, *Competitive Strategy,* pp. 241–46.

to improve labor efficiency, creating self-directed work teams, reengineering the manufacturing portion of the value chain, and increasing use of advanced technology (robotics, computerized controls, and automatic guided vehicles). Japanese firms have become remarkably adept at using manufacturing process innovation to become lower-cost producers of higher-quality products.

A Stronger Focus on Cost Reduction   Stiffening price competition gives firms extra incentive to reduce unit costs. Such efforts can cover a broad front: companies can push suppliers for better prices, switch to lower-priced components, develop more economical product designs, cut low-value activities out of the value chain, streamline distribution channels, and reengineer internal processes.

Increasing Sales to Present Customers   In a mature market, growing by taking customers away from rivals may not be as appealing as expanding sales to existing customers. Strategies to increase purchases by existing customers can involve providing complementary items and ancillary services, and finding more ways for customers to use the product. Convenience food stores, for example, have boosted average sales per customer by adding video rentals, automatic bank tellers, and deli counters.

Purchasing Rival Firms at Bargain Prices   Sometimes the facilities and assets of distressed rivals can be acquired cheaply. Bargain-priced acquisitions can help create a low-cost position if they also present opportunities for greater operating efficiency. In addition, an acquired firm's customer base can provide expanded market coverage. The most desirable acquisitions are those that will significantly enhance the acquiring firm's competitive strength.

Expanding Internationally   As its domestic market matures, a firm may seek to enter foreign markets where attractive growth potential still exists and competitive pressures are not so strong. Several manufacturers in highly industrialized nations found international expansion attractive because equipment no longer suitable for domestic operations could be used in plants in less-developed foreign markets (a condition that lowered entry costs). Such possibilities arise when (1) foreign buyers have less sophisticated needs and have simpler, old-fashioned, end-use applications, and (2) foreign competitors are smaller, less formidable, and do not employ the latest production technology. Strategies to expand internationally also make sense when a domestic firm's skills, reputation, and product are readily transferable to foreign markets. Even though the U.S. market for soft drinks is mature, Coca-Cola has remained a growth company by upping its efforts to penetrate foreign markets where soft-drink sales are expanding rapidly.

STRATEGIC PITFALLS

Perhaps the biggest strategic mistake a company can make as an industry matures is steering a middle course between low cost, differentiation, and focusing. Such strategic compromises guarantee that a firm will end up stuck in the middle with a fuzzy strategy, a lack of commitment to winning a competitive advantage based on either low cost or differentiation, an average image with buyers, and little chance of springing into the ranks of the industry leaders. Other strategic pitfalls include sacrificing long-term competitive position for short-term profit, waiting too long to respond to

One of the greatest strategic mistakes a firm can make in a maturing industry is pursuing a compromise between low-cost, differentiation, and focusing such that it ends up "stuck in the middle" with a fuzzy strategy, an average image, an ill-defined market identity, no competitive advantage, and little prospect of becoming an industry leader.

price-cutting, getting caught with too much capacity as growth slows, overspending on marketing efforts to boost sales growth, and failing to pursue cost reduction soon enough and aggressively enough.

STRATEGIES FOR FIRMS IN STAGNANT OR DECLINING INDUSTRIES

Many firms operate in industries where demand is growing more slowly than the economywide average or is even declining. Although harvesting the business to obtain the greatest cash flow, selling out, or closing down are obvious end-game strategies for uncommitted competitors with dim long-term prospects, strong competitors may be able to achieve good performance in a stagnant market environment.[7] Stagnant demand by itself is not enough to make an industry unattractive. Selling out may or may not be practical, and closing operations is always a last resort.

Businesses competing in slow-growth/declining industries have to accept the difficult realities of an environment of continuing stagnation, and they must resign themselves to performance targets consistent with available market opportunities. Cash flow and return-on-investment criteria are more appropriate than growth-oriented performance measures, but sales and market share growth are by no means ruled out. Strong competitors may be able to take sales from weaker rivals, and the acquisition or exit of weaker firms creates opportunities for the remaining companies to capture greater market share.

In general, companies that succeed in stagnant industries rely heavily on one of the following three strategic themes:[8]

Achieving competitive advantage in stagnant or declining industries usually requires pursuing one of three competitive approaches: focusing on growing market segments within the industry, differentiating on the basis of better quality and frequent product innovation, or becoming a lower cost producer.

1. *Pursue a focused strategy by identifying, creating, and exploiting the growth segments within the industry.* Stagnant or declining markets, like other markets, are composed of numerous segments or niches. Frequently, one or more of these segments is growing rapidly, despite stagnation in the industry as a whole. An astute competitor who is first to concentrate on the attractive growth segments can escape stagnating sales and profits and possibly achieve competitive advantage in the target segments.

2. *Stress differentiation based on quality improvement and product innovation.* Either enhanced quality or innovation can rejuvenate demand by creating important new growth segments or inducing buyers to trade up. Successful product innovation opens up an avenue for competing besides meeting or beating rivals' prices. Differentiation based on successful innovation has the additional advantage of being difficult and expensive for rival firms to imitate.

3. *Work diligently and persistently to drive costs down.* When increases in sales cannot be counted on to generate increases in earnings, companies can improve profit margins and return on investment by continuous productivity improvement and cost reduction year after year. Potential cost-saving actions include (a) outsourcing functions and activities that can be performed more

---

[7]R. G. Hamermesh and S. B. Silk, "How to Compete in Stagnant Industries," *Harvard Business Review* 57, no. 5 (September–October 1979), p. 161.
[8]Ibid., p. 162.

ILLUSTRATION CAPSULE 18

YAMAHA'S STRATEGY IN THE PIANO INDUSTRY

For some years now, worldwide demand for pianos has been declining—in the mid-1980s the decline was 10% annually. Modern-day parents have not put the same stress on music lessons for their children as prior generations of parents did. In an effort to see if it could revitalize its piano business, Yamaha conducted a market research survey to learn what use was being made of pianos in households that owned one. The survey revealed that the overwhelming majority of the 40 million pianos in American, European, and Japanese households were seldom used. In most cases, the reasons the piano had been purchased no longer applied. Children had either stopped taking piano lessons or were grown and had left the household; adult household members played their pianos sparingly, if at all—only a small percentage were accomplished piano players. Most pianos were serving as a piece of fine

furniture and were in good condition despite not being tuned regularly. The survey also confirmed that the income levels of piano owners were well above average.

Yamaha's piano strategists saw the idle pianos in these upscale households as a potential market opportunity. The strategy that emerged entailed marketing an attachment that would convert the piano into an old-fashioned automatic player piano capable of playing a wide number of selections recorded on 3½-inch floppy disks (the same kind used to store computer data). The player piano conversion attachment carried a $2,500 price tag. Concurrently, Yamaha introduced Disklavier, an upright acoustic player piano model that could play *and record* performances up to 90 minutes long; the Disklavier retailed for $8,000. At year-end 1988 Yamaha offered 30 prerecorded disks for $29.95 each and planned to release a continuing stream of new selections. Yamaha believed that these new high-tech products held potential to reverse the downtrend in piano sales.

---

cheaply by outsiders, (b) completely redesigning internal business processes, (c) consolidating underutilized production facilities, (d) adding more distribution channels to ensure the unit volume needed for low-cost production, (e) closing low-volume, high-cost distribution outlets, and (f) cutting marginally beneficial activities out of the value chain.

These three strategic themes are not mutually exclusive.[9] Introducing new, innovative versions of a product can *create* a fast-growing market segment. Similarly, relentless pursuit of greater operating efficiencies permits price reductions that create price-conscious growth segments. Note that all three themes are spinoffs of the generic competitive strategies, adjusted to fit the circumstances of a tough industry environment.

The most attractive declining industries are those in which sales are eroding only slowly, there is large built-in demand, and some profitable niches remain. The most common strategic mistakes companies make in stagnating or declining markets are (1) getting trapped in a profitless war of attrition, (2) diverting too much cash out of the business too quickly (thus accelerating a company's demise), and (3) being overly optimistic about the industry's future and waiting complacently for things to get better.

Illustration Capsule 18 describes the creative approach taken by Yamaha to reverse declining market demand for pianos.

---

[9]Ibid., p. 165.

STRATEGIES FOR COMPETING IN FRAGMENTED INDUSTRIES

INSURANCE

A number of industries are populated by hundreds, even thousands, of small and medium-sized companies, many privately held and none with a substantial share of total industry sales.[10] The standout competitive feature of a fragmented industry is the absence of market leaders with king-sized market shares or widespread buyer recognition. Examples of fragmented industries include book publishing, landscaping and plant nurseries, kitchen cabinets, oil tanker shipping, auto repair, restaurants and fast-food, public accounting, women's dresses, metal foundries, meat packing, paper-board boxes, log homes, hotels and motels, and furniture.

Any of several reasons can account for why the supply side of an industry is fragmented:

- Low entry barriers allow small firms to enter quickly and cheaply.
- An absence of large-scale production economies permits small companies to compete on an equal cost footing with larger firms.
- Buyers require relatively small quantities of customized products (as in business forms, interior design, and advertising); because demand for any particular product version is small, sales volumes are not adequate to support producing, distributing, or marketing on a scale that yields advantages to a large firm.
- The market for the industry's product/service is local (dry cleaning, residential construction, medical services, automotive repair), giving competitive advantage to local businesses familiar with local buyers and local market conditions.
- Market demand is so large and so diverse that it takes very large numbers of firms to accommodate buyer requirements (restaurants, energy, apparel).
- High transportation costs limit the radius a plant can economically service—as in concrete blocks, mobile homes, milk, and gravel.
- Local regulations make each geographic area somewhat unique.
- The industry is so new that no firms have yet developed the skills and resources to command a significant market share.

In fragmented industries competitors usually have the strategic latitude (1) to compete broadly or to focus and (2) to pursue either a low-cost or a differentiation-based competitive advantage.

Some fragmented industries consolidate naturally as they mature. The stiffer competition that accompanies slower growth produces a shake-out of weak, inefficient firms and a greater concentration of larger, more visible sellers. Other fragmented industries remain atomistically competitive because it is inherent in the nature of their businesses. And still others remain stuck in a fragmented state because existing firms lack the resources or ingenuity to employ a strategy powerful enough to drive industry consolidation.

Competitive rivalry in fragmented industries can vary from moderately strong to fierce. Low barriers make entry of new competitors an ongoing threat. Competition from substitutes may or may not be a major factor. The relatively small size of companies in fragmented industries puts them in a weak position to bargain with powerful suppliers and buyers, although sometimes they can become members of a

---

[10]This section is summarized from Porter, *Competitive Strategy,* chapter 9.

cooperative formed for the purpose of using their combined leverage to negotiate better sales and purchase terms. In such an environment, the best a firm can expect is to cultivate a loyal customer base and grow a bit faster than the industry average. Competitive strategies based either on low cost or product differentiation are viable unless the industry's product is highly standardized. Focusing on a well-defined market niche or buyer segment usually offers more competitive advantage potential than striving for broad market appeal. Suitable competitive strategy options in a fragmented industry include

- **Constructing and operating "formula" facilities**—This strategic approach is frequently employed in restaurant and retailing businesses operating at multiple locations. It involves constructing standardized outlets in favorable locations at minimum cost and then polishing to a science how to operate all outlets in a superefficient manner. McDonald's, Home Depot, and 7-Eleven have pursued this strategy to perfection, earning excellent profits in their respective industries.

- **Becoming a low-cost operator**—When price competition is intense and profit margins are under constant pressure, companies can stress no-frills operations featuring low overhead, high-productivity/low-cost labor, lean capital budgets, and dedicated pursuit of total operating efficiency. Successful low-cost producers in a fragmented industry can play the price-cutting game and still earn profits above the industry average.

- **Increasing customer value through integration**—Backward or forward integration may contain opportunities to lower costs or enhance the value provided to customers. Examples include assembling components before shipment to customers, providing technical advice, or opening regional distribution centers.

- **Specializing by product type**—When a fragmented industry's products include a range of styles or services, a strategy to focus on one product/service category can be very effective. Some firms in the furniture industry specialize in only one furniture type such as brass beds, rattan and wicker, lawn and garden, or early American. In auto repair, companies specialize in transmission repair, body work, or speedy oil changes.

- **Specialization by customer type**—A firm can cope with the intense competition of a fragmented industry by catering to those customers (1) who have the least bargaining leverage (because they are small in size or purchase small amounts), (2) who are the least price sensitive, or (3) who are interested in unique product attributes, a customized product/service, or other "extras."

- **Focusing on a limited geographic area**—Even though a firm in a fragmented industry can't win a big share of total industrywide sales, it can still try to dominate a local/regional geographic area. Concentrating company efforts on a limited territory can produce greater operating efficiency, speed delivery and customer services, promote strong brand awareness, and permit saturation advertising, while avoiding the diseconomies of stretching operations out over a much wider area. Supermarkets, banks, and sporting goods retailers successfully operate multiple locations within a limited geographic area.

In fragmented industries, firms generally have the strategic freedom to pursue broad or narrow market targets and low-cost or differentiation-based competitive advantages. Many different strategic approaches can exist side by side.

STRATEGIES FOR COMPETING IN INTERNATIONAL MARKETS

Companies are motivated to expand into international markets for any of three basic reasons: a desire to seek out new markets, a competitive need to achieve lower costs, or a desire to access natural resource deposits in other countries. Whatever the reason, an international strategy has to be situation-driven. Special attention has to be paid to how national markets differ in buyer needs and habits, distribution channels, long-run growth potential, driving forces, and competitive pressures. In addition to the basic market differences from country to country, there are four other situational considerations unique to international operations: cost variations among countries, fluctuating exchange rates, host government trade policies, and the pattern of international competition.

Competing in international markets poses a bigger strategy-making challenge than competing in only the company's home market.

Country-to-Country Cost Variations   Differences in wage rates, worker productivity, inflation rates, energy costs, tax rates, government regulations, and the like create sizable variations in manufacturing costs from country to country. Plants in some countries have major manufacturing cost advantages because of lower input costs (especially labor), relaxed government regulations, or unique natural resources. In such cases, the low-cost countries become principal production sites, and most of the output is exported to markets in other parts of the world. Companies with facilities in these locations (or that source their products from contract manufacturers in these countries) have a competitive advantage. The competitive role of low manufacturing costs is most evident in low-wage countries like Taiwan, South Korea, Mexico, and Brazil, which have become production havens for goods with high labor content.

Another important manufacturing cost consideration in international competition is the concept of *manufacturing share* as distinct from brand share or market share. For example, although less than 40 percent of all the video recorders sold in the United States carry a Japanese brand, Japanese companies do 100 percent of the manufacturing—all sellers source their video recorders from Japanese manufacturers.[11] In microwave ovens, Japanese brands have less than a 50 percent share of the U.S. market, but the manufacturing share of Japanese companies is over 85 percent. *Manufacturing share is significant because it is a better indicator than market share of the industry's low-cost producer.* In a globally competitive industry where some competitors are intent on global dominance, being the worldwide low-cost producer is a powerful competitive advantage. Achieving low-cost producer status often requires a company to have the largest worldwide manufacturing share, with production centralized in one or a few superefficient plants. However, important marketing and distribution economies associated with multinational operations can also yield low-cost leadership.

Fluctuating Exchange Rates   The volatility of exchange rates greatly complicates the issue of geographic cost advantages. Exchange rates often fluctuate as much as 20 to 40 percent annually. Changes of this magnitude can totally wipe out a country's low-cost advantage or transform a former high-cost location into a competitive-cost location. A strong U.S. dollar makes it more attractive for U.S. companies to manufacture

---

[11]C. K. Prahalad and Yves L. Doz, *The Multinational Mission* (New York: Free Press, 1987), p. 60.

in foreign countries. Declines in the value of the dollar against foreign currencies can eliminate much of the cost advantage that foreign manufacturers have over U.S. manufacturers and can even prompt foreign companies to establish production plants in the United States.

Host Government Trade Policies   National governments enact all kinds of measures affecting international trade and the operation of foreign companies in their markets. Host governments may impose import tariffs and quotas, set local content requirements on goods made inside their borders by foreign-based companies, and regulate the prices of imported goods. In addition, outsiders may face a web of regulations regarding technical standards, product certification, prior approval of capital spending projects, withdrawal of funds from the country, and minority (sometimes majority) ownership by local citizens. Some governments also provide subsidies and low-interest loans to domestic companies to help them compete against foreign-based companies. Other governments, anxious to obtain new plants and jobs, offer foreign companies a helping hand in the form of subsidies, privileged market access, and technical assistance.

MULTICOUNTRY COMPETITION VERSUS GLOBAL COMPETITION

There are important differences in the patterns of international competition from industry to industry.[12] At one extreme, competition can be termed *multicountry* or *multidomestic* because it takes place country by country; competition in each national market is essentially independent of competition in other national markets. For example, there is a banking industry in France, one in Brazil, and one in Japan, but competitive conditions in banking differ markedly in all three countries. Moreover, a bank's reputation, customer base, and competitive position in one nation have little or no bearing on its ability to compete successfully in another. In industries where multicountry competition prevails, the power of a company's strategy in any one nation and any competitive advantage it yields are largely confined to that nation and do not spill over to other countries where it operates. With multicountry competition there is no "international market," just a collection of self-contained country markets. Industries characterized by multicountry competition include beer, life insurance, apparel, metals fabrication, many types of food products (coffee, cereals, canned goods, frozen foods), and many types of retailing.

> *Multicountry* (or *multidomestic*) *competition* exists when competition in one national market is independent of competition in another national market—there is no "international market," just a collection of self-contained country markets.

At the other extreme is *global competition* where prices and competitive conditions across country markets are strongly linked together and the term international or global market has true meaning. In a globally competitive industry, a company's competitive position in one country both affects and is affected by its position in other countries. Rival companies compete against each other in many different countries, but especially so in countries where sales volumes are large and where having a competitive presence is strategically important to building a strong global position in the industry. In global competition, a firm's overall competitive advantage grows out of its entire worldwide operations; the competitive advantage it creates at its home base is supplemented by advantages growing out of its operations in other countries (having plants in low-wage countries, a capability to serve customers with multinational operations of their own, and a brand reputation that is transferable from

> *Global competition* exists when competitive conditions across national markets are linked strongly enough to form a true international market and when leading competitors compete head-to-head in many different countries.

---

[12]Michael E. Porter, *The Competitive Advantage of Nations* (New York: Free Press, 1990), pp. 53–54.

country to country). *A global competitor's market strength is directly proportional to its portfolio of country-based competitive advantages.* Global competition exists in automobiles, television sets, tires, telecommunications equipment, copiers, watches, and commercial aircraft.

An industry can have segments that are globally competitive and segments where competition is country by country.[13] In the hotel-motel industry, for example, the low- and medium-priced segments are characterized by multicountry competition because competitors mainly serve travelers within the same country. In the business and luxury segments, however, competition is more globalized. Companies like Nikki, Marriott, Sheraton, and Hilton have hotels at many international locations and use worldwide reservation systems and common quality and service standards to gain marketing advantages in serving businesspeople and travelers who make frequent international trips.

In lubricants, the marine engine segment is globally competitive because ships move from port to port and require the same oil everywhere they stop. Brand reputations have a global scope, and successful marine engine lubricant producers (Exxon, British Petroleum, and Shell) operate globally. In automotive motor oil, however, multicountry competition dominates. Countries have different weather conditions and driving patterns, production is subject to limited scale economies and shipping costs are high, and retail distribution channels differ markedly from country to country. Thus domestic firms, like Quaker State and Pennzoil in the U.S. and Castrol in Great Britain, can be leaders in their home markets without competing globally.

All these situational considerations, along with the obvious cultural and political differences between countries, shape a company's strategic approach in international markets.

> In multicountry competition, rival firms vie for national market leadership. In globally competitive industries, rival firms vie for worldwide leadership.

TYPES OF INTERNATIONAL STRATEGIES

There are six distinct strategic options for a company participating in international markets. It can

1. *License foreign firms to use the company's technology or produce and distribute the company's products* (in which case international revenues will equal the royalty income from the licensing agreement).

2. *Maintain a national (one-country) production base and export goods to foreign markets* using either company-owned or foreign-controlled forward distribution channels.

3. *Follow a multicountry strategy* whereby a company's international strategy is crafted country by country to be responsive to buyer needs and competitive conditions in each country where it operates. Strategic moves in one country are made independent of actions taken in another country; strategy coordination across countries is secondary to matching company strategy to individual country conditions.

4. *Follow a global low-cost strategy* where the company strives to be a low-cost supplier to buyers in most or all strategically important markets of the world. The company's strategic efforts are coordinated worldwide to achieve a low-cost position relative to all competitors.

---

[13] Ibid., p. 61.

5. *Follow a global differentiation strategy* whereby a firm differentiates its product on the same attributes in all countries to create a globally consistent image and a consistent competitive theme. The firm's strategic moves are coordinated across countries to achieve consistent differentiation worldwide.

6. *Follow a global focus strategy* where company strategy is aimed at serving the same identifiable niche in each of many strategically important country markets. Strategic actions are coordinated globally to achieve a consistent low-cost or differentiation-based competitive approach in the target niche worldwide.

Licensing makes sense when a firm with valuable technical know-how or a unique patented product has neither the internal organizational capability nor the resources in foreign markets. By licensing the technology or the production rights to foreign-based firms, the firm at least realizes income from royalties.

Using domestic plants as a production base for exporting goods to foreign markets is an excellent initial strategy for pursuing international sales. It minimizes both risk and capital requirements, and it is a conservative way to test the international waters. With an export strategy, a manufacturer can limit its involvement in foreign markets by contracting with foreign wholesalers experienced in importing to handle the entire distribution and marketing function in their countries or regions of the world. If it is more advantageous to maintain control over these functions, a manufacturer can establish its own distribution and sales organizations in some or all of the target foreign markets. Either way, a firm minimizes its direct investments in foreign countries because of its home-based production and export strategy. Such strategies are commonly favored by Korean and Italian companies—products are designed and manufactured at home and only marketing activities are performed abroad. Whether such a strategy can be pursued successfully over the long run hinges on the relative cost competitiveness of a home-country production base. In some industries, firms gain additional scale economies and experience curve benefits from centralizing production in one or several giant plants whose output capability exceeds demand in any one country market; obviously, to capture such economies a company must export to markets in other countries. However, this strategy is vulnerable when manufacturing costs in the home country are substantially higher than in foreign countries where rivals have plants.

The pros and cons of a multicountry strategy versus a global strategy are a bit more complex.

A MULTICOUNTRY STRATEGY OR A GLOBAL STRATEGY?

The need for a multicountry strategy derives from the sometimes vast differences in cultural, economic, political, and competitive conditions in different countries. The more diverse national market conditions are, the stronger the case for a *multicountry strategy* where the company tailors its strategic approach to fit each host country's market situation. In such cases, the company's overall international strategy is a collection of its individual country strategies.

While multicountry strategies are best suited for industries where multicountry competition dominates, global strategies are best suited for globally competitive industries. A *global strategy* is one where the company's strategy for competing is mostly the same in all countries. Although *minor* country-to-country differences in strategy do exist to accommodate specific competitive conditions in host countries, the company's fundamental competitive approach (low-cost, differentiation, or

A multicountry strategy is appropriate for industries where multicountry competition dominates, but a global strategy works best in markets that are globally competitive or beginning to globalize.

focused) remains the same worldwide. Moreover, a global strategy involves (1) integrating and coordinating the company's strategic moves worldwide and (2) selling in many if not all nations where there is significant buyer demand. Table 6–1 provides a point-by-point comparison of multicountry versus global strategies. The question of which of these two strategies to pursue is the foremost strategic issue firms face when they compete in international markets.

The strength of a multicountry strategy is that it matches the company's competitive approach to host country circumstances. A multicountry strategy is essential when there are significant country-to-country differences in customers' needs and buying habits (see Illustration Capsule 19), when buyers in a country insist on special-order or highly customized products, when buyer demand for the product exists in comparatively few national markets, when host governments enact regulations requiring that products sold locally meet strict manufacturing specifications or performance standards, and when the trade restrictions of host governments are so diverse and complicated they preclude a uniform, coordinated worldwide market approach. However, a multicountry strategy has two big drawbacks: it entails very

T A B L E 6–1 | *Differences between Multicountry and Global Strategies*

	Multicountry Strategy	Global Strategy
Strategic Arena	• Selected target countries and trading areas.	• Most countries which constitute critical markets for the product, at least North America, the European Community, and the Pacific Rim (Australia, Japan, South Korea, and Southeast Asia).
Business Strategy	• Custom strategies to fit the circumstances of each host country situation; little or no strategy coordination across countries.	• Same basic strategy worldwide; minor country-by-country variations where essential.
Product-line Strategy	• Adapted to local needs.	• Mostly standardized products sold worldwide.
Production Strategy	• Plants scattered across many host countries.	• Plants located on the basis of maximum competitive advantage (in low-cost countries, close to major markets, geographically scattered to minimize shipping costs, or use of a few world-scale plants to maximize economies of scale—as most appropriate).
Source of Supply for Raw Materials and Components	• Suppliers in host country preferred (local facilities meeting local buyer needs; some local sourcing may be required by host government).	• Attractive suppliers from anywhere in the world.
Marketing and Distribution	• Adapted to practices and culture of each host country.	• Much more worldwide coordination; minor adaptation to host country situations if required.
Company Organization	• Form subsidiary companies to handle operations in each host country; each subsidiary operates more or less autonomously to fit host country conditions.	• All major strategic decisions are closely coordinated at global headquarters; a global organizational structure is used to unify the operations in each country.

NESTLÉ'S MULTICOUNTRY STRATEGY IN INSTANT COFFEE

Nestlé is the world's largest food company with over $33 billion in revenues, market penetration on all major continents, and plants in over 60 countries. The star performer in Nestlé's food products lineup is coffee, with sales of over $5 billion and operating profits of $600 million. Nestlé is the world's largest producer of coffee. It is also the world's market leader in mineral water (Perrier), condensed milk, frozen food, candies, and infant food.

In 1992 the company's Nescafé brand was the leader in the instant coffee segment in virtually every national market but the U.S., where it ranked number two behind Maxwell House. Nestlé produced 200 types of instant coffee, from lighter blends for the U.S. market to dark espressos for Latin America. To keep its instant coffees matched to consumer tastes in different countries (and areas within some countries), Nestlé operated four coffee research labs, with a combined budget of $50 million annually, to experiment with new blends in aroma, flavor, and color. The strategy was to match the blends marketed in each country to the tastes and preferences of coffee drinkers in that country, introducing new blends to develop new segments when opportunities appeared and altering blends as needed to respond to changing tastes and buyer habits.

Although instant coffee sales were declining worldwide due to the introduction of new style automatic coffeemakers, sales were rising in two tea-drinking countries, Britain and Japan. In Britain, Nescafé was promoted extensively to build a wider base of instant coffee drinkers. In Japan, where Nescafé was considered a luxury item, the company made its Japanese blends available in fancy containers suitable for gift-giving. In 1993 Nestlé began introducing Nescafé instant coffee and Coffee-Mate creamer in several large cities in China.

Sources: Shawn Tully, "Nestlé Shows How to Gobble Markets," *Fortune,* January 16, 1989, pp. 74–78; "Nestlé: A Giant in a Hurry," *Business Week,* March 22, 1993, pp. 50–54; and company annual reports.

little strategic coordination across country boundaries, and it is not tied tightly to competitive advantage. The primary orientation of a multicountry strategy is responsiveness to local country conditions, not building a multinational competitive advantage over other international competitors and the domestic companies of host countries.

A global strategy, because it is more uniform from country to country, can concentrate on securing a sustainable low-cost or differentiation-based competitive advantage over both international and domestic rivals. Whenever country-to-country differences are small enough to be accommodated within the framework of a global strategy, a global strategy is preferable to a multicountry strategy because of the value of uniting a company's competitive efforts worldwide to pursue lower cost or differentiation.

GLOBAL STRATEGY AND COMPETITIVE ADVANTAGE

There are two ways in which a firm can gain competitive advantage (or offset domestic disadvantages) with a global strategy.[14] One way exploits a global competitor's ability to deploy R&D, parts manufacture, assembly, distribution centers, sales and marketing, customer service centers and other activities among nations in a manner that lowers costs or achieves greater product differentiation; the other way draws on a global competitor's ability to coordinate its dispersed activities in ways that a domestic-only competitor cannot.

---

[14]Ibid., p. 54.

Locating Activities   To use location to build competitive advantage, a global firm must consider two issues: (1) whether to concentrate each activity it performs in one or two countries or to disperse performance of the activity to many nations and (2) in which countries to locate particular activities. Activities tend to be concentrated in one or two locations when there are significant economies of scale in performing an activity, when there are advantages in locating related activities in the same area to achieve better coordination, and when there is a steep learning or experience curve associated with performing an activity in a single location. Thus in some industries scale economies in parts manufacture or assembly are so great that a company establishes one large plant from which it serves the world market. Where just-in-time inventory practices yield big cost savings and/or where the assembly firm has long-term partnering arrangements with its key suppliers, parts manufacturing plants may be clustered around final assembly plants.

On the other hand, dispersing activities is more advantageous than concentrating them in several instances. Buyer-related activities—such as distribution to dealers, sales and advertising, and after-sale service—usually must take place close to buyers. This means physically locating the capability to perform such activities in every country market where a global firm has major customers (unless buyers in several adjoining countries can be served quickly from a nearby central location). For example, firms that make mining and oil drilling equipment maintain operations in many international locations to support customers' needs for speedy equipment repair and technical assistance. Large public accounting firms have numerous international offices to service the foreign operations of their multinational corporate clients. A global competitor that effectively disperses its buyer-related activities can gain a service-based competitive edge in world markets over rivals whose buyer-related activities are more concentrated—this is one reason the Big Six public accounting firms have been so successful relative to second-tier firms. Dispersing activities to many locations is also competitively advantageous when high transportation costs, diseconomies of large size, and trade barriers make it too expensive to operate from a central location. Many companies distribute their products from multiple locations to shorten delivery times to customers. In addition, it is strategically advantageous to disperse activities to hedge against the risks of fluctuating exchange rates, supply interruptions (due to strikes, mechanical failures, and transportation delays), and adverse political developments. Such risks are greater when activities are concentrated in a single location.

The classic reason for locating an activity in a particular country is lower costs.[15] Even though a global firm has strong reason to disperse buyer-related activities to many international locations, such activities as materials procurement, parts manufacture, finished goods assembly, technology research, and new-product development can frequently be decoupled from buyer locations and performed wherever advantage lies. Components can be made in Mexico, technology research done in Frankfurt, new products developed and tested in Phoenix, and assembly plants located in Spain, Brazil, Taiwan, and South Carolina. Capital can be raised in whatever country it is available on the best terms.

Low front-end cost is not the only locational consideration, however. A research unit may be situated in a particular nation because of its pool of technically trained

A global strategy enables a firm to pursue sustainable competitive advantage by locating activities in the most advantageous nations and coordinating its strategic actions worldwide; a domestic-only competitor forfeits such opportunities.

[15]Ibid., p. 57.

personnel. A customer service center or sales office may be opened in a particular country to help develop strong relationships with pivotal customers. An assembly plant may be located in a country in return for the host government's allowing freer import of components from large-scale, centralized parts plants located elsewhere.

Coordinating Activities and Strategic Moves   Aligning and coordinating company activities located in different countries contributes to sustainable competitive advantage in several different ways. If a firm learns how to assemble its product more efficiently at its Brazilian plant, the accumulated knowledge and expertise can be transferred to its assembly plant in Spain. Knowledge gained in marketing a company's product in Great Britain can be used to introduce the product in New Zealand and Australia. A company can shift production from one country to another to take advantage of exchange rate fluctuations, to enhance its leverage with host country governments, and to respond to changing wage rates, energy costs, or trade restrictions. A company can enhance its brand reputation by consistently incorporating the same differentiating attributes in its products in all worldwide markets where it competes. The reputation for quality that Honda established worldwide first in motorcycles and then in automobiles gave it competitive advantage in positioning Honda lawnmowers at the upper end of the market—the Honda name gave the company instant credibility with buyers.

A global competitor can choose where and how to challenge rivals. It may decide to retaliate against aggressive rivals in the country market where the rival has its biggest sales volume or its best profit margins in order to reduce the rival's financial resources for competing in other country markets. It may decide to wage a price-cutting offensive against weak rivals in their home markets, capturing greater market share and subsidizing any short-term losses with profits earned in other country markets.

A company that competes only in its home country has access to none of the competitive advantage opportunities associated with international locations or coordination. By shifting from a domestic strategy to a global strategy, a domestic company that finds itself at a competitive disadvantage against global companies can begin to restore its competitiveness.

STRATEGIC ALLIANCES

Strategic alliances are cooperative agreements between firms that go beyond normal company-to-company dealings but that fall short of merger or full partnership.[16] An alliance can involve joint research efforts, technology sharing, joint use of production facilities, marketing one another's products, or joining forces to manufacture components or assemble finished products. Strategic alliances are a means for firms in the same industry yet based in different countries to compete on a more global scale while still preserving their independence. Historically, export minded firms in industrialized nations sought alliances with firms in less-developed countries to import and market their products locally—such arrangements were often necessary to gain access to the less-developed country's market. More recently, leading companies from different parts of the world have formed strategic alliances to strengthen their

Strategic alliances can help companies in globally competitive industries strengthen their competitive positions while still preserving their independence.

---

[16]Ibid., p. 65. See also Kenichi Ohmae, "The Global Logic of Strategic Alliances," *Harvard Business Review* 89, no. 2 (March–April 1989), pp. 143–54.

mutual ability to serve whole continental areas and move toward more global market participation. Both Japanese and American companies are actively forming alliances with European companies to strengthen their ability to compete in the 12-nation European Community and to capitalize on the opening up of Eastern European markets. Illustration Capsule 20 describes Toshiba's successful use of strategic alliances and joint ventures to pursue related technologies and product markets.

Companies enter into alliances for several strategically beneficial reasons.[17] The three most important are to gain economies of scale in production and/or marketing, to fill gaps in their technical and manufacturing expertise, and to acquire market access. By joining forces in producing components, assembling models, and marketing their products, companies can realize cost savings not achievable with their own small volumes. Allies learn much from one another in performing joint research, sharing technological know-how, and studying one another's manufacturing methods. Alliances are often used by outsiders to meet governmental requirements for local ownership, and allies can share distribution facilities and dealer networks, thus mutually strengthening their access to buyers. In addition, alliances affect competition; not only can alliances offset competitive disadvantages but they also can result in the allied companies' directing their competitive energies more toward mutual rivals and less toward one another. Many runner-up companies, wanting to preserve their independence, resort to alliances rather than merger to try to close the competitive gap on leading companies.

Alliances have their pitfalls, however. Achieving effective coordination between independent companies, each with different motives and perhaps conflicting objectives, is a challenging task. It requires many meetings of many people over a period of time to iron out what is to be shared, what is to remain proprietary, and how the cooperative arrangements will work. Allies may have to overcome language and cultural barriers as well. The communication, trust-building, and coordination costs are high in terms of management time. Often, once the bloom is off the rose, partners discover they have deep differences of opinion about how to proceed and conflicting objectives and strategies. Tensions build up, working relationships cool, and the hoped-for benefits never materialize.[18] Many times, allies find it difficult to collaborate effectively in competitively sensitive areas, thus raising questions about mutual trust and forthright exchanges of information and expertise. There can also be clashes of egos and company cultures. The key people on whom success or failure depends may have little personal chemistry, be unable to work closely together or form a partnership, or be unable to come to consensus.

> Strategic alliances are more effective in combating competitive disadvantage than in gaining competitive advantage.

Most important, though, is the danger of depending on another company for essential expertise and capabilities over the long term. To be a serious market contender, a company must ultimately develop internal capabilities in all areas important to strengthening its competitive position and building a sustainable competitive advantage. Where this is not feasible, merger is a better solution than strategic alliance. Strategic alliances are best used as a transitional way to combat competitive disadvantage in international markets; rarely if ever can they be relied on as a means for creating competitive advantage. Illustration Capsule 21 relates the experiences of companies with strategic alliances.

---

[17]Porter, *The Competitive Advantage of Nations,* p. 66; see also Jeremy Main, "Making Global Alliances Work," *Fortune,* December 17, 1990, pp. 121–26.

[18]Jeremy Main, "Making Global Alliances Work," p. 125.

TOSHIBA'S USE OF STRATEGIC ALLIANCES AND JOINT VENTURES

Toshiba, Japan's oldest and third largest electronics company (after Hitachi and Matsushita), over the years has made technology licensing agreements, joint ventures, and strategic alliances cornerstones of its corporate strategy. Using such partnerships to complement its own manufacturing and product innovation capabilities, it has become a $37 billion maker of electrical and electronics products—from home appliances to computer memory chips to telecommunications equipment to electric power generation equipment.

Fumio Sato, Toshiba's CEO, contends that joint ventures and strategic alliances are a necessary component of strategy for a high-tech electronics company with global ambitions:

> It is no longer an era in which a single company can dominate any technology or business by itself. The technology has become so advanced, and the markets so complex, that you simply can't expect to be the best at the whole process any longer.

Among Toshiba's two dozen major joint ventures and strategic alliances are

- A five-year-old joint venture with Motorola to design and make dynamic random access memory chips (DRAMs) for Toshiba and microprocessors for Motorola. Initially the two partners invested $125 million apiece in the venture and have since invested another $480 million each.
- A joint venture with IBM to make flat-panel liquid crystal displays in color for portable computers.
- Two other joint ventures with IBM to develop computer memory chips (one a "flash" memory chip that remembers data even after the power is turned off).
- An alliance with Sweden-based Ericsson, one of the world's biggest telecommunications manufacturers, to develop new mobile telecommunications equipment.

- A partnership with Sun Microsystems, the leading maker of microprocessor-based workstations, to provide portable versions of the workstations to Sun and to incorporate Sun's equipment in Toshiba products to control power plants, route highway traffic, and monitor automated manufacturing processes.
- A $1 billion strategic alliance with IBM and Siemens to develop and produce the next-generation DRAM—a single chip capable of holding 256 million bits of information (approximately 8,000 typewritten pages).
- An alliance with Apple Computer to develop CD-ROM-based multimedia players that plug into a TV set.
- A joint project with the entertainment division of Time Warner to design advanced interactive cable television technology.

Other alliances and joint ventures with General Electric, United Technologies, National Semiconductor, Samsung (Korea), LSI Logic (Canada), and European companies like Olivetti, SCS-Thomson, Rhone-Poulenc, Thomson Consumer Electronics, and GEC Alstholm are turning out such products as fax machines, copiers, medical equipment, computers, rechargeable batteries, home appliances, and nuclear and steam power generating equipment.

So far, none of Toshiba's relationships with partners have gone sour despite potential conflicts among related projects with competitors (Toshiba has partnerships with nine other chip makers to develop or produce semiconductors). Toshiba attributes this to its approach to alliances: choosing partners carefully, being open about Toshiba's connections with other companies, carefully defining the role and rights of each partner in the original pact (including who gets what if the alliance doesn't work out), and cultivating easy relations and good friendships with each partner. Toshiba's management believes that strategic alliances and joint ventures are an effective way for the company to move into new businesses quickly, share the design and development costs of ambitious new products with competent partners, and achieve greater access to important geographic markets outside Japan.

Source: Based on Brenton R. Schlender, "How Toshiba Makes Alliances Work," *Fortune,* October 4, 1993, pp. 116–20.

ILLUSTRATION CAPSULE 21

COMPANY EXPERIENCES WITH STRATEGIC ALLIANCES

As the chairman of British Aerospace recently observed, a strategic alliance with a foreign company is "one of the quickest and cheapest ways to develop a global strategy." AT&T formed joint ventures with many of the world's largest telephone and electronics companies. Boeing, the world's premier manufacturer of commercial aircraft, partnered with Kawasaki, Mitsubishi, and Fuji to produce a long-range, wide-body jet for delivery in 1995. General Electric and Snecma, a French maker of jet engines, have a 50-50 partnership to make jet engines to power aircraft made by Boeing, McDonnell-Douglas, and Airbus Industrie (Airbus, the leading European maker of commercial aircraft, was formed by an alliance of aerospace companies from Britain, Spain, Germany, and France). The GE/Snecma alliance is regarded as a model because it existed for 17 years and it produced orders for 10,300 engines, totaling $38 billion.

Since the early 1980s, hundreds of strategic alliances have been formed in the motor vehicle industry as car and truck manufacturers and automotive parts suppliers moved aggressively to get in stronger position to compete globally. Not only have there been alliances between automakers strong in one region of the world and automakers strong in another region but there have also been strategic alliances between vehicle makers and key parts suppliers (especially those with high-quality parts and strong technological capabilities). General Motors and Toyota in 1984 formed a 50-50 partnership called New United Motor Manufacturing Inc. (NUMMI) to produce cars for both companies at an old GM plant in Fremont, California. The strategic value of the GM-Toyota alliance was that Toyota would learn how to deal with suppliers and workers in the U.S. (as a prelude to building its own plants in the U.S.) while GM would learn about Toyota's approaches to manufacturing and management. Each company sent managers to the NUMMI plant to work for two or three years to learn and absorb all they could, then transferred their NUMMI "graduates" to jobs where they could be instrumental in helping their companies apply what they learned. Toyota moved quickly to capitalize on its experiences at NUMMI. By 1991 Toyota had opened two plants on its own in North America, was constructing a third plant, and was producing 50% of the vehicles it sold in North America in its North American plants. While General Motors incorporated much of its NUMMI learning into the management practices and manufacturing methods it was using at its newly opened Saturn plant in Tennessee, it proceeded more slowly than Toyota. American and European companies are generally regarded as less skilled than the Japanese in transferring the learning from strategic alliances into their own operations.

Many alliances fail or are terminated when one partner ends up acquiring the other. A 1990 survey of 150 companies involved in terminated alliances found that three-fourths of the alliances had been taken over by Japanese partners. A nine-year alliance between Fujitsu and International Computers, Ltd., a British manufacturer, ended when Fujitsu acquired 80% of ICL. According to one observer, Fujitsu deliberately maneuvered ICL into a position of having no better choice than to sell out to its partner. Fujitsu began as a supplier of components for ICL's mainframe computers, then expanded its role over the next nine years to the point where it was ICL's only source of new technology. When ICL's parent, a large British electronics firm, saw the mainframe computer business starting to decline and decided to sell, Fujitsu was the only buyer it could find.

Source: Jeremy Main, "Making Global Alliances Work," *Fortune,* December 17, 1990, pp. 121–26.

To realize the most from strategic alliance, companies should observe five guidelines:[19]

1. Pick a compatible partner; take the time to build strong bridges of communication and trust and don't expect immediate payoffs.
2. Choose an ally whose products and market strongholds *complement* rather than compete directly with the company's own products and customer base.

---

[19]Ibid.

3. Learn thoroughly and rapidly about a partner's technology and management; transfer valuable ideas and practices into one's own operations promptly.

4. Be careful not to divulge competitively sensitive information to a partner.

5. View the alliance as temporary (5 to 10 years); continue longer if it's beneficial but don't hesitate to terminate the alliance and go it alone when the payoffs run out.

STRATEGIC INTENT, PROROFIT SANCTUARIES, AND CROSS-SUBSIDIZATION

Competitors in international markets can be distinguished not only by their strategies but also by their long-term strategic objectives and strategic intent. Four types of competitors stand out:[20]

- Firms whose strategic intent is *global dominance* or, at least, high rank among the global market leaders; such firms pursue some form of global strategy.

- Firms whose primary strategic objective is *defending domestic dominance* in their home market, even though they derive some of their sales internationally (usually under 20 percent) and have operations in several or many foreign markets.

- Firms who aspire to a growing share of worldwide sales and whose primary strategic orientation is *host country responsiveness;* such firms have a multicountry strategy and may already derive a large fraction of their revenues from foreign operations.

- *Domestic-only firms* whose strategic intent does not extend beyond building a strong competitive position in their home country market; such firms base their competitive strategies on domestic market conditions and watch events in the international market only for their impact on the domestic situation.

The types of firms are *not* equally well-positioned to be successful in markets where they compete head-on. Consider the case of a purely domestic U.S. company in competition with a Japanese company operating in many country markets and aspiring to global dominance. The Japanese company can cut its prices in the U.S. market to gain market share at the expense of the U.S. company, subsidizing any losses with profits earned in its home sanctuary and in other foreign markets. The U.S. company has no effective way to retaliate. It is vulnerable even if it is the U.S. market leader. However, if the U.S. company is a multinational competitor and operates in Japan as well as elsewhere, it can counter Japanese pricing in the United States with retaliatory price cuts in its competitor's main profit sanctuary, Japan, and in other countries where it competes against the same Japanese company.

Thus, a domestic-only competitor is not on a level playing field in competing against a multinational rival. When aggressive global competitors enter a domestic-only company's market, one of the domestic-only competitor's best strategic defenses is to switch to a multinational or global strategy to give it the same cross-subsidizing capabilities the aggressors have.

Profit Sanctuaries and Critical Markets   *Profit sanctuaries* are country markets where a company has a strong or protected market position and derives substantial profits.

---

[20]Prahalad and Doz, *The Multinational Mission,* p. 52.

Japan, for example, is a profit sanctuary for most Japanese companies because trade barriers erected around Japanese industries by the Japanese government effectively block foreign companies from competing for a large share of Japanese sales. Protected from the threat of foreign competition in their home market, Japanese companies can safely charge somewhat higher prices to their Japanese customers and thus earn attractively large profits on sales made in Japan. In most cases, a company's biggest and most strategically crucial profit sanctuary is its home market, but multinational companies also have profit sanctuaries in those country markets where they have strong competitive positions, big sales volumes, and attractive profit margins.

Profit sanctuaries are valuable competitive assets in global industries. Companies with large, protected profit sanctuaries have competitive advantage over companies that don't have a dependable sanctuary. Companies with multiple profit sanctuaries are more favorably positioned than companies with a single sanctuary. Normally, a global competitor with multiple profit sanctuaries can successfully attack and beat a domestic competitor whose only profit sanctuary is its home market.

To defend against global competitors, companies don't have to compete in all or even most foreign markets, but they do have to compete in all critical markets. *Critical markets* are markets in countries

- That are the profit sanctuaries of key competitors.
- That have big sales volumes.
- That contain prestigious customers whose business it is strategically important to have.
- That offer exceptionally good profit margins due to weak competitive pressures.[21]

The more critical markets a company participates in, the greater its ability to use cross-subsidization as a defense against competitors intent on global dominance.

The Competitive Power of Cross-Subsidization   Cross-subsidization is a powerful competitive weapon. It involves using profits earned in one or more country markets to support a competitive offensive against key rivals or to gain increased penetration of a critical market. A typical offensive involves matching (or nearly matching) rivals on product quality and service, then charging a low enough price to draw customers away from rivals. While price-cutting may result in a challenger's earning lower profits (or even incurring losses) in the critical market it is attacking, it may still realize acceptable overall profits when the above-average earnings from its profit sanctuaries are added in.

Cross-subsidization is most powerful when a global firm with multiple profit sanctuaries is aggressively intent on achieving global market dominance over the long term. Both a domestic-only competitor and a multicountry competitor with no strategic coordination between its locally responsive country strategies are vulnerable to competition from rivals intent on global dominance. A global strategy can defeat a domestic-only strategy because a one-country competitor cannot effectively defend its market share over the long term against a global competitor with cross-subsidization capability. The global company can use lower prices to siphon off the domestic company's customers, all the while gaining market share, building name recognition, and supporting its strategic offensive with profits earned in its other critical markets.

A particular nation is a company's profit sanctuary *when the company, either because of its strong competitive position or protective governmental trade policies, derives a substantial part of its total profits from sales in that nation.*

A competent global competitor with multiple profit sanctuaries can wage and generally win a competitive offensive against a domestic competitor whose only profit sanctuary is its home market.

---

[21]Ibid., p. 61.

It can adjust the depth of its price-cutting to move in and capture market share quickly, or it can shave prices slightly to make gradual market inroads over a decade or more so as not to threaten domestic firms precipitously and perhaps trigger protectionist government actions. When attacked in this manner, a domestic company's best short-term hope is to pursue immediate and perhaps dramatic cost reduction and, if the situation warrants, to seek government protection in the form of tariff barriers, import quotas, and antidumping penalties. In the long term, the domestic company has to find ways to compete on a more equal footing—a difficult task when it must charge a price to cover full unit costs plus a margin for profit while the global competitor can charge a price only high enough to cover the incremental costs of selling in the domestic company's profit sanctuary. The best long-term strategic defenses for a domestic company are to enter into strategic alliances with foreign firms or to adopt a global approach to strategy and compete on an international scale, although sometimes it is possible to drive enough costs out of the business over the long term to survive with a domestic-only strategy. As a rule, however, competing only domestically is a perilous strategy in an industry populated with global competitors.

> To defend against aggressive international competitors intent on global dominance, a domestic-only competitor usually has to abandon its domestic focus, become a multinational competitor, and craft a multinational competitive strategy.

While a company with a multicountry strategy has some cross-subsidy defense against a company with a global strategy, its vulnerability comes from a lack of competitive advantage and a probable cost disadvantage. A global competitor with a big manufacturing share and world-scale state-of-the-art plants is almost certain to be a lower-cost producer than a multicountry strategist with many small plants and short production runs turning out specialized products country by country. Companies pursuing a multicountry strategy thus need differentiation and focus-based advantages keyed to local responsiveness in order to defend against a global competitor. Such a defense is adequate in industries with significant enough national differences to impede use of a global strategy. But if an international rival can accommodate necessary local needs within a global strategy and still retain a cost edge, then a global strategy can defeat a multicountry strategy.

STRATEGIES FOR INDUSTRY LEADERS

The competitive positions of industry leaders normally range from stronger-than-average to powerful. Leaders typically are well-known, and strongly entrenched leaders have proven strategies (keyed either to low-cost leadership or to differentiation). Some of the best-known industry leaders are Anheuser-Busch (beer), IBM (mainframe computers), McDonald's (fast-food), Gillette (razor blades), Campbell's Soup (canned soups), Gerber (baby food), AT&T (long-distance telephone service), Eastman Kodak (camera film), and Levi Strauss (jeans). The main strategic concern for a leader revolves around how to sustain a leadership position, perhaps becoming the *dominant* leader as opposed to *a* leader. However, the pursuit of industry leadership and large market share per se is primarily important because of the competitive advantage and profitability that accrue to being the industry's biggest company.

Three contrasting strategic postures are open to industry leaders and dominant firms:[22]

---

[22]Kotler, *Marketing Management,* chapter 23; Michael E. Porter, *Competitive Advantage* (New York: Free Press, 1985), chapter 14; and Ian C. MacMillan, "Seizing Competitive Initiative," *The Journal of Business Strategy* 2, no. 4 (Spring 1982), pp. 43–57.

1. **Stay-on-the-offensive strategy**—This strategy rests on the principle that the best defense is a good offense. Offensive-minded leaders stress being first-movers to sustain their competitive advantage (lower cost or differentiation) and to reinforce their reputation as *the* leader. A low-cost provider aggressively pursues cost reduction, and a differentiator constantly tries new ways to set its product apart from rivals' brands. The theme of a stay-on-the-offensive strategy is relentless pursuit of continuous improvement and innovation. Striving to be first with new products, better performance features, quality enhancements, improved customer services, or ways to cut production costs not only helps a leader avoid complacency but it also keeps rivals on the defensive scrambling to keep up. The array of offensive options can also include initiatives to expand overall industry demand—discovering new uses for the product, attracting new users of the product, and promoting more frequent use. In addition, a clever offensive leader stays alert for ways to make it easier and less costly for potential customers to switch their purchases from runner-up firms to its own products. Unless a leader's market share is already so dominant that it presents a threat of antitrust action (a market share under 60 percent is usually "safe"), a stay-on-the-offensive strategy means trying to grow *faster* than the industry as a whole and wrest market share from rivals. A leader whose growth does not equal or outpace the industry average is losing ground to competitors.

2. **Fortify-and-defend strategy**—The essence of "fortify and defend" is to make it harder for new firms to enter and for challengers to gain ground. The goals of a strong defense are to hold onto the present market share, strengthen current market position, and protect whatever competitive advantage the firm has. Specific defensive actions can include

   - Attempting to raise the competitive ante for challengers and new entrants via increased spending for advertising, higher levels of customer service, and bigger R&D outlays.
   - Introducing more of the company's own brands to match the product attributes that challenger brands have or could employ.
   - Adding personalized services and other "extras" that boost customer loyalty and make it harder or more costly for customers to switch to rival products.
   - Broadening the product line to close off possible vacant niches for competitors to slip into.
   - Keeping prices reasonable and quality attractive.
   - Building new capacity ahead of market demand to try to block the market expansion potential of smaller competitors.
   - Investing enough to remain cost competitive and technologically progressive.
   - Patenting the feasible alternative technologies.
   - Signing exclusive contracts with the best suppliers and dealer distributors.

   A fortify-and-defend strategy best suits firms that have already achieved industry dominance and don't wish to risk antitrust action. It is also well-suited to situations where a firm wishes to milk its present position for profits and cash flow because the industry's prospects for growth are low or because further gains in market share do not appear profitable enough to go after. But the fortify-and-defend strategy always entails trying to grow as fast as the

Industry leaders can strengthen their long-term competitive positions with strategies keyed to aggressive offense, aggressive defense, or muscling smaller rivals into a follow-the-leader role.

market as a whole (to stave off market share slippage) and requires reinvesting enough capital in the business to protect the leader's ability to compete.

3. **Follow-the-leader strategy**—Here the leader's strategic posture involves using its competitive muscle (ethically and fairly!) to encourage runner-up firms to be content followers rather than aggressive challengers. The leader plays competitive hardball when smaller rivals rock the boat with price cuts or mount new market offensives that directly threaten its position. Specific responses can include quickly matching and perhaps exceeding challengers' price cuts, using large promotional campaigns to counter challengers' moves to gain market share, and offering better deals to the major customers of maverick firms. Leaders can also court distributors assiduously to dissuade them from carrying rivals' products, provide salespersons with documented information about the weaknesses of an aggressor's products, or try to fill any vacant positions in their own firms by making attractive offers to the better executives of rivals that "get out of line." When a leader consistently meets any moves to cut into its business with strong retaliatory tactics, it sends clear signals that offensive attacks on the leader's position will be met head-on and probably won't pay off. However, leaders pursuing this strategic approach should choose their battles. It may be more strategically productive to assume a hands-off posture and not respond in hardball fashion when smaller rivals attack each other's customer base in ways that don't affect its own.

STRATEGIES FOR RUNNER-UP FIRMS

Runner-up firms occupy weaker market positions than the industry leader(s). Some runner-up firms are up-and-coming *market challengers,* employing offensive strategies to gain market share and a stronger market position. Others behave as *content followers,* willing to coast along in their current positions because profits are adequate. Follower firms have no urgent strategic issue to confront beyond "What kinds of strategic changes are the leaders initiating and what do we need to do to follow along?"

A challenger firm interested in improving its market standing needs a strategy aimed at building a competitive advantage of its own. *Rarely can a runner-up firm improve its competitive position by imitating the strategies of leading firms. A cardinal rule in offensive strategy is to avoid attacking a leader head-on with an imitative strategy, regardless of the resources and staying power an underdog may have.*[23] Moreover, if a challenger has a 5 percent market share and needs a 20 percent share to earn attractive returns, it needs a more creative approach to competing than just "try harder."

In industries where large size yields significantly lower unit costs and gives large-share competitors an important cost advantage, small-share firms have only two viable strategic options: try to increase their market share (and achieve cost parity with larger rivals) or withdraw from the business (gradually or quickly). The competitive strategies most underdogs use to build market share are based on (1) becoming a lower-cost producer and using lower price to win customers from weak, higher-cost rivals and (2) using differentiation strategies based on quality, technological superiority, better customer service, best cost, or innovation. Achieving low-cost leadership is

Rarely can a runner-up firm successfully challenge an industry leader with a copycat strategy.

---

[23]Porter, *Competitive Advantage,* p. 514.

usually open to an underdog only when one of the market leaders is not already solidly positioned as the industry's low-cost producer. But a small-share firm may still be able to reduce its cost disadvantage by merging with or acquiring smaller firms; the combined market shares may provide the needed access to size-related economies. Other options include revamping its value chain to produce the needed cost savings and finding ways to better manage executional cost drivers.

In situations where scale economies or experience curve effects are small and a large market share produces no cost advantage, runner-up companies have more strategic flexibility and can consider any of the following six approaches:[24]

1. **Vacant-niche strategy**—This version of a focused strategy involves concentrating on customer or end-use applications that market leaders have bypassed or neglected. An ideal vacant niche is of sufficient size and scope to be profitable, has some growth potential, is well-suited to a firm's own capabilities and skills, and for one reason or another is not interesting to leading firms. Two examples where vacant-niche strategies worked successfully are regional commuter airlines serving cities with too few passengers to attract the interest of major airlines and health foods producers (like Health Valley, Hain, and Tree of Life) that cater to local health food stores—a market segment traditionally ignored by Pillsbury, Kraft General Foods, Heinz, Nabisco, Campbell's Soup, and other leading food products firms.

2. **Specialist strategy**—A specialist firm trains its competitive effort on one market segment: a single product, a particular end use, or buyers with special needs. The aim is to build competitive advantage through product uniqueness, expertise in special-purpose products, or specialized customer services. Smaller companies that successfully use a specialist focused strategy include Formby's (a specialist in stains and finishes for wood furniture, especially refinishing), Liquid Paper Co. (a leader in correction fluid for writers and typists), Canada Dry (known for its ginger ale, tonic water, and carbonated soda water), and American Tobacco (a leader in chewing tobacco and snuff).

3. **Ours-is-better-than-theirs strategy**—The approach here is to use a differentiation-based focused strategy keyed to superior product quality or unique attributes. Sales and marketing efforts are aimed directly at quality-conscious and performance-oriented buyers. Fine craftsmanship, prestige quality, frequent product innovations, and/or close contact with customers to solicit their input in developing a better product usually undergird this "superior product" approach. Some examples include Beefeater and Tanqueray in gin, Tiffany in diamonds and jewelry, Chicago Cutlery in premium-quality kitchen knives, Baccarat in fine crystal, Cannondale in mountain bikes, Bally in shoes, and Patagonia in apparel for outdoor recreation enthusiasts.

4. **Content-follower strategy**—Follower firms deliberately refrain from initiating trendsetting strategic moves and from aggressive attempts to steal customers away from the leaders. Followers prefer approaches that will not provoke competitive retaliation, often opting for focus and differentiation strategies that keep them out of the leaders' paths. They react and respond

---

[24]For more details, see Kotler, *Marketing Management,* pp. 397–412; R. G. Hamermesh, M. J. Anderson, Jr., and J. E. Harris, "Strategies for Low Market Share Businesses," *Harvard Business Review* 56, no. 3 (May–June 1978), pp. 95–102; and Porter, *Competitive Advantage,* chapter 15.

rather than initiate and challenge. They prefer defense to offense. And they rarely get out of line with the leaders on price. Union Camp (in paper products) has been a successful market follower by consciously concentrating on selected product uses and applications for specific customer groups, focused R&D, profits rather than market share, and cautious but efficient management.

5. **Growth-via-acquisition strategy**—One way to strengthen a company's position is to merge with or acquire weaker rivals to form an enterprise that has more competitive strength and a larger share of the market. Commercial airline companies such as Northwest, USAir, and Delta owe their market share growth during the past decade to acquisition of smaller, regional airlines. Likewise, the Big Six public accounting firms enhanced their national and international coverage by merging or forming alliances with smaller CPA firms at home and abroad.

6. **Distinctive-image strategy**—Some runner-up companies build their strategies around ways to make themselves stand out from competitors. A variety of strategic approaches can be used: creating a reputation for charging the lowest prices, providing prestige quality at a good price, going all out to give superior customer service, designing unique product attributes, being a leader in new product introduction, or devising unusually creative advertising. Examples include Dr Pepper's strategy in calling attention to its distinctive taste, Apple Computer's making it easier and more interesting for people to use a personal computer, and Mary Kay Cosmetics' distinctive use of the color pink.

In industries where big size is definitely a key success factor, firms with low market shares have some obstacles to overcome: (1) less access to economies of scale in manufacturing, distribution, or sales promotion; (2) difficulty in gaining customer recognition; (3) an inability to afford mass media advertising on a grand scale; and (4) difficulty in funding capital requirements.[25] But *it is erroneous to view runner-up firms as inherently less profitable or unable to hold their own against the biggest firms.* Many firms with small market shares earn healthy profits and enjoy good reputations with customers. Often, the handicaps of smaller size can be surmounted and a profitable competitive position established by (1) focusing on a few market segments where the company's strengths can yield a competitive edge; (2) developing technical expertise that will be highly valued by customers; (3) aggressively pursuing the development of new products for customers in the target market segments; and (4) using innovative/"dare to be different"/"beat the odds" entrepreneurial approaches to outmanage stodgy, slow-to-change market leaders. Runner-up companies have a golden opportunity to gain market share if they make a leapfrog technological breakthrough, if the leaders stumble or become complacent, or if they have the patience to nibble away at the leaders and build up their customer base over a long period of time.

STRATEGIES FOR WEAK BUSINESSES

A firm in an also-ran or declining competitive position has four basic strategic options. If it has the financial resources, it can launch an *offensive turnaround strat-*

---

[25]Hamermesh, Anderson, and Harris, "Strategies for Low Market Share Businesses," p. 102.

The strategic options for a competitively weak company include waging a modest offensive to improve its position, defending its present position, being acquired by another company, or employing a harvest strategy.

egy keyed either to low-cost or "new" differentiation themes, pouring enough money and talent into the effort to move up a notch or two in the industry rankings and become a respectable market contender within five years or so. It can employ a *fortify-and-defend* strategy, using variations of its present strategy and fighting hard to keep sales, market share, profitability, and competitive position at current levels. It can opt for an *immediate abandonment strategy* and get out of the business, either by selling out to another firm or by closing down operations if a buyer cannot be found. Or it can employ a *harvest strategy,* keeping reinvestment to a bare-bones minimum and taking actions to maximize short-term cash flows in preparation for an orderly market exit. The gist of the first three options is self-explanatory. The fourth merits more discussion.

A *harvest strategy* steers a middle course between preserving the status quo and exiting as soon as possible. Harvesting is a phasing down or endgame strategy that involves sacrificing market position in return for improved cash flows or short-term profitability. The overriding financial objective is to reap the greatest possible harvest of cash to deploy to other business endeavors.

The measures taken in a harvest strategy are fairly clear-cut. The operating budget is chopped to a rock-bottom level; reinvestment in the business is held to a bare minimum. Capital expenditures for new equipment are put on hold or given low financial priority (unless replacement needs are unusually urgent); instead, efforts are made to stretch the life of existing equipment and make do with present facilities as long as possible. Price may be raised gradually, promotional expenses slowly cut, quality reduced in not-so-visible ways, nonessential customer services curtailed, and the like. Although harvesting results in shrinking sales and market share, if cash expenses can be cut even faster, then after-tax cash flows may rise (at least temporarily) and the company's profits will erode slowly rather than rapidly.

Harvesting is a reasonable strategic option for a weak business in the following circumstances:[26]

1. When the industry's long-term prospects are unattractive.
2. When rejuvenating the business would be too costly or at best marginally profitable.
3. When the firm's market share is becoming increasingly costly to maintain or defend.
4. When reduced levels of competitive effort will not trigger an immediate or rapid falloff in sales.
5. When the enterprise can redeploy the freed resources in higher opportunity areas.
6. When the business is *not* a crucial or core component of a diversified company's portfolio of business interests (harvesting a noncore business is strategically preferable to harvesting a core business).
7. When the business does not contribute other desired features (sales stability, prestige, a well-rounded product line) to a company's overall business portfolio.

The more of these seven conditions present, the more ideal the business is for harvesting.

---

[26]Phillip Kotler, "Harvesting Strategies for Weak Products," *Business Horizons* 21, no. 5 (August 1978), pp. 17–18.

Harvesting strategies make the most sense for diversified companies that have sideline or noncore business units in weak competitive positions or in unattractive industries. Such companies can take the cash flows from harvesting unattractive, noncore business units and reallocate them to business units with greater profit potential or to the acquisition of new businesses.

TURNAROUND STRATEGIES FOR BUSINESSES IN CRISIS

Turnaround strategies are needed when a business worth rescuing goes into crisis; the objective is to arrest and reverse the sources of competitive and financial weakness as quickly as possible. Management's first task in formulating a suitable turnaround strategy is to diagnose what lies at the root of poor performance. Is it an unexpected downturn in sales brought on by a weak economy? An ill-chosen competitive strategy? Poor execution of an otherwise workable strategy? An overload of debt? Can the business be saved, or is the situation hopeless? Understanding what is wrong with the business and how serious its strategic problems are is essential because different diagnoses lead to different turnaround strategies.

Some of the most common causes of business trouble are taking on too much debt, overestimating the potential for sales growth, ignoring the profit-depressing effects of an overly aggressive effort to "buy" market share with deep price-cuts, being burdened with heavy fixed costs because of an inability to utilize plant capacity, betting on R&D efforts to boost competitive position and profitability and failing to come up with effective innovations, betting on technological long shots, being too optimistic about the ability to penetrate new markets, making frequent changes in strategy (because the previous strategy didn't work out), and being overpowered by the competitive advantages enjoyed by more successful rivals. Curing these kinds of problems and achieving a successful business turnaround can involve any of the following actions:

- Revising the existing strategy.
- Launching efforts to boost revenues.
- Pursuing cost reduction.
- Selling off assets to raise cash to save the remaining part of the business.
- Using a combination of these efforts.

Strategy Revision   When weak performance is caused by bad strategy, the task of strategy overhaul can proceed along any of several paths: (1) shifting to a new competitive approach to rebuild the firm's market position; (2) overhauling internal operations and functional area strategies to better support the same overall business strategy; (3) merging with another firm in the industry and forging a new strategy keyed to the newly merged firm's strengths; and (4) retrenching into a reduced core of products and customers more closely matched to the firm's strengths. The most appealing path depends on prevailing industry conditions, the firm's particular strengths and weaknesses, its competitive capabilities vis-à-vis rival firms, and the severity of the crisis. Situation analysis of the industry, major competitors, and the firm's own competitive position and its skills and resources are prerequisites for action. As a rule, successful strategy revision must be tied to the ailing firm's strengths and near-term competitive capabilities and directed at its best market opportunities.

Boosting Revenues   Revenue-increasing turnaround efforts aim at generating increased sales volume. There are a number of revenue-building options: price cuts, increased promotion, a bigger sales force, added customer services, and quickly achieved product improvements. Attempts to increase revenues and sales volumes are necessary (1) when there is little or no room in the operating budget to cut expenses and still break even and (2) when the key to restoring profitability is increased utilization of existing capacity. If buyer demand is not especially price sensitive because of differentiating features, the quickest way to boost short-term revenues may be to raise prices rather than opt for volume-building price cuts.

Cutting Costs   Cost-reducing turnaround strategies work best when an ailing firm's value chain and cost structure are flexible enough to permit radical surgery, when operating inefficiencies are identifiable and readily correctable, when the firm's costs are obviously bloated and there are many places where savings can be quickly achieved, and when the firm is relatively close to its break-even point. Accompanying a general belt-tightening can be an increased emphasis on paring administrative overheads, elimination of nonessential and low value-added activities in the firm's value chain, modernization of existing plant and equipment to gain greater productivity, delay of nonessential capital expenditures, and debt restructuring to reduce interest costs and stretch out repayments.

Selling Off Assets   Assets reduction/retrenchment strategies are essential when cash flow is a critical consideration and when the most practical ways to generate cash are (1) through sale of some of the firm's assets (plant and equipment, land, patents, inventories, or profitable subsidiaries) and (2) through retrenchment (pruning of marginal products from the product line, closing or selling older plants, reducing the workforce, withdrawing from outlying markets, cutting back customer service, and the like). Sometimes crisis-ridden companies sell off assets not so much to unload losing operations and to stem cash drains as to raise funds to save and strengthen the remaining business activities. In such cases, the choice is usually to dispose of non-core business assets to support strategy renewal in the firm's core business(es).

Combination Efforts   Combination turnaround strategies are usually essential in grim situations that require fast action on a broad front. Likewise, combination actions frequently come into play when new managers are brought in and given a free hand to make whatever changes they see fit. The tougher the problems, the more likely the solutions will involve multiple strategic initiatives.

Turnaround efforts tend to be high-risk undertakings, and they often fail. A landmark study of 64 companies found no successful turnarounds among the most troubled companies in eight basic industries.[27] Many of the troubled businesses waited too long to begin a turnaround. Others found themselves short of both the cash and entrepreneurial talent needed to compete in a slow-growth industry characterized by a fierce battle for market share. Better-positioned rivals simply proved too strong to defeat in a long, head-to-head contest. Even when successful, many troubled companies go through a series of turnaround attempts and management changes before long-term competitive viability and profitability are finally restored.

---

[27]William K. Hall, "Survival Strategies in a Hostile Environment," *Harvard Business Review* 58, no. 5 (September–October 1980), pp. 75–85. See also Frederick M. Zimmerman, *The Turnaround Experience: Real-World Lessons in Revitalizing Corporations* (New York: McGraw-Hill, 1991), and Gary J. Castrogiovanni, B. R. Baliga, and Roland E. Kidwell, "Curing Sick Businesses: Changing CEOs in Turnaround Efforts," *Academy of Management Executive* 6, no. 3 (August 1992), pp. 26–41.

THIRTEEN COMMANDMENTS FOR CRAFTING SUCCESSFUL BUSINESS STRATEGIES

Business experiences over the years prove again and again that disastrous courses of action can be avoided by adhering to good strategy-making principles. The wisdom gained from these past experiences can be distilled into 13 commandments which, if faithfully observed, can help strategists craft better strategic action plans.

1. *Place top priority on crafting and executing strategic moves that enhance the company's competitive position for the long term.* An ever stronger competitive position pays off year after year, but the glory of meeting one quarter's and one year's financial performance targets quickly fades. Shareholders are never well-served by managers who let short-term financial performance considerations rule out strategic initiatives that will meaningfully bolster the company's long-term competitive position and competitive strength. The best way to protect a company's long-term profitability is with a strategy that strengthens the company's long-term competitiveness.

2. *Understand that a clear, consistent competitive strategy, when well-crafted and well-executed, builds reputation and recognizable industry position; a frequently changed strategy aimed at capturing momentary market opportunities yields fleeting benefits.* Short-run financial opportunism, absent any long-term strategic consistency, tends to produce the worst kind of profits: one-shot rewards that are unrepeatable. Over the long haul, a company that has a well-conceived, consistent competitive strategy aimed at securing an ever stronger market position will outperform and defeat a rival whose strategic decisions are driven by a desire to meet Wall Street's short-term financial performance expectations. In an ongoing enterprise, the game of competition ought to be played for the long term, not the short term.

3. *Avoid "stuck in the middle" strategies that represent compromises between lower costs and greater differentiation and between broad and narrow market appeal.* Compromise strategies rarely produce sustainable competitive advantage or a distinctive competitive position—well-executed best-cost producer strategies are the only exception where a compromise between low cost and differentiation succeeds. Usually, companies with compromise or middle-of-the-road strategies end up with average costs, average differentiation, an average image and reputation, a middle-of-the-pack industry ranking, and little prospect of climbing into the ranks of the industry leaders.

4. *Invest in creating a sustainable competitive advantage.* It is the single most dependable contributor to above-average profitability.

5. *Play aggressive offense to build competitive advantage and aggressive defense to protect it.*

6. *Avoid strategies capable of succeeding only in the most optimistic circumstances.* Expect competitors to employ countermeasures and expect times of unfavorable market conditions.

7. *Be cautious in pursuing a rigid or inflexible strategy that locks the company in for the long term with little room to maneuver—inflexible strategies can be made obsolete by changing market conditions.* Strategies to achieve top quality or lowest cost should be interpreted as *relative to competitors'* and/or customers' needs rather than based on arbitrary management absolutes. While

long-term strategic consistency is usually a virtue, strategic absolutes and constants are usually flaws—some adapting to changing circumstances and some discovery of ways to improve are normal and necessary.

8. *Don't underestimate the reactions and the commitment of rival firms.* Rivals are most dangerous when they are pushed into a corner and their well-being is threatened.

9. *Be wary of attacking strong, resourceful rivals without solid competitive advantage and ample financial strength.*

10. *Consider that attacking competitive weakness is usually more profitable than attacking competitive strength.*

11. *Be judicious in cutting prices without an established cost advantage.* Only a low-cost producer can win at price-cutting over the long term.

12. *Be aware that aggressive moves to wrest market share away from rivals often provoke aggressive retaliation in the form of a marketing "arms race" and/or price wars*—to the detriment of everyone's profits. Aggressive moves to capture a bigger market share invite cutthroat competition, particularly when the market is plagued with high inventories and excess production capacity.

13. *Strive to open up very meaningful gaps in quality or service or performance features when pursuing a differentiation strategy.* Tiny differences between rivals' product offerings may not be visible or important to buyers.

KEY POINTS

It is not enough to understand that a company's basic competitive strategy options are overall low-cost leadership, broad differentiation, best cost, focused low cost, and focused differentiation and that there are a variety of offensive, defensive, first-mover, and late-mover initiatives and actions to choose from. Managers must also understand that the array of strategic options is narrowed and shaped by (1) the nature of industry and competitive conditions and (2) a firm's own competitive capabilities, market position, and best opportunities. Some strategic options are better suited to certain specific industry and competitive environments than others. Some strategic options are better suited to certain specific company situations than others. This chapter portrays the multifaceted task of matching strategy to a firm's external and internal situations by considering five classic types of industry environments and three classic types of company situations.

Rather than try to summarize the main points we made about choosing strategies for these eight sets of circumstances (the relevant principles can't really be encapsulated in three or four sentences each), we think it more useful to conclude by outlining a broader framework for matching strategy to *any* industry and company situation. Table 6–2 provides a summary checklist of the most important situational considerations and strategic options. Matching strategy to the situation starts with an overview of the industry environment and the firm's competitive standing in the industry (columns 1 and 2 in Table 6–2):

1. What basic type of industry environment does the company operate in (emerging, rapid growth, mature, fragmented, global, commodity-product)? What strategic options and strategic postures are usually best suited to this generic type of environment?

T A B L E 6-2 | **Matching Strategy to the Situation** (*A checklist of optional strategies and generic situations*)

Industry Environments	Company Positions/ Situations	Situational Considerations	Market Share and Investment Options	Strategy Options
• Young, emerging industry	• Dominant leader	• External	• Grow and build	• Competitive approach
• Rapid growth	— Global	— Driving forces	— Capture a bigger market	— Overall low-cost
• Consolidating to a smaller	— National	— Competitive pressures	share by growing faster than	— Differentiation
group of competitors	— Regional	— Anticipated moves of key	industry as a whole	— Best-cost
• Mature/slow growth	— Local	rivals	— Invest heavily to capture	— Focused low-cost
• Aging/declining	• Leader	— Key success factors	growth potential	— Focused differentiation
• Fragmented	• Aggressive challenger	— Industry attractiveness	• Fortify and defend	• Offensive initiatives
• International/global	• Content follower	• Internal	— Protect market share; grow	— Competitor strengths
• Commodity product orientation	• Weak/distressed candidate for	— Current company	at least as fast as whole	— Competitor weaknesses
• High technology/rapid changes	turnaround or exit	performance	industry	— End run
	• "Stuck in the middle"/no clear	— Strengths and weaknesses	— Invest enough resources to	— Guerrilla warfare
	strategy or market image	— Opportunities and threats	maintain competitive	— Preemptive strikes
		— Cost position	strength and market	• Defensive initiatives
		— Competitive strength	position	— Fortify/protect
		— Strategic issues and	• Retrench and retreat	— Retaliatory
		problems	— Surrender weakly held	— Harvest
			positions when forced to,	• International initiatives
			but fight hard to defend	— Licensing
			core markets/customer	— Export
			base	— Multicountry
			— Maximize short-term cash	— Global
			flow	• Vertical integration initiatives
			— Minimize reinvestment of	— Forward
			capital in the business	— Backward
			• Overhaul and reposition	
			— Pursue a turnaround	
			• Abandon/liquidate	
			— Sell out	
			— Close down	

2. What position does the firm have in the industry (strong vs. weak vs. crisis-ridden; leader vs. runner-up vs. also-ran)? How does the firm's standing influence its strategic options given the stage of the industry's development—in particular, which options have to be ruled out?

Next, strategists need to factor in the primary external and internal situational considerations (column 3) and decide how all the factors add up. This should narrow the firm's basic market share and investment options (column 4) and strategic options (column 5).

The final step is to custom-tailor the chosen generic strategic approaches (columns 4 and 5) to fit *both* the industry environment and the firm's standing vis-à-vis competitors. Here, it is important to be sure that (1) the customized aspects of the proposed strategy are well-matched to the firm's competencies and competitive capabilities and (2) the strategy addresses all strategic issues the firm confronts.

In weeding out weak strategies and weighing the pros and cons of the most attractive ones, the answers to the following questions often indicate the way to go:

- What kind of competitive edge can the company realistically hope to have and what strategic moves/approaches will it need take to secure this edge?
- Does the company have the organizational capabilities and financial resources to succeed in these moves and approaches? If not, can they be acquired?
- Once built, how can the competitive advantage be protected? What defensive strategies need to be employed? Will rivals counterattack? What will it take to blunt their efforts?
- Are any rivals particularly vulnerable? Should the firm mount an offensive to capitalize on these vulnerabilities? What offensive moves need to be employed?
- What additional strategic moves are needed to deal with driving forces in the industry, specific threats and weaknesses, and any other issues/problems unique to the firm?

As the choice of strategic initiatives is developed, there are several pitfalls to avoid:

- Designing an overly ambitious strategic plan—one that calls for a lot of different strategic moves and/or that overtaxes the company's resources and capabilities.
- Selecting a strategy that represents a radical departure from or abandonment of the cornerstones of the company's prior success—a radical strategy change need not be rejected automatically, but it should be pursued only after careful risk assessment.
- Choosing a strategy that goes against the grain of the organization's culture or that conflicts with the values and philosophies of the most senior executives.
- Being unwilling to make a decisive *choice* about how to compete. Trying to achieve competitive advantage through several means simultaneously often produces so many compromises and inconsistent actions that the company fails to achieve any of them and ends up stuck in the middle.

Table 6–3 suggests a generic format for presenting a strategic action plan for a single-business enterprise.

TABLE 6-3 | **Sample Format for a Strategic Action Plan**

1. Strategic Vision and Mission	**5. Supporting Functional Strategies** • Production • Marketing/sales • Finance • Personnel/human resources • Other
2. Strategic Objectives • Short term • Long term	
3. Financial Objectives • Short term • Long term	**6. Recommended Actions** • Immediate • Longer-range
4. Overall Business Strategy	

SUGGESTED READINGS

Bleeke, Joel A. "Strategic Choices for Newly Opened Markets." *Harvard Business Review* 68, no. 5 (September–October 1990), pp. 158–65.

Bolt, James F. "Global Competitors: Some Criteria for Success." *Business Horizons* 31, no. 1 (January–February 1988), pp. 34–41.

Cooper, Arnold C., and Clayton G. Smith. "How Established Firms Respond to Threatening Technologies." *Academy of Management Executive* 6, no. 2 (May 1992), pp. 55–57.

D'Aveni, Richard A. *Hypercompetition: Managing the Dynamics of Strategic Maneuvering.* New York: Free Press, 1994, chaps. 3 and 4.

Feldman, Lawrence P., and Albert L. Page. "Harvesting: The Misunderstood Market Exit Strategy." *Journal of Business Strategy* 5, no. 4 (Spring 1985), pp. 79–85.

Finkin, Eugene F. "Company Turnaround." *Journal of Business Strategy* 5, no. 4 (Spring 1985), pp. 14–25.

Gordon, Geoffrey L., Roger J. Calantrone, and C. Anthony di Benedetto. "Mature Markets and Revitalization Strategies: An American Fable." *Business Horizons* (May–June 1991), pp. 39–50.

Hall, William K. "Survival Strategies in a Hostile Environment." *Harvard Business Review* 58, no. 5 (September–October 1980), pp. 75–85.

Hamermesh, R. G., and S. B. Silk. "How to Compete in Stagnant Industries." *Harvard Business Review* 57, no. 5 (September–October 1979), pp. 161–68.

Heany, Donald F. "Businesses in Profit Trouble." *Journal of Business Strategy* 5, no. 4 (Spring 1985), pp. 4–13.

Hofer, Charles W. "Turnaround Strategies." *Journal of Business Strategy* 1, no. 1 (Summer 1980), pp. 19–31.

Lei, David. "Strategies for Global Competition." *Long Range Planning* 22, no. 1 (February 1989), pp. 102–9.

Mayer, Robert J. "Winning Strategies for Manufacturers in Mature Industries." *Journal of Business Strategy* 8, no. 2 (Fall 1987), pp. 23–31.

Ohmae, Kenichi. "The Global Logic of Strategic Alliances." *Harvard Business Review* 67, no. 2 (March–April 1989), pp. 143–54.

Porter, Michael E. *Competitive Strategy: Techniques for Analyzing Industries and Competitors.* New York: Free Press, 1980, chaps. 9–13.

Porter, Michael E. *The Competitive Advantage of Nations.* New York: Free Press, 1990, chap. 2.

Sugiura, Hideo, "How Honda Localizes Its Global Strategy." *Sloan Management Review* 33 (Fall 1990), pp. 77–82.

Yip, George S. *Total Global Strategy.* Englewood Cliffs, N.J.: Prentice-Hall, 1992, chaps. 1, 2, 3, 5, and 7.

Zimmerman, Frederick M. *The Turnaround Experience: Real-World Lessons in Revitalizing Corporations.* New York: McGraw-Hill, 1991.

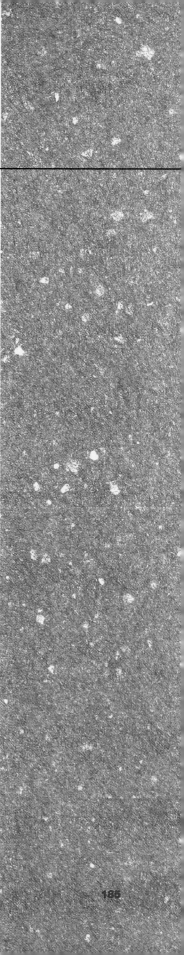

CHAPTER SEVEN

CORPORATE DIVERSIFICATION STRATEGIES

. . . to acquire or not to acquire: that is the question.

Robert J. Terry

Strategy is a deliberate search for a plan of action that will develop a business's competitive advantage and compound it.

Bruce D. Henderson

In this chapter and the next, we move up one level in the strategy-making hierarchy. Attention shifts from formulating strategy for a single-business enterprise to formulating strategy for a diversified enterprise. Because a diversified company is a collection of individual businesses, corporate strategy-making is a bigger-picture exercise than crafting line-of-business strategy. In a single-business enterprise, management has to contend with only one industry environment and the question of how to compete successfully in it. But in a diversified company corporate managers have to craft a multibusiness, multi-industry strategic action plan for a number of different business divisions competing in diverse industry environments.

As explained in Chapter 2, the task of crafting corporate strategy for a diversified company concerns

1. Deciding on moves to position the company in the industries chosen for diversification (the basic strategic options here are to acquire a company in the target industry, form a joint venture with another company to enter the target industry, or start a new company internally and try to grow it from the ground up).

2. Devising actions to improve the long-term performance of the corporation's portfolio of businesses once diversification is achieved (helping to strengthen the competitive positions of existing businesses, divesting businesses that no

longer fit into management's long-range plans, and adding new businesses to the portfolio).

3. Trying to capture whatever strategic-fit benefits exist within the portfolio of businesses and turn them into competitive advantage.

4. Evaluating the profit prospects of each business unit and steering corporate resources into the most attractive strategic opportunities.

These four tasks are sufficiently time-consuming and demanding that corporate-level decision-makers generally refrain from becoming immersed in the details of crafting and implementing business-level strategies, preferring instead to delegate lead responsibility for business strategy to the heads of each business unit.

In this chapter we survey the generic types of corporate diversification strategies and describe how a company can use diversification to create or compound competitive advantage for its business units. In Chapter 8 we will examine the techniques and procedures for assessing the strategic attractiveness of a diversified company's business portfolio.

FROM SINGLE-BUSINESS CONCENTRATION TO DIVERSIFICATION

Most companies begin as small single-business enterprises serving a local or regional market. During a company's early years, its product line tends to be limited, its capital base thin, and its competitive position vulnerable. Usually, a young company's strategic emphasis is on increasing sales volume, boosting market share, and cultivating a loyal clientele. Profits are reinvested and new debt is taken on to grow the business as fast as conditions permit. Price, quality, service, and promotion are tailored more precisely to customer needs. As soon as practical, the product line is broadened to meet variations in customer wants and to capture sales opportunities in related end-use applications.

Opportunities for geographic market expansion are normally pursued next. The natural sequence of geographic expansion proceeds from local to regional to national to international markets, though the degree of penetration may be uneven from area to area because of varying profit potentials. Geographic expansion may, of course, stop well short of global or even national proportions because of intense competition, lack of resources, or the unattractiveness of further market coverage.

Somewhere along the way, the potential of vertical integration, either backward to sources of supply or forward to the ultimate consumer, may become a strategic consideration. Generally, vertical integration makes strategic sense only if it significantly enhances a company's profitability and competitive strength.

So long as the company has its hands full trying to capitalize on profitable growth opportunities in its present industry, there is no urgency to pursue diversification. But when company growth potential starts to wane, the strategic options are either to become more aggressive in taking market share away from rivals or to pursue diversification into other lines of businesses. A decision to diversify raises the question "What kind and how much diversification?" The strategic possibilities are wide open. A company can diversify into closely related businesses or into totally unrelated businesses. It can diversify to a small extent (less than 10 percent of total revenues and profits) or to a large extent (up to 50 percent of revenues and profits). It can move into one or two large new businesses or a greater number of small ones. And once

Diversification doesn't need to become a strategic priority until a company begins to run out of growth opportunities in its core business.

once diversification is achieved, the time may come when management has to consider divesting or liquidating businesses that are no longer attractive.

WHY A SINGLE-BUSINESS STRATEGY IS ATTRACTIVE

Companies that concentrate on a single business can achieve enviable success over many decades without relying upon diversification to sustain their growth. McDonald's, Delta Airlines, Coca-Cola, Domino's Pizza, Apple Computer, Wal-Mart, Federal Express, Timex, Campbell's Soup, Anheuser-Busch, Xerox, Gerber, and Polaroid all won their reputations in a single business. In the nonprofit sector, continued emphasis on a single activity has proved successful for the Red Cross, Salvation Army, Christian Children's Fund, Girl Scouts, Phi Beta Kappa, and American Civil Liberties Union.

Concentrating on a single line of business (totally or with a small dose of diversification) has some useful organizational and managerial advantages. First, single-business concentration entails less ambiguity about "who we are and what we do." The energies of the *total* organization are directed down *one* business path. There is less chance that senior management's time or limited organizational resources will be stretched too thin over too many diverse activities. Entrepreneurial efforts can be trained exclusively on keeping the firm's business strategy and competitive approach responsive to industry change and fine-tuned to customer needs. All the firm's managers, especially top executives, can have hands-on contact with the core business and in-depth knowledge of operations. Most senior officers will usually have risen through the ranks and possess firsthand experience in field operations. (In broadly diversified enterprises, corporate managers seldom have had the opportunity to work in more than one or two of the company's businesses.) Furthermore, concentrating on one business carries a heftier built-in incentive for managers to direct the company toward capturing a stronger long-term competitive position in the industry rather than pursuing the fleeting benefits of juggling corporate assets to produce higher short-term profits. The company can devote the full force of its organizational resources to becoming better at what it does. Important competencies and competitive skills are more likely to emerge. With management's attention focused exclusively on one business, the probability is higher that good ideas will emerge on how to improve production technology, better meet customer needs with innovative new product features, and enhance efficiencies or differentiation capabilities along the value chain. The more successful a single-business enterprise is, the more able it is to parlay its accumulated experience and distinctive expertise into a sustainable competitive advantage and a prominent leadership position in its industry.

There are important organizational and managerial advantages to concentrating on just one business.

THE RISK OF A SINGLE-BUSINESS STRATEGY

The big risk of single-business concentration is putting all of a firm's eggs in one industry basket. If the industry stagnates or becomes competitively unattractive, company prospects dim, and superior profit performance is much harder to achieve. At times, changing customer needs, technological innovation, or new substitute products can undermine or wipe out a single-business firm—consider, for example, what the word processing capabilities of personal computers have done to the electric typewriter business and what compact disk technology is doing to the market for cassette tapes and records. For this reason most single-business companies turn their strategic attention to diversification when their business starts to show signs of peaking out.

WHEN DIVERSIFICATION STARTS TO MAKE SENSE

To analyze when diversification makes the most strategic sense, consider Figure 7–1 where the variable of competitive position is plotted against various rates of market growth to create four distinct strategic situations that might be occupied by an undiversified company.[1] Firms that fall into the rapid market growth/strong competitive position box have several logical strategy options, the strongest of which in the near term may be continuing to pursue single-business concentration. Given the industry's high growth rate (and implicit long-term attractiveness), it makes sense for firms in this position to push hard to maintain or increase their market shares, further develop core competencies, and make whatever capital investments are necessary to continue in a strong industry position. At some juncture, a company in this box may contemplate vertical integration if this would add to its competitive strength. Later, when market growth starts to slow, it can consider a diversification strategy to spread business risk and transfer the skills or expertise the company has built up into closely *related* businesses.

Firms in the rapid growth/weak position category should first address the questions of (1) why their current approach to the market has resulted in a weak competitive position and (2) what it will take to become an effective competitor. Second they should consider their options for rejuvenating their present competitive strategy (given the high rate of market growth). In a rapidly expanding market, even weak firms should be able to improve their performance and make headway in building a stronger market position. If the firm is young and struggling to develop, it usually has a better chance for survival in a growing market where plenty of new business is up for grabs than in a stable or declining industry. However, if a weakly positioned company in a rapid-growth market lacks the resources and skills to hold its own, its best option is merger either with another company in the industry that has the missing pieces or with an outsider having the cash and resources to support the firm's development. Vertical integration, either forward or backward or both, is an option for a weakly positioned firm whenever it can materially strengthen the firm's competitive position. A third option is diversification into related or unrelated businesses (if adequate financing can be found). If all else fails, abandonment—divestiture in the case of a multibusiness firm or liquidation in the case of a single-business firm—has to become an active strategic option. While abandonment may seem extreme because of the high growth potential, a company unable to make a profit in a booming market probably does not have the ability to make a profit at all—particularly if competition stiffens or industry conditions sour.

Companies with a weak competitive position in a relatively slow-growth market should look at (1) initiating actions to create a more attractive competitive position, (2) merging with or being acquired by a rival to build a stronger base for competing, (3) diversifying into related or unrelated areas if ample financial resources are available, (4) integrating forward or backward if such actions will boost profits and long-term competitive strength, (5) employing a harvest-then-divest strategy, and (6) liquidating their position in the business by either selling out to another firm or closing down operations.

Companies that are strongly positioned in a slow-growth industry should consider taking the excess cash flow from their existing business to finance a diversification

[1]C. Roland Christensen, Norman A. Berg, and Malcolm S. Salter, *Policy Formulation and Administration,* 7th ed. (Homewood, Ill.: Richard D. Irwin, 1976), pp. 16–18.

When to diversify depends partly on a company's growth opportunities in its present industry and partly on its competitive position.

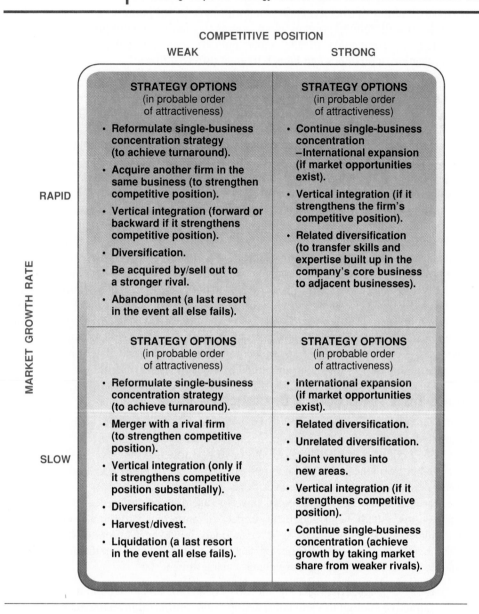

strategy. Diversification into businesses where a firm can leverage its core competencies and competitive strengths is usually the best strategy. But diversification into totally unrelated businesses has to be considered if none of its related business opportunities offer attractive profit prospects. Joint ventures with other organizations into new fields of endeavor are another logical possibility. Vertical integration should be a last resort (since it provides no escape from the industry's slow-growth condition) and makes strategic sense only if a firm can expect sizable profit gains. Unless it sees important growth *segments* within the industry that merit further invest-and-build actions, a strong company in a slow-growth industry usually needs to curtail new investment in its present business to free cash for new endeavors.

Companies with strong competitive positions in slow-growth industries are prime candidates for diversifying into new businesses.

When to diversify is therefore partly a function of a firm's competitive position and partly a function of the remaining opportunities in its home-base industry. There really is no well-defined point at which companies in the same industry should diversify. Indeed, companies in the same industry can rationally choose different diversification approaches and launch them at different times.

BUILDING SHAREHOLDER VALUE: THE ULTIMATE JUSTIFICATION FOR DIVERSIFYING

The overriding purpose of corporate diversification is to build shareholder value. For diversification to enhance shareholder value, corporate strategy must do more than simply diversify the company's business risk by investing in more than one industry. Shareholders can achieve the same risk diversification on their own by purchasing stock in companies in different industries. Strictly speaking, *diversification does not create shareholder value unless a diversified group of businesses perform better under a single corporate umbrella than they would perform operating as independent, stand-alone businesses.* For example, if company A diversifies by purchasing company B and if A and B's consolidated profits in the years to come prove no greater than what each would have earned on its own, then A's diversification into business B won't provide its shareholders with added value. Company A's shareholders could have achieved the same 2 + 2 = 4 result on their own accord by purchasing stock in company B. Shareholder value is not *created* by diversification unless it produces a 2 + 2 = 5 effect where sister businesses perform better together as part of the same firm than they could have performed as independent companies.

> To create shareholder value, a diversifying company must get into businesses that can perform better under common management than they could perform as stand-alone enterprises.

THREE TESTS FOR JUDGING A DIVERSIFICATION MOVE

The problem with such a strict benchmark of whether diversification has enhanced shareholder value is that it requires speculative judgments about how well a diversified company's businesses would have performed on their own. Comparisons of actual performance against the hypothetical of what performance might have been under other circumstances are never very satisfactory and, besides, they represent after-the-fact assessments. Strategists have to base diversification decisions on future expectations. Attempts to gauge the impact of particular diversification moves on shareholder value do not have to be abandoned, however. Corporate strategists can make before-the-fact assessments of whether a particular diversification move is capable of increasing shareholder value by using three tests:[2]

1. **The attractiveness test:** The industry chosen for diversification must be attractive enough to yield consistently good returns on investment. Whether an industry is attractive depends chiefly on the presence of favorable competitive conditions and a market environment conducive to long-term profitability. Such indicators as rapid growth or a sexy product are unreliable proxies of attractiveness.

2. **The cost-of-entry test:** The cost to enter the target industry must not be so high as to erode the potential for good profitability. A catch-22 situation can

---

[2]Michael E. Porter, "From Competitive Advantage to Corporate Strategy," *Harvard Business Review* 45, no. 3 (May–June 1987), pp. 46–49.

prevail here, however. The more attractive the industry, the more expensive it can be to get into. Entry barriers for start-up companies are nearly always high—were barriers low, a rush of new entrants would soon erode the potential for high profitability. And buying a company already in the business typically entails a high acquisition cost because of the industry's strong appeal. Costly entry undermines the potential for enhancing shareholder value.

3. **The better-off test:** The diversifying company must bring some potential for competitive advantage to the new business it enters, or the new business must offer added competitive advantage potential to the company's present businesses. The opportunity to create sustainable competitive advantage where none existed before means there is also opportunity for added profitability and shareholder value.

Diversification moves that satisfy all three tests have the greatest potential to build shareholder value over the long term. Diversification moves that can pass only one or two tests are suspect.

DIVERSIFICATION STRATEGIES

Once the decision is made to pursue diversification, any of several different paths can be taken. There is plenty of room for varied strategic approaches. Figure 7–2 shows the paths a company can take in moving from a single-business enterprise to a diversified enterprise. Vertical integration strategies may or may not enter the picture depending on the extent to which forward or backward integration strengthens a firm's competitive position or helps it secure a competitive advantage. When diversification becomes a serious strategic option, a choice must be made whether to pursue related diversification, unrelated diversification, or some mix of both. Once diversification is accomplished, management's task is to figure out how to manage the collection of businesses the company has invested in—the six fundamental strategic options are shown in the last box of Figure 7–2.

We can better understand the strategic issues corporate managers face in creating and managing a diversified group of businesses by looking at six diversification-related strategies:

1. Strategies for entering new industries—acquisition, start-up, and joint ventures.
2. Related diversification strategies.
3. Unrelated diversification strategies.
4. Divestiture and liquidation strategies.
5. Corporate turnaround, retrenchment, and restructuring strategies.
6. Multinational diversification strategies.

The first three are ways to diversify; the last three are strategies to strengthen the positions and performance of companies that have already diversified.

STRATEGIES FOR ENTERING NEW BUSINESSES

Entry into new businesses can take any of three forms: acquisition, internal start-up, and joint ventures. *Acquisition of an existing business* is the most popular means of diversifying into another industry and has the advantage of much quicker entry into

| **Corporate Strategy Alternatives**

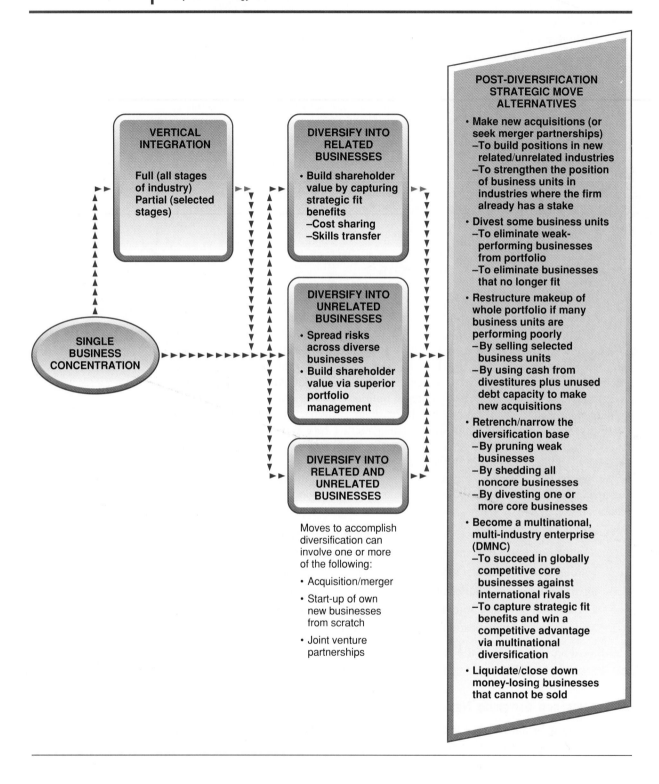

the target market.[3] At the same time, it helps a diversifier overcome such entry barriers as acquiring technological experience, establishing supplier relationships, becoming big enough to match rivals' efficiency and unit costs, having to spend large sums on introductory advertising and promotions to gain market visibility and brand recognition, and getting adequate distribution. In many industries, going the internal start-up route and trying to develop the knowledge, resources, scale of operation, and market reputation necessary to become an effective competitor can take years and entail all the problems of getting a brand new company off the ground and operating.

However, finding the right kind of company to acquire sometimes presents a challenge.[4] The big dilemma an acquisition-minded firm faces is whether to buy a successful company at a high price or a struggling company at a bargain price. If the buying firm has little knowledge of the industry but ample capital, it is often better off purchasing a capable, strongly positioned firm—unless the acquisition price is unreasonably high. On the other hand, when the acquirer sees promising ways to transform a weak firm into a strong one and has the money, the know-how, and the patience to do it, a struggling company can be the better long-term investment.

The cost-of-entry test requires that the expected profit stream of an acquired business provide an attractive return on the total acquisition cost and on any new capital investment needed to sustain or expand its operations. A high acquisition price can make meeting that test improbable or difficult. For instance, suppose that the price to purchase a company is $3 million and that the business is earning after-tax profits of $200,000 on an equity investment of $1 million (a 20 percent annual return). Simple arithmetic requires that the acquired business's profits be tripled for the purchaser to earn the same 20 percent return on the $3 million acquisition price that the previous owners were getting on their $1 million equity investment. Building the acquired firm's earnings from $200,000 to $600,000 annually could take several years—and require additional investment on which the purchaser would also have to earn a 20 percent return. Since the owners of a successful and growing company usually demand a price that reflects their business's future profit prospects, it's easy for such an acquisition to flunk the cost-of-entry test. A would-be diversifier can't count on being able to acquire a desirable company in an appealing industry at a price that still permits attractive returns on investment.

Achieving diversification through *internal start-up* involves creating a new company under the corporate umbrella to compete in the desired industry. A newly formed organization not only has to overcome entry barriers, it also has to invest in new production capacity, develop sources of supply, hire and train employees, build channels of distribution, grow a customer base, and so on. Generally, forming a start-up company to enter a new industry is more attractive when (1) there is ample time to launch the business from the ground up, (2) incumbent firms are likely to be slow or ineffective in responding to a new entrant's efforts to crack the market, (3) internal entry has lower costs than entry via acquisition, (4) the company already has in-house most or all of the skills it needs to compete effectively, (5) adding new production capacity will not adversely impact the supply-demand balance in the industry,

One of the big stumbling blocks to entering attractive industries by acquisition is the difficulty of finding a suitable company at a price that satisfies the cost-of-entry test.

The biggest drawbacks to entering an industry by forming a start-up company internally are the costs of overcoming entry barriers and the extra time it takes to build a strong and profitable competitive position.

---

[3]In recent years, hostile takeovers have become a hotly debated and sometimes abused approach to acquisition. The term *takeover* refers to the attempt (often sprung as a surprise) of one firm to acquire ownership or control over another firm against the wishes of the latter's management (and perhaps some of its stockholders).

[4]Michael E. Porter, *Competitive Strategy: Techniques for Analyzing Industries and Competitors* (New York: Free Press, 1980), p. 354–55.

and (6) the targeted industry is populated with many relatively small firms so the new start-up does not have to compete head-to-head against larger, more powerful rivals.[5]

Joint ventures are a useful way to gain access to a new business in at least three types of situations.[6] First, a joint venture is a good way to do something that is uneconomical or risky for an organization to do alone. Second, joint ventures make sense when pooling the resources and competencies of two or more independent organizations produces an organization with more of the skills needed to be a strong competitor. In such cases, each partner brings special talents or resources that the other doesn't have and that are important for success. Third, joint ventures with foreign partners are sometimes the only or best way to surmount import quotas, tariffs, nationalistic political interests, and cultural roadblocks. The economic, competitive, and political realities of nationalism often require a foreign company to team up with a domestic partner in order to gain access to the national market in which the domestic partner is located. Domestic partners offer outside companies the benefits of local knowledge, managerial and marketing personnel, and access to distribution channels. However, such joint ventures often pose complicated questions about how to divide efforts among the partners and about who has effective control.[7] Conflicts between foreign and domestic partners can arise over whether to use local sourcing of components, how much production to export, whether operating procedures should conform to the foreign company's standards or to local preferences, who has control of cash flows, and how to distribute profits.

RELATED DIVERSIFICATION STRATEGIES

In choosing which industries to diversify into, the two basic options are to pick industries *related* to or *unrelated* to the organization's core business and what the organization already does. A related diversification strategy involves diversifying into businesses that possess some kind of "strategic fit." *Strategic fit* exists when different businesses have sufficiently related value chains that there are important opportunities for (1) transferring skills and expertise from one business to another or (2) combining the related activities of separate businesses into a single operation and reducing costs.[8] *A diversified firm that exploits these value-chain interrelationships and captures the benefits of strategic fit achieves a consolidated performance greater than the sum of what the businesses can earn pursuing independent strategies.* The presence of strategic fit within a diversified firm's business portfolio, together with corporate management's deftness and skill in capturing the benefits of the interrelationships, makes related diversification a 2 + 2 = 5 phenomenon and becomes a basis for competitive advantage. The bigger the strategic-fit benefits, the bigger the competitive advantage of related diversification and the more that related diversification satisfies the better-off test for building shareholder value.

Related diversification involves diversifying into businesses whose value chains have appealing strategic fits.

---

[5]Ibid., pp. 344–45.

[6]Peter Drucker, *Management: Tasks, Responsibilities, Practices* (New York: Harper & Row, 1974), pp. 720–24. Strategic alliances offer much the same benefits as joint ventures, but represent a weaker commitment to entering a new business.

[7]Porter, *Competitive Strategy,* p. 340.

[8]Michael E. Porter, *Competitive Advantage* (New York: Free Press, 1985), pp. 318–19 and pp. 337–53; Kenichi Ohmae, *The Mind of the Strategist* (New York: Penguin Books, 1983), pp. 121–24; and Porter, "From Competitive Advantage to Corporate Strategy," pp. 53–57.

Strategic-fit relationships can arise out of the opportunity for technology sharing, the existence of common labor skills and requirements, use of common suppliers and raw materials sources, the potential for joint manufacture of parts and components, the presence of similar operating methods and similar managerial know-how, reliance on the same types of marketing and merchandising skills, the possibility of sharing a common sales force and using the same wholesale distributors or retail dealers, the potential for combining after-sale service activities, or the advantages and synergistic effects of a common brand name. The fit or relatedness can occur anywhere along the businesses' respective value chains. Strategic-fit relationships are important because they represent opportunities for cost-saving efficiencies, technology or skills transfers, added differentiation, or brand name advantages, all of which are avenues for gaining competitive advantages over business rivals that have not diversified or that have diversified but not in ways that give them access to such strategic-fit benefits.

> What makes related diversification attractive is the opportunity to turn strategic fits into competitive advantage.

Some of the most commonly used approaches to related diversification are

- Entering businesses where sales force, advertising, and distribution activities can be shared (a bread bakery buying a maker of crackers and salty snack foods).

- Exploiting closely related technologies (a marketer of agricultural seeds and fertilizers diversifying into chemicals for insect and plant disease control).

- Transferring know-how and expertise from one business to another (a successful operator of hamburger outlets acquiring a chain specializing in Mexican fast-foods).

- Transferring the organization's brand name and reputation with consumers to a new product/service (a tire manufacturer diversifying into automotive repair centers).

- Acquiring new businesses that will uniquely help the firm's position in its existing businesses (a cable TV broadcaster purchasing a sports team or purchasing a movie production company to provide original programming).

Examples of related diversification abound. BIC Pen, which pioneered inexpensive disposable ballpoint pens, used its core competencies in low-cost manufacturing and mass merchandising as its basis for diversifying into disposable cigarette lighters and disposable razors—both of which required low-cost production know-how and skilled consumer marketing for success. Tandy Corp. practiced related diversification when its chain of Radio Shack outlets, which originally handled mostly radio and stereo equipment, added telephones, intercoms, calculators, clocks, electronic and scientific toys, personal computers, and peripheral computer equipment. The Tandy strategy was to use the marketing access provided by its thousands of Radio Shack locations to become one of the world's leading retailers of electronic technology to individual consumers. Philip Morris, a leading cigarette manufacturer, employed a marketing-related diversification strategy when it purchased Miller Brewing, General Foods, and Kraft and transferred its skills in cigarette marketing to the marketing of beer and food products. Lockheed pursued a customer needs-based diversification strategy in creating business units to supply the Department of Defense with missiles, rocket engines, aircraft, electronic equipment, ships, and contract R&D for weapons. Procter & Gamble's lineup of products includes Jif peanut butter, Duncan Hines cake mixes, Folger's coffee, Tide laundry detergent, Crisco vegetable oil, Crest toothpaste, Ivory soap, Charmin toilet tissue, and Head and Shoulders shampoo—all different businesses with different competi-

EXAMPLES OF COMPANIES WITH RELATED BUSINESS PORTFOLIOS

Presented below are the business portfolios of four companies that have pursued some form of related diversification:

Gillette

- Blades and razors
- Toiletries (Right Guard, Silkience, Foamy, Dry Idea, Soft & Dry, Oral-B toothbrushes, White Rain, Toni)
- Writing instruments and stationery products (Paper Mate pens, Liquid Paper correction fluids, Waterman pens)
- Braun shavers, cordless curlers, coffeemakers, alarm clocks, and electric toothbrushes

PepsiCo

- Soft drinks (Pepsi, Mountain Dew, Slice)
- Kentucky Fried Chicken
- Pizza Hut
- Taco Bell
- Frito-Lay
- 7UP International (non-US sales of 7UP)

Philip Morris Companies

- Cigarettes (Marlboro, Virginia Slims, Benson & Hedges, and Merit)
- Miller Brewing Company
- Kraft General Foods (Maxwell House, Sanka, Oscar Mayer, Kool-Aid, Jell-O, Post cereals, Birds-Eye frozen foods, Kraft cheeses, Sealtest dairy products, Breyer's ice cream)
- Mission Viejo Realty

Johnson & Johnson

- Baby products (powder, shampoo, oil, lotion)
- Disposable diapers
- Band-Aids and wound care products
- Stayfree, Carefree, Sure & Natural, and Modess feminine hygiene products
- Tylenol
- Prescription drugs
- Surgical and hospital products
- Dental products
- Oral contraceptives
- Veterinary and animal health products

Source: Company annual reports.

tors and different production requirements. But P&G's products still represent related diversification because they all move through the same wholesale distribution systems, are sold in common retail settings to the same shoppers, are advertised and promoted in the same ways, and utilize the same marketing and merchandising skills. Illustration Capsule 22 shows the business portfolios of several companies that have pursued a strategy of related diversification.

STRATEGIC FIT, ECONOMIES OF SCOPE, AND COMPETITIVE ADVANTAGE

A related diversification strategy clearly has considerable appeal. It allows a firm to preserve a degree of unity in its business activities, reap the competitive advantage benefits of skills transfer or lower costs, and still spread investor risks over a broader business base.

Diversifying into businesses where technology, facilities, functional activities, or distribution channels can be shared can lead to lower costs because of economies of

Strategic fits among related businesses offer the competitive advantage potential of (a) lower costs, (b) efficient transfer of key skills, technological expertise, or managerial know-how from one business to another, or (c) ability to share a common brand name.

scope. *Economies of scope* exist whenever it is less costly for two or more businesses to be operated under centralized management than to function as independent businesses. The economies of operating over a wider range of businesses or product lines can arise from cost-saving opportunities to share resources or combine activities anywhere along the respective value chains of the businesses and from shared use of an established brand name. The greater the economies of scope associated with the particular businesses a company has diversified into, the greater the potential for creating a competitive advantage based on lower costs.

Both skills transfer and activity sharing enable the diversifier to earn greater profits from its businesses than the businesses could earn operating independently. Thus the economies of scope. The key to activity sharing and skills transfer opportunities and thus to cost saving is diversification into businesses with strategic fit. While strategic-fit relationships can occur throughout the value chain, most fall into one of three broad categories.

Economies of scope arise from the ability to eliminate costs by operating two or more businesses under the same corporate umbrella; the cost-saving opportunities can stem from interrelationships anywhere along the businesses' value chains.

Market-Related Fit   When the value chains of different businesses overlap such that the products are used by the same customers, distributed through common dealers and retailers, or marketed and promoted in similar ways, then the businesses enjoy *market-related strategic fit*. A variety of cost-saving opportunities (or economies of scope) spring from market-related strategic fit: using a single sales force for all related products rather than having separate sales forces for each business, advertising the related products in the same ads and brochures, using the same brand names, coordinating delivery and shipping, combining after-sale service and repair organizations, coordinating order processing and billing, using common promotional tie-ins (cents-off couponing, free samples and trial offers, seasonal specials, and the like), and combining dealer networks. Such market-related strategic fits usually allow a firm to economize on its marketing, selling, and distribution costs.

In addition to economies of scope, market-related fit can generate opportunities to transfer selling skills, promotional skills, advertising skills, and product differentiation skills from one business to another. Moreover, a company's brand name and reputation in one product can often be transferred to other products. Honda's name in motorcycles and automobiles gave it instant credibility and recognition in entering the lawnmower business without spending large sums on advertising. Canon's reputation in photographic equipment was a competitive asset that facilitated the company's diversification into copying equipment. Panasonic's name in consumer electronics (radios, TVs) was readily transferred to microwave ovens, making it easier and cheaper for Panasonic to diversify into the microwave oven market.

Operating Fit   Different businesses have *operating fit* when there is potential for activity sharing or skills transfer in procuring materials, conducting R&D, mastering a new technology, manufacturing components, assembling finished goods, or performing administrative support functions. Sharing-related operating fits usually present cost-saving opportunities; some derive from the economies of combining activities into a larger-scale operation *(economies of scale),* and some derive from the ability to eliminate costs by performing activities together rather than independently *(economies of scope).* The bigger the proportion of cost that a shared activity represents, the more significant the shared cost savings become and the bigger the cost advantage that can result. With operating fit, the most important skills transfer opportunities usually relate to situations where technological or manufacturing expertise in one business has beneficial applications in another.

Management Fit   This type of fit emerges when different business units have comparable types of entrepreneurial, administrative, or operating problems, thereby allowing managerial know-how in one line of business to be transferred to another. Transfers of managerial expertise can occur anywhere in the value chain. Ford transferred its automobile financing and credit management know-how to the savings and loan industry when it acquired some failing savings and loan associations during the 1989 bailout of the crisis-ridden S&L industry. Emerson Electric transferred its skills in low-cost manufacture to its newly acquired Beaird-Poulan chain saw business division; the transfer of management know-how drove Beaird-Poulan's new strategy, changed the way its chain saws were designed and manufactured, and paved the way for new pricing and distribution emphasis.

Capturing Strategic-Fit Benefits   It is one thing to diversify into industries with strategic fit and another to actually realize the benefits. To capture the benefits of activity sharing, related activities must be merged into a single functional unit and coordinated; then the cost savings (or differentiation advantages) must be squeezed out. Merged functions and coordination can entail reorganization costs, and management must determine that the benefit of *some* centralized strategic control is great enough to warrant sacrifice of business-unit autonomy. Likewise, where skills transfer is the cornerstone of strategic fit, managers must find a way to make the transfer effective without stripping too many skilled personnel from the business with the expertise. The more a company's diversification strategy is tied to skills transfer, the more it has to develop a big enough and talented enough pool of specialized personnel not only to supply new businesses with the skill but also to master the skill sufficiently to create competitive advantage.

> Competitive advantage achieved through strategic fits among related businesses adds to the performance potential of the firm's individual businesses; this extra source of competitive advantage allows related diversification to have a 2 + 2 = 5 effect on shareholder value.

UNRELATED DIVERSIFICATION STRATEGIES

Despite the strategic-fit benefits associated with related diversification, a number of companies opt for unrelated diversification strategies—they exhibit a willingness to diversify into *any industry* with a good profit opportunity. Corporate managers exert no deliberate effort to seek out businesses having strategic fit with the firm's other businesses. While companies pursuing unrelated diversification may try to make certain their diversification targets meet the industry-attractiveness and cost-of-entry tests, the conditions needed for the better-off test are either disregarded or relegated to secondary status. Decisions to diversify into one industry versus another are the product of an opportunistic search for "good" companies to acquire—*the basic premise of unrelated diversification is that any company that can be acquired on good financial terms and that has satisfactory profit prospects represents a good business to diversify into.* Much time and effort goes into finding and screening acquisition candidates. Typically, corporate strategists screen candidate companies using such criteria as

> A strategy of unrelated diversification involves diversifying into whatever industries and businesses hold promise for attractive financial gain; exploiting strategic-fit relationships is secondary.

- Whether the business can meet corporate targets for profitability and return on investment.
- Whether the new business will require substantial infusions of capital to replace fixed assets, fund expansion, and provide working capital.
- Whether the business is in an industry with significant growth potential.
- Whether the business is big enough to contribute significantly to the parent firm's bottom line.

- Whether there is a potential for union difficulties or adverse government regulations concerning product safety or the environment.
- Whether there is industry vulnerability to recession, inflation, high interest rates, or shifts in government policy.

Sometimes, companies with unrelated diversification strategies concentrate on identifying acquisition candidates that offer quick opportunities for financial gain because of their "special situation." Three types of businesses may hold such attraction:

- *Companies whose assets are undervalued*—opportunities may exist to acquire such companies for less than full market value and make substantial capital gains by reselling their assets and businesses for more than their acquired costs.
- *Companies that are financially distressed*—such businesses can often be purchased at a bargain price, their operations turned around with the aid of the parent companies' financial resources and managerial know-how, and then either held as long-term investments in the acquirers' business portfolios (because of their strong earnings or cash flow potential) or sold at a profit, whichever is more attractive.
- *Companies that have bright growth prospects but are short on investment capital*—capital-poor, opportunity-rich companies are usually coveted diversification candidates for a financially strong, opportunity-seeking firm.

Companies that pursue unrelated diversification nearly always enter new businesses by acquiring an established company rather than by forming a start-up subsidiary within their own corporate structures. Their premise is that growth by acquisition translates into enhanced shareholder value. Suspending application of the better-off test is seen as justifiable so long as unrelated diversification results in sustained growth in corporate revenues and earnings and so long as none of the acquired businesses end up performing badly.

Illustration Capsule 23 shows the business portfolios of several companies that have pursued unrelated diversification. Such companies are frequently labeled *conglomerates* because there is no strategic theme in their diversification makeup and because their business interests range broadly across diverse industries.

THE PROS AND CONS OF UNRELATED DIVERSIFICATION

Unrelated or conglomerate diversification has appeal from several financial angles:

1. Business risk is scattered over a variety of industries, making the company less dependent on any one business. While the same can be said for related diversification, unrelated diversification places no restraint on how risk is spread. An argument can be made that unrelated diversification is a superior way to diversify financial risk as compared to related diversification because the company's investments can span a bigger variety of totally different businesses.
2. Capital resources can be invested in whatever industries offer the best profit prospects; cash flows from company businesses with lower profit prospects can be diverted to acquiring and expanding business units with higher growth and profit potentials. Corporate financial resources are thus employed to maximum advantage.

ILLUSTRATION CAPSULE 23

DIVERSIFIED COMPANIES WITH UNRELATED BUSINESS PORTFOLIOS

Union Pacific Corporation

- Railroad operations (Union Pacific Railroad Company)
- Oil and gas exploration
- Mining
- Microwave and fiber optic transportation information and control systems
- Hazardous waste management disposal
- Trucking (Overnite Transportation Company)
- Oil refining
- Real estate

United Technologies, Inc.

- Pratt & Whitney aircraft engines
- Carrier heating and air-conditioning equipment
- Otis elevators
- Sikorsky helicopters
- Essex wire and cable products
- Norden defense systems)
- Hamilton Standard controls
- Space transportation systems
- Automotive components

Westinghouse Electric Corporation

- Electric utility power generation equipment
- Nuclear fuel
- Electric transmission and distribution products
- Commercial and residential real estate financing
- Equipment leasing
- Receivables and fixed asset financing
- Radio and television broadcasting
- Longines-Wittnauer Watch Co.
- Beverage bottling
- Elevators and escalators
- Defense electronic systems (missile launch equipment, marine propulsion)
- Commercial furniture
- Community land development

Textron, Inc.

- Bell helicopters
- Paul Revere Insurance
- Missile reentry systems
- Lycoming gas turbine engines and jet propulsion systems
- E-Z-Go golf carts
- Homelite chain saws and lawn and garden equipment
- Davidson automotive parts and trims
- Specialty fasteners
- Avco Financial Services
- Jacobsen turf care equipment
- Tanks and armored vehicles

Source: Company annual reports.

3. Company profitability is somewhat more stable because hard times in one industry may be partially offset by good times in another—ideally, cyclical downswings in some of the company's businesses are counterbalanced by cyclical upswings in other businesses the company has diversified into.

4. To the extent that corporate managers are exceptionally astute at spotting bargain-priced companies with big upside profit potential, shareholder wealth can be enhanced.

While entry into an unrelated business can often pass the attractiveness and the cost-of-entry tests (and sometimes even the better-off test), a strategy of unrelated diversification has drawbacks. One Achilles' heel of conglomerate diversification is the big demand it places on corporate-level management to make sound decisions regarding fundamentally different businesses operating in fundamentally different industry and competitive environments. The greater the number of businesses a company is in and the more diverse they are, the harder it is for corporate managers to oversee each subsidiary and spot problems early, to have real expertise in evaluating the attractiveness of each business's industry and competitive environment, and to judge the calibre of strategic actions and plans proposed by business-level managers. As one president of a diversified firm expressed it:

> . . . we've got to make sure that our core businesses are properly managed for solid, long-term earnings. We can't just sit back and watch the numbers. We've got to know what the real issues are out there in the profit centers. Otherwise, we're not even in a position to check out our managers on the big decisions.[9]

With broad diversification, corporate managers have to be shrewd and talented enough to (1) discern a good acquisition from a bad acquisition, (2) select capable managers to run each of many different businesses, (3) discern when the major strategic proposals of business-unit managers are sound, and (4) know what to do if a business unit stumbles. Because every business tends to encounter rough sledding, a good way to gauge the risk of diversifying into new unrelated areas is to ask, "If the new business got into trouble, would we know how to bail it out?" When the answer is no, unrelated diversification can pose significant financial risk and the business's profit prospects are more chancy.[10] As the former chairman of a Fortune 500 company advised, "Never acquire a business you don't know how to run." It takes only one or two big strategic mistakes (misjudging industry attractiveness, encountering unexpected problems in a newly acquired business, or being too optimistic about how hard it will be to turn a struggling subsidiary around) to cause a precipitous drop in corporate earnings and crash the parent company's stock price.

Second, without the competitive advantage potential of strategic fit, consolidated performance of an unrelated multibusiness portfolio tends to be no better than the sum of what the individual business units could achieve if they were independent, and it may be worse to the extent that corporate managers meddle unwisely in business-unit operations or hamstring them with corporate policies. Except, perhaps, for the added financial backing that a cash-rich corporate parent can provide, a strategy of unrelated diversification does nothing for the competitive strength of the individual business units. Each business is on its own in trying to build a competitive edge—the unrelated nature of sister businesses offers no basis for cost reduction, skills transfer, or technology sharing. In a widely diversified firm, the value added by corporate managers depends primarily on how good they are at deciding what new businesses to add, which ones to get rid of, how best to deploy available financial resources to build a higher-performing collection of businesses, and the quality of the decision-making guidance they give to the general managers of their business subsidiaries.

Third, although in theory unrelated diversification offers the potential for greater sales-profit stability over the course of the business cycle, in practice attempts at countercyclical diversification fall short of the mark. Few attractive businesses have

> The two biggest drawbacks to unrelated diversification are the difficulties of competently managing many different businesses and being without the added source of competitive advantage that strategic fit provides.

---

[9]Carter F. Bales, "Strategic Control: The President's Paradox," *Business Horizons* 20, no. 4 (August 1977), p. 17.

[10]Of course, management may be willing to assume the risk that trouble will not strike before it has had time to learn the business well enough to bail it out of almost any difficulty. See Peter Drucker, *Management: Tasks, Responsibilities, Practices,* p. 709.

opposite up-and-down cycles; the great majority of businesses are similarly affected by economic good times and hard times. There's no convincing evidence that the consolidated profits of broadly diversified firms are more stable or less subject to reversal in periods of recession and economic stress than the profits of less diversified firms.[11]

Despite these drawbacks, unrelated diversification can sometimes be a desirable corporate strategy. It certainly merits consideration when a firm needs to diversify away from an endangered or unattractive industry and has no distinctive skills it can transfer to an adjacent industry. There's also a rationale for pure diversification to the extent owners have a strong preference for investing in several unrelated businesses instead of a family of related ones. Otherwise, the argument for unrelated diversification hinges on the case-by-case prospects for financial gain.

A key issue in unrelated diversification is how wide a net to cast in building the business portfolio. In other words, should the corporate portfolio contain few or many unrelated businesses? How much business diversity can corporate executives successfully manage? A reasonable way to resolve the issue of how much diversification comes from answering two questions: "What is the least diversification it will take to achieve acceptable growth and profitability?" and "What is the most diversification that can be managed given the complexity it adds?"[12] The optimal amount of diversification usually lies between these two extremes.

UNRELATED DIVERSIFICATION AND SHAREHOLDER VALUE

Unrelated diversification is fundamentally a finance-driven approach to creating shareholder value whereas related diversification is fundamentally strategy-driven. *Related diversification represents a strategic approach to building shareholder value* because it is predicated on exploiting the linkages between the value chains of different businesses to lower costs, transfer skills and technological expertise across businesses, and gain other strategic-fit benefits. The objective is to convert the strategic fits among the firm's businesses into an extra measure of competitive advantage that goes beyond what business subsidiaries are able to achieve on their own. The added competitive advantage a firm achieves through related diversification is the driver for building greater shareholder value.

In contrast, *unrelated diversification is principally a financial approach to creating shareholder value* because it is predicated on astute deployment of corporate financial resources and executive skill in spotting financially attractive business opportunities. Since unrelated diversification produces no strategic-fit opportunities of consequence, corporate strategists can't build shareholder value by acquiring companies that create or compound competitive advantage for its business subsidiaries— in a conglomerate, competitive advantage doesn't go beyond what each business subsidiary can achieve independently through its own competitive strategy. Consequently, for unrelated diversification to result in enhanced shareholder value (above the $2 + 2 = 4$ effect that the subsidiary businesses could produce through independent operations and that shareholders could obtain by purchasing ownership interests in a variety of businesses to spread investment risk on their own behalf),

---

Unrelated diversification is a financial approach to creating shareholder value; related diversification, in contrast, represents a strategic approach.

For corporate strategists to build shareholder value in some way other than through strategic fits and competitive advantage, they must be smart enough to produce financial results from a group of businesses that exceed what business-level managers can produce.

---

[11]Ibid., p. 767. Research studies in the interval since 1974, when Drucker made his observation, uphold his conclusion—on the whole, broadly diversified firms do not outperform less diversified firms over the course of the business cycle.
[12]Ibid., pp. 692–93.

corporate strategists must exhibit superior skills in creating and managing a portfolio of diversified business interests. This specifically means

- Doing a superior job of diversifying into new businesses that can produce consistently good returns on investment (satisfying the attractiveness test).
- Doing an excellent job of negotiating favorable acquisition prices (satisfying the cost-of-entry test).
- Making astute moves to sell previously acquired business subsidiaries at their peak and getting premium prices (this requires skills in discerning when a business subsidiary is on the verge of confronting adverse industry and competitive conditions and probable declines in long-term profitability).
- Being shrewd in shifting corporate financial resources out of businesses where profit opportunities are dim and into businesses where rapid earnings growth and high returns on investment are occurring.
- Doing such a good job overseeing the firm's business subsidiaries and contributing to how they are managed (by providing expert problem-solving skills, creative strategy suggestions, and decision-making guidance to business-level managers) that the businesses perform at a higher level than they would otherwise be able to do (a possible way to satisfy the better-off test).

To the extent that corporate executives are able to craft and execute a strategy of unrelated diversification that produces enough of the above outcomes for an enterprise to consistently outperform other firms in generating dividends and capital gains for stockholders, then a case can be made that shareholder value has truly been enhanced. Achieving such results consistently requires supertalented corporate executives, however. Without them, unrelated diversification is a very dubious and unreliable way to try to build shareholder value—there are far more who have tried it and failed than who have tried and succeeded.

DIVESTITURE AND LIQUIDATION STRATEGIES

Even a shrewd corporate diversification strategy can result in the acquisition of business units that, down the road, just do not work out. Misfits or partial fits cannot be completely avoided because it is impossible to predict precisely how getting into a new line of business will actually work out. In addition, long-term industry attractiveness changes with the times; what was once a good diversification move into an attractive industry may later turn sour. Subpar performance by some business units is bound to occur, thereby raising questions of whether to keep them or divest them. Other business units, despite adequate financial performance, may not mesh as well with the rest of the firm as was originally thought.

> A business needs to be considered for divestiture when corporate strategists conclude it no longer fits or is an attractive investment.

Sometimes, a diversification move that seems sensible from a strategic-fit standpoint turns out to lack the compatibility of values essential to a *cultural fit*.[13] Several pharmaceutical companies had just this experience. When they diversified into cosmetics and perfume, they discovered their personnel had little respect for the "frivolous" nature of such products compared to the far nobler task of developing miracle drugs to cure the ill. The absence of shared values and cultural compatibility between the medical research and chemical-compounding expertise of the pharmaceutical

[13]Ibid., p. 709.

companies and the fashion-marketing orientation of the cosmetics business was the undoing of what otherwise was diversification into businesses with technology-sharing potential, product-development fit, and some overlap in distribution channels.

When a particular line of business loses its appeal, the most attractive solution usually is to sell it. Normally such businesses should be divested as fast as is practical. To drag things out serves no purpose unless time is needed to get it into better shape to sell. The more business units in a diversified firm's portfolio, the more likely that it will have occasion to divest poor performers, "dogs," and misfits. A useful guide to determine if and when to divest a business subsidiary is to ask the question, "If we were not in this business today, would we want to get into it now?"[14] When the answer is no or probably not, divestiture should be considered.

Divestiture can take either of two forms. The parent can spin off a business as a financially and managerially independent company in which the parent company may or may not retain partial ownership. Or the parent may sell the unit outright, in which case a buyer needs to be found. As a rule, divestiture should not be approached from the angle of "Who can we pawn this business off on and what is the most we can get for it?"[15] Instead, it is wiser to ask "For what sort of organization would this business be a good fit, and under what conditions would it be viewed as a good deal?" Organizations for which the business is a good fit are likely to pay the highest price.

Of all the strategic alternatives, liquidation is the most unpleasant and painful, especially for a single-business enterprise where it means the organization ceases to exist. For a multi-industry, multibusiness firm to liquidate one of its lines of business is less traumatic. The hardships of job eliminations, plant closings, and so on, while not to be minimized, still leave an ongoing organization, perhaps one that is healthier after its pruning. In hopeless situations, an early liquidation effort usually serves owner-stockholder interests better than an inevitable bankruptcy. Prolonging the pursuit of a lost cause exhausts an organization's resources and leaves less to liquidate; it can also mar reputations and ruin management careers. Unfortunately, it is seldom simple for management to differentiate between when a turnaround is achievable and when it isn't. This is particularly true when emotions and pride overcome sound business judgment—as often they do.

CORPORATE TURNAROUND, RETRENCHMENT, AND PORTFOLIO RESTRUCTURING STRATEGIES

Turnaround, retrenchment, and portfolio restructuring strategies come into play when corporate management has to restore an ailing business portfolio to good health. Poor performance can be caused by large losses in one or more business units that pull the corporation's overall financial performance down, a disproportionate number of businesses in unattractive industries, a bad economy adversely impacting many of the firm's business units, an excessive debt burden, or ill-chosen acquisitions that haven't lived up to expectations.

Corporate turnaround strategies focus on efforts to restore money-losing businesses to profitability instead of divesting them. The intent is to get the whole company back in the black by curing the problems of those businesses in the portfolio

---

[14]Ibid., p. 94.
[15]Ibid., p. 719.

that are most responsible for pulling overall performance down. Turnaround strategies are most appropriate in situations where the reasons for poor performance are short-term, the ailing businesses are in attractive industries, and divesting the money-losers does not make long-term strategic sense.

Corporate retrenchment strategies involve reducing the scope of diversification to a smaller number of businesses. Retrenchment is usually undertaken when corporate management concludes that the company is in too many businesses and needs to concentrate its efforts on a few core businesses. Sometimes diversified firms retrench because they can't make certain businesses profitable after several frustrating years of trying or because they lack funds to support the investment needs of all of their business subsidiaries. More commonly, however, corporate executives conclude that the firm's diversification efforts have ranged too far afield and that the key to improved long-term performance lies in concentrating on building strong positions in a smaller number of businesses. Retrenchment is usually accomplished by divesting businesses that are too small to make a sizable contribution to earnings or that have little or no strategic fit with the company's core businesses. Divesting such businesses frees resources that can be used to reduce debt or support expansion of the company's core businesses.

Portfolio restructuring strategies involve radical surgery on the mix and percentage makeup of the types of businesses in the portfolio. For instance, one company over a two-year period divested 4 business units, closed down the operations of 4 others, and added 25 new lines of business to its portfolio, 16 through acquisition and 9 through internal start-up. Restructuring can be prompted by any of several conditions: (1) when a strategy review reveals that the firm's long-term performance prospects have become unattractive because the portfolio contains too many slow-growth, declining, or competitively weak business units; (2) when one or more of the firm's core businesses fall prey to hard times; (3) when a new CEO takes over and decides to redirect where the company is headed; (4) when "wave of the future" technologies or products emerge and a major shakeup of the portfolio is needed to build a position in a potentially big new industry; (5) when the firm has a unique opportunity to make an acquisition so big that it has to sell several existing business units to finance the new acquisition; or (6) when major businesses in the portfolio have become more and more unattractive, forcing a shakeup in the portfolio in order to produce satisfactory long-term corporate performance.

> Portfolio restructuring involves bold strategic action to revamp the diversified company's business makeup through a series of divestitures and new acquisitions.

Portfolio restructuring typically involves both divestitures and new acquisitions. Candidates for divestiture include not only weak or up-and-down performers or those in unattractive industries, but also those that no longer fit (even though they may be profitable and in attractive-enough industries). Many broadly diversified companies, disenchanted with the performance of some acquisitions and having only mixed success in overseeing so many unrelated business units, restructure their business portfolios to a narrower core of activities. Business units incompatible with newly established related diversification criteria are divested, the remaining units regrouped and aligned to capture more strategic fit benefits, and new acquisitions made to strengthen the parent company's business position in the industries it has chosen to emphasize.

The recent trend among broadly diversified companies to demerge and deconglomerate is being driven by a growing preference for building diversification around the creation of strong competitive positions in a few, well-selected industries. Indeed, in response to investor disenchantment with the conglomerate approach to diversification (evident in the fact that conglomerates often have *lower* price-earnings ratios than companies with related diversification strategies), some conglomerates have undertaken portfolio restructuring and retrenchment in a deliberate effort to escape being regarded as a conglomerate.

MULTINATIONAL DIVERSIFICATION STRATEGIES

The distinguishing characteristics of a multinational diversification strategy are a *diversity of businesses* and a *diversity of national markets.*[16] Here, corporate managers have to conceive and execute a substantial number of strategies—at least one for each industry, with as many multinational variations as is appropriate for the situation. At the same time, managers of diversified multinational corporations (DMNCs) need to be alert for beneficial ways to coordinate their firms' strategic actions across industries and countries. The goal of strategic coordination at the headquarters level is to bring the full force of corporate resources and capabilities to the task of securing sustainable competitive advantages in each business and national market.[17]

THE EMERGENCE OF MULTINATIONAL DIVERSIFICATION

Until the 1960s, multinational companies (MNCs) operated fairly autonomous subsidiaries in each host country, each catering to the special requirements of its own national market.[18] Management tasks at company headquarters primarily involved finance functions, technology transfer, and export coordination. In pursuing a national responsiveness strategy, the primary competitive advantage of an MNC was grounded in its ability to transfer technology, manufacturing know-how, brand name identification, and marketing and management skills from country to country quite efficiently, allowing them to beat out smaller host country competitors on price, quality, and management know-how. Standardized administrative procedures helped minimize overhead costs, and once an initial organization for managing foreign subsidiaries was put in place, entry into additional national markets could be accomplished at low incremental costs. Frequently, an MNC's presence and market position in a country was negotiated with the host government rather than driven by international competition.

During the 1970s, however, multicountry strategies based on national responsiveness began to lose their effectiveness. Competition broke out on a global scale in more and more industries as Japanese, European, and U.S. companies pursued international expansion in the wake of trade liberalization and the opening up of market opportunities in both industrialized and less-developed countries.[19] The relevant market arena in many industries shifted from national to global principally because the strategies of global competitors, most notably the Japanese companies, involved gaining a market foothold in host country markets via lower-priced, higher-quality offerings than established companies. To fend off global competitors, traditional MNCs were driven to integrate their operations across national borders in a quest for better efficiencies and lower manufacturing costs. Instead of separately manufacturing a complete product range in each country, plants became more specialized in their production operations to gain the economies of longer production runs, to per-

---

[16]C. K. Prahalad and Yves L. Doz, *The Multinational Mission* (New York: Free Press, 1987), p. 2.
[17]Ibid., p. 15.
[18]Yves L. Doz, *Strategic Management in Multinational Companies* (New York: Pergamon Press, 1985), p. 1.
[19]Ibid., pp. 2–3.

their production operations to gain the economies of longer production runs, to permit use of faster automated equipment, and to capture experience curve effects. Country subsidiaries obtained the rest of the product range they needed from sister plants in other countries. Gains in manufacturing efficiencies from converting to state-of-the-art, world-scale manufacturing plants more than offset increased international shipping costs, especially in light of the other advantages globalized strategies offered. With a global strategy, an MNC could locate plants in countries with low labor costs—a key consideration in industries whose products have high labor content. With a global strategy, an MNC could also exploit differences in tax rates, setting transfer prices in its integrated operations to produce higher profits in low-tax countries and lower profits in high-tax countries. Global strategic coordination also gave MNCs increased ability to take advantage of country-to-country differences in interest rates, exchange rates, credit terms, government subsidies, and export guarantees. As a consequence of these advantages, it became increasingly difficult for a company that produced and sold its product in only one country to succeed in an industry populated with aggressive competitors intent on achieving global dominance.

During the 1980s another source of competitive advantage began to emerge: using the strategic fit advantages of related diversification to build stronger competitive positions in several related global industries simultaneously. Being a diversified MNC (DMNC) became competitively superior to being a single-business MNC in cases where strategic fits existed across global industries. Related diversification is most capable of producing competitive advantage for a multinational company where expertise in a core technology can be applied in different industries (at least one of which is global) and where there are important economies of scope and brand name advantages to being in a family of related businesses.[20] Illustration Capsule 24 indicates Honda's strategy in exploiting gasoline engine technology and its well-known name by diversifying into a variety of products with engines.

A multinational corporation can gain competitive advantage by diversifying into global industries having related technologies.

Sources of Competitive Advantage for a DMNC

When a multinational company has expertise in a core technology and has diversified into a series of related products and businesses to exploit that core, a centralized R&D effort coordinated at the headquarters level holds real potential for competitive advantage. By channeling corporate resources directly into a strategically coordinated R&D/technology effort, as opposed to letting each business unit perform its own R&D function, the DMNC can launch a world-class, global-scale assault to advance the core technology, generate technology-based manufacturing economies within and across product/business lines, make across-the-board product improvements, and develop complementary products—all significant advantages in a globally competitive marketplace. In the absence of centralized coordination, R&D/technology investments are likely to be scaled down to match each business's product-market perspective, setting the stage for lost opportunity as the strategic-fit benefits of coordinated technology management slip through the cracks and go uncaptured.[21]

The second source of competitive advantage for a DMNC concerns the distribution and brand name advantages that can accrue from diversifying into related global industries. Consider, for instance, the competitive strength of such Japanese DMNCs

---

[20]Pralahad and Doz, *The Multinational Mission*, pp. 62–63.
[21]Ibid.

ILLUSTRATION CAPSULE 24

HONDA'S COMPETITIVE ADVANTAGE
THE TECHNOLOGY OF ENGINES

At first blush anyone looking at Honda's lineup of products—cars, motorcycles, lawn mowers, power generators, outboard motors, snowmobiles, snowblowers, and garden tillers—might conclude that Honda has pursued unrelated diversification. But underlying the obvious product diversity is a common core: the technology of engines.

The basic Honda strategy is to exploit the company's expertise in engine technology and manufacturing and to capitalize on its brand recognition. One Honda ad teases consumers with the question, "How do you put six Hondas in a two-car garage?" It then shows a garage containing a Honda car, a Honda motorcycle, a Honda snowmobile, a Honda lawnmower, a Honda power generator, and a Honda outboard motor.

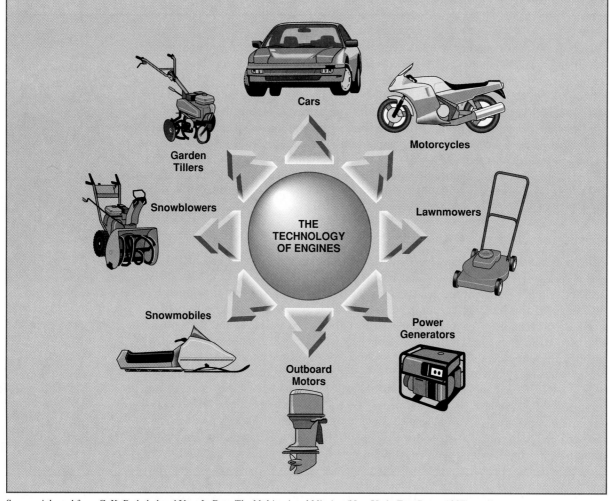

Source: Adapted from C. K. Prahalad and Yves L. Doz, *The Multinational Mission* (New York: Free Press, 1987), p. 62.

as Sanyo and Matsushita. Both have diversified into a range of globally competitive consumer goods industries—TVs, stereo equipment, radios, VCRs, small domestic appliances (microwave ovens, for example), and personal computers. By widening their scope of operations in products marketed through similar distribution channels, Sanyo and Matsushita have not only exploited related technologies but also built stronger distribution capabilities, captured logistical and distribution-related economies, and established greater brand awareness for their products.[22] Such competitive advantages are not available to a domestic-only company pursuing single-business concentration. Moreover, with a well-diversified product line and a multinational market base, a DMNC can enter new country markets or new product markets and gain market share via below-market pricing (and below-average cost pricing if need be), subsidizing the entry with earnings from one or more of its country market profit sanctuaries and/or earnings in other businesses.

Both a one-business multinational company and a one-business domestic company are weakly positioned to defend their market positions against a determined DMNC willing to accept lower short-term profits in order to win long-term competitive position in a desirable new market. A one-business domestic company has only one profit sanctuary—its home market. A one-business multinational company may have profit sanctuaries in several country markets but all are in the same business. Each is vulnerable to a DMNC that launches a major strategic offensive in their profit sanctuaries and low-balls its prices to win market share at their expense. A DMNC's ability to keep hammering away at competitors with low-ball prices year after year may reflect either a cost advantage growing out of its related diversification strategy or a willingness to cross-subsidize low profits or even losses with earnings from its profit sanctuaries in other country markets and/or its earnings from other businesses. Sanyo, for example, by pursuing related diversification keyed to product-distribution-technology strategic fit and managing its product families on a global scale, has the ability to encircle domestic companies like Zenith (which manufactures TVs and small computer systems) and Maytag (which manufactures home appliances) and put them under serious competitive pressure. In Zenith's case, Sanyo can peck away at Zenith's market share in TVs and in the process weaken the loyalty of TV retailers to the Zenith brand. In Maytag's case, Sanyo can diversify into large home appliances (by acquiring an established appliance maker or manufacturing on its own) and cross-subsidize a low-priced market entry against Maytag and other less-diversified home appliance firms with earnings from its many other business and product lines. If Sanyo chooses, it can keep its prices low for several years to gain market share at the expense of domestic rivals, turning its attention to profits after the battle for market share and competitive position is won.[23] Some additional aspects of the competitive power of broadly diversified enterprises is described in Illustration Capsule 25.

The competitive principle is clear: A DMNC has a strategic arsenal capable of defeating both a single-business MNC and a single-business domestic company over the long term. The competitive advantages of a DMNC, however, depend on employing a related diversification strategy in industries that are already globally competitive or are on the verge of becoming so. Then the related businesses have to be managed so as to capture strategic-fit benefits. DMNCs have the biggest competitive advantage potential in industries with technology-sharing and

A multinational corporation can also gain competitive advantage by diversifying into related global industries where the strategic fits produce economies of scope and the benefits of brand name transfer.

A multinational corporation that diversifies into related global industries is well-positioned to outcompete both a one-business domestic company and a one-business multinational company.

A DMNC's most potent advantages usually derive from technology sharing, economies of scope, shared brand names, and its potential to employ cross-subsidization tactics.

---

[22]Ibid., p. 64.
[23]Ibid.

ILLUSTRATION CAPSULE 25

MITSUBISHI: THE COMPETITIVE POWER OF A KEIRETSU

Mitsubishi is Japan's largest *keiretsu*—a family of affiliated companies. With combined 1992 sales of $175 billion, the Mitsubishi keiretsu consists of 28 core companies: Mitsubishi Corp. (the trading company), Mitsubishi Heavy Industries (the group's biggest manufacturer—shipbuilding, air conditioners, forklifts, robots, gas turbines), Mitsubishi Motors, Mitsubishi Steel, Mitsubishi Aluminum, Mitsubishi Oil, Mitsubishi Petrochemical, Mitsubishi Gas Chemical, Mitsubishi Plastics, Mitsubishi Cable, Mitsubishi Electric, Mitsubishi Construction, Mitsubishi Paper Mills, Mitsubishi Mining and Cement, Mitsubishi Rayon, Nikon, Asahi Glass, Kirin Brewery, Mitsubishi Bank (the world's fifth largest bank and the lead bank for family companies), Tokio Marine and Fire Insurance (one of the world's largest insurance companies), and eight others. Beyond this core group are hundreds of other Mitsubishi-related subsidiaries and affiliates.

The 28 core companies of the Mitsubishi keiretsu are bound together by cross-ownership of each other's stock (the percentage of shares of each core company owned by other members ranges from 17% to 100%, with an average of 27%), by interlocking directorships (it is standard for officers of one company to sit on the boards of other keiretsu members), joint ventures, and long-term business relationships. They use each other's products and services in many instances—among the suppliers to Mitsubishi Motor's Diamond Star plant in Bloomington, Illinois, are 25 Mitsubishi and Mitsubishi-related suppliers. It is common for them to join forces to make acquisitions—five Mitsubishi companies teamed to buy a cement plant in California; Mitsubishi Corp. bought an $880 million chemical company in Pittsburgh with financial assistance from Mitsubishi Bank and Mitsubishi Trust, then sold pieces to Mitsubishi Gas Chemical, Mitsubishi Rayon, Mitsubishi Petrochemical, and Mitsubishi Kasei. Mitsubishi Bank and occasionally other Mitsubishi financial enterprises serve as a primary financing source for new ventures and as a financial safety net if keiretsu members encounter tough market conditions or have financial problems.

Despite these links, there's no grand Mitsubishi strategy. Each company operates independently, pursuing its own strategy and markets. On occasion, group members find themselves going after the same markets competing with each other. Nor do member companies usually get sweetheart deals from other members; for example, Mitsubishi Heavy Industries lost out to Siemens in competing to supply gas turbines to a new power plant that Mitsubishi Corp.'s wholly owned Diamond Energy subsidiary constructed in Virginia. But operating independence does not prevent them from recognizing their mutual interests, cooperating voluntarily without formal controls, or turning inward to

(continued)

technology-transfer opportunities and where there are important economies of scope and brand name benefits associated with competing in related product families.

A DMNC also has important cross-subsidization potential for winning its way into attractive new markets. However, while DMNCs have significant cross-subsidization powers, they rarely use them in the extreme. It is one thing to use a *portion* of the profits and cash flows from existing businesses to cover reasonable short-term losses to gain entry to a new business or a new country market; it is quite another to drain corporate profits indiscriminately (and thus impair overall company performance) to support either deep price discounting and quick market penetration in the short term or continuing losses over the longer term. At some juncture, every business and every market entered has to make a profit contribution or become a candidate for abandonment. Moreover, the company has to wring consistently acceptable overall performance from the whole business portfolio. So there are limits to cross-subsidization. As a general rule, cross-subsidization is justified only if there is a good chance that short-term losses can be amply recouped in some way over the long term.

(concluded)

keiretsu members for business partnerships on ventures perceived as strategically important.

A President's Council, consisting of 49 chairmen and presidents, meets monthly, usually the second Friday of the month. While the formal agenda typically includes a discussion of joint philanthropical and public relations projects and a lecture by an expert on some current topic, participants report instances where strategic problems or opportunities affecting several group members are discussed and major decisions made. It is common for a Mitsubishi company involved in a major undertaking (initiating its first foray into the U.S. or European markets or developing a new technology) to ask for support from other members. In such cases, group members who can take business actions that contribute to solutions are expected to do so. The President's Council meetings also serve to cement personal ties, exchange information, identify mutual interests, and set up follow-on actions by subordinates. Other ways that Mitsubishi uses to foster an active informal network of contacts, information sharing, cooperation, and business relationships among member companies include regular get-togethers of Mitsubishi-America and Mitsubishi-Europe executives and even a matchmaking club where member company employees can meet prospective spouses.

In recent years, Mitsubishi companies introduced a number of consumer products in the U.S. and elsewhere, all branded with a three-diamond logo derived from the crest of the founding samurai family—cars and trucks made by Mitsubishi Motors, big-screen TVs and mobile phones made by Mitsubishi Electric, and air conditioners produced by Mitsubishi Heavy Industries. Mitsubishi executives believe common logo usage has produced added brand awareness; for example, in the U.S. Mitsubishi Motors' efforts to advertise and market its cars and trucks helped boost brand awareness of Mitsubishi TVs. In several product categories one or more Mitsubishi companies operate in stages all along the industry value chain—from components production to assembly to shipping, warehousing, and distribution.

Similar practices exist in the other five of the six largest Japanese keiretsu: Dai-Ichi Kangin with 47 core companies, Mitsui Group with 24 core companies (including Toyota and Toshiba), Sanwa with 44 core companies, Sumitomo with 20 core companies (including NEC, a maker of telecommunications equipment and personal computers), and Fuyo with 29 core companies (including Nissan and Canon). Most observers agree that Japan's keiretsu model gives Japanese companies major competitive advantages in international markets. According to a Japanese economics professor at Osaka University, "Using group power, they can engage in cutthroat competition."

Source: Based on information in "Mighty Mitsubishi Is on the Move" and "Hands across America: The Rise of Mitsubishi," *Business Week,* September 24, 1990, pp. 98–107.

COMBINATION DIVERSIFICATION STRATEGIES

The six corporate diversification approaches described above are not mutually exclusive. They can be pursued in combination and in varying sequences, allowing ample room for companies to customize their diversification strategies to fit their own circumstances. The most common business portfolios created by corporate diversification strategies are

- A dominant-business enterprise with sales concentrated in one major core business but with a modestly diversified portfolio of either related or unrelated businesses (amounting to one-third or less of total corporatewide sales).
- A narrowly diversified enterprise having a *few* (two to five) *related core* business units.
- A broadly diversified enterprise made up of *many* mostly *related* business units.
- A narrowly diversified enterprise composed of a *few* (two to five) *core* business units in *unrelated* industries.

- A broadly diversified enterprise having *many* business units in mostly *unrelated* industries.
- A multibusiness enterprise that has diversified into unrelated areas but that has a portfolio of related businesses within each area—thus giving it *several unrelated groups of related businesses.*

In each case, the geographic markets of individual businesses within the portfolio can range from local to regional to national to multinational to global. Thus, a company can be competing locally in some businesses, nationally in others, and globally in still others.

KEY POINTS

Most companies have their business roots in a single industry. Even though they may have since diversified into other industries, a substantial part of their revenues and profits still usually comes from the original or core business. Diversification becomes an attractive strategy when a company runs out of profitable growth opportunities in its core business (including any opportunities to integrate backward or forward to strengthen its competitive position). The purpose of diversification is to build shareholder value. Diversification builds shareholder value when a diversified group of businesses can perform better under the auspices of a single corporate parent than they would as independent, stand-alone businesses. Whether a particular diversification move is capable of increasing shareholder value hinges on the attractiveness test, the cost-of-entry test, and the better-off test.

There are two fundamental approaches to diversification—into related businesses and into unrelated businesses. The rationale for related diversification is *strategic:* diversify into businesses with strategic fit, capitalize on strategic-fit relationships to gain competitive advantage, then use competitive advantage to achieve the desired 2 + 2 = 5 impact on shareholder value. Businesses have strategic fit when their value chains offer potential (1) for realizing economies of scope or cost-saving efficiencies associated with sharing technology, facilities, functional activities, distribution outlets, or brand names; (2) for skills transfers or technology transfers; and/or (3) for added differentiation. Such competitive advantage potentials can exist anywhere along the value chains of related businesses.

The basic premise of unrelated diversification is that any business that has good profit prospects and can be acquired on good financial terms is a good business to diversify into. Unrelated diversification is basically a *financial* approach to diversification; strategic fit is a secondary consideration compared to the expectation of financial gain. Unrelated diversification surrenders the competitive advantage potential of strategic fit in return for such advantages as (1) spreading business risk over a variety of industries and (2) gaining opportunities for quick financial gain (if candidate acquisitions have undervalued assets, are bargain-priced and have good upside potential given the right management, or need the backing of a financially strong parent to capitalize on attractive opportunities). In theory, unrelated diversification also offers greater earnings stability over the business cycle, a third advantage. However, achieving these three outcomes consistently requires corporate executives who are smart enough to avoid the considerable disadvantages of unrelated diversification. The greater the number of businesses a conglomerate company is in and the more diverse these businesses are, the more that corporate executives are stretched to know enough about each business to distinguish a good acquisition from a risky one, select capable managers to run each business, know when the major strategic proposals of business units are sound, or wisely decide what to do when a business unit stumbles. Unless corporate managers are exceptionally shrewd and talented, unrelated diversification is a dubious and unreliable approach to building shareholder value when compared to related diversification.

Once diversification is accomplished, corporate management's task is to manage the firm's business portfolio for maximum long-term performance. There are six different strategic options for improving a diversified company's performance: (1) make new acquisitions, (2) divest weak-performing business units or those that no longer fit, (3) restructure the makeup of the portfolio when overall performance is poor and future prospects are bleak, (4) retrench to a narrower diversification base, (5) pursue multinational diversification, and (6) liquidate money-losing businesses with poor turnaround potential.

The most popular option for getting out of a business that is unattractive or doesn't fit is to sell it—ideally to a buyer for whom the business has attractive fit. Sometimes a business can be divested by spinning it off as a financially and managerially independent enterprise in which the parent company may or may not retain an ownership interest.

Corporate turnaround, retrenchment, and restructuring strategies are used when corporate management has to restore an ailing business portfolio to good health. Poor performance can be caused by large losses in one or more businesses that pull overall corporate performance down, by too many business units in unattractive industries, by an excessive debt burden, or by ill-chosen acquisitions that haven't lived up to expectations. Corporate turnaround strategies aim at restoring money-losing businesses to profitability instead of divesting them. Retrenchment involves reducing the scope of diversification to a smaller number of businesses by divesting those that are too small to make a sizable contribution to corporate earnings or those that don't fit with the narrower business base on which corporate management wants to concentrate company resources and energies. Restructuring strategies involve radical portfolio shakeups, divestiture of some businesses and acquisition of others to create a group of businesses with much improved performance potential.

Multinational diversification strategies feature a diversity of businesses and a diversity of national markets. Despite the complexity of having to devise and manage so many strategies (at least one for each industry, with as many variations for country markets as may be needed), multinational diversification can be a competitively advantageous strategy. DMNCs can use the strategic-fit advantages of related diversification (economies of scope, skills transfer, and shared brand names) to build competitively strong positions in several related global industries simultaneously. Such advantages, if competently exploited, can allow a DMNC to outcompete a one-business domestic rival or a one-business multinational rival over time. A one-business domestic company has only one profit sanctuary—its home market. A single-business multinational company may have profit sanctuaries in several countries, but all are in the same business. Both are vulnerable to a DMNC that launches offensive campaigns in their profit sanctuaries. The DMNC can use its lower-cost advantage growing out of its economies of scope to underprice rivals and gain market share at their expense. Even without a cost advantage, the DMNC can decide to underprice such rivals and subsidize its lower profit margins (or even losses) with the profits earned in its other businesses. A well-financed and competently managed DMNC can sap the financial and competitive strength of one-business domestic-only and multi-national rivals. DMNCs have the biggest competitive advantage potential in industries with significant economies of scope, shared brand name benefits, and technology-sharing opportunities.

SUGGESTED READINGS

Buzzell, Robert D. "Is Vertical Integration Profitable?" *Harvard Business Review* 61, no. 1 (January–February 1983), pp. 92–102.

Goold, Michael, and Kathleen Luchs. "Why Diversify? Four Decades of Management Thinking." *Academy of Management Executive* 7, no. 3 (August 1993), pp. 7–25.

Harrigan, Kathryn R. "Matching Vertical Integration Strategies to Competitive Conditions." *Strategic Management Journal* 7, no. 6 (November–December 1986), pp. 535–56.

Hax, Arnoldo, and Nicolas S. Majluf. *The Strategy Concept and Process.* Englewood Cliffs, N.J.: Prentice-Hall, 1991, chaps. 9, 11, and 15.

Hofer, Charles W. "Turnaround Strategies." *Journal of Business Strategy* 1, no. 1 (Summer 1980), pp. 19–31.

Hoffman, Richard C. "Strategies for Corporate Turnarounds: What Do We Know about Them?" *Journal of General Management* 14, no. 3 (Spring 1989), pp. 46–66.

Kumpe, Ted, and Piet T. Bolwijn. "Manufacturing: The New Case for Vertical Integration." *Harvard Business Review* 88, no. 2 (March–April 1988), pp. 75–82.

Ohmae, Kenichi. *The Mind of the Strategist.* New York: Penguin Books, 1983, chaps. 10 and 12.

Prahalad, C. K., and Yves L. Doz. *The Multinational Mission.* New York: Free Press, 1987, chaps. 1 and 2.

CHAPTER EIGHT

STRATEGIC ANALYSIS OF DIVERSIFIED COMPANIES

If we can know where we are and something about how we got there, we might see where we are trending—and if the outcomes which lie naturally in our course are unacceptable, to make timely change.

Abraham Lincoln

No company can afford everything it would like to do. Resources have to be allocated. The essence of strategic planning is to allocate resources to those areas that have the greatest future potential.

Reginald Jones

Once a company diversifies, three strategic issues emerge to challenge corporate strategy-makers:

- How attractive is the group of businesses the company is in?
- Assuming the company sticks with its present lineup of businesses, how good is its performance outlook in the years ahead?
- If the previous two answers are not satisfactory, what should the company do to get out of some businesses, strengthen the positions of remaining businesses, and get into new businesses to boost the performance prospects of its business portfolio?

Crafting and implementing action plans to improve the attractiveness and competitive strength of a company's business-unit portfolio is the heart of corporate-level strategic management.

Strategic analysis of diversified companies builds on the concepts and methods used for single-business companies. But there are also new aspects to consider and additional analytical approaches to master. To evaluate the strategy of a diversified company, assess the caliber and potential of its businesses, and decide what strategic actions to take next, managers need to adhere closely to the following eight-step procedure:

1. Identify the present corporate strategy.
2. Construct one or more business portfolio matrices to reveal the character of the company's business portfolio.
3. Compare the long-term attractiveness of each industry the company is in.
4. Compare the competitive strength of the company's business units to see which ones are strong contenders in their respective industries.
5. Rate each business unit on the basis of its historical performance and future prospects.
6. Assess each business unit's compatibility with corporate strategy and determine the value of any strategic-fit relationships among existing business units.
7. Rank the business units in terms of priority for new capital investment and decide whether the strategic posture for each business unit should be aggressive expansion, fortify and defend, overhaul and reposition, or harvest/divest. (The task of initiating *specific* business-unit strategies to improve the business unit's competitive position is usually delegated to business-level managers, with corporate-level managers offering suggestions and having authority for final approval.)
8. Craft new strategic moves to improve overall corporate performance— change the makeup of the portfolio via acquisitions and divestitures, improve coordination among the activities of related business units to achieve greater cost-sharing and skills-transfer benefits, and steer corporate resources into the areas of greatest opportunity.

The rest of this chapter describes this eight-step process and introduces analytical techniques needed to arrive at sound corporate strategy appraisals.

IDENTIFYING THE PRESENT CORPORATE STRATEGY

Evaluating a diversified firm's business portfolio needs to begin with a clear identification of the firm's diversification strategy.

Strategic analysis of a diversified company starts by probing the organization's present strategy and business makeup. Recall from Figure 2–2 in Chapter 2 that a good overall perspective of a diversified company's corporate strategy comes from looking at

- The extent to which the firm is diversified (as measured by the proportion of total sales and operating profits contributed by each business unit and by whether the diversification base is broad or narrow).
- Whether the firm's portfolio is keyed to related or unrelated diversification, or a mixture of both.
- Whether the scope of company operations is mostly domestic, increasingly multinational, or global.
- The nature of recent moves to boost performance of key business units and/or strengthen existing business positions.
- Any moves to add new businesses to the portfolio and build positions in new industries.
- Any moves to divest weak or unattractive business units.
- Management efforts to realize the benefits of strategic-fit relationships and use diversification to create competitive advantage.
- The proportion of capital expenditures going to each business unit.

Getting a clear fix on the current corporate strategy and its rationale sets the stage for a thorough strategy analysis and, subsequently, for making whatever refinements or major alterations management deems appropriate.

MATRIX TECHNIQUES FOR EVALUATING DIVERSIFIED PORTFOLIOS

One of the most-used techniques for assessing the quality of a diversified company's businesses is portfolio matrix analysis. *A business portfolio matrix* is a two-dimensional display comparing the strategic positions of each business a diversified company is in. Matrices can be constructed using any pair of strategic position indicators. The most revealing indicators are industry growth rate, market share, long-term industry attractiveness, competitive strength, and stage of product/market evolution. Usually one dimension of the matrix relates to the attractiveness of the industry environment and the other to the strength of a business within the industry. Three types of business portfolio matrices are used most frequently—the growth-share matrix developed by the Boston Consulting Group, the industry attractiveness–business strength matrix pioneered at General Electric, and the Hofer–A. D. Little industry life-cycle matrix.

> A business portfolio matrix is a two-dimensional display comparing the strategic positions of every business a diversified company is in.

THE GROWTH-SHARE MATRIX

The first business portfolio matrix to receive widespread use was a four-square grid devised by the Boston Consulting Group (BCG), a leading management consulting firm.[1] Figure 8–1 illustrates a BCG-type matrix. The matrix is formed using *industry growth rate* and *relative market share* as the axes. Each business unit in the corporate portfolio appears as a "bubble" on the four-cell matrix, with the size of each bubble or circle scaled to the percent of revenues it represents in the overall corporate portfolio.

> The BCG portfolio matrix compares a diversified company's businesses on the basis of industry growth rate and relative market share.

Early BCG methodology arbitrarily placed the dividing line between "high" and "low" industry growth rates at around twice the real GNP growth rate plus inflation, but the boundary can be set at any percentage (5 percent, 10 percent, or whatever) managers consider appropriate. Business units in industries growing faster than the economy as a whole should end up in the "high-growth" cells and those in industries growing slower in the "low-growth" cells ("low-growth" industries are those that are mature, aging, stagnant, or declining). Rarely does it make sense to put the dividing line between high growth and low growth at less than 5 percent.

Relative market share is the ratio of a business's market share to the market share held by the largest rival firm in the industry, with market share measured in unit volume, not dollars. For instance, if business A has a 15 percent share of its industry's total volume and A's largest rival has 30 percent, A's relative market share is 0.5. If business B has a market-leading share of 40 percent and its largest rival has 30 percent, B's relative market share is 1.33. Given this definition, only business units that are market share leaders in their respective industries will have relative market shares

---

[1]The original presentation is Bruce D. Henderson, "The Experience Curve—Reviewed. IV. The Growth Share Matrix of the Product Portfolio" (Boston: The Boston Consulting Group, 1973), Perspectives No. 135. For an excellent chapter-length treatment of the use of the BCG growth-share matrix in strategic portfolio analysis, see Arnoldo C. Hax and Nicolas S. Majluf, *Strategic Management: An Integrative Perspective* (Englewood Cliffs, N.J.: Prentice-Hall, 1984), chapter 7.

FIGURE 8–1 | **The BCG Growth-Share Business Portfolio Matrix**

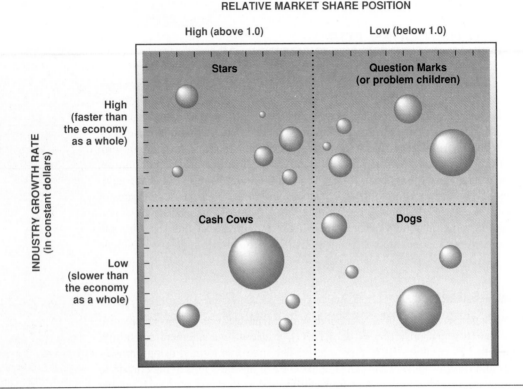

Note: *Relative* market share is defined by the ratio of a company's own market share to the market share held by its largest rival. When the vertical dividing line is set at 1.0, the only way a firm can achieve a star or cash cow position in the growth-share matrix is to have the largest market share in the industry. Since this is a very stringent criterion, it may be "fairer" and more revealing to locate the vertical dividing line in the matrix at about 0.75 or 0.80.

greater than 1.0. Business units that trail rivals in market share will have ratios below 1.0.

BCG's original standard put the border between "high" and "low" relative market share at 1.0, as shown in Figure 8–1. When the boundary is set at 1.0, circles in the two left-side cells of the matrix represent businesses that are market share leaders in their industries. Circles in the two right-side cells identify businesses that are runners-up in their industries. The degree to which they trail is indicated by the size of the relative market share ratio. A ratio of .10 indicates that the business has a market share only one-tenth that of the largest firm in the market; a ratio of .80 indicates a market share four-fifths or 80 percent as big as the leading firm's. Many portfolio analysts think that putting the boundary between high and low relative market share at 1.0 is unreasonably stringent because only businesses with the largest market share in their industry qualify for the two left-side cells of the matrix. They advocate putting the boundary at about 0.75 or 0.80 so businesses to the left have *strong* or above-average market positions (even though they are not *the* leader) and businesses to the right are clearly in underdog or below-average positions.

Using *relative* market share instead of *actual* market share to construct the growth-share matrix is analytically superior because the former measure is a better indicator of comparative market strength and competitive position. A 10 percent market share is much stronger if the leader's share is 12 percent than if it is 50 percent; the use of relative market share captures this difference. Equally important, relative market share is likely to reflect relative cost based on experience in producing the product and economies of large-scale production. Large businesses may be able to operate at lower unit costs than smaller firms because of technological and efficiency gains that attach to larger size. But the Boston Consulting Group accumulated evidence that the phenomenon of lower unit costs went beyond just the effects of scale economies; they found that, as the cumulative volume of production increased, the knowledge gained from the firm's growing production experience often led to the discovery of additional efficiencies and ways to reduce costs even further. BCG labeled the relationship between *cumulative production volume* and lower unit costs *the experience curve effect* (for more details, see Figure 3–1 in Chapter 3). A sizable experience curve effect in an industry's value chain places a strategic premium on market share: the competitor that gains the largest market share tends to realize important cost advantages which, in turn, can be used to lower prices and gain still additional customers, sales, market share, and profit. The stronger the experience curve effect in a business, the more dominant its role in strategy-making.[2]

> Relative market share is a better indicator of a business's competitive strength and market position than a simple percentage measure of market share.

With these features of the BCG growth-share matrix in mind, we are ready to explore the portfolio implications for businesses in each cell of the matrix in Figure 8–1.

Question Marks and Problem Children   Business units in the upper-right quadrant of the growth-share matrix were labeled by BCG as "question marks" or "problem children." Rapid market growth makes such business units attractive from an industry standpoint. But their low relative market share (and thus reduced access to experience curve effects) raises a question about whether they have the strength to compete successfully against larger, more cost-efficient rivals—hence, the question mark or problem child designation. Question mark businesses, moreover, are typically "cash hogs"—so labeled because their cash needs are high (owing to the large investment needed to finance rapid growth and new product development) and their internal cash generation is low (owing to low market share, less access to experience curve effects and scale economies, and consequently thinner profit margins). A question mark/cash hog business in a fast-growing industry may require large infusions of cash just to keep up with rapid market growth—and even bigger cash infusions if it must outgrow the market and gain enough market share to become an industry leader. The corporate parent of a cash hog/question mark has to decide whether it is worthwhile to fund the perhaps considerable investment requirements of such a business.

> A "cash hog" business is one whose internal cash flows are inadequate to fully fund its needs for working capital and new capital investment.

BCG has argued that the two best strategic options for a question mark business are (1) an aggressive invest-and-expand strategy to capitalize on the industry's rapid-growth opportunities or (2) divestiture, in the event that the costs of expanding capacity and building market share outweigh the potential payoff and financial risk. Pursuit of a fast-growth strategy is imperative any time an attractive question mark business is in an industry characterized by a strong experience curve effect; in such

---

[2]For two insightful discussions of the strategic importance of the experience curve, see Pankoy Ghemawat, "Building Strategy on the Experience Curve," *Harvard Business Review* 64, no. 2 (March–April 1985), pp. 143–49, and Bruce D. Henderson, "The Application and Misapplication of the Experience Curve," *Journal of Business Strategy* 4, no. 3 (Winter 1984), pp. 3–9.

cases it takes major gains in market share to begin to match the lower costs of firms with greater cumulative production experience and bigger market shares. The stronger the experience curve effect, the more potent the cost advantages of rivals with larger relative market shares. Consequently, so the BCG thesis goes, unless a question mark/problem child business can successfully pursue a fast-growth strategy and win major market share gains, it cannot hope to become cost competitive with large-volume firms that are further down the experience curve. Divestiture then becomes the only other viable long-run alternative. BCG's corporate strategy prescriptions for question mark/problem child businesses are straightforward: divest those that are weaker and have less chance to catch the leaders on the experience curve; invest heavily in high-potential question marks and groom them to become tomorrow's "stars."

Stars   Businesses with high relative market share positions in high-growth markets rank as stars in the BCG grid because they offer excellent profit and growth opportunities. They are the business units an enterprise depends on to boost overall performance of the total portfolio.

Given their dominant market-share position and rapid growth environment, stars typically require large cash investments to expand production facilities and meet working capital needs. But they also tend to generate their own large internal cash flows due to the low-cost advantage of scale economies and cumulative production experience. Star businesses vary as to their cash hog status. Some can cover their investment needs with self-generated cash flows; others require capital infusions from their corporate parents to stay abreast of rapid industry growth. Normally, strongly positioned star businesses in industries where growth is beginning to slow tend to be self-sustaining in terms of cash flow and make little claim on the corporate parent's treasury. Young stars, however, typically require substantial investment capital *beyond what they can generate on their own* and are thus cash hogs.

Cash Cows   Businesses with a high relative market share in a low growth market are designated "cash cows" in the BCG scheme. A *cash cow business* generates substantial cash surpluses over what is needed for reinvestment and growth. There are two reasons why a business in this box tends to be a cash cow. Because of the business's high relative market share and industry leadership position, it has the sales volumes and reputation to earn attractive profits. Because it is in a slow-growth industry, cash flows from current operations typically exceed what is needed for capital reinvestment and competitive maneuvers to sustain its present market position.

Many of today's cash cows are yesterday's stars, having gradually moved down on the vertical scale (dropping from the top cell into the bottom cell) as industry demand matured. Cash cows, though less attractive from a growth standpoint, are valuable businesses. The surplus cash flows they generate can be used to pay corporate dividends, finance acquisitions, and provide funds for investing in emerging stars and problem children being groomed as future stars. Every effort should be made to keep strong cash cow businesses in healthy condition to preserve their cash-generating capability over the long term. The goal should be to fortify and defend a cash cow's market position while efficiently generating dollars to redeploy elsewhere. Weakening cash cows (those drifting toward the lower right corner of the cash cow cell) may become candidates for harvesting and eventual divestiture if stiffer competition or increased capital requirements (stemming from new technology) cause cash flow surpluses to dry up or, in the worst case, become negative.

The standard strategy prescriptions for a "question mark" business are to either invest aggressively and grow it into a star performer or else divest it and shift resources to businesses with better prospects.

"Star" businesses have strong competitive positions in rapidly growing industries, are major contributors to corporate revenue and profit growth, and may or may not be cash hogs.

A "cash cow" business is a valuable part of a diversified company's business portfolio because it generates cash for financing new acquisitions, funding the capital requirements of cash hog businesses, and paying dividends.

Dogs   Businesses with a low relative market share in a slow-growth industry are called "dogs" because of their dim growth prospects, their trailing market position, and the squeeze that trailing the experience curve leaders puts on their profit margins. Weak dog businesses (those positioned in the lower right corner of the dog cell) often cannot generate attractive long-term cash flows. Sometimes they cannot produce enough cash to support a rear-guard fortify-and-defend strategy—especially if competition is brutal and profit margins are chronically thin. Consequently, except in unusual cases, BCG prescribes that weaker-performing dog businesses be harvested, divested, or liquidated, depending on which alternative yields the most cash.

Weaker "dog" businesses should be harvested, divested, or liquidated; stronger dogs can be retained as long as their profits and cash flows remain acceptable.

Implications for Corporate Strategy   The chief contribution of the BCG growth-share matrix is the attention it draws to the cash flow and investment characteristics of various types of businesses and how corporate financial resources can be shifted between business subsidiaries to optimize the performance of the whole corporate portfolio. According to BCG analysis, a sound, long-term corporate strategy should utilize the excess cash generated by cash cow business units to finance market share increases for cash hog businesses—the young stars unable to finance their own growth internally and problem children with the best potential to grow into stars. If successful, the cash hogs eventually become self-supporting stars. Then, when stars' markets begin to mature and their growth slows, they become cash cows. The "success sequence" is thus problem child/question mark to young star (but perhaps still a cash hog) to self-supporting star to cash cow.

The BCG growth-share matrix highlights the cash flow, investment, and profitability characteristics of various types of businesses and the benefits of shifting a diversified company's financial resources between them to optimize the whole portfolio's performance.

Weaker, less-attractive question mark businesses unworthy of a long-term invest-and-expand strategy are often a liability to a diversified company because of the high cost economics associated with their low relative market share and because their cash hog nature typically requires the corporate parent to keep pumping more capital into the business to keep abreast of fast-paced market growth. According to BCG prescriptions, weaker question marks should be prime divestiture candidates *unless* (1) they can be kept profitable and viable with their own internally generated funds or (2) the capital infusions needed from the corporate parent are quite modest.

Not every question mark business is a cash hog or a disadvantaged competitor, however. Those in industries with small capital requirements, few scale economies, and weak experience curve effects can often compete ably against larger industry leaders and contribute enough to corporate earnings and return on investment to justify retention. Clearly, though, weaker question marks still have a low-priority claim on corporate resources and a tenuous role in the portfolio. Question mark businesses unable to become stars are destined to drift vertically downward in the matrix, becoming dogs as their industry growth slows and market demand matures.

Dogs should be retained only as long as they contribute adequately to overall company performance. Strong dogs may produce a positive cash flow and show average profitability. But the further a dog business moves toward the bottom right corner of the BCG matrix, the more likely it is tying up assets that could be redeployed more profitably elsewhere. BCG recommends harvesting a weakening or already weak dog. When a harvesting strategy is no longer attractive, a weak dog should be eliminated from the portfolio.

There are two "disaster sequences" in the BCG scheme of things: (1) when a star's position in the matrix erodes over time to that of a problem child and then is dragged by slowing industry growth into the dog category and (2) when a cash cow loses market leadership to the point where it becomes a dog on the decline. Other strategic mistakes include overinvesting in a safe cash cow; underinvesting in a high-potential question mark so instead of moving into the star category it tumbles into a dog; and scattering resources thinly over many question marks rather than concentrating on the best question marks to boost their chances of becoming stars.

Strengths and Weaknesses in the Growth-Share Matrix Approach   The BCG business portfolio matrix makes a definite contribution to the corporate strategist's toolkit when it comes to evaluating the attractiveness of a diversified company's businesses and devising general prescriptions for strategy and direction for each business unit in the portfolio. Viewing a diversified group of businesses as a collection of cash flows and cash requirements (present and future) is a major step forward in understanding the financial aspects of corporate strategy. The BCG matrix highlights the financial interaction within a corporate portfolio, shows the kinds of financial considerations that must be dealt with, and explains why priorities for corporate resource allocation can differ from business to business. It also provides good rationalizations for both invest-and-expand strategies and divestiture. Yet, it is analytically incomplete and potentially misleading:

> *The growth-share matrix has significant shortcomings.*

1. A four-cell matrix based on high-low classifications hides the fact that many businesses (the majority?) are in markets with an average growth rate and have relative market shares that are neither high nor low but in between or intermediate. In which cells do these average businesses belong?

2. While viewing businesses as stars, cash cows, dogs, or question marks does have communicative appeal, it is a misleading simplification to classify all businesses into one of four categories. Some market-share leaders are never really stars in terms of profitability. All businesses with low relative market shares are not dogs or question marks—in many cases, runner-up firms have proven track records in terms of growth, profitability, and competitive ability, even gaining on the so-called leaders. Hence, a key characteristic to assess is the *trend* in a firm's relative market share. Is it gaining ground or losing ground and why? This weakness of the matrix can be solved by placing directional arrows on each of the circles in the matrix—see Figure 8–2.

3. The BCG matrix is not a reliable indicator of relative investment opportunities across business units.[3] For example, investing in a star is not necessarily more attractive than investing in a lucrative cash cow. The matrix doesn't indicate if a question mark business is a potential winner or a likely loser. It says nothing about whether shrewd investment can turn a strong dog into a cash cow.

4. Being a market leader in a slow-growth industry does not guarantee cash cow status because *(a)* the investment requirements of a fortify-and-defend strategy, given the impact of inflation and changing technology on the costs of replacing worn-out facilities and equipment, can soak up much or all of the available internal cash flows and *(b)* as markets mature, competitive forces often stiffen and the ensuing vigorous battle for volume and market share can shrink profit margins and wipe out any surplus cash flows.

5. To thoroughly assess the relative long-term attractiveness of a group of businesses, corporate strategists need to examine more than just industry growth and relative market share—as our discussion in Chapter 3 clearly indicated.

[3]Derek F. Abell and John S. Hammond, *Strategic Market Planning* (Englewood Cliffs, N.J.: Prentice-Hall, 1979), p. 212.

F I G U R E 8-2 | **Present versus Future Positions in the Portfolio Matrix**

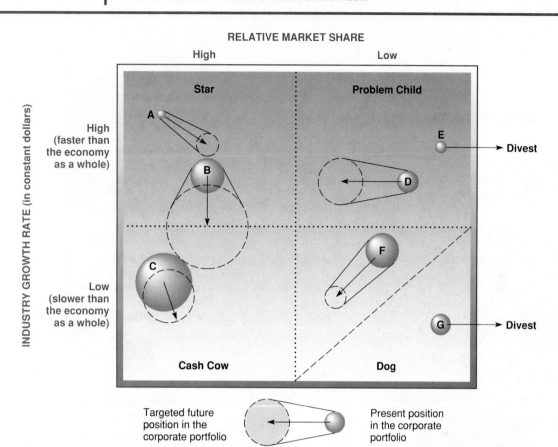

6. The connection between relative market share and profitability is not as tight as the experience curve effect implies. The importance of cumulative production experience in lowering unit costs varies from industry to industry. Sometimes, a larger market share translates into a unit-cost advantage; sometimes it doesn't. Hence, it is wise to be cautious when prescribing strategy based on the assumption that experience curve effects are strong enough and cost differences among competitors big enough to totally drive competitive advantage (there are more sources of competitive advantage than just experience curve economics).

THE INDUSTRY ATTRACTIVENESS–BUSINESS STRENGTH MATRIX

An alternative approach that avoids some of the shortcomings of the BCG growth-share matrix was pioneered by General Electric with help from the consulting firm of McKinsey and Company. GE's effort to analyze its broadly diversified portfolio produced a nine-cell matrix based on the two dimensions of long-term industry attractiveness and business strength/competitive position (see Figure 8–3).[4] Both dimensions of

In the attractiveness-strength matrix, each business's location is plotted using quantitative measures of long-term industry attractiveness and business strength/competitive position.

[4]For an expanded treatment, see Michael G. Allen, "Diagramming GE's Planning for What's WATT," in *Corporate Planning: Techniques and Applications,* ed. Robert J. Allio and Malcolm W. Pennington (New York: AMACOM, 1979), and Hax and Majluf, *Strategic Management: An Integrative Perspective,* chapter 8.

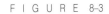 **General Electric's Industry Attractiveness–Business Strength Matrix**

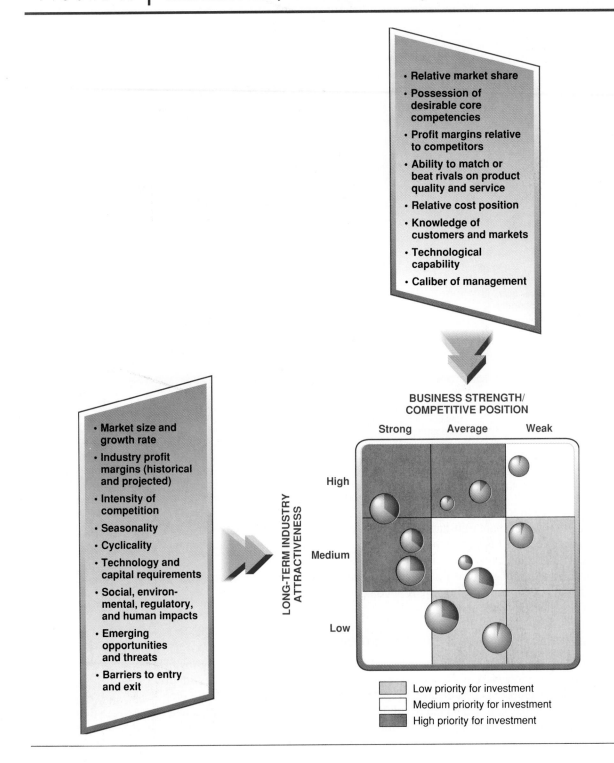

the matrix are a composite of several factors as opposed to a single factor. The criteria for determining long-term industry attractiveness include market size and growth rate; technological requirements; the intensity of competition; entry and exit barriers; seasonality and cyclical influences; capital requirements; emerging industry threats and opportunities; historical and projected industry profitability; and social, environmental, and regulatory influences. To arrive at a formal, quantitative measure of long-term industry attractiveness, the chosen measures are assigned weights based on their importance to corporate management and their role in the diversification strategy. The sum of the weights must add up to 1.0. Weighted attractiveness ratings are calculated by multiplying the industry's rating on each factor (using a 1 to 5 or 1 to 10 rating scale) by the factor's weight. For example, a rating score of 8 times a weight of .25 gives a weighted rating of 2.0. The sum of weighted ratings for all the attractiveness factors yields the industry's long-term attractiveness. The procedure is shown below:

Industry Attractiveness Factor	Weight	Rating	Weighted Industry Rating
Market size and projected growth	.15	5	0.75
Seasonality and cyclical influences	.10	8	0.80
Technological considerations	.10	1	0.10
Intensity of competition	.25	4	1.00
Emerging opportunities and threats	.15	1	0.15
Capital requirements	.05	2	0.10
Industry profitability	.10	3	0.30
Social, political, regulatory, and environmental factors	.10	7	0.70
Industry Attractiveness Rating	1.00		3.90

Attractiveness ratings are calculated for each industry represented in the corporate portfolio. Each industry's attractiveness score determines its position on the vertical scale in Figure 8–3.

To arrive at a quantitative measure of business strength/competitive position, each business in the corporate portfolio is rated using the same kind of approach as for industry attractiveness. The factors used to assess business strength/competitive position include such criteria as market share, relative cost position, ability to match rival firms on product quality, knowledge of customers and markets, possession of desirable core competencies, adequacy of technological know-how, caliber of management, and profitability relative to competitors (as specified in the box in Figure 8–3). Analysts have a choice between rating each business unit on the same generic factors (which strengthens the basis for interindustry comparisons) or rating each business unit's strength on the factors most pertinent to its industry (which gives a sharper measure of competitive position than a generic set of factors). Each business's strength/position rating determines its position along the horizontal axis of the matrix—that is, whether it merits a strong, average, or weak designation.[5]

---

[5]Essentially the same procedure is used in company situation analysis to do a competitive strength assessment (see Table 4–3 in Chapter 4). The only difference is that in the GE methodology the same set of competitive strength factors is used for every industry to provide a common benchmark for making comparisons across industries. In strategic analysis at the business level, the strength measures are *always* industry specific, never generic generalizations.

The industry attractiveness and business strength scores provide the basis for locating a business in one of the nine cells of the matrix. In the GE attractiveness-strength matrix, the area of the circles is proportional to the size of the industry, and the pie slices within the circle reflect the business's market share.

Corporate Strategy Implications   The most important strategic implications from the attractiveness-strength matrix concern the assignment of investment priorities to each of the company's business units. Businesses in the three cells at the upper left, where long-term industry attractiveness and business strength/competitive position are favorable, are accorded top investment priority. The strategic prescription for businesses falling in these three cells is "grow and build," with businesses in the high-strong cell having the highest claim on investment funds. Next in priority come businesses positioned in the three diagonal cells stretching from the lower left to the upper right. These businesses are usually given medium priority. They merit steady reinvestment to maintain and protect their industry positions; however, if such a business has an unusually attractive opportunity, it can win a higher investment priority and be given the go-ahead to employ a more aggressive strategic approach. The strategy prescription for businesses in the three cells in the lower right corner of the matrix is typically harvest or divest (in exceptional cases where good turnaround potential exists, it can be "overhaul and reposition" using some type of turnaround approach).[6]

The nine-cell attractiveness-strength approach has three desirable attributes. First, it allows for intermediate rankings between high and low and between strong and weak. Second, it incorporates explicit consideration of a much wider variety of strategically relevant variables. The BCG matrix is based on only two considerations—industry growth rate and relative market share; the nine-cell GE matrix takes many factors into account to determine long-term industry attractiveness and business strength/competitive position. Third, and most important, the nine-cell matrix stresses the channeling of corporate resources to businesses with the greatest probability of achieving competitive advantage and superior performance. It is hard to argue against the logic of concentrating resources in those businesses that enjoy a higher degree of attractiveness and competitive strength, being very selective in making investments in businesses with intermediate positions, and withdrawing resources from businesses that are lower in attractiveness and strength unless they offer exceptional turnaround potential.

However, the nine-cell GE matrix, like the four-cell growth-share matrix, provides no real guidance on the specifics of business strategy; the most that can be concluded from the GE matrix analysis is what *general* strategic posture to take: aggressive expansion, fortify and defend, or harvest-divest. Such prescriptions, though valuable from an overall portfolio management perspective, ignore the issue of strategic coordination across related businesses as well as the issue of what specific competitive approaches and strategic actions to take at the business-unit level. Another weakness is that the attractiveness-strength matrix effectively hides businesses that are about to emerge as winners because their industries are entering the takeoff stage.[7]

The nine-cell attractiveness-strength matrix has a stronger conceptual basis than the four-cell growth-share matrix.

---

[6]At General Electric, each business actually ended up in one of five types of categories: (1) *high-growth potential* businesses deserving top investment priority, (2) *stable base* businesses deserving steady reinvestment to maintain position, (3) *support* businesses deserving periodic investment funding, (4) *selective pruning or rejuvenation* businesses deserving reduced investment funding, and (5) *venture* businesses deserving heavy R&D investment.

[7]Charles W. Hofer and Dan Schendel, *Strategy Formulation: Analytical Concepts* (St. Paul, Minn.: West Publishing, 1978), p. 33.

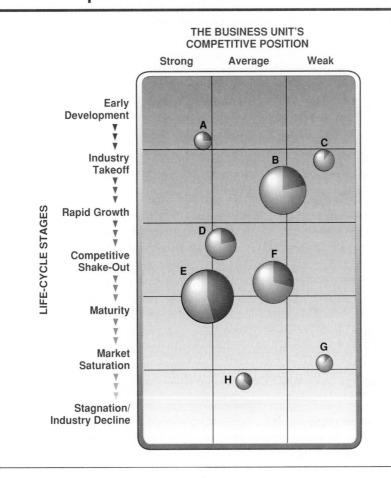

THE LIFE-CYCLE MATRIX

To better identify a *developing winner* business, analysts can use a 15-cell matrix where business units are plotted based on stage of industry evolution and strength of competitive position, as shown in Figure 8–4.[8] Again, the circles represent the sizes of the industries involved, and pie wedges denote the business's market share. In Figure 8–4, business A could be labeled a *developing winner;* business C a *potential loser,* business E an *established winner,* business F a cash cow, and business G a loser or a dog. The power of the life-cycle matrix is the story it tells about the distribution of a diversified company's businesses across the stages of industry evolution.

The life-cycle matrix highlights how a diversified firm's businesses are distributed across the stages of the industry life-cycle.

DECIDING WHICH PORTFOLIO MATRIX TO CONSTRUCT

Restricting portfolio analysis to just one type of matrix is unwise. Each matrix has its pros and cons, and each tells a different story about the portfolio's strengths and weaknesses. Provided adequate data is available, all three matrices should be con-

---

[8]Ibid., p. 34. This approach to business portfolio analysis was reportedly first used in actual practice by consultants at Arthur D. Little, Inc. For a full-scale review of this portfolio matrix approach, see Hax and Majluf, *Strategic Management: An Integrative Perspective,* chapter 9.

structed since there's merit in assessing the company's business portfolio from different perspectives. Corporate managers need to understand the mix of industries represented in the portfolio, the strategic position each business has in its industry, the portfolio's performance potential, and the kinds of financial and resource allocation considerations that have to be dealt with. Using all three matrices to view a diversified portfolio enhances such understanding.

COMPARING INDUSTRY ATTRACTIVENESS

The more attractive the industries that a company has diversified into, the better its performance prospects.

A principal consideration in evaluating a diversified company's strategy is the attractiveness of the industries it has diversified into. The more attractive these industries, the better the company's long-term profit prospects. Industry attractiveness needs to be evaluated from three perspectives:

1. *The attractiveness of each industry represented in the business portfolio.* The relevant question is "Is this a good industry for the company to be in?" Ideally, each industry the firm has diversified into can pass the attractiveness test.

2. *Each industry's attractiveness relative to the others.* The question to answer here is "Which industries in the portfolio are the most attractive and which are the least attractive?" Ranking the industries from most attractive to least attractive is a prerequisite for deciding how to allocate corporate resources.

3. *The attractiveness of all the industries as a group.* The question here is "How appealing is the mix of industries?" A company whose revenues and profits come chiefly from businesses in unattractive industries probably needs to consider restructuring its business portfolio.

All the industry attractiveness considerations discussed in Chapter 3 have application in this analytical phase.

An industry attractiveness-business strength portfolio matrix provides a strong, systematic basis for judging which business units are in the most attractive industries. If such a matrix has not been constructed, quantitative rankings of industry attractiveness can be developed using the same procedure described earlier for the nine-cell GE portfolio matrix. As a rule, all the industries represented in the business portfolio should, at minimum, be judged on the following attractiveness factors:

- *Market size and projected growth rate*—faster-growing industries tend to be more attractive than slow-growing industries, other things being equal.

- *The intensity of competition*—industries where competitive pressures are relatively weak are more attractive than industries where competitive pressures are strong.

- *Technological and production skills required*—industries where the skill requirements are closely matched to company capabilities are more attractive than industries where the company's technical and/or manufacturing know-how is limited.

- *Capital requirements*—industries with low capital requirements (or amounts within the company's reach) are relatively more attractive than industries where investment requirements could strain corporate financial resources.

- *Seasonal and cyclical factors*—industries where demand is relatively stable and dependable are more attractive than industries where there are wide swings in buyer demand.

- *Industry profitability*—industries with healthy profit margins and high rates of return on investment are generally more attractive than industries where profits have historically been low or where the business risks are high.
- *Social, political, regulatory, and environmental factors*—industries with significant problems in these areas are less attractive than industries where such problems are no worse than most businesses encounter.
- *Strategic fits with other industries the firm has diversified into*—an industry can be attractive simply because it has valuable strategic-fit relationships with other industries represented in the portfolio.

Calculation of industry attractiveness ratings for all industries in the corporate portfolio provides a basis for ranking the industries from most to least attractive. If formal industry attractiveness ratings seem too cumbersome or tedious to calculate, corporate managers can rely on their knowledge of conditions in each industry to classify individual industries as having "high," "medium," or "low" attractiveness. However, the validity of such subjective assessments depends on whether management has probed industry conditions sufficiently to make dependable judgments.

For a diversified company to be a strong performer, a substantial portion of its revenues and profits must come from business units judged to be in attractive industries. It is particularly important that core businesses be in industries with a good outlook for growth and above-average profitability. Business units in the least attractive industries may be divestiture candidates, unless they are positioned strongly enough to overcome the adverse industry environment or they are a strategically important component of the portfolio.

COMPARING BUSINESS-UNIT STRENGTH

Doing an appraisal of each business unit's strength and competitive position in its industry helps corporate managers judge a business unit's chances for success. The task here is to evaluate whether the business is well-positioned in its industry and the extent to which it already is or can become a strong market contender. The two most revealing techniques for evaluating a business's position in its industry are SWOT analysis and competitive strength assessment. Quantitative rankings of the strength/position of the various business units in the corporate portfolio can be calculated using either the procedure described in constructing the attractiveness-strength matrix or the procedure presented in Chapter 4. Assessments of how a diversified company's business subsidiaries compare in competitive strength should be based on such factors as

- *Relative market share*—business units with higher relative market shares normally have greater competitive strength than those with lower shares.
- *Ability to compete on price and/or quality*—business units that are very cost competitive and/or have established brand names and reputations for excellent product quality tend to be more strongly positioned in their industries than business units struggling to establish recognized names or to achieve cost parity with major rivals.
- *Technology and innovation capabilities*—business units recognized for their technological leadership and track record in innovation are usually strong competitors in their industry.

- *How well the business unit's skills and competences match industry key success factors*—the more a business unit's strengths match the industry's key success factors, the stronger its competitive position tends to be.
- *Profitability relative to competitors*—business units that consistently earn above-average returns on investment and have bigger profit margins than their rivals usually have stronger competitive positions than business units with below-average profitability for their industry. Moreover, above-average profitability signals competitive advantage while below-average profitability usually denotes competitive disadvantage.

Other competitive strength indicators that can be employed include knowledge of customers and markets, production capabilities, marketing skills, reputation and brand name awareness, and the caliber of management.

Calculation of competitive strength ratings for each business unit provides a basis for judging which ones are in strong positions in their industries and which are in weak positions. If analysts lack sufficient data, they can rely on their knowledge of each business unit's competitive situation to classify it as being in a "strong," "average," or "weak" competitive position. If trustworthy, such subjective assessments of business-unit strength can substitute for quantitative measures.

Managerial evaluations of which businesses in the portfolio enjoy the strongest competitive positions add further rationale and justification for corporate resource allocation. A company may earn larger profits over the long term by investing in a business with a competitively strong position in a moderately attractive industry than by investing in a weak business in a glamour industry. This is why a diversified company needs to consider *both* industry attractiveness and business strength in deciding where to steer resources.

Many diversified companies concentrate their resources on industries where they can be strong market contenders and divest businesses that are not good candidates for becoming leaders. At General Electric, the whole thrust of corporate strategy and corporate resource allocation is to put GE's businesses into a number one or two position in both the United States and globally—see Illustration Capsule 26.

> Shareholder interests are generally best served by concentrating corporate resources on businesses that can contend for market leadership in their industries.

COMPARING BUSINESS-UNIT PERFORMANCE

Once each business subsidiary is rated on the basis of industry attractiveness and competitive strength, the next step is to evaluate which businesses have the best performance prospects and which ones the worst. The most important considerations in judging business-unit performance are sales growth, profit growth, contribution to company earnings, and the return on capital invested in the business; sometimes, cash flow generation is a big consideration, especially for cash cow businesses or businesses with potential for harvesting. Information on each business's past performance can be gleaned from financial records. While past performance is not necessarily a good predictor of future performance, it does signal which businesses have been strong performers and which have been weak performers. The industry attractiveness-business strength evaluations should provide a solid basis for judging future prospects. Normally, strong business units in attractive industries have significantly better prospects than weak businesses in unattractive industries.

The growth and profit outlooks for the company's core businesses generally determine whether the portfolio as a whole will turn in a strong or weak performance. Noncore businesses with subpar track records and little expectation for improvement

PORTFOLIO MANAGEMENT AT GENERAL ELECTRIC

When Jack Welch became CEO of General Electric in 1981, he launched a corporate strategy effort to reshape the company's diversified business portfolio. Early on he issued a challenge to GE's business-unit managers to become number one or number two in their industry; failing that, the business units either had to capture a

Sears), and Kidder Peabody (a Wall Street investment banking firm). Internally, many of the company's smaller business operations were put under the direction of larger "strategic business units." But, most significantly, in 1989, 12 of GE's 14 strategic business units were market leaders in the United States and globally (the company's financial services and communications units served markets too fragmented to rank).

In 1989, having divested most of the weak businesses and having built existing businesses into leading

GE Strategic Business Units	Market Standing in the United States	Market Standing in the World
Aircraft engines	First	First
Broadcasting (NBC)	First	Not applicable
Circuit breakers	Tied for first with two others	Tied for first with three others
Defense electronics	Second	Second
Electric motors	First	First
Engineering plastics	First	First
Factory automation	Second	Third
Industrial and power systems	First	First
Lighting	First	Second
Locomotives	First	Tied for first
Major home appliances	First	Tied for second
Medical diagnostic imaging	First	First

decided technological advantage translatable into a competitive edge or face possible divestiture.

By 1989, GE was a different company. Under Welch's prodding, GE divested operations worth $9 billion—TV operations, small appliances, a mining business, and computer chips. It spent a total of $24 billion acquiring new businesses, most notably RCA, Roper (a maker of major appliances whose biggest customer was

contenders, Welch launched a new initiative within GE to dramatically boost productivity and reduce the size of GE's bureaucracy. Welch argued that for GE to continue to be successful in a global marketplace, the company had to press hard for continuous cost reduction in each of its businesses and cut through bureaucratic procedures to shorten response times to changing market conditions.

Source: Developed from information in Stratford P. Sherman, "Inside the Mind of Jack Welch," *Fortune,* March 27, 1989, pp. 39–50.

are logical candidates for divestiture. Business subsidiaries with the brightest profit and growth prospects generally should head the list for capital investment.

STRATEGIC-FIT ANALYSIS

The next analytical step is to determine how well each business unit fits into the company's overall business picture. Fit needs to be looked at from two angles: (1) whether a business unit has valuable strategic fit with other businesses the firm has diversified into (or has an opportunity to diversify into) and (2) whether the business unit meshes well with corporate strategy or adds a beneficial dimension to the corporate portfolio. A business is more attractive *strategically* when it has activity-sharing, skills transfer, or brand-name transfer opportunities that enhance competitive advantage, and when it fits in with the firm's strategic direction. A business is more valuable *financially* when it is capable of contributing heavily to corporate performance objectives (sales growth, profit growth, above-average return on investment, and so on) and when it materially enhances the company's overall worth. Just as businesses with poor profit prospects ought to become divestiture candidates, so should businesses that don't fit strategically into the company's overall business picture. Firms that emphasize related diversification probably should divest businesses with little or no strategic fit unless such businesses are unusually good financial performers or offer superior growth opportunities.

> Business subsidiaries that don't fit strategically should be considered for divestiture unless their financial performance is outstanding.

RANKING THE BUSINESS UNITS ON INVESTMENT PRIORITY

Using the information and results of the preceding evaluation steps, corporate strategists can rank business units in terms of priority for new capital investment and decide on a general strategic direction for each business unit. The task is to determine where the corporation should be investing its financial resources. Which business units should have top priority for new capital investment and financial support? Which business units should carry the lowest priority for new investment? The ranking process should clarify management thinking about what the basic strategic approach for each business unit should be—invest-and-grow (aggressive expansion), fortify-and-defend (protect current position with new investments as needed), overhaul-and-reposition (try to move the business into a more desirable industry position and to a better spot in the business portfolio matrix), or harvest-divest. In deciding whether to divest a business unit, corporate managers should rely on a number of evaluating criteria: industry attractiveness, competitive strength, strategic fit with other businesses, performance potential (profit, return on capital employed, contribution to cash flow), compatibility with corporate priorities, capital requirements, and value to the overall portfolio.

> Improving a diversified company's long-term financial performance entails concentrating company resources on businesses with good to excellent prospects and investing minimally, if at all, in businesses with subpar prospects.

In ranking the business units on investment priority, consideration needs to be given to whether and how corporate resources and skills can be used to enhance the competitive standing of particular business units.[9] The potential for skills transfer and infusion of new capital becomes especially important when the firm has business units in less than desirable competitive positions and/or where improvement in some key success area could make a big difference to the business unit's performance. It is also important when corporate strategy is predicated on strategic fits that involve transferring corporate skills to recently acquired business units to strengthen their competitive capabilities.[10]

CRAFTING A CORPORATE STRATEGY

The preceding analysis sets the stage for crafting strategic moves to improve a diversified company's overall performance. The basic issue of "what to do" hinges on the

---

[9]Hofer and Schendel, *Strategy Formulation: Analytical Concepts,* p. 80.
[10]Michael E. Porter, *Competitive Advantage* (New York: Free Press, 1985), chapter 9.

conclusions drawn about the overall *mix* of businesses in the portfolio.[11] Key considerations here are: Does the portfolio contain enough businesses in very attractive industries? Does the portfolio contain too many marginal businesses or question marks? Is the proportion of mature or declining businesses so great that corporate growth will be sluggish? Does the firm have enough cash cows to finance the stars and emerging winners? Can the company's core businesses be counted on to generate dependable profits and/or cash flow? Is the portfolio overly vulnerable to seasonal or recessionary influences? Does the portfolio contain businesses that the company really doesn't need to be in? Is the firm burdened with too many businesses in average-to-weak competitive positions? Does the makeup of the business portfolio put the company in good position for the future? Answers to these questions indicate whether corporate strategists should consider divesting certain businesses, making new acquisitions, or restructuring the makeup of the portfolio.

THE PERFORMANCE TEST

A good test of the strategic and financial attractiveness of a diversified firm's business portfolio is whether the company can attain its performance objectives with its current lineup of businesses. If so, no major corporate strategy changes are indicated. However, if a performance shortfall is probable, corporate strategists can take any of several actions to close the gap:[12]

1. *Alter the strategic plans for some (or all) of the businesses in the portfolio.* This option involves renewed corporate efforts to get better performance out of its present business units. Corporate managers can push business-level managers for better business-unit performance. However, pursuing better short-term performance, if done too zealously, can impair a business's potential for performing better over the long term. Cancelling expenditures that will bolster a business's long-term competitive position in order to squeeze out better short-term financial performance is a perilous strategy. In any case there are limits on how much extra performance can be squeezed out to reach established targets.

2. *Add new business units to the corporate portfolio.* Boosting overall performance by making new acquisitions and/or starting new businesses internally raises some new strategy issues. Expanding the corporate portfolio means taking a close look at *(a)* whether to acquire related or unrelated businesses, *(b)* what size acquisition(s) to make, *(c)* how the new unit(s) will fit into the present corporate structure, *(d)* what specific features to look for in an acquisition candidate, and *(e)* whether acquisitions can be financed without shortchanging present business units on their new investment requirements. Nonetheless, adding new businesses is a major strategic option, one frequently used by diversified companies to escape sluggish earnings performance.

3. *Divest weak-performing or money-losing businesses.* The most likely candidates for divestiture are businesses in a weak competitive position, in a relatively unattractive industry, or in an industry that does not "fit." Funds from

---

[11]Barry Hedley, "Strategy and the Business Portfolio," *Long Range Planning* 10, no. 1 (February 1977), p. 13; and Hofer and Schendel, *Strategy Formulation,* pp. 82–86.
[12]Hofer and Schendel, *Strategy Formulation: Analytical Concepts,* pp. 93–100.

divestitures can, of course, be used to finance new acquisitions, pay down corporate debt, or fund new strategic thrusts in the remaining businesses.

4. *Form alliances to try to alter conditions responsible for subpar performance potentials.* In some situations, alliances with domestic or foreign firms, trade associations, suppliers, customers, or special interest groups may help ameliorate adverse performance prospects.[13] Forming or supporting a political action group may be an effective way of lobbying for solutions to import-export problems, tax disincentives, and onerous regulatory requirements.

5. *Lower corporate performance objectives.* Adverse market circumstances or declining fortunes in one or more core business units can render companywide performance targets unreachable. So can overly ambitious objective-setting. Closing the gap between actual and desired performance may then require revision of corporate objectives to bring them more in line with reality. Lowering performance objectives is usually a "last resort" option, used only after other options come up short.

Finding Additional Diversification Opportunities

One of the major corporate strategy-making concerns in a diversified company is whether to pursue further diversification and, if so, how to identify the "right" kinds of industries and businesses to get into. For firms pursuing unrelated diversification, the issue of where to diversify next always remains wide open—the search for acquisition candidates is based more on financial criteria than on industry or strategic criteria. Decisions to add unrelated businesses to the firm's portfolio are usually based on such considerations as whether the firm has the financial ability to make another acquisition, whether new acquisitions are badly needed to boost overall corporate performance, whether one or more acquisition opportunities have to be acted on before they are purchased by other firms, and whether the timing is right for another acquisition (corporate management may have its hands full dealing with the current portfolio of businesses).

> Firms with unrelated diversification strategies hunt for businesses that offer attractive financial returns—regardless of what industry they're in.

With a related diversification strategy, however, the search for new industries is aimed at identifying industries whose value chains have fits with the value chains of one or more businesses represented in the company's business portfolio.[14] The interrelationships can concern (1) product or process R&D, (2) opportunities for joint manufacturing and assembly, (3) marketing, distribution channel, or common brand-name usage, (4) customer overlaps, (5) opportunities for joint after-sale service, or (6) common managerial know-how requirements—essentially any area where market-related, operating, or management fits can occur.

> Firms with related diversification strategies look for an attractive industry with good strategic fit.

Once strategic-fit opportunities outside a diversified firm's related business portfolio are identified, corporate strategists have to distinguish between opportunities where important competitive advantage potential exists (through cost savings, skill transfers, and so on) and those where the strategic-fit benefits are minor. The size of the competitive advantage potential depends on whether the strategic-fit benefits are competitively significant, how much it will cost to capture the benefits, and how

---

[13]For an excellent discussion of the benefits of alliances among competitors in global industries, see Kenichi Ohmae, "The Global Logic of Strategic Alliances," *Harvard Business Review* 67, no. 2 (March–April 1989), pp. 143–54.

[14]Porter, *Competitive Advantage,* pp. 370–371.

difficult it will be to merge or coordinate the business unit interrelationships.[15] Often, careful analysis reveals that while there are many actual and potential business unit interrelationships and linkages, only a few have enough strategic importance to generate meaningful competitive advantage.

DEPLOYING CORPORATE RESOURCES

To get ever-higher levels of performance out of a diversified company's business portfolio, corporate managers also have to do an effective job of allocating corporate resources. They have to steer resources out of low-opportunity areas into high-opportunity areas. Divesting marginal businesses is one of the best ways of freeing unproductive assets for redeployment. Surplus funds from cash cow businesses and businesses being harvested also add to the corporate treasury. Options for allocating these funds include (1) investing in ways to strengthen or expand existing businesses, (2) making acquisitions to establish positions in new industries, (3) funding long-range R&D ventures, (4) paying off existing long-term debt, (5) increasing dividends, and (6) repurchasing the company's stock. The first three are *strategic* actions; the last three are *financial* moves. Ideally, a company will have enough funds to serve both its strategic and financial purposes. If not, strategic uses of corporate resources should take precedence over financial uses except in unusual and compelling circumstances.

GUIDELINES FOR MANAGING THE PROCESS OF CRAFTING CORPORATE STRATEGY

Although formal analysis and entrepreneurial brainstorming normally undergird the corporate strategy-making process, there is more to where corporate strategy comes from and how it evolves. Rarely is there an all-inclusive grand formulation of the total corporate strategy. Instead, corporate strategy in major enterprises emerges incrementally from the unfolding of many different internal and external events, the result of probing the future, experimenting, gathering more information, sensing problems, building awareness of the various options, spotting new opportunities, developing ad hoc responses to unexpected crises, communicating consensus as it emerges, and acquiring a feel for all the strategically relevant factors, their importance, and their interrelationships.[16]

Strategic analysis is not something that the executives of diversified companies do all at once in comprehensive fashion. Such big reviews are sometimes scheduled, but research indicates that major strategic decisions emerge gradually rather than from periodic, full-scale analysis followed by prompt decision. Typically, top executives approach major strategic decisions a step at a time, often starting from broad, intuitive conceptions and then embellishing, fine-tuning, and modifying their original thinking as more information is gathered, as formal analysis confirms or modifies their judgments about the situation, and as confidence and consensus build for what strategic moves need to be made. Often attention and resources are concentrated on a few critical strategic thrusts that illuminate and integrate corporate direction, objectives, and strategies.

[15]Ibid., pp. 371–72.
[16]Ibid., pp. 58 and 196.

KEY POINTS

Strategic analysis in diversified companies is an eight-step process:

Step 1: *Get a clear fix on the present strategy*—whether the emphasis is on related or unrelated diversification; whether the scope of company operations is mostly domestic, increasingly multinational, or global; recent moves to add new businesses and build positions in new industries; recent divestitures; any efforts to capture strategic fits and create competitive advantage based on economies of scope, skills transfer, or shared brand name; and how much capital is being invested in each business. This step sets the stage for thorough evaluation of the need for strategy changes.

Step 2: *Construct a four-cell growth-share matrix, a nine-cell attractiveness-business strength matrix, and/or a life-cycle matrix to expose the strategic quality of the company's portfolio and the relative positions of its different businesses.* The nine-cell attractiveness-business strength matrix is conceptually and methodologically superior to the four-cell growth-share matrix, mainly because it incorporates consideration of a richer variety of strategically relevant considerations.

Step 3: *Evaluate the relative attractiveness of each industry represented in the company's portfolio.* If a nine-cell industry attractiveness-business strength matrix was constructed in Step 2, then the information is already available. Quantitative ratings of industry attractiveness, using the methodology described, are more systematic and reliable than qualitative subjective judgments.

Step 4: *Evaluate the relative competitive positions and business strength of each of the company's business units.* Again, this is a simple step if a nine-cell industry attractiveness-business strength matrix has been constructed. As always, quantitative ratings of competitive strength, using the same methodology as for industry attractiveness or the methodology presented in Table 4–4 in Chapter 4, are preferable to subjective judgments.

Step 5: *Rank the past performance of different business units from best to worst and rank their future performance prospects from best to worst.* Normally, strong business units in attractive industries have significantly better prospects than weak businesses or businesses in unattractive industries. This step provides a basis for concluding how well the portfolio as a whole should perform in the future.

Step 6: *Determine which businesses have important strategic fits with other businesses in the portfolio and how well each business fits in with the parent company's direction and strategy.* A business is more attractive *strategically* if it contributes economies of scope, skills transfer opportunities, and shared brand-name opportunities and if it is a business the parent company should be in for the foreseeable future. A business is more attractive *financially* if it is capable of contributing heavily to the firm's future financial performance.

Step 7: *Rank the business units from highest to lowest in investment priority,* thereby determining where the parent company should concentrate new capital investments. Also, determine a general strategic direction for each business unit (invest-and-expand, fortify-and-defend, overhaul-and-reposition, harvest, or divest).

Step 8: *Use the preceding analysis to craft a series of moves to improve overall corporate performance.* The most advantageous actions include

- Making acquisitions, starting new businesses from within, and divesting marginal businesses or businesses that no longer match the corporate direction and strategy.
- Devising moves to strengthen the long-term competitive positions of the company's core businesses.
- Acting to create strategic-fit opportunities and turn them into long-term competitive advantage.
- Steering corporate resources out of low-opportunity areas into high-opportunity areas.

SUGGESTED READINGS

Bettis, Richard A., and William K. Hall. "Strategic Portfolio Management in the Multibusiness Firm." *California Management Review* 24 (Fall 1981), pp. 23–38.

_____. "The Business Portfolio Approach—Where It Falls Down in Practice." *Long Range Planning* 16, no. 2 (April 1983), pp. 95–104.

Christensen, H. Kurt, Arnold C. Cooper, and Cornelius A. Dekluyuer. "The Dog Business: A Reexamination." *Business Horizons* 25, no. 6 (November–December 1982), pp. 12–18.

Haspeslagh, Phillippe. "Portfolio Planning: Uses and Limits." *Harvard Business Review* 60, no. 1 (January–February 1982), pp. 58–73.

Haspeslagh, Phillippe C., and David B. Jamison. *Managing Acquisitions: Creating Value through Corporate Renewal.* New York: Free Press, 1991.

Hax, Arnoldo, and Nicolas S. Majluf. *Strategic Management: An Integrative Perspective.* Englewood Cliffs, N.J.: Prentice-Hall, 1984, chaps. 7–9.

_____. *The Strategy Concept and Process.* Englewood Cliffs, N.J.: Prentice-Hall, 1991, chaps. 8–11 and 15.

Henderson, Bruce D. "The Application and Misapplication of the Experience Curve." *Journal of Business Strategy* 4, no. 3 (Winter 1984), pp. 3–9.

Naugle, David G., and Garret A. Davies. "Strategic-Skill Pools and Competitive Advantage." *Business Horizons* 30, no. 6 (November–December 1987), pp. 35–42.

Porter, Michael E. *Competitive Advantage.* New York: Free Press, 1985, chaps. 9–11.

_____. "From Competitive Advantage to Corporate Strategy." *Harvard Business Review* 65, no. 3 (May–June 1987), pp. 43–59.

CHAPTER NINE

IMPLEMENTING STRATEGY: CORE COMPETENCIES, REENGINEERING, AND STRUCTURE

We strategize beautifully, we implement pathetically.

An auto-parts firm executive

Just being able to conceive bold new strategies is not enough. The general manager must also be able to translate his or her strategic vision into concrete steps that "get things done."

Richard G. Hamermesh

Organizing is what you do before you do something, so that when you do it, it is not all mixed up.

A. A. Milne

Once managers have decided on a strategy, the next step is to convert it into actions and good results. Putting a strategy into place and getting the organization to execute it well call for a different set of managerial tasks and skills. Whereas crafting strategy is largely a market-driven entrepreneurial activity, implementing strategy is primarily an operations-driven activity revolving around the management of people and business processes. Whereas successful strategy-making depends on business vision, shrewd industry and competitive analysis, and entrepreneurial creativity, successful strategy implementation depends on leading, motivating, and working with and through others to create strong "fits" between how the organization performs its core business activities and the requirements for good strategy execution. Implementing strategy is an action-oriented, make-things-happen task that tests a manager's ability to direct organizational change, design and supervise business processes, motivate people, and achieve performance targets.

Experienced managers, savvy in strategy-making and strategy-implementing, are emphatic in declaring that it is a whole lot easier to develop a sound strategic plan than it is to make it happen. According to one executive, "It's been rather easy for us to decide where we wanted to go. The hard part is to get the organization to act on the new priorities."[1] What makes strategy implementation a tougher, more time-consuming management challenge than crafting strategy is the wide array of managerial activities that have to be attended to, the many ways managers can proceed, the demanding people-management skills required, the perseverance it takes to get a variety of initiatives launched and moving, the number of bedeviling issues that must be worked out, and the resistance to change that must be overcome. *Just because managers announce a new strategy doesn't mean that subordinates will agree with it or cooperate in implementing it.* Some may be skeptical about the merits of the strategy, seeing it as contrary to the organization's best interests, unlikely to succeed, or threatening to their own careers. Moreover, company personnel may interpret the new strategy differently, be uncertain about how their departments will fare, and have different ideas about the internal changes the new strategy will entail. Long-standing attitudes, vested interests, inertia, and ingrained organizational practices don't melt away when managers decide on a new strategy and start to implement it. It takes adept managerial leadership to overcome pockets of doubt and disagreement, build consensus for how to proceed, secure the commitment and cooperation of concerned parties, and get all the implementation pieces into place. Depending on how much consensus building and organizational change is involved, the implementation process can take several months to several years.

> The strategy-implementer's task is to convert the strategic plan into action and get on with what needs to be done to achieve the targeted strategic and financial objectives.

> Companies don't implement strategies, people do.

A FRAMEWORK FOR IMPLEMENTING STRATEGY

Implementing strategy entails converting the organization's strategic plan into action and then into results. Like crafting strategy, it's a job for the whole management team, not a few senior managers. While an organization's chief executive officer and the heads of major organizational units (business divisions, functional departments, and key operating units) are ultimately responsible for seeing that strategy is implemented successfully, the implementation process typically impacts every part of the organizational structure, from the biggest operating unit to the smallest frontline work group. Every manager has to think through the answer to "What has to be done in my area to implement our part of the strategic plan, and what should I do to get these things accomplished?" In this sense, all managers become strategy-implementers in their areas of authority and responsibility, and all employees are participants. One of the keys to successful implementation is communication. Management must present the case for organizational change so clearly and persuasively that there is determined commitment throughout the ranks to carry out the strategy and meet performance targets. Ideally, managers turn the implementation process into a companywide crusade. When they achieve the strategic objectives and financial and operating performance targets, they can consider the implementation successful.

> Every manager has an active role in the process of implementing and executing the firm's strategic plan.

Unfortunately, there are no 10-step checklists, no proven paths, and few concrete guidelines for tackling the job—strategy implementation is the least charted, most open-ended part of strategic management. The best evidence on do's and don'ts comes from personal experiences, anecdotal reports, and case studies—and the wisdom they yield is inconsistent. What's worked well for some managers has been tried by others and found lacking. The reasons are understandable. Not only are some managers more effective than others in employing this or that recommended

> Managing strategy implementation is more art than science.

---

[1] As quoted in Steven W. Floyd and Bill Wooldridge, "Managing Strategic Consensus: The Foundation of Effective Implementation," *Academy of Management Executive* 6, no. 4 (November 1992), p. 27.

approach to organizational change but each instance of strategy implementation takes place in a different organizational context. Different business practices and competitive circumstances, different work environments and cultures, different policies, different compensation incentives, and different mixes of personalities and organizational histories require a customized approach to strategy implementation—one based on individual situations and circumstances, the strategy-implementer's best judgment, and the implementer's ability to use particular change techniques adeptly.

THE PRINCIPAL TASKS

While managers' approaches should be tailor-made for the situation, certain bases have to be covered no matter what the organization's circumstances; these include

- Building an organization capable of carrying out the strategy successfully.
- Developing budgets to steer ample resources into those value-chain activities critical to strategic success.
- Establishing strategically appropriate policies and procedures.
- Instituting best practices and mechanisms for continuous improvement.
- Installing support systems that enable company personnel to carry out their strategic roles successfully day in and day out.
- Tying rewards and incentives to the achievement of performance objectives and good strategy execution.
- Creating a strategy-supportive work environment and corporate culture.
- Exerting the internal leadership needed to drive implementation forward and to keep improving on how the strategy is being executed.

These managerial tasks crop up repeatedly in the strategy implementation process, no matter what the specifics of the situation, and drive the priorities on the strategy-implementer's agenda—as depicted in Figure 9–1. One or two of these tasks usually end up being more crucial or time-consuming than others, depending on the organization's financial condition and competitive capabilities, the nature and extent of the strategic change involved, the requirements for creating sustainable competitive advantage, the strength of ingrained behavior patterns that have to be changed, whether there are important weaknesses to correct or new competencies to develop, the configuration of personal and organizational relationships in the firm's history, any pressures for quick results and near-term financial improvements, and all other relevant factors.

In devising an action agenda, strategy-implementers should begin with a probing assessment of what the organization must do differently and better to carry out the strategy successfully, then consider how to make the necessary internal changes as rapidly as practical. The strategy-implementer's action priorities should concentrate on fitting how the organization performs its value-chain activities and conducts its internal business to what it takes for first-rate strategy execution. A series of "fits" are needed. Organizational skills and capabilities must be carefully matched to the requirements of strategy—especially if the chosen strategy is predicated on a competence-based competitive advantage. Resources must be allocated in a manner calculated to provide departments with the people and operating budgets needed to execute their strategic roles effectively. The company's reward structure, policies, information systems, and operating practices need to push for strategy execution, rather than playing a merely passive role or, even worse, acting as obstacles. Equally important, is the need for managers to do things in a manner and style that create and nurture a strategy-supportive work environment and corporate culture. The stronger such fits, the better the chances for successful strategy implementation. Systematic management

F I G U R E 9-1 | The Eight Big Managerial Components of Implementing Strategy

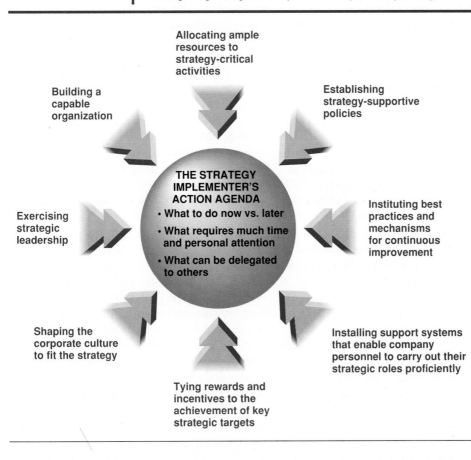

efforts to match how the organization goes about its business with the needs of good strategy execution help unite the organization in a team effort to achieve the intended performance outcomes. Successful strategy-implementers have a knack for diagnosing what their organizations need to do to execute the chosen strategy well, and they are creative in finding ways to perform key value-chain activities effectively.

LEADING THE IMPLEMENTATION PROCESS

One make-or-break determinant of successful strategy implementation is how well management leads the process. Managers can exercise leadership in many ways. They can play an active, visible role or a low-key, behind-the-scenes one. They can make decisions authoritatively or on the basis of consensus; delegate much or little; be personally involved in the details of implementation or stand on the sidelines and coach others; proceed swiftly (launching implementation initiatives on many fronts) or deliberately (remaining content with gradual progress over a long time frame). How managers lead the implementation task tends to be a function of (1) their experience and knowledge about the business; (2) whether they are new to the job or veterans; (3) their network of personal relationships with others in the organization; (4) their own diagnostic, administrative, interpersonal, and problem-solving skills; (5) the authority they've been given; (6) the leadership style they're comfortable with; and (7) their view of the role they need to play to get things done.

Although major initiatives to implement corporate and business strategies usually have to be led by the CEO and other senior officers, top-level managers still have to rely on the active support and cooperation of middle and lower managers to push strategy changes into functional areas and operating units and to carry out the strategy effectively on a daily basis. Middle- and lower-level managers not only are responsible for initiating and supervising the implementation process in their areas of authority but they also are instrumental in seeing that performance targets are met and in working closely with employees to improve strategy execution on the front lines where key value-chain activities are performed.

The action agenda of senior-level strategy-implementers, especially in big organizations with geographically scattered operating units, mostly involves communicating the case for change to others, building consensus for how to proceed, installing strong allies in positions where they can push implementation along in key organizational units, urging and empowering subordinates to get the process moving, establishing measures of progress and deadlines, recognizing and rewarding those who achieve implementation milestones, reallocating resources, and personally presiding over the strategic change process. Thus, the bigger the organization, the more the success of the chief strategy-implementer depends on the cooperation and implementing skills of operating managers who can push needed changes at the lowest organizational levels. In small organizations, the chief strategy-implementer doesn't have to work through middle managers and can deal directly with frontline managers and employees, personally orchestrating the action steps and implementation sequence, observing firsthand how implementation is progressing, and deciding how hard and how fast to push the process along. Irrespective of organization size and whether implementation involves sweeping or minor changes, the most important leadership trait is a strong, confident sense of "what to do" to achieve the desired results. Knowing "what to do" comes from a savvy understanding of the business and the organization's circumstances.

In the remainder of this chapter and the next two chapters, we survey the ins and outs of the manager's role as chief strategy-implementer. The discussion is framed around the eight managerial components of the strategy implementation process and the most often-encountered issues associated with each. This chapter explores the management tasks of building a capable organization. Chapter 10 looks at budget allocations, policies, best practices, internal support systems, and strategically appropriate reward structures. Chapter 11 deals with creating a strategy-supportive corporate culture and exercising strategic leadership.

> The real strategy-implementing skill is being good at figuring out what it will take to execute the strategy proficiently.

BUILDING A CAPABLE ORGANIZATION

Proficient strategy execution depends heavily on competent personnel, better-than-adequate skills and competitive capabilities, and effective internal organization. Building a capable organization is thus always a top strategy-implementing priority. Three types of organization-building actions are paramount:

1. Selecting able people for key positions.
2. Making certain that the organization has the skills, core competencies, managerial talents, technical know-how, and competitive capabilities it needs.
3. Organizing business processes and decision-making in a manner that is conducive to successful strategy execution.

SELECTING PEOPLE FOR KEY POSITIONS

Assembling a capable management team is one of the first cornerstones of the organization-building task. Strategy-implementers must determine the kind of core management team they need to execute the strategy successfully and then find the right people to fill each slot. Sometimes the existing management team is suitable; sometimes it needs to be strengthened and/or expanded by promoting qualified people from within or by bringing in outsiders whose backgrounds, ways of thinking, and leadership styles suit the situation. In turnaround and rapid-growth situations, and in instances when a company doesn't have insiders with the requisite experience and management know-how, filling key management slots from the outside is a fairly standard organization-building approach.

The important skill in assembling a core executive group is discerning what mix of backgrounds, experiences, know-how, values, beliefs, management styles, and personalities will reinforce and contribute to successful strategy execution. As with any kind of team-building exercise, it is important to put together a compatible group of managers who possess the full set of skills to get things done. The personal chemistry needs to be right, and the talent base needs to be appropriate for the chosen strategy. Picking a solid management team is an essential organization-building function— often the first strategy implementation step to take.[2] Until key slots are filled with able people, it is hard for strategy implementation to proceed at full speed.

> Putting together a strong management team with the right personal chemistry and mix of skills is one of the first strategy-implementing steps.

BUILDING CORE COMPETENCIES

An equally important organization-building concern is that of staffing operating units with the specialized talents, skills, and technical expertise needed to give the firm a competitive edge over rivals in performing one or more critical activities in the value chain. When it is difficult or impossible to outstrategize rivals (beat them on the basis of a superior strategy), the other main avenue to industry leadership is to outexecute them (beat them with superior strategy implementation). Superior strategy execution is essential in situations where rival firms have very similar strategies and can readily imitate one another's strategic maneuvers. Building core competencies and organizational capabilities that rivals can't match is one of the best ways to outexecute them. This is why one of management's most important strategy-implementing tasks is to guide the building of core competencies in competitively advantageous ways.

> **Strategic Management Principle**
> Building core competencies and organizational capabilities that rivals can't match is a sound foundation for sustainable competitive advantage.

Core competencies can relate to any strategically relevant factor: greater proficiency in product development, better manufacturing know-how, the capability to provide customers better after-sale services, faster response to changing customer requirements, superior performance in minimizing costs, the capacity to reengineer and redesign products faster than rivals, superior inventory management systems, strong marketing and merchandising skills, specialized depth in unique technologies, or greater effectiveness in promoting union-management cooperation. Honda's core competence is its depth of expertise in gasoline engine technology and small engine design. Intel's is in the design of complex chips for personal computers. Procter & Gamble's core competencies reside in its superb marketing-distribution skills and its R&D capabilities in five core technologies—fats, oils, skin chemistry, surfactants, and emulsifiers.[3] Sony's core competencies are its expertise in electronic technology and its ability to translate that expertise into innovative products (miniaturized radios and video cameras, TVs and VCRs with unique features). Most often, a company's core competencies emerge incrementally as it moves either to bolster skills that contributed to earlier successes or to respond to customer problems, new tech-

---

[2]For an analytical framework in top-management team analysis, see Donald C. Hambrick, "The Top Management Team: Key to Strategic Success," *California Management Review* 30, no. 1 (Fall 1987), pp. 88–108.

[3]James Brian Quinn, *Intelligent Enterprise* (New York: Free Press, 1992), p. 76.

technological and market opportunities, and the competitive maneuverings of rivals.[4] Occasionally, company managers may foresee coming changes in customer-market requirements and proactively build up new sets of competencies that offer a competitive edge.

Four traits concerning core competencies are important to a strategy-implementer's organization-building task:[5]

- Core competencies rarely consist of narrow skills or the work efforts of a single department. Rather, they are composites of skills and activities performed at different locations in the firm's value chain that, when linked, create unique organizational capability.
- Because core competencies typically originate in the combined efforts of different work groups and departments, individual supervisors and department heads can't be expected to see building the overall corporation's core competencies as their responsibility.
- The key to leveraging a company's core competencies into long-term competitive advantage is concentrating more effort and more talent than rivals on deepening and strengthening these competencies.
- Because customers' needs change in often unpredictable ways and the specific skills needed for competitive success cannot always be accurately forecasted, a company's selected bases of competence need to be broad enough and flexible enough to respond to an unknown future.

The multiskill, multiactivity character of core competencies makes building and strengthening them an exercise in (1) managing human skills, knowledge bases, and intellect and (2) coordinating and networking the efforts of different work groups and departments at every related place in the value chain. It's an exercise best orchestrated by senior managers who understand how the organization's core competencies are created and who can enforce the necessary networking and cooperation among functional departments and managers protective of their turf. Moreover, organization builders have to concentrate enough resources and management attention on core competence-related activities to achieve the *dominating depth* needed for competitive advantage.[6] This does not necessarily mean spending more money on competence-related activities than present or potential competitors. It does mean consciously focusing more talent on them and making appropriate internal and external benchmarking comparisons to move toward best-in-industry, if not best-in-world, status. To achieve dominance on lean financial resources, companies like Cray in large computers, Lotus in software, and Honda in small engines leveraged the expertise of their talent pool by frequently re-forming high-intensity teams and reusing key people on special projects.[7] In leveraging internal knowledge and skills rather than physical assets or market position, it is superior selection, training, powerful cultural influences, cooperative networking, motivation, empowerment, attractive incentives, organizational flexibility, short deadlines, and good databases—not big operating budgets—that are the usual keys to success.[8]

Core competencies don't come into being or reach strategic fruition without conscious management attention.

---

[4]Ibid.
[5]Quinn, *Intelligent Enterprise,* pp. 52–53, 55, 73, and 76.
[6]Ibid., p. 73.
[7]Ibid.
[8]Ibid., pp. 73–74.

Strategy-implementers can't afford to become complacent once core competencies are in place and functioning. It's a constant organization-building challenge to broaden, deepen, or modify them in response to ongoing customer-market changes. But it's a task worth pursuing. Core competencies that are finely honed and kept current with shifting circumstances can provide a big executional advantage. Distinctive core competencies and organizational capabilities are not easily duplicated by rival firms; thus any competitive advantage that results from them is likely to be sustainable, paving the way for above-average organizational performance. Dedicated management attention to the task of building strategically relevant internal skills and capabilities is always one of the keys to of effective strategy implementation.

Employee Training   Training and retraining are important parts of the strategy implementation process when a company shifts to a strategy requiring different skills, managerial approaches, and operating methods. Training is also strategically important in organizational efforts to build skills-based competencies. And it is a key activity in businesses where technical know-how is changing so rapidly that a company loses its ability to compete unless its skilled people have cutting-edge knowledge and expertise. Successful strategy-implementers see that the training function is adequately funded and that effective training programs are in place. If the chosen strategy calls for new skills or different know-how, training should be placed near the top of the action agenda because it needs to be done early in the strategy implementation process.

MATCHING ORGANIZATION STRUCTURE TO STRATEGY

There are few hard-and-fast rules for organizing the work effort in a strategy-supportive fashion. Every firm's organization chart is idiosyncratic, reflecting prior organizational patterns, executive judgments about how best to arrange reporting relationships, the politics of who to give which assignments, and varying internal circumstances. Moreover, every strategy is grounded in its own set of key success factors and value-chain activities. So a customized organization structure is appropriate. The following four guidelines can be helpful in fitting structure to strategy:

1. Pinpoint the primary activities and key tasks in the value chain that are pivotal to successful strategy execution and make them the main building blocks in the organization structure.
2. If all facets of a strategy-related activity cannot, for some reason, be placed under the authority of a single manager, establish ways to bridge departmental lines and achieve the necessary coordination.
3. Determine the degrees of authority needed to manage each organizational unit, endeavoring to strike an effective balance between capturing the advantages of both centralization and decentralization.
4. Determine whether noncritical activities can be outsourced more efficiently or effectively than they can be performed internally.

Pinpointing Strategy-Critical Activities   In any business, some activities in the value chain are always more critical to strategic success than others. From a strategy perspective, a certain portion of an organization's work involves routine administrative housekeeping (doing the payroll, managing cash flows, handling grievances and the usual assortment of people problems, providing corporate security, managing stockholder relations, maintaining fleet vehicles, and complying with regulations). Other activities are support functions (data processing, accounting, training, public relations, market research, legal and legislative affairs, and purchasing). Among the primary value-chain activities are certain crucial business processes that have to be performed exceedingly well for the strategy succeed. For instance, hotel/motel enterprises have to be good at fast check in/check out, room maintenance, food service, and creating a pleasant ambiance. A manufacturer of chocolate bars must be skilled in purchasing quality cocoa beans at low prices, efficient production (a fraction of a cent in cost savings per bar can mean seven-figure improvement in the bottom line), merchandising, and promotional activities. In discount stock brokerage, the strategy-critical activities are fast access to information, accurate order execution, efficient record-keeping and transactions processing, and good customer service. In specialty chemicals, the critical activities are R&D, product innovation, getting new products onto the market quickly, effective marketing, and expertise in assisting customers. Strategy-critical activities vary according to the particulars of a firm's strategy, value-chain makeup, and competitive requirements.

Two questions help identify what an organization's strategy-critical activities are: "What functions have to be performed extra well or in timely fashion to achieve sustainable competitive advantage?" and "In what value-chain activities would malperformance seriously endanger strategic success?"[9] The answers generally point to the crucial activities and organizational areas on which to concentrate organization-building efforts.

The rationale for making strategy-critical activities the main building blocks in the organization structure is compelling: if activities crucial to strategic success are to get the attention and organizational support they merit, they have to be centerpieces in the organizational scheme. When key business units and strategy-critical functions are put on a par with or, worse, superseded by less important activities, they usually end up with fewer resources and less clout in the organization's power structure than they deserve. On the other hand, when the primary value-creating activities form the core of a company's organization structure and their managers hold key positions on the organization chart, their role and power is ingrained in daily operations and decision-making. Senior executives seldom send a stronger signal about what is strategically important than by making key business units and critical activities prominent organizational building blocks and, further, giving the managers of these units a visible, influential position in the organizational pecking order. In many cases, there is merit in operating each of these main organizational units as profit centers.

In deciding how to graft routine and staff support activities onto the basic building block structure, company managers must understand the strategic relationships among the primary and support functions that make up its value chain. Activities can be related by the flow of work along the value chain, by the type of customer served, by the distribution channels used, by the technical skills and know-how needed to perform them, by their contribution to building a core competence, by their role in a work process that spans traditional departmental lines, by their role in how customer value is created, by their sequence in the value chain, by the skills-transfer opportunities they present, and by the potential for combining or coordinating them in a manner that will reduce total costs, to mention some of the most obvious. Such relationships are important because one or more such linkages usually signal how to

Strategic Management Principle

Matching structure to strategy requires making strategy-critical activities and strategy-critical organizational units the main building blocks in the organization structure.

---

[9]Peter F. Drucker, *Management: Tasks, Responsibilities, Practices* (New York: Harper & Row, 1974), pp. 530, 535.

structure reporting relationships and where there's a need for close cross-functional coordination. If the needs of successful strategy execution are to drive organization design, then the relationships to look for are those that (1) link one work unit's performance to another and (2) can be melded into a core competence.

Managers need to be particularly alert to the fact that in traditional functionally organized structures, pieces of strategically relevant activities are often scattered across many departments. The process of filling customer orders accurately and promptly is a case in point. The order fulfillment process begins when a customer places an order, ends when the goods are delivered, and typically includes a dozen or so steps performed by different people in different departments.[10] Someone in customer service receives the order, logs it in, and checks it for accuracy and completeness. It may then go to the finance department, where someone runs a credit check on the customer. Another person may be needed to approve credit terms or special financing. Someone in sales calculates or verifies the correct pricing. When the order gets to inventory control, someone has to determine if the goods are in stock. If not, a back order may be issued or the order routed to production planning so that it can be factored into the production schedule. When the goods are ready, warehouse operations prepares a shipment schedule. Personnel in the traffic department determine the shipment method (rail, truck, air, water) and choose the route and carrier. Product handling picks the product from the warehouse, verifies the picking against the order, and packages the goods for shipment. Traffic releases the goods to the carrier, which takes responsibility for delivery to the customer. Each handoff from one department to the next entails queues and wait times. Although such organization incorporates Adam Smith's division of labor principle (every person involved has specific responsibility for performing one simple task) and allows for tight management control (everyone in the process is accountable to a manager for efficiency and adherence to procedures), *no one oversees the whole process and its result*.[11] Accurate, timely order fulfillment, despite its relevance to effective strategy execution, ends up being neither a single person's job nor the job of any one functional department.[12]

> Functional specialization can result in the pieces of strategically relevant activities being scattered across many different departments.

Managers have to guard against organization designs that unduly fragment strategically relevant activities. Parceling strategy-critical work efforts across many specialized departments contributes to an obsession with activity (performing the assigned tasks in the prescribed manner) rather than result (customer satisfaction, competitive advantage, lower costs). So many handoffs lengthen completion time and frequently drive up overhead costs since coordinating the fragmented pieces can soak up hours of effort on the parts of many people. Nonetheless, some fragmentation is necessary, even desirable, in the case of support activities like finance and accounting, human resource management, engineering, technology development, and information systems where functional centralization works to good advantage. The key in weaving support activities into the organization design is to establish reporting and coordinating arrangements that

- Maximize how support activities contribute to enhanced performance of the primary, strategy-critical tasks in the firm's value chain.
- Contain the costs of support activities and minimize the time and energy internal units have to spend doing business with each other.

---

[10]Michael Hammer and James Champy, *Reengineering the Corporation* (New York: HarperBusiness, 1993), pp. 26–27.
[11]Ibid.
[12]Ibid., pp. 27–28.

Without such arrangements, the cost of transacting business internally becomes excessive, and functional managers, forever diligent in guarding their turf and protecting their prerogatives to run their areas as they see fit, can weaken the strategy execution effort and become part of the strategy-implementing problem rather than part of the solution.

Reporting Relationships and Cross-Functional Coordination   The classic way to coordinate the activities of organizational units is to position them in the hierarchy so that those most closely related report to a single person. Managers higher up in the pecking order generally have authority over more organizational units and thus the clout to coordinate, integrate, and arrange for the cooperation of units under their supervision. In such structures, the chief executive officer, chief operating officer, and business-level managers end up as central points of coordination because of their positions of authority over the whole unit. When a firm is pursuing a related diversification strategy, coordinating the related activities of independent business units often requires the centralizing authority of a single corporate-level officer. Also, companies with either related or unrelated diversification strategies commonly centralize such staff support functions as public relations, finance and accounting, employee benefits, and data processing at the corporate level.

But, as the customer order fulfillment example illustrates, it isn't always feasible to position closely related value-chain activities and/or organizational units vertically under the coordinating authority of a single executive. Formal reporting relationships have to be supplemented. Options for unifying the strategic efforts of interrelated organizational units include the use of coordinating teams, cross-functional task forces, dual reporting relationships, informal organizational networking, voluntary cooperation, incentive compensation tied to group performance measures, and strong executive-level insistence on teamwork and interdepartmental cooperation (including removal of recalcitrant managers who stonewall cooperative efforts).

Determining the Degree of Authority and Independence to Give Each Unit   Companies must decide how much authority and decision-making latitude to give managers of each organization unit, especially the heads of business subsidiaries and functional departments. In a highly centralized organization structure, top executives retain authority for most strategic and operating decisions and keep a tight rein on business-unit heads and department heads; comparatively little discretionary authority is granted to subordinate managers. The weakness of centralized organization is that its vertical, hierarchical character tends to foster excessive bureaucracy and stall decision-making until the review-approval process runs its course through the management layers. In a highly decentralized organization, managers (and, increasingly, many nonmanagerial employees) are empowered to act on their own in their areas of responsibility. In a diversified company operating on the principle of decentralized decision-making, for example, business unit heads have broad authority to run the subsidiary with comparatively little interference from corporate headquarters. Moreover, the business head gives functional department heads considerable decision-making latitude. Employees with customer contact are empowered to do what it takes to please customers.

Delegating greater authority to subordinate managers and employees creates a more horizontal organization structure with fewer management layers. Whereas in a centralized vertical structure managers and workers have to go up the ladder of

Resolving which decisions to centralize and which to decentralize is always a big issue in organization design.

authority for an answer, in a decentralized horizontal structure they develop their own answers and action plans—making decisions and being accountable for results is part of their job. Streamlining the decision-making process usually shortens the time it takes to respond to competitors' actions, changing customer preferences, and other market developments. And it spurs new ideas, creative thinking, innovation, and greater involvement on the part of subordinate managers and employees.

In recent years, there's been a decided shift from authoritarian, multilayered hierarchical structures to flatter, more decentralized structures that stress employee empowerment. The new preference for leaner management structures and empowered employees is grounded in two tenets. (1) Decision-making authority should be pushed down to the lowest organizational level capable of making timely, informed, competent decisions—those people (managers or nonmanagers) nearest the scene who are knowledgeable about the issues and trained to weigh all the factors. Insofar as strategic management is concerned, decentralization means that the managers of each organizational unit should not only lead the crafting of their unit's strategy but also lead the decision-making on how to implement it. Decentralization thus requires selecting strong managers to head each organizational unit and holding them accountable for crafting and executing appropriate strategies for their units. Managers who consistently produce unsatisfactory results and have poor track records in strategy-making and strategy-implementing have to be weeded out. (2) Employees below the management ranks should be empowered to exercise judgement on matters pertaining to their jobs. The case for empowering employees to make decisions and be accountable for their performance is based on the belief that a company that draws on the combined brainpower of all its employees can outperform a company where the approach to people management consists of transferring ideas from the heads of bosses into the actions of workers-doers. To ensure that the decisions of empowered people are as well-informed as possible, great pains have to be taken to put accurate, timely data into everyone's hands and make sure they understand the links between their performance and company performance. Delayered corporate hierarchies and rapid diffusion of information technologies make greater empowerment feasible. It's possible now to create "a wired company" where people have direct electronic access to data and other employees and managers, allowing them to access information quickly, check with superiors as needed and take responsible action. Typically, there are genuine morale gains when people are well-informed and allowed to operate in a self-directed way.

One of the biggest exceptions to decentralizing strategy-related decisions and giving lower-level managers more operating rein arises in diversified companies with related businesses. In such cases, strategic-fit benefits are often best captured by either centralizing decision-making authority or enforcing close cooperation and shared decision-making. For example, if businesses with overlapping process and product technologies have their own independent R&D departments, each pursuing their own priorities, projects, and strategic agendas, it's hard for the corporate parent to prevent duplication of effort, capture either economies of scale or economies of scope, or broaden the vision of the company's R&D efforts to include new technological pathways, product families, end-use applications, and customer groups. Likewise, centralizing control over the related activities of separate businesses makes sense when there are opportunities to share a common sales force, utilize common distribution channels, rely upon a common field service organization to handle customer requests for technical assistance or provide maintenance and repair services, and so on. And for reasons previously discussed, limits also have to be placed on the

Centralizing strategy-implementing authority at the corporate level has merit when the related activities of related businesses need to be tightly coordinated.

independence of functional managers when pieces of strategy-critical processes are located in different organizational units and require close coordination for maximum effectiveness.

Reasons to Consider Outsourcing Noncritical Activities   Each supporting activity in a firm's value chain and within its traditional staff groups can be considered a "service."[13] Most overheads, for example, are just services the company chooses to produce internally. Often, such services are readily purchased from outside vendors. An outsider, by concentrating specialists and technology in its area of expertise, can sometimes perform these services better or more cheaply than a company that performs the activities only for itself. Outsourcing activities not crucial to its strategy allows a company to concentrate its own energies and resources on those value-chain activities where it can create unique value, where it can be best in the industry (or, better still, best in the world), and where it needs strategic control to build core competencies, achieve competitive advantage, and manage key customer-supplier relationships.[14] Managers too often spend inordinate amounts of time, psychic energy, and resources wrestling with functional support groups and other internal bureaucracies, diverting attention from the company's strategy-critical activities. Approached from a strategic point of view, outsourcing noncrucial support activities (and maybe a few selected primary activities in the value chain if they are not a basis for competitive advantage) can decrease internal bureaucracies, flatten the organization structure, provide the company with heightened strategic focus, and increase competitive responsiveness.[15]

Critics contend that extensive outsourcing can hollow out a company, leaving it at the mercy of outside suppliers and barren of the skills and organizational capabilities needed to be master of its own destiny.[16] However, a number of companies have successfully relied on outside components suppliers, product designers, distribution channels, advertising agencies, and financial services firms. For years Polaroid Corporation bought its film medium from Eastman Kodak, its electronics from Texas Instruments, and its cameras from Timex and others, while it concentrated on producing its unique self-developing film packets and designing its next generation of cameras and films. Nike concentrates on design, marketing, and distribution to retailers, while outsourcing virtually all production of its shoes and sporting apparel. Many mining companies outsource geological work, assaying, and drilling. Ernest and Julio Gallo Winery outsources 95 percent of its grape production, letting farmers take on the weather and other grape-growing risks while it concentrates on wine production and the marketing-sales function.[17] The major airlines outsource their in-flight meals even though food quality is important to travelers' perception of overall service quality. Eastman Kodak, Ford, Exxon, Merrill Lynch, and Chevron have outsourced their data processing activities to computer service firms, believing that outside specialists can perform the needed services at lower costs and equal or better quality. Outsourcing certain value-chain activities makes strategic sense whenever outsiders can perform them at lower cost and/or with higher value-added than the buyer company can perform them internally.[18]

Outsourcing noncritical activities has many advantages.

---

[13]Quinn, *Intelligent Enterprise*, p. 32.
[14]Ibid., p. 37.
[15]Ibid., pp. 33 and 89.
[16]Ibid., pp. 39–40.
[17]Ibid., p. 43.
[18]Ibid., p. 47.

WHY STRUCTURE FOLLOWS STRATEGY

Research confirms the merits of matching organization design and structure to the particular needs of strategy. A landmark study by Alfred Chandler found that changes in an organization's strategy bring about new administrative problems which, in turn, require a new or refashioned structure for the new strategy to be successfully implemented.[19] Chandler's study of 70 large corporations revealed that structure tends to follow the growth strategy of the firm—but often not until inefficiency and internal operating problems provoke a structural adjustment. The experiences of these firms followed a consistent sequential pattern: new strategy creation, emergence of new administrative problems, a decline in profitability and performance, a shift to a more appropriate organizational structure, and then recovery to more profitable levels and improved strategy execution. That managers should reassess their company's internal organization whenever strategy changes is pretty much common sense. A new strategy is likely to entail new or different skills and key activities; if these go unrecognized, the resulting mismatch between strategy and structure can open the door to implementation and performance problems.

Strategic Management Principle

Attempting to carry out a new strategy with an old organizational structure is usually unwise.

How Structure Evolves as Strategy Evolves As firms develop from small, single-business companies into more complex enterprises employing vertical integration, geographic expansion, and diversification strategies, their organizational structures tend to evolve from one-person management to functional departments to divisions to decentralized business units. Single-business companies are usually organized around functional departments. In vertically integrated firms, the major building blocks are divisional units, each of which performs one (or more) of the major processing steps along the value chain (raw materials production, components manufacture, assembly, wholesale distribution, retail store operations); each division in the value-chain sequence may operate as a profit center for performance measurement purposes. Companies with broad geographic coverage typically are divided into regional operating units, each of which has profit-loss responsibility for its assigned geographic area. The typical building blocks of a diversified company are its individual businesses; the authority for business-unit decisions is delegated to business-level managers. Each business unit operates as an independent profit center, with corporate headquarters performing assorted support functions for all the businesses.

THE STRATEGIC ADVANTAGES AND DISADVANTAGES OF DIFFERENT ORGANIZATIONAL STRUCTURES

There are five formal approaches to matching structure to strategy: (1) functional specialization, (2) geographic organization, (3) decentralized business divisions, (4) strategic business units, and (5) matrix structures featuring dual lines of authority and strategic priority. Each has strategic advantages and disadvantages, and each usually needs to be supplemented with formal or informal organizational arrangements to fully coordinate the work effort.

---

[19] Alfred Chandler, *Strategy and Structure* (Cambridge, Mass.: MIT Press, 1962). Although the stress here is on matching structure to strategy, it is worth noting that structure can and does influence the choice of strategy. A good strategy must be doable. When an organization's present structure is so far out of line with the requirements of a particular strategy that the organization would have to be turned upside down to implement it, the strategy may not be doable and should not be given further consideration. In such cases, structure shapes the choice of strategy. The point here, however, is that once strategy is chosen, structure must be modified to fit the strategy if, in fact, an approximate fit does not already exist. Any influences of structure on strategy should, logically, come before the point of strategy selection rather than after it.

Functional Organization Structures   Organizational structures anchored around functionally specialized departments are far and away the most popular form for matching structure to strategy in single-business enterprises. However, just what form the functional specialization takes varies according to customer-product-technology considerations. For instance, a technical instruments manufacturer may be organized around research and development, engineering, production, technical services, quality control, marketing, personnel, and finance and accounting. A hotel may have an organization based on front-desk operations, housekeeping, building maintenance, food service, convention services and special events, guest services, personnel and training, and accounting. A discount retailer may divide its organizational units into purchasing, warehousing and distribution, store operations, advertising, merchandising and promotion, and corporate administrative services. Two types of functional organizational approaches are diagrammed in Figure 9–2.

Making specialized functions the main organizational building blocks works best when a firm's value chain consists of a series of discipline-specific activities, each requiring a fairly extensive set of specialized skills, experience, and know-how. In such instances, departmental units staffed with experts in every facet of the activity is an attractive way (1) to exploit any learning/experience curve benefits or economy-of-scale opportunities associated with division of labor and the use of specialized technology and equipment and (2) to develop deep expertise in an important business function. When dominating depth in one or more functional specialties enhances operating efficiency and/or organizational know-how, it becomes a basis for competitive advantage (lower cost or unique capability). Functional structures work quite satisfactorily so long as strategy-critical activities closely match functional specialties, there's minimal need for interdepartmental cooperation, and top-level management is able to short-circuit departmental rivalries and create a spirit of teamwork, trust, and interdepartmental cooperation.

A functional structure has two Achilles' heels: excessive functional myopia and fragmentation of strategy-critical business processes across traditional departmental lines. It's tough to achieve tight strategic coordination across strongly entrenched functional bureaucracies that don't "talk the same language" and that prefer to do their own thing without outside interference. Functional specialists are prone to focus inward on departmental matters and upward at their boss's priorities but not outward on the business, the customer, or the industry.[20] Members of functional departments usually have strong departmental loyalties and are protective of departmental interests. There's a natural tendency for each functional department to push for solutions and decisions that advance its well-being and organizational influence (despite the lip service given to cooperation and "what's best for the company"). All this creates an organizational environment where functional departments operate as vertical silos, or stovepipes, and a breeding ground for departmental bureaucracies, excessive layers of management, authoritarian decision-making, and narrow perspectives. In addition, functionally dominated structures, because of preoccupation with developing deeper expertise and improving functional performance, have tunnel vision when it comes to devising entrepreneurially creative responses to major customer-market-technological changes. They are quick to kill ideas or discard alternatives that aren't compatible with the present functional structure. Classical functional structures also exacerbate the problems of process fragmentation whenever a firm's value chain includes strat-

Functional departments develop strong functional mindsets and are prone to approach strategic issues more from a functional than a business perspective.

---

[20]Hammer and Champy, *Reengineering the Corporation,* p. 28.

FIGURE 9-2 | **Functional Organizational Structures**

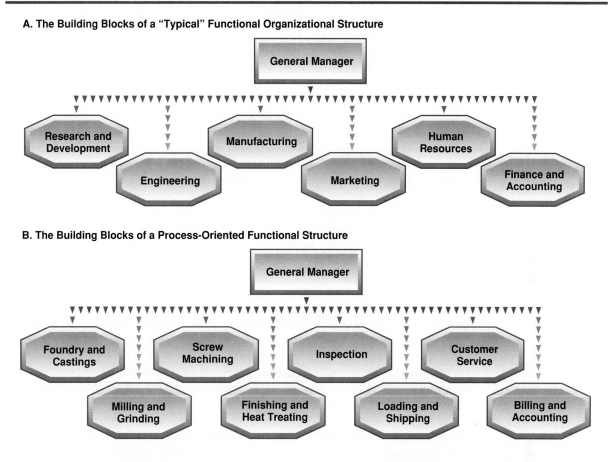

A. The Building Blocks of a "Typical" Functional Organizational Structure

General Manager

Research and Development · Engineering · Manufacturing · Marketing · Human Resources · Finance and Accounting

B. The Building Blocks of a Process-Oriented Functional Structure

General Manager

Foundry and Castings · Milling and Grinding · Screw Machining · Finishing and Heat Treating · Inspection · Loading and Shipping · Customer Service · Billing and Accounting

STRATEGIC ADVANTAGES	STRATEGIC DISADVANTAGES
• Centralized control of strategic results.	• Excessive fragmentation of strategy-critical processes.
• Very well suited for structuring a single business.	• Can lead to interfunctional rivalry and conflict, rather than team-play and cooperation—GM must referee functional politics.
• Structure is linked tightly to strategy by designating key activities as functional departments.	• Multilayered management bureaucracies and centralized decision-making slow response times.
• Promotes in-depth functional expertise.	• Hinders development of managers with cross-functional experience because the ladder of advancement is up the ranks within the same functional area.
• Well suited to developing functional skills and functional-based competencies.	• Forces profit responsibility to the top.
• Conducive to exploiting learning/experience curve effects associated with functional specialization.	• Functional specialists often attach more importance to what's best for the functional area than to what's best for the whole business—can lead to functional empire-building.
• Enhances operating efficiency where tasks are routine and repetitive.	• Functional myopia often works against creative entrepreneurship, adapting to change, and attempts to create cross-functional core competencies.

egy-critical activities that, by their very nature, are cross-functional rather than discipline specific. Process fragmentation not only complicates the problems of achieving interdepartmental coordination but also poses serious hurdles to developing cross-functional core competencies.

Interdepartmental politics, functional empire-building, functional myopia, and process fragmentation can impose a time-consuming administrative burden on the general manager, who is the only person on the organization chart with authority to resolve cross-functional differences and to enforce interdepartmental cooperation. In a functional structure, much of a GM's time and energy is spent opening lines of communication across departments, tempering departmental rivalries, convincing stovepipe thinkers of the merits of broader solutions, devising ways to secure cooperation, and working to mold desirable cross-functional core competencies. To be successful, a GM has to be tough and uncompromising in insisting that department heads be team players and that functional specialists work together closely as needed; failure to cooperate fully has to carry negative consequences (specifically, a lower job performance evaluation and maybe even reassignment).

To strike a good balance between being function-driven and team-driven, the formal functional structure has to be supplemented with coordinating mechanisms—frequent use of interdisciplinary task forces to work out procedures for coordinating fragmented processes and strategy-critical activities, incentive compensation schemes tied to joint performance measures, empowerment of cross-functional teams that possess all the skills needed to perform strategy-critical processes in a unified, timely manner, and the formation of interdisciplinary teams charged with building the internal organizational bridges needed to create cross-functional organizational capabilities. On occasion, rather than continuing to scatter related pieces of a business process across several functional departments and scrambling to integrate their efforts, it may be better to reengineer the work effort and create *process* departments by pulling the people who performed the pieces in functional departments into a group that works together to perform the whole process.[21] Bell Atlantic did so in cutting through its bureaucratic procedures for connecting a telephone customer to its long-distance carrier.[22] In Bell Atlantic's functional structure, when a business customer requested a connection between its telephone system and a long-distance carrier for data services, the request traveled from department to department, taking two to four weeks to complete all the internal processing steps. In reengineering that process, Bell Atlantic pulled workers doing the pieces of the process from the many functional departments and put them on teams that, working together, could handle most customer requests in a matter of days and sometimes hours. Because the work was recurring—similar customer requests had to be processed daily—the teams were permanently grouped into a "process department."

A geographic organization structure is well-suited to firms pursuing different strategies in different geographic regions.

Geographic Forms of Organization   Organizing on the basis of geographic areas or territories is a common structural form for enterprises operating in diverse geographic markets or serving an expansive geographic area. As indicated in Figure 9–3, geographic organization has advantages and disadvantages, but the chief reason for its popularity is that it promotes improved performance.

---

[21]Ibid., p. 66.
[22]Ibid., pp. 66–67.

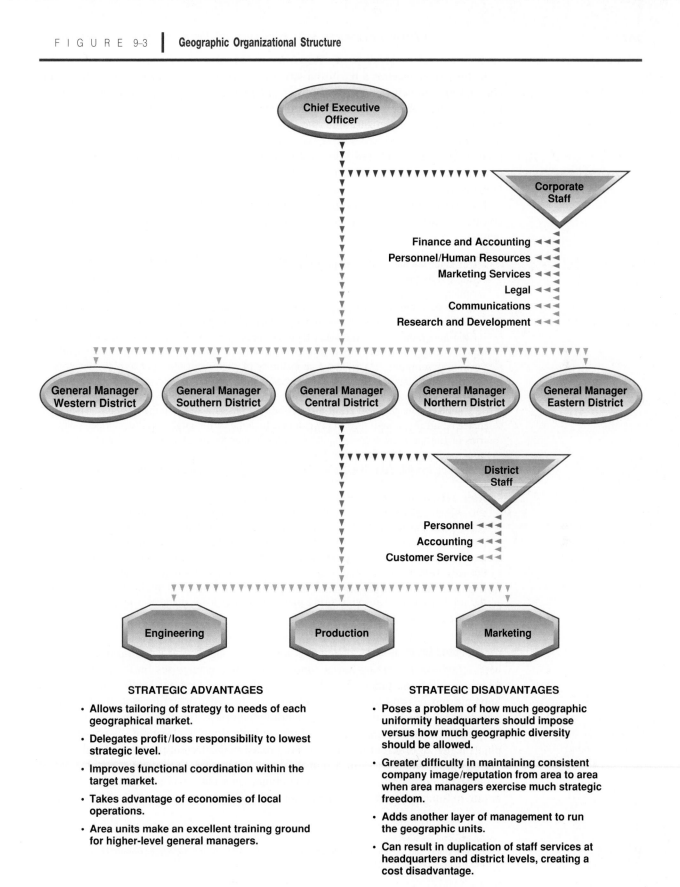

STRATEGIC ADVANTAGES

- Allows tailoring of strategy to needs of each geographical market.
- Delegates profit/loss responsibility to lowest strategic level.
- Improves functional coordination within the target market.
- Takes advantage of economies of local operations.
- Area units make an excellent training ground for higher-level general managers.

STRATEGIC DISADVANTAGES

- Poses a problem of how much geographic uniformity headquarters should impose versus how much geographic diversity should be allowed.
- Greater difficulty in maintaining consistent company image/reputation from area to area when area managers exercise much strategic freedom.
- Adds another layer of management to run the geographic units.
- Can result in duplication of staff services at headquarters and district levels, creating a cost disadvantage.

In the private sector, a territorial structure is typically utilized by discount retail-ers, power companies, cement firms, restaurant chains, and dairy products enter-prises. In the public sector, such organizations as the Internal Revenue Service, the Social Security Administration, the federal courts, the U.S. Postal Service, state troopers, and the Red Cross have adopted territorial structures in order to be directly accessible to geographically dispersed clienteles. Multinational enterprises use geo-graphic structures to manage the diversity they encounter operating across national boundaries.

Raymond Corey and Steven Star cite Pfizer International as a good example of a company whose strategic requirements made geographic decentralization advanta-geous:

> Pfizer International operated plants in 27 countries and marketed in more than 100 countries. Its product lines included pharmaceuticals (antibiotics and other ethical pre-scription drugs), agricultural and veterinary products (such as animal feed supplements and vaccines and pesticides), chemicals (fine chemicals, bulk pharmaceuticals, petro-chemicals, and plastics), and consumer products (cosmetics and toiletries).
>
> Ten geographic Area Managers reported directly to the President of Pfizer Interna-tional and exercised line supervision over Country Managers. According to a company position description, it was "the responsibility of each Area Manager to plan, develop, and carry out Pfizer International's business in the assigned foreign area in keeping with company policies and goals."
>
> Country Managers had profit responsibility. In most cases a single Country Manager managed all Pfizer activities in his country. In some of the larger, well-developed coun-tries of Europe there were separate Country Managers for pharmaceutical and agricul-tural products and for consumer lines.
>
> Except for the fact that New York headquarters exercised control over the to-the-market prices of certain products, especially prices of widely used pharmaceuticals, Area and Country Managers had considerable autonomy in planning and managing the Pfizer International business in their respective geographic areas. This was appropriate because each area, and some countries within areas, provided unique market and regula-tory environments. In the case of pharmaceuticals and agricultural and veterinary prod-ucts (Pfizer International's most important lines), national laws affected formulations, dosages, labeling, distribution, and often price. Trade restrictions affected the flow of bulk pharmaceuticals and chemicals and packaged products, and might in effect require the establishment of manufacturing plants to supply local markets. Competition, too, varied significantly from area to area.[23]

Decentralized Business Units   Grouping activities along business and product lines has been a favored organizing device among diversified enterprises for the past 70 years, beginning with the pioneering efforts of DuPont and General Motors in the 1920s. Separate business/product divisions emerged because diversification made a func-tionally specialized manager's job incredibly complex. Imagine the problems a man-ufacturing executive and his/her staff would have if put in charge of, say, 50 different plants using 20 different technologies to produce 30 different products in eight differ-ent businesses/industries. In a multibusiness enterprise, the practical organizational sequence is corporate to business to functional area within a business rather than cor-porate to functional area (aggregated for all businesses).

---

[23]Raymond Corey and Steven H. Star, *Organization Strategy: A Marketing Approach* (Boston: Harvard Business School, 1971), pp. 23–24.

Thus while functional departments and geographic divisions are the standard organizational building blocks in a single-business enterprise, in a multibusiness corporation the basic building blocks are the individual businesses. Authority over each business unit is typically delegated to a business-level manager. The approach is to put entrepreneurial general managers in charge of each business unit, give them authority to formulate and implement a business strategy, motivate them with performance-based incentives, and hold them accountable for results. Each business unit then operates as a stand-alone profit center and is organized around whatever functional departments and geographic units suit the business's strategy, key activities, and operating requirements.

> In a diversified firm, the basic organizational building blocks are its business units; each business is operated as a stand-alone profit center.

Fully independent business units, however, pose an organizational obstacle to companies pursuing related diversification: *there is no mechanism for coordinating related activities across business units.* It can be tough to get autonomy-conscious business-unit managers to coordinate and share related activities. They are prone to argue about turf and about being held accountable for activities outside their control. To capture strategic-fit benefits in a diversified company, corporate headquarters must devise some internal organizational means for achieving strategic coordination across related business-unit activities. One option is to centralize related functions at the corporate level—e.g., maintaining a corporate R&D department if there are technology and product development fits, creating a special corporate sales force to call on customers who purchase from several of the company's business units, combining the dealer networks and sales force organizations of closely related businesses, merging the order processing and shipping functions of businesses with common customers, and consolidating the production of related components and products into fewer, more efficient plants. Alternatively, corporate officers can develop bonus arrangements that give business-unit managers strong incentives to work together to achieve the full benefits of strategic fit. If the strategic-fit relationships involve skills or technology transfers across businesses, corporate headquarters can arrange to transfer people with the requisite skills and know-how from one business to another and can create interbusiness teams to open the flow of proprietary technology, managerial know-how, and related skills between businesses.

> **Strategic Management Principle**
> A decentralized business-unit structure can block success of a related diversification strategy unless specific organizational arrangements are devised to coordinate the related activities of related businesses.

A typical line-of-business organization structure is shown in Figure 9–4, along with the strategy-related pros and cons of this organizational form.

Strategic Business Units   In broadly diversified companies, the number of decentralized business units can be so great that the span of control is too much for a single chief executive. Then it may be useful to group related businesses and to delegate authority over them to a senior executive who reports directly to the chief executive officer. While this imposes a layer of management between business-level managers and the chief executive, it may nonetheless improve strategic planning and top-management coordination of diverse business interests. This explains both the popularity of the group vice president concept among multibusiness companies and the creation of strategic business units.

A *strategic business unit* (SBU) is a grouping of business subsidiaries based on some important strategic elements common to all. The elements can be an overlapping set of competitors, closely related value-chain activities, a common need to compete globally, emphasis on the same kind of competitive advantage (low cost or differentiation), common key success factors, or technologically related growth opportunities. At General Electric, a pioneer in the concept of SBUs, 190 businesses

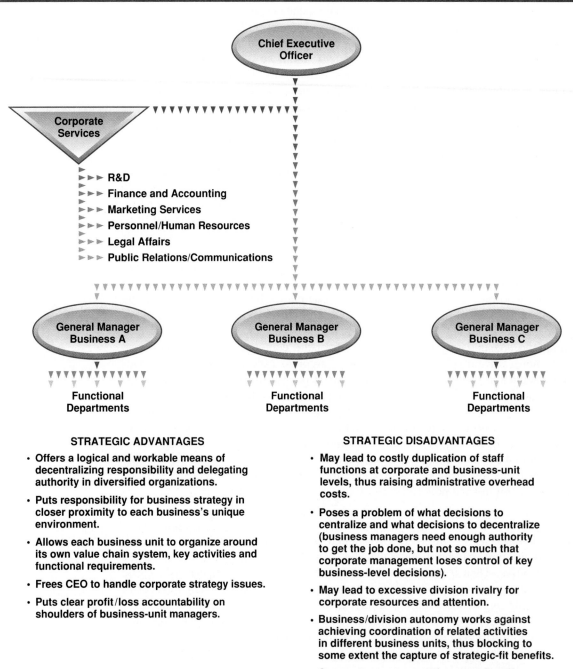

STRATEGIC ADVANTAGES

- Offers a logical and workable means of decentralizing responsibility and delegating authority in diversified organizations.

- Puts responsibility for business strategy in closer proximity to each business's unique environment.

- Allows each business unit to organize around its own value chain system, key activities and functional requirements.

- Frees CEO to handle corporate strategy issues.

- Puts clear profit/loss accountability on shoulders of business-unit managers.

STRATEGIC DISADVANTAGES

- May lead to costly duplication of staff functions at corporate and business-unit levels, thus raising administrative overhead costs.

- Poses a problem of what decisions to centralize and what decisions to decentralize (business managers need enough authority to get the job done, but not so much that corporate management loses control of key business-level decisions).

- May lead to excessive division rivalry for corporate resources and attention.

- Business/division autonomy works against achieving coordination of related activities in different business units, thus blocking to some extent the capture of strategic-fit benefits.

- Corporate management becomes heavily dependent on business-unit managers.

- Corporate managers can lose touch with business-unit situations, end up surprised when problems arise, and not know much about how to fix such problems.

were grouped into 43 SBUs and then aggregated further into six "sectors."[24] At Union Carbide, 15 groups and divisions were decomposed into 150 "strategic planning units" and then regrouped and combined into 9 new "aggregate planning units." At General Foods, SBUs were originally defined on a product-line basis but were later redefined according to menu segments (breakfast foods, beverages, main meal products, desserts, and pet foods). SBUs make headquarters' reviews of the strategies of lower-level units less imposing (there is no practical way for a CEO to conduct in-depth reviews of a hundred or more different businesses). A CEO can, however, effectively review the strategic plans of a lesser number of SBUs, leaving detailed business strategy reviews and direct supervision of individual businesses to the SBU heads. Figure 9–5 illustrates the SBU form of organization, along with its strategy-related pros and cons.

The SBU concept provides broadly diversified companies with a way to rationalize the organization of many different businesses and a management arrangement for capturing strategic-fit benefits and streamlining strategic planning and budgeting processes. The strategic function of the group vice president is to provide the SBU with some cohesive direction, enforce strategic coordination across related businesses, and keep an eye out for trouble at the business-unit level, providing counsel and additional corporate support as needed. The group vice president, as strategic coordinator for all businesses in the SBU, can facilitate resource sharing and skills transfers where appropriate and unify the strategic decisions and actions of businesses in the SBU. The SBU, in effect, becomes a strategy-making, strategy-implementing unit with a wider field of vision and operations than a single business unit. It serves as a diversified company's organizational mechanism for capturing strategic-fit benefits across businesses and adding to the competitive advantage that each business in the SBU is able to build on its own. Moreover, it affords opportunity to "cross-pollinate" the activities of separate businesses, ideally creating enough new capability to stretch a company's strategic reach into adjacent products, technologies, and markets. Aggressive pursuit of resource-sharing, skills-transfer, and cross-pollination opportunities is one of the best avenues companies can use to develop the internal capabilities needed to enter new business areas.

Matrix Forms of Organization   A matrix organization is a structure with two (or more) channels of command, two lines of budget authority, and two sources of performance and reward. The key feature of the matrix is that authority for a business/product/project/venture and authority for a function or business process are overlaid (to form a matrix or grid), and decision-making responsibility in each unit/cell of the matrix is shared between the business/project/venture team manager and the functional/process manager—as shown in Figure 9–6. In a matrix structure, subordinates have a continuing dual assignment: to the business/project/process/venture and to their home-base function. The outcome is a compromise between functional specialization (engineering, R&D, manufacturing, marketing, finance) and product line, project, process, line-of-business or special venture divisions (where all of the specialized talent needed for the product line/project/line-of-business/venture are assigned to the same divisional or departmental unit).

---

[24]William K. Hall, "SBUs: Hot, New Topic in the Management of Diversification," *Business Horizons* 21, no. 1 (February 1978), p. 19. For an excellent discussion of the problems of implementing the SBU concept at 13 companies, see Richard A. Bettis and William K. Hall, "The Business Portfolio Approach—Where It Falls Down in Practice," *Long Range Planning* 16, no. 2 (April 1983), pp. 95–104.

Basic Concept
A strategic business unit (SBU) is a grouping of related businesses under the supervision of a senior executive.

SBU structures are a means for managing broad diversification and enforcing strategic coordination across related businesses.

Matrix structures, although complex to manage and sometimes unwieldy, allow a firm to be organized in two different strategy-supportive ways at the same time.

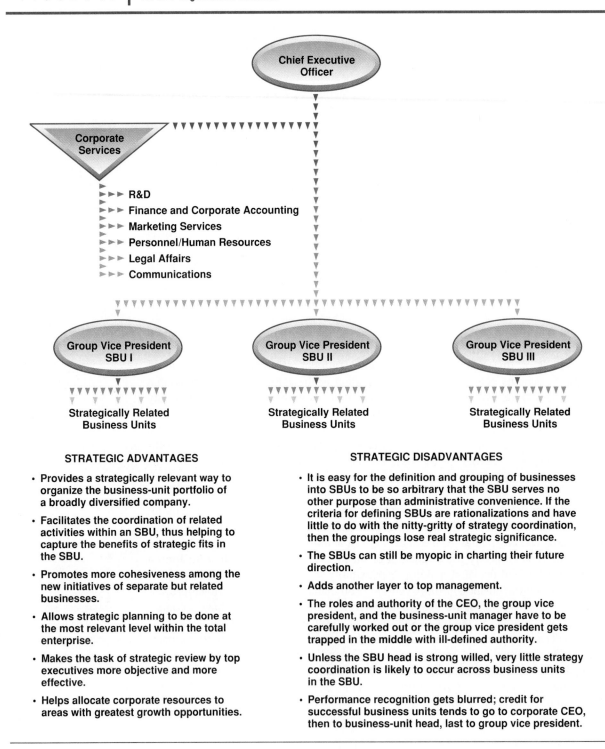

STRATEGIC ADVANTAGES

- Provides a strategically relevant way to organize the business-unit portfolio of a broadly diversified company.

- Facilitates the coordination of related activities within an SBU, thus helping to capture the benefits of strategic fits in the SBU.

- Promotes more cohesiveness among the new initiatives of separate but related businesses.

- Allows strategic planning to be done at the most relevant level within the total enterprise.

- Makes the task of strategic review by top executives more objective and more effective.

- Helps allocate corporate resources to areas with greatest growth opportunities.

STRATEGIC DISADVANTAGES

- It is easy for the definition and grouping of businesses into SBUs to be so arbitrary that the SBU serves no other purpose than administrative convenience. If the criteria for defining SBUs are rationalizations and have little to do with the nitty-gritty of strategy coordination, then the groupings lose real strategic significance.

- The SBUs can still be myopic in charting their future direction.

- Adds another layer to top management.

- The roles and authority of the CEO, the group vice president, and the business-unit manager have to be carefully worked out or the group vice president gets trapped in the middle with ill-defined authority.

- Unless the SBU head is strong willed, very little strategy coordination is likely to occur across business units in the SBU.

- Performance recognition gets blurred; credit for successful business units tends to go to corporate CEO, then to business-unit head, last to group vice president.

FIGURE 9-6 | **A Matrix Organization Structure***

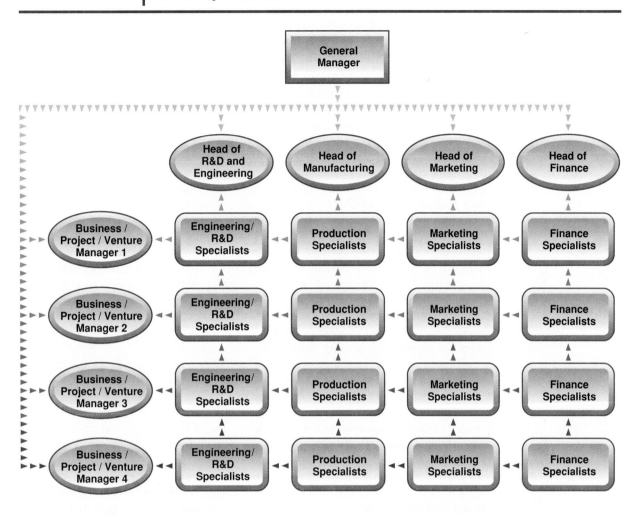

STRATEGIC ADVANTAGES

- Gives formal attention to each dimension of strategic priority.
- Creates checks and balances among competing viewpoints.
- Facilitates capture of functionally based strategic fits in diversified companies.
- Promotes making trade-off decisions on the basis of "what's best for the organization as a whole."
- Encourages cooperation, consensus-building, conflict resolution. and coordination of related activities.

STRATEGIC DISADVANTAGES

- Very complex to manage.
- Hard to maintain "balance" between the two lines of authority.
- So much shared authority can result in a transactions logjam and disproportionate amounts of time being spent on communications.
- It is hard to move quickly and decisively without getting clearance from many other people.
- Promotes an organizational bureaucracy and hamstrings creative entrepreneurship.

*Arrows indicate reporting channels.

A matrix-type organization is a genuinely different structural form and represents a "new way of life." It breaks the unity-of-command principle; two reporting channels, two bosses, and shared authority create a new kind of organizational climate. In essence, the matrix is a conflict resolution system through which strategic and operating priorities are negotiated, power is shared, and resources are allocated internally on the basis of "strongest case for what is best overall for the unit.[25]

The impetus for matrix organizations stems from growing use of strategies that create a simultaneous need for process teams, special project managers, product managers, functional managers, geographic area managers, new-venture managers, and business-level managers—all of whom have important strategic responsibilities. When at least two of several variables (product, customer, technology, geography, functional area, business process, and market segment) have roughly equal strategic priorities, a matrix organization can be an effective structural form. A matrix structure promotes internal checks and balances among competing viewpoints and perspectives, with separate managers for different dimensions of strategic initiative. A matrix arrangement thus allows each of several strategic considerations to be managed directly and to be formally represented in the organization structure. In this sense, it helps middle managers make trade-off decisions from an organizationwide perspective.[26] The other big advantage of matrix organization is that it can serve as a mechanism for capturing strategic fit. When the strategic fits in a diversified company are related to a specific functional area (R&D, technology, marketing), or cross traditional functional lines, matrix organization can be a reasonable structural arrangement for coordinating activity sharing and skills transfer.

Companies using matrix structures include General Electric, Texas Instruments, Citibank, Shell Oil, TRW, Bechtel, Boeing, and Dow Chemical. Illustration Capsule 27 on p. 264–265 describes how one broadly diversified company with global strategies in each of its businesses developed a matrix-type structure to manage its operations worldwide. However, in most companies, use of matrix organization is confined to a portion of what the firm does (certain important functions) rather than its whole organizing scheme.

Many companies and managers shun matrix organization because of its chief weaknesses.[27] It is a complex structure to manage; people end up confused or frustrated over who to report to for what. Moreover, because the matrix signals a need for communication and consensus, a "transactions logjam" can result. People in one area are pushed into transacting business with people in another area and networking their way through internal bureaucracies. Action turns into paralysis since, with shared authority, it is hard to move decisively without first checking with other people and getting clearance. Much time and psychic energy get eaten up in meetings and communicating back and forth. Sizable transactions costs and longer decision times can result with little value-added work accomplished. Even so, in some situations the benefits of conflict resolution, consensus building, and coordination outweigh these weaknesses, as the ABB example in Illustration Capsule 27 indicates.

---

[25]For two excellent critiques of matrix organizations, see Stanley M. Davis and Paul R. Lawrence, "Problems of Matrix Organizations," *Harvard Business Review* 56, no. 3 (May–June 1978), pp. 131–42, and Erik W. Larson and David H. Gobeli, "Matrix Management: Contradictions and Insights," *California Management Review* 29, no. 4 (Summer 1987), pp. 126–38.

[26]Davis and Lawrence, "Problems of Matrix Organizations," p. 132.

[27]Thomas J. Peters and Robert H. Waterman, Jr., *In Search of Excellence* (New York: Harper & Row, 1982), pp. 306–7.

Supplementing the Basic Organization Structure   None of the basic structural designs is wholly adequate for organizing the total work effort in strategy-supportive ways. Some weaknesses can be corrected by using two or more of the structural designs simultaneously—many companies are large enough and diverse enough to have SBUs, functionally organized business units, geographic organizational structures in one or more businesses, units employing matrix principles, and several functionally specialized departments. But in many companies strategy-supportive organization requires supplementing the formal structure with special coordinating mechanisms and "creative disorganization"—cross-functional task forces, project teams, venture teams, self-sufficient work teams to perform whole processes, and special empowerment of key individuals to cut through red tape and get things done quickly when necessary. Six of the most frequently used devices for supplementing the formal organization structure are:

1. *Special project teams*—creating a separate, largely self-sufficient work group to oversee the completion of a special activity (setting up a new technological process, bringing out a new product, starting up a new venture, consummating a merger with another company, seeing through the completion of a government contract, supervising the construction and opening of a new plant). Project teams are especially suitable for one-of-a-kind situations with a finite life expectancy when the normal organization is not equipped to achieve the same results in addition to regular duties.

2. *Cross-functional task forces*—bringing a number of top-level executives and/or specialists together to solve problems requiring specialized expertise from several parts of the organization, coordinating strategy-related activities that span departmental boundaries, or exploring ways to leverage the skills of different functional specialists into broader core competencies. Task forces seem to be most effective when they have less than 10 members, membership is voluntary, the seniority of the members is proportional to the importance of the problem, the task force moves swiftly to deal with its assignment, they are used sparingly—only on an as-needed basis, no staff is assigned, and documentation is scant.[28] Companies that have used task forces successfully form them to solve pressing problems, produce some solutions efficiently, and then disband them.

3. *Venture teams*—forming a group of individuals to manage the launch of a new product, entry into a new geographic market, or creation of a specific new business. Dow, General Mills, Westinghouse, General Electric, and Monsanto used the venture-team approach to regenerate an entrepreneurial spirit. The difficulties with venture teams include deciding who the venture manager should report to; whether funding for ventures should come from corporate, business, or departmental budgets; how to keep the venture clear of bureaucratic and vested interests; and how to coordinate large numbers of different ventures.

4. *Self-contained work teams*—forming a group of people drawn from different disciplines who work together on a semipermanent basis to continuously improve organizational performance in specific strategy-related areas— shortening the lab-to-market cycle time, boosting product quality, improving

---

[28]Ibid., pp. 127–32.

MATRIX ORGANIZATION IN A DIVERSIFIED GLOBAL COMPANY
THE CASE OF ASEA BROWN BOVERI

Asea Brown Boveri (ABB) is a diversified multinational corporation headquartered in Zurich, Switzerland. ABB was formed in 1987 through the merger of Asea, one of Sweden's largest industrial enterprises, and Brown Boveri, a major Swiss company. Both companies manufactured electrical products and equipment. Following the merger, ABB acquired or took minority positions in 60 companies, mostly outside Europe. In 1991 ABB had annual revenues of $25 billion and employed 240,000 people around the world, including 150,000 in Western Europe, 40,000 in North America, 10,000 in South America, and 10,000 in India. The company was a world leader in the global markets for electrical products, electrical installations and service, and power-generation equipment and was the dominant European producer. European sales accounted for 60% of revenues, while North America accounted for 30% and Asia 15%.

To manage its global operations, ABB had devised a matrix organization that leveraged its core competencies in electrical-power technologies and its ability to achieve global economies of scale while, at the same time, maximizing its national market visibility and responsiveness. At the top of ABB's corporate organi-

zation structure was an executive committee composed of the CEO, Percy Barnevik, and 12 colleagues; the committee consisted of Swedes, Swiss, Germans, and Americans, several of whom were based outside Switzerland. The group, which met every three weeks at various locations around the world, was responsible for ABB's corporate strategy and performance.

Along one dimension of ABB's global matrix were 50 or so business areas (BAs), each representing a closely related set of products and services. The BAs were grouped into eight "business segments"; each segment was supervised by a different member of the executive committee. Each BA had a leader charged with responsibility for (1) devising and championing a global strategy, (2) setting quality and cost standards for the BA's factories worldwide, (3) deciding which factories would export to which country markets, (4) rotating people across borders to share technical expertise, create mixed-nationality teams to solve BA problems, and build a culture of trust and communication, and (5) pooling expertise and research funds for the benefit of the BA worldwide. BA leaders worked out of whatever world location made the most sense for their BA. For example, the BA leader for power transformers, who had responsibility for 25 factories in 16 countries, was a Swede who worked out of Mannheim, Germany; the BA leader for electric metering was an American based in North Carolina.

(continued)

customer service, cutting delivery times, eliminating stockouts, reducing the costs of purchased materials and components, increasing assembly-line productivity, trimming equipment downtime and maintenance expenses, or designing new models. American Express cut out three layers of hierarchy when it developed self-managed teams to handle all types of customer inquiries in a single-call, quick-resolution manner.[29]

5. *Process teams*—putting functional specialists who perform pieces of a business process together on a team instead of assigning them to their home-base functional department. Such teams can be empowered to reengineer the process, held accountable for results, and rewarded on the basis of how well the process is performed. Much of Chrysler's revitalization is due to dramatically revamping its new-model development process using "platform teams."[30] Each platform team consists of members from engineering, design, finance, purchasing, and marketing. The team is responsible for the car's design from beginning to end, has broad decision-making power, and is held

---

[29]Quinn, *Intelligent Enterprise,* p. 163.
[30]"Can Jack Smith Fix GM?" *Business Week,* November 1, 1993, pp. 130–31.

(concluded)

Along the other dimension of the matrix was a group of national enterprises with presidents, boards of directors, financial statements, and career ladders. The presidents of ABB's national enterprises had responsibility for maximizing the performance and effectiveness of all ABB activities within their country's borders. Country presidents worked closely with the BA leaders to evaluate and improve what was happening in ABB's business areas in their countries.

Inside the matrix were 1,200 "local" ABB companies with an average of 200 employees, each headed by a president. The local company president reported both to the national president in whose country the local company operated and to the leader of the BA to which its products/services were assigned. Each local company was a subsidiary of the ABB national enterprise where it was located. Thus, all of ABB's local companies in Norway were subsidiaries of ABB Norway, the national company for Norway; all ABB operations in Portugal were subsidiaries of ABB Portugal, and so on. The 1,200 presidents of ABB's local companies were expected to be excellent profit center managers, able to answer to two bosses effectively. The local president's

global boss was the BA manager who established the local company's role in ABB's global strategy and, also, the rules a local company had to observe in supporting this strategy. The local president's country boss was the national CEO, with whom it was necessary to cooperate on local issues.

ABB believed that its matrix structure allowed it to optimize its pursuit of global business strategies and, at the same time, maximize its performance in every country market where it operated. The matrix was a way of being global and big strategically, yet small and local operationally. Decision-making was decentralized (to BA leaders, country presidents, and local company presidents), but reporting and control was centralized (through the BA leaders, the country presidents, and the executive committee). ABB saw itself as a federation of national companies with a global coordination center.

Only 100 professionals were located in ABB's corporate headquarters in Zurich. A management information system collected data on all profit centers monthly, comparing actual performance against budgets and forecasts. Data was collected in local currencies but translated into U.S. dollars to allow for cross-border analysis. ABB's corporate financial statements were reported in U.S. dollars, and English was ABB's official language. All high-level meetings were conducted in English.

Source: Compiled from information in William Taylor, "The Logic of Global Business: An Interview with ABB's Percy Barnevik," *Harvard Business Review* 69, no. 2 (March–April 1991), pp. 90–105.

accountable for the success or failure of their design. Teams coordinate their designs with manufacturing so that the models will be easier to build and consult regularly with purchasing agents regarding parts quality. In one case Chrysler purchasing agents elected to pay 30 percent more for a better part because the engineer on the platform team believed the added cost would be offset by the time saved during assembly.

6. *Contact managers*—providing a single point of contact for customers when the steps of a process either are so complex or are dispersed in such a way that integrating them for a single person or team to perform is impractical.[31] Acting as a buffer between internal processes and the customer, the contact person endeavors to answer customer questions and solve customer problems as if he or she were responsible for performing the called-for activities. To perform this role, contact persons need access to all the information systems that the persons actually performing the process use and the ability to contact those people with questions and requests for further assistance when necessary. The

---

[31]Hammer and Champy, *Reengineering the Corporation*, pp. 62–63.

best results are achieved when contact persons are empowered to use their own judgment to get things done in a manner that will please customers. Duke Power, a Charlotte-based electric utility, uses empowered customer service representatives to resolve the problems of residential customers while shielding them from whatever goes on "behind the scenes" to produce solutions.

PERSPECTIVES ON ORGANIZING THE WORK EFFORT

There's no perfect or ideal organization structure. All the basic designs have their strategy-related strengths and weaknesses. To do a good job of matching structure to strategy, strategy-implementers have to pick a basic design, modify it as needed to fit the company's particular business makeup, and then supplement it with whatever coordinating mechanisms and communication arrangements it takes to support effective execution of the firm's strategy. While practical realities often dictate giving some consideration to existing reporting relationships, to the personalities involved, to internal politics, and to other situational idiosyncrasies, strategy-structure factors have to predominate.

Peter Drucker, one of the foremost authorities on managing, sums up the intricacies of organization design:

> The simplest organization structure that will do the job is the best one. What makes an organization structure "good" is the problems it does not create. The simpler the structure, the less that can go wrong.
>
> Some design principles are more difficult and problematic than others. But none is without difficulties and problems. None is primarily people-focused rather than task-focused; none is more "creative," "free," or "democratic." Design principles are tools; and tools are neither good nor bad in themselves. They can be used properly or improperly; and that is all. To obtain both the greatest possible simplicity and the greatest "fit," organization design has to start out with a clear focus on *key activities* needed to produce *key results*. They have to be structured and positioned in the simplest possible design. Above all, the architect of organization needs to keep in mind the purpose of the structure he is designing.[32]

Current Organizational Trends   Many of today's companies are remodeling their traditional hierarchical structures built around functional specialization and centralized authority. Such structures make good strategic and organizational sense so long as (1) activities can be divided into simple, repeatable tasks that can be mastered quickly and then efficiently performed in mass quantity, (2) there are important benefits to deep functional expertise in each managerial discipline, and (3) customer needs are sufficiently standardized that it is easy to prescribe procedures for satisfying them. But traditional hierarchies become a liability in businesses where customer preferences are shifting from standardized products to custom orders and special features, product life-cycles are growing shorter, flexible manufacturing methods are replacing mass production techniques, customers want to be treated as individuals, the pace of technological change is accelerating, and market conditions are fluid. Multilayered management hierarchies and functionalized bureaucracies that require people to look upward in the organizational structure for answers tend to bog down in such environments. They can't deliver responsive customer service or adapt fast enough to changing conditions. Functional silos, task-oriented work, process fragmentation, layered

---

[32]Drucker, *Management: Tasks, Responsibilities, Practices,* pp. 601–2.

management hierarchies, centralized decision-making, growing functional and middle-management bureaucracies, lots of checks and controls, and long response times can undermine competitive success in fluid or volatile business environments. Success in fast-changing markets depends on strategies featuring important organizational capabilities: quick response to shifting customer preferences, short design-to-market cycles, make-it-right-the-first-time quality, custom-order and multiversion production, expedited delivery, personalized customer service, accurate order filling, rapid assimilation of new technologies, creativity and innovativeness, and speedy reactions to external competitive developments.

These new components of business strategy are driving a revolution in corporate organization.[33] Much of the corporate downsizing movement is aimed at busting up functional and middle management bureaucracies and recasting authoritarian pyramidal organizational structures into flatter, decentralized structures. The latest organizational designs for matching structure to strategy feature fewer layers of management authority, small-scale business units, reengineered work processes to cut back on fragmentation across functional department lines, creation of process teams and interdisciplinary work groups, lean staffing of corporate support functions, partnerships with key suppliers, empowerment of firstline supervisors and nonmanagement employees, open communications vertically and laterally, computers and telecommunications technologies to provide fast access to and dissemination of information, and accountability for results rather than emphasis on activity. The new organizational themes are lean, flat, responsive, and innovative. The new tools of organizational design are managers and workers empowered to act on their own judgments, reengineered work processes, and self-directed work teams.

The command-and-control paradigm of vertically layered structures assumes that the people actually performing work have neither the time nor the inclination to monitor and control it and that they lack the knowledge to make informed decisions about how best to do it; hence, the need for prescribed procedures, close supervision, and managerial control of decision-making. In flat, decentralized structures, these assumptions are discarded. Jobs are defined more broadly; several tasks are integrated into a single job where possible. People operate in a more self-directed fashion, armed with the information they need to get things done. Fewer managers are needed because deciding how to do things becomes part of each person's or team's job.

Reengineering Can Promote Better Implementation   Reengineering strategy-critical business processes to reduce fragmentation across traditional departmental lines and cut bureaucratic overheads has proven to be a legitimate organization design tool. It's not a passing fad or another management program of the month. Process organization is every bit as valid an organizing principle as functional specialization. Strategy execution is improved when the pieces of strategy-critical activities and core business processes performed by different departments are properly integrated and coordinated.

Companies that have reengineered some of their business processes have ended up compressing formerly separate steps and tasks into jobs performed by a single person and integrating jobs into team activities. Reorganization then follows, a natural consequence of task synthesis and job redesign. The experiences of companies that have successfully reengineered and restructured their operations in strategy-supportive

---

[33]Evidence to this effect is contained in the scores of examples reported in Tom Peters, *Liberation Management* (New York: Alfred A. Knopf, 1992); Quinn, *Intelligent Enterprise;* and Hammer and Champy, *Reengineering the Corporation.*

ways suggest attacking process fragmentation and overhead reduction in the following fashion:[34]

Reengineer, then reorganize.

- Develop a flow chart of the total business process, including its interfaces with other value-chain activities.
- Try to simplify the process first, eliminating tasks and steps where possible and analyzing how to streamline the performance of what remains.
- Determine which parts of the process can be automated (usually those that are repetitive, time-consuming, and require little thought or decision); consider introducing advanced technologies that can be upgraded to achieve next-generation capability and provide a basis for further productivity gains down the road.
- Evaluate each activity in the process to determine whether it is strategy-critical or not. Strategy-critical activities are candidates for benchmarking to achieve best-in-industry or best-in-world performance status.
- Weigh the pros and cons of outsourcing activities that are noncritical or that contribute little to organizational capabilities and core competencies.
- Design a structure for performing the activities that remain; reorganize the personnel and groups who perform these activities into the new structure.

Reengineering can produce dramatic gains in productivity and organizational capability when done properly. In the order-processing section of General Electric's circuit breaker division, elapsed time from order receipt to delivery was cut from three weeks to three days by consolidating six production units into one, reducing a variety of former inventory and handling steps, automating the design system to replace a human custom-design process, and cutting the organizational layers between managers and workers from three to one.[35] Productivity rose 20 percent in one year, and unit manufacturing costs dropped 30 percent.

There's no escaping the conclusion that reengineering, in concert with advanced office technologies, empowerment, and the use of self-directed work teams, provides company managers with important new organization design options. Organizational hierarchies can be flattened and middle-management layers removed. Responsibility and decision-making authority can be pushed downward and outward to those places in the organization where customer contacts are made. Strategy-critical processes can be unified, performed more quickly and at lower cost, and made more responsive to changing customer preferences and expectations. Used properly, these new design approaches can trigger big gains in organizational creativity and employee productivity.

Illustration Capsule 28 reports the results of a study of trends in organizational arrangements in multinational and global companies.

KEY POINTS

The job of strategy implementation is to convert strategic plans into actions and good results. The test of successful strategy implementation is whether actual organization performance matches or exceeds the targets spelled out in the strategic plan. Shortfalls in performance signal weak strategy, weak implementation, or both.

---

[34]Quinn, *Intelligent Enterprise,* p. 162.
[35]T. Stuart, "GE Keeps Those Ideas Coming," *Fortune,* August 12, 1991. For other examples, see Gene Hall, Jim Rosenthal, and Judy Wade, "How to Make Reengineering Really Work," *Harvard Business Review* 71, no. 6 (November–December 1993), pp. 119–31.

ORGANIZATIONAL APPROACHES FOR INTERNATIONAL AND GLOBAL MARKETS

A 1993 study of 43 large U.S.-based consumer products companies conducted by McKinsey & Co., a leading management consulting firm, identified internal organizational actions with the strongest and weakest links to rapidly growing sales and profits in international and global markets.

Organizational Actions Strongly Linked to International Success

- Centralizing international decision-making in every area except new product development.
- Having a worldwide management development program and more foreigners in senior management posts.
- Requiring international experience for advancement into top management.
- Linking global managers with video-conferencing and electronic mail.
- Having product managers of foreign subsidiaries report to a country general manager.
- Using local executives to head operations in foreign

countries (however, this is rapidly ceasing to distinguish successful companies because nearly everyone has implemented such a practice).

Organizational Actions Weakly Linked to International Success

- Creating global divisions.
- Forming international strategic business units.
- Establishing centers of excellence (where a single company facility takes global responsibility for a key product or emerging technology (too new to evaluate pro or con).
- Using cross-border task forces to resolve problems and issues.
- Creating globally-integrated management information systems.

However, the lists of organizational do's and don'ts are far from decisive. In general, the study found that internal organizational structure "doesn't matter that much" as compared to having products with attractive prices and features. It is wrong to expect good results just because of good organization. Moreover, certain organizational arrangements, such as centers of excellence, are too new to determine whether they positively affect sales and profit growth.

Source: Based on information reported by Joann S. Lublin, "Study Sees U.S. Businesses Stumbling on the Road to Globalization," *The Wall Street Journal,* March 22, 1993, p. B4B.

In deciding how to implement strategy, managers have to determine what internal conditions are needed to execute the strategic plan successfully. Then they must create these conditions as rapidly as practical. The process involves creating a series of tight fits:

- Between strategy and the organization's skills, competencies, and structure.
- Between strategy and budgetary allocations.
- Between strategy and policy.
- Between strategy and internal support systems.
- Between strategy and the reward structure.
- Between strategy and the corporate culture.

The tighter the fits, the more powerful strategy execution becomes and the more likely targeted performance can actually be achieved.

Implementing strategy is not just a top-management function; it is a job for the whole management team. All managers function as strategy-implementers in their respective areas of authority and responsibility. All managers have to consider what actions to take in their areas to achieve the intended results—they each need an *action agenda*.

The three major organization-building actions are (1) filling key positions with able people, (2) seeing that the organization has the skills, know-how, core competencies, and internal capabilities needed to perform its value-chain activities proficiently, and (3) structuring the work effort and deciding what the organization chart should look like. Selecting able people for key positions tends to be one of the earliest strategy implementation steps because it takes a full complement of capable managers to get changes in place and functioning smoothly.

Building strategy-critical core competencies is one of the best ways to outexecute rivals with similar strategies. Core competencies emerge from skills and activities performed at different points in the value chain that, when linked, create unique organizational capability. The key to leveraging a company's core competencies into long-term competitive advantage is to concentrate more effort and more talent than rivals do on strengthening and deepening these competencies. The multiskill, multi-activity character of core competencies makes achieving dominating depth an exercise in (1) managing human skills, knowledge bases, and intellect and (2) coordinating and networking the efforts of different work groups and departments at every place in the value chain related to such competencies.

Matching structure to strategy centers around making strategy-critical activities the main organizational building blocks and finding effective ways to bridge organizational lines of authority and coordinate the related efforts of separate units and individuals. Other big considerations include what decisions to centralize and what decisions to decentralize and whether noncritical activities can be outsourced more effectively or efficiently than they can be performed internally.

All organization structures have strategic advantages and disadvantages; there is no one best way to organize. Functionally specialized organization structures have traditionally been the most popular way to organize single-business companies. Functional organization works well where strategy-critical activities closely match discipline-specific activities and minimal interdepartmental cooperation is needed. But it has significant drawbacks: functional myopia and empire-building, interdepartmental rivalries, excessive process fragmentation, and vertically layered management hierarchies.

Geographic organization structures are favored by enterprises operating in diverse geographic markets or across expansive geographic areas. SBU structures are well-suited to companies pursuing related diversification. Decentralized business-unit structures are well-suited to companies pursuing unrelated diversification. Matrix structures work well for companies that need separate lines of authority and managers for each of several strategic dimensions (products, buyer segments, functional departments, projects or ventures, technologies, core business processes, geographic areas) yet also need close cooperation between these managers to coordinate related value-chain activities, share or transfer skills, and perform certain related activities jointly.

Whatever formal organization structure is chosen, it usually has to be supplemented with interdisciplinary task forces, incentive compensation schemes tied to measures of joint performance, empowerment of cross-functional teams to perform and unify fragmented processes and strategy-critical activities, special project and venture teams, self-contained work teams, and contact managers.

New strategic priorities like short design-to-market cycles, multiversion production, and personalized customer service are promoting a revolution in organization-building featuring lean, flat, horizontal structures that are responsive and innovative. Such designs for matching structure to strategy involve fewer layers of management authority, small-scale business units, reengineering work processes to reduce fragmentation across departmental lines, the creation of process teams and cross-functional work groups, managers and workers empowered to act on their own judgments, partnerships with key suppliers and increased outsourcing of noncritical activities, lean staffing of internal support functions, and use of computers and telecommunications technologies to provide fast access to and information.

SUGGESTED READINGS

Aaker, David A. "Managing Assets and Skills: The Key to a Sustainable Competitive Advantage." *California Management Review* 31 (Winter 1989), pp. 91–106.

Bartlett, Christopher A., and Sumantra Ghoshal. "Matrix Management: Not a Structure, a Frame of Mind." *Harvard Business Review* 68, no. 4 (July–August 1990), pp. 138–45.

Bettis, Richard A., and William K. Hall. "The Business Portfolio Approach—Where It Falls Down in Practice." *Long Range Planning* 16, no. 2 (April 1983), pp. 95–104.

Chandler, Alfred D. *Strategy and Structure.* Cambridge, Mass.: MIT Press, 1962.

Hall, Gene, Jim Rosenthal, and Judy Wade. "How to Make Reengineering Really Work." *Harvard Business Review* 71, no. 6 (November–December 1993), pp. 119–31.

Hambrick, Donald C. "The Top Management Team: Key to Strategic Success." *California Management Review* 30, no. 1 (Fall 1987), pp. 88–108.

Hammer, Michael, and James Champy. *Reengineering the Corporation.* New York: HarperBusiness, 1993, chaps. 2 and 3.

Howard, Robert. "The CEO as Organizational Architect: An Interview with Xerox's Paul Allaire." *Harvard Business Review* 70, no. 5 (September–October 1992), pp. 107–19.

Katzenbach, Jon R., and Douglas K. Smith. "The Discipline of Teams." *Harvard Business Review* 71, no. 2 (March–April 1993), pp. 111–24.

Larson, Erik W., and David H. Gobeli. "Matrix Management: Contradictions and Insights." *California Management Review* 29, no. 4 (Summer 1987), pp. 126–27.

Powell, Walter W. "Hybrid Organizational Arrangements: New Form or Transitional Development?" *California Management Review* 30, no. 1 (Fall 1987), pp. 67–87.

Prahalad, C. K., and Gary Hamel. "The Core Competence of the Corporation." *Harvard Business Review* 68 (May–June 1990), pp. 79–93.

Quinn, James Brian. *Intelligent Enterprise.* New York: Free Press, 1992, chaps. 2 and 3.

Stalk, George, Philip Evans, and Lawrence E. Shulman. "Competing on Capabilities: The New Rules of Corporate Strategy." *Harvard Business Review* 70, no. 2 (March–April 1992), pp. 57–69.

Yip, George S. *Total Global Strategy: Managing for Worldwide Competitive Advantage.* Englewood Cliffs, N.J.: Prentice-Hall, 1992, chap. 8.

CHAPTER TEN

IMPLEMENTING STRATEGY: BUDGETS, POLICIES, BEST PRACTICES, SUPPORT SYSTEMS, AND REWARDS

If you talk about change but don't change the reward and recognition system, nothing changes.

Paul Allaire
CEO, Xerox Corporation

. . . Winning companies know how to do their work better.

Michael Hammer and James Champy

. . . While a corporation can come up with a plan for the future, it takes everybody's help—and commitment—to implement it.

Ronald W. Allen
CEO, Delta Airlines

In the previous chapter we emphasized the importance of building an organization capable of performing strategy-critical activities in a coordinated and highly competent manner. In this chapter we discuss five additional strategy-implementing tasks:

1. Reallocating resources to match the budgetary and staffing requirements of the new strategy.
2. Establishing strategy-supportive policies.
3. Instituting best practices and mechanisms for continuous improvement.
4. Installing support systems that enable company personnel to carry out their strategic roles proficiently day in and day out.
5. Employing motivational practices and incentive compensation methods that enhance organizationwide commitment to good strategy execution.

LINKING BUDGETS TO STRATEGY

Implementing strategy forces a manager into the budget-making process. Organizational units need enough resources to carry out their parts of the strategic plan. This includes having enough of the right kinds of people and having sufficient operating funds for organizational units to do their work successfully. Strategy-implementers must screen subordinates' requests for new capital projects and bigger operating budgets, distinguishing between what would be nice and what can make a cost-justified contribution to strategy execution. Moreover, implementers have to make a persuasive, documented case to superiors on what additional resources, if any, it will take to execute their assigned pieces of company strategy.

How well a strategy-implementer links budget allocations to the needs of strategy can either promote or impede the implementation process. Too little funding slows progress and impedes the ability of organizational units to execute their pieces of the strategic plan proficiently. Too much funding wastes organizational resources and reduces financial performance. Both outcomes argue for the strategy-implementer to be deeply involved in the budgeting process, closely reviewing the programs and budget proposals of strategy-critical organization units.

Implementers must also be willing to shift resources from one area to another to support new strategic initiatives and priorities. A change in strategy nearly always calls for budget reallocations. Units important in the old strategy may now be oversized and overfunded. Units that now have a bigger and more critical strategic role may need more people, new equipment, additional facilities, and above-average increases in their operating budgets. Strategy-implementers need to be active and forceful in shifting resources, downsizing some areas, upsizing others, and amply funding activities with a critical role in the new strategy. They have to exercise their power to allocate resources to make things happen and make the tough decisions to kill projects and activities that are no longer justified. The essential condition is that the funding requirements of the new strategy must drive how capital allocations are made and the size of each unit's operating budgets. Underfunding organizational units and activities pivotal to strategic success can defeat the whole implementation process.

Aggressive resource reallocation can have a positive strategic payoff. For example, at Harris Corporation where the strategy was to diffuse research ideas into areas that were commercially viable, top management regularly shifted groups of engineers out of government projects and moved them (as a group) into new commercial venture divisions. Boeing used a similar approach to reallocating ideas and talent; according to one Boeing officer, "We can do it (create a big new unit) in two weeks. We couldn't do it in two years at International Harvester."[1] Forceful actions to reallocate operating funds and move people into new organizational units signal a strong commitment to implementing strategic change and are frequently needed to catalyze the implementation process and give it credibility.

Fine-tuning the implementation of a company's existing strategy seldom requires big movements of people and money from one area to another. The desired improvements can usually be accomplished through above-average budget increases to organizational units where new initiatives are contemplated and below-average increases

Strategic Management Principle

Depriving strategy-critical groups of the funds needed to execute their pieces of the strategy can undermine the implementation process.

New strategies usually call for significant budget reallocations.

---

[1] Thomas J. Peters and Robert H. Waterman, Jr., *In Search of Excellence* (New York: Harper & Row, 1980), p. 125.

(or even small cuts) for the remaining organizational units. The chief exception occurs where a prime ingredient of corporate/business strategy is to generate fresh, new products and business opportunities within the existing budget. Then, as proposals and business plans worth pursuing bubble up from below, decisions have to be made regarding where the needed capital expenditures, operating budgets, and personnel will come from. Companies like 3M, GE, and Boeing shift resources and people from area to area on an as-needed basis to support the launch of new products and new business ventures. They empower "product champions" and small bands of would-be entrepreneurs by giving them financial and technical support and by setting up organizational units and programs to help new ventures blossom more quickly.

CREATING STRATEGY-SUPPORTIVE POLICIES AND PROCEDURES

Changes in strategy generally call for some changes in work practices and how internal operations are conducted. Asking people to alter established procedures and behavior always upsets the internal order of things. It is normal for pockets of resistance to develop and for people to exhibit some degree of stress and anxiety about how the changes will affect them, especially when the changes may eliminate jobs. Questions are also likely to arise over what needs to be done in like fashion and where there ought to be leeway for independent action.

Prescribing policies and operating procedures aids the task of implementing strategy in several ways:

1. New or freshly revised policies and procedures provide top-down guidance to operating managers, supervisory personnel, and employees regarding how certain things now need to be done and what behavior is expected, thus establishing some degree of regularity, stability, and dependability in how management has decided to try to execute the strategy and operate the business on a daily basis.

2. Policies and procedures help align actions and behavior with strategy throughout the organization, placing limits on independent action and channeling individual and group efforts along the intended path. Policies and procedures counteract tendencies for some people to resist or reject common approaches—most people refrain from violating company policy or ignoring established practices without first gaining clearance or having strong justification.

3. Policies and standardized operating procedures help enforce needed consistency in how particular strategy-critical activities are performed in geographically scattered operating units (different plants, sales regions, customer service centers, or the individual outlets in a chain operation). Eliminating significant differences in the operating practices and procedures of organizational units performing common functions is necessary to avoid sending mixed messages to internal personnel and to customers who do business with the company at multiple locations.

4. Because dismantling old policies and procedures and instituting new ones invariably alter the character of the internal work climate, strategy-implementers can use the policy-changing process as a powerful lever for changing the corporate culture in ways that produce a stronger fit with the new strategy.

ILLUSTRATION CAPSULE 29

NIKE'S MANUFACTURING POLICIES AND PRACTICES

When Nike decided on a strategy of outsourcing 100% of its athletic footwear from independent manufacturers (all of which turned out, for reasons of low cost, to be located in Taiwan, South Korea, Thailand, Indonesia, and China), it developed a series of policies and production practices to govern its working relationships with its "production partners" (a term Nike carefully nurtured because it implied joint responsibilities):

- Nike personnel were stationed on-site at all key manufacturing facilities; each Nike representative tended to stay at the same factory site for several years to get to know the partner's people and processes in detail. They functioned as liaisons with Nike headquarters, working to match Nike's R&D and new product design efforts with factory capabilities and to keep monthly orders for new production in line with the latest sales forecasts.

- Nike instituted a quality assurance program at each factory site to enforce up-to-date and effective quality management practices.

- Nike endeavored to minimize ups and downs in monthly production orders at factory sites making Nike's premium-priced top-of-the-line models (volumes typically ran 20,000 to 25,000 pairs daily); the policy was to keep month-to-month variations in order quantity under 20%. These factories made Nike footwear exclusively and were expected to codevelop new models and to coinvest in new technologies.

- Factory sites that made mid-to-low-end Nike products in large quantities (usually 70,000 to 85,000 pairs per day), known as "volume producers," were expected to handle most ups and downs in monthly orders themselves; these factories usually produced shoes for five to eight other buyers, giving them the flexibility to juggle orders and stabilize their production.

- It was strict Nike policy to pay its bills from production partners on time, providing them with predictable cash flows.

Source: Based on information in James Brian Quinn, *Intelligent Enterprise* (New York: Free Press, 1992), pp. 60–64.

From a strategy implementation perspective, therefore, company managers need to be inventive in devising policies and practices that can provide vital support to effective strategy implementation. McDonald's policy manual, in an attempt to steer "crew members" into stronger quality and service behavior patterns, spells out such detailed procedures as "Cooks must turn, never flip, hamburgers. If they haven't been purchased, Big Macs must be discarded in 10 minutes after being cooked and french fries in 7 minutes. Cashiers must make eye contact with and smile at every customer." At Delta Airlines, it is corporate policy to test the aptitudes of all applicants for flight attendants' positions for friendliness, cooperativeness, and teamwork. Caterpillar Tractor has a policy of guaranteeing its customers 24-hour parts delivery anywhere in the world; if it fails to fulfill the promise, it supplies the part free. Hewlett-Packard requires R&D people to make regular visits to customers to learn about their problems, talk about new product applications, and, in general, keep the company's R&D programs customer-oriented. Illustration Capsule 29 describes Nike's manufacturing policies and practices in some detail.

> Well-conceived policies and procedures aid implementation; out-of-sync policies are barriers.

Thus there is a definite role for new and revised policies and procedures in the strategy implementation process. Wisely constructed policies and procedures help enforce strategy implementation by channeling actions, behavior, decisions, and practices in directions that improve strategy execution. When policies and practices aren't strategy-supportive, they become a barrier to the kinds of attitudinal and behavioral changes strategy-implementers are trying to promote. Often, people opposed to certain elements of the strategy or certain implementation approaches will hide behind or vigorously defend long-standing policies and operating procedures in an effort to stall implementation or divert the approach to implementation along a different route. Any time a company alters its strategy, managers should review existing policies and operating procedures, proactively revise or discard those that are out of sync, and formulate new ones to facilitate execution of new strategic initiatives.

None of this implies that companies need huge policy manuals. Too much policy can be as stifling as wrong policy or as chaotic as no policy. Sometimes, the best policy for implementing strategy is a willingness to empower subordinates and let them do it any way they want if it makes sense and works. A little "structured chaos" can be a good thing when individual creativity and initiative are more essential to good strategy execution than standardization and strict conformity. When Rene McPherson became CEO at Dana Corp., he dramatically threw out 22½ inches of policy manuals and replaced them with a one-page statement of philosophy focusing on "productive people."[2] Creating a strong supportive fit between strategy and policy can mean more policies, less policies, or different policies. It can mean policies that require things to be done a certain way or policies that give employees leeway to do activities the way they think best.

INSTITUTING BEST PRACTICES AND A COMMITMENT TO CONTINUOUS IMPROVEMENT

Identifying and implementing best practices is a journey not a destination.

If value-chain activities are to be performed as effectively and efficiently as possible, each department and organizational unit needs to benchmark how it performs specific tasks and activities against best-in-industry or best-in-world performers. A strong commitment to searching out and adopting best practices is integral to effective strategy implementation—especially for strategy-critical and big-dollar activities where better quality performance or lower costs can translate into a sizable bottom-line impact.

The benchmarking movement to search out, study, and implement best practices has spawned a number of spinoff efforts—reengineering (the redesign of business processes), continuous improvement programs, and total quality management (TQM). A 1991 survey by The Conference Board showed 93 percent of manufacturing companies and 69 percent of service companies have implemented some form of quality improvement program.[3] Another survey found that 55 percent of American executives and 70 percent of Japanese executives used quality improvement information at least monthly as part of their assessment of overall business performance.[4] Indeed, quality improvement processes have now become part of the fabric of implementing strategies keyed to defect-free manufacture, superior product quality, superior customer service, and total customer satisfaction.

Management interest in quality improvement programs typically originates in a company's production areas—fabrication and assembly in manufacturing enterprises, teller transactions in banks, order picking and shipping at catalog firms, or customer-

---

[2]Ibid., p. 65.
[3]Judy D. Olian and Sara L. Rynes, "Making Total Quality Work: Aligning Organizational Processes, Performance Measures, and Stakeholders," *Human Resource Management* 30, no. 3 (Fall 1991), p. 303.
[4]Ibid.

contact interfaces in service organizations. Other times, initial interest begins with executives who hear TQM presentations, read about TQM, or talk to people in other companies that have benefited from total quality programs. Usually, interested managers have quality and customer-satisfaction problems they are struggling to solve.

While TQM concentrates on the production of quality goods and the delivery of excellent customer service, to succeed it must extend organizationwide to employee efforts in all departments—HR, billing, R&D, engineering, accounting and records, and information systems—that may lack less-pressing customer-driven incentives to improve. This is because the institution of best practices and continuous improvement programs involves reforming the corporate culture and shifting to a total quality/continuous improvement business philosophy that permeates every facet of the organization. TQM aims at instilling enthusiasm and commitment to doing things right from top to bottom of the organization. It entails a restless search for continuing improvement, the little steps forward each day that the Japanese call *kaizen*. TQM is a race without a finish. The managerial objective is to kindle an innate, burning desire in people to use their ingenuity and initiative to progressively improve on how tasks and value-chain activities are performed. TQM preaches that there's no such thing as good enough and that everyone has a responsibility to participate in continuous improvement—see Illustration Capsule 30 describing Motorola's approach to involving employees in the TQM effort.

TQM entails creating a total quality culture bent on continuously improving the performance of every task and value-chain activity.

Best practices, reengineering, and continuous improvement efforts like TQM all aim at improved efficiency and reduced costs, better product quality, and greater customer satisfaction. The essential difference between reengineering and TQM is that reengineering aims at quantum gains on the order of 30 to 50 percent or more whereas total quality programs stress incremental progress, striving for inch-by-inch gains again and again in a never-ending stream. The two approaches to improved performance of value-chain activities are not mutually exclusive; it makes sense to use them in tandem. Reengineering can be used first to produce a good basic design that yields dramatic improvements in performing a business process. Total quality programs can then be used as a follow-on to work out bugs, perfect the process, and gradually improve both efficiency and effectiveness. Such a two-pronged approach to implementing organizational change is like a marathon race where you run the first four laps as fast as you can, then gradually pick up speed the remainder of the way.

Reengineering seeks one-time quantum improvement; TQM seeks ongoing incremental improvement.

Surveys indicate that some companies benefit from reengineering and TQM and some do not.[5] Usually, the biggest beneficiaries are companies that view such programs not as ends in themselves but as tools for implementing and executing company strategy more effectively. The skimpiest payoffs from best practices, TQM, and reengineering occur when company managers seize them as something worth trying, novel ideas that could improve things; in most such instances, they result in strategy-blind efforts to simply manage better. There's an important lesson here. Best practices, TQM, and reengineering all need to be seen and used as part of a bigger-picture effort to execute strategy proficiently. Only strategy can point to which activities matter and what performance targets make the most sense. Absent a strategic framework, managers lack the context in which to fix things that really matter to business-unit performance and competitive success.

When best practices, reengineering, and TQM are not part of a wider-scale effort to improve strategy execution and business performance, they deteriorate into strategy-blind efforts to manage better.

---

[5]See, for example, Gene Hall, Jim Rosenthal, and Judy Wade, "How to Make Reengineering Really Work," *Harvard Business Review* 71, no. 6 (November–December 1993), pp. 119–31.

MOTOROLA'S APPROACH TO TQM AND TEAMWORK

Motorola is rated as one of the best companies in measuring performance against its strategic targets and in promoting total quality practices that lead to continuous improvement. Motorola was selected in 1988 as one of the first winners of the Malcolm Baldrige Quality Award and has since improved on its own award-winning efforts. In 1993, the company estimated it was saving about $2.2 billion annually from its team-oriented approach to TQM and continuous improvement.

A central feature of Motorola's approach is a year-long contest highlighting the successes of employee teams from around the world in improving internal company practices, making better products, saving money, pleasing customers, and sharing best practices with other Motorola groups. The contest, known as the Total Customer Satisfaction Team Competition, in 1992 attracted entries from nearly 4,000 teams involving nearly 40,000 of Motorola's 107,000 employees. Preliminary judging eventually reduced the 1992 finalists to 24 teams from around the world, all of which were invited to Chicago in January 1993 to make a 12-minute presentation to a panel of 15 senior executives, including the CEO. Twelve teams were awarded gold medals and 12 silver medals. The gold medalists are listed below.

Motorola does not track the costs of the contest because "the benefits are so overwhelming." It has sent hundreds of videos about the contests to other companies wanting details. However, TQM consultants are skeptical whether other companies have progressed far enough in establishing a team-based quality culture to benefit from a companywide contest. The downsides to such elaborate contests, they say, are the added costs (preparation, travel, presentation, and judging) and the risks to the morale of those who don't win.

Gold Medal Teams	Work Location	Achievement
B.E.A.P. Goes On	Florida	Removed bottleneck in testing pagers by using robots.
The Expedition	Malaysia	Designed and delivered a new chip for Apple Computer in six months.
Operation Paging Storm	Singapore	Eliminated component alignment defect in papers.
ET/EV=1	Illinois	Streamlined order process for auto electronics.
The Mission	Arizona	Developed quality system for design of iridium satellites.
Class Act	Illinois	Cut training program from 5 years to 2 with better results.
Dyna-Attackers	Dublin	Cut production time and defect rate on new battery part.
Orient Express	Malaysia	Cut response time on tooling orders from 23 days to 4.
The Dandles	Japan	Improved efficiency of boiler operations.
Cool Blue Racers	Arizona	Cut product development time in half to win IBM contract.
IO Plastics Misload	Manila	Eliminated resin seepage in modulator assembly.

Source: Based on information reported in Barnaby J. Feder, "At Motorola, Quality Is a Team Sport," *New York Times,* January 21, 1993, pp. C1 and C6.

To get the most from benchmarking, best practices, reengineering, TQM, and related tools for enhancing organizational competence in executing strategy, managers have to start with a clear fix on the indicators of successful strategy execution—defect-free manufacture, on-time delivery, low overall costs, exceeding customers' expectations, faster cycle time, increased product innovation, or some other specific performance measure. Benchmarking best-in-industry and best-in-world performance of most or all value-chain activities provides a realistic basis for setting internal performance milestones and longer-range targets.

Then comes the managerial task of building a total quality culture and instilling the necessary commitment to achieving the targets and performance measures that the strategy requires. The action steps managers can take include[6]

- Visible, unequivocal, and unyielding commitment to total quality and continuous improvement, including a quality vision and specific, measurable quality goals.
- Nudging people toward TQ-supportive behaviors by initiating such organizational programs as

  – Screening job applicants rigorously and hiring only those with attitudes and aptitudes right for quality-based performance.
  – Quality training for most employees.
  – Using teams and team-building exercises to reinforce and nurture individual effort (expansion of a TQ culture is facilitated when teams become more cross-functional, multitask, and increasingly self-managed).
  – Recognizing and rewarding individual and team efforts regularly and systematically.
  – Stressing prevention (doing it right the first time) not inspection (instituting ways to correct mistakes).

- Empowering employees so that authority for delivering great service or improving products is in the hands of the doers rather than the overseers.
- Providing quick electronic information access to doers so that real-time data can drive actions and decisions and feedback can continuously improve value-chain activities.
- Preaching that performance can, and must, be improved because competitors are not resting on past laurels and customers are always looking for something better.

If the targeted performance measures are appropriate to the strategy and if all organizational members (top executives, middle managers, professional staff, and line employees) buy into the process of continuous improvement, then the work climate will be conducive to proficient strategy execution and good bottom-line business performance.

INSTALLING SUPPORT SYSTEMS

Company strategies can't be implemented or executed well without a number of support systems for business operations. American, United, Delta, and other major airlines cannot hope to provide world-class passenger service without a computerized reservation system, an accurate and expeditious baggage handling system, and a strong aircraft maintenance program. Federal Express has a computerized parcel-tracking system that can instantly report the location of any given package in its transit-delivery process; it has communication systems that allow it to coordinate its 21,000 vans nationwide to make an average of 720,000 stops per day to pick up customer packages; and it has leading-edge flight operations systems that allow a single controller to direct as many as 200 FedEx aircraft simultaneously, overriding their

---

[6]Olian and Rynes, "Making Total Quality Work," pp. 305–6 and 310–11.

flight plans should weather or special emergencies arise—all these operations essential to FedEx's strategy of next-day delivery of a package that "absolutely, positively has to be there."[7]

Otis Elevator has a sophisticated support system called OtisLine to coordinate its maintenance efforts nationwide.[8] Trained operators take all trouble calls, input critical information on a computer screen, and dispatch people directly via a beeper system to the local trouble spot. From the trouble-call inputs, problem patterns can be identified nationally and the information communicated to design and manufacturing personnel, allowing them to quickly alter design specifications or manufacturing procedures when needed to correct recurring problems. Also, much of the information needed for repairs is provided directly from faulty elevators through internally installed microcomputer monitors, further lowering outage time.

Procter & Gamble codes the more than 900,000 call-in inquiries it receives annually on its toll-free 800 number to obtain early warning signals of product problems and changing tastes.[9] Domino's Pizza has computerized systems at each outlet to facilitate ordering, inventory, payroll, cash flow, and work control functions, thereby freeing managers to spend more time on supervision, customer service, and business development activities.[10] Most telephone companies, electric utilities, and TV broadcasting systems have on-line monitoring systems to spot transmission problems within seconds and increase the reliability of their services. At Mrs. Fields' Cookies, systems can monitor sales at 15-minute intervals and suggest product mix changes, promotional tactics, or operating adjustments to improve customer response—see Illustration Capsule 31.

Well-conceived, state-of-the art support systems not only facilitate better strategy execution, they also can strengthen organizational capabilities enough to provide a competitive edge over rivals. For example, a company with a differentiation strategy based on superior quality needs systems for training personnel in quality techniques, tracking product quality at each production step, and ensuring that all goods shipped meet quality standards. A company striving to be a low-cost provider needs systems that exploit opportunities to drive costs out of the business. Fast-growing companies need employee recruiting systems to attract and hire qualified employees in large numbers. In businesses such as public accounting and management consulting where large numbers of professional staffers need cutting-edge technical know-how, companies have to install systems to train and retrain employees regularly and keep them supplied with up-to-date information.

INSTITUTING FORMAL REPORTING OF STRATEGIC INFORMATION

Accurate information is an essential guide to action. Every organization needs systems for gathering and reporting strategy-critical information and tracking key performance measures over time. Telephone companies have elaborate information systems to measure signal quality, connection times, interrupts, wrong connections, billing errors, and other measures of reliability. To track and manage the quality of passenger service, airlines have information systems to monitor gate delays, on-time

---

Strategic Management Principle

Innovative, state-of-the-art support systems can be a basis for competitive advantage if they give a firm capabilities that rivals

---

Accurate, timely information allows organizational members to monitor progress and take corrective action promptly.

---

[7]James Brian Quinn, *Intelligent Enterprise* (New York: Free Press, 1992) pp. 114–15.
[8]Ibid., p. 181.
[9]Ibid., p. 186.
[10]Ibid., p. 111.

OPERATING PRACTICES AND SUPPORT SYSTEMS AT MRS. FIELDS' COOKIES, INC.

Mrs. Fields' Cookies is one of the best known specialty foods companies in the United States with over 500 outlets in operation in malls, airports, and other high pedestrian-traffic locations; the company also has over 250 outlets retailing other bakery and cookie products. Debbi Fields, age 37, is the company's founder and CEO. Her business concept for Mrs. Fields' Cookies is "to serve absolutely fresh, warm cookies as though you'd stopped by my house and caught me just taking a batch from the oven." Cookies not sold within two hours are removed from the case and given to charity. The company's major form of advertising is sampling; store employees walk around the shopping mall giving away cookie samples. People are hired for store crews on the basis of warmth, friendliness, and the ability to have a good time giving away samples, baking fresh batches, and talking to customers during the course of a sale.

To implement its strategy, the company developed several novel practices and a customized computer support system. One key practice is giving each store an *hourly* sales quota. Another is for Fields to make unannounced visits to her stores, where she masquerades as a casual shopper to test the enthusiasm and sales techniques of store crews, sample the quality of the cookies they are baking, and observe customer reactions.

Debbi's husband Randy developed a software program that keeps headquarters and stores in close contact. Via the computer network, each store manager receives a daily sales goal (broken down by the hour) based on the store's recent performance history and on such special factors as special promotions, mall activities, weekdays vs. weekends, holiday shopping patterns, and the weather forecast. With the hourly sales quotas also comes a schedule of the number of cookies to bake and when to bake them. As the day progresses, store managers type in actual hourly sales figures and customer counts. If customer counts are up but sales are lagging, the computer is programmed to recommend more aggressive sampling or more suggestive selling. If it becomes obvious the day is going to be a bust for the store, the computer automatically revises the sales projections for the day, reducing hourly quotas and instructing how much to cut back cookie baking. To facilitate crew scheduling by the store manager, sales projections are also provided for two weeks in advance. All job applicants must sit at the store's terminal and answer a computerized set of questions as part of the interview process.

In addition, the computer software contains a menu giving store staff immediate access to company personnel policies, maintenance schedules for store equipment, and repair instructions. If a store manager has a specific problem, it can be entered on the system and routed to the appropriate person. Messages can be sent directly to Debbi Fields via the computer; even if she is on a store inspection trip, her promise is to respond to all inquiries within 48 hours.

The computerized information support system serves several objectives: (1) it gives store managers more time to work with their crews and achieve sales quotas as opposed to handling administrative chores and (2) it gives headquarters instantaneous information on store performance and a means of controlling store operations. Debbi Fields sees the system as a tool for projecting her influence and enthusiasm into more stores more frequently than she could otherwise reach.

Source: Developed from information in Mike Korologos, "Debbi Fields," *Sky Magazine,* July 1988, pp. 42–50.

---

departures and arrivals, baggage handling times, lost baggage complaints, stockouts on meals and drinks, overbookings, and maintenance delays and failures. Many companies have provided customer-contact personnel with instant electronic access to customer databases so that they can respond effectively to customer inquiries and personalize customer services.

To properly oversee strategy implementation, company managers need prompt feedback on implementation initiatives to steer them to a successful conclusion in case early steps don't produce the expected progress or things seem to be drifting off course. Such monitoring (1) allows managers to detect problems early and adjust either the strategy or how it is being implemented and (2) provides some assurance that things are moving ahead as planned.[11] Early experiences are sometimes difficult to assess, but they yield the first hard data and should be closely scrutinized as a basis for corrective action.

Information systems need to cover four broad areas: (1) customer data, (2) operations data, (3) employee data, and (4) financial performance data. All key strategic performance indicators have to be measured as often as practical. Many retail companies generate daily sales reports for each store and maintain up-to-the-minute inventory and sales records on each item. Manufacturing plants typically generate daily production reports and track labor productivity on every shift. Monthly profit-and-loss statements are common, as are monthly statistical summaries.

In designing formal reports to monitor strategic progress, five guidelines should be observed:[12]

1. Information and reporting systems should involve no more data and reporting than is needed to give a reliable picture. The data gathered should emphasize strategically meaningful outcomes and symptoms of potentially significant developments. Temptations to supplement "what managers need to know" with other "interesting" but marginally useful information should be avoided.

2. Reports and statistical data-gathering have to be timely—not too late to take corrective action or so often as to overburden.

3. The flow of information and statistics should be kept simple. Complicated reports confound readers and divert attention to methodological issues; long or overly-detailed reports run the risk of going unread; and too many reports consume unnecessary amounts of managerial time.

4. Information and reporting systems should aim at "no surprises"; i.e., they should point out early warning signs rather than just produce information. It is debatable whether reports should receive wide distribution ("for your information"); but they should always be provided to managers who are in a position to act when trouble signs appear.

5. Statistical reports should flag exceptions and big or unusual variances from plan, thus directing management attention to significant departures from targeted performance.

Statistical information gives the strategy-implementer a feel for the numbers; reports and meetings provide a feel for new developments and problems; and personal contacts add a feel for the people dimension. All are good barometers of overall performance and good indicators of which things are on and off track. Managers have to identify problem areas and deviations from plan before they can take actions either to improve implementation or fine-tune strategy.

DESIGNING STRATEGY-SUPPORTIVE REWARD SYSTEMS

It is important for organizational subunits and for individuals to be committed to implementing strategy and achieving performance targets. Company managers typi-

---

[11]Boris Yavitz and William H. Newman, *Strategy in Action* (New York: Free Press, 1982), pp. 209–10.

[12]Peter F. Drucker, *Management: Tasks, Responsibilities, Practices* (New York: Harper & Row, 1974), pp. 498–504; Harold Koontz, "Management Control: A Suggested Formulation of Principles," *California Management Review* 2, no. 2 (Winter 1959), pp. 50–55; and William H. Sihler, "Toward Better Management Control Systems," *California Management Review* 14, no. 2 (Winter 1971), pp. 33–39.

cally try to enlist organizationwide commitment to carrying out the strategic plan by motivating people and rewarding them for good performance. The range of options includes offering people the chance to be part of something exciting, giving them an opportunity for greater personal satisfaction, challenging them with ambitious performance targets for them, using the carrot of promotion and the stick of being "sidelined" in a routine or dead-end job, giving praise, recognition, constructive criticism, more (or less) responsibility, increased (or decreased) job control and decision-making autonomy, offering a better shot at assignments in attractive locations, the intangible bonds of group acceptance, greater job security, and the promise of sizable financial rewards (salary increases, performance bonuses, stock options, and retirement packages). But motivational techniques and rewards have to be used *creatively* and linked tightly to the factors and targets necessary for good strategy execution.

MOTIVATIONAL PRACTICES

Successful strategy-implementers inspire and challenge employees to do their best. They get employees to buy into the strategy and commit to making it work. They allow employees to participate in making decisions about how to perform their jobs, and they try to make jobs interesting and satisfying. As Frederick Herzberg said, "If you want people motivated to do a good job, give them a good job to do." They structure individual efforts into teams and work groups in order to facilitate an exchange of ideas and a climate of support. They devise strategy-supportive motivational approaches and use them effectively. Consider some actual examples:[13]

> One of the biggest strategy-implementing challenges is to employ motivational techniques that build whole-hearted commitment and winning attitudes among employees.

- At Mars Inc. (best known for its candy bars), every employee, including the president, gets a weekly 10 percent bonus by coming to work on time each day that week. This on-time incentive is designed to minimize absenteeism and tardiness and to boost worker productivity in order to produce the greatest number of candy bars during each available minute of machine time.

- In a number of Japanese companies, employees meet regularly to hear inspirational speeches, sing company songs, and chant the corporate litany. In the United States, Tupperware conducts a weekly Monday night rally to honor, applaud, and fire up its salespeople who conduct Tupperware parties. Amway and Mary Kay Cosmetics hold similar inspirational get-togethers for their sales force organizations.

- A San Diego area company assembles its 2,000 employees at its six plants the first thing every workday to listen to a management talk about the state of the company. Then they engage in brisk calisthenics. This company's management believes "that by doing one thing together each day, it reinforces the unity of the company. It's also fun. It gets the blood up." Managers take turns making the presentations. Many of the speeches "are very personal and emotional, not approved beforehand or screened by anybody."

- Texas Instruments and Dana Corp. insist that teams and divisions set their own goals and have regular peer reviews.

- Procter & Gamble's brand managers are asked to compete fiercely against each other; the official policy is "a free-for-all among brands with no holds barred." P&G's system of purposeful internal competition breeds people who love to

---

[13]Alfie Kohn, "Rethinking Rewards," *Harvard Business Review* 71, no. 6 (November–December 1993), p. 49.

compete and excel. Those who win become corporate heroes, and around them emerges a folklore of war stories of valiant brand managers who waged uphill struggles against great odds and made market successes out of their brands.

These motivational approaches accentuate the positive; others blend positive and negative features. Consider the way Harold Geneen, former president and chief executive officer of ITT, allegedly combined the use of money, tension, and fear:

> Geneen provides his managers with enough incentives to make them tolerate the system. Salaries all the way through ITT are higher than average—Geneen reckons 10 percent higher—so that few people can leave without taking a drop. As one employee put it: "We're all paid just a bit more than we think we're worth." At the very top, where the demands are greatest, the salaries and stock options are sufficient to compensate for the rigors. As someone said, "He's got them by their limousines."
>
> Having bound his [managers] to him with chains of gold, Geneen can induce the tension that drives the machine. "The key to the system," one of his [managers] explains, "is the profit forecast. Once the forecast has been gone over, revised, and agreed on, the managing director has a personal commitment to Geneen to carry it out. That's how he produces the tension on which the success depends." The tension goes through the company, inducing ambition, perhaps exhilaration, but always with some sense of fear: what happens if the target is missed?[14]

If a strategy-implementer's motivational approach and reward structure induces too much stress, internal competitiveness, and job insecurity, the results can be counterproductive. For a healthy work environment, positive reinforcement needs to outweigh negative reinforcement. Yet it is unwise to completely eliminate pressure for performance and the anxiety it evokes. There is no evidence that a no-pressure work environment leads to superior strategy execution or sustained high performance. As the CEO of a major bank put it, "There's a deliberate policy here to create a level of anxiety. Winners usually play like they're one touchdown behind."[15] High-performing organizations need a cadre of ambitious people who relish the opportunity to climb the ladder of success, love a challenge, thrive in a performance-oriented environment, and find some competition and pressure useful to satisfy their own drives for personal recognition, accomplishment, and self-satisfaction. Unless meaningful incentive and career consequences are associated with successfully implementing strategic initiatives and hitting strategic performance targets, few people will attach much significance to the company's strategic plan.

Positive motivational approaches generally work better than negative ones.

REWARDS AND INCENTIVES

The conventional view is that a manager's push for strategy implementation should incorporate more positive than negative motivational elements because when cooperation is positively enlisted and rewarded, rather than strong-armed by a boss's orders, people tend to respond with more enthusiasm and more effort. Nevertheless, how much of which incentives to use depends on how hard the task of strategy implementation will be. A manager has to do more than just talk to everyone about how important new strategic practices and performance targets are to the organization's future well-being. No matter how inspiring, talk seldom commands people's best efforts for

---

[14]Anthony Sampson, *The Sovereign State of ITT* (New York: Stein and Day, 1973), p. 132.

[15]As quoted in John P. Kotter and James L. Heskett, *Corporate Culture and Performance* (New York: Free Press, 1992), p. 91.

long. To get employees' sustained, energetic commitment, management has to be resourceful in designing and using motivational incentives—both monetary and non-monetary. The more a manager understands what motivates subordinates and the more he or she relies on motivational incentives as a tool for implementing strategy, the greater will be employees' commitment to good day in, day out execution of their roles in the company's strategic plan.

Linking Work Assignments to Performance Targets   The first step in creating a strategy-supportive system of rewards and incentives is to define jobs and assignments in terms of the *results to be accomplished,* not the duties and functions to be performed. Focusing the jobholder's attention and energy on what to *achieve* as opposed to what activities to perform boosts the chances of reaching agreed-on outcomes. It is flawed thinking to stress duties and activities in job descriptions in hopes that the by-products will be the desired kinds of accomplishments. In any job, performing assigned tasks is not equivalent to achieving intended outcomes. Working hard, staying busy, and diligently attending to assigned duties do not guarantee results. Stressing "what to accomplish" instead of "what to do" is an important difference. As any student knows, just because an instructor teaches doesn't mean students are learning. Teaching and learning are different things—the first is an activity and the second is a result.

Emphasizing what to accomplish—that is, performance targets for individual jobs, work groups, departments, businesses, and the entire company—has the larger purpose of making the work environment results-oriented. Without target objectives, individuals and work groups can become so engrossed in the details of performing assigned functions on schedule that they lose sight of what the tasks are intended to accomplish. By regularly tracking actual achievement versus targeted performance (monthly, weekly, or daily if need be), managers can proactively concentrate on making the right things happen rather than supervising people closely in hopes that the right outcomes will materialize if every activity is performed according to the book. Making the right things happen is what results-oriented management is all about.

To create a tight fit between carrying out work assignments and accomplishing the strategic plan, managers must use strategic and financial objectives as the basis for incentive compensation. If the details of strategy have been fleshed out thoroughly from the corporate level down to the operating level, appropriate measures of performance either exist or can be developed for the whole company, for each business unit, for each functional department, for each operating unit, and for each work group. These become the targets that strategy-implementers aim at achieving, and they form the basis for deciding on the necessary jobs, skills, expertise, funding, and time frame.

Usually a number of performance measures are needed at each level. At the corporate and line-of-business levels, performance objectives typically revolve around measures of profitability (total profit, return on equity investment, return on total assets, return on sales, operating profit, and so on), sales and earnings growth, market share, product quality, customer satisfaction, and other hard measures that market position, overall competitiveness, and future prospects have improved. In the manufacturing area, the strategy-relevant performance measures may focus on unit manufacturing costs, employee productivity, on-time production and shipping, defect rates, the number and extent of work stoppages due to labor disagreements and equipment breakdowns, and so on. In the marketing area, measures may include unit selling costs, dollar sales and unit volume, sales penetration of each target customer group, market share, the fate of newly introduced products, the frequency of customer

Job assignments should stress the results to be achieved rather than the duties and activities to be performed.

complaints, the number of new accounts acquired, and customer satisfaction surveys. While most performance measures are quantitative, several may have elements of subjectivity—the state of labor-management relations, employee morale, the effectiveness of advertising campaigns, and how far the firm is ahead of or behind rivals on quality, service, and technological capability.

Strategic Management Principle

The strategy-implementer's standard for judging whether individuals and organizational units have done a good job must be whether they achieved their performance targets.

Rewarding Performance   The most dependable way to keep people focused on the objectives laid out in the strategic plan and to make achieving these objectives a way of life up and down the organization is to generously reward individuals and groups who achieve their assigned targets and deny rewards to those who don't. For strategy-implementers, doing a good job needs to mean one thing: achieving the agreed-on performance targets. Any other standard undermines implementation of the strategic plan and condones the diversion of time and energy into activities that don't much matter (if such activities are really important, they deserve a place in the strategic plan). The pressure to achieve the targeted strategic performance should be unrelenting. A "no excuses" standard has to prevail.[16]

With the pressure to perform must come deserving and meaningful rewards. Without an ample payoff, the system breaks down, and the strategy-implementer is left with the unworkable option of barking orders and pleading for compliance. Some of the best performing companies—Wal-Mart, Nucor Steel, Lincoln Electric, Electronic Data Systems, Remington Products, and Mary Kay Cosmetics—owe much of their success to a set of incentives and rewards that induce people to do the things needed to hit performance targets and execute strategy well enough for the companies to become leaders in their industries.

Nucor's strategy was (and is) to be *the* low-cost producer of steel products. Because labor costs are a significant fraction of total cost in the steel business, successful implementation of Nucor's low-cost strategy requires achieving lower labor costs per ton of steel than competitors'. To drive its labor costs per ton below rivals', Nucor management utilizes production incentives that give workers bonuses roughly equal to their regular wages if their production teams meet or exceed weekly production targets; the regular wage scale is set at levels comparable to wages for similar manufacturing jobs in the local areas where Nucor has plants. Bonuses are paid every two weeks based on the prior weeks' actual production levels measured against the targets. The results of Nucor's piece-rate incentive plan are impressive. Nucor's labor productivity (in output per worker) runs over 50% above the average of the unionized workforces of the industry's major producers. Nucor enjoys about a $50 to $75 per ton cost advantage over large, integrated steel producers like U.S. Steel and Bethlehem Steel (a substantial part of which comes from its labor cost advantage), and Nucor workers are the highest-paid workers in the steel industry.

At Remington Products, only 65 percent of factory workers' paychecks is salary; the rest is based on piece-work incentives. The company conducts 100 percent inspections of products, and rejected items are counted against incentive pay for the responsible worker. Top-level managers earn more from bonuses than from their salaries. During the first four years of Remington's incentive program, productivity rose 17 percent.

---

[16]Tom Peters and Nancy Austin, *A Passion for Excellence* (New York: Random House, 1985), p. xix.

These and other experiences demonstrate some important lessons about designing rewards and incentives:

1. *The performance payoff must be a major, not minor, piece of the total compensation package.* Incentives that amount to 20 percent or more of total compensation are big attention-getters and are capable of driving individual effort.

2. *The incentive plan should extend to all managers and all workers,* not just be restricted to top management. It is a gross miscalculation to expect that lower-level managers and employees will work their tails off to hit performance targets just so a few senior executives can get lucrative rewards!

3. *The reward system must be administered with scrupulous care and fairness.* If performance standards are set unrealistically high or if individual performance evaluations are not accurate and well-documented, dissatisfaction and disgruntlement with the system will overcome any positive benefits.

4. *The incentives must be tightly linked to achieving only those performance targets spelled out in the strategic plan* and not to any other factors that get thrown in because they are thought to be nice occurrences. Performance evaluation based on factors not related to the strategy signal that either the strategic plan is incomplete (because important performance targets were left out) or management's real agenda is something other than what was stated in the strategic plan.

5. *The performance targets each individual is expected to achieve should involve outcomes that the individual can personally affect.* The role of incentives is to enhance individual commitment and channel behavior in beneficial directions. This role is not well-served when the performance measures an individual is judged by are outside his/her arena of influence.

Aside from these general guidelines it is hard to prescribe what kinds of incentives and rewards to develop except to say that the payoff must be directly attached to performance measures that indicate the strategy is working and implementation is on track. If the company's strategy is to be a low-cost provider, the incentive system must reward performance that lowers costs. If the company has a differentiation strategy predicated on superior quality and service, the incentive system must reward such outcomes as zero defects, infrequent need for product repair, low numbers of customer complaints, and speedy order processing and delivery. If a company's growth is predicated on a strategy of new product innovation, incentives should be tied to factors such as the percentages of revenues and profits coming from newly introduced products.

Why the Performance-Reward Link Is Important

The use of incentives and rewards is the single most powerful tool management has to win strong employee commitment to carrying out the strategic plan. Failure to use this tool wisely and powerfully will weaken the entire implementation process. *Decisions on salary increases, incentive compensation, promotions, who gets which key assignments, and the ways and means of awarding praise and recognition are the strategy-implementer's foremost attention-getting, commitment-generating devices.* How a company's incentives are structured signals what sorts of behavior and

Strategic Management Principle

The reward structure is management's most powerful

performance management wants; how managers parcel out raises, promotions, and praise says more about who is considered to be doing a good job than any other factor. Such matters seldom escape the closest employee scrutiny. A company's system of incentives and rewards thus ends up being the vehicle by which its strategy is emotionally ratified in the form of real commitment. Incentives make it in employees' self-interest to do what is needed to achieve the performance targets spelled out in the strategic plan.

Making Performance-Driven Compensation Work

Creating a tight fit between strategy and the reward structure is generally best accomplished by agreeing on strategy-critical performance objectives, fixing responsibility and deadlines for achieving them, and treating their achievement as a pay-for-performance *contract*. From a strategy-implementation perspective, the key is to make strategically relevant measures of performance the dominating basis for designing incentives, evaluating individual efforts, and handing out rewards. Every organizational unit, every manager, every team or work group, and ideally every employee needs to have clearly defined performance targets to aim at that reflect measurable progress in implementing the strategic game plan, and then they must be held accountable for achieving them. For example, at Banc One, the fifth largest U.S. bank and the second most profitable bank in the world (based on return on assets), a high level of customer satisfaction is a key performance objective. To enhance employee commitment to the task of pleasing customers, Banc One ties the pay scales in each branch office to that branch's customer satisfaction rating—the higher the branch's ratings, the higher that branch's pay scales. By shifting from a theme of equal pay for equal work to one of equal pay for equal performance, Banc One has focused the attention of branch employees on the task of pleasing, even delighting, their customers.

To prevent undermining and undoing pay-for-performance approaches to strategy implementation, companies must be scrupulously fair in comparing actual performance against agreed-on performance targets. Everybody needs to understand how their incentive compensation is calculated and how their individual performance targets contribute to organizational performance targets. The reasons for anyone's failure or deviations from targets have to be explored fully to determine whether the causes are attributable to poor individual performance or to circumstances beyond the individual's control. Skirting the system to find ways to reward nonperformers must be absolutely avoided. It is debatable whether exceptions should be made for people who've tried hard, gone the extra mile, yet still come up short because of circumstances beyond their control—a good case can be made either way. The problem with making exceptions for unknowable, uncontrollable, or unforeseeable circumstances is that once "good" excuses start to creep into justifying rewards for nonperformers, the door is open for all kinds of "legitimate" reasons why actual performance failed to match targeted performance. In short, people at all levels have to be held accountable for carrying out their assigned parts of the strategic plan, and they have to know their rewards are based on the caliber of their strategic accomplishments.

KEY POINTS

A change in strategy nearly always calls for budget reallocations. Reworking the budget to make it more strategy-supportive is a crucial part of the implementation process because every organization unit needs to have the people, equipment, facilities, and other resources to carry out its part of the strategic plan (but no *more* than what it really needs!). Implementing a new strategy often entails shifting resources from one area to another—downsizing units that are overstaffed and overfunded, upsizing those more critical to strategic success, and killing projects and activities that are no longer justified.

Anytime a company alters its strategy, company managers are well-advised to review existing policies and operating procedures, revising those that are out of sync and devising new ones. Prescribing new or freshly revised policies and operating procedures aids the task of implementation (1) by providing top-down guidance to operating managers, supervisory personnel, and employees regarding how certain things now need to be done and what behavior is expected; (2) by placing limits on independent actions and decisions; (3) by enforcing needed consistency in how particular strategy-critical activities are performed in geographically scattered operating units; and (4) by helping to create a strategy-supportive work climate and corporate culture. Huge policy manuals are uncalled for. Indeed, when individual creativity and initiative are more essential to good execution than standardization and conformity, it is often wise to give people the freedom to do things however they see fit and hold them accountable for good results. Hence, creating a supportive fit between strategy and policy can mean more policies, fewer policies, or different policies.

Competent strategy execution entails visible, unyielding managerial commitment to best practices and continuous improvement. Benchmarking, instituting best practices, reengineering core business processes, and total quality management programs all aim at improved efficiency, lower costs, better product quality, and greater customer satisfaction. All these techniques are important tools for learning how to execute a strategy more proficiently. Benchmarking provides a realistic basis for setting performance targets. Instituting "best-in-industry" or "best-in-world" operating practices in most or all value-chain activities is essential to create a total quality, high-performance work environment. Reengineering is a way to make quantum progress in being world class while TQM instills a commitment to continuous improvement. Typically, such techniques involve organizing the work effort around cross-functional, multitask teams and work groups that are self-directed and/or self-managed.

Company strategies can't be implemented or executed well without a number of support systems to carry on business operations. Well-conceived, state-of-the-support systems not only facilitate better strategy execution, they can also strengthen organizational capabilities enough to provide a competitive edge over rivals. In an age of computers, computerized monitoring and control systems, and expanding communications capabilities, companies can't hope to outexecute their competitors without elaborate information systems and technologically sophisticated operating capabilities that allow people to perform their jobs effectively and efficiently.

Strategy-supportive motivational practices and reward systems are powerful management tools for gaining employee buy-in and commitment. Positive motivational practices generally work better than negative ones, but there is a place for both. There's also a place for both monetary and nonmonetary incentives. For monetary incentives to work well (1) the monetary payoff should be a major percentage of the compensation package, (2) the incentive plan should extend to all managers and workers, (3) the system should be administered with care and fairness, (4) the incentives should be linked to performance targets spelled out in the strategic plan, and (5) each individual's performance targets should involve outcomes the person can personally affect.

SUGGESTED READINGS

Grant, Robert M., Rami Shani, and R. Krishnan, "TQM's Challenge to Management Theory and Practice." *Sloan Management Review* (Winter 1994), pp. 25–35.

Herzberg, Frederick. "One More Time: How Do You Motivate Employees?" *Harvard Business Review* 65, no. 4 (September–October 1987), pp. 109–20.

Johnson, H. Thomas. *Relevance Regained.* New York: Free Press, 1992.

Kiernan, Matthew J. "The New Strategic Architecture: Learning to Compete in the Twenty-First Century." *Academy of Management Executive* 7, no. 1 (February 1993), pp. 7–21.

Kohn, Alfie. "Why Incentive Plans Cannot Work." *Harvard Business Review* 71, no. 5 (September–October 1993), pp. 54–63.

Olian, Judy D. and Sara L. Rynes, "Making Total Quality Work: Aligning Organizational Processes, Performance Measures, and Stakeholders," *Human Resource Management* 30, no. 3 (Fall 1991), pp. 303–333.

Wiley, Carolyn. "Incentive Plan Pushes Production." *Personnel Journal* (August 1993), pp. 86–91.

Quinn, James Brian. *Intelligent Enterprise.* New York: Free Press, 1992, chap. 4.

Shetty, Y. K. "Aiming High: Competitive Benchmarking for Superior Performance." *Long-Range Planning* 26, no. 1 (February 1993), pp. 39–44.

CHAPTER ELEVEN

IMPLEMENTING STRATEGY: CULTURE AND LEADERSHIP

Weak leadership can wreck the soundest strategy; forceful execution of even a poor plan can often bring victory.

Sun Zi

Effective leaders do not just reward achievement, they celebrate it.

Shelley A. Kirkpatrick and Edwin A. Locke

Ethics is the moral courage to do what we know is right, and not to do what we know is wrong.

C. J. Silas
CEO, Philips Petroleum

. . . A leader lives in the field with his troops.

H. Ross Perot

In the previous two chapters we examined six of the strategy-implementer's tasks—building a capable organization, steering ample resources into strategy-critical activities and operating units, establishing strategy-supportive policies, instituting best practices and programs for continuous improvement, creating internal support systems to enable better execution, and employing appropriate motivational practices and compensation incentives. In this chapter we explore the two remaining implementation tasks: creating a strategy-supportive corporate culture and exerting the internal leadership needed to drive implementation forward.

BUILDING A STRATEGY-SUPPORTIVE CORPORATE CULTURE

Every company has a unique organizational culture. Each has its own business philosophy and principles, its own ways of approaching problems and making decisions, its own embedded patterns of "how we do things around here," its own lore (stories

THE CULTURE AT NORDSTROM

The culture at Nordstrom, a department store retailer noted for exceptional commitment to its customers, revolves around the company's motto: "Respond to Unreasonable Customer Requests." Living up to the company's motto is so strongly ingrained in behavior that employees learn to relish the challenges that some customer requests pose. Usually, meeting customer demands in pleasing fashion entails little more than gracious compliance and a little extra personal attention. But occasionally it means paying a customer's parking ticket when in-store gift wrapping takes longer than normal or hand delivering items purchased by phone to the airport for a customer with an emergency need.

At Nordstrom, each out-of-the-ordinary customer request is seen as an opportunity for a "heroic" act by an employee and a way to build the company's reputation for great service. Nordstrom encourages these acts by promoting employees noted for outstanding service, keeping scrapbooks of "heroic" acts, and paying its salespeople entirely on commission (it is not unusual for good salespeople at Nordstrom to earn double what they would at other department store retailers). For go-getters who truly enjoy retail selling and pleasing customers, Nordstrom is a great company to work for. But the culture weeds out those who can't meet Nordstrom's demanding standards and rewards those who are prepared to be what Nordstrom stands for.

Source: Based on information in Tracy Goss, Richard Pascale, and Anthony Athos, "Risking the Present for a Powerful Future," *Harvard Business Review* 71, no. 6 (November–December 1993), pp. 101–2.

told over and over to illustrate company values and what they mean to employees), its own taboos and political don'ts—in other words, its own ingrained beliefs, behavior and thought patterns, business practices, and personality. The bedrock of Wal-Mart's culture is dedication to customer satisfaction, zealous pursuit of low costs, a strong work ethic, Sam Walton's legendary frugality, the ritualistic Saturday morning headquarters meetings to exchange ideas and review problems, and company executives' commitment to visiting stores, talking to customers, and soliciting suggestions from employees. At Frito-Lay, stories abound of potato chip route salesmen slogging through mud and snow to uphold the company's 99.5 percent service level. At McDonald's the constant message from management is the overriding importance of quality, service, cleanliness, and value; employees are drilled over and over on the need for attention to detail and perfection in every fundamental of the business. Illustration Capsule 32 describes the culture of Nordstrom's.

> Corporate culture refers to a company's values, beliefs, traditions, operating style, and internal work environment.

WHERE DOES CORPORATE CULTURE COME FROM?

The taproot of corporate culture is the organization's beliefs and philosophy about how its affairs ought to be conducted—the reasons why it does things the way it does. A company's culture is manifested in the values and business principles that management preaches and practices, in its ethical standards and official policies, in its stakeholder relationships (especially its dealings with employees, unions, stockholders, vendors, and the communities in which it operates), in the traditions the organization maintains, in its supervisory practices, in employees' attitudes and behavior, in the legends people repeat about happenings in the organization, in the peer pressures that exist, in the organization's politics, and in the "chemistry" and the "vibrations" that permeate the work environment. All these sociological forces, some of which operate quite subtly, combine to define an organization's culture.

Beliefs and practices that become embedded in a company's culture can originate anywhere: from one influential individual, work group, department, or division, from the bottom of the organizational hierarchy or the top.[1] Very often, many components of the culture are associated with a founder or other early leaders who articulated them as a company philosophy, a set of principles which the organization should rigidly adhere to, company policies, a vision, a business strategy, or a combination of these. Over time, these cultural underpinnings come to be shared by company managers and employees and then persist as new employees are encouraged to adopt and follow the professed values and practices. A company's culture is a product of internal social forces; it represents an interdependent set of values and behavioral norms that prevail across the organization.

Once established, company cultures can be perpetuated by continuity of leadership, by screening and selecting new group members according to how well their values and behavior fit in, by systematic indoctrination of new members in the culture's fundamentals, by the efforts of senior group members to reiterate core values in daily conversations and pronouncements, by the telling and retelling of company legends, by regular ceremonies honoring members who display cultural ideals, and by visibly rewarding those who follow cultural norms and penalizing those who don't.[2] However, even stable cultures aren't static. Crises and new challenges evolve into new ways of doing things. Arrival of new leaders and turnover of key members often spawn new or different values and practices that alter the culture. Diversification into new businesses, expansion into different geographical areas, and rapid growth that adds new employees can all cause a culture to evolve.

Although it is common to speak about corporate culture in the singular, companies typically have multiple cultures (or subcultures).[3] Values, beliefs, and practices can vary significantly by department, geographic location, division, or business unit. A company's subcultures can clash, or at least not mesh well, if recently acquired business units have not yet been assimilated or if different organizational units have conflicting managerial styles, business philosophies, and operating approaches.

THE POWER OF CULTURE

Most managers, as a consequence of their own experiences and of reading case studies in the business press, accept that an organization's culture is an important contributor (or obstacle) to successful strategy execution. Thomas Watson, Jr., who succeeded his father as CEO at IBM, stated the case for a culture-performance link eloquently in a 1962 speech at Columbia University:

> The basic philosophy, spirit, and desire of an organization have far more to do with its relative achievements than do technological or economic resources, organization structure, innovation, and timing. All these things weigh heavily on success. But they are, I think, transcended by how strongly the people in the organization believe in its basic precepts and how faithfully they carry them out.[4]

The beliefs, goals, and practices called for in a strategy may be compatible with a firm's culture or they may not. When they are not, a company usually finds it difficult to implement the strategy successfully.[5] A close culture-strategy match that energizes people throughout the company to do their jobs in a strategy-supportive manner adds

---

[1]John P. Kotter and James L. Heskett, *Corporate Culture and Performance* (New York: Free Press, 1992), p. 7.
[2]Ibid., pp. 7–8.
[3]Ibid., p. 5.
[4]"A Business and Its Beliefs," McKinsey Foundation Lecture (New York: McGraw-Hill, 1963), as quoted in Kotter and Heskett, *Corporate Culture and Performance*, p. 17.
[5]Kotter and Heskett, *Corporate Culture and Performance*, p. 5.

significantly to the power and effectiveness of strategy execution. Strong cultures promote good long-term performance when there's fit and hurt performance when there's little fit. When a company's culture is out of sync with what is needed for strategic success, the culture has to be changed as rapidly as can be managed; the more entrenched the culture, the greater the difficulty of implementing new or different strategies. A sizable and prolonged strategy-culture conflict weakens and may even defeat managerial efforts to make the strategy work.

A strong culture and a tight strategy-culture fit are powerful levers for influencing people to do their jobs better.

A tight culture-strategy alignment is a powerful lever for channeling behavior and helping employees do their jobs in a more strategy-supportive manner; this occurs in two ways:[6]

- *A work environment where the culture matches well with the conditions for good strategy execution provides a system of informal rules and peer pressures regarding how to conduct business internally and how to go about doing one's job.* Culturally approved behavior thrives, while culturally disapproved behavior gets squashed and often penalized. In a company where strategy and culture are misaligned, ingrained values and operating philosophies don't cultivate strategy-supportive work habits; often, the very kinds of behavior needed to execute strategy successfully run afoul of the culture and attract negative recognition rather than praise and reward.

- *A strong strategy-supportive culture nurtures and motivates people to their best; it provides structure, standards, and a value system in which to operate; and it promotes strong company identification among employees.* All this makes employees feel genuinely better about their jobs and work environment and, more often than not, stimulates them to perform closer to the best of their abilities.

This says something important about the task of leading strategy implementation: *anything so fundamental as implementing a strategic plan involves moving the organization's culture into close alignment with the requirements for proficient strategy execution.* The optimal condition is a work environment that enlists and encourages people to perform strategy-critical activities in superior fashion. As one observer noted:

> It has not been just strategy that led to big Japanese wins in the American auto market. It is a cultu+re that enspirits workers to excel at fits and finishes, to produce moldings that match and doors that don't sag. It is a culture in which Toyota can use that most sophisticated of management tools, the suggestion box, and in two years increase the number of worker suggestions from under 10,000 to over 1 million with resultant savings of $250 million.[7]

Strong versus Weak Cultures

Company cultures vary widely in the degree to which they are embedded in company practices and behavioral norms. A company's culture can be weak and fragmented in the sense that many subcultures exist, few values and behavioral norms are widely shared, and there are few traditions. In such cases, organizational members typically have no deeply felt sense of company identity; they view their company as merely a place to work and their job only as a way to make a living. While they may have some feelings of loyalty toward their department, their colleagues, their union, or their boss, they usually have no strong emotional allegiance to the company or its

---

[6]Ibid., pp. 15–16.
[7]Robert H. Waterman, Jr., "The Seven Elements of Strategic Fit," *Journal of Business Strategy* 2, no. 3 (Winter 1982), p. 70.

business mission. On the other hand, a company's culture can be strong and cohesive in the sense that the company conducts its business according to a clear and explicit set of principles and values, that management devotes considerable time to communicating these principles and values to organizational members and explaining how they relate to its business environment, and that the values are shared widely across the company—by senior executives and rank-and-file employees alike.[8] Strong-culture companies typically have creeds or values statements, and executives regularly stress the importance of using these values and principles as the basis for decisions and actions taken throughout the organization. In strong culture companies values and behavioral norms are so deeply rooted that they don't change much when a new CEO takes over—although they can erode over time if the CEO ceases to nurture them.

Three factors contribute to the development of strategically supportive strong cultures: (1) a founder or strong leader who establishes values, principles, and practices that are consistent and sensible in light of customer needs, competitive conditions, and strategic requirements; (2) a sincere, long-standing company commitment to operating the business according to these established traditions, thereby creating an internal environment that supports decision-making based on cultural norms; and (3) a genuine concern for the well-being of the organization's three biggest constituencies—customers, employees, and shareholders. Continuity of leadership, small group size, stable group membership, geographic concentration, and considerable success all contribute to the emergence of a strong culture.[9]

LOW-PERFORMANCE OR UNHEALTHY CULTURES

There are a number of unhealthy cultural characteristics that can undermine a company's business performance.[10] One unhealthy organizational trait is a politicized internal environment that allows influential managers to operate their fiefdoms autonomously and resist needed change. In politically dominated cultures, many issues get resolved on the basis of turf, vocal support or opposition by powerful executives, personal lobbying by a key executive, and coalitions among individuals or departments with vested interests in a particular outcome. What's best for the company plays second fiddle to personal aggrandizement.

A second unhealthy cultural trait, one that can plague companies suddenly confronted with fast-changing business conditions, is hostility to change and to people who champion new ways of doing things. Executives who don't value managers or employees with initiative or new ideas put a damper on experimentation and on efforts to improve the status quo. Avoiding risks and not screwing up become more important to a person's career advancement than entrepreneurial successes and innovative accomplishments. This trait is most often found in companies with multilayered management bureaucracies that have enjoyed considerable market success and whose business environments have been hit with accelerating change. General Motors, IBM, Sears, and Eastman Kodak are classic examples; all four gradually became burdened by a stifling bureaucracy that rejected innovation. Now, they are struggling to reinvent the cultural approaches that caused them to succeed in the first place.

A third unhealthy characteristc is promoting managers who understand structures, systems, budgets, and controls better than they understand vision, strategies, inspiration, and culture-building. While the former are adept at solving internal organiza-

A strong culture is a valuable asset when it matches strategy and a dreaded liability when it doesn't.

[8]Terrence E. Deal and Allen A. Kennedy, *Corporate Cultures* (Reading, Mass.: Addison-Wesley, 1982), p. 22.

[9]Vijay Sathe, *Culture and Related Corporate Realities* (Homewood, Ill.: Richard D. Irwin, 1985).

[10]Kotter and Heskett, *Corporate Culture and Performance,* chapter 6.

tional challenges, if they ascend to senior executive positions, the company can find itself short on the entrepreneurial skills and leadership needed to manage strategic change—a condition that ultimately erodes long-term performance.

A fourth characteristic of low-performance cultures is an aversion to looking outside the company for superior practices and approaches. Sometimes a company enjoys such great market success and reigns as an industry leader for so long that its management becomes inbred and arrogant. It believes it has all the answers or can develop them on its own. Insular thinking, inward-looking solutions, and a must-be-invented-here syndrome often precede a decline in company performance. Kotter and Heskett cite Avon, BankAmerica, Citicorp, Coors, Ford, General Motors, Kmart, Kroger, Sears, Texaco, and Xerox as examples of companies that had low-performance cultures during the late 1970s and early 1980s.[11]

Changing problem cultures is very difficult because of the heavy anchor of deeply held values, habits, and the emotional clinging of people to the old and familiar. Sometimes executives succeed in changing the values and behaviors of small groups of managers and even whole departments or divisions, only to find the changes eroded over time by the actions of the rest of the organization. What is communicated, praised, supported, and penalized by the entrenched majority undermines the new emergent culture and halts its progress. Executives can revamp formal organization charts, announce new strategies, bring in managers from the outside, introduce new technologies, and open new plants, yet fail at altering embedded cultural traits and behaviors because of skepticism about the new directions and covert resistance to altering traditional methods.

ADAPTIVE CULTURES

In fast-changing business environments, the capacity to introduce new strategies and organizational practices is a necessity if a company is to achieve superior performance over long periods of time.[12] This requires a culture that *helps* the company adapt to environmental change rather than a culture that has to be coaxed and cajoled to change. The hallmarks of an adaptive culture are: (1) leaders who have a greater commitment to timeless business principles and to organizational stakeholders—customers, employees, shareowners, suppliers, and the communities where the company operates—than to any specific business strategy or operating practice; and (2) group members who are receptive to risk-taking, experimentation, innovation, and changing strategies and practices whenever necessary to satisfy the legitimate interests of stakeholders.

In adaptive cultures, members share a feeling of confidence that the organization can deal with whatever threats and opportunities come down the pike. Hence, members willingly embrace a proactive approach to identifying issues, evaluating the implications and options, and implementing workable solutions—there's a spirit of doing what's necessary to ensure long-term organizational success *provided core values and business principles are upheld in the process.* Managers habitually fund product development initiatives, evaluate new ideas openly, and take prudent risks to create new business positions. Entrepreneurship is encouraged and rewarded. Strategies and traditional operating practices are modified as needed to adjust to or take advantage of changes in the business environment. The leaders of adaptive cultures

Adaptive cultures are a strategy-implementer's best ally.

---

[11]Ibid., p. 68.
[12]This section draws heavily from Kotter and Heskett, *Corporate Culture and Performance,* chapter 4.

are adept at changing the right things in the right ways, not changing for the sake of change and not compromising core values or business principles. Adaptive cultures are very supportive of managers and employees at all ranks who propose or help initiate useful change; indeed, executives consciously seek, train, and promote individuals who display these leadership traits.

In adaptive cultures, top management genuinely cares about the well-being of all key constituencies—customers, employees, stockholders, major suppliers, and the communities where the company operates—and tries to satisfy all their legitimate interests simultaneously. No group is ignored, and fairness to all constituencies is a decision-making principle—a commitment often described as "doing the right thing."[13] In less-adaptive cultures where resistance to change is the norm, managers often behave conservatively and politically to protect or advance their own careers, the interests of their immediate work groups, or their pet projects. They avoid risk-taking and prefer following to leading when it comes to technological change and new product innovation.[14]

CREATING THE FIT BETWEEN STRATEGY AND CULTURE

It is the *strategy-maker's* responsibility to select a strategy compatible with the "sacred" or unchangeable parts of prevailing corporate culture. It is the *strategy-implementer's* task, once strategy is chosen, to change whatever facets of the corporate culture hinder effective execution.

Changing a company's culture and aligning it with strategy are among the toughest management tasks—easier to talk about than do. The first step is to diagnose which facets of the present culture are strategy-supportive and which are not. Then, managers have to talk openly and forthrightly to all concerned about those aspects of the culture that have to be changed. The talk has to be followed swiftly by visible actions to modify the culture—actions that everyone will understand are intended to establish a new culture more in tune with the strategy.

Symbolic Actions and Substantive Actions   Managerial actions to tighten the culture-strategy fit need to be both symbolic and substantive. Symbolic actions are valuable for the signals they send about the kinds of behavior and performance strategy-implementers wish to encourage. The most important symbolic actions are those that top executives take to serve as role models—leading cost reduction efforts by curtailing executive perks; emphasizing the importance of responding to customers' needs by requiring *all* officers and executives to spend a significant portion of each week talking with customers and understanding their requirements; and initiating efforts to alter policies and practices identified as hindrances in executing the new strategy. Another category of symbolic actions includes the events organizations hold to designate and honor people whose actions and performance exemplify what is called for in the new culture. Many universities give outstanding teacher awards each year to symbolize their commitment to and esteem for instructors who display exceptional classroom talents. Numerous businesses have employee-of-the-month awards. The military has a long-standing custom of awarding ribbons and medals for exemplary actions. Mary Kay Cosmetics awards an array of prizes—from ribbons to pink automobiles—to its beauty consultants for reaching various sales plateaus.

---

[13]Ibid., p. 52.
[14]Ibid., p. 50.

The best companies and the best executives expertly use symbols, role models, ceremonial occasions, and group gatherings to tighten the strategy-culture fit. Low-cost leaders like Wal-Mart and Nucor are renowned for their Spartan facilities, executive frugality, intolerance of waste, and zealous control of costs. Executives sensitive to their role in promoting strategy-culture fits make a habit of appearing at ceremonial functions to praise individuals and groups that "get with the program." They honor individuals who exhibit cultural norms and reward those who achieve strategic milestones. They participate in employee training programs to stress strategic priorities, values, ethical principles, and cultural norms. Every group gathering is seen as an opportunity to implant values, praise good deeds, reinforce cultural norms, and promote changes that assist strategy implementation. Sensitive executives make sure that current decisions and policy changes will be construed by organizational members as consistent with and supportive of the company's new strategic direction.[15]

> Awards ceremonies, role models, and symbols are a fundamental part of a strategy-implementer's culture-shaping effort.

In addition to being out front personally and symbolically leading the push for new behaviors and communicating the reasons for new approaches, strategy-implementers have to convince all those concerned that the effort is more than cosmetic. Talk and plans have to be complemented by substantive actions and real movement. The actions taken have to be credible, highly visible, and unmistakably indicative of the seriousness of management's commitment to new strategic initiatives and the associated cultural changes. There are several ways to accomplish this. One is to engineer some quick successes that highlight the benefits of strategy-culture changes, thus making enthusiasm for the changes contagious. However, instant results are usually not as important as having the will and patience to create a solid, competent team psychologically committed to pursuing the strategy in a superior fashion. The strongest signs that management is truly committed to creating a new culture include: replacing old-culture traditionalist managers with "new breed" managers, changing long-standing policies and operating practices that are dysfunctional or that impede new initiatives, undertaking major reorganizational moves that bring structure into better alignment with strategy, tying compensation incentives directly to the new measures of strategic performance, and making major budgetary reallocations that shift substantial resources from old-strategy projects and programs to new-strategy projects and programs.

> Senior executives must personally lead efforts to align culture with strategy.

At the same time, chief strategy-implementers must be careful to *lead by example*. For instance, if the organization's strategy involves a drive to become the industry's low-cost producer, senior managers must display frugality in their own actions and decisions: Spartan decorations in the executive suite, conservative expense accounts and entertainment allowances, a lean staff in the corporate office, scrutiny of budget requests, and so on. The CEO of SAS Airlines, Jan Carlzon, symbolically reinforced the primacy of quality service for business customers by flying coach instead of first class and by giving up his seat to waitlisted travelers.[16]

Implanting the needed culture-building values and behavior depends on a sincere, sustained commitment by the chief executive coupled with extraordinary persistence in reinforcing the culture at every opportunity through both word and deed. Neither charisma nor personal magnetism are essential. However, personally talking to many departmental groups about the reasons for change *is* essential; organizational changes are seldom accomplished successfully from an office. Moreover, creating and sustaining a strategy-supportive culture is a job for the whole management team. Major

---

[15]Judy D. Olian and Sara L. Rynes, "Making Total Quality Work: Aligning Organizational Processes, Performance Measures, and Stakeholders," *Human Resource Management* 30, no. 3 (Fall 1991), p. 324.
[16]Ibid.

cultural change requires many initiatives from many people. Senior officers, department heads, and middle managers have to reiterate values, "walk the talk," and translate the organization's philosophy into everyday practice. In addition, for the culture-building effort to be successful, strategy-implementers must enlist the support of firstline supervisors and employee opinion-leaders, convincing them of the merits of practicing and enforcing cultural norms at the lowest levels in the organization. Until a big majority of employees join the new culture and share an emotional commitment to its basic values and behavioral norms, there's considerably more work to be done in both instilling the culture and tightening the culture-strategy fit.

The task of making culture supportive of strategy is not a short-term exercise. It takes time for a new culture to emerge and prevail; it's unrealistic to expect an overnight transformation. The bigger the organization and the greater the cultural shift needed to produce a culture-strategy fit, the longer it takes. In large companies, changing the corporate culture in significant ways can take three to five years at minimum. In fact, it is usually tougher to reshape a deeply ingrained culture that is not strategy-supportive than it is to instill a strategy-supportive culture from scratch in a brand new organization.

ESTABLISHING ETHICAL STANDARDS AND VALUES

A strong corporate culture founded on ethical business principles and moral values is a vital driving force behind continued strategic success. Many executives are convinced that a company must care about *how* it does business; otherwise a company's reputation, and ultimately its performance, is put at risk. Corporate ethics and values programs are not window dressing; they are undertaken to create an environment of strongly held values and convictions and to make ethical conduct a way of life. Morally upstanding values and high ethical standards nurture the corporate culture in a very positive way—they connote integrity, "doing the right thing," and genuine concern for stakeholders.

> An ethical corporate culture has a positive impact on a company's long-term strategic success; an unethical culture can undermine it.

Companies establish values and ethical standards in a number of different ways.[17] Companies steeped in tradition with a rich folklore to draw on rely on word-of-mouth indoctrination and the power of tradition to instill values and enforce ethical conduct. But many companies today set forth their values and codes of ethics in written documents. Table 11–1 indicates the kinds of topics such statements cover. Written statements have the advantage of explicitly stating what the company intends and expects, and they serve as benchmarks for judging both company policies and actions and individual conduct. They put a stake in the ground and define the company's position. Value statements serve as a cornerstone for culture-building; a code of ethics serves as a cornerstone for developing a corporate conscience. Illustration Capsule 33 presents the Johnson & Johnson Credo, the most publicized and celebrated code of ethics and values among U.S. companies. J&J's CEO calls the credo "the unifying force for our corporation." Illustration Capsule 34 presents the pledge that Bristol-Myers Squibb makes to all of its stakeholders.

Once values and ethical standards have been formally set forth, they must be institutionalized and ingrained in the company's policies, practices, and actual conduct. Implementing the values and code of ethics entails several actions:

> Values and ethical standards must not only be explicitly stated but they must also be ingrained into the corporate culture.

- Incorporation of the statement of values and the code of ethics into employee training and educational programs.

---

[17]The Business Roundtable, *Corporate Ethics: A Prime Asset,* February 1988, pp. 4–10.

T A B L E 11–1 | **Topics Generally Covered in Value Statements and Codes of Ethics**

Topics Covered in Values Statements	Topics Covered in Codes of Ethics
• Importance of customers and customer service	• Honesty and observance of the law
• Commitment to quality	• Conflicts of interest
• Commitment to innovation	• Fairness in selling and marketing practices
• Respect for the individual employee and the duty the company has to employees	• Using inside information and securities trading
• Importance of honesty, integrity, and ethical standards	• Supplier relationships and purchasing practices
• Duty to stockholders	• Payments to obtain business/Foreign Corrupt Practices Act
• Duty to suppliers	• Acquiring and using information about others
• Corporate citizenship	• Political activities
• Importance of protecting the environment	• Use of company assets, resources, and property
	• Protection of proprietary information
	• Pricing, contracting, and billing

ILLUSTRATION CAPSULE 33

THE JOHNSON & JOHNSON CREDO

- We believe our first responsibility is to the doctors, nurses, and patients, to mothers and all others who use our products and services.
- In meeting their needs everything we do must be of high quality.
- We must constantly strive to reduce our costs in order to maintain reasonable prices.
- Customers' orders must be serviced promptly and accurately.
- Our suppliers and distributors must have an opportunity to make a fair profit.
- We are responsible to our employees, the men and women who work with us throughout the world.
- Everyone must be considered as an individual.
- We must respect their dignity and recognize their merit.
- They must have a sense of security in their jobs.
- Compensation must be fair and adequate, and working conditions clean, orderly, and safe.
- Employees must feel free to make suggestions and complaints.

- There must be equal opportunity for employment, development, and advancement for those qualified.
- We must provide competent management, and their actions must be just and ethical.
- We are responsible to the communities in which we live and work and to the world community as well.
- We must be good citizens—support good works and charities and bear our fair share of taxes.
- We must encourage civic improvements and better health and education.
- We must maintain in good order the property we are privileged to use, protecting the environment and natural resources.
- Our final responsibility is to our stockholders.
- Business must make a sound profit.
- We must experiment with new ideas.
- Research must be carried on, innovative programs developed, and mistakes paid for.
- New equipment must be purchased, new facilities provided, and new products launched.
- Reserves must be created to provide for adverse times.
- When we operate according to these principles, the stockholders should realize a fair return.

Source: 1982 Annual Report.

ILLUSTRATION CAPSULE 34

THE BRISTOL-MYERS SQUIBB PLEDGE

To those who use our products . . .
We affirm Bristol-Myers Squibb's commitment to the highest standards of excellence, safety, and reliability in everything we make. We pledge to offer products of the highest quality and to work diligently to keep improving them.

To our employees and those who may join us . . .
We pledge personal respect, fair compensation, and equal treatment. We acknowledge our obligation to provide able and humane leadership throughout the organization, within a clean and safe working environment. To all who qualify for advancement, we will make every effort to provide opportunity.

To our suppliers and customers . . .
We pledge an open door, courteous, efficient, and ethical dealing, and appreciation for their right to a fair profit.

To our shareholders . . .
We pledge a companywide dedication to continued profitable growth, sustained by strong finances, a high level of research and development, and facilities second to none.

To the communities where we have plants and offices . . .
We pledge conscientious citizenship, a helping hand for worthwhile causes, and constructive action in support of civic and environmental progress.

To the countries where we do business . . .
We pledge ourselves to be a good citizen and to show full consideration for the rights of others while reserving the right to stand up for our own.

Above all, to the world we live in . . .
We pledge Bristol-Myers Squibb to policies and practices which fully embody the responsibility, integrity, and decency required of free enterprise if it is to merit and maintain the confidence of our society.

Source: 1990 Annual Report.

- Explicit attention to values and ethics in recruiting and hiring to screen out applicants who do not exhibit compatible character traits.
- Communication of the values and ethics code to all employees and explaining compliance procedures.
- Management involvement and oversight, from the CEO down to firstline supervisors.
- Strong endorsements by the CEO.
- Word-of-mouth indoctrination.

In the case of codes of ethics, special attention must be given to sections of the company that are particularly sensitive and vulnerable—purchasing, sales, and political lobbying.[18] Employees who deal with external parties are in ethically sensitive positions and often are drawn into compromising situations. Procedures for enforcing ethical standards and handling potential violations have to be developed.

The compliance effort must permeate the company, extending into every organizational unit. The attitudes, character, and work history of prospective employees must be scrutinized. Every employee must receive adequate training. Line managers at all levels must give serious and continuous attention to the task of explaining how the values and ethical code apply in their areas. In addition, they must insist that company values and ethical standards become a way of life. In general, instilling values and insisting on ethical conduct must be looked on as a continuous culture-building,

---

[18]Ibid, p. 7.

culture-nurturing exercise. Whether the effort succeeds or fails depends largely on how well corporate values and ethical standards are visibly integrated into company policies, managerial practices, and actions at all levels.

BUILDING A SPIRIT OF HIGH PERFORMANCE INTO THE CULTURE

An ability to instill strong individual commitment to strategic success and to create an atmosphere in which there is constructive pressure to perform is one of the most valuable strategy-implementing skills. When an organization performs consistently at or near peak capability, the outcome is not only improved strategic success but also an organizational culture permeated with a spirit of high performance. Such a spirit of performance should not be confused with whether employees are "happy" or "satisfied" or whether they "get along well together." An organization with a spirit of high performance emphasizes achievement and excellence. Its culture is results-oriented, and its management pursues policies and practices that inspire people to do their best.

> A results-oriented culture that inspires people to do their best is conducive to superior strategy execution.

Companies with a spirit of high performance typically are intensely people-oriented, and they reinforce their concern for individual employees on every conceivable occasion in every conceivable way. They treat employees with dignity and respect, train each employee thoroughly, encourage employees to use their own initiative and creativity in performing their work, set reasonable and clear performance expectations, utilize the full range of rewards and punishment to enforce high-performance standards, hold managers at every level responsible for developing the people who report to them, and grant employees enough autonomy to stand out, excel, and contribute. To create a results-oriented organizational culture, a company must make champions out of the people who turn in winning performances:[19]

- At Boeing, General Electric, and 3M Corporation, top executives make a point of ceremoniously honoring individuals who believe so strongly in their ideas that they take it on themselves to hurdle the bureaucracy, maneuver their projects through the system, and turn them into improved services, new products, or even new businesses. In these companies, "product champions" are given high visibility, room to push their ideas, and strong executive support. Champions whose ideas prove out are usually handsomely rewarded; those whose ideas don't pan out still have secure jobs and are given chances to try again.

- The manager of a New York area sales office rented the Meadowlands Stadium (home field of the New York Giants) for an evening. After work, the salespeople were all assembled at the stadium and asked to run one at a time through the players' tunnel onto the field. As each one emerged, the electronic scoreboard flashed the person's name to those gathered in the stands— executives from corporate headquarters, employees from the office, family, and friends. Their role was to cheer loudly in honor of the individual's sales accomplishments. The company involved was IBM. The occasion for this action was to reaffirm IBM's commitment to satisfy an individual's need to be part of something great and to reiterate IBM's concern for championing individual accomplishment.

- Some companies upgrade the importance and status of individual employees by referring to them as Cast Members (Disney), crew members (McDonald's), or

---

[19]Thomas J. Peters and Robert H. Waterman, Jr., *In Search of Excellence* (New York: Harper & Row, 1982), pp. xviii, 240, and 269, and Thomas J. Peters and Nancy Austin, *A Passion for Excellence* (New York: Random House, 1985), pp. 304–7.

associates (Wal-Mart and J. C. Penney). Companies like Mary Kay Cosmetics, Tupperware, and McDonald's actively seek out reasons and opportunities to give pins, buttons, badges, and medals for good showings by average performers—the idea being to express appreciation and give a motivational boost to people who stand out doing "ordinary" jobs.

- McDonald's has a contest to determine the best hamburger cooker in its entire chain. It begins with a competition to determine the best hamburger cooker in each store. Store winners go on to compete in regional championships, and regional winners go on to the "All-American" contest. The winners get trophies and an All-American patch to wear on their shirts.

- Milliken & Co. holds Corporate Sharing Rallies once every three months; teams come from all over the company to swap success stories and ideas. A hundred or more teams make five-minute presentations over a two-day period. Each rally has a major theme—quality, cost reduction, and so on. No criticisms and negatives are allowed, and there is no such thing as a big idea or a small one. Quantitative measures of success are used to gauge improvement. All those present vote on the best presentation and several ascending grades of awards are handed out. Everyone, however, receives a framed certificate for participating.

What makes a spirit of high performance come alive is a complex network of practices, words, symbols, styles, values, and policies pulling together that produces extraordinary results with ordinary people. The drivers of the system are a belief in the worth of the individual, strong company commitment to job security and promotion from within, managerial practices that encourage employees to exercise individual initiative and creativity in doing their jobs, and pride in doing the "itty-bitty, teeny-tiny things" right. A company that treats its employees well generally benefits from increased teamwork, higher morale, and greater employee loyalty.

While emphasizing a spirit of high performance nearly always accentuates the positive, there are negative reinforcers too. Managers whose units consistently perform poorly have to be removed. Aside from the organizational benefits, weak-performing managers should be reassigned for their own good—people who find themselves in a job they cannot handle are usually frustrated, anxiety-ridden, harassed, and unhappy.[20] Moreover, subordinates have a right to be managed with competence, dedication, and achievement. Unless their boss performs well, they themselves cannot perform well. In addition, weak-performing workers and people who reject the cultural emphasis on dedication and high performance have to be weeded out. Recruitment practices need to aim at selecting highly motivated, ambitious applicants whose attitudes and work habits mesh well with a results-oriented corporate culture.

EXERTING STRATEGIC LEADERSHIP

The litany of good strategic management is simple enough: formulate a sound strategic plan, implement it, execute it to the fullest, win! But it's easier said than done. Exerting take-charge leadership, being a "spark plug," ramrodding things through, and getting things done by coaching others to do them are difficult tasks. Moreover, a strategy manager has many different leadership roles to play: chief entrepreneur and strategist, chief administrator and strategy-implementer, culture builder, supervisor,

---

[20] Peter Drucker, *Management: Tasks, Responsibilities, Practices* (New York: Harper & Row, 1974), p. 457.

crisis solver, taskmaster, spokesperson, resource allocator, negotiator, motivator, adviser, arbitrator, consensus builder, policymaker, policy enforcer, mentor, and head cheerleader. Sometimes it is useful to be authoritarian and hardnosed; sometimes it is best to be a perceptive listener and a compromising decision-maker; and sometimes a strongly participative, collegial approach works best. Many occasions call for a highly visible role and extensive time commitments, while others entail a brief cere-monial performance with the details delegated to subordinates.

In general, the problem of strategic leadership is one of diagnosing the situation and choosing from any of several ways to handle it. Six leadership roles dominate the strategy-implementer's action agenda:

1. Staying on top of what is happening and how well things are going.
2. Promoting a culture in which the organization is "energized" to accomplish strategy and perform at a high level.
3. Keeping the organization responsive to changing conditions, alert for new opportunities, and bubbling with innovative ideas.
4. Building consensus, containing "power struggles," and dealing with the politics of crafting and implementing strategy.
5. Enforcing ethical standards.
6. Pushing corrective actions to improve strategy execution and overall strategic performance.

MANAGING BY WALKING AROUND (MBWA)

To stay on top of how well the implementation process is going, a manager needs to develop a broad network of contacts and sources of information, both formal and informal. The regular channels include talking with key subordinates, reviewing reports and the latest operating results, talking to customers, watching the·competitive reactions of rival firms, tapping into the grapevine, listening to rank-and-file employ-ees, and observing the situation firsthand. However, some information tends to be more trustworthy than the rest. Written reports may represent "the truth but not the whole truth." Bad news may be covered up, minimized, or not reported at all. Some-times subordinates delay conveying failures and problems in hopes that more time will give them room to turn things around. As information flows up an organization, there is a tendency for it to get censored and sterilized to the point that it may fail to reveal strategy-critical information. Hence, there is reason for strategy managers to guard against major surprises by making sure that they have accurate information and a "feel" for the existing situation. The chief way this is done is by regular visits "to the field" and talking with many different people at many different levels. The tech-nique of *managing by walking around* (MBWA) is practiced in a variety of styles:[21]

> *MBWA is one of the tech-niques effective leaders use.*

- At Hewlett-Packard, there are weekly beer busts in each division, attended by both executives and employees, to create a regular opportunity to keep in touch. Tidbits of information flow freely between down-the-line employees and executives—facilitated in part because "the HP Way" is for people at all ranks to be addressed by their first names. Bill Hewlett, one of HP's cofounders, had a companywide reputation for getting out of his office and "wandering around" the plant greeting people, listening to what was on their minds, and asking questions. He found this so valuable that he made MBWA a standard practice

---

[21]Ibid., pp. xx, 15, 120–23, 191, 242–43, 246–47, 287–90. For an extensive report on the benefits of MBWA, see Peters and Austin, *A Passion for Excellence,* chapters 2, 3, and 19.

for all HP managers. Furthermore, ad hoc meetings of people from different departments spontaneously arise; they gather in rooms with blackboards and work out solutions informally.

• McDonald's founder Ray Kroc regularly visited store units and did his own personal inspection on Q.S.C.&V. (Quality, Service, Cleanliness, and Value)—the themes he preached regularly. There are stories of his pulling into a unit's parking lot, seeing litter lying on the pavement, getting out of his limousine to pick it up himself, and then lecturing the store staff at length on the subject of cleanliness.

• The CEO of a small manufacturing company spends much of his time riding around the factory in a golf cart, waving to and joking with workers, listening to them, and calling all 2,000 employees by their first names. In addition, he spends a lot of time with union officials, inviting them to meetings and keeping them well-informed about what is going on.

• Wal-Mart executives have had a long-standing practice of spending two to three days every week visiting Wal-Mart's stores and talking with store managers and employees. Sam Walton, Wal-Mart's founder, insisted "The key is to get out into the store and listen to what the associates have to say. Our best ideas come from clerks and stockboys."

• When Ed Carlson became CEO of United Airlines, he traveled about 200,000 miles a year talking with United's employees. He observed, "I wanted these people to identify me and to feel sufficiently comfortable to make suggestions or even argue with me if that's what they felt like doing . . . Whenever I picked up some information, I would call the senior officer of the division and say that I had just gotten back from visiting Oakland, Reno, and Las Vegas, and here is what I found."

• At Marriott Corp. Bill Marriott personally inspects Marriott hotels. He also invites all Marriott guests to send him their evaluations of Marriott's facilities and services; he personally reads every customer complaint and has been known to telephone hotel managers about them.

Managers at many companies attach great importance to informal communications. They report that it is essential to have a "feel" for situations and to have the ability to gain quick, easy access to information. When executives stay in their offices, they tend to become isolated and often surround themselves with people who are not likely to offer criticism and different perspectives. The information they get is secondhand, screened and filtered, and sometimes dated.

FOSTERING A STRATEGY-SUPPORTIVE CLIMATE AND CULTURE

Strategy-implementers have to be out front in promoting a strategy-supportive organizational climate and culture. When major strategic changes are being implemented, a manager's time is best spent personally leading the changes and promoting needed cultural adjustments. In general, organizational cultures need major overhaul every 5 to 25 years, depending on how fast events in the company's business environment move.[22] When only strategic fine-tuning is being implemented, it takes less time and effort to bring values and culture into alignment with strategy, but there is still a lead role for the manager to play in pushing ahead and prodding for continuous improve-

---

[22]Kotter and Heskett, *Corporate Culture and Performance*, p. 91.

ments. Successful strategy leaders recognize it is their responsibility to convince people that the chosen strategy is right and that implementing it to the best of the organization's ability is top priority.

The single most visible factor that distinguishes successful culture-change efforts from failed attempts is competent leadership at the top. Effective management action to match culture and strategy has several attributes:[23]

- A stakeholders-are-king philosophy that links the need to change to the need to serve the long-term best interests of all key constituencies.

- An openness to new ideas.

- Challenging the status quo with very basic questions: Are we giving customers what they really need and want? How can we be more competitive on cost? Why can't design-to-market cycle time be halved? How can we grow the company instead of downsizing it? Where will the company be five years from now if it sticks with just its present business?

- Persuading individuals and groups to commit themselves to the new direction and energizing individuals and departments sufficiently to make it happen despite the obstacles.

- Repeating the new messages again and again, explaining the rationale for change, and convincing skeptics that all is not well and must be changed.

- Recognizing and generously rewarding those who exhibit new cultural norms and who lead successful change efforts—this helps cultivate expansion of the coalition for change.

- Creating events where everyone in management is forced to listen to angry customers, dissatisfied stockholders, and alienated employees to keep management informed and to help them realistically assess organizational strengths and weaknesses.

Only top management has the power to bring about major cultural change.

Great power is needed to force major cultural change—to overcome the springback resistance of entrenched cultures—and great power normally resides only at the top. Moreover, the interdependence of values, strategies, practices, and behaviors inside organizations makes it difficult to change anything fundamental without simultaneously undertaking wider-scale changes. Usually the people with the power to effect change of that scope are those at the top.

Both words and deeds play a part in strategic leadership. Words inspire people, infuse spirit and drive, define strategy-supportive cultural norms and values, articulate the reasons for strategic and organizational change, legitimize new viewpoints and new priorities, urge and reinforce commitment, and arouse confidence in the new strategy. Deeds add credibility to the words, create strategy-supportive symbols, set examples, give meaning and content to the language, and teach the organization what sort of behavior is needed and expected.

Highly visible symbols and imagery are needed to complement substantive actions. One General Motors manager explained how symbolism and managerial style accounted for the striking difference in performance between two large plants:[24]

At the poorly performing plant, the plant manager probably ventured out on the floor once a week, always in a suit. His comments were distant and perfunctory. At South

---

[23]Ibid., pp. 84, 144, and 148.
[24]As quoted in Peters and Waterman, *In Search of Excellence,* p. 262.

Gate, the better plant, the plant manager was on the floor all the time. He wore a base-ball cap and a UAW jacket. By the way, whose plant do you think was spotless? Whose looked like a junkyard?

As a rule, the greater the degree of strategic change being implemented and/or the greater the shift in cultural norms needed to accommodate a new strategy, the more visible and unequivocal the strategy-implementer's words and deeds need to be. Lessons from well-managed companies show that what the strategy leader says and does has a significant bearing on down-the-line strategy implementation and execution.[25] According to one view, "It is not so much the articulation . . . about what an [organization] should be doing that creates new practice. It's the imagery that creates the understanding, the compelling moral necessity that the new way is right."[26] Moreover, the actions and images, both substantive and symbolic, have to be ham-mered out regularly, not just restricted to ceremonial speeches and special occasions. This is where a high profile and "managing by walking around" come into play. As a Hewlett-Packard official expresses it in the company publication *The HP Way:*

> Once a division or department has developed a plan of its own—a set of working objec-tives—it's important for managers and supervisors to keep it in operating condition. This is where observation, measurement, feedback, and guidance come in. It's our "management by wandering around." That's how you find out whether you're on track and heading at the right speed and in the right direction. If you don't constantly monitor how people are operating, not only will they tend to wander off track but also they will begin to believe you weren't serious about the plan in the first place. It has the extra benefit of getting you off your chair and moving around your area. By wandering around, I literally mean moving around and talking to people. It's all done on a very informal and spontaneous basis, but it's important in the course of time to cover the whole territory. You start out by being accessible and approachable, but the main thing is to realize you're there to listen. The second reason for MBWA is that it is vital to keep people informed about what's going on in the company, especially those things that are important to them. The third reason for doing this is because it is just plain fun.

Such contacts give the manager a "feel" for how things are progressing, and they provide opportunity to speak with encouragement, lift spirits, shift attention from the old to the new priorities, create some excitement, and project an atmosphere of infor-mality and fun—all of which drive implementation in a positive fashion and intensify the organizational energy behind strategy execution. John Welch of General Electric sums up the hands-on role and motivational approach well: "I'm here every day, or out into a factory, smelling it, feeling it, touching it, challenging the people."[27]

The vast majority of companies probably don't have strong, adaptive cultures capable of producing excellent long-term performance in a fast-paced market and competitive environment. In such companies, managers have to do more than show incremental progress. Conservative incrementalism seldom leads to major cultural adaptations; more usually, gradualism is defeated by the resilience of entrenched cul-tures and the ability of vested interests to thwart or minimize the impact of piecemeal change. Only with bold leadership and concerted action on many fronts can a com-pany succeed in tackling so large and difficult a task as major cultural change.

---

[25]Ibid., chapter 9.

[26]Warren Bennis, *The Unconscious Conspiracy: Why Leaders Can't Lead* (New York: AMACOM, 1987), p. 93.

[27]As quoted in Ann M. Morrison, "Trying to Bring GE to Life," *Fortune,* January 25, 1982, p. 52.

KEEPING THE INTERNAL ORGANIZATION RESPONSIVE AND INNOVATIVE

While formulating and implementing strategy is a manager's responsibility, the task of generating fresh ideas, identifying new opportunities, and being responsive to changing conditions cannot be accomplished by a single person. It is an organization-wide task, particularly in large corporations. One of the toughest parts of exerting strategic leadership is generating a dependable supply of fresh ideas from the rank and file, managers and employees alike, and promoting an entrepreneurial, opportunistic spirit that permits continuous adaptation to changing conditions. A flexible, responsive, innovative internal environment is critical in fast-moving high-technology industries, in businesses where products have short life-cycles and growth depends on new product innovation, in companies with widely diversified business portfolios (where opportunities are varied and scattered), in markets where successful product differentiation depends on out-innovating the competition, and in situations where low-cost leadership hinges on continuous improvement and new ways to drive costs out of the business. Managers cannot mandate such an environment by simply exhorting people to "be creative."

One useful leadership approach is to take special pains to foster, nourish, and support people who are willing to champion new ideas, better services, new products, and new product applications and are eager for a chance to try turning their ideas into new divisions, new businesses, and even new industries. When Texas Instruments reviewed 50 or so successful and unsuccessful new product introductions, one factor marked every failure: "Without exception we found we hadn't had a volunteer champion. There was someone we had cajoled into taking on the task."[28] The rule seems to be that an idea either finds a champion or dies. The best champions are persistent, competitive, tenacious, committed, and fanatic about the idea and seeing it through to success.

Empowering Champions   In order to promote an organizational climate where champion innovators can blossom and thrive, strategy managers need to do several things. First, individuals and groups have to be encouraged to bring their ideas forward, be creative, and exercise initiative. The culture has to nurture, even celebrate, experimentation and innovation. Everybody must be expected to contribute ideas and seek out continuous improvement. The trick is to keep a sense of urgency alive in the business so that people see change and innovation as a necessity. Second, the champion's maverick style has to be tolerated and given room to operate. People's imaginations need to be encouraged to fly in all directions. Freedom to experiment and a practice of informal brainstorming sessions need to become ingrained. Above all, people with creative ideas must not be looked on as disruptive or troublesome. Third, managers have to induce and promote lots of "tries" and be willing to tolerate mistakes and failures. Most ideas don't pan out, but the organization learns from a good attempt even when it fails. Fourth, strategy managers should be willing to use all kinds of ad hoc organizational forms to support ideas and experimentation—venture teams, task forces, "performance shootouts" among different groups working on competing approaches, informal "bootlegged" projects composed of volunteers, and so on. Fifth, strategy managers have to see that the rewards for successful champions are large and visible and that people who champion an unsuccessful idea are encouraged to try again rather than punished or sidelined. In effect, the leadership task is to create an adaptive, innovative culture that embraces organizational responses to

High-performance cultures make champions out of people who excel.

The faster a company's business environment changes, the more attention managers must pay to keeping the organization innovative and responsive.

---

[28] As quoted in Peters and Waterman, *In Search of Excellence,* pp. 203–4.

changing conditions rather than fearing the new conditions or seeking to minimize them. Companies with conspicuously innovative cultures include Sony, 3M, Motorola, and Levi Strauss. All four inspire their employees with strategic visions to excel and be world-class at what they do.

Dealing with Company Politics

A manager can't effectively formulate and implement strategy without being perceptive about company politics and being adept at political maneuvering.[29] Politics virtually always comes into play in formulating the strategic plan. Inevitably, key individuals and groups form coalitions, and each group presses the benefits and potential of its own ideas and vested interests. Political considerations enter into decisions about which objectives take precedence and which lines of business in the corporate portfolio have top priority in resource allocation. Internal politics is a factor in building a consensus for one strategic option over another.

As a rule, there is even more politics in implementing strategy than in formulating it. Typically, internal political considerations affect practical issues such as whose areas of responsibility get reorganized, who reports to whom, who has how much authority over subunits, what individuals should fill key positions and head strategy-critical activities, and which organizational units will get the biggest budget increases. As a case in point, Quinn cites a situation where three strong managers who fought each other constantly formed a potent coalition to resist a reorganization scheme that would have coordinated the very things that caused their friction.[30]

In short, political considerations and the forming of individual and group alliances are integral parts of building organizationwide support for the strategic plan and gaining consensus on how to implement it. Political skills are a definite, maybe even necessary, asset for managers in orchestrating the whole strategic process.

A strategy manager must understand how an organization's power structure works, who wields influence in the executive ranks, which groups and individuals are "activists" and which are defenders of the status quo, who can be helpful and who may not be in a showdown on key decisions, and which direction the political winds are blowing on a given issue. When major decisions have to be made, strategy managers need to be especially sensitive to the politics of managing coalitions and reaching consensus. As the chairman of a major British corporation expressed it:

> I've never taken a major decision without consulting my colleagues. It would be unimaginable to me, unimaginable. First, they help me make a better decision in most cases. Second, if they know about it and agree with it, they'll back it. Otherwise, they might challenge it, not openly, but subconsciously.[31]

The politics of strategy centers chiefly around stimulating options, nurturing support for strong proposals and killing weak ones, guiding the formation of coalitions on particular issues, and achieving consensus and commitment. A recent study of strategy management in nine large corporations showed that successful executives relied upon the following political tactics:[32]

Company politics presents strategy leaders with the challenge of building consensus for the strategy and how to implement it.

---

[29]For further discussion of this point see Abraham Zaleznik, "Power and Politics in Organizational Life," *Harvard Business Review* 48, no. 3 (May–June 1970), pp. 47–60; R. M. Cyert, H. A. Simon, and D. B. Trow, "Observation of a Business Decision," *Journal of Business,* October 1956, pp. 237–48; and James Brian Quinn, *Strategies for Change: Logical Incrementalism* (Homewood, Ill.: Richard D. Irwin, 1980).

[30]Quinn, *Strategies for Change,* p. 68.

[31]Ibid., p. 65. This statement was made by Sir Alastair Pilkington, Chairman, Pilkington Brothers, Ltd.

[32]Ibid., pp. 128–45.

- Letting weakly supported ideas and proposals die through inaction.
- Establishing additional hurdles or tests for strongly supported ideas that the manager views as unacceptable but that are best not opposed openly.
- Keeping a low political profile on unacceptable proposals by getting subordinate managers to say no.
- Letting most negative decisions come from a group consensus that the manager merely confirms, thereby reserving personal veto for big issues and crucial moments.
- Leading the strategy but not dictating it—giving few orders, announcing few decisions, depending heavily on informal questioning, and seeking to probe and clarify until a consensus emerges.
- Staying alert to the symbolic impact of one's actions and statements lest a false signal stimulate proposals and movements in unwanted directions.
- Ensuring that all major power bases within the organization have representation in or access to top management.
- Injecting new faces and new views into considerations of major changes to preclude those involved from coming to see the world the same way and then acting as systematic screens against other views.
- Minimizing political exposure on issues that are highly controversial and in circumstances where opposition from major power centers can trigger a "shootout."

The politics of strategy implementation is especially critical when it comes to introducing a new strategy against the resistance of those who support the old one. Except for crisis situations where the old strategy is plainly revealed as out-of-date, it is usually bad politics to push the new strategy via attacks on the old one.[33] Bad-mouthing old strategy can easily be interpreted as an attack on those who formulated it and those who supported it. The old strategy and the judgments behind it may have been well-suited to the organization's earlier circumstances, and the people who made these judgments may still be influential.

In addition, the new strategy and/or the plans for implementing it may not have been the first choices of others, and lingering doubts may remain. Good arguments may exist for pursuing other actions. Consequently, in trying to surmount resistance, nothing is gained by knocking the arguments for alternative approaches. Such attacks often produce alienation instead of cooperation.

In short, to bring the full force of an organization behind a strategic plan, the strategy manager must assess and deal with the most important centers of potential support for and opposition to new strategic thrusts.[34] He or she needs to secure the support of key people, co-opt or neutralize serious opposition and resistance when and where necessary, learn where the zones of indifference are, and build as much consensus as possible.

ENFORCING ETHICAL BEHAVIOR

For an organization to display consistently high ethical standards, the CEO and those around the CEO must be openly and unequivocally committed to ethical and moral conduct.[35] In companies that strive hard to make high ethical standards a reality, top

---

[33]Ibid., pp. 118–19.
[34]Ibid., p. 205.
[35]The Business Roundtable, *Corporate Ethics,* pp. 4–10.

management communicates its commitment in a code of ethics, in speeches and company publications, in policies concerning the consequences of unethical behavior, in the deeds of senior executives, and in the actions taken to ensure compliance. Senior management iterates and reiterates to employees that it is not only their duty to observe ethical codes but also to report ethical violations. While such companies have provisions for disciplining violators, the main purpose of enforcement is to encourage compliance rather than administer punishment. Although the CEO leads the enforcement process, all managers are expected to make a personal contribution by stressing ethical conduct with their subordinates and by involving themselves in the process of monitoring compliance with the code of ethics. "Gray areas" must be identified and openly discussed with employees, and procedures created for offering guidance when issues arise, for investigating possible violations, and for resolving individual cases. The lesson from these companies is that it is never enough to assume activities are being conducted ethically, nor can it be assumed that employees understand they are expected to act with integrity.

> High ethical standards cannot be enforced without the open and unequivocal commitment of the chief executive.

There are several concrete things managers can do to exercise ethics leadership.[36] First and foremost, they must set an excellent ethical example in their own behavior and establish a tradition of integrity. Company decisions have to be seen as ethical—"actions speak louder than words." Second, managers and employees have to be educated about what is ethical and what is not; ethics training programs may have to be established and gray areas pointed out and discussed. Everyone must be encouraged to raise issues with ethical dimensions, and such discussions should be treated as a legitimate topic. Third, top management should regularly reiterate its unequivocal support of the company's ethical code and take a strong stand on ethical issues. Fourth, top management must be prepared to act as the final arbiter on hard calls; this means removing people from a key position or terminating them when they are guilty of a violation. It also means reprimanding those who have been lax in monitoring and enforcing ethical compliance. Failure to act swiftly and decisively in punishing ethical misconduct is interpreted as a lack of real commitment.

A well-developed program to ensure compliance with ethical standards typically includes (1) an oversight committee of the board of directors, usually made up of outside directors; (2) a committee of senior managers to direct ongoing training, implementation, and compliance; (3) an annual audit of each manager's efforts to uphold ethical standards and formal reports on the actions taken by managers to remedy deficient conduct; and (4) periodically requiring people to sign documents certifying compliance with ethical standards.[37]

LEADING THE PROCESS OF MAKING CORRECTIVE ADJUSTMENTS

No strategic plan and no scheme for strategy implementation can foresee all the events and problems that will arise. Making adjustments and mid-course corrections is a normal and necessary part of strategic management.

When responding to new conditions involving either the strategy or its implementation, prompt action is often needed. In a crisis, the typical approach is to push key subordinates to gather information and formulate recommendations, personally preside over extended discussions of the proposed responses, and try to build a quick consensus among members of the executive inner circle. If no consensus emerges or

> Corrective adjustments in the company's approach to strategy implementation should be made on an as-needed basis.

---

[36]Ibid.
[37]Ibid.

if several key subordinates remain divided, the burden falls on the strategy manager to choose the response and urge its support.

When time permits a full-fledged evaluation, strategy managers seem to prefer a process of incrementally solidifying commitment to a response.[38] The approach involves

1. Staying flexible and keeping a number of options open.
2. Asking a lot of questions.
3. Gaining in-depth information from specialists.
4. Encouraging subordinates to participate in developing alternatives and proposing solutions.
5. Getting the reactions of many different people to proposed solutions to test their potential and political acceptability.
6. Seeking to build commitment to a response by gradually moving toward a consensus solution.

The governing principle seems to be to make a final decision as late as possible to (1) bring as much information to bear as needed, (2) let the situation clarify enough to know what to do, and (3) allow the various political constituencies and power bases within the organization to move toward a consensus solution. Executives are often wary of committing themselves to a major change too soon because it limits the time for further fact-finding and analysis, discourages others from asking questions that need to be raised, and precludes thorough airing of all the options.

Corrective adjustments to strategy need not be just reactive, however. Proactive adjustments can improve the strategy or its implementation. The distinctive feature of a proactive adjustment is that it arises from management initiatives rather than from forced reactions. Successful strategy managers employ a variety of proactive tactics:[39]

1. Commissioning studies to explore and amplify areas where they have a "gut feeling" or sense a need exists.
2. Shopping ideas among trusted colleagues and putting forth trial concepts.
3. Teaming people with different skills, interests, and experiences and letting them push and tug on interesting ideas to expand the variety of approaches considered.
4. Contacting a variety of people inside and outside the organization to sample viewpoints, probe, and listen, thereby deliberating short-circuiting all the careful screens of information flowing up from below.
5. Stimulating proposals for improvement from lower levels, encouraging the development of competing ideas and approaches, and letting the momentum for change come from below, with final choices postponed until it is apparent which option best matches the organization's situation.
6. Seeking new options and solutions that go beyond extrapolations from the status quo.
7. Accepting and committing to partial steps forward as a way of building comfort levels before going on ahead.
8. Managing the politics of change to promote managerial consensus and solidify management's commitment to whatever course of action is chosen.

Strategy leaders should be proactive as well as reactive in reshaping strategy and how it is implemented.

---

[38] Quinn, *Strategies for Change,* pp. 20–22.
[39] Ibid., chapter 4.

The process leaders go through in deciding on corrective adjustments is essentially the same for both proactive and reactive changes; they sense needs, gather information, amplify understanding and awareness, put forth trial concepts, develop options, explore the pros and cons, test proposals, generate partial (comfort-level) solutions, empower champions, build a managerial consensus, and finally formally adopt an agreed-on course of action.[40] The ultimate managerial prescription may have been given by Rene McPherson, former CEO at Dana Corporation. Speaking to a class of students at Stanford University, he said, "You just keep pushing. You just keep pushing. I made every mistake that could be made. But I just kept pushing."[41]

All this, once again, highlights the fundamental nature of strategic management: the job of formulating and implementing strategy is not one of steering a clear-cut, linear course while carrying out the original strategy intact according to some preconceived and highly detailed implementation plan. Rather, it is one of creatively (1) adapting and reshaping strategy to unfolding events and (2) drawing upon whatever managerial techniques are needed to align internal activities and behaviors with strategy. The process is interactive, with much looping and recycling to fine-tune and adjust visions, objectives, strategies, implementation approaches, and cultures to one another in a continuously evolving process where the conceptually separate acts of crafting and implementing strategy blur and join together.

KEY POINTS

Building a strategy-supportive corporate culture is important to successful implementation because it produces a work climate and organizational esprit de corps that thrive on meeting performance targets and being part of a winning effort. An organization's culture emerges from why and how it does things the way it does, the values and beliefs that senior managers espouse, the ethical standards expected of all, the tone and philosophy underlying key policies, and the traditions the organization maintains. Culture thus concerns the atmosphere and "feeling" a company has and the style in which it gets things done.

Very often, the elements of company culture originate with a founder or other early influential leaders who articulate certain values, beliefs, and principles the company should adhere to, which then get incorporated into company policies, a creed or values statement, strategies, and operating practices. Over time, these values and practices become shared by company employees and managers. Cultures are perpetuated as new leaders act to reinforce them, as new employees are encouraged to adopt and follow them, as legendary stories that exemplify them are told and retold, and as organizational members are honored and rewarded for displaying the cultural norms.

Company cultures vary widely in strength and in makeup. Some cultures are strongly embedded, while others are weak and fragmented in the sense that many subcultures exist, few values and behavioral norms are shared companywide, and there are few strong traditions. Some cultures are unhealthy, dominated by self-serving politics, resistant to change, and too inwardly focused; such cultural traits are often precursors to declining company performance. In fast-changing business environments, adaptive cultures are best because the internal environment is receptive to change, experimentation, innovation, new strategies, and new operating practices needed to respond to changing stakeholder requirements. One significant defining

---

[40]Ibid., p. 146.
[41]As quoted in Peters and Waterman, *In Search of Excellence*, p. 319.

trait of adaptive cultures is that top management genuinely cares about the well-being of all key constituencies—customers, employees, stockholders, major suppliers, and the communities where it operates—and tries to satisfy all their legitimate interests simultaneously.

The philosophy, goals, and practices implicit or explicit in a new strategy may or may not be compatible with a firm's culture. A close strategy-culture alignment promotes implementation and good execution; a mismatch poses real obstacles. Changing a company's culture, especially a strong one with traits that don't fit a new strategy's requirements, is one of the toughest management challenges. Changing a culture requires competent leadership at the top. It requires symbolic actions (leading by example) and substantive actions that unmistakably indicate top management is seriously committed. The stronger the fit between culture and strategy, the less managers have to depend on policies, rules, procedures, and supervision to enforce what people should and should not do; rather, cultural norms are so well-observed that they automatically guide behavior.

Healthy corporate cultures are also grounded in ethical business principles and moral values. Such standards connote integrity, "doing the right thing," and genuine concern for stakeholders and for how the company does business. To be effective, corporate ethics and values programs have to become a way of life through training, strict compliance and enforcement procedures, and reiterated management endorsements.

Successful strategy-implementers exercise an important leadership role. They stay on top of how well things are going by spending considerable time outside their offices, wandering around the organization, listening, coaching, cheerleading, picking up important information, and keeping their fingers on the organization's pulse. They take pains to reinforce the corporate culture through the things they say and do. They encourage people to be creative and innovative in order to keep the organization responsive to changing conditions, alert to new opportunities, and anxious to pursue fresh initiatives. They support "champions" of new approaches or ideas who are willing to stick their necks out and try something innovative. They work hard at building consensus on how to proceed, on what to change and what not to change. They enforce high ethical standards. And they push corrective action to improve strategy execution and overall strategic performance.

A manager's action agenda for implementing and executing strategy is thus expansive and creative. As we indicated at the beginning of our discussion of strategy implementation (Chapter 9), eight bases need to be covered:

1. Building an organization capable of carrying out the strategy successfully.
2. Developing budgets to steer ample resources into those value-chain activities critical to strategic success.
3. Establishing strategically appropriate policies and procedures.
4. Instituting best practices and mechanisms for continuous improvement.
5. Installing support systems that enable company personnel to carry out their strategic roles successfully day in and day out.
6. Tying rewards and incentives tightly to the achievement of performance objectives and good strategy execution.
7. Creating a strategy-supportive work environment and corporate culture.
8. Leading and monitoring the process of driving implementation forward and improving on how the strategy is being executed.

Making progress on these eight tasks sweeps broadly across virtually every aspect of administrative and managerial work.

Because each instance of strategy implementation occurs under different organizational circumstances, a strategy-implementer's action agenda always needs to be situation specific—there's no neat generic procedure to follow. And, as we said at the beginning, implementing strategy is an action-oriented, make-the-right-things-happen task that challenges a manager's ability to lead and direct organizational change, create or reinvent business processes, manage and motivate people, and achieve performance targets. If you now better understand the nature of the challenge, the range of available approaches, and the issues that need to be considered, we will look upon our discussion in these last three chapter as a success.

SUGGESTED READINGS

Bettinger, Cass. "Use Corporate Culture to Trigger High Performance." *Journal of Business Strategy* 10, no. 2 (March–April 1989), pp. 38–42.

Bower, Joseph L., and Martha W. Weinberg. "Statecraft, Strategy, and Corporate Leadership." *California Management Review* 30, no. 2 (Winter 1988), pp. 39–56.

Deal, Terrence E., and Allen A. Kennedy. *Corporate Cultures*. Reading, Mass.: Addison-Wesley, 1982, especially chaps. 1 and 2.

Eccles, Robert G. "The Performance Measurement Manifesto." *Harvard Business Review* 69 (January–February 1991), pp. 131–37.

Floyd, Steven W., and Bill Wooldridge. "Managing Strategic Consensus: The Foundation of Effective Implementation." *Academy of Management Executive* 6, no. 4 (November 1992), pp. 27–39.

Freeman, R. Edward, and Daniel R. Gilbert, Jr. *Corporate Strategy and the Search for Ethics*. Englewood Cliffs, N.J.: Prentice-Hall, 1988.

Gabarro, J. J. "When a New Manager Takes Charge." *Harvard Business Review* 64, no. 3 (May–June 1985), pp. 110–23.

Ginsburg, Lee and Neil Miller, "Value-Driven Management," *Business Horizons* (May–June 1992), pp. 25–27.

Green, Sebastian. "Strategy, Organizational Culture, and Symbolism." *Long Range Planning* 21, no. 4 (August 1988), pp. 121–29.

Kirkpatrick, Shelley A., and Edwin A. Locke. "Leadership: Do Traits Matter?" *Academy of Management Executive* 5, no. 2 (May 1991), pp. 48–60.

Kotter, John P. "What Leaders Really Do." *Harvard Business Review* 68 (May–June 1990), pp. 103–11.

——————, and James L. Heskett. *Corporate Culture and Performance*. New York: Free Press, 1992.

O'Toole, James. "Employee Practices at the Best-Managed Companies." *California Management Review* 28, no. 1 (Fall 1985), pp. 35–66.

Paine, Lynn Sharp. "Managing for Organizational Integrity." *Harvard Business Review* 72, no. 2 (March–April 1994), pp. 106–117.

Pascale, Richard. "The Paradox of 'Corporate Culture': Reconciling Ourselves to Socialization." *California Management Review* 27, no. 2 (Winter 1985), pp. 26–41.

Quinn, James Brian. *Strategies for Change: Logical Incrementalism*. Homewood, Ill.: Richard D. Irwin, 1980, chap. 4.

——————. "Managing Innovation: Controlled Chaos." *Harvard Business Review* 64, no. 3 (May–June 1985), pp. 73–84.

Reimann, Bernard C., and Yoash Wiener. "Corporate Culture: Avoiding the Elitest Trap." *Business Horizons* 31, no. 2 (March–April 1988), pp. 36–44.

Scholz, Christian. "Corporate Culture and Strategy—The Problem of Strategic Fit." *Long Range Planning* 20 (August 1987), pp. 78–87.

PART TWO

READINGS IN
STRATEGIC MANAGEMENT

STRATEGIC INTENT

Gary Hamel, London Business School
C. K. Prahalad, University of Michigan

Today managers in many industries are working hard to match the competitive advantages of their new global rivals. They are moving manufacturing offshore in search of lower labor costs, rationalizing product lines to capture global scale economies, instituting quality circles and just-in-time production, and adopting Japanese human resource practices. When competitiveness still seems out of reach, they form strategic alliances—often with the very companies that upset the competitive balance in the first place.

Important as these initiatives are, few of them go beyond mere imitation. Too many companies are expending enormous energy simply to reproduce the cost and quality advantages their global competitors already enjoy. Imitation may be the sincerest form of flattery, but it will not lead to competitive revitalization. Strategies based on imitation are transparent to competitors who have already mastered them. Moreover, successful competitors rarely stand still. So it is not surprising that many executives feel trapped in a seemingly endless game of catch-up—regularly surprised by the new accomplishments of their rivals.

For these executives and their companies, regaining competitiveness will mean rethinking many of the basic concepts of strategy.[1] As "strategy" has blossomed, the competitiveness of Western companies has withered. This may be coincidence, but we think not. We believe that the application of concepts such as "strategic fit" (between resources and opportunities), "generic strategies" (low cost versus differentiation versus focus), and the "strategy hierarchy" (goals, strategies, and tactics) has often abetted the process of competitive decline. The new global competitors

---

Source: Reprinted by permission of *Harvard Business Review.* "Strategic Intent," by Gary Hamel and C. K. Prahalad, May–June 1989, pp. 63–76. Copyright © 1989 by the President and Fellows of Harvard College; all rights reserved.

[1]Among the first to apply the concept of strategy to management were H. Igor Ansoff in *Corporate Strategy: An Analytic Approach to Business Policy for Growth and Expansion* (New York: McGraw-Hill, 1965) and Kenneth R. Andrews in *The Concept of Corporate Strategy* (Homewood, Ill.: Dow Jones-Irwin, 1971).

approach strategy from a perspective that is fundamentally different from that which underpins Western management thought. Against such competitors, marginal adjustments to current orthodoxies are no more likely to produce competitive revitalization than are marginal improvements in operating efficiency. (The box, "Remaking Strategy," describes our research and summarizes the two contrasting approaches to strategy we see in large, multinational companies.)

Few Western companies have an enviable track record anticipating the moves of new global competitors. Why? The explanation begins with the way most companies have approached competitor analysis. Typically, competitor analysis focuses on the existing resources (human, technical, and financial) of present competitors. The only companies seen as threats are those with the resources to erode margins and market share in the next planning period. Resourcefulness, the pace at which new competitive advantages are being built, rarely enters in.

In this respect, traditional competitor analysis is like a snapshot of a moving car. By itself, the photograph yields little information about the car's speed or direction—whether the driver is out for a quiet Sunday drive or warming up for the Grand Prix. Yet many managers have learned through painful experience that a business's initial resource endowment (whether bountiful or meager) is an unreliable predictor of future global success.

Think back. In 1970, few Japanese companies possessed the resource base, manufacturing volume, or technical prowess of U.S. and European industry leaders. Komatsu was less than 35 percent as large as Caterpillar (measured by sales), was scarcely represented outside Japan, and relied on just one product line—small bulldozers—for most of its revenue. Honda was smaller than American Motors and had not yet begun to export cars to the United States. Canon's first halting steps in the reprographics business looked pitifully small compared with the $4 billion Xerox powerhouse.

If Western managers had extended their competitor analysis to include these companies, it would merely have underlined how dramatic the resource discrepancies between them were. Yet by 1985, Komatsu was a $2.8 billion company with a product scope encompassing a broad range of earth-moving equipment, industrial robots, and semiconductors. Honda manufactured almost as many cars worldwide in 1987 as Chrysler. Canon had matched Xerox's global unit market share.

The lesson is clear: assessing the current tactical advantages of known competitors will not help you understand the resolution, stamina, and inventiveness of potential competitors. Sun-tzu, a Chinese military strategist, made the point 3,000 years ago: "All men can see the tactics whereby I conquer," he wrote, "but what none can see is the strategy out of which great victory is evolved."

Companies that have risen to global leadership over the past 20 years invariably began with ambitions that were out of all proportion to their resources and capabilities. But they created an obsession with winning at all levels of the organization and then sustained that obsession over the 10- to 20-year quest for global leadership. We term this obsession "strategic intent."

On the one hand, strategic intent envisions a desired leadership position and establishes the criterion the organization will use to chart its progress. Komatsu set out to "Encircle Caterpillar." Canon sought to "Beat Xerox." Honda strove to become a second Ford—an automotive pioneer. All are expressions of strategic intent.

At the same time, strategic intent is more than simply unfettered ambition. (Many companies possess an ambitious strategic intent yet fall short of their goals.) The concept also encompasses an active management process that includes focusing the

REMAKING STRATEGY

Over the last 10 years, our research on global competition, international alliances, and multinational management has brought us into close contact with senior managers in America, Europe, and Japan. As we tried to unravel the reasons for success and surrender in global markets, we became more and more suspicious that executives in Western and Far Eastern companies often operated with very different conceptions of competitive strategy. Understanding these differences, we thought, might help explain the conduct and outcome of competitive battles as well as supplement traditional explanations for Japan's ascendance and the West's decline.

We began by mapping the implicit strategy models of managers who had participated in our research. Then we built detailed histories of selected competitive battles. We searched for evidence of divergent views of strategy, competitive advantage, and the role of top management.

Two contrasting models of strategy emerged. One, which most Western managers will recognize, centers on the problem of maintaining strategic fit. The other centers on the problem of leveraging resources. The two are not mutually exclusive, but they represent a significant difference in emphasis—an emphasis that deeply affects how competitive battles get played out over time.

Both models recognize the problem of competing in a hostile environment with limited resources. But while the emphasis in the first is on trimming ambitions to match available resources, the emphasis in the second is on leveraging resources to reach seemingly unattainable goals.

Both models recognize that relative competitive advantage determines relative profitability. The first emphasizes the search for advantages that are inherently sustainable, the second emphasizes the need to accelerate organizational learning to outpace competitors in building new advantages.

Both models recognize the difficulty of competing against larger competitors. But while the first leads to a search for niches (or simply dissuades the company from challenging an entrenched competitor), the second produces a quest for new rules that can devalue the incumbent's advantages.

Both models recognize that balance in the scope of an organization's activities reduces risk. The first seeks to reduce financial risk by building a balanced portfolio of cash-generating and cash-consuming businesses. The second seeks to reduce competitive risk by ensuring a well-balanced and sufficiently broad portfolio of advantages.

Both models recognize the need to disaggregate the organization in a way that allows top management to differentiate among the investment needs of various planning units. In the first model, resources are allocated to product-market units in which relatedness is defined by common products, channels, and customers. Each business is assumed to own all the critical skills it needs to execute its strategy successfully. In the second, investments are made in core competencies (microprocessor controls or electronic imaging, for example) as well as in product-market units. By tracking these investments across business, top management works to assure that the plans of individual strategic units don't undermine future developments by default.

Both models recognize the need for consistency in action across organizational levels. In the first, consistency between corporate and business levels is largely a matter of conforming to financial objectives. Consistency between business and functional levels comes by tightly restricting the means the business uses to achieve its strategy—establishing standard operating procedures, defining the served market, adhering to accepted industry practices. In the second model, business-corporate consistency comes from allegiance to a particular strategic intent. Business-functional consistency comes from allegiance to intermediate-term goals, or challenges, with lower-level employees encouraged to invent how those goals will be achieved.

organization's attention on the essence of winning; motivating people by communicating the value of the target; leaving room for individual and team contributions; sustaining enthusiasm by providing new operational definitions as circumstances change; and using intent consistently to guide resource allocations.

Strategic intent captures the essence of winning. The Apollo program—landing a man on the moon ahead of the Soviets—was as competitively focused as Komatsu's drive against Caterpillar. The space program became the scorecard for America's technology race with the USSR. In the turbulent information technology industry, it was hard to pick a single competitor as a target, so NEC's strategic intent, set in the early 1970s, was to acquire the technologies that would put it in the best position to exploit the convergence ·of computing and telecommunications. Other industry observers foresaw this convergence, but only NEC made convergence the guiding theme for subsequent strategic decisions by adopting "computing and communications" as its intent. For Coca-Cola, strategic intent has been to put a Coke within "arm's reach" of every consumer in the world.

Strategic intent is stable over time. In battles for global leadership, one of the most critical tasks is to lengthen the organization's attention span. Strategic intent provides consistency to short-term action, while leaving room for reinterpretation as new opportunities emerge. At Komatsu, encircling Caterpillar encompassed a succession of medium-term programs aimed at exploiting specific weaknesses in Caterpillar or building particular competitive advantages. When Caterpillar threatened Komatsu in Japan, for example, Komatsu responded by first improving quality, then driving down costs, then cultivating export markets, and then underwriting new product development.

Strategic intent sets a target that deserves personal effort and commitment. Ask the chairmen of many American corporations how they measure their contributions to their companies' success and you're likely to get an answer expressed in terms of shareholder wealth. In a company that possesses a strategic intent, top management is more likely to talk in terms of global market leadership. Market share leadership typically yields shareholder wealth, to be sure. But the two goals do not have the same motivational impact. It is hard to imagine middle managers, let alone blue-collar employees, waking up each day with the sole thought of creating more shareholder wealth. But mightn't they feel different given the challenge to "Beat Benz"—the rallying cry at one Japanese auto producer? Strategic intent gives employees the only goal that is worthy of commitment: to unseat the best or remain the best, worldwide.

Many companies are more familiar with strategic planning than they are with strategic intent. The planning process typically acts as a "feasibility sieve." Strategies are accepted or rejected on the basis of whether managers can be precise about the "how" as well as the "what" of their plans. Are the milestones clear? Do we have the necessary skills and resources? How will competitors react? Has the market been thoroughly researched? In one form or another, the admonition "Be realistic!" is given to line managers at almost every turn.

But can you *plan* for global leadership? Did Komatsu, Canon, and Honda have detailed, 20-year "strategies" for attacking Western markets? Are Japanese and Korean managers better planners than their Western counterparts? No. As valuable as strategic planning is, global leadership is an objective that lies outside the range of planning. We know of few companies with highly developed planning systems that have managed to set a strategic intent. As tests of strategic fit become more stringent, goals that cannot be planned for fall by the wayside. Yet companies that are afraid to commit to goals that lie outside the range of planning are unlikely to become global leaders.

Although strategic planning is billed as a way of becoming more future oriented, most managers, when pressed, will admit that their strategic plans reveal more about today's problems than tomorrow's opportunities. With a fresh set of problems confronting managers at the beginning of every planning cycle, focus often shifts dramatically from year to year. And with the pace of change accelerating in most industries, the predictive horizon is becoming shorter and shorter. So plans do little more than project the present forward incrementally. The goal of strategic intent is to fold the future back into the present. The important question is not "How will next year be different from this year?" but "What must we do differently next year to get closer to our strategic intent?" Only with a carefully articulated and adhered to strategic intent will a succession of year-on-year plans sum up to global leadership.

Just as you cannot plan a 10- to 20-year quest for global leadership, the chance of falling into a leadership position by accident is also remote. We don't believe that global leadership comes from an undirected process of intrapreneurship. Nor is it the product of a skunkworks or other techniques for internal venturing. Behind such programs lies a nihilistic assumption: the organization is so hidebound, so orthodox that the only way to innovate is to put a few bright people in a dark room, pour in some money, and hope that something wonderful will happen. In this "Silicon Valley" approach to innovation, the only role for top managers is to retrofit their corporate strategy to the entrepreneurial successes that emerge from below. Here the value added of top management is low indeed.

Sadly, this view of innovation may be consistent with the reality in many large companies.[2] On the one hand, top management lacks any particular point of view about desirable ends beyond satisfying shareholders and keeping raiders at bay. On the other, the planning format, reward criteria, definition of served market, and belief in accepted industry practice all work together to tightly constrain the range of available means. As a result, innovation is necessarily an isolated activity. Growth depends more on the inventive capacity of individuals and small teams than on the ability of top management to aggregate the efforts of multiple teams toward an ambitious strategic intent.

In companies that overcame resource constraints to build leadership positions, we see a different relationship between means and ends. While strategic intent is clear about ends, it is flexible as to means—it leaves room for improvisation. Achieving strategic intent requires enormous creativity with respect to means: witness Fujitsu's use of strategic alliances in Europe to attack IBM. But this creativity comes in the service of a clearly prescribed end. Creativity is unbridled, but not uncorralled, because top management establishes the criterion against which employees can pretest the logic of their initiatives. Middle managers must do more than deliver on promised financial targets; they must also deliver on the broad direction implicit in their organization's strategic intent.

Strategic intent implies a sizable stretch for an organization. Current capabilities and resources will not suffice. This forces the organization to be more inventive, to make the most of limited resources. Whereas the traditional view of strategy focuses on the degree of fit between existing resources and current opportunities, strategic intent creates an extreme misfit between resources and ambitions. Top management then challenges the organization to close the gap by systematically building new advantages. For Canon this meant first understanding Xerox's patents, then licensing technology to create a product that would yield early market experience, then gearing up internal R&D efforts, then licensing its own technology to other manufacturers to fund further R&D, then entering market segments in Japan and Europe where Xerox was weak, and so on.

In this respect, strategic intent is like a marathon run in 400-meter sprints. No one knows what the terrain will look like at mile 26, so the role of top management is to focus the organization's attention on the ground to be covered in the next 400 meters.

---

[2]Robert A. Burgelman, "A Process Model of Internal Corporate Venturing in the Diversified Major Firm," *Administrative Science Quarterly,* June 1983.

In several companies, management did this by presenting the organization with a series of corporate challenges, each specifying the next hill in the race to achieve strategic intent. One year the challenge might be quality, the next total customer care, the next entry into new markets, the next a rejuvenated product line. As this example indicates, corporate challenges are a way to stage the acquisition of new competitive advantages, a way to identify the focal point for employees' efforts in the near to medium term. As with strategic intent, top management is specific about the ends (reducing product development times by 75 percent for example) but less prescriptive about the means.

Like strategic intent, challenges stretch the organization. To preempt Xerox in the personal copier business, Canon set its engineers a target price of $1,000 for a home copier. At the time, Canon's least expensive copier sold for several thousand dollars. Trying to reduce the cost of existing models would not have given Canon the radical price-performance improvement it needed to delay or deter Xerox's entry into personal copiers. Instead, Canon engineers were challenged to reinvent the copier—a challenge they met by substituting a disposable cartridge for the complex image-transfer mechanism used in other copiers.

Corporate challenges come from analyzing competitors as well as from the foreseeable pattern of industry evolution. Together these reveal potential competitive openings and identify the new skills the organization will need to take the initiative away from better-positioned players. The box, "Building Competitive Advantage at Komatsu," illustrates the way challenges helped that company achieve its intent.

For a challenge to be effective, individuals and teams throughout the organization must understand it and see its implications for their own jobs. Companies that set corporate challenges to create new competitive advantages (as Ford and IBM did with quality improvement) quickly discover that engaging the entire organization requires top management to:

Create a sense of urgency, or quasi-crisis, by amplifying weak signals in the environment that point up the need to improve, instead of allowing inaction to precipitate a real crisis. (Komatsu, for example, budgeted on the basis of worst case exchange rates that overvalued the yen.)

Develop a competitor focus at every level through widespread use of competitive intelligence. Every employee should be able to benchmark his or her efforts against best-in-class competitors so that the challenge becomes personal. (For example, Ford showed production-line workers videotapes of operations at Mazda's most efficient plant.)

Provide employees with the skills they need to work effectively—training in statistical tools, problem solving, value engineering, and team building, for example.

Give the organization time to digest one challenge before launching another. When competing initiatives overload the organization, middle managers often try to protect their people from the whipsaw of shifting priorities. But this "wait and see if they're serious this time" attitude ultimately destroys the credibility of corporate challenges.

Establish clear milestones and review mechanisms to track progress and ensure that internal recognition and rewards reinforce desired behavior. The goal is to make the challenge inescapable for everyone in the company.

It is important to distinguish between the process of managing corporate challenges and the advantages that the process creates. Whatever the actual challenge may be—quality, cost, value engineering, or something else—there is the same need to engage employees intellectually and emotionally in the development of new skills.

BUILDING COMPETITIVE ADVANTAGE AT KOMATSU

Corporate Challenge	Protect Komatsu's Home Market Against Caterpillar		Reduce Costs While Maintaining Quality		Make Komatsu An International Enterprise And Build Export Markets		Respond To External Shocks That Threaten Markets		Create New Products And Markets	
Programs	early 1960s	Licensing deals with Cummins Engine, international Harvester, and Bucyrus-Erie to acquire technology and establish benchmarks	1965	CD (Cost Down) program	early 1960s	Develop Eastern bloc countries	1975	¥10 program to reduce costs by 10% while maintaining quality; reduce parts by 20%; rationalize manufacturing system	late 1970s	Accelerate product development to expand line
	1961	Project A (for Ace) to advance the product quality of Komatsu's small- and medium-size bulldozers above Caterpillar's	1966	Total CD program	1967	Komatsu Europe marketing subsidiary established			1979	Future and Frontiers program to identify new businesses based on society's needs and company's know-how
	1962	Quality Circles companywide to provide training for all employees			1970	Komatsu America established	1977	¥180 program to budget companywide for 180 yen to the dollar when exchange rate was 240	1981	EPOCHS program to reconcile greater product variety with improved production efficiencies
					1972	Project B to improve the durability and reliability and to reduce costs of large bulldozers	1979	Project E to establish teams to redouble cost and quality efforts in response to oil crisis		
					1972	Project C to improve payloaders				
					1972	Project D to improve hydraulic excavators				
					1974	Establish presales and service department to assist newly industrializing countries in construction projects				

In each case, the challenge will take root only if senior executives and lower-level employees feel a reciprocal responsibility for competitiveness.

We believe workers in many companies have been asked to take a disproportionate share of the blame for competitive failure. In one U.S. company, for example, management had sought a 40 percent wage-package concession from hourly employees to bring labor costs into line with Far Eastern competitors. The result was a long strike and, ultimately, a 10 percent wage concession from employees on the line. However, direct labor costs in manufacturing accounted for less than 15 percent of total value-added. The company thus succeeded in demoralizing its entire blue-collar workforce for the sake of a 1.5 percent reduction in total costs. Ironically, further analysis showed that their competitors' most significant cost savings came not from lower hourly wages but from better work methods invented by employees. You can imagine how eager the U.S. workers were to make similar contributions after the strike and concessions. Contrast this situation with what happened at Nissan when the yen strengthened: top management took a big pay cut and then asked middle managers and line employees to sacrifice relatively less.

Reciprocal responsibility means shared gain and shared pain. In too many companies, the pain of revitalization falls almost exclusively on the employees least responsible for the enterprise's decline. Too often, workers are asked to commit to corporate goals without any matching commitment from top management—be it employment security, gain sharing, or an ability to influence the direction of the business. This one-sided approach to regaining competitiveness keeps many companies from harnessing the intellectual horsepower of their employees.

Creating a sense of reciprocal responsibility is crucial because competitiveness ultimately depends on the pace at which a company embeds new advantages deep within its organization, not on its stock of advantages at any given time. Thus we need to expand the concept of competitive advantage beyond the scorecard many managers now use: Are my costs lower? Will my product command a price premium?

Few competitive advantages are long lasting. Uncovering a new competitive advantage is a bit like getting a hot tip on a stock: The first person to act on the insight makes more money than the last. When the experience curve was young, a company that built capacity ahead of competitors, dropped prices to fill plants, and reduced costs as volume rose went to the bank. The first mover traded on the fact that competitors undervalued market share—they didn't price to capture additional market share because they didn't understand how market share leadership could be translated into lower costs and better margins. But there is no more undervalued market share when each of 20 semiconductor companies builds enough capacity to serve 10 percent of the world market.

Keeping score of existing advantages is not the same as building new advantages. The essence of strategy lies in creating tomorrow's competitive advantages faster than competitors mimic the ones you possess today. In the 1960s, Japanese producers relied on labor and capital cost advantages. As Western manufacturers began to move production offshore, Japanese companies accelerated their investment in process technology and created scale and quality advantages. Then as their U.S. and European competitors rationalized manufacturing, they added another string to their bow by accelerating the rate of product development. Then they built global brands. Then they deskilled competitors through alliances and outsourcing deals. The moral? An organization's capacity to improve existing skills and learn new ones is the most defensible competitive advantage of all.

To achieve a strategic intent, a company must usually take on larger, better-financed competitors. That means carefully managing competitive engagements so that scarce resources are conserved. Managers cannot do that simply by playing the same game better—making marginal improvements to competitors' technology and business practices. Instead, they must fundamentally change the game in ways that disadvantage incumbents—devising novel approaches to market entry, advantage building, and competitive warfare. For smart competitors, the goal is not competitive imitation but competitive innovation, the art of containing competitive risks within manageable proportions.

Four approaches to competitive innovation are evident in the global expansion of Japanese companies. These are building layers of advantage, searching for loose bricks, changing the terms of engagement, and competing through collaboration.

The wider a company's portfolio of advantages, the less risk it faces in competitive battles. New global competitors have built such portfolios by steadily expanding their arsenals of competitive weapons. They have moved inexorably from less-defensible advantages such as low wage costs to more defensible advantages like global brands. The Japanese color television industry illustrates this layering process.

By 1967, Japan had become the largest producer of black-and-white television sets. By 1970, it was closing the gap in color televisions. Japanese manufacturers used their competitive advantage—at that time, primarily, low labor costs—to build a base in the private-label business, then moved quickly to establish world-scale plants. This investment gave them additional layers of advantage—quality and reliability—as well as further cost reductions from process improvements. At the same time, they recognized that these cost-based advantages were vulnerable to changes in labor costs, process and product technology, exchange rates, and trade policy. So throughout the 1970s, they also invested heavily in building channels and brands, thus creating another layer of advantage, a global franchise. In the late 1970s, they enlarged the scope of their products and businesses to amortize these grand investments, and by 1980 all the major players—Matsushita, Sharp, Toshiba, Hitachi, Sanyo—had established related sets of businesses that could support global marketing investments. More recently, they have been investing in regional manufacturing and design centers to tailor their products more closely to national markets.

These manufacturers thought of the various sources of competitive advantage as mutually desirable layers, not mutually exclusive choices. What some call competitive suicide—pursuing both cost and differentiation—is exactly what many competitors strive for.[3] Using flexible manufacturing technologies and better marketing intelligence, they are moving away from standardized "world products" to products like Mazda's minivan, developed in California expressly for the U.S. market.

Another approach to competitive innovation—searching for loose bricks—exploits the benefits of surprise, which is just as useful in business battles as it is in war. Particularly in the early stages of a war for global markets, successful new competitors work to stay below the response threshold of their larger, more powerful rivals. Staking out underdefended territory is one way to do this.

To find loose bricks, managers must have few orthodoxies about how to break into a market or challenge a competitor. For example, in one large U.S. multinational, we asked several country managers to describe what a Japanese competitor was doing in the local market. The first executive said, "They're coming at us in the low end. Japanese companies always come in at the bottom." The second speaker found the comment interesting but disagreed: "They don't offer any low-end products in my market, but they have some exciting stuff at the top end. We really should reverse engineer that thing." Another colleague told still another story. "They haven't taken any business away from me," he said, "but they've just made me a great offer to supply components." In each country, their Japanese competitor had found a different loose brick.

---

[3]For example, see Michael E. Porter, *Competitive Strategy* (New York: Free Press, 1980).

The search for loose bricks begins with a careful analysis of the competitor's conventional wisdom: How does the company define its "served market"? What activities are most profitable? Which geographic markets are too troublesome to enter? The objective is not to find a corner of the industry (or niche) where larger competitors seldom tread but to build a base of attack just outside the market territory that industry leaders currently occupy. The goal is an uncontested profit sanctuary, which could be a particular product segment (the "low end" in motorcycles), a slice of the value chain (components in the computer industry), or a particular geographic market (Eastern Europe).

When Honda took on leaders in the motorcycle industry, for example, it began with products that were just outside the conventional definition of the leaders' product-market domains. As a result, it could build a base of operations in underdefended territory and then use that base to launch an expanded attack. What many competitors failed to see was Honda's strategic intent and its growing competence in engines and power trains. Yet even as Honda was selling 50cc motorcycles in the United States, it was already racing larger bikes in Europe—assembling the design skills and technology it would need for a systematic expansion across the entire spectrum of motor-related businesses.

Honda's progress in creating a core competence in engines should have warned competitors that it might enter a series of seemingly unrelated industries—automobiles, lawn mowers, marine engines, generators. But with each company fixated on its own market, the threat of Honda's horizontal diversification went unnoticed. Today companies like Matsushita and Toshiba are similarly poised to move in unexpected ways across industry boundaries. In protecting loose bricks, companies must extend their peripheral vision by tracking and anticipating the migration of global competitors across product segments, businesses, national markets, value-added stages, and distribution channels.

Changing the terms of engagement—refusing to accept the front-runner's definition of industry and segment boundaries—represents still another form of competitive innovation. Canon's entry into the copier business illustrates this approach.

During the 1970s, both Kodak and IBM tried to match Xerox's business system in terms of segmentation, products, distribution, service, and pricing. As a result, Xerox had no trouble decoding the new entrants' intentions and developing countermoves. IBM eventually withdrew from the copier business, while Kodak remains a distant second in the large copier market that Xerox still dominates.

Canon, on the other hand, changed the terms of competitive engagement. While Xerox built a wide range of copiers, Canon standardized machines and components to reduce costs. Canon chose to distribute through office-product dealers rather than try to match Xerox's huge direct sales force. It also avoided the need to create a national service network by designing reliability and serviceability into its product and then delegating service responsibility to the dealers. Canon copiers were sold rather than leased, freeing Canon from the burden of financing the lease base. Finally, instead of selling to the heads of corporate duplicating departments, Canon appealed to secretaries and department managers who wanted distributed copying. At each stage, Canon neatly sidestepped a potential barrier to entry.

Canon's experience suggests that there is an important distinction between barriers to entry and barriers to imitation. Competitors that tried to match Xerox's business system had to pay the same entry costs—the barriers to imitation were high. But Canon dramatically reduced the barriers to entry by changing the rules of the game.

Changing the rules also short-circuited Xerox's ability to retaliate quickly against its new rival. Confronted with the need to rethink its business strategy and organization, Xerox was paralyzed for a time. Xerox managers realized that the faster they downsized the product line, developed new channels, and improved reliability, the faster they would erode the company's traditional profit base. What might have been seen as critical success factors—Xerox's national sales force and service network, its large installed base of leased machines, and its reliance on service revenues—instead became barriers to retaliation. In this sense, competitive innovation is like judo: The goal is to use a larger competitor's weight against it. And that happens not by matching the leader's capabilities but by developing contrasting capabilities of one's own.

Competitive innovation works on the premise that a successful competitor is likely to be wedded to a "recipe" for success. That's why the most effective weapon new competitors possess is probably a clean sheet of paper. And why an incumbent's greatest vulnerability is its belief in accepted practice.

Through licensing, outsourcing agreements, and joint ventures, it is sometimes possible to win without fighting. For example, Fujitsu's alliances in Europe with Siemens and STC (Britain's largest computer maker) and in the United States with Amdahl yield manufacturing volume and access to Western markets. In the early 1980s, Matsushita established a joint venture with Thorn (in the United Kingdom), Telefunken (in Germany), and Thomson (in France), which allowed it to quickly multiply the forces arrayed against Philips in the battle for leadership in the European VCR business. In fighting larger global rivals by proxy, Japanese companies have adopted a maxim as old as human conflict itself: My enemy's enemy is my friend.

Hijacking the development efforts of potential rivals is another goal of competitive collaboration. In the consumer electronics war, Japanese competitors attacked traditional businesses like TVs and hi-fis while volunteering to manufacture "next generation" products like VCRs, camcorders, and compact disk players for Western rivals. They hoped their rivals would ratchet down development spending, and in most cases that is precisely what happened. But companies that abandoned their own development efforts seldom reemerged as serious competitors in subsequent new product battles.

Collaboration can also be used to calibrate competitors' strengths and weaknesses. Toyota's joint venture with GM, and Mazda's with Ford, give these automakers an invaluable vantage point for assessing the progress their U.S. rivals have made in cost reduction, quality, and technology. They can also learn how GM and Ford compete—when they will fight and when they won't. Of course, the reverse is also true: Ford and GM have an equal opportunity to learn from their partner-competitors.

The route to competitive revitalization we have been mapping implies a new view of strategy. Strategic intent assures consistency in resource allocation over the long term. Clearly articulated corporate challenges focus the efforts of individuals in the medium term. Finally, competitive innovation helps reduce competitive risk in the short term. This consistency in the long term, focus in the medium term, and inventiveness and involvement in the short term provide the key to leveraging limited resources in pursuit of ambitious goals. But just as there is a process of winning, so there is a process of surrender. Revitalization requires understanding that process too.

Given their technological leadership and access to large regional markets, how did U.S. and European companies lose their apparent birthright to dominate global industries? There is no simple answer. Few companies recognize the value of documenting failure. Fewer still search their own managerial orthodoxies for the seeds for compet-

THE PROCESS OF SURRENDER

In the battles for global leadership that have taken place during the last two decades, we have seen a pattern of competitive attack and retrenchment that was remarkably similar across industries. We call this the process of surrender.

The process started with unseen intent. Not possessing long-term, competitor-focused goals themselves, Western companies did not ascribe such intentions to their rivals. They also calculated the threat posed by potential competitors in terms of their existing resources rather than their resourcefulness. This led to systematic underestimation of smaller rivals who were fast gaining technology through licensing arrangements, acquiring market understanding from downstream OEM partners, and improving product quality and manufacturing productivity through companywide employee involvement programs. Oblivious of the strategic intent and intangible advantages of their rivals, American and European businesses were caught off guard.

Adding to the competitive surprise was the fact that the new entrants typically attacked the periphery of a market (Honda in small motorcycles, Yamaha in grand pianos, Toshiba in small black-and-white televisions) before going head-to-head with incumbents. Incumbents often misread these attacks, seeing them as part of a niche strategy and not as a search for "loose bricks." Unconventional market entry strategies (minority holdings in less developed countries, use of nontraditional channels, extensive corporate advertising) were ignored or dismissed as quirky. For example, managers we spoke with said Japanese companies' position in the European computer industry was nonexistent. In terms of brand share that's nearly true, but the Japanese control as much as one-third of the manufacturing value added in the hardware sales of European-based computer businesses. Similarly, German auto producers claimed to feel unconcerned over the proclivity of Japanese producers to move upmarket. But with its low-end models under tremendous pressure from Japanese producers, Porsche has now announced that it will no longer make "entry level" cars.

Western managers often misinterpreted their rivals' tactics. They believed that Japanese and Korean companies were competing solely on the basis of cost and quality. This typically produced a partial response to those competitors' initiatives: moving manufacturing offshore, outsourcing, or instituting a quality program. Seldom was the full extent of the competitive threat appreciated—the multiple layers of advantage, the expansion across related product segments, the development of global brand positions. Imitating the currently visible tactics of rivals put Western businesses into a perpetual catch-up trap. One by one, companies lost battles and came to see surrender as inevitable. Surrender was not inevitable, of course, but the attack was staged in a way that disguised ultimate intentions and sidestepped direct confrontation.

itive surrender. But we believe there is a pathology of surrender (summarized in the box "The Process of Surrender") that gives some important clues.

It is not very comforting to think that the essence of Western strategic thought can be reduced to eight rules for excellence, seven S's, five competitive forces, four product life-cycle stages, three generic strategies, and innumerable two-by-two matrices.[4]

Yet for the past 20 years, "advances" in strategy have taken the form of ever more typologies, heuristics, and laundry lists, often with dubious empirical bases. Moreover, even reasonable concepts like the product life cycle, experience curve, product portfolios, and generic strategies often have toxic side effects: They reduce the number of strategic options management is willing to consider. They create a preference

---

[4]Strategic frameworks for resource allocation in diversified companies are summarized in Charles W. Hofer and Dan E. Schendel, *Strategy Formulation: Analytical Concepts* (St. Paul, Minn.: West Publishing, 1978).

for selling businesses rather than defending them. They yield predictable strategies that rivals easily decode.

Strategy "recipes" limit opportunities for competitive innovation. A company may have 40 businesses and only four strategies—invest, hold, harvest, or divest. Too often strategy is seen as a positioning exercise in which options are tested by how they fit the existing industry structure. But current industry structure reflects the strengths of the industry leader, and playing by the leader's rules is usually competitive suicide.

Armed with concepts like segmentation, the value chain, competitor benchmarking, strategic groups, and mobility barriers, many managers have become better and better at drawing industry maps. But while they have been busy mapmaking, their competitors have been moving entire continents. The strategist's goal is not to find a niche within the existing industry space but to create new space that is uniquely suited to the company's own strengths, space that is off the map.

This is particularly true now that industry boundaries are becoming more and more unstable. In industries such as financial services and communications, rapidly changing technology, deregulation, and globalization have undermined the value of traditional industry analysis. Mapmaking skills are worth little in the epicenter of an earthquake. But an industry in upheaval presents opportunities for ambitious companies to redraw the map in their favor, so long as they can think outside traditional industry boundaries.

Concepts like "mature" and "declining" are largely definitional. What most executives mean when they label a business mature is that sales growth has stagnated in their current geographic markets for existing products sold through existing channels. In such cases, it's not the industry that is mature, but the executives' conception of the industry. Asked if the piano business was mature, a senior executive at Yamaha replied, "Only if we can't take any market share from anybody anywhere in the world and still make money. And anyway, we're not in the 'piano' business, we're in the 'keyboard' business." Year after year, Sony has revitalized its radio and tape recorder businesses, despite the fact that other manufacturers long ago abandoned these businesses as mature.

A narrow concept of maturity can foreclose a company from a broad stream of future opportunities. In the 1970s, several U.S. companies thought that consumer electronics had become a mature industry. What could possibly top the color TV? they asked themselves. RCA and GE, distracted by opportunities in more "attractive" industries like mainframe computers, left Japanese products with a virtual monopoly in VCRs, camcorders, and compact disk players. Ironically, the TV business, once thought mature, is on the verge of a dramatic renaissance. A $20 billion-a-year business will be created when high-definition television is launched in the United States. But the pioneers of television may capture only a small part of this bonanza.

Most of the tools of strategic analysis are focused domestically. Few force managers to consider global opportunities and threats. For example, portfolio planning portrays top management's investment options as an array of businesses rather than as an array of geographic markets. The result is predictable: As businesses come under attack from foreign competitors, the company attempts to abandon them and enter others in which the forces of global competition are not yet so strong. In the short term, this may be an appropriate response to waning competitiveness, but there are fewer and fewer businesses in which a domestic-oriented company can find refuge. We seldom hear such companies asking: Can we move into emerging markets overseas ahead of our global rivals and prolong the profitability of this business? Can we counterattack in our global competitors' home markets and slow the pace of their expansion? A senior executive in one successful global company made a telling comment: "We're glad to find a competitor managing by the portfolio concept—we can almost predict how much share we'll have to take away to put the business on the CEO's 'sell list.'"

Companies can also be overcommitted to organizational recipes, such as strategic business units and the decentralization an SBU structure implies. Decentralization is seductive because it places the responsibility for success or failure squarely on the shoulders of line managers. Each business is assumed to have all the resources it needs to execute its strategies successfully, and in this no-excuses environment, it is hard for top management to fail. But desirable as clear lines of responsibility and accountability are, competitive revitalization requires positive value added from top management.

Few companies with a strong SBU orientation have built successful global distribution and brand positions. Investments in a global brand franchise typically transcend the resources and risk propensity of a single business. While some Western companies have had global brand positions for 30 or 40 years or more (Heinz, Siemens, IBM, Ford, and Kodak, for example), it is hard to identify any American or European company that has created a new global brand franchise in the last 10 to 15 years. Yet Japanese companies have created a score or more—NEC, Fujitsu, Panasonic (Matsushita), Toshiba, Sony, Seiko, Epson, Canon, Minolta, and Honda, among them.

General Electric's situation is typical. In many of its businesses, this American giant has been almost unknown in Europe and Asia. GE made no coordinated effort to build a global corporate franchise. Any GE business with international ambitions had to bear the burden of establishing its credibility and credentials in the new market alone. Not surprisingly, some once-strong GE businesses opted out of the difficult task of building a global brand position. In contrast, smaller Korean companies like Samsung, Daewoo, and Lucky Gold Star are busy building global-brand umbrellas that will ease market entry for a whole range of businesses. The underlying principle is simple: Economies of scope may be as important as economies of scale in entering global markets. But capturing economies of scope demands interbusiness coordination that only top management can provide.

We believe that inflexible SBU-type organizations have also contributed to the deskilling of some companies. For a single SBU, incapable of sustaining investment in a core competence such as semiconductors, optical media, or combustion engines, the only way to remain competitive is to purchase key components from potential (often Japanese or Korean) competitors. For an SBU defined in product-market terms, competitiveness means offering an end product that is competitive in price and performance. But that gives an SBU manager little incentive to distinguish between external sourcing that achieves "product embodied" competitiveness and internal development that yields deeply embedded organizational competences that can be exploited across multiple businesses. Where upstream component manufacturing activities are seen as cost centers with cost-plus transfer pricing, additional investment in the core activity may seem a less profitable use of capital than investment in downstream activities. To make matters worse, internal accounting data may not reflect the competitive value of retaining control over core competence.

Together a shared global corporate brand franchise and shared core competence act as mortar in many Japanese companies. Lacking this mortar, a company's businesses are truly loose bricks—easily knocked out by global competitors that steadily invest in core competences. Such competitors can co-opt domestically oriented companies into long-term sourcing dependence and capture the economies of scope of global brand investment through interbusiness coordination.

Last in decentralization's list of dangers is the standard of managerial performance typically used in SBU organizations. In many companies, business unit managers are rewarded solely on the basis of their performance against return on investment targets. Unfortunately, that often leads to denominator management because executives soon discover that reductions in investment and head count—the denominator—"improve" the financial ratios by which they are measured more easily than growth in the numerator—revenues. It also fosters a hair-trigger sensitivity to industry downturns that can be very costly. Managers who are quick to reduce investment and dismiss workers find it takes much longer to regain lost skills and catch up on investment when the industry turns upward again. As a result, they lose market share in every business cycle. Particularly in industries where there is fierce competition for the best people and where competitors invest relentlessly, denominator management creates a retrenchment ratchet.

The concept of the general manager as a movable peg reinforces the problem of denominator management. Business schools are guilty here because they have perpetuated the notion that a manager with net present value calculations in one hand and portfolio planning in the other can manage any business anywhere.

In many diversified companies, top management evaluates line managers on numbers alone because no other basis for dialogue exists. Managers move so many times as part of their "career development" that they often do not understand the nuances of the businesses they are managing. At GE, for example, one fast-track manager heading an important new venture had moved across five businesses in five years. His series of quick successes finally came to an end when he confronted a Japanese competitor whose managers had been plodding along in the same business for more than a decade.

Regardless of ability and effort, fast-track managers are unlikely to develop the deep business knowledge they need to discuss technology options, competitors' strategies, and global opportunities substantively. Invariably, therefore, discussions gravitate to "the numbers," while the value added of managers is limited to the financial and planning savvy they carry from job to job. Knowledge of the company's internal planning and accounting systems substitutes for substantive knowledge of the business, making competitive innovation unlikely.

When managers know that their assignments have a two-to three-year time frame, they feel great pressure to create a good track record fast. This pressure often takes one of two forms. Either the manager does not commit to goals whose time line extends beyond his or her expected tenure, or ambitious goals are adopted and squeezed into an unrealistically short time frame. Aiming to be number one in a business is the essence of strategic intent; but imposing a three- to four-year horizon on the effort simply invites disaster. Acquisitions are made with little attention to the problems of integration. The organization becomes overloaded with initiatives. Collaborative ventures are formed without adequate attention to competitive consequences.

Almost every strategic management theory and nearly every corporate planning system is premised on a strategy hierarchy in which corporate goals guide business unit strategies and business unit strategies guide functional tactics.[5] In this hierarchy,

---

[5]For example, see Peter Lorange and Richard E. Vancil, *Strategic Planning Systems* (Englewood Cliffs, N.J.: Prentice Hall, 1977).

senior management makes strategy and lower levels execute it. The dichotomy between formulation and implementation is familiar and widely accepted. But the strategy hierarchy undermines competitiveness by fostering an elitist view of management that tends to disenfranchise most of the organization. Employees fail to identify with corporate goals or involve themselves deeply in the work of becoming more competitive.

The strategy hierarchy isn't the only explanation for an elitist view of management, of course. The myths that grow up around successful top managers—"Lee Iacocca saved Chrysler," "De Benedetti rescued Olivetti," "John Sculley turned Apple around"—perpetuate it. So does the turbulent business environment. Middle managers buffeted by circumstances that seem to be beyond their control desperately want to believe that top management has all the answers. And top management, in turn, hesitates to admit it does not for fear of demoralizing lower-level employees.

The result of all this is often a code of silence in which the full extent of a company's competitiveness problem is not widely shared. We interviewed business unit managers in one company, for example, who were extremely anxious because top management wasn't talking openly about the competitive challenges the company faced. They assumed the lack of communication indicated a lack of awareness on their senior managers' part. But when asked whether they were open with their own employees, these same managers replied that while they could face up to the problems, the people below them could not. Indeed, the only time the workforce heard about the company's competitiveness problems was during wage negotiations when problems were used to extract concessions.

Unfortunately, a threat that everyone perceives but no one talks about creates more anxiety than a threat that has been clearly identified and made the focal point for the problem-solving efforts of the entire company. That is one reason honesty and humility on the part of top management may be the first prerequisite of revitalization. Another reason is the need to make participation more than a buzzword.

Programs such as quality circles and total customer service often fall short of expectations because management does not recognize that successful implementation requires more than administrative structures. Difficulties in embedding new capabilities are typically put down to "communication" problems, with the unstated assumption that if only downward communication were more effective—"if only middle management would get the message straight"—the new program would quickly take root. The need for upward communication is often ignored, or assumed to mean nothing more than feedback. In contrast, Japanese companies win, not because they have smarter managers, but because they have developed ways to harness the "wisdom of the anthill." They realize that top managers are a bit like the astronauts who circle the earth in the space shuttle. It may be the astronauts who get all the glory, but everyone knows that the real intelligence behind the mission is located firmly on the ground.

Where strategy formulation is an elitist activity it is also difficult to produce truly creative strategies. For one thing, there are not enough heads and points of view in divisional or corporate planning departments to challenge conventional wisdom. For another, creative strategies seldom emerge from the annual planning ritual. The starting point for next year's strategy is almost always this year's strategy. Improvements are incremental. The company sticks to the segments and territories it knows, even though the real opportunities may be elsewhere. The impetus for Canon's pioneering entry into the personal copier business came from an overseas sales subsidiary—not from planners in Japan.

The goal of the strategy hierarchy remains valid—to ensure consistency up and down the organization. But this consistency is better derived from a clearly articulated strategic intent than from inflexibly applied top-down plans. In the 1990s, the challenge will be to enfranchise employees to invent the means to accomplish ambitious ends.

We seldom found cautious administrators among the top managements of companies that came from behind to challenge incumbents for global leadership. But in studying organizations that had surrendered, we invariably found senior managers who, for whatever reason, lacked the courage to commit their companies to heroic goals—goals that lay beyond the reach of planning and existing resources. The conservative goals they set failed to generate pressure and enthusiasm for competitive innovation or give the organization much useful guidance. Financial targets and vague mission statements just cannot provide the consistent direction that is a prerequisite for winning a global competitive war.

This kind of conservatism is usually blamed on the financial markets. But we believe that in most cases investors' so-called short-term orientation simply reflects their lack of confidence in the ability of senior managers to conceive and deliver stretch goals. The chairman of one company complained bitterly that even after improving return on capital employed to over 40 percent (by ruthlessly divesting lackluster businesses and downsizing others), the stock market held the company to an 8:1 price/earnings ratio. Of course the market's message was clear: "We don't trust you. You've shown no ability to achieve profitable growth. Just cut out the slack, manage the denominators, and perhaps you'll be taken over by a company that can use your resources more creatively." Very little in the track record of most large Western companies warrants the confidence of the stock market. Investors aren't hopelessly short term, they're justifiably skeptical.

We believe that top management's caution reflects a lack of confidence in its own ability to involve the entire organization in revitalization—as opposed to simply raising financial targets. Developing faith in the organization's ability to deliver on tough goals, motivating it to do so, focusing its attention long enough to internalize new capabilities—this is the real challenge for top management. Only by rising to this challenge will senior managers gain the courage they need to commit themselves and their companies to global leadership.

STRATEGIC PLANNING: ITS ROLE IN ORGANIZATIONAL POLITICS

Ken Peattie, Cardiff Business School

One of the great themes of corporate planning during the 1980s and one that is predicted by Taylor to be "the most important new frontier" for the 1990s[1] is the challenge of implementation. Ansoff[2] suggests that the practice and theory of strategic management has been hindered by three underlying assumptions about implementation:

1. That *reasonable people will do reasonable things.* If people are asked to plan and are given the relevent information and analytical tools, they will select the "right" strategy and support its formulation and implementation.

2. That a correctly formulated strategic plan will be straightforward to implement. So the "right" strategy will somehow be easier to implement than the "wrong" one.

3. That strategy formulation and implementation are separate and sequential activities.

This article centers around a fourth assumption, which has significant implications for strategic planning, but which has received less attention. This is the assumption that *written strategic plans are an accurate reflection of a company's strategic intent.* In other words, we assume that what people want to do, and what they say they want to do, are much the same thing.

In an earlier article the author helped to demonstrate that the presentation of planned strategies is influenced by their perceived acceptability, visibility, and priority

Source: *Long Range Planning* 26, no. 3 (1993), pp. 10–17. Reprinted with permission.

Ken Peattie joined Cardiff Business School's marketing and strategy group in 1986 after working as a systems and business analyst with an American multinational and for two years as a corporate planner in the U.K. electronics industry.

[1]B. Taylor, "Corporate Planning for the 1990s: The New Frontiers," *Long Range Planning* 19 (1986), pp. 13–18.

[2]H. I. Ansoff, *Implanting Strategic Management* (Englewood Cliffs, N.J.: Prentice Hall, 1984).

in relation to the prevailing corporate culture.[3] This reading pursues a similar theme by examining how organizational politics influences the strategic planning process to render our fourth assumption both incorrect and dangerous. The work which forms the basis of this study is a byproduct of a practical involvement in the introduction of formalized business planning to 15 British companies. The companies ranged in size from a turnover of £1m to over £200m. They represented a wide range of businesses including electronic and electromechanical components, electronic assemblies, automotive products, telecommunications, aerospace, distribution services, and educational products.

The study began with an observation that a range of managers in all the companies were happy to admit (during confidential interviews) that there were considerable differences between what we can identify as their strategic intent, and their recorded contribution to the strategic plan. This prompted the question Why? which was pursued during subsequent interviews; the insights gained are presented here.

RATIONAL ASSUMPTIONS ABOUT STRATEGIC PLANNING

Much of the prescriptive literature about strategy makes several rationally based assumptions about the relationship between strategic planning, strategy, and plans—i.e., that:

1. The main reason for the introduction of formalized strategic planning is to improve company performance through the development and implementation of better strategies.

2. A written plan is a strategy. Mintzberg proposes that a plan (in the sense of a consciously intended course of action) is one conception of strategy, but that such strategies may be formally documented or remain informally in the strategist's head.[4] Although it is recognized that a firm does not have to have a written plan to have a strategy, it is usually assumed that if a written plan exists, it will be a fair reflection of the strategy.

3. Strategy formulation is preceded by an objective corporate appraisal.

4. Contingency planning is an important element of a strategic plan. With increasing environmental turbulence the importance of contingency planning is increasingly being stressed.[5] It is assumed that a plan is strengthened by the flexibility that thorough contingency planning brings.

5. The strategy that is implemented is a combination of the "intended strategy" and of a series of unplanned actions that form an "emergent strategy." This is demonstrated by Figure 2–1 showing the model proposed by Mintzberg.[6]

It is worth reexamining these assumptions in the light of one company's experience of introducing formalized strategic planning.

---

[3]N. F. Piercy and K. J. Peattie, "Matching Marketing Strategies to Corporate Culture: The Parcel and the Wall," *Journal of General Management* 13, no. 4 (Summer 1988), pp. 33–44.

[4]H. Mintzberg, "Opening Up the Definition of Strategy," in *The Strategy Process: Concepts, Contexts, and Cases,* ed. J. B. Quinn, H. Mintzberg, and R. M. James (Englewood Cliffs, N.J.: Prentice Hall, 1988).

[5]D. D. McConkey, "Planning for Uncertainty," *Business Horizons* 30, no. 1 (1987), pp. 40–45.

[6]Mintzberg, "Opening Up the Definition of Strategy."

FIGURE 2–1 | **Forms of Strategy**

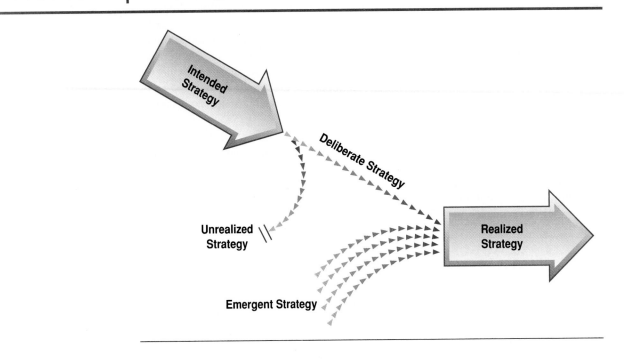

The company had a conglomerate structure, and the strategic planning process was partly a mechanism for senior corporate management to assess the results and potential of each subsidiary or strategic business unit (SBU). This assessment was then fed into the process of allocating corporate resources. The subsidiaries' management quickly learned that plans were assessed more on their forecast results than on their realism. Failure to implement an overoptimistic plan led to criticism, but a defense based on *changing market circumstances* was usually acceptable. Submitting a realistically conservative plan was punished by a cut in resources and a step toward a downward spiral. The result was a set of SBU plans containing "hockey-stick" results, where the future success of an SBU was usually inversely proportional to its current overdraft situation.

SBU strategic audits turned into benefit/benefit analysis of their favored strategies, where no negative outcomes existed and no positive ones were mutually exclusive. One manager demonstrated this dominance of political realities over good planning practice when it was suggested that he should append a contingency plan to his business plan. He replied, "You seriously expect me to write down all the things that could go wrong with this project after a two year fight to get it authorized?"

At the corporate level, senior managers believed that the introduction of formal planning and the development of a corporate plan were a good opportunity to produce a definitive document explaining the current position and future direction of a very diverse company. This was achieved primarily by editing together the SBU plans in a way that emphasized the more glamorous and dynamic aspects of the company. This "corporate plan" was then used externally to impress the financial community and internally as an "inspirational" idealized picture of the business and its future. This process of drafting the plan gradually edited out the problems that the company faced, and failed to mention some of its solid but less glamorous strengths.

Similar issues in the relationships between corporate and subsidiary management have been detailed by Goold and Campbell.[7] Hussey also concluded that in practice most companies usually either omit searching corporate appraisals, or simply gloss over many important factors.[8] Taylor observed that many strategic decisions are made outside companies' formal planning processes.[9]

This company's experience raises some interesting points:

1. Strategic planning in reality is often much more than a process for developing and implementing strategies. Taylor concludes that in large companies "the perspective of planning as a central control system tends to dominate management thinking about corporate planning."[10] Mintzberg[11] and Pettigrew[12] suggest that planning can be more about the interplay of political forces than about the formulation of explicit strategies. Reid and Hinkley show that planning processes fulfill a wide range of roles,[13] including acting as:

   • A process of control and conflict resolution.
   • A resource-bidding process.
   • A communication process.

2. If plans are used to help in allocating resources and as a means of communicating with internal and external stakeholders, then there will be pressure to remove strategically important information that might send the wrong messages to senior managers or other stakeholders. The potential for such errors was underlined by one manager who declined any help in developing his first formal plan, saying, "I know exactly what to write, because I know exactly what the managing director wants to hear—good news!"

3. A plan is not necessarily a full and explicit summary of the planning that has actually taken place. In all the companies that were studied, the final plans omitted some significant alternatives, risks, possible outcomes, and contingencies. The reasons given for this were "lack of space," "to keep things simple," or "because senior managers would not really understand."

4. An important dimension of any strategy when considering its adoption, documentation, and presentation is its internal and external acceptability.[14]

---

[7]M. Goold and A. Campbell, *Strategies and Styles: The Role of the Center in Managing Diversified Corporations* (Oxford: Blackwell, 1988).

[8]D.E. Hussey, *Corporate Planning: Theory and Practice* (Oxford: Pergamon, 1974).

[9]B. Taylor, "New Dimensions in Corporate Planning," in B. Taylor and D.E. Hussey, *The Realities of Planning* (Oxford: Pergamon, 1982).

[10]Ibid.

[11]H. Mintzberg, "What is Planning Anyway?" *Strategic Management Journal* 2 (1981), pp. 319–24.

[12]A.M. Pettigrew, "Strategy Formulation as a Political Process," *International Studies of Management and Organization* 7, no. 9 (1977).

[13]D. M. Reid and L. C. Hinkley, "Strategic Planning: The Cultural Impact," *MIP* 7, no. 11/12 (1989), pp. 4–12.

[14]Piercy and Peattie, "Matching Marketing Strategies to Corporate Culture."

STRATEGIC PLANNING
AS A DOCUMENTATION PROCESS

Documenting strategies allows them to be crystallized in detail, communicated, and stored for security and future reference. Managing a large business without a plan is like trying to organize a car rally without a map; not impossible, but difficult. It is tempting to assume that a written plan will be an objective, comprehensive, and explicit summary of intended strategy. Capturing strategy on paper can be far from straightforward, and the process of strategy documentation is an important step in the planning process. It is this documentation process that frequently forms the watershed between strategy formulation and implementation, helping to separate and sequence them in the way observed by Ansoff.[15] During documentation the problems of distilling a comprehensive and dynamic strategy into a succinct and static plan are compounded by the pressures to package or screen out information for political purposes. Our interviews with managers revealed a consistent pattern of concern about the whole process of documenting strategies. *At a corporate level* the following threats were identified regarding the preparation and presentation of plans:

1. *Once a strategy is fully explicit and documented it can more easily be communicated to competitors.* The relatively "incestuous" career developments patterns within industries like electronics (where managers frequently move between close rivals) increases sensitivity about what any given staff member might walk away with.

2. *The exposure of a self-critical strategic plan could prejudice any attempts to raise money from the financial community.*

3. *A strategy may have to remain covert if it would be unpopular with shareholders, customers, trade unions,* or any form of regulatory body. The scandals concerning Guiness and Maxwell provide startling examples of strategies that could not be committed to paper.

4. *There may be internal political repercussions* if the strategy is perceived as favoring some areas of the business over others in terms of resource distribution. The strategic logic of planning techniques such as portfolio analysis promotes the transfer of resources from established cash generating SBUs into emerging cash-hungry SBUs. In practice, investing in new and unproven businesses is unpopular with the managers of the "cash cows" who usually lobby for corporate management to "invest in success."

The concern about documenting strategy can introduce a degree of security consciousness that actually hampers the planning process. At one company the attitude toward the security of planning information bordered on paranoia. It resulted in a blanket ban on plans being communicated between subsidiaries. Access to subsidiary plans was limited to the subsidiary's board and certain key corporate directors. One of the four reasons justifying their adoption of strategic planning was to "improve internal coordination and communication"; yet corporate management reacted to the existence of strategic plans like the Government faced with a boxed set of M15 memoirs.

---

[15] Ansoff, *Implanting Strategic Management.*

Subsidiary or SBU managers also expressed concerns about fully revealing their strategic hand:

1. *Realistic projected results may not be good enough to gain acceptance for the plan* and to secure the resources needed to maintain future growth.
2. *The optimum strategies for the subsidiaries may be in conflict with a corporate policy, strategy, or philosophy.*
3. *The more detail which senior management have about a business and its plans, the more ability they would have to monitor its progress and intervene if necessary.* Subsidiary managers with a "Give us the money and let us get on with it" attitude try to reveal as little as possible to minimize corporate assistance, which is typically viewed as counterproductive.[16]

THE EMERGENCE OF "INVISIBLE PLANS"

Two sets of forces can be seen acting on those involved in the planning process: rational forces concerned with contributing to the performance of the business, which call for openness, communication, objectivity, and self-analysis. There are also political forces concerned with internal rivalry and protecting parochial interests, personal power, and prospects. These call for caution and the retention and selective presentation of information. The planning process must produce strategies to enhance performance, and also plans to help secure resources and political advantage. As soon as these roles begin to conflict, the planning becomes split between the politically acceptable elements that end up as an explicit strategy in the written plan and the less acceptable elements that become part of an "invisible plan" containing the implicit strategy. Planning systems, like any man-made structures, become more vulnerable to collapse once their foundations are split.

THE NATURE OF INVISIBLE PLANS

Corporate planning aims to make strategy explicit and visible and therefore open to scrutiny and available for communication. The formal plans produced should summarize managers' strategic thinking, turning the invisible plan into a visible written one. However, at best, written plans only represent a partial and periodic summary of the many aspects of a business and its future that a manager will consider. An invisible plan may exist inside the strategist's head or as an uncirculated document. It is likely to contain some or all of the following elements not present in the formal written plan:

1. A full and frank assessment of forecast results, potential external changes, implementation schedules, costs, and risks.
2. A full picture of the less glamorous strengths of the business.
3. A strategy freed from perceived constraints of corporate goals, philosophies, or fads, and instead aimed at generating the best results in terms of the criteria used for assessing the performance of an SBU and its management.

---

[16]Goold and Campbell, *Strategies and Styles.*

4. The contingency plans for dealing with the "unthinkables." O'Connor found that most companies only formulated explicit plans for about six significant contingencies.[17] Since companies usually face many more than six significant potential problems, the other contingency plans remain invisible.

IMPLICIT AND EXPLICIT STRATEGIES

Interviewing managers confidentially about their plans revealed that the explicit plan is not always representative of the invisible plan and the implicit strategy that lies behind it. The most extreme gap between the two belonged to a management maverick running a successful distribution business inside a larger organization. When asked about his formal five-year plan he replied, "Yes, it's very useful. It performs two important tasks. First, it keeps the Board of Directors happy. Second, it's fixed the wobbly leg of this coffee table. The plan I run the business with was written over a year ago, by me, in my own way, for my business. There's only one copy, it's locked in my drawer, and that is where it's going to stay."

A gap between the written and invisible plans does not necessarily cause problems if the invisible plan is complementary, thorough, and can be implemented as required. Strategy is often spoken of as being implicit or explicit as if it makes little difference which it is. Tregoe and Zimmerman suggest that the presence of more effective strategic thinking, rather than strategic plans, is the key to corporate survival.[18] If Eisenhower was right when he said that "planning is everything, plans are nothing," then it follows that it does not matter if part of the strategy remains invisible, provided that it has been planned. Or does it? Invisible plans do contain inherent dangers:

1. They may be weakened by the absence of formal discussions and a methodical approach in their development.
2. They will often deal with the most difficult (and therefore important) problems that the business will face.
3. If strategies remain invisible to the extent of remaining in managers' heads, they may remain vague, and vulnerable to fallible memories or the departure of the manager in question.
4. The explicit visible and implicit invisible strategies can conflict. In the most extreme instances strategies and strengths around which the actual success of a company is based can end up having to compete for resources against a rhetorical explicit strategy and image, which managers wished to promote.

Conflict between the explicit and invisible strategies can cause serious problems:

1. *The structure may be changed to follow the explicit strategy, in a way that hampers the invisible strategy.* For example, at one company a proposal to appoint a particular troubleshooter was vetoed on the basis that "the problem didn't officially exist." Another company followed its new "market-led" strategy by reorganizing its SBUs into a set of market-defined product groups. However, these new labels did not match the actual product/market mix of the SBUs

---

[17] R. O'Connor, *Planning under Uncertainty: Multiple Scenario and Contingency Planning,* Conference Board Report no. 471 (New York: Conference Board, 1978).

[18] B. B. Tregoe and J. W. Zimmerman, "Strategic Thinking Key to Corporate Survival," *Management Review* 88, no. 2 (1979), p. 8.

involved and were meaningless in view of the company's continuing focus on products and technology. The result was confusion and in some cases direct competition between SBUs in supposedly different product/market groups.

2. *If you say something often enough you end up believing it.* In several cases explicit strategies seemed to gain increasing weight despite an obvious lack of success, and in contrast to some of the obvious successes of the implicit strategies. One manager, when questioned about his continued pursuit of one unsuccessful strategy, announced, "We've said we're going to penetrate this market, therefore we will!"

3. *Key players can be misled by strategic rhetoric.* "Sticking to the knitting" is a very sound piece of strategic advice. Unfortunately it does not sound very dynamic, especially if your knitting is army socks rather than designer knitwear. One marketing director took at face value his managing director's new strategy of "bold steps into new markets" and adjusted his marketing strategy accordingly. He ended up severely criticized for spreading marketing resources too thinly and for failing to protect and maintain the company's core market (the less dynamic sounding implicit strategy).

4. *An issue may be placed in the explicit plan as a smokescreen for an invisible strategy.* One manufacturer suffered from over 80 percent dependency on one customer. This left the business very exposed despite good profitability. Each year reducing this dependency was the number one priority of the strategic plan, but each year no progress was made and further business was sought and won from the key customer. When questioned about this the managing director replied, "Well, this year we've been too busy making money, but next year . . ." Needless to say, following the implicit strategy of staying close to the one dominant customer ended in disaster after several lucrative years.

Authors such as Warren,[19] Steiner,[20] Hussey,[21] and Taylor and Hussey[22] who have examined the shortcomings of formal planning systems illustrate how gaps can emerge between explicit plans and the reality of the business. Having an explicit/implicit strategy gap that is bridged by an invisible plan produces a situation reminiscent of "the emperor's new clothes." Most of the managers realize that the company described in the plan and the one they work for are significantly different, but nobody dares to admit it. As one manager confided, "I know I'd be shot for saying this, but despite all this proactive planning palaver, we're still an opportunistic subcontractor, just as we've always been!"

CONCLUSIONS

We should redress the balance of this discussion by stressing the positive aspects of the planning experiences of the managers interviewed. Almost all of them felt that, despite the problems, planning was a worthwhile effort producing tangible benefits. Also, virtually all the companies recorded improved results following the introduction of formal strategic planning (although whether such performance improvements can be directly attributed to formal planning is a moot point). Almost without excep-

[19]E. K. Warren, *Long Range Planning—The Executive Viewpoint.* (Englewood Cliffs, N.J.: Prentice Hall, 1966).

[20]G. Steiner, *Pitfalls in Comprehensive Long Range Planning* (Planning Executives Institute, 1972).

[21]Hussey, *Corporate Planning.*

[22]Taylor and Hussey, *The Realities of Planning.*

tion the managers emphasized that the benefits they perceived would have been far greater if the planning process could have become somehow less entangled with organizational politics.

Keeping the politics out of planning may sound appealing, but most managers accepted the political nature of the planning process as a fact of managerial life. Some even viewed it positively, seeing opportunities to outplan their internal rivals, even if they could not outperform them. Others saw the planning process as a good forum for debating fundamental organizational issues, and the formal plans as useful mechanisms for informing and structuring the debate.

HIDDEN AGENDAS AND INVISIBLE PLANS

However rational and scientific a planning process appears, it has to exist within the realities of organizational politics. This is particularly evident in the relationship between corporate and subsidiary management within the planning process (a relationship neatly captured by Goold and Campbell).[23] When corporate managers launch planning initiatives and when SBU managers prepare plans, they both approach the planning process with a hidden agenda. *SBU managers seek to:*

- *Justify their current position and direction.*
- *Gain approval for their explicit strategy* and as much corporate resource as possible on the basis of it.
- *Gain the freedom needed to implement their invisible plan,* whether or not this coincides with the explicit plan. This requires allaying any fears that senior management may have about the written plan, to keep the strings and monitoring devices attached to it to a minimum.

Corporate managers seek to:

- *Use the plans as a shortcut* to actually understanding the full complexities of SBUs and their markets.
- *Use plans as a stick* with which to beat SBUs which stray from their planned path in an unprofitable direction (as Unterman[24] notes, nobody seems to object to profitable excursions, even when the profit involved is strictly short term).
- *Use the SBU plans as a basis for the corporate strategic audit and plan.* This use of a "strategic edit" in place of a strategic audit will tend to compound any optimism present in the SBU plans.
- *Use the planning process as a symbol of sophistication.* As one manager put it, "It isn't so much that we really need formal strategic planning, but we need to be seen to be planning."

A strategic planning system has to fulfill its explicit role in the development and implementation of strategies, and also to resolve the issues on these hidden agendas. The irony is that it is the formal explicit plans that (because of their high profile) tend to get caught up in the political process. The invisible plans, because of their low profile, can continue their role in running a business much as they did before the advent of formal planning.

---

[23]Goold and Campbell, *Strategies and Styles.*
[24]I. Unterman, "American Finance: Three Views of Strategy." *Journal of General Management* 1, no. 3 (1974).

A NEW MODEL FOR STRATEGIC PLANNING

Mintzberg proposes *five concepts of strategy* as.[25]

1. *A plan* of written or remembered intentions.
2. *A pattern* of consistent actions which emerge.
3. *A perspective;* a view of the world or philosophy.
4. *A position* that the firm occupies in relation to its environment.
5. *A ploy* to outwit competitors by announcing an intention that the company does not actually intend to implement.

In view of the perspectives presented in this article, we would replace the concept of strategy as a ploy, with: *strategy as a pronouncement, an intention announced to outwit competitors externally, to help to secure resources or to influence key stakeholders,* which the company does not intend *to implement.* This means that as well as genuine strategic intent, formal plans will contain a certain degree of strategic rhetoric.

Mintzberg's model of the strategy process (Figure 2–1) can be adapted to take account of the presence of strategic rhetoric and invisible plans. This adaptation is presented in Figure 2–2. What it lacks in terms of the lost simple elegance of the original, it perhaps gains in added realism.

ELIMINATING POLITICAL DISTORTION

Using the output of a planning process to paint a picture of the company's future that will inspire staff and attract investors is logical and potentially beneficial. Developing a planning process from which such a picture is the only explicit output is fraught with danger. So what can companies do to safeguard themselves against gaps appearing between the rhetoric and reality of strategic plans? When managers were asked what could be done to free the planning process from political distortion, a consensus of five points emerged:

1. *Emphasis should be placed on the need for a thorough and objective strategic audit* as the starting point for any planning process.
2. *Plans should be assessed on their realism* as well as their forecast results. An index could be used to weight forecast results for subsidiaries by a factor reflecting the perceived probability of those results being achieved. The use of such an "index of realism" should encourage subsidiaries to avoid unsubstantiated and overoptimistic forecasts.
3. *The performance of SBUs and managers needs to be partly assessed on factors like achievement of strategic objectives,* quality of planning, conformance to plan, and long-term prospects, as well as on bottom-line results.
4. *Uncut strategic plans should not be used as a document for external consumption.* Such plans make a useful source of information for external presentations, but a potential role as a PR handout will compromise the plan's more important role in helping to develop the corporate strategy.
5. *Managers at all levels need to recognize explicitly the political nature of the planning process, and the influence that managers' personal ambitions and values can have on it.* Several managers complained that senior management

---

[25]Mintzberg, "Opening Up the Definition of Strategy."

F I G U R E 2-2 | **Planning as Strategic Rhetoric**

F I G U R E 2-2 | **Planning as Strategic Rhetoric**

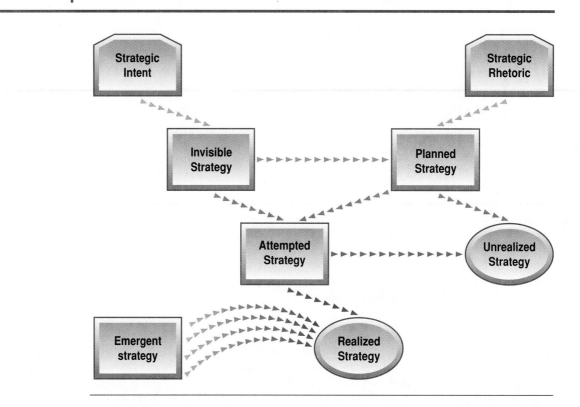

"pretend that planning is a totally rational affair, when everyone knows that it is overtly political." Guth and Tagiuri proposed that if managers' personal values were made explicit, their influence on strategy could be brought into the open.[26] Over 25 years later it seems that the hidden political agenda for planning still remains as dangerously submerged as ever.

Invisible plans will always exist. They existed long before formal corporate plans, and in many cases they are more realistic, more comprehensive, and more flexible than formal plans could ever hope to be. There are many benefits that formalized strategic planning can offer companies in terms of improved decision-making, communication, resource allocation, and monitoring. Formalizing the planning process introduces a structure, a level of consistency, an external long-term focus, and a methodological approach that are frequently weak in informal planning processes and the resulting invisible plans.

Talking to managers reveals that even a carefully designed and implemented planning process can become hijacked by the political process of resource bartering, by the need of corporate management to control subsidiaries, or simply by a desire to impress people both inside and outside the company. The result of such a process is a set of formal plans often divorced from or in conflict with the reality of the business. Invisible plans are left to bridge the gap between the reality and the rhetoric and to deal with some of the key issues that confront the business.

[26]W. D. Guth and R. Tagiuri, "Personal Values and Corporate Strategy," *Harvard Business Review* 43, no. 5 (1965), pp. 123–32.

BLIND SPOTS IN COMPETITIVE ANALYSIS

Shaker A. Zahra, Georgia State University
Sherry S. Chaples, Science Applications International Corp.

There is no resting place for an enterprise in a competitive economy.

Alfred P. Sloan

Consider the following two cases:

- A chief executive officer (CEO) of a large U.S. manufacturing corporation of heavy equipment and machinery was astounded: his rivals were almost invisible; they were Japanese and Korean firms of whom he had never heard—and they continued to multiply. "Where did they come from? Why didn't we see them coming? How could we get blindsided like this!" the CEO asked his strategic planning staff.

- A manufacturing company launched an intensive marketing campaign to promote its new product. Senior executives described the product as a breakthrough that would strengthen their firm's market position, propelling it to unquestionable industry dominance. Executives boasted that the technology embedded in their product was so advanced that it would be several years before competitors could catch up with it. However, as soon as the company announced its product, a lesser-known and much smaller firm introduced a product that clearly preempted the leader's claim of technological superiority. The substitute was cheaper and easier to use than the product of the self-proclaimed industry leader.

These examples illustrate flaws in competitive analysis—areas that have been ignored in identifying competitors and their possible moves. Although the literature is full of similar cases of corporate disasters resulting from faulty competitive analysis, little is known about the nature and sources of these flaws. This article identifies six such flaws, discusses their causes, and offers recommendations to avoid them. To appreciate the role of competitive analysis in determining a company's success or failure, its objectives must be discussed.

Source: © *Academy of Management Executive 7*, no. 2 (1993), pp. 7–28. Reprinted with permission.

STRATEGIC SIGNIFICANCE OF COMPETITIVE ANALYSIS

Competitive analysis is the process by which a company attempts to define and understand its industry, identify its competitors, determine the strengths and weaknesses of its rivals, and anticipate their moves. It embodies both competitive intelligence to collect data on rivals and the analysis and interpretation of the data for managerial decision-making. This analysis provides rich data that help a company to avoid surprises in the marketplace by anticipating its competitors' moves, and shorten the time required to respond to them. The analysis also offers a forum for executives to discuss and evaluate their assumptions about the firm's capabilities, market position, and the competition. It also helps in selecting viable strategies that position the firm strongly in its market. Therefore, competitive analysis serves as the foundation for a firm's strategy-formulation processes.

Competitive analysis also contributes to the successful implementation of a company's strategy. In a recent study, corporate competitive intelligence professionals reported that they spent their time about evenly on projects relating to strategy formulation and execution.[1] Competitive analysis enables companies to learn from rivals, as occurred when Xerox analyzed its Japanese rivals, concluding that product quality was a key factor of their global success. Consequently, Xerox then embarked on a massive corporatewide project to establish excellence in quality as the core of its strategy, helping the company to regain its market leadership. A factor that contributed to the success of this strategy's implementation was employees' recognition of the competitive challenge facing the company. Awareness of, and learning from, rivals' actions can be a major motivator that eases the successful implementation of the strategy. As Roger Smith, former CEO of General Motors (GM), observed, discussions of the company's Japanese rivals brought employees and executives closer, alerting the company's labor force to the changing forces of global competition.[2]

Besides serving as a motivator, the analysis aids in building consensus among executives on the company's goals and capabilities, thus increasing their commitment to the chosen strategy. Finally, it provides timely information on rivals' countermoves that create bottlenecks in executing the strategy and options to resolve problems quickly—leading to the effective implementation of the strategy.

Competitive analysis requires several steps, each of which provides insights into competitors' thinking, motives, skills, and potential moves. Typically, a competitive analysis system should help to determine the competition and examine the factors that influence rivalry in the industry, the power of buyers, power of suppliers, the threat of substitutes, and the threat of new entry into the industry.[3] Because no single

---

[1] For an extensive discussion of the importance of competitive analysis, see Raphael Amit, Ian Domowitz, and Chaim Fershtman, "Thinking One Step Ahead: The Use of Conjectures in Competitors' Analysis," *Strategic Management Journal* 9, no. 5 (1988), pp. 431–42; B. Gilad, "The Role of Organized Competitive Intelligence in Corporate Strategy," *Columbia Journal of World Business* 24, no. 4 (1989), pp. 29–35; John E. Prescott and D. C. Smith, "A Project-Based Approach to Competitive Analysis," *Strategic Management Journal* 8, no. 5 (1987), pp. 411–23; John E. Prescott and D. C. Smith, "The Largest Survey of 'Leading-Edge' Competitor Intelligence Managers," *Planning Review* 17, no. 3 (1989), pp. 6–13; Daniel C. Smith and John E. Prescott, "Demystifying Competitive Analysis," *Planning Review* 15 (1987), p. 7; and M. A. Young, "Sources of Competitive Data for the Management Strategist," *Strategic Management Journal* 10, no. 3 (1987), pp. 285–93.

[2] J. Treece, "GM Faces Reality," *Business Week,* May 9, 1988, pp. 114–22.

[3] For a comprehensive discussion of the processes involved in competitive analysis, see Michael E. Porter, *Competitive Strategy* (New York, N.Y.: Free Press, 1980). For a more expanded discussion and illustration, see Robert M. Grant, *Contemporary Strategy Analysis: Concepts, Techniques, Applications* (Cambridge, Mass.: Basil Blackwell, 1991), and S. Oster, *Modern Competitive Analysis* (New York, N.Y.: Oxford University).

TABLE 3-1 | **Competitive Analysis Flaws and Managerial Actions**

Flaws	Executive Actions
1. Misjudging industry boundaries	Change view of the competition by focusing on competitors' intent; seeing the industry from the entrant's eye; examining the reason for an entrant's failure; and performing an autopsy on failing competitors.
2. Poor identification of the competition	Study competitors' response pattern and blind spots. Survey customers and suppliers. Focus on competitors' capabilities, not only form.
3. Overemphasis on competitor's visible competence	Study competitors' response patterns. Analyze rivals' invisible functions.
4. Overemphasis on where, not how	Study competitors' strategic intent. See the industry from the competitors' eyes.
5. Faulty assumptions about the competition	Transform the cliché that competition is good into a living reality. Study competitors' actions and response patterns. Ensure representation of different groups in the competitive analysis process. Teach your employees about your competition. Validate your assumptions by discussing them with suppliers and customers.
6. Paralysis by analysis	Pay attention to the staffing, organization, and mission of the competitive analysis unit. Integrate competitive analysis with managerial decision-making process. Use your own invisible functions.

competitive analysis system is universally valid, executives should match these steps with the specific situations of their industries and companies. Since most industries are constantly changing, the process of competitive analysis should also be continuous, guaranteeing accurate and timely data for executive decision-making.

To be useful, the analysis should be thorough, providing timely data on competitors' goals, plans, capabilities, and intended moves. It should also help in predicting competitors' actions and their timing. Performed in this spirit, the analysis can offer a basis for understanding the forces of competition in an industry and help to position the firm in its market.

BLIND SPOTS

Observation of companies' strategic moves suggests that flaws exist in some competitive analyses. These flaws or blind spots result from a company's mistaken or incomplete view of its industry and competition, the poor design of the competitive analysis system, inaccurate managerial perceptions, or ineffective organizational processes.

Six such blind spots are particularly serious: (1) misjudging industry boundaries; (2) poor identification of the competition; (3) overemphasis on competitors' visible competence; (4) overemphasis on where, not how, rivals will compete; (5) faulty assumptions about the competition; and (6) paralysis by analysis (see Table 3–1). These blind spots reflect flaws in a company's perception and understanding of its rivals. Blind spots are the "areas where a competitor will either not see the significance of events at all, will perceive them incorrectly, or will perceive them very

---

[4]Michael E. Porter, *Competitive Strategy* p. 59. For a detailed discussion of the manifestations of competitive blind spots, see E. J. Zajac and M. H. Bazerman, "Blind Spots in Industry and Competitor Analysis: Implications of Interfirm (Mis)perception for Strategic Decisions," *Academy of Management Review* 16, no. 1 (1991), pp. 37–56.

or even cause the selection of the wrong competitive approach. Blind spots also lead some companies to underestimate the ability of their rivals. Flawed competitive analysis, resulting from these blind spots, weakens a company's capacity to seize opportunities or interact effectively with its rivals, ultimately leading to an erosion in the company's market position and profitability.

Misjudging Industry Boundaries

A major contribution of competitive analysis is the clear definition of a firm's industry and its boundaries. This definition is usually the starting point in determining the competition, formulating a company's strategy, and allocating resources among businesses. Surprisingly, misjudging industry boundaries has handicapped well-known companies. Consider the following examples:

- Once considered one of America's most venerable industries, the newspaper industry is currently in a state of disarray because of the success of cable television. Cable news, financial, sports, style, and home shopping services have caused a major decline in readership. It has taken nearly a decade for well-established giants such as the *New York Times,* the *Washington Post,* the *Chicago Tribune,* and the *Los Angeles Times* to recognize that their concept of the printed newspaper has become outdated and that they must reexamine their definition of the industry's boundaries. Although newspapers still play a major role in society, the emerging boundaries of the industry are broader, covering printed, broadcast, and telecast media.

- ABC, CBS, and NBC were startled by the success of Turner Broadcasting System (TBS) and other cable companies. For years, the three giants dismissed the threat of cable television (including TBS) to their operations, believing that cable companies were fringe businesses. Today, because of serious declines in their shares of news viewers and entertainment services, ABC, CBS, and NBC are actively seeking joint ventures and acquisition targets in the cable industry, realizing that their traditional definition of the broadcasting industry has become outdated.

- Pharmaceutical companies have been surprised at the increased entry of chemical firms into their industry. Faced with industry maturity, fierce competition, and declining margins, several leading chemical companies entered the profitable pharmaceutical industry by forming strategic alliances with upstart biotechnology companies. For years, pharmaceutical companies fiercely jockeyed for position within their traditionally defined industry, and ignored the threat posed by young biotechnology companies. Recognizing the significant changes in their industry, some pharmaceutical companies have recently created their own biotechnology divisions or formed strategic alliances with start-up biotechnology firms. Clearly, the alliance between chemical and biotechnology companies has profoundly transformed the pharmaceutical industry, forcing incumbents to rethink their industry's definition.

The genesis of misjudging industry boundaries may lie in environmental enactment, defined as the process by which a company selects the sectors of its external environment it plans to emphasize. While these sectors are numerous, a company typically emphasizes a limited definition of its industry's boundaries. For instance, although a firm may view its industry broadly (e.g., medical instruments), it defines that industry in much narrower terms (e.g., particular instruments for certain procedures). This definition determines the market a company serves. Obviously, "Companies do not offer every product or service that they conceivably could, or sell to all of the customers that they could."[5] Instead, executives focus on the market segment where they believe the firm has a suitable product and possesses appropriate skills and resources. As a result some executives ignore other areas in its industries—areas that can undergo major changes over time. Typically, executives focus on their served market and they give other parts of the industry less attention in their analysis, leading to a possible delay in spotting changes in boundaries.

An effective definition of industry boundaries requires consideration of four interrelated issues: domain (where does the industry begin and end); customer groups (sectors to be served and their specific needs); customer functions (customer needs and purchasing patterns); and critical technologies (production, marketing, and administrative systems).[6] These factors should be considered simultaneously, otherwise the firm will err in selecting its competitive arena.

Focusing solely on defining the industry's domain will lead executives to believe that their competition consists of all firms that, currently or potentially, offer a product that satisfies a particular customer. Yet this broad definition should be viewed only as a start in defining the competition. Executives should also consider the customer groups of interest to their company, thus focusing the analysis on a smaller set of viable competitors who similarly define their target market(s). Still, by considering customer groups of interest, executives can further refine their definition of the competition. Accordingly, competitors are those companies that, currently or potentially, offer a product targeted to a specific segment with the goal of satisfying a specific need. Finally, definition of the business and competition would be incomplete without consideration of alternative technologies employed in the creation and distribution of the product. Typically, executives consider companies that use similar technologies to offer a product that meets the needs of their target market as competitors.

In addition to considering the domain, customer groups, customer functions, and alternative technologies, executives should also reevaluate the firm's definition of business and served market over time. Not only technologies, customer groups, and consumer needs change over time but so do companies' skills and competencies, compelling executives to redraw their definition of the business. Clearly, the environmental enactment process unfolds over time, building primarily on executives' perceptions of the changes in the industry. It benefits also from data gathered through environmental scanning—the process by which a company collects, analyzes, and interprets data on its industry. This data can help to spot the forces that cause a change in the industry's boundaries.

The process of environmental enactment is often affected by the evolutionary changes industries undergo. With time, industries change, producing many potential new industries. This evolution results from the actions and strategies of companies in an industry. For example, during the past two decades the electronics industry has grown rapidly to include semiconductors, connectors, office equipment, measuring and testing tools, office automation, audio and video products, electronic games and toys, home computers, and home automation products. Each field can be viewed as a seg-

---

[5]Robert D. Buzzell and Bradley T. Gale, *The PIMS Principles: Linking Strategy to Performance* (New York, Free Press, 1987).

[6]One of the landmark studies on defining industry boundaries is presented in Derek E. Abell, *Defining the Business* (Englewood Cliffs, N.J.: Prentice Hall, 1980).

The following authors provide a detailed discussion of the issues: John F. Cady and Robert D. Buzzell, *Strategic Marketing* (Boston, Mass.: Little, Brown, 1986). A recent study warns against excessive reliance on the military metaphor which can encourage unethical behavior in collecting data about the competition: Shaker A. Zahra, "Unethical Practices in Competitive Analysis," *Journal of Business Ethics,* 1993, in press.

ment of an industry or a distinct industry in its own right. When companies compete in an industry similar to the electronics industry, the chances for errors in misjudging boundaries increase because the segments are related and participants in one segment may opt to penetrate others, almost without being detected. Penetration can occur through product and market expansion or through diversification strategies. For example, driven by overcapacity and declining margins, electric utility companies have diversified into lucrative growth industries such as cable television, travel agencies, and resort areas. Few could have foreseen the entry of utility companies into these markets.

Changing technologies lead to radical changes in an industry, causing a firm to misjudge its industry's boundaries. Currently, cable companies are concerned about the potential entry by the "baby Bells," which can use their phone networks to offer state-of-the-art interactive programming. Similarly, telephone companies are currently considering the possibility of offering information services, thus significantly broadening their own business concept. Technological advances have aided companies' venturing into new industries, surprising incumbents.

The profound effect of changing technology is especially visible in emerging industries where boundaries are fuzzy. What are the boundaries of the biotechnology industry? The multimedia industry? Establishing precise boundaries for these and similar industries is a matter of convenience at best; these industries are in a state of flux. The ingenuity of companies—in finding links between their industry and other fields—makes a definition of industry boundaries only temporary. A firm must frequently check its definition of those boundaries to ensure its accuracy and currency.

Executives become aware of their firm's poor definition of its boundaries when wide disagreements persist among key officers about the scope and nature of the arena in which the firm participates. This occurs when myopia prevails among executives who refuse to revise their firm's traditional concept of the industry. This is likely to happen when the company holds a position of market leadership. Here, well-intended dedication to a successful business concept becomes a dogma that prevents executives from seeing the connection between their existing product lines and emerging industry trends. Executives will resist change also if their experience and beliefs support the idea that their markets do not reward radical changes in the business concept or competitive approach.

Misjudging industry boundaries can be a devastating flaw in competitive analysis. It occurs because of flawed managerial perceptions of the environment, and failure to adjust a firm's view to reflect current status of the industry. Misjudging boundaries leads to the poor identification of the competition.

Poor Identification of Competitors

One of the most damaging (if not puzzling) flaws of competitive analysis is the poor identification of the competition, as the following examples illustrate:

- In 1982, Apple paused for only a minute when IBM announced its entry into the PC market. Apple executives quickly dismissed IBM as a serious contender. Steve Jobs, Apple's founder and first CEO, stated "When IBM entered the market, we did not take it seriously enough. It was a pretty heady time at Apple. We were shipping tens of thousands of machines a month—more computers than

---

[7]"Jobs and Gates Together," *Fortune,* August 26, 1991, p. 50.

mitment to the industry. Apple could not see IBM as a credible rival, who within five years emerged as the industry's leader.

- The MIT Commission on Industrial Productivity concluded that myopic thinking caused the failure of the executives of the largest U.S. integrated steel mills to see the potential threat of imports and domestic minimills in the 1980s. Efficient and innovative domestic minimills and foreign producers took away market share from the established steelmakers, forcing them to retrench or enter other industries.[8]

Poor identification of competitors has several dimensions. One of the most serious is the exclusive focus on well-known companies while ignoring other potentially viable organizations. This tendency has been blamed for contributing to the eroding competitive position of U.S. and European firms' market leadership. In these companies, "Typically competitive analysis focuses on the existing resources . . . of present competitors. The only companies seen as a threat are those with the resources to erode margins and market share in the next planning period."[9] This faulty focus has caused companies to ignore their foreign rivals. With the globalization of industries, it is difficult to identify relevant competitors to keep abreast of their strategic moves. Globalization introduces additional potential product varieties, entrants, and competitors, thus complicating the task of the strategist. Today, executives in the electronics, software, multimedia, and biotechnology industries must monitor the actions of many firms around the globe.

Overemphasis on a regional identification of the competition—when a national or international focus is essential—is another serious flaw. For a decade, Coors—a successful U.S. brewer—proclaimed it had no competitors because of its regional market focus. By the end of the 1980s, Coors faced several domestic and international brands that targeted its segments. Coors's executives apparently overlooked the changing competitive arena with its trend toward a national beer market.

Why do some competitive analysis systems err in identifying a firm's competitors? One reason is the faulty definition of industry boundaries. Another reason lies in managerial cognition (i.e., their thinking patterns and perceptions) and personality, on one hand, and the process of competitive analysis on the other. These factors are so intertwined that one can only speculate about the contributing cause.

Research shows that executives develop cognitive taxonomies (classifications) of their competitive environments, focusing on those companies that are similar to their own in goals and resources. Companies that are similar in resources and goals are said to have the same "form."[10] In selecting competitors, executives typically focus on only a few companies that match their definition of organizational form. This process limits the number of credible rivals to two or three, thus ignoring other potential rivals. Because executives focus on existing and known competitors, sometimes less-known companies or those that possess a different form are ignored, as happened in the following cases:

---

[8]The MIT Commission on Industrial Productivity, *The Working Papers of the MIT Commission on Industrial Productivity,* vol. 1 (Cambridge, Mass.: MIT Press, 1989).

[9]G. Hamel and C. K. Prahalad, "Strategic Intent," *Harvard Business Review,* 67, no. 3 (1989), pp. 63–76.

[10]J. Porac and H. Thomas, "Competitive Groups as Cognitive Communities: The Case of Scottish Knitwear Manufacturers," *Journal of Management Studies* 26, no. 4 (1989), pp. 397–416; and Joseph F. Porac and H. Thomas, "Taxonomic Mental Models in Competitor Definition," *Academy of Management Review* 15, no. 2 (1990), pp. 224–40. Additional insights can be found in W. C. Bogner and H. Thomas, "The Role of Competitive Groups in Strategy Formulation: A Dynamic Integration of Two Competing Models," *Journal of Management Studies,* 1993, in press.

- In the 1960s, Xerox was one of the best-publicized success stories in the United States. It capitalized on a growing market by emphasizing product introduction and expansion in Europe and Japan, retaining two overseas subsidiaries. However, perhaps lulled by its success, Xerox ignored some disturbing trends both at home and abroad. Early in the 1970s, Xerox was not threatened by IBM's entry into the copier market. However, Kodak, a company similar to Xerox in organizational form, introduced the Ektaprint copier hoping to penetrate the upper-middle segment of the market, long cherished by Xerox. This caught Xerox's attention; it promptly counterattacked Kodak's moves. The battle between Kodak and Xerox allowed emerging Japanese competitors (including Canon, Minolta, and Ricoh) to develop better-quality copiers and strengthen their market positions. By the 1980s, it was clear that Xerox had not taken the Japanese threat seriously. Fuji (a former Xerox subsidiary) and others had already made significant inroads in the Japanese, U.S., and other markets.[11] Yet, apparently, Xerox mistakenly dismissed its then smaller Japanese competitors as weak rivals who could not possibly challenge its market leadership. Instead, Xerox devoted considerable resources and energy to repelling Kodak—a well-known, rich company with a similar "form" to its own.

- Honda took on leaders in the motorcycle industry by first introducing innovative product designs, and a wide assortment of models. From there Honda started to expand its activities. "Yet, even as Honda was selling 50cc motorcycles in the United States, it was already racing larger bikes in Europe—assembling the designs, skills, and technologies it would need for a systematic expansion across the entire spectrum of motor-related businesses."[12] To complicate things, for two decades, Honda entered a series of seemingly unrelated businesses—automobiles, lawn mowers, marine engines, and generators. This occurred at a time when U.S. car companies focused on tracking each other's moves, giving occasional attention only to European producers who had the same form—that is, they used similar production techniques and managerial processes. U.S. companies ignored Honda because it competed differently, emphasizing different managerial and manufacturing philosophies. Honda was finally taken seriously a decade later when it emerged as a renowned global competitor.

But why and how do executives retain these cognitive taxonomies, even after they have become outdated? *Consistency theory* offers an explanation. It suggests that "decision makers' goals relate to maintaining consistency among their images of themselves, their attitudes, and their decisions."[13] This means that executives will more readily accept industry and competitive information that supports their existing beliefs. Conversely, they may discount data that is different from their beliefs or that challenges their values. For instance, few in the 1960s thought Honda could become a major global quality car producer. Even fewer Xerox executives believed that Japanese companies could successfully enter U.S. markets, let alone become truly global firms. Thus, executives of established companies ignored potential rivals who had a different form from their own organizations.

---

[11]For a detailed account of this example, see Douglas K. Ramsey, *The Corporate Warriors: Six Classic Cases in American Business* (Boston, Mass.: Houghton Mifflin, 1987).

[12]G. Hamel and C. K. Prahalad, "Strategic Intent," *Harvard Business Review* 67, no. 3 (1989), p. 70.

[13]Sara Kiesler and Lee Sproull, "Managerial Responses to Changing Environments: Perspectives on Problem Sensing from Social Cognition." *Administrative Science Quarterly* 27 (1982), p. 558.

This error was magnified by another flaw that sometimes plagues managerial cognition: inflexible commitment to the historical key factors for success (KFS) in the industry. KFS are the factors that determine successful performance in an industry. Companies that possess the skills and resources required for KFS are considered viable members of an industry. But KFS change as an industry evolves. Thus, when executives rely on historical KFS, they contribute to a flawed analysis. Historical KFS may not fully capture emerging competitors who possess different organizational forms or use different competitive approaches.

Research suggests that executives' reliance on historical KFS may occur because some established companies become less vigilant in monitoring their environment.[14] Believing that they are well protected because of their resources and reputation, established companies do not analyze the environment effectively. Lack of current—especially contrary—data on competitors perpetuates executives' outdated cognitive taxonomies.

Cognitive factors contribute to flawed competitive analysis also by causing executives to make incorrect attributions about environmental and competitive shifts. For instance, for a decade major U.S. frozen-food producers dismissed as "small-time" players their thriving domestic-niche producers who targeted ethnic groups and institutional markets. Only recently did major food producers awaken to the great potential of these niches. How did this happen? The principles of discounting and augmentation offer an explanation. At a time when domestic-niche players were thriving, the industry leaders were besieged by the entry of foreign producers. The *discounting principle* states that "if one powerful facilitative cause is present, other plausible causes will seem less influential."[15] This meant that executives would focus on the most powerful causal agent (strong foreign companies) and ignore secondary ones (small niche players). Likewise, the *augmentation principle* helps to explain incumbents' moves. It asserts that when two factors simultaneously affect a particular outcome, the stronger factor will receive greater attention. This meant that U.S. companies would focus primarily on the perceived greater threat—strong, foreign competitors—rather than on the less-known, small domestic producers. The two principles seem to apply also to Xerox's lack of initial response to its foreign rivals. Xerox felt more threatened by the actions of IBM and Kodak—two very powerful corporations—than by their lesser-known foreign entrants.

---

[14]M. Tushman and E. Romanelli, "Organizational Evolution: A Metamorphosis Model of Convergence and Reorientation," in L. L. Cummings and B. M. Staw, eds., *Research in Organizational Behavior,* vol. 7 (Greenwich, CT: JAI Press, 1985), pp. 171–222.

[15]Kiesler and Sproull, "Managerial Responses," p. 552. There is a large body of research on how executives view and interpret their environment or events in their industries; see, Robert M. Billings, Thomas W. Milburn, and Mary Lou Shaalman, "A Model of Crisis Perception: A Theoretical and Empirical Analysis," *Administrative Science Quarterly* 25 (1980), pp. 330–46; Gifford W. Bradley, "Self-Serving Biases in the Attribution Process: A Reexamination of the Fact or Fiction Question," *Journal of Personality and Social Psychology* 36 (1978), pp. 56–71; Richard L. Daft and Karl E. Weick, "Toward a Model of Organizations as Interpretation Systems," *Academy of Management Review* 9, no. 2 (1984), pp. 284–95; C. J. Fombrun and E. J. Zajac, "Structural and Perceptual Influences on Intra-industry Stratification," *Academy of Management Journal* 30, no. 1 (1987), pp. 33–50; T. Gilovich, "Seeing the Past in the Present: The Effect of Associations to Familiar Events in Judgments and Decisions," *Journal of Personality and Social Psychology* 40 (1981), pp. 797–808; F. J. Milliken, "Perceiving and Interpreting Environmental Changes: An Examination of College Administrators' Interpretations of Changing Demographics," *Academy of Management Journal* 33, no. 1 (1990), pp. 42–63; J. B. Thomas and R. R. McDaniel, Jr., "Interpreting Strategic Issues: Effects of Strategy and the Information-Processing Structure of Top Management Teams," *Academy of Management Journal* 33, no. 2 (1990), pp. 286–306; S. Waddock and L. Isabella, "Strategy, Beliefs about the Environment, Performance in a Banking Simulation," *Journal of Management* 15 (1989), pp. 617–32; and J. P. Walsh "Selectivity and Selective Perception: An Investigation of Managers' Belief Structures and Information Processing," *Academy of Management Journal* 31, no. 4 (1988), pp. 873–96.

Besides faulty cognition, executives with dysfunctional (or pathological) personality styles also contribute to flawed competitive analysis. Executives with a pathologically *paranoid* personality type will see everyone as their potential rival, leading to a poor definition of viable competitors. The competitive analysis will be overwhelmed with collecting almost every piece of data on every potential rival. When senior executives have a *melodramatic* personality type, they pay attention to the most visible rivals, possibly ignoring smaller and less visible firms.[16] In these cases, the analysis fails to identify viable competitors.

The risk of ignoring some potentially viable competitors is very real, especially in view of the nature of industry changes. Radical changes are infrequent because they are risky, time-consuming, and painful. However, their infrequency lulls some into believing that they will not occur. Consider, for instance, the recent transformation of the Gerber Products Company, a well-known baby food manufacturer. Forced to rethink its strategy because of stiff competition and declining birth rates, it broadened its business definition to become a child care company. Gerber added new lines of business centering on children's toys, furniture, and clothing, and day care centers. An effective analysis by Gerber's rivals should have explored this radical move. Yet, because these dramatic strategic changes are infrequent, they were ignored in rivals' analyses.

Industry changes, poor managerial cognition, and dysfunctional personality types contribute to flawed competitive analysis. They lead to the misspecification of a company's competitors and their strength. This can erode a company's competitive position, especially when the analysis overemphasizes competitors' visible capabilities, ignoring rivals' potent but invisible functions.

EMPHASIS ON COMPETITORS' VISIBLE FUNCTIONS

This flaw occurs when the analysis centers primarily on competitors' most visible resources while deemphasizing their less-visible but potentially more important functions. Typically, manufacturing companies focus on their competitors' finance, R&D, and production functions. Other functions such as product design, logistics, and human resources do not always receive the same attention. In a study of 308 firms, Sutton found that companies were interested primarily in collecting information on competitors' pricing, sales, strategic plans, market share, key customers, new products, and expansion plans.[17] The companies paid little attention to their competitors' less visible aspects such as organization, structure, and culture, possibly leading to an incomplete assessment of their strengths and weaknesses. Of course, successful firms have used their invisible characteristics to achieve market eminence. For example, Pfizer, Inc., has benefitted greatly from its international operations as a major source of information about the new competitors, their product offerings, and their distribution channels. Pfizer uses this information in identifying its international rivals and developing its competitive strategy.

Unfortunately, companies become aware of the importance of invisible functions *after* the fact. They notice that competitors use those functions to pursue a chosen strategy, and perhaps alter the KFS. Three factors cause companies' tendencies to ignore competitors' invisible functions. The first is the difficulty in securing data on

---

[16]For a look into the interplay between personality and competitive analysis, see M. R. Kets de Vries and D. Miller, *Unstable at the Top: Inside the Troubled Organization* (New York, N.Y.: New American Library, 1987).
[17]H. Sutton, *Competitive Intelligence* (New York, N.Y.: The Conference Board, Report no. 913, 1988).

competitors' invisible functions. Although data on different product models, their features, and prices are readily available in many industries, information on rivals' R&D projects and organizational culture is not as easily accessible.

Second, the augmentation and discounting principles of cognition, discussed earlier, explain some firms' tendencies to overlook competitors' invisible functions. For one thing, it is difficult to document the effect of these functions on rivals' success. Accordingly these functions are not thoroughly examined. Fortunately, this practice is changing. Successful companies increasingly make good use of their rivals' flawed, exclusive focus on visible functions. For example, a study of 670 companies in 350 industries found that successful companies recognize the danger of patents in leaking information to competitors. To counteract this weakness, some companies rely on proprietary processes to protect their technological superiority. Proprietary processes are less visible than patents and receive less analysis from rivals.[18]

Third, not only are data on invisible functions scarce, but also the analytical tools for estimating their value are lacking. For instance, companies such as Merck and IBM are increasingly attentive to the potential advantage they can derive from capitalizing on their intellectual capital—the specialized skills and capabilities of their personnel—in developing strategic choices. However, there are few guidelines for measuring and evaluating the value of this capital. The same problem applies to the value of companies' brands, product design, name recognition, and similar functions.

Despite these difficulties, rivals' invisible functions must be analyzed because they can be the foundation for effective strategic moves. Companies should contact rivals' suppliers, buyers, and former managers to collect as much data as feasible on their invisible functions. Companies should focus on locating competitors' idiosyncrasies, rather than their easily quantifiable, common attributes.[19] These idiosyncrasies are the source of an enduring competitive advantage, defined as the unique position an organization develops relative to its rivals. Ignoring rivals' invisible functions leads to faulty assumptions about the competition—assumptions that understate their competence.

EMPHASIS ON WHERE, NOT HOW, TO COMPETE

Sometimes, competitive analysis focuses primarily on defining the markets where a firm will face intensive competition, ignoring *how* competitors intend to position themselves. Consider the following examples:

- Texas Instruments (TI) and Motorola took the market away from the well-established germanium producers like Hughes and Sylvania by introducing new semiconductor silicon-based technology. The new technology was cheaper, easier to process, and more reliable. Existing companies were slow in responding, believing that TI and Motorola would focus on the low end of the market; they ignored *how* these companies would compete—by using the new technology to attack different segments of the market.

- The success of Nike as a major producer of athletic shoes is explained by its ability to work closely with athletes, coaches, shoe retailers, and distributors. Close contact with these groups gave the company clues about the desirable changes in the design of shoes to make them comfortable and to quickly posi-

---

[18]R. Levin, A. K. Klevorick, R. R. Nelson, and S. G. Winter, "Appropriating the Returns from Industrial Research and Development," *Brookings Papers on Economic Activity* 3 (1987), pp. 783–820.
[19]D. Smith and J. Prescott, "Demystifying Competitive Analysis," *Planning Review* 15 (1987), p. 9.

tion itself, by sponsoring promotional marathons, when the national trend toward fitness appeared. Nike capitalized on a major flaw in the way the industry leaders (Adidas and Puma) marketed their products. For decades, the leaders had designed their shoes and pushed them through the distribution channels without close contact with distributors. In contrast, Nike listened to distributors' suggestions in developing company production plans and even made special financial arrangements to reduce their inventory cost. Adidas and Puma ignored Nike's innovative competitive approach.

These examples show that competitive analyses sometimes fail to determine their rivals' strategic intent, defined as competitors' approach to winning in the marketplace and plans for allocating resources over time to build or acquire capabilities.[20] Obviously, predicting how a competitor may reconfigure its skills over time is difficult. However, an effective analysis should focus on what rivals *can* do with their skills, considering potentially radical moves. What a firm may do in the future should not be viewed as an extension of its current actions; possible radical departures from its existing strategies must be considered.

Research on strategic change offers an explanation for some companies' tendencies to focus on logical extensions in competitors' strategies. It shows that most strategic changes are incremental in nature; quantum changes are few and short-lived.[21] Because radical strategic changes are infrequent, some competitive analysis systems may overlook these shifts. To safeguard against this flaw, analysts should explore radical scenarios, focusing on potentially revolutionary changes. They should also collect, analyze, and interpret data about competitors' potential moves (What will they do next?), location (Where?), and competitive weapons (How will they do it?). An analysis that does not address these fundamental issues about the competition is flawed.

Finally, even when a company identifies its rival's next move ("where"), it is difficult to determine how it can use this information. In the examples cited earlier, some incumbents were aware of the arena of their rivals' next move. Still, they were taken by surprise at the ingenuity of their rivals, who were also adept at innovation, working around the assumptions of existing firms. TBS, Nike, and Honda revolutionized their industries by creatively destroying incumbents' assumptions, thus revising the industry's KFS to their advantage, placing established firms in a defensive posture.

A symptom of misjudging competitors' competence is when the persistent attacks by a company on its rivals do not trigger expected reactions based on competitors' presumed competence. For instance, a consumer goods company defined its major competitor's competence as speedy new-product introduction. However, executives

[20]G. Hamel and C. K. Prahalad, "Strategic Intent," *Harvard Business Review* 82, no. 2 (1989), pp. 63–76.

[21]A. Ginsberg, "Measuring and Modeling Changes in Strategy: Theoretical Foundations and Empirical Directions," *Strategic Management Journal* 9, no. 6 (1988), pp. 559–75; D. Miller and P. H. Friesen, "Archetypes of Organizational Transition," *Administrative Science Quarterly* 25 (1980a), pp. 268–99; D. Miller and P. H. Friesen, "Momentum and Revolution in Organizational Adaptation," *Academy of Management Journal* 23 (1980b), pp. 591–614; D. Miller and P. H. Friesen, "The Longitudinal Analysis of Organizations: A Methodological Perspective," *Management Science* 28 (1982), pp. 1013–34; D. Miller and P. H. Friesen, "Strategy-Making and Environment: The Third Link," *Strategic Management Journal* 4 (1983), pp. 221–35; D. Miller and P. H. Friesen, *Organizations: A Quantum View* (Englewood Cliffs, N.J.: Prentice Hall, 1984); J. B. Quinn, "Strategic Change: Logical Incrementalism," *Sloan Management Review* 20 (1978), pp. 7–12; E. Romanelli and M. L. Tushman, "Inertia, Environments, and Strategic Choice: A Quasi-Experimental Design for Comparative-Longitudinal Research," *Management Science* 32 (1986), pp. 608–21; K. G. Smith and C. M. Grimm, "Environmental Variation, Strategic Change, and Firm Performance: A Study of Railroad Deregulation," *Strategic Management Journal* 8, no. 4 (1987), pp. 363–76.

observed that when there were repeated assaults on this basis, the competitor's countermoves were based solely on price. Further analysis of intelligence data revealed serious problems in the coordination of the rival's R&D, marketing, and manufacturing functions. This finding became the basis for reevaluating the competitor's ability to continue its speedy product innovation.

Another symptom of misjudging a competitor's competence is when a company is forced to compete in a totally new arena, using new tools and facing almost new competitors. A classic example is Addressograph Multigraph and A.B. Dick, who faced this situation in the office products industry. These two firms did not see that, while they held leadership positions in the industry, xerography was fast becoming the new basis of competitive advantage in the industry. Multigraph and A.B. Dick did not see that new competitive rules were being introduced—rules that transformed the very texture of their industry.

A final symptom is executives' failure to see the limits of their firm's competitive advantage. For example, in 1984, AT&T's reputation for technological innovation was viewed as a good reason for its entering the personal computer industry. However, during the first five years after its entry, its track record was dismal. Apparently, AT&T believed that its reputation for technological innovation in one industry would carry forward to other technology-based industries. AT&T tended to underestimate the technical innovation competence of its existing competitors. Only after AT&T redefined its niche and entered into global strategic alliances did it start to reap the rewards of its presence in the industry.

Misjudging competitors' competence results from the lack of reliable intelligence data on rivals and from outdated assumptions about their capabilities, as discussed earlier. Lack of data reflects operational deficiencies in the competitive analysis system: it does not provide timely information about competitors' assets, capabilities, and skills. Further, it does not isolate the *idiosyncratic* qualities that can form the basis of establishing an enduring competitive advantage. These factors lead to yet another flaw in competitive analysis: holding faulty assumptions about the competition.

FAULTY ASSUMPTIONS ABOUT THE COMPETITION

Underestimating rivals' competence can create and reinforce faulty assumptions about these companies, as the following example illustrates.

U.S. semiconductor producers believed that their Japanese competitors had an advantage in the form of low wages. As a result, these producers relocated their production facilities to Southeast Asia. However, these producers failed to recognize two emerging trends: technological and production improvements introduced by their Japanese counterparts have become a major source of competitive advantage for foreign producers, and there was an ongoing change in industry dynamics—away from low cost to being capital intensive.

The MIT Commission on Industrial Productivity concluded: "Contrary to popular opinion, in the 1960s and early 1970s the U.S. spent amounts equal to Japan's expenditures for research and new equipment."[22] The Commission also noted that the problem in managerial attitudes made adoption of innovations in American companies difficult. While some U.S. executives may believe that higher U.S. stamping costs are

---

[22]MIT Commission on Industrial Productivity, *The Working Papers of the MIT Commission on Industrial Productivity,* vol. 2 (Cambridge, Mass.: The MIT Press, 1990).

steel and auto makers in the U.S. and the lack of technical assistance by steel makers for steel stamping. U.S. firms held similar faulty beliefs and assumptions about their foreign rivals in the electronics, chemical, and textile industries, contributing to a significant erosion in domestic producers' market shares.

When competitors behave in a significantly different way from a company's predictions, it is likely that the firm's assumptions are inaccurate. For example, as Honda proceeded to build its distribution channels, increase the breadth of its product offering, and invest in new technology and up-to-date facilities, these were not the actions of a firm that had only casual interest in the car industry. But, when some companies became alarmed by some of these actions, they alleviated their fears by reverting to long-held assumptions about Honda. Most U.S. producers then believed that Japanese producers (including Honda) were incapable of offering high-quality products and that U.S. customers would not accept Japanese-made small cars. These outdated beliefs were rooted in the early encounters of American companies with Japanese and other Far Eastern competitors who, at that time, offered low-quality products. Even as foreign rivals improved their quality, offered innovative products, and adopted different competitive postures, it was difficult for U.S. companies to alter these views. By continuing to believe that the Japanese threat was a minor annoyance, U.S. firms erred badly in judging their competitors' skills.

Executives develop and maintain questionable assumptions about their competitors for several reasons. One is a lack of accurate competitive data because strategic moves often require secrecy, making them difficult to anticipate. Lack of current data may reinforce long-held beliefs about the competition. As mentioned, established companies become less vigilant in tracking environmental changes, including shifts in rivals' competitive approaches. Another reason for flawed perceptions of the competition is the dogmatic belief system of some executives. Dogmatic beliefs—arising from experience, lack of fresh data, or rigid beliefs—limit executives' span of attention and prevent them from seeing emerging trends.

Sometimes, organizational cultures also encourage stereotyping of competitors and perpetuate faulty assumptions about them. As firms orient their employees, it is common for some to imply their own superiority over rivals. This practice may carry over in identifying and interpreting competitive moves. For example, in one firm, the CEO complained about the invisible competitors who penetrated the heavy-equipment and machinery industry without warning. Yet, the employee orientation programs touted the superior financial, technological, and marketing resources of the company without ever mentioning the firm's competitors or their products. Failing to mention competitors may have been only a symbol of an inward focus of that firm's culture, reinforcing a belief that the firm had "no competitors."

The power of organizational culture in perpetuating faulty assumptions about rivals is subtle but can be deadly. It conditions managerial action through learning and the creation of an organizational memory. Nystrom and colleagues suggest that top managers cannot be expected to go beyond their past experiences because they become captives of these experiences.[23] Equally serious, executives may overestimate the value of (and generalize) their experiences; they will continue to cherish and apply certain beliefs even as they face new competitive issues, or rivals. In strong organizational cultures these collective experiences, faulty or not, become the

---

[23]P. C. Nystrom and W. H. Starbuck, "To Avoid Organizational Crises—Unlearn," *Organizational Dynamics* 12, no. 4 (1984) pp. 53–65.

basis of *organizational memory* that guides the thinking and actions of executives as they understand and engage their competitors.[24] This flawed memory may encourage a routine response when a nonroutine action is necessary, as was the case with ABC's, NBC's, and CBS's response to TBS's market entry. In other cases, flawed memory invites a radical response, when only a routine action is needed, as occasionally happens in a company's overreaction to price reduction by a rival. When organizational memory is flawed, outdated assumptions about rivals are perpetuated.

Some firms' acceptance of the military metaphor in thinking about their strategy also contributes to flawed assumptions about the competition.[25] Some executives see competition as a warlike, zero-sum game; to win, competitors must lose. They appear to accept founder of Revlon, Inc., Charles Revlon's statement, "I don't meet competition. I crush it." Obviously, this thinking ignores possible opportunities for collaboration among companies through strategic alliances. Open-minded executives, on the other hand, see opportunities by being alert to the rhythms of the market, deciphering competitors' moves, and building their own skills and capabilities. Unshackled by faulty assumptions about their rivals, they have a broad perspective of the industry and how to compete.

Dysfunctional obsession with the military metaphor manifests itself in the fierce, brutal reaction by existing companies to newcomers. While justified in some cases, these moves obscure the incumbents' ability to see the possible contributions of newcomers. The success of Ted Turner in the cable industry has attracted the attention of ABC, CBS, and NBC to the great potential of this new industry. Similarly, the threat of entry into the cable industry itself has forced existing companies to explore innovative technology such as fiber optics to compete with direct broadcast technology.

Finally, poor environmental scanning perpetuates faulty assumptions about the competition. Research shows that environmental scanning functions are often poorly staffed and lack alignments with the needs of executives.[26] Poor scanning results in overlooking fundamental industry shifts and changes in the composition of the competition, leading to organizational paralysis.

PARALYSIS BY ANALYSIS

Effective competitive analysis requires extensive data collection, analysis, and interpretation—giving data meaning that enables executives to understand or develop specific strategic moves. One cause of this paralysis is obsessive data collection. Several executives have expressed serious concerns in this regard. A survey by Sutton concluded that "one of the main inhibitions to competitive analysis is that there's far too much information, and it's hard to separate the essential from the inessential."[27] This information overload reduces the contribution of competitive analysis to managerial action. For example, Coors Company executives reported that a frequent problem was that the majority of competitive intelligence efforts centered on collecting rather than analyzing and disseminating data. In response, Coors redefined the priorities of its competitive analysis staff, by allocating 40 percent of their time to data collection and 60 percent to analysis and reporting. Similarly, Prescott and Smith's research on

[24]J. P. Walsh and G. R. Ungson, "Organization Memory," *Academy of Management Review* 16, no. 1 (1991), pp. 57–91.

[25]Al Ries and J. Trout, *Marketing Warfare* (New York, N.Y.: McGraw-Hill, 1986); and R. Duro and B. Sandstrom, *The Basic Principles of Marketing Warfare* (New York, N.Y.: John Wiley & Sons, 1987).

[26]R. Lenz and J. Engledow, "Environmental Analysis Units and Strategic Decision-Making Analysis: A Field Study of Selected 'Leading-Edge' Corporations," *Strategic Management Journal* 7, no. 1 (1988), pp. 69–89.

[27]Sutton, *Competitive Intelligence,* p. 4.

the time allocation among the different activities of competitive intelligence documents a serious mismatch between this function and managerial needs. More than 75 percent of the competitive analysis effort was devoted to data planning, collection, and analysis. Even in premier companies, little attention is given to offering thoughtful interpretations of data to guide managerial action.[28]

Obsessive data collection results from the poor definition of industry boundary or misspecification of rivals and their competence; an overreliance on elaborate statistical analyses to impress senior executives of the rigor of the process; and a lack of clarity about the ultimate use of the results of the analysis.

Paralysis by analysis can handicap a company's ability to seize opportunities and dictate the rules of competition, as happened in the following two cases:

- GM's delay in teaming up with Swatch, a well-known Swiss manufacturer who revolutionized the watchmaking industry in the 1980s, is a case in point. In 1991, Swatch announced a joint venture with Volkswagen (VW) to produce an electric car and introduce it to the market within the next two and a half years. For years, GM and Swatch discussed a similar plan to produce an electric car. But Swatch has been frustrated by the slowness of GM caused by excessive analysis of competitive trends.[29]

- In the 1980s, Procter & Gamble Company (P&G) tested and retested a new chocolate-chip cookie. Although pretests were successful, the company continued to analyze the market and retest the product. Consumed with these pretests, P&G found itself facing a slew of competing brands introduced by powerful companies such as Nabisco, Keebler, and PepsiCo. Likewise, this paralysis may have also handicapped P&G's Crest toothpaste response to Colgate's gel and pump-dispenser innovations.

Sometimes, the organizational structure of the firm contributes to paralysis by analysis. Research shows that most competitive analysis units are poorly placed within their companies' formal structures.[30] For instance, Sutton found that while there was agreement that competitive intelligence should be directed by the group that is responsible for a company's strategy, 59 percent of the 308 companies he studied indicated that competitive intelligence was directed by managers of the marketing, market research, or sales units in their organizations. Only 4 percent reported that strategic-planning managers directed competitive-analysis activities while only 3 percent indicated that it was the responsibility of the general manager. Clearly, the crucial task of competitive analysis was assigned to middle managers. Only 16 percent of the firms indicated that it is the responsibility of the vice president, senior vice president, or general manager. Consequently, competitive analysis did not receive the necessary political support, resources, or recognition.

There are several symptoms of paralysis by analysis: the firm always behind in tracking competitors' moves; number crunching rapidly replacing "what if" scenario developments that outline potential moves by competitors and their likely impact on the company; the emergence of rapidly growing staff who are highly specialized in

---

[28]These figures are based on an empirical study by Prescott and Smith, 1987. These results are supported by the findings of a survey of 340 companies: John Prescott and Craig Fleisher, *Society of Competitive Intelligence Professionals: Who We are and What We Do* (Pittsburgh, Penn.: University of Pittsburgh, 1991).

[29]M. Fisher, "How Long a Wait for the Car of the Future?" *Washington Post,* August 11, 1991, p. H5.

[30]H. Sutton, *Competitive Intelligence,* 1988. These results are corroborated by the Prescott and Fleisher survey cited in n. 28.

functional analyses; and the tendency to confuse operational and strategic data. This last problem occurs when data on competitors' activities—rather than their goals, strategies, strengths and weaknesses, and the quality of their senior executives—predominate. Confusing operational and strategic data are clear signs of disorientation.

SAFEGUARDING AGAINST FAULTY COMPETITIVE ANALYSIS

Executives can help avoid (or reduce) flaws in competitive analysis by paying special attention to the staffing, organization, and mission of that activity; using the company's own invisible functions; changing views of the competition; studying competitors' response patterns; and studying rivals' blind spots.

PAY SPECIAL ATTENTION TO THE STAFFING, ORGANIZATION, AND MISSION OF THE COMPETITIVE-ANALYSIS UNIT

Often, companies expect way too much from their poorly staffed, poorly funded, and poorly organized competitive-analysis units. Research highlights several deficiencies in managing competitive-analysis units. One study shows that the units experienced serious shortages in personnel, averaging three people in the largest U.S. companies. The units also experienced difficulties in integrating their findings into their companies' decision-making processes, receiving only limited feedback from senior executives. In fact, respondents reported that senior executives lacked an awareness of their units' purpose. They also complained that they lacked an internal champion to promote their mission. Finally, organizational political problems caused confusion about the status and usefulness of competitive-intelligence units. These findings led Prescott and Smith to conclude, "At many of the 'role model' companies, competitive intelligence is still conducted sporadically by many different functions and transmitted to 'customers without a plan for the organization as a whole.'"[31] Poor organization and staffing contribute to these shortcomings.

Another major source of flawed analysis is the absence of a clear mission for that function. A reason for this problem is the informality that characterizes competitive-analysis activities in many companies. Most existing programs are loosely organized and informal.[32]

Executives can use several approaches to address these shortcomings. First, they should study the need for a formal unit that conducts competitive analysis. If a formal unit is established, it should be placed close to senior executives while, at the same time, interacting with different business units. Thus the unit can function as a linchpin, funneling information and offering recommendations for managerial action. Besides closeness to senior executives and business-unit leadership, the units should be better staffed. Finally, the mission of these units should be formalized. Indeed, some progressive firms have recognized the need for a formal mission for their competitive-analysis units, as the following two examples illustrate.

---

[31]See the Prescott and Smith study cited in n. 28. Other researchers support this conclusion; see B. D. Gelb, M. J. Saxton, G. M. Zinkhan, and N. D. Albers, "Competitive Intelligence: Insights from Executives," *Business Horizons* 34, no. 1 (1991), pp. 43–47; and A. G. Gib and R. A. Margulies, "Making Competitive Intelligence Relevant to the User," *Planning Review* 19, no. 3 (1991), pp. 16–22.

[32]Research shows that most competitive-analysis systems are informally organized; see, S. Ghoshal and D. E. Westney, "Organizing Competitor Analysis Systems," *Strategic Management Journal* 12, no. 1 (1991), pp. 17–31.

- Corning Inc. has formalized the mission of its competitive-analysis function, emphasizing the need to supply different units with timely information on competitive forces.
- RHH Home Equity has also formalized the objectives of the competitive-analysis unit, focusing on meeting the needs of business planning. The company also requires the unit to promote awareness of competitive intelligence and the need for employees' involvement in the process.

Setting a formal mission for the competitive analysis unit clarifies the scope of its activities and creates a sense of accountability among its staff. A study by Tetlock and Kim concluded that "accountability motivates subjects to process . . . information in more analytic and complex ways that can substantially reduce judgment biases . . ."[33] Having a formal mission also creates a measurement by which executives can evaluate the contribution of the unit.

USE YOUR OWN INVISIBLE FUNCTIONS IN CONDUCTING COMPETITIVE ANALYSIS

As companies recognize the importance of their own invisible functions in developing their strategic moves, executives must learn to use them in understanding their competition. For example, Pfizer, Inc., used its invisible functions in identifying its generic drug producers. It started with its credit department, developing a list of wholesalers to whom Pfizer sold products. The company then contacted wholesalers who were also buying from the generic drug producers. This helped Pfizer develop a strategy to deal with generic drug makers. Clearly, a company should use its invisible functions to complement its formal competitive-analysis activities.

CHANGE YOUR VIEWS OF THE COMPETITION

Ohmae notes that without competition, there is no need for strategy.[34] A company that understands its competitors is well positioned to succeed. Success hinges on appreciating the uniqueness and resourcefulness of the competition, and their success formula. As mentioned, the roots of flawed competitive analysis lie in executives' perceptions and views of the competition. Executives can remedy this flaw by using the following approaches:

Transform the cliché that "competition is good" into a living reality. Sometimes executives overlook the value of competitors in enhancing the status of the industry, maintaining technological innovation and progress, meeting customer needs, and keeping the company alert and focused. Remembering these contributions helps an executive to adopt a healthy view of the competition. It opens the door for accepting the diversity of rivals and their possible roles.[35]

Executives should also teach their employees about competitors, as Xerox did successfully by studying Fuji's quality program—widely touted as a key factor in Fuji's global market success. Ford also showed its employees and workers films of its competitors' manufacturing facilities and processes to make them aware of the seriousness of the company's competitive challenge. Awareness of the competition

---

[33]P. Tetlock and J. Kim, "Accountability and Judgment Processes in a Personality Prediction Task," *Journal of Personality and Social Psychology* 52 (1987), p. 707.

[34]Kenichi Ohmae, *The Mind of the Strategist: Business Planning for Competitive Advantage* (New York, N.Y.: Penguin Books, 1982).

[35]M. E. Porter, *Competitive Advantage* (New York: Free Press, 1985), pp. 201–28.

can enhance organizational learning and employee motivation. Understanding and recognizing the competition should thus become an integral component of the firm's culture.

Develop an ability to see the industry from the eye of the competitor. Viewing the industry from the perspective of competition requires several actions:

1. Executives and analysts should focus on current competitors' strategic intent, which is the driving force behind their market moves. Focusing on strategic intent requires attention to competitors' core skills and how they can be leveraged in the pursuit of new applications, especially in radically different industries. This can help the executives probe their own (and their staff's) cognitive taxonomies. These discussions can promote consideration of divergent views of the evolution of the industry and the competition.

2. Analysts should learn to see the industry from the entrant's eye. One of the most useful ways to visualize an industry's changing boundaries is to see it from the perspective of the potential entrant: What are the areas that have been overlooked by existing rivals? Where do these companies fail to meet customer needs? What will alter the balance of power in the industry? What can a new company do differently to succeed in the industry? How will it alter the traditional KFS? How can I alter these KFS and succeed?

3. Executives should study the reason for a potential entrant's failure. Executives can learn much from examining the reason for a company's failure to enter the market, and can gain valuable clues from studying who responded to that entry, the timing, seriousness, and nature of their actions. These clues can help in understanding how existing competitors define their boundaries and their strategy. Observing failed entrants can help in learning what not to do, thus avoiding some competitive minefields.

4. Executives should perform an autopsy on failing companies. The failure of existing rivals offers an opportunity to study the causes of success and failure in one's marketplace. It might be useful to pause and examine the reasons for the demise of one's rivals: Where did they err? Which market signals did they ignore? What are the implications of their exit for the firm's market definition? Will their customers switch to our products? An autopsy of a failing rival also can serve as a foundation for reexamining one's assumptions about the industry's KFS and the remaining competitors.

Executives should also encourage their staff to consider radical scenarios of industry changes, and competitors' entry or exit. They should examine subindustries within the industry, and how they may connect over time. Examining these scenarios promotes discussions and controversy about the firm's definition of the industry's boundaries of rivals. Executives should ask: Which companies (current and potential) find our business attractive? When, where, and how will they enter? An accurate answer to these questions would require testing one's assumptions about the industry boundaries by probing suppliers and customers' perceptions of substitutes and newcomers to the industry.

Executives can also infuse competitive-analysis teams with new individuals to ensure that new perspectives are introduced into the process; provoke controversy and debate to maximize exposure to different perspectives; and train other executives in creativity techniques to increase openness to ideas and attention to the not-so-obvious concerns. In addition, the executive should ensure broad participation in the process. Senior and middle managers, staff, and employees can contribute to competitive analysis. Executives should create a forum where these groups can contribute to their companies' competitive analyses, thus capturing their diverse views and opinions. This can be achieved by formally soliciting their ideas; sharing preliminary results of competitive analysis with as many individuals within the company as possible; and tying the analysis to existing environmental scanning systems.

STUDY COMPETITORS' RESPONSE PATTERNS

Executives can gain important insights about their competitors' thinking patterns by examining rivals' responses to the company's (or others') moves.[36] Research by Smith, Grimm, and Gannon in different industries shows that managers should examine rivals' particular actions (moves and countermoves) and the order of these countermoves (what they did versus what they could have done). Typically, rivals have several alternatives from which to select their response. The choice of a particular response can be revealing because it shows how the competitor sees its strengths. In addition to the type and order of response, executives should examine the speed of competitors' countermoves. A speedy, visible, and forceful move signals a rival's strong commitment to a particular segment or market. Conversely, a slower response may signal, among other things, a lack of commitment by the competitor or a paralyzed organization. Of course, appropriate interpretations of the specific actions by rivals can be made only based on a thorough understanding of their capabilities and industry conditions.

STUDY RIVALS' BLIND SPOTS

Executives can learn a great deal from studying their competitors' blind spots.[37] These blind spots can be inferred from the actions rivals take, as in the winner's curse, escalation of commitment, and overconfidence about the views they hold about the industry. The winner's curse occurs when some firms "consistently and voluntarily enter into loss-making purchases," as happens in consistently overpaying for acquisition targets. These companies tend to hold more optimistic estimates of the commodity (in this case the acquisition target) than competitors. These optimistic estimates reflect a poor understanding of competitors' motives or capabilities. Moreover, they show a nonrational escalation of commitment because of a lack of consideration of competitors' positions. Misjudging the competitors' competence or interest can lead to this almost paranoid behavior. Another contributing factor is the rivals' overconfidence in their judgment about the dynamics of competition. Flawed analysis often contributes to this overconfidence and to some companies' mistaken beliefs that rivals will have similar aspirations. Possessing similar organizational forms does not mean that companies will act alike in every regard. Generally, analyzing competitors' blind spots can reveal much about their perceptions of the dynamics of rivalry.

---

[36]These authors' decade-long empirical research appears in several references, including Ken G. Smith, Curtis M. Grimm, Martin J. Gannon and Ming-Jer Chen, "Organizational Information Processing, Competitive Responses, and Performance in the U.S. Domestic Airline Industry," *Academy of Management Journal* 34, (1991), pp. 60–85; K. G. Smith, C. M. Grimm, M. J. Chen, and M. J. Gannon, "Predictors of Competitive Strategic Actions: Theory and Preliminary Evidence," *Journal of Business Research* 18 (1989), pp. 245–58; K. G. Smith, C. M. Grimm, and M. J. Gannon, *Dynamics of Competitive Strategy* (Beverly Hills, Calif.: Sage Publications, 1992); and Ken G. Smith and Curtis M. Grimm, "A Communication-Information Model of Competitive Response Timing," *Journal of Management* 17, no. 1 (1991), pp. 5–23.

[37]E. J. Zajac and M. H. Bazerman, "Blind Spots in Industry and Competitor Analysis: Implications of Interfirm (Mis)perception for Strategic Decisions," *Academy of Management Review* 16, no. 1 (1991), pp. 37–56.

Obviously, information gleaned from these analyses can help in developing a company's strategy to maximize the element of surprise, thus minimizing the likelihood of a rival's response.

CONCLUSION

Competitive analysis is the cornerstone of effective strategy formulation and implementation. It helps executives to identify their competitors, and to understand, interpret, and predict their actions. This reading identified six potential blind spots in conducting this analysis and discussed several remedies for faulty competitive analysis. Understanding and addressing the root causes behind these flaws is only one step toward building an effective system for competitive analysis. This system should become an integral component of senior executives' decision-making processes, stimulating (and sometimes challenging) their thinking about their firm's mission and views of the industry and competition. Effective competitive analysis should help track competitors' moves and also stretch executives' thinking about their companies' new opportunities and how to create and sustain a competitive advantage in today's dynamic marketplace.

COMPETING ON CAPABILITIES: THE NEW RULES OF CORPORATE STRATEGY

George Stalk, Philip Evans, and Lawrence E. Shulman
The Boston Consulting Group

In the 1980s, companies discovered time as a new source of competitive advantage. In the 1990s, they will learn that time is just one piece of a more far-reaching transformation in the logic of competition.

Companies that compete effectively on time—speeding new products to market, manufacturing just in time, or responding promptly to customer complaints—tend to be good at other things as well: for instance, the consistency of their product quality, the acuity of their insight into evolving customer needs, the ability to exploit emerging markets, enter new businesses, or generate new ideas and incorporate them in innovations. But all these qualities are mere reflections of a more fundamental characteristic: a new conception of corporate strategy that we call "capabilities-based competition."

For a glimpse of the new world of capabilities-based competition, consider the astonishing reversal of fortunes represented by Kmart and Wal-Mart:

In 1979, Kmart was king of the discount retailing industry, an industry it had virtually created. With 1,891 stores and average revenues per store of $7.25 million, Kmart enjoyed enormous size advantages. This allowed economies of scale in purchasing, distribution, and marketing that, according to just about any management textbook, are crucial to competitive success in a mature and low-growth industry. By contrast, Wal-Mart was a small niche retailer in the South with only 229 stores and average revenues about half of those of Kmart stores—hardly a serious competitor.

And yet, only 10 years later, Wal-Mart had transformed itself and the discount retailing industry. Growing nearly 25 percent a year, the company achieved the highest sales per square foot, inventory turns, and operating profit of any discount retailer. Its 1989 pretax return on sales was 8 percent, nearly double that of Kmart.

Today Wal-Mart is the largest and highest-profit retailer in the world—a performance that has translated into a 32 percent return on equity and a market valuation more than 10 times book value. What's more, Wal-Mart's growth has been concentrated in half the United States, leaving ample room for further expansion. If Wal-Mart continues to gain market share at just one-half its historical rate, by 1995 the company will have eliminated all competitors from discount retailing with the exception of Kmart and Target.

THE SECRET OF WAL-MART'S SUCCESS

What accounts for Wal-Mart's remarkable success? Most explanations focus on a few familiar and highly visible factors: the genius of founder Sam Walton, who inspires his employees and has molded a culture of service excellence; the "greeters" who welcome customers at the door; the motivational power of allowing employees to own part of the business; the strategy of "everyday low prices" that offers the customer a better deal and saves on merchandising and advertising costs. Economists also point to Wal-Mart's big stores, which offer economies of scale and a wider choice of merchandise.

But such explanations only redefine the question. *Why* is Wal-Mart able to justify building bigger stores? Why does Wal-Mart alone have a cost structure low enough to accommodate everyday low prices and greeters? And what has enabled the company to continue to grow far beyond the direct reach of Sam Walton's magnetic personality? The real secret of Wal-Mart's success lies deeper, in a set of strategic business decisions that transformed the company into a capabilities-based competitor.

The starting point was a relentless focus on satisfying customer needs. Wal-Mart's goals were simple to define but hard to execute: to provide customers access to quality goods, to make these goods available when and where customers want them, to develop a cost structure that enables competitive pricing, and to build and maintain a reputation for absolute trustworthiness. The key to achieving these goals was to make the way the company replenished inventory the centerpiece of its competitive strategy.

This strategic vision reached its fullest expression in a largely invisible logistics technique known as "cross-docking." In this system, goods are continuously delivered to Wal-Mart's warehouses, where they are selected, repacked, and then dispatched to stores, often without ever sitting in inventory. Instead of spending valuable time in the warehouse, goods just cross from one loading dock to another in 48 hours or less.

Cross-docking enables Wal-Mart to achieve the economies that come with purchasing full truckloads of goods while avoiding the usual inventory and handling costs. Wal-Mart runs a full 85 percent of its goods through its warehouse system—as opposed to only 50 percent for Kmart. This reduces Wal-Mart's costs of sales by 2 percent to 3 percent compared with the industry average. That cost difference makes possible the everyday low prices.

But that's not all. Low prices in turn mean that Wal-Mart can save even more by eliminating the expense of frequent promotions. Stable prices also make sales more predictable, thus reducing stockouts and excess inventory. Finally, everyday low prices bring in the customers, which translates into higher sales per retail square foot. These advantages in basic economics make the greeters and the profit sharing easy to afford.

With such obvious benefits, why don't all retailers use cross-docking? The reason: it is extremely difficult to manage. To make cross-docking work, Wal-Mart has had to make strategic investments in a variety of interlocking support systems far beyond what could be justified by conventional ROI criteria.

For example, cross-docking requires continuous contact among Wal-Mart's distribution centers, suppliers, and every point of sale in every store to ensure that orders can flow in and be consolidated and executed within a matter of hours. So Wal-Mart operates a private satellite-communication system that daily sends point-of-sale data directly to Wal-Mart's 4,000 vendors.

Another key component of Wal-Mart's logistics infrastructure is the company's fast and responsive transportation system. The company's 19 distribution centers are serviced by nearly 2,000 company-owned trucks. This dedicated truck fleet permits Wal-Mart to ship goods from warehouse to store in less than 48 hours and to replenish its store shelves twice a week on average. By contrast, the industry norm is once every two weeks.

To gain the full benefits of cross-docking, Wal-Mart has also had to make fundamental changes in its approach to managerial control. Traditionally in the retail industry, decisions about merchandising, pricing, and promotions have been highly centralized and made at the corporate level. Cross-docking, however, turns this command-and-control logic on its head. Instead of the retailer pushing products into the system, customers "pull" products when and where they need them. This approach places a premium on frequent, informal cooperation among stores, distribution centers, and suppliers—with far less centralized control.

The job of senior management at Wal-Mart, then, is not to tell individual store managers what to do but to create an environment where they can learn from the market—and from each other. The company's information systems, for example, provide store managers with detailed information about customer behavior, while a fleet of airplanes regularly ferries store managers to Bentonville, Arkansas, headquarters for meetings on market trends and merchandising.

F I G U R E 4-1 | **Capabilities Help Wal-Mart Outperform Its Industry**

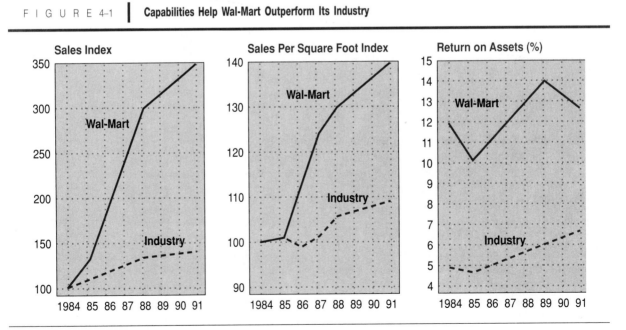

Source: The Boston Consulting Group.

As the company has grown and its stores have multiplied, even Wal-Mart's own private air force hasn't been enough to maintain the necessary contacts among store managers. So Wal-Mart has installed a video link connecting all its stores to corporate headquarters and to each other. Store managers frequently hold videoconferences to exchange information on what's happening in the field, like which products are selling and which ones aren't, which promotions work and which don't.

The final piece of this capabilities mosaic is Wal-Mart's human resources system. The company realizes that its frontline employees play a significant role in satisfying customer needs. So it set out to enhance its organizational capability with programs like stock ownership and profit sharing geared toward making its personnel more responsive to customers. Even the way Wal-Mart stores are organized contributes to this goal. Where Kmart has 5 separate merchandise departments in each store, Wal-Mart has 36. This means that training can be more focused and more effective, and employees can be more attuned to customers.

Kmart did not see its business this way. While Wal-Mart was fine-tuning its business processes and organizational practices, Kmart was following the classic text-book approach that had accounted for its original success. Kmart managed its business by focusing on a few product-centered strategic business units, each a profit center under strong centralized line management. Each SBU made strategy—selecting merchandise, setting prices, and deciding which products to promote. Senior management spent most of its time and resources making line decisions rather than investing in a support infrastructure.

Similarly, Kmart evaluated its competitive advantage at each stage along a value chain and subcontracted activities that managers concluded others could do better. While Wal-Mart was building its ground transportation fleet, Kmart was moving out of trucking because a subcontracted fleet was cheaper. While Wal-Mart was building close relationships with its suppliers, Kmart was constantly switching suppliers in search of price improvements. While Wal-Mart was controlling all the departments in its stores, Kmart was leasing out many of its departments to other companies on the theory that it could make more per square foot in rent than through its own efforts.

This is not to say that Kmart managers do not care about their business processes. After all, they have quality programs too. Nor is it that Wal-Mart managers ignore the structural dimension of strategy: they focus on the same consumer segments as Kmart and still have to make traditional strategic decisions like where to open new stores. The difference is that Wal-Mart emphasizes behavior—the organizational practices and business processes in which capabilities are rooted—as the primary object of strategy and therefore focuses its managerial attention on the infrastructure that supports capabilities. This subtle distinction has made all the difference between exceptional and average performance.

FOUR PRINCIPLES OF CAPABILITIES-BASED COMPETITION

The story of Kmart and Wal-Mart illustrates the new paradigm of competition in the 1990s. In industry after industry, established competitors are being outmaneuvered and overtaken by more dynamic rivals.

- In the years after World War II, Honda was a modest manufacturer of a 50 cc engine designed to be attached to a bicycle. Today it is challenging General Motors and Ford for dominance of the global automobile industry.

- Xerox invented xerography and the office copier market. But between 1976 and 1982, Canon introduced more than 90 new models, cutting Xerox's share of the mid-range copier market in half.[1] Today Canon is a key competitor not only in mid-range copiers but also in high-end color copiers.
- The greatest challenge to department store giants like Macy's comes neither from other large department stores nor from small boutiques but from The Limited, a $5.25 billion design, procurement, delivery, and retailing machine that exploits dozens of consumer segments with the agility of many small boutiques.
- Citicorp may still be the largest U.S. bank in terms of assets, but Banc One has consistently enjoyed the highest return on assets in the U.S. banking industry and now enjoys a market capitalization greater than Citicorp's.

These examples represent more than just the triumph of individual companies. They signal a fundamental shift in the logic of competition, a shift that is revolutionizing corporate strategy.

When the economy was relatively static, strategy could afford to be static. In a world characterized by durable products, stable customer needs, well-defined national and regional markets, and clearly identified competitors, competition was a "war of position" in which companies occupied competitive space like squares on a chessboard, building and defending market share in clearly defined product or market segments. The key to competitive advantage was *where* a company chose to compete. *How* it chose to compete was also important but secondary, a matter of execution.

Few managers need reminding of the changes that have made this traditional approach obsolete. As markets fragment and proliferate, "owning" any particular market segment becomes simultaneously more difficult and less valuable. As product life cycles accelerate, dominating existing product segments becomes less important than being able to create new products and exploit them quickly. Meanwhile, as globalization breaks down barriers between national and regional markets, competitors are multiplying and reducing the value of national market share.

In this more dynamic business environment, strategy has to become correspondingly more dynamic. Competition is now a "war of movement" in which success depends on anticipation of market trends and quick response to changing customer needs. Successful competitors move quickly in and out of products, markets, and sometimes even entire businesses—a process more akin to an interactive video game than to chess. In such an environment, the essence of strategy is *not* the structure of a company's products and markets but the dynamics of its behavior. And the goal is to identify and develop the hard-to-imitate organizational capabilities that distinguish a company from its competitors in the eyes of customers.

Companies like Wal-Mart, Honda, Canon, The Limited, or Banc One have learned this lesson. Their experience and that of other successful companies suggest four basic principles of capabilities-based competition:

1. The building blocks of corporate strategy are not products and markets but business processes.
2. Competitive success depends on transforming a company's key processes into strategic capabilities that consistently provide superior value to the customer.
3. Companies create these capabilities by making strategic investments in a

---

[1]See T. Michael Nevens, Gregory L. Summe, and Bro Uttal, "Commercializing Technology: What the Best Companies Do," *Harvard Business Review,* May–June, 1990, p. 154.

support infrastructure that links together and transcends traditional SBUs and functions.

4. Because capabilities necessarily cross functions, the champion of a capabilities-based strategy is the CEO.

A capability is a set of business processes strategically understood. Every company has business processes that deliver value to the customer. But few think of them as the primary object of strategy. Capabilities-based competitors identify their key business processes, manage them centrally, and invest in them heavily, looking for a long-term payback.

Take the example of cross-docking at Wal-Mart. Cross-docking is not the cheapest or the easiest way to run a warehouse. But seen in the broader context of Wal-Mart's inventory-replenishment capability, it is an essential part of the overall process of keeping retail shelves filled while also minimizing inventory and purchasing in truckload quantities.

What transforms a set of individual business processes like cross-docking into a strategic capability? The key is to connect them to real customer needs. A capability is strategic only when it begins and ends with the customer.

Of course, just about every company these days claims to be "close to the customer." But there is a qualitative difference in the customer focus of capabilities-driven competitors. These companies conceive of the organization as a giant feedback loop that begins with identifying the needs of the customer and ends with satisfying them.

As managers have grasped the importance of time-based competition, for example, they have increasingly focused on the speed of new product development. But as a unit of analysis, new product *development* is too narrow. It is only part of what is necessary to satisfy a customer and, therefore, to build an organizational capability. Better to think in terms of new product *realization,* a capability that includes the way a product is not only developed but also marketed and serviced. The longer and more complex the string of business processes, the harder it is to transform them into a capability—but the greater the value of that capability once built because competitors have more difficulty imitating it.

Weaving business processes together into organizational capabilities in this way also mandates a new logic of vertical integration. At a time when cost pressures are pushing many companies to outsource more and more activities, capabilities-based competitors are integrating vertically to ensure that they, not a supplier or distributor, control the performance of key business processes. Remember Wal-Mart's decision to own its transportation fleet in contrast to Kmart's decision to subcontract.

Even when a company doesn't actually own every link of the capability chain, the capabilities-based competitor works to tie these parts into its own business systems. Consider Wal-Mart's relationships with its suppliers. In order for Wal-Mart's inventory-replenishment capability to work, vendors have to change their own business processes to be more responsive to the Wal-Mart system. In exchange, they get far better payment terms from Wal-Mart than they do from other discount retailers. At Wal-Mart, the average "days payable," the time between the receipt of an invoice from a supplier and its payment, is 29 days. At Kmart, it is 45.

Another attribute of capabilities is that they are collective and cross-functional— a small part of many people's jobs, not a large part of a few. This helps explain why most companies underexploit capabilities-based competition. Because a capability is "everywhere and nowhere," no one executive controls it entirely. Moreover, leveraging capabilities requires a panoply of strategic investments across SBUs and functions far beyond what traditional cost-benefit metrics can justify. Traditional internal accounting and control systems often miss the strategic nature of such invest-ments. For these reasons, building strategic capabilities cannot be treated as an oper-ating matter and left to operating managers, to corporate staff, or still less to SBU heads. It is the primary agenda of the CEO.

Only the CEO can focus the entire company's attention on creating capabilities that serve customers. Only the CEO can identify and authorize the infrastructure investments on which strategic capabilities depend. Only the CEO can insulate indi-vidual managers from any short-term penalties to the P&Ls of their operating units that such investments might bring about.

Indeed, a CEO's success in building and managing capabilities will be the chief test of management skill in the 1990s. The prize will be companies that combine scale and flexibility to outperform the competition along five dimensions:

- *Speed.* The ability to respond quickly to customer or market demands and to incorporate new ideas and technologies quickly into products.
- *Consistency.* The ability to produce a product that unfailingly satisfies customers' expectations.
- *Acuity.* The ability to see the competitive environment clearly and thus to anticipate and respond to customers' evolving needs and wants.
- *Agility.* The ability to adapt simultaneously to many different business environments.
- *Innovativeness.* The ability to generate new ideas and to combine existing elements to create new sources of value.

BECOMING A CAPABILITIES-BASED COMPETITOR

Few companies are fortunate enough to begin as capabilities-based competitors. For most, the challenge is to become one.

The starting point is for senior managers to undergo the fundamental shift in per-ception that allows them to see their business in terms of strategic capabilities. Then they can begin to identify and link together essential business processes to serve cus-tomer needs. Finally, they can reshape the organization—including managerial roles and responsibilities—to encourage the new kind of behavior necessary to make capa-bilities-based competition work.

The experience of a medical-equipment company we'll call Medequip illustrates this change process. An established competitor, Medequip recently found itself strug-gling to regain market share it had lost to a new competitor. The rival had introduced a lower-priced, lower-performance version of the company's most popular product. Medequip had developed a similar product in response, but senior managers were hesitant to launch it.

Their reasoning made perfect sense according to the traditional competitive logic. As managers saw it, the company faced a classic no-win situation. The new product was lower priced but also lower profit. If the company promoted it aggressively to regain market share, overall profitability would suffer.

But when Medequip managers began to investigate their competitive situation more carefully, they stopped defining the problem in terms of static products and markets. Increasingly, they saw it in terms of the organization's business processes.

Traditionally, the company's functions had operated autonomously. Manufacturing was separate from sales, which was separate from field service. What's more, the company managed field service the way most companies do—as a classic profit center whose resources were deployed to reduce costs and maximize profitability. For instance, Medequip assigned full-time service personnel only to those customers who bought enough equipment to justify the additional cost.

However, a closer look at the company's experience with these steady customers led to a fresh insight: at accounts where Medequip had placed one or more full-time service representatives on-site, the company renewed its highly profitable service contracts at three times the rate of its other accounts. When these accounts needed new equipment, they chose Medequip twice as often as other accounts did and tended to buy the broadest mix of Medequip products as well.

The reason was simple. Medequip's on-site service representatives had become expert in the operations of their customers. They knew what equipment mix best suited the customer and what additional equipment the customer needed. So they had teamed up informally with Medequip's salespeople to become part of the selling process. Because the service reps were on-site full-time, they were also able to respond quickly to equipment problems. And of course, whenever a competitor's equipment broke down, the Medequip reps were on hand to point out the product's shortcomings.

This new knowledge about the dynamics of service delivery inspired top managers to rethink how their company should compete. Specifically, they redefined field service from a stand-alone function to one part of an integrated sales and service capability. They crystallized this new approach in three key business decisions.

First, Medequip decided to use its service personnel *not* to keep costs low but to maximize the life-cycle profitability of a set of targeted accounts. This decision took the form of a dramatic commitment to place at least one service rep on-site with selected customers—no matter how little business each account currently represented.

The decision to guarantee on-site service was expensive, so choosing which customers to target was crucial; there had to be potential for considerable additional business. The company divided its accounts into three categories: those it dominated, those where a single competitor dominated, and those where several competitors were present. Medequip protected the accounts it dominated by maintaining the already high level of service and by offering attractive terms for renewing service contracts. The company ignored those customers dominated by a single competitor —unless the competitor was having serious problems. All the remaining resources were focused on those accounts where no single competitor had the upper hand.

Next Medequip combined its sales, service, and order-entry organizations into cross-functional teams that concentrated almost exclusively on the needs of the targeted accounts. The company trained service reps in sales techniques so they could take full responsibility for generating new sales leads. This freed up the sales staff to focus on the more strategic role of understanding the long-term needs of the customer's business. Finally, to emphasize Medequip's new commitment to total service, the company even taught its service reps how to fix competitors' equipment.

Once this new organizational structure was in place, Medequip finally introduced its new low-priced product. The result: the company has not only stopped its decline in market share but also *increased* share by almost 50 percent. The addition of the lower-priced product has reduced profit margins, but the overall mix still includes many higher-priced products. And absolute profits are much higher than before.

This story suggests four steps by which any company can transform itself into a capabilities-based competitor.

Shift the strategic framework to achieve aggressive goals. At Medequip, managers transformed what looked like a no-win situation—either lose share or lose profits—

into an opportunity for a major competitive victory. They did so by abandoning the company's traditional function, cost, and profit-center orientation and by identifying and managing the capabilities that link customer need to customer satisfaction. The chief expression of this new capabilities-based strategy was the decision to provide on-site service reps to targeted accounts and to create cross-functional sales and service teams.

Organize around the chosen capability and make sure employees have the necessary skills and resources to achieve it. Having set this ambitious competitive goal, Medequip managers next set about reshaping the company in terms of it. Rather than retaining the existing functional structure and trying to encourage coordination through some kind of matrix, they created a brand new organization—Customer Sales and Service—and divided it into "cells" with overall responsibility for specific customers. The company also provided the necessary training so that employees could understand how their new roles would help achieve new business goals. Finally, Medequip created systems to support employees in their new roles. For example, one information system uses CD-ROMs to give field-service personnel quick access to information about Medequip's product line as well as those of competitors.

Make progress visible and bring measurements and reward into alignment. Medequip also made sure that the company's measurement and reward systems reflected the new competitive strategy. Like most companies, the company had never known the profitability of individual customers. Traditionally, field-service employees were measured on overall service profitability. With the shift to the new approach, however, the company had to develop a whole new set of measures—for example, Medequip's "share-by-customer-by-product," the amount of money the company invested in servicing a particular customer, and the customer's current and estimated lifetime profitability. Team members' compensation was calculated according to these new measures.

Do not delegate the leadership of the transformation. Becoming a capabilities-based competitor requires an enormous amount of change. For that reason, it is a process extremely difficult to delegate. Because capabilities are cross-functional, the change process can't be left to middle managers. It requires the hands-on guidance of the CEO and the active involvement of top-line managers. At Medequip, the heads of sales, service, and order entry led the subteams that made the actual recommendations, but it was the CEO who oversaw the change process, evaluated their proposals, and made the final decision. His leading role ensured senior management's commitment to the recommended changes.

This top-down change process has the paradoxical result of driving business decision-making down to those directly participating in key processes—for example, Medequip's sales and service staff. This leads to a high measure of operational flexibility and an almost reflex-like responsiveness to external change.

A NEW LOGIC OF GROWTH: THE CAPABILITIES PREDATOR

Once managers reshape the company in terms of its underlying capabilities, they can use these capabilities to define a growth path for the corporation. At the center of capabilities-based competition is a new logic of growth.

In the 1960s, most managers assumed that when growth in a company's basic business slowed, the company should turn to diversification. This was the age of the multibusiness conglomerate. In the 1970s and 1980s, however, it became clear that growth through diversification was difficult. And so, the pendulum of management thinking swung once again. Companies were urged to "stick to their knitting"—that is, to focus on their core business, identify where the profit was, and get rid of everything else. The idea of the corporation became increasingly narrow.

Competing on capabilities provides a way for companies to gain the benefits of both focus and diversification. Put another way, a company that focuses on its strategic capabilities can compete in a remarkable diversity of regions, products, and businesses and do it far more coherently than the typical conglomerate can. Such a company is a "capabilities predator"—able to come out of nowhere and move rapidly from nonparticipant to major player and even to industry leader.

Capabilities-based companies grow by transferring their essential business processes—first to new geographic areas and then to new businesses. Wal-Mart CEO David Glass alludes to this method of growth when he characterizes Wal-Mart as "always pushing from the inside out; we never jump and backfill."

Strategic advantages built on capabilities are easier to transfer geographically than more traditional competitive advantages. Honda, for example, has become a manufacturer in Europe and the United States with relatively few problems. The quality of its cars made in the United States is so good that the company is exporting some of them back to Japan.

In many respects, Wal-Mart's move from small towns in the South to large, urban, northern cities spans as great a cultural gap as Honda's move beyond Japan. And yet, Wal-Mart has done it with barely a hiccup. While the stores are much bigger and the product lines different, the capabilities are exactly the same. Wal-Mart simply replicates its system as soon as the required people are trained. The company estimates that it can train enough new employees to grow about 25 percent a year.

But the big payoff for capabilities-led growth comes not through geographical expansion but through rapid entry into whole new businesses. Capabilities-based companies do this in at least two ways. The first is by "cloning" their key business processes. Again, Honda is a typical example.

Most people attribute Honda's success to the innovative design of its products or the way the company manufactures them. These factors are certainly important. But the company's growth has been spearheaded by visible capabilities.

For example, a big part of Honda's original success in motorcycles was due to the company's distinctive capability in "dealer management," which departed from the traditional relationship between motorcycle manufacturers and dealers. Typically, local dealers were motorcycle enthusiasts who were more concerned with finding a way to support their hobby than with building a strong business. They were not particularly interested in marketing, parts-inventory management, or other business systems.

Honda, by contrast, managed its dealers to ensure that they would become successful businesspeople. The company provided operating procedures and policies for merchandising, selling, floor planning, and service management. It trained all its dealers and their entire staffs in these new management systems and supported them with a computerized dealer-management information system. The part-time dealers of competitors were no match for the better-prepared and better-financed Honda dealers.

Honda's move into new businesses, including lawn mowers, outboard motors, and automobiles, has depended on recreating this same dealer-management capability in each new sector. Even in segments like luxury cars, where local dealers are generally more service-oriented than those in the motorcycle business, Honda's skill at managing its dealers is transforming service standards. Honda dealers consistently receive the highest ratings for customer satisfaction among auto companies selling in the

United States. One reason is that Honda gives its dealers far more autonomy to decide on the spot whether a needed repair is covered by warranty. (See the box, "How Capabilities Differ from Core Competences: The Case of Honda.")

But the ultimate form of growth in the capabilities-based company may not be cloning business processes so much as creating processes so flexible and robust that the same set can serve many different businesses. This is the case with Wal-Mart. The company uses the same inventory-replenishment system that makes its discount stores so successful to propel itself into new and traditionally distinct retail sectors.

Take the example of warehouse clubs, no-frills stores that sell products in bulk at a deep discount. In 1983, Wal-Mart created Sam's Club to compete with industry founder Price Club and Kmart's own PACE Membership Warehouse. Within four years, Sam's Club sales had passed those of both Price and PACE, making it the largest wholesale club in the country. Sam's 1990 sales were $5.3 billion, compared with $4.9 billion for Price and $1.6 billion for PACE. What's more, Wal-Mart has repeated this rapid penetration strategy in other retail sectors, including pharmacies, European-style hypermarkets, and large, no-frills grocery stores known as superstores.

While Wal-Mart has been growing by quickly entering these new businesses, Kmart has tried to grow by acquisition, with mixed success. In the past decade, Kmart has bought and sold a number of companies in unrelated businesses such as restaurants and insurance—an indication the company has had difficulty adding value.

How Capabilities Differ from Core Competencies: The Case of Honda

In their influential 1990 *Harvard Business Review* article, "The Core Competence of the Corporation," Gary Hamel and C. K. Prahalad mount an attack on traditional notions of strategy that is not so dissimilar from what we are arguing here. For Hamel and Prahalad, however, the central building block of corporate strategy is "core competence." How is a competence different from a capability, and how do the two concepts relate to each other?

Hamel and Prahalad define core competence as the combination of individual technologies and production skills that underly a company's myriad product lines. Sony's core competence in miniaturization, for example, allows the company to make everything from the Sony Walkman to videocameras to notebook computers. Canon's core competencies in optics, imaging, and microprocessor controls have enabled it to enter markets as seemingly diverse as copiers, laser printers, cameras, and image scanners.

As the above examples suggest, Hamel and Prahalad use core competence to explain the ease with which successful competitors are able to enter new and seemingly unrelated businesses. But a closer look reveals that competencies are not the whole story.

Consider Honda's move from motorcycles into other businesses, including lawn mowers, outboard motors, and automobiles. Hamel and Prahalad attribute Honda's success to its underlying competence in engines and power trains. While Honda's engine competence is certainly important, it alone cannot explain the speed with which the company has successfully moved into a wide range of businesses over the past 20 years. After all, General Motors (to take just one example) is also an accomplished designer and manufacturer of engines. What distinguishes Honda from its competitors is its focus on capabilities.

One important but largely invisible capability is Honda's expertise in "dealer management"—its ability to train and support its dealer network with operating procedures and policies for merchandising, selling, floor planning, and service management. First developed for its motorcycle business, this set of business processes has since been replicated in each new business the company has entered.

Another capability central to Honda's success has been its skill at "product realization." Traditional product development separates planning, proving, and executing into three sequential activities:

This is not to suggest that growth by acquisition is necessarily doomed to failure. Indeed, the company that is focused on its capabilities is often better able to target sensible acquisitions and then integrate them successfully. For example, Wal-Mart has recently begun to supplement its growth "from the inside out" by acquiring companies—for example, other small warehouse clubs and a retail and grocery distributor—whose operations can be folded into the Wal-Mart system.

It is interesting to speculate where Wal-Mart will strike next. The company's inventory-replenishment capability could prove to be a strong competitive advantage in a wide variety of retail businesses. In the past decade, Wal-Mart came out of nowhere to challenge Kmart. In the next decade, companies such as Toys "Я" Us (Wal-Mart already controls as much as 10 percent of the $13 billion toy market) and Circuit City (consumer electronics) may find themselves in the sights of this capabilities predator.

THE FUTURE OF CAPABILITIES-BASED COMPETITION

For the moment, capabilities-based companies have the advantage of competing against rivals still locked into the old way of seeing the competitive environment. But such a situation won't last forever. As more and more companies make the transition to capabilities-based competition, the simple fact of competing on capabilities will become less important than the specific capabilities a company has chosen to build.

---

assessing the market's needs and whether existing products are meeting those needs; testing the proposed product; then building a prototype. The end result of this process is a new factory or organization to introduce the new product. This traditional approach takes a long time—and with time goes money.

Honda has arranged these activities differently. First, planning and proving go on continuously and in parallel. Second, these activities are clearly separated from execution. At Honda, the highly disciplined execution cycle schedules major product revisions every four years and minor revisions every two years. The 1990 Honda Accord, for example, which is the first major redesign of that model since 1986, incorporates a power train developed two years earlier and first used in the 1988 Accord. Finally, when a new product is ready, it is released to *existing* factories and organizations, which dramatically shortens the amount of time needed to launch it. As time is reduced, so are cost and risk.

Consider the following comparison between Honda and GM. In 1984, Honda launched its Acura division; one year later, GM created Saturn. Honda chose to integrate Acura into its existing organization and facilities. In Europe, for example, the Acura Legend is sold through the same sales force as the Honda Legend. The Acura division now makes three models—the Legend, Integra, and Vigor—and is turning out 300,000 cars a year. At the end of 1991, seven years after it was launched, the division had produced a total of 800,000 vehicles. More important, it had already introduced eight variations of its product line.

By contrast, GM created a separate organization and a separate facility for Saturn. Production began in late 1990, and 1991 will be its first full model year. If GM is lucky, it will be producing 240,000 vehicles in the next year or two and will have two models out.

As the Honda example suggests, competencies and capabilities represent two different but complementary dimensions of an emerging paradigm for corporate strategy. Both concepts emphasize "behavioral" aspects of strategy in contrast to the traditional structural model. But whereas core competence emphasizes technological and production expertise at specific points along the value chain, capabilities are more broadly based, encompassing the entire value chain. In this respect, capabilities are visible to the customer in a way that core competencies rarely are.

Like the "grand unified theory" that modern day physicists are searching for to explain physical behavior at both the subatomic level and that of the entire cosmos, the combination of core competence and capabilities may define the universal model for corporate strategy in the 1990s and beyond.

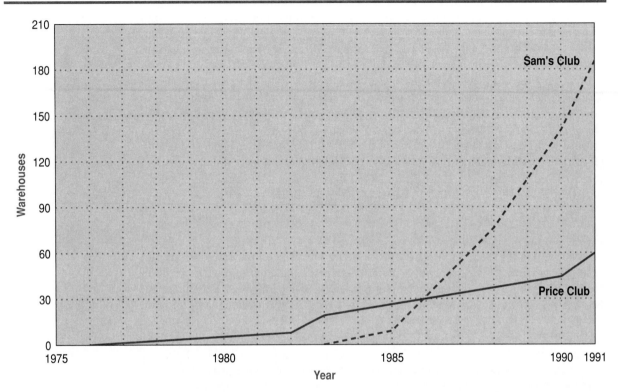

By applying capabilities developed in its core business, Wal-Mart was able to penetrate the wholesale club market quickly. Its unit, Sam's Club, overtook industry leader Price Club in a mere four years.

Source: The Boston Consulting Group.

Given the necessary long-term investments, the strategic choices managers make will end up determining a company's fate.

If Wal-Mart and Kmart are a good example of the present state of capabilities-based competition, the story of two fast-growing regional banks suggests its future. Wachovia Corporation, with dual headquarters in Winston-Salem, North Carolina, and Atlanta, Georgia, has superior returns and growing market share throughout its core markets in both states. Banc One, based in Columbus, Ohio, has consistently enjoyed the highest return on assets in the U.S. banking industry. Both banks compete on capabilities, but they do it in very different ways.

Wachovia competes on its ability to understand and serve the needs of individual customers, a skill that manifests itself in probably the highest "cross-sell ratio"—the average number of products per customer—of any bank in the country. The linchpin of this capability is the company's roughly 600 "personal bankers," frontline employees who provide Wachovia's mass-market customers with a degree of personalized service approaching what has traditionally been available only to private banking clients. The company's specialized support systems allow each personal banker to serve about 1,200 customers. Among those systems: an integrated customer-information file, simplified work processes that allow the bank to respond to almost all customer requests by the end of business that day, and a five-year personal banker training program.

Where Wachovia focuses on meeting the needs of individual customers, Bank One's distinctive ability is to understand and respond to the needs of entire *communities*. To do community banking effectively, a bank has to have deep roots in the local community. But traditionally, local banks have not been able to muster the professional expertise, state-of-the-art products, and highly competitive cost structure of large national banks like Citicorp. Bank One competes by offering its customers the best of both these worlds. Or in the words of one company slogan, Banc One "out-locals the national banks and out-nationals the local banks."

Striking this balance depends on two factors. One is local autonomy. The central organizational role in the Bank One business system is played not by frontline employees but by the presidents of the 51 affiliate banks in the Bank One network. Affiliate presidents have exceptional power within their own region. They select products, establish prices and marketing strategy, make credit decisions, and set internal management policies. They can even overrule the activities of Bank One's centralized direct-marketing businesses. But while Banc One's affiliate system is highly decentralized, its success also depends on an elaborate, and highly centralized, process of continuous organizational learning. Affiliate presidents have the authority to mold bank products and services to local conditions, but they are also expected to learn from best practice throughout the Bank One system and to adapt it to their own operations.

Banc One collects an extraordinary amount of detailed and current information on each affiliate bank's internal and external performance. For example, the bank regularly publishes "league tables" on numerous measures of operating performance, with the worst performers listed first. This encourages collaboration to improve the weakest affiliates rather than competition to be the best. The bank also continuously engages in workflow reengineering and process simplification. The 100 most successful projects, known as the "Best of the Best," are documented and circulated among affiliates.

Wachovia and Banc One both compete on capabilities. Both banks focus on key business processes and place critical decision-making authority with the people directly responsible for them. Both manage these processes through a support system that spans the traditional functional structure, and senior managers concentrate on managing this system rather than controlling decisions. Both are decentralized but focused, single-minded but flexible.

But there the similarities end. Wachovia responds to individual customers en masse with personalization akin to that of a private banker. Banc One responds to local markets en masse with the flexibility and canniness of the traditional community bank. As a result, they focus on different business processes: Wachovia on the transfer of customer-specific information across numerous points of customer contact; Banc One on the transfer of best practices across affiliate banks. They also empower different levels in the organization: the personal banker at Wachovia, the affiliate president at Bank One.

Most important, they grow differently. Because so much of Wachovia's capability is embedded in the training of the personal bankers, the bank has made few acquisitions and can integrate them only very slowly. Banc One's capabilities, by contrast, are especially easy to transfer to new acquisitions. All the company needs to do is install its corporate MIS and intensively train the acquired bank's senior officers, a process that can be done in a few months, as opposed to the much longer period it takes Wachovia to train a new cadre of frontline bankers. Banc One has therefore made acquisitions almost a separate line of business.

If Banc One and Wachovia were to compete against each other, it is not clear who would win. Each would have strengths that the other could not match. Wachovia's capability to serve individual customers by cross-selling a wide range of banking products will in the long term probably allow the company to extract more profit per customer than Banc One. On the other hand, Wachovia cannot adapt its products, pricing, and promotion to local market conditions the way Bank One can. And Wachovia's growth rate is limited by the amount of time it takes to train new personal bankers.

Moreover, these differences are deep-seated. They define each of the two companies in ways that are not easy to change. Capabilities are often mutually exclusive. Choosing the right ones is the essence of strategy.

HONDA AND THE ART OF COMPETITIVE MANEUVER

Chris Benjamin, Itochu Europe

Now that "enterprise" and "entrepreneur"—already mildewed—have been devalued by academics and politicians, and by the fall of the heroes of the 1980s, we need refocusing on what business is really all about. A company that has grown from a turnover in 1949 of $230,000 to $30.5 billion in 1991 should offer a few guidelines: in fact Pascale remarks that Honda Motor Company "is arguably the best managed company in the world." But such plaudits (see Appendix)—however surely merited—rarely give credit to Honda's special competitive style.

Honda's ethos stems from the two personalities who, from an almost chance meeting, guided the company until they jointly retired in 1973. For Soichiro Honda, who had already shown his flair in engine design, "there is no end to the pursuit of technology." Apart from a flow of new motorcycle and car models, success in all classes of the Isle of Man TT, a Formula 1 win and engines powering many subsequent winners, and a string of "firsts" in engine, emission, and body design attest to this spirit.

Takeo Fujisawa—recalled informally by Sir Graham Day as "the nearest to genius in the commercial world"—had said to his friend that he would find the money "to launch your technology." But in viewing the future of the company, his concern was that "those who flourish are destined to fall into decline," and "Honda Motor would sooner or later be governed by the same law." In short, the more successful, the more vulnerable, echoed by President Kawamoto in the company's 1991 annual report: "We have been successful, but our success has brought some negative aspects, such as our declining ability to keep pace with the changes in our operating environment . . . I am sure we will face many challenges, but it is impossible to say exactly what they will be . . . We must be able to respond appropriately and rapidly."

These underlying themes of technology and wary vulnerability are well illustrated by the company's behavior at some crucial moments of its history.

Source: *Long Range Planning* 26, no. 4 (1993), pp. 22–31. Reprinted with permission.

MOTORCYCLE LEADERSHIP IN JAPAN

In 1949 Honda had been one of some 200 producers of motorized transport, many larger and financially stronger. But steadily the quality and inventiveness of its products were gaining market. In 1952–54, Honda undertook a major best-practice investment program, and it survived a crisis while there was general labor unrest in 1954. In 1955, while Japan was enjoying an unprecedented economic boom, rather than increase production and boost profit, Fujisawa started a program to streamline production, stock controls, clerical work, to upgrade skills, to reduce costs and to raise technical competence. "Increasing production is the easiest method of reducing costs. But if you seek to achieve simultaneously the three goals of streamlining production, elevating technical standards, and increasing production, you will end up not fully achieving any of the goals. That is why I chose the most difficult path of reducing costs without increasing production."

At the same time, Fujisawa took advantage of the relative scarcity of Honda's products to "cultivate distributors who were reliable and loyal," stopping delivery to those who were in arrears. This ensured that sales would be met with immediate payment. The Japanese discount rate was raised in March 1957, and then in May, as Japan's trade went into deficit, Honda lowered its prices, in all by some 20 percent as a result of the cost improvements. Fujisawa confirmed that his sales forces were ready to exploit the increased production capacity available, and, "as the recession started, Honda Motor moved to increase production." The two and a half years of restraint paid off as, during the recession, Honda captured 80 percent of the Japanese motorcycle market. In sales terms, between March 1953 and March 1958, sales doubled to ¥14,188 million with inventories halved.

U.S. MOTORCYCLE MARKET

In the 1950s the U.S. represented about half of the world market, and over two-thirds for larger machines: the latter were more expensive, but had the image of being big, bad, and dangerous. Meanwhile, Honda's experience in racing enabled them to design a 50 cc engine capable of 4.5 horsepower. The Super Cub was developed around this engine, and with its unconventional step-through chassis, proved popular in Japan. Honda went ahead with a new plant to produce 30,000 units a month—10 times the rate of other models.

Initial attempts to market a range of models through the existing U.S. network were not successful, but the Super Cub aroused immediate interest. After some problems with exchange controls, American Honda Company was founded in 1960, allowing Honda to develop its own network for selling the Super Cub through sports shops, hobby stores, etc., backed by a popular advertising campaign: "The Nicest Things Happen on a Honda." As BCG remarked, "Honda created the market—in the U.S. and elsewhere for . . . motorcycling as a fun activity," broadening its appeal to a new market of high-school kids, shopping, beach-bikes, etc.

From this foothold, U.S. sales by Honda, followed by other Japanese manufacturers, rose from 6,300 units in 1959 to 148,000 in 1963. This breakthrough opened the final chapter in the collapse of the British motorcycle industry, which eventually fell from 60 percent of the market above 440 cc bikes in 1968 to 4 percent in 1974 (see Figure 5–1). The essential elements of this collapse were:

FIGURE 5-1 | **Market Shares of Motorcycles ≥440 cc in the United States, 1968–1974**

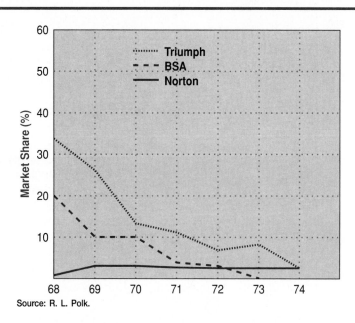

Source: R. L. Polk.

1. Honda, followed by other Japanese makers, established a strong market position in smaller displacement segments through new models that had higher quality and performance, and were keenly priced.

2. With a tendency for customers to trade up to a larger model every 12 to 18 months, Honda led the way in offering attractive new models and terms to entice its customers up-market.

3. The orientation of British manufacturers was to seek "model-by-model profit levels . . . prices are set at the levels necessary to achieve profitability—and would be raised higher if possible . . . plans and objectives are primarily oriented to earning a profit on the existing business and facilities of the company" (BCG).

4. Lacking the production efficiencies and flexibility (British models could not even employ the latest production machinery), and design resources to match the flow of Japanese models, the British producers were offered the sole choice of fighting on price. But given their "tendency toward short-term profit," in effect the only option was retreat to the higher value-added ranges, where for a time they were not under Japanese pressure. This became a progressive retreat up-market, until there was no market up which to go. Figure 5–2 illustrates stages of this withdrawal.

5. The "last Citadel" was the largest capacity segment, where the shift in relative market shares is shown in Figures 5–3A and 5–3B. Harley Davidson and BMW were also affected, and subsequently required radical restructuring.

6. Comparative figures at the end of the process were striking: output per man in British factories was 10 to 18 motorbikes, whereas Honda's company average was 106 bikes and 26 cars, with the Suzuka factory alone making 350 bikes per man year; while British manufacturers had made only one engine upgrading during 1968–75, and reduced their models in the large-bike range from 8 to 3, Japanese producers had increased theirs from 3 to 13, of which Honda alone

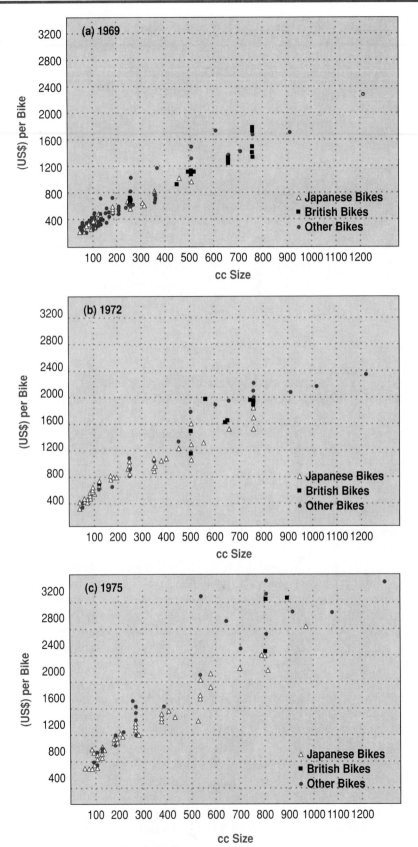

Source: NADA Motorcycle Appraisal Guide.

| **Market Shares by Manufacturers: 450-749 cc, 1968-1974**

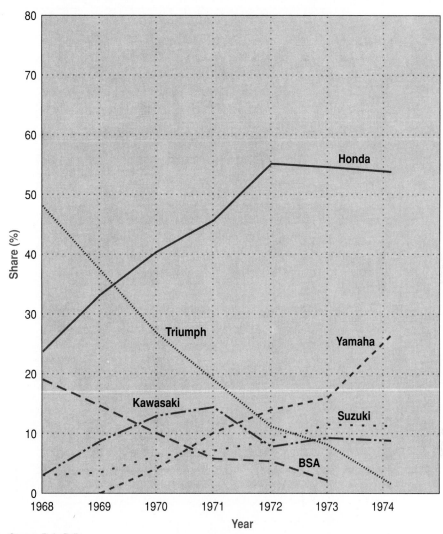

Source: R. L. Polk.

accounted for 5; overall there were 79 Japanese models in 1974 against 18 from all other producers; where Honda had 1,300 staff on R&D, and 1,400 in engineering and design (in all some 20 percent of manpower), British companies' R&D staff totalled 100; with their market advance the Honda franchise became more attractive, so that by 1974 Honda had built up nearly 2,000 U.S. dealers, 84 percent of whom were sole distributors, whereas the British manufacturers had 400, with 4 percent exclusive.

While there was a high level of opportunism in Honda's approach, as the sectoral advance took place, such opportunism could be exploited only with manufacturing efficiencies, volumes, and flexibility; the development flair for timely new models; expansion of market presence and dedicated dealer network; availability of financing to take rapid advantage of the trade-up bias of customers; reliable servicing; etc. As the market advance took place, Honda became relatively stronger through efficiencies of volume

F I G U R E 5–3B | **Market Shares by Manufacturers: ≥750 cc, 1968–1974**

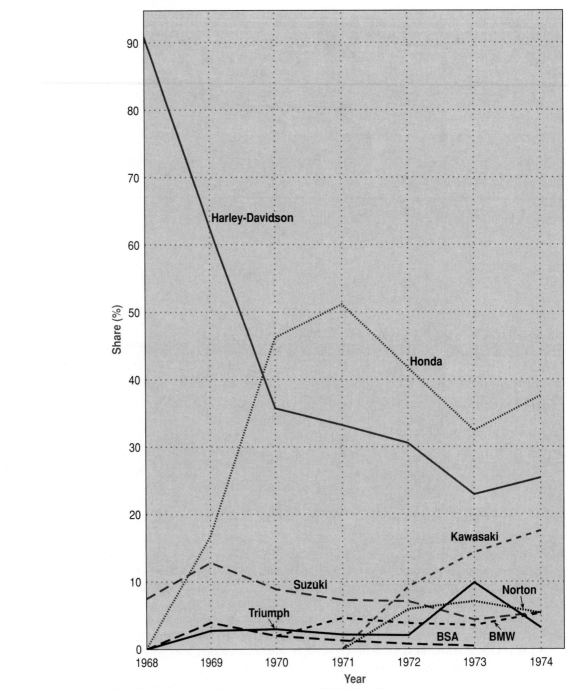

Note: Yamaha was removed for clarity. From zero in 1971 it follows Triumph very closely.
Source: R. L. Polk.

and education, increasing profits, whereas British and other competitors were forced into the confused inefficiencies of retreat—layoffs, factory closures, strikes, boardroom reshuffles, reviews of corporate strategy, takeovers, receiverships, etc.

DEALING WITH THREATS

Abegglen and Stalk recall Yamaha's attempt to unseat Honda's leadership in motorcycles in 1981–1983: with Honda apparently preoccupied with getting a position in the tough car market, by 1981 its production share of motorbikes in Japan had fallen from a high of 65 percent to 40 percent, while Yamaha's had risen from 10 percent to 35 percent, and the relative market shares in Japan were 38 percent Honda and 37 percent Yamaha.

Yamaha embarked on a major expansion to produce another 1 million units, so bringing its capacity to 4 million, exceeding Honda's. And in January 1982, Yamaha's president declared that in one year his company would be the domestic leader, and in two years the world leader. By June, Yamaha announced historic records of sales and profits. But Yamaha had borrowed heavily to finance its new factory, pushing its debt/equity ratio to 3:1.

At the command "Slaughter Yamaha," Honda introduced 81 new models over the next 18 months, with increased production and stocks, and price reductions of more than a third—"it was possible to buy a 50 cc motorcycle—the large-volume cycle in Japan—for less than the cost of a 10-speed bicycle." Yamaha could manage "only 34" new models, and its sales halved, with unsold stocks by early 1983 at about a year's output.

Honda's production share increased from 38 to 47 percent, while Yamaha's fell from 37 to 23 percent. Yamaha faced substantial losses, and under continuing pressure from Honda had to make successive cuts in production capacity, with large redundancies, and eventually sued for peace.

Perhaps this was the most virtuoso display of product variation yet seen, but coupled with an awesome production flexibility, illustrating again the latent power of a "drawer" or "refrigerator" of models designed ready for production, noted earlier by BCG; and again the resolution to strike quickly when the opportunity offers to gain a decisive competitive advance.

THE HONDA MAGIC

All the praise for Honda's management misses its special magic unless seen in the context of this blend of *technological creativity and verve, production and marketing disciplines, judgment of opportunities, courage to act, and suppleness in doing so.* The legacy of the founders lies in creating the moral cohesion and spirit to sustain this dynamic, which now extends across national boundaries—while Pascale's analysis is focused mainly on Honda America, plants also operate as far apart as U.K., Italy, Spain, Canada, Brazil, Mexico, Australia, New Zealand, Indonesia, and Thailand.

As the examples have shown, the features are so securely bound together that they respond autonomously and in mutual harmony. So, trying to explain each element risks distorting the cohesion of the whole, which stems from the fundamental insight that the classical "military" hierarchical structure was inappropriate to an enterprise that would have to respond rapidly to technology and competitive demands: Fujisawa's ideal was *an organization where "employees would take their own initiative in making judgments and taking specific actions,"* within "an organizational structure in which every human resource and skill would be utilized to the fullest extent" with *"true leadership"* becoming *"doing nothing at all."* This required radical shifts in approach, and Honda led the way in matrix organization—a "spider's web"—communication flows, multidisciplinary project development (SED—sales, engineering, and development), cross-movements of staff, even to Fujisawa's "musical chairs"—a single room for directors with insufficient desks to go around.

This enhanced fluidity evolved alongside tight controls—shares are farmed around to allies to avoid external threats of takeover or disruptive shareholder demands; key suppliers have been developed into a "group" for closer involvement in development but also to ensure their quality, reliability, and responsiveness, which, with loyal distribution, are essential for such an adaptive and competitive style.

Within this dynamic pallisade, there are contrasting priorities. Recalling Fujisawa again: *"We cannot be assured of continued corporate activity unless we have not one but many Soichiro Hondas. We must foster experts in various fields. And we want to establish an organizational structure in which such experts can fully exercise their skills"*—an organization that did not inhibit "experts from advancement or waste their potential." Notably, "there were fundamental differences between a research and development department, whose mission was to study advanced technologies and be prepared to face many trials and failure, and a production department, whose purpose was to mass-produce goods, accumulate profits, and not make mistakes." These two departments, he thought, "cannot and must not be operated under the same financial or organizational structure." Sure enough, BCG noted the difference in "research projects, in which totally new designs had been developed as the basis for new product offerings, 99 percent failure is permitted to achieve 1 percent success," whereas for "the detailed development of products for production and sale, not even 1 percent failure is permitted."

Fujisawa viewed *the creation of Honda R&D as a separate entity* as a way of achieving this—classed with setting up Honda America as an "offensive measure." But the spirit of creativity is stimulated across the company—Pascale notes the toleration, indeed encouragement, of internal challenge—not least by the *invention competitions* where staff can use facilities to work up ideas, however bizarre. The tradition of "a drawer" of ready new designs continues in cars—again Sir Graham Day remarked informally, "they design more cars each year than the rest of the world's car industry put together." At the same time, Honda is at the forefront of production engineering, with *Honda Engineering also a separate subsidiary:* long before "lean production" became a buzz-phrase, Honda, noted by BCG, were *demanding suppliers deliveries "to the minute,"* model changes on the line took *"of the order of 5 to 10 minutes,"* and links with suppliers keep their costs and responsiveness up to scratch, with guidance and finance from Honda if needed.

These structures have not remained static, but adapted to the increasing global spread of the business, changing those that might have become inappropriate (*Financial Times,* August 12, 1991). In the product area, a typical example is the new Beat miniroadster, aimed at the youth market—and the parking pressures of Japan—which was designed by a team whose average age was 28 and with less assessment review (*Nikkei Weekly,* March 31, 1992). (All the Japanese car producers have sophisticated minimodels for this rising demand, but they also offer insurance against any other producers challenging in the small-car market.)

JUST HISTORY?

Honda has refreshed and increased its range of motorcycles, most recently adding the NR luxury model—incorporating an exotic light metal structure and a 747 cc engine with oval pistons, originally developed for road racing 14 years ago (*Nikkei Weekly,* April 18, 1992)—retaining its position as the world's leading producer. In cars, the same process of refreshment has taken place, though replacement models have often been new designs, and the range extended, especially into the luxury ranges through the Acura marque, including the NSX in the sport category applying racing engine technology but also the first production car to have an aluminum structure. As in motorcycles, Honda was the first Japanese producer to set up manufacturing in the U.S. No sign that the old spirit has declined.

In 1991, while the domestic output of U.S. domestic car producers declined, that of Japanese-owned plants in the U.S. increased, taking their market share of U.S.-produced cars to 18.5 percent. Of these, Honda's Accord was the best-selling car in the U.S.—their U.S. plant also has the distinction of designing its own version of the Accord—an Estate—and is also the largest U.S. exporter of vehicles to Japan, exceeding all U.S.-owned makers put together. Coupled with Japanese and other imports, the U.S.-owned producers have been coming under pressure across the whole model range; symptomatically, Renault and Daihatsu have exited the market.

Figure 5–4 depicts recent market share movements in the luxury segment. Notice anything familiar? Honda led into this segment with the Acura Legend and Integra in 1986, achieving sales of 128,000 by 1988, just over an 11 percent share. Honda was followed by Toyota (Lexus) and Nissan (Infiniti). Though there are more producers than in the superbike class in 1975, the rising share of Japanese models and the decline of others shows a similar trend (Volvo 940 had a rise to a very small share following introduction in 1990, as the only modest exception). 1992 will be an interesting year, with the market still depressed. Intriguingly, the U.S. government's pressure for greater voluntary restraint may well focus Japanese suppliers on this higher value-added segment. But we shall see.

The U.S. producers, with rising losses, cries from shareholders to reinstate profits, downsizing, redundancies, disputes, with very limited markets for their domestic products outside the U.S., and management turbulence, seem set on emulating their erstwhile predecessors in the British motorcycle industry, despite having had a ringside seat to the motorbike saga. BMW, among those who suffered in the motorcycle story, seem to have learned the lesson of not becoming overdependent on a single market, with a wide global coverage, including Japan.

CHALLENGES

Honda, like any business, faces an array of opportunities and threats: it cannot take advantage of the former without containing the latter. If Honda's style is unique, the principles are at least 2000 years old (see Appendix). Strategy starts from the need for security in an uncertain and vulnerable world: in a market led by producers who sustain high levels of in-house R&D, fast rates of model change, always improving efficiency and flexibility in production, retain and train their members, free of pressures from uncommitted shareholders, mutual tries and development with suppliers, etc., Honda has no choice but to be better in these respects if it wants to survive, let alone grow. In turn, countermoves by competitors need vigilance and speed of response. And so the competitive dynamic works. But if of a Schumpeterian mind, this style of competition poses a few questions for Anglo-Saxon notions of economic and commercial efficiency.

Not least, *R&D to build up a reserve of products*—to be deployed rapidly or held for many years against the best moment—appears "heretical"[1] in a corporate setting

---

[1]Kevin Jones and Tatsuo Ohbora, "Managing the Heretical Company," *McKinsey Quarterly* 3 (November 1990).

F I G U R E 5-4 | **Market Shares by Manufacturers: U.S. Luxury Cars, 1987–1992**

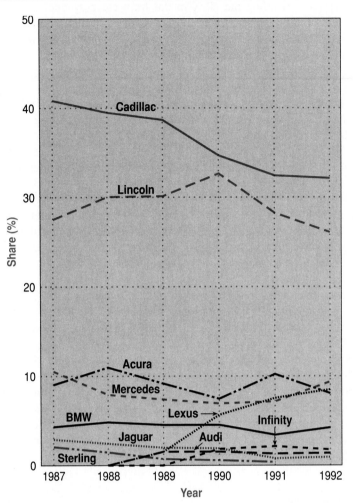

Note: Rolls Royce removed for clarity: from 0.2% in 1987, fell to 0.1% in 1992.
Source : *Automotive News,* market classification.

expecting every investment to show some reasonable prospect of return. Rapid product churning—effectively making one's own product obsolete before someone else does—itself influencing the customer's concept of the product, occurs over a wide range, including soft drinks, consumer electronics, microcomputers, sports kit at the most obvious consumer level, but applies also in the relative rate of new variants in office design, machinery, and vehicles. Even if there are calls to slow down in the interests of squeezing more profits out of each model, the capability for rapid shifts remains, and it is still to be seen whether the competitive tempo will relax.

It is false condescension to suggest, as some are prone, that Japan's strengths are confined to production processes. For manufacturing capability is the basic plank—only by driving costs always lower and saving time and stocks through flexibility can the resources be created for the high levels of R&D (industry accounts for more than 80 percent of national R&D), investment, and marketing.

But ensuring enough flexible capacity puts a premium on people—"a sense of satisfaction for Honda would come only when an independent individual meets a challenge without fear of failure and achieves his goal." This style of engaging people—everyone—to use their creativity is a special feature of Japan's approach: measured by participation in suggestions, some companies have millions of ideas a year from their members, with striking results: ". . . the goal of increasing productivity by 3 percent per month throughout the organization, which they achieve without laying off a single permanent worker," while, as Imai illustrates, continuous improvements in processes feed back to create new options for product innovations.

Or how do we see the function of a company? President Kawamoto remarks in his 1991 annual report, *"Honda was built on a core philosophy of the three joys: joy for those who buy our products, sell our products, and manufacture our products."* Joy? When was the last time your CEO used the word, let alone in an annual report?

More fundamentally, to the extent that other Japanese companies—whatever Honda's special blend—follow a similar organization and competitive style, and as the motorcycle pattern is replicated in other product fields, Thurow aptly depicts the fate of the U.S. consumer-electronics industry as "a profit-maximizing strategic retreat into oblivion," but similar trends are to be seen in cameras, memory chips, machine tools, microcomputers, faxes, etc.

And as other rising economies see the success of Japan as their ideal model, maybe we are watching a phase of "creative destruction" where the system that more efficiently applies creative talent is displacing another, which, in failing to adapt—or hanging onto obsolete attitudes for "conviction," or because it suits a minority with influence—becomes self-destructive.

Yet, this apparently novel style—whatever its antecedents—is probably closer to the origins of capitalism, where endeavor evolved from communities with benefits shared among those who directly participated, or where competition was sharpest within those communities. Intrigued by why Yamaha had taken on an opponent with Honda's track record, I put the point to an eminent Japanese banker, who replied, with a shrug, "They are both Hamamatsu companies."

As for Honda, no one—not least anyone in the company—can be sure how they will fare; they are going through some rough water at the moment. But it has a great entrepreneurial tradition among its members to drive the enterprise. With such an adventurous past, one thing is for sure. It will not stand still or stop fighting. After all,

REFERENCES

its members have something to fight for.

Tetsuo Sakiya, *Honda Motor* (Kodansha).

Boston Consulting Group (BCG), *Strategy Alternatives for the British Motorcycle Industry* (HMSO, 1975).

James C. Abegglen and George Stalk, Jr., *Kaisha: The Japanese Corporation* (New York: Harper and Row).

Richard Tanner Pascale, *Managing on the Edge* (New York: Viking).

George Stalk, Jr., and Thomas H. Hout, *Competing against Time* (New York: Free Press).

Womack, Jones, and Roos, *The Machine That Changed the World* (Rawson Associates).

Masaaki Imai, *Kaizen* (New York: McGraw-Hill).

Robert L. Shook, *Honda—An American Success Story* (Englewood Cliffs, N.J.: Prentice Hall).

Setsuo Mito, *The Honda Book of Management* (Kogan Page).

Mark Payne, *The Internationalization of the Japanese Automotive Industry*, Financial Times Business Information (1991).

Hiroyuki Odagiri, *Growth through Competition, Competition through Growth* (Oxford).

A P P E N D I X | **Sun Tzu—The Art of War[2]**

Unpredictability

As water has no constant form, there are in war no constant conditions. (VI.29)

Organization

Pay heed to nourishing the troops; do not unnecessarily fatigue them. Unite them in spirit; conserve their strength. Make unfathomable plans for the movements of the army.

Throw the troops into a position from which there is no escape and even when faced with death they will not flee. For if prepared to die, what can they not achieve? Then officers and men together put forth their utmost efforts . . . Thus, such troops need no encouragement to be vigilant. Without exhorting their support the general obtains it; without inviting their affection he gains it; without demanding their trust he wins it. (XI.32–34)

Spirit

By moral influence I mean that which causes the people to be in harmony with their leaders, so that they will accompany them in life and unto death without fear of mortal peril. (I.4)

Strategy

For to win one hundred victories in one hundred battles is not the acme of skill. To subdue the enemy without fighting is the acme of skill.— Thus, what is of supreme importance in war is to attack the enemy's strategy. (III.3–4)

Opportunism

Thus, those skilled at making the enemy move do so by creating a situation to which he must conform . . .

Therefore a skilled commander seeks victory from the situation. (V.20–21)

To a surrounded enemy, you must leave a way of escape. (VII.31)

Latent and Focused Power

When torrential water tosses boulders, it is because of its momentum; when the strike of the hawk breaks the body of its prey, it is because of timing. Thus the momentum of one skilled in war is overwhelming, and his attack precisely regulated. His potential is that of a fully drawn crossbow; his timing, the release of the trigger. (V.13–16)

As a hundred-weight balanced against a grain . . . the effect of pent-up waters. (IV.19–20)

When the enemy gives you an opening be swift as a hare and he will be unable to withstand you. (XI.61)

Dispositions

Invincibility depends on oneself; the enemy's vulnerability on him . . . invincibility lies in the defense; the possibility of victory in the attack. (IV.1, 5)

Generally, in battle, use the normal force to engage; use the extraordinary to win. (V.5)

Alliances

Disrupt his alliances. (III.5) . . . prevent allies from grouping. (XI.52)

Intelligence

Now the reason the enlightened prince and the wise general conquer the enemy wherever they move and their achievements surpass those of ordinary men is foreknowledge. (XIII.3)

Adaptability

Now an army may be likened to water, for just as flowing water avoids the heights and hastens to the lowlands, so an army avoids strength and strikes weakness. And as water shapes its flow in accordance with the ground, so an army manages its victory in accordance with the situation of the enemy. (XI.27–28)

Disruption

All warfare is based on deception . . . keep him under a strain and wear him down . . . When he is united divide him . . . Attack when he is unprepared: sally out when he does not expect you. (I.17–26)

---

[2]Trans.: Samuel B. Griffith, Oxford University Press.

WHY SOME STRATEGIC ALLIANCES SUCCEED AND OTHERS FAIL

Peter Lorange, University of Pennsylvania
Johan Roos, Norweigian School of Management

A key competitive precondition for any organization involved in any of today's multinational businesses is speed and pace in implementing strategies. Although one's organization may offer superior products or services today, it may quickly lag behind its competitors if it is not adept at *implementing* critical decisions.

An important approach to this requirement is the increasing use of strategic alliances.

In the last decade, the world was commonly viewed by managers and scholars in terms of a "competitive arena," even, at times, in terms of analogies from military strategy and warfare.

Today's decision maker needs not only to function in a competitive and hostile environment but also to be able to cooperate with other companies, perhaps even with one that, in other respects, may be a competitor.

For many multinational firms, strategic alliances have become increasingly important tools for ensuring speed and flexibility in carrying out multinational strategies. A typical example is SEVEL (Societa Europea Veicoli Leggeri), the 1978 strategic alliance between Fiat and Peugeot for the production of a new light van, labeled Ducato.

Both parties were short on resources and saved time and energy by combining their R&D and manufacturing efforts. Marketing and sales remained in the hands of each partner. However, both parties were able to benefit from the scale advantage that accrued from the cooperation.

Strategic alliances can be effective ways to diffuse new technologies rapidly, to enter a new market, to bypass governmental restrictions expeditiously, and/or to learn quickly from the leading firms in a given field. Many early U.S. joint ventures in Japan, for instance, can be characterized in terms of having been driven by several of these rationales (e.g., CPC International and Ajinomoto within the food industry in

Source: Reprinted by permission Faulkner & Gray, 11 Penn Plaza, New York 10001. "Why Some Strategic Alliances Succeed and Others Fail," by Peter Lorange and Johan Roos, *Journal of Business Strategy* (January-February 1991).

1963 and Hewlett-Packard and Yokogawa Electric within the electronics industry in 1971). These ventures allowed U.S. firms to disseminate new products rapidly into the otherwise exceedingly demanding Japanese market.

A more recent example that not only incorporates several of the above rationales but also illustrates the advent of *global* strategic alliances is the pair of strategic alliances between Hitachi Construction Machineries (HCM) and Fiat-Geotech and between HCM and John Deere & Co. In the early 1980s, the worldwide earth-moving-machinery industry was characterized by overcapacity, low margins, and strong global competitors.

In this situation, FiatGeotech saw the need to change its strategy to one of cooperation with others. To avoid anticipated increase in European protectionism and to attempt to enlarge its market share, HCM began to search actively for a joint venture partner in Europe. This resulted in 1987 in Fiat-Hitachi Excavator S.p.a.—a 51-49 joint venture to manufacture and market a new line of hydraulic excavators in Europe. To supply its U.S. market with hydraulic excavators, John Deere had also forged an initial link with HCM, the latter being its original equipment-manufacturing supplier of such products.

This cooperation evolved into a 50-50 joint venture between the two, with manufacturing carried out in the United States. More recently, Deere and FiatGeotech have entered into a joint development agreement for certain new products. Thus, we see a network of strategic relationships spanning the globe. To develop a wholly owned global strategy, an alternative on paper would probably have been outside the resource limits for the partners and would also have taken much more time.

It would be an overstatement to say that all strategic alliances are successful. Some of the reasons for failure often emphasize matters such as "lack of trust" and "incompatible personal chemistry"—for example:

- "We could not get along, which destroyed the cooperative spirit."
- "We came from too disparate corporate cultures."
- "Managers within the joint venture could not work with the owners' managers."
- "The contribution of our partner did not meet our expectations."
- "We could not get our personnel down the line to deliver what we had promised."

An example of a strategic alliance that seems to have had many such problems is SAAB-Fairchild, established in the late 1970s for the manufacture and sale of the SF-340 commercial airplane. This alliance was subsequently dissolved, and SAAB assumed Fairchild's responsibilities.

Another example is Agfa-Gaevert, a 1964 alliance in the filmmaking industry. During the 1970s, this alliance was restructured twice. With the sudden increase in silver prices in 1979, Agfa's parent, Bayer, took over full ownership while leaving the important managerial roles with it former partner. It is now very successful.

These examples demonstrate that at times strategic alliances can be more difficult to operate than wholly owned business ventures. Indeed, they involve challenges that require new types of managerial capabilities when it comes to living with ambiguity and displaying a mature attitude. There are at least three fundamental reasons: (1) More than one organization is usually involved in the decision making, often leading to slower, more complex decision making. This is further accentuated by (2) the merging of separate corporate cultures in which (3) the parent firms may have different, even ultimately conflicting, strategic intents.

At least two additional complicating factors can influence implementation. First, one may often have to develop more strategic alliances to increase the territorial coverage and speed of implementation. For example, ARCO Chemicals entered a series of strategic alliances in various countries in the Far East to increase its penetration of these markets within the gasoline-additives business. This approach can put an added burden on management's capacity to master such a strategy.

Second, experience shows that, typically, one must permit strategic alliances to evolve over time into more independent and freestanding entities. This evolutionary process simplifies more adaptive decision making, reflecting that knowledge transfer has taken place, and, therefore, retains its place in tackling new implementation challenges. It also implies that traditional "hands-on" involvement and control typically may have to ease up over time—to permit the strategic alliance to "grow up."

Given these challenges and difficulties, how can one track the way a strategic alliance is formed in order to up the ante for success in its implementation? First of all, we have to modify traditional attitudes toward cooperative strategies. Very often, firms view strategic alliances as a second-best option that they would prefer to do without. Strategic alliances receive attention only after one's wholly owned business has been dealt with, often through the assignment of one's less-than-strongest executives.

Because of uncertainty and discomfort, the feeling remains that these alliances must be closely managed and controlled so as not to "get out of hand." This is a counterproductive attitude that often leads to an unsatisfactory outcome for at least one partner.

The upside rationale for cooperating—namely, to achieve a "win-win" result that none of the parties could have achieved alone—is foregone. Thus, a strategic alliance must be structured so that it is the *intent* of both parties that it will actually succeed—through the need for speed, adaptation, and facilitated evolution. The foundation of a successful strategic alliance is laid during the internal formation process.

TWO POLITICAL CONSIDERATIONS

STAKEHOLDER BLESSING

A first political consideration is how to ensure that the most important external and internal stakeholders will see the general benefits from the strategic alliance and thus sponsor it. Questions that need to be addressed include the following:

- Are relevant ownership groups convinced that the venture will be desirable from their stockholder viewpoint?
- What will be the effects on the company's reputation and the response of the stock market?
- Are key members of the top-management team likely to be willing to pursue the venture—by seeing how the alliance will *not* be a threat to their own power and careers?
- To the extent that the alliance could represent a threat to any person or group, how can they be convinced to work toward the alliance's subsequent success?
- How will customers, suppliers, existing alliance partners, financiers, and competitors react?

It is important to carry out initial preparatory efforts to increase the likelihood that major stakeholders accept and promote the idea of a particular cooperative strategy.

These considerations are dependent, of course, on previous positive experiences, reputations, and old contacts. The purpose here is to ensure that key individuals and groups see the overall rationale for the alliance. If these stakeholders, at least tacitly, "bless" the venture at an early stage, the chances for smooth implementation increase. Consequently, if active resistance emerges among key stakeholders at an early stage, it is probably wise to call off the formation efforts then and there. A great deal of time and energy can be saved by exercising such realism.

An example of a strategic alliance in which both parties apparently established broad early stakeholder blessing would be the previously mentioned Fiat-Geotech-HCM-John Deere venture. The alliance idea was "bought into" at the top management level of all the firms. A major external stakeholder, Sumitomo Corporation, acted as a catalyst in helping the parties to view the major aspects of the strategic-alliance idea in a positive light.

INTERNAL SUPPORT

A second political consideration, which should occur later, during the more intense formation stages, involves ensuring that a broad range of people within the organization is committed to and enthusiastic about the venture. This consideration concerns managers in various operational functions who might be actively involved in contributing to the strategic alliance. Key questions to ask follow:

- Has the venture idea been sufficiently explained throughout the organization?
- Has it been presented with sufficient detail to ensure that everyone sees the tasks ahead and can focus on them as an opportunity and not as a threat?
- Are relevant specialists motivated to carry out their specific tasks in a cooperative mode?
- Do the operational staffs have sufficiently complementary styles to simplify their working contacts with the partner organization?

Thus, in order for the entire organization to be prepared for quick task actions during the venture's implementation, everyone must be "sold" on the concept early on. This might diminish the likelihood of a rejection later. A study of U.S.-Japanese strategic alliances found that the Japanese partners often were more forthright at informing their own organizations, and they did so at an earlier stage in the process.

Confidentiality considerations concerning early information about a business deal may, of course, create problems if too many people are involved early in forming the organization. In certain cases, it simply may not be possible to disseminate the venture plans to a broad range of people before the plans are already a fait accompli.

A typical example of this is the 1987 strategic alliance between the Swedish firm ASEA and the Swiss firm Brown Bovery, resulting in ABB. Only a handful of the top executives initiated and implemented the entire deal due to a fear of insider trading in the two firms' stocks. Undoubtedly, this might have created organizational integration challenges and problems that could have been eased in the face of a more gradual and broader dissemination of information to the two organizations. Early and gradual information dissemination can be implemented more readily in those strategic-alliance negotiations where stock market disclosure constraints are of little concern.

TWO ANALYTICAL CONSIDERATIONS

STRATEGIC MATCH

An initial strategic consideration is the early assessment of the overall strategic potential for cooperation. The analytical effort should yield answers to questions such as these:

- What are the broad, readily apparent objectives of this strategic alliance for each partner?
- How can the two parties complement each other to create common strengths from which both can benefit?
- How important is the strategic alliance within each partner's corporate portfolio?
- Are there any problems with the alliance due to its relative closeness to the core business of the partners?
- Are the partners "leaders" or "followers" within the particular business segment?
- Do they combine to create strength, or is this a case of the "sick joining the sick"?
- Are the partners sufficiently culturally similar?

In short, is there an obvious resulting strategic "win-win" match between the two partners? To obtain answers, it is important also to place oneself in the partner's position and assess one's own strategic considerations in these respects.

The analysis at this stage should involve broad strategic matters. If an apparent win-win match emerges, the chances for success in implementation increase. If this cannot be seen readily by most of the people involved, one should reflect on whether it is worthwhile and appropriate to continue.

An example of establishing a clear win-win perspective is the strategic alliance between Yokogawa Electric and General Electric Medical Systems. The strategic alliance, Yokogawa Medical Systems, underscores the need to reestablish a new win-win strategy as the alliance evolves over time.

This alliance emerged from a successful sales-agent agreement in the early 1970s. Yokogawa was carefully selected because General Electric Medical Systems planned to make available its latest technology. By the early 1980s, Yokogawa had learned so much about the technology that the firm suggested the development of a more cost-efficient and customer-adapted generation of products.

Following new negotiations, the two firms agreed to form a 50-50 joint venture company in 1982 that would develop, manufacture, market, distribute, and service this new line of products. The new product line was immediately successful, and the operations grew rapidly. In fact, these operations subsequently became so important that General Electric Medical Systems gained clear benefits in integrating the joint venture operation further into its global strategy. In 1988, the partners agreed to increase General Electric Medical Systems's ownership share in the joint venture.

The win-win strategic-match issue received a great deal of attention during the move from one evolutionary phase to the next. The complementary benefits of continued cooperation for both partners were carefully reassessed at each phase. In each case, a meaningful continuation of a win-win posture led to a modification in each party's role, including the ownership split.

DELINEATION OF STRATEGIC PLAN

The second analytical phase involves the development of an overall strategic plan for the strategic alliance as it emerges as a *continued* effort by the two parties. This phase may involve more detailed information gathering by the two prospective partners, taking into consideration the following questions:

- How do the prospective partners view the market potential?
- Whom do they view as the key competitors, and how will they want to compete with them?

- What is the worst-case scenario, particularly for achieving planned revenue levels?

In total, how viable is the strategic-alliance idea as a business plan?
Turning, then, to internal implementation issues, one must ask:

- What are each partner's relevant and available resources over the short term and the long term?
- Is it sufficiently clear *who* is expected to do *what* and by *when?*
- What are the partners' attitudes toward long-term cooperation?
- How can this cooperation evolve harmoniously over time without conflicting with other strategic concerns of either partner?

These considerations involve more detailed assessments regarding operational and tactical matters. If a realistic and favorable picture emerges, implementation efforts will be facilitated.

Nippon Steel exemplifies a firm that emphasized analytical considerations before it entered into a joint venture with IBM. Due to the steel industry decline in the early 1980s, the firm made a strategic decision to diversify into several new business areas, one of which was information systems.

This decision resulted in the formation of several alliances, all announced in late 1988. One of them was NS&I, a relatively small venture with IBM. Nippon Steel contacted IBM directly with an invitation to form this strategic alliance. During the year prior to this invitation, however, Nippon Steel had conducted *thorough* assessments of the strategic match and operational details.

Failure to do the more detailed analytical work will probably lead to problems, as illustrated by the 1973 strategic alliance between Joseph Seagram and Kirin in Japan. This alliance was the result of, on the one hand, Seagram's wish to enter the promising Japanese market and, on the other hand, Kirin's wish to link up with a well-known and reputable foreign partner with complementary products.

Both partners had their relevant stakeholders' blessings for the alliance and made thorough assessments of the strategic match. However, they appeared to have put less emphasis on a detailed analysis of the market and the development of a business plan during the formation phase. Difficulties, including less-than-expected sales, subsequently occurred.

One reason was that the alliance's main product, spirits, turned out to be difficult to market through Kirin's existing distribution network for beers. Over the last few years, however, sales improved significantly after a separate distribution plan was developed. Today, the venture generates a substantial profit, with new products being added to the assortment.

To ensure smooth implementation of a cooperative strategy, decision makers must carefully address the four considerations discussed in this article *before* entering into substantive discussions with the partner. A thorough formation process will facilitate implementation of the strategic alliance and, therefore, increase the likelihood of its subsequent success.

An experienced strategic-alliance negotiation team must consider the major judgments of such a process and should play out the negotiation scenario in their minds even before actual negotiations begin.

WHEN AND WHEN *NOT* TO VERTICALLY INTEGRATE

John Stuckey and David White, McKinsey & Company

Vertical integration can be a highly important strategy, but it is notoriously difficult to implement successfully and—when it turns out to be the wrong strategy—costly to fix. Management's track record on vertical integration decisions is not good.[1] Our purpose in this paper is to help managers make better integration decisions. We discuss when to vertically integrate, when not to integrate, and when to use alternative, quasi-integration strategies. Then we present a framework for making the decision.

WHEN TO INTEGRATE

"Vertical integration" is simply a means of coordinating the different stages of an industry chain when bilateral trading is not beneficial. Consider hot-metal production and steel making, two stages in the traditional steel industry chain. Hot metal is produced in blast furnaces, tapped into insulated ladles, and transported in molten form at about 2,500 degrees perhaps 500 yards to the steel shop, where it is poured into steel-making vessels. These two processes are almost always under common ownership, although occasionally hot metal is traded; for several months in 1991, Weirton Steel sold hot metal to Wheeling-Pittsburgh, almost 10 miles away.

Such trading is rare, however. The fixed asset technologies and frequency of transactions would dictate a market structure of tightly bound pairs of buyers and sellers that would need to negotiate an almost continuous stream of transactions. Transaction costs and the risk of exploitation would be high. It is more effective, lower cost, and lower risk to combine these two stages under common ownership.

Table 7–1 lists the kinds of costs, risks, and coordination issues that should be weighed in the integration decision. The tough part is that these criteria are often at

Source: Reprinted from "When and When *Not* to Vertically Integrate," by John Stuckey and David White, *Sloan Management Review,* Spring 1993, pp. 71-83, by permission of publisher. Copyright © 1993 by the Sloan Management Review Association. All rights reserved.

[1]See, for instance, R. P. Rumelt, *Strategy, Structure, and Economic Performance* (Cambridge, Mass.: Harvard University Press, 1974).

TABLE 7-1 | Criteria for Integration Decisions

Setup Costs	Transaction Costs	Risk	Coordination Effectiveness
Capital (e.g., equipment, acquisitions)	Information collection and processing	Possibility for unreasonable price changes	Run lengths, inventory levels
Systems development	Legal	Supply or outlet foreclosure	Capacity utilization
Training	Sales and purchasing	Insulation from market (e.g., from technical changes, new products)	Delivery performance
			Quality

odds with each other. Vertical integration typically reduces some risks and transaction costs, but it requires heavy setup costs, and its coordination effectiveness is often dubious.

There are four reasons to vertically integrate:

1. The market is too risky and unreliable—it "fails."
2. Companies in adjacent stages of the industry chain have more market power than companies in your stage.
3. Integration would create or exploit market power by raising barriers to entry or allowing price discrimination across customer segments.
4. The market is young and the company must forward integrate to develop a market, or the market is declining and independents are pulling out of adjacent stages.

Some of these are better reasons than others. The first reason—vertical market failure—is the most important one.

VERTICAL MARKET FAILURE

A vertical market "fails" when transactions within it are too risky and the contracts designed to overcome these risks are too costly (or impossible) to write and administer. The typical features of a failed vertical market are (1) a small number of buyers and sellers; (2) high asset specificity, durability, and intensity; and (3) frequent transactions. In addition, broader issues that affect all markets—uncertainty, bounded rationality, and opportunism—play a special part in a failed vertical market. None of these features, taken individually, necessarily signifies a vertical market failure (VMF), but when they are all present, chances are good the market has failed.

Buyers and Sellers The number of buyers and sellers in a market is the most critical—although the least permanent—variable determining VMF. Problems arise when the market has only one buyer and one seller (bilateral monopoly) or only a few buyers and a few sellers (bilateral oligopoly). Figure 7–1 illustrates the possible market structures.

Microeconomists have realized that rational supply and demand forces alone do not set transaction prices and volumes deterministically in such markets, as they do

F I G U R E 7–1 | **Vertical Market Structures**

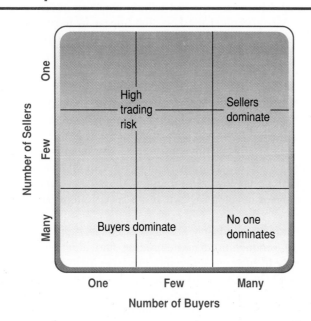

in all other vertical market structures. Rather, the terms of transactions, especially price, are determined by the balance of power between buyers and sellers—a balance that is unpredictable and unstable.

Where there is only one buyer and one supplier (especially in long-term relationships that involve frequent transactions), each attempts to leverage its monopoly status. As commercial conditions change unpredictably over time, this leads to a lot of haggling and attempts at exploitation, which are costly and risky.

Bilateral obligopolies have especially complex coordination problems. If, for example, there are three suppliers and three customers, each player sees five other players with whom the collective economic surplus must be shared. If players are not careful, they will collectively compete away all the surplus and pass it along to customers. In order to avoid this, they might try to create monopolies at each stage of the chain, but antitrust laws prevent them. So players merge vertically, creating, in this case, three players instead of six. When each then sees only two other players seeking slices of the surplus, they have a better chance of behaving rationally.

We relied on this concept to advise a company on whether to continue to run an in-house shop that supplied machining services to the company's steel plant. An analysis showed that the shop was very costly, relative to outside contractors. Some managers wanted to close the shop. Others countered that this would leave the plant vulnerable to disruptions; there was a small number of potential outside suppliers, including only one heavy machine shop within 100 kilometers.

We recommended that the shop be closed if it failed to be competitive on scheduled work and most light machining jobs. This work was predictable, used standardized machines, and could be done by several outside suppliers. Therefore, it was low risk and had low transaction costs. However, we recommended that a slimmed-down heavy machine shop be maintained in-house for breakdown work requiring very large lathes and vertical borers. This work was unpredictable, only one outside supplier could provide it, and the costs of any delay in bringing the plant back on stream were enormous.

Assets   If this combination of problems occurs only in bilateral monopolies or close-knit bilateral oligopolies, aren't we just talking about an oddity with little practical significance? No. Many vertical markets that appear to have numerous players on each side are, in effect, composed of groups of bilateral oligopolists tightly bound together. The groupings arise because asset specificity, durability, and intensity raise switching costs to the point where only a small segment of the apparent universe of buyers is truly available to the sellers, and vice versa.

There are three principal types of asset specificity that compartmentalize industries into bilateral monopolies and oligopolies. *Site specificity* occurs when buyers and sellers locate fixed assets, such as a coal mine and power station, in close proximity to minimize transport and inventory costs. *Technical specificity* occurs when one or both parties to a transaction invest in equipment that can be used only by one or both parties and that has low value in alternative uses. *Human capital specificity* occurs when employees develop skills that are specific to a particular buyer or customer relationship.

The upstream aluminum industry has high asset specificity. This industry has two principal stages of production: bauxite mining and alumina refining. Mines and refineries are usually located close together (site specificity) because of the high cost of transporting bauxite, relative to its value, and the 60 percent to 70 percent volume reduction typically achieved during refining. Refineries are tailored to process their own bauxite, with its unique chemical and physical properties; switching suppliers or customers is either impossible or prohibitively expensive (technical specificity). Consequently, mine-refinery pairs are locked together economically.

These bilateral monopolies exist despite the apparent presence of dozens of buyers and sellers. In fact, the preinvestment phase of the transaction relationship between a mine and a refinery does not suffer from bilateral monopoly. A number of bauxite miners and alumina refiners around the world line up and bid whenever a greenfield mine and refinery are in the offing. However, the market quickly becomes a bilateral monopoly in the postinvestment phase. The miner and the refiner who exploit the greenfield opportunity are locked together economically by asset specificity.

Because industry participants realize the perils of VMF, the mine and the refinery usually end up under common ownership. Around 90 percent of bauxite transactions occur under vertical integration or quasi-vertical arrangements, such as joint ventures.

Auto assemblers and their component suppliers can also be locked together, as when a component is specific to a particular make and model. When the amount of research and development (R&D) investment in the component is high (asset intensity), it is risky for the component supplier and auto assembler to be independent. Either side is vulnerable to opportunistic recontracting, especially if, for example, the model is a surprising success or failure. To avoid the dangers of bilateral monopolies and oligopolies in such cases, auto assemblers tend to backward integrate or, following the example of the Japanese, enter into close-knit contractual arrangements with carefully chosen suppliers—where the strength of relationships and contracts prevents risks of opportunistic exploitation inherent in arm's-length sales between "compatible" parties.

Postinvestment-phase bilateral monopolies and oligopolies caused by asset specificity are the most frequent cause of VMF. The effect of asset specificity is magnified when the assets are also capital intensive and durable and when they give rise to high fixed-cost structures. While the existence of a bilateral oligopoly increases the *risk* of supply or outlet disruption, high capital intensity and high fixed costs increase the *costs* of any production disruption because of the magnitude of both cash and opportunity costs incurred during the interruption. Asset durability increases the time horizon over which the risks and costs are relevant.

Taken together, high asset specificity, intensity, and durability often cause high switching costs for both suppliers and customers. Their presence is one of the most important contributing factors to decisions to vertically integrate.

Transaction Frequency   High transaction frequency is another factor that will promote VMF, when it is accompanied by bilateral oligopolies and high asset specificity. Frequent transactions raise costs for the simple reason that haggling and negotiating occur more often and allow for frequent exploitation.

Figure 7–2 plots transaction frequency and asset characteristics on a matrix that suggests appropriate vertical coordination mechanisms. When buyers and sellers seldom need to interact, vertical integration is usually not necessary, whether asset specificity is low or high. When asset specificity is low, markets can operate effectively using standard contracts such as leases and credit sale agreements. And when asset specificity is high, the contracts may be quite complicated but integration is still not necessary. An example would be major public construction projects.

Even if transaction frequency is high, low asset specificity will mitigate its effects. For example, trips to the grocery store don't usually require complicated negotiations. But when assets are specific, durable, and intensive, and transactions are frequent, vertical integration is likely to be warranted. Otherwise, transaction costs and risks will be too high, and complete contracts to eliminate these uncertainties will be difficult to write.

Uncertainty, Bounded Rationality, and Opportunism   Three additional factors have subtle but important implications for vertical strategy. Uncertainties make it difficult for companies to draw up contracts that will guide them as circumstances change. In the machine shop example, the major *uncertainties* included the timing, nature, and

F I G U R E 7-2 | **Transaction-Asset Matrix**

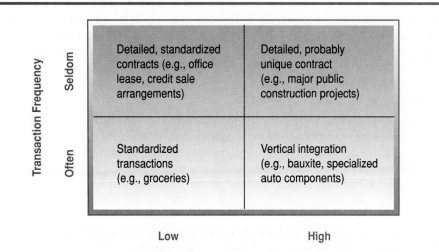

	Low	High
Seldom	Detailed, standardized contracts (e.g., office lease, credit sale arrangements)	Detailed, probably unique contract (e.g., major public construction projects)
Often	Standardized transactions (e.g., groceries)	Vertical integration (e.g., bauxite, specialized auto components)

Transaction Frequency (vertical axis)

Asset Specificity, Durability, and Intensity

severity of plant breakdowns and the supply and demand balance in the local markets for machining services. With such a high level of uncertainty, the company was better off maintaining its in-house shop for breakdown work. The work will proceed more smoothly, cheaply, and with a lower risk if this part of the chain is integrated.

Bounded rationality also inhibits companies from writing contracts that fully describe transactions under all future possibilities. This concept, formalized by economist Herbert Simon, is that human beings have a limited ability to solve complex problems.[2] One of Simon's students, Oliver Williamson, noted the effect of bounded rationality on market failure.[3] Williamson also introduced the notion of *opportunism:* when given the chance, people will often cheat and deceive in commercial dealings when they perceive that it is in their long-term interest to do so. Uncertainty and opportunism can often be seen to drive vertical integration outcomes in the markets for R&D services and the markets for new products and processes generated by R&D. These markets often fail because the end product of R&D is largely information about new products and processes. In a world of uncertainty, the value of new products and processes to a purchaser is not known until it has been observed. But the seller is reluctant to disclose information before payment because a preview could give the product away. The situation is ripe for opportunism.

When specific assets are required in the development and application of the new ideas or when the originator cannot protect its property rights through patents, companies will probably benefit from vertical integration. For buyers that would mean developing their own R&D departments; for sellers that would mean forward integrating. For example, EMI, the developer of the first CAT scanner, should have forward integrated into specialized distribution and servicing, as producers of sophisticated medical equipment typically do.[4] But it did not have these assets at the time, and they are slow and costly to build. General Electric and Siemens, which were integrated across R&D, engineering, and marketing, reverse-engineered the scanner, improved on it, provided more training, support, and servicing, and captured the major share of the market.

While uncertainty, bounded rationality, and opportunism are ubiquitous, they do not always have the same intensity. This observation may explain some interesting patterns in vertical integration across countries, industries, and time. For example, Japanese manufacturers in industries like steel and autos are less backward integrated into supplier industries, such as components and engineering services, than are their Western counterparts. Instead, they rely on relatively few contractors with whom they enjoy fairly stable, nonadversarial relationships. One of the possible reasons for Japanese manufacturers' willingness to rely on outsiders is that opportunism is not as rife in Japanese culture as it is in Western culture.

DEFENDING AGAINST MARKET POWER

Vertical market failure is the most important reason to vertically integrate. But companies sometimes integrate because a company in an adjacent stage of the industry chain has more market power. If one stage of an industry chain exerts market power over another and thereby achieves abnormally high returns, it may be attractive for participants in the dominated industry to enter the dominating industry. In other

[2]H. A. Simon, *Models of Man: Social and Rational* (New York: John Wiley & Sons, 1957), p. 198.
[3]O. E. Williamson, *Markets and Hierarchies: Analysis and Antitrust Implications* (New York: Free Press, 1975).
[4]D. J. Teece, "Profiting from Technological Innovation," *Research Policy* 15 (1986), pp. 285–305.

words, the industry is attractive in its own right and might attract prospective entrants from within the industry chain and outside it.

The Australian ready-mix concrete industry is notoriously competitive because there are low barriers to entry and because there is cyclical demand for what is essentially a commodity product. Participants often engage in price wars and generally earn low returns.

By contrast, the quarry industry, which supplies sand and stone to the ready-mix manufacturers, is extremely profitable. Limited quarry sites in each region and high transport costs from other regions create high barriers to entry. The few players, recognizing their mutual interests, charge prices well above what would occur in a competitive marketplace and earn an attractive economic surplus. These high-priced quarry products are an important input cost for ready-mix concrete. Therefore, the concrete companies have backward integrated into quarries, largely via acquisitions, and now three large players control about 75 percent of both the concrete and quarry industries.

It is important to note that entry via acquisitions will not create value if the acquirer has to hand over the capitalized value of the economic surplus in the form of an inflated acquisition price. Often, the existing players in the less powerful stages of an industry chain pay too much for businesses in the powerful stages. In the Australian concrete business, at least some of the quarry acquisitions would seem to have destroyed value. Recently one of the large concrete makers acquired a small, integrated quarrying and concrete-making operator at an inferred price cash flow multiple of 20. It is very difficult to justify such a premium, given that the acquirer's real cost of capital is about 10 percent.

While players in weak stages of an industry chain have clear incentives to move into the powerful stages, the key issue is whether they can achieve integration at a cost less than the value of the benefits to be achieved. Unfortunately, in our experience, they often cannot.

Managers often mistakenly believe that, as an existing player in the industry, their entry into a more attractive business within the chain is easier than it is for outsiders. However, the key skills along an industry chain usually differ so substantially that outsiders with analogous skills from other industries are often superior entrants. (Outsiders, too, can dissipate the stage's value; if one firm can scale the barriers and enter the attractive stage, other new entrants may be able to do the same.)

CREATING AND EXPLOITING MARKET POWER

Vertical integration also makes strategic sense when used to create or exploit market power.

Barriers to Entry   When most competitors in an industry are vertically integrated, it can be difficult for nonintegrated players to enter. Potential entrants may have to enter all stages to compete. This increases capital costs and the minimum efficient scale of operations, thus raising barriers to entry.

One industry where vertical integration added to entry barriers was the upstream aluminum industry. Until the 1970s, the industry's three stages—bauxite mining, alumina refining, and metal smelting—were dominated by the six vertically integrated majors: Alcoa, Alcan, Pechiney, Reynolds, Kaiser, and Alusuisse. The markets for the intermediate products, bauxite and alumina, were too thin for a nonintegrated trader. Even integrated entrants were repelled by the $2 billion price tag (in 1988 figures) for efficient-scale entry as a vertically integrated player.

Even if this barrier could be scaled, an entrant would need to find immediate markets for the roughly 4 percent it would be adding to world capacity—not an easy task in an industry growing at about 5 percent annually. Not surprisingly, the vertical integration strategies of the majors were the predominant cause of the industry's sizable barriers to entry.

Similar entry barriers exist in the automobile industry. Auto manufacturers are usually forward-integrated into distribution and franchised dealerships. Those with strong dealer networks tend to have exclusive dealerships. This means that new entrants must establish widespread dealer networks, which is expensive and time-consuming. Without their "inherited" dealer networks, manufacturers like General Motors would have lost more market share than they already have to the Japanese.

Using vertical integration to build entry barriers is often, however, an expensive ploy. Furthermore, success is not guaranteed, as inventive entrants ultimately find chinks in the armor if the economic surplus is large enough. For example, the aluminum companies eventually lost control of their industry, mainly as a result of new entrants using joint ventures.

Price Discrimination   Forward integration into selected customer segments can allow a company to benefit from price discrimination. Consider a supplier with market power that sells a commodity product to two customer segments with different price sensitivities. The supplier would like to maximize its total profits by charging a high price to the price-insensitive segment and a low price to the price-sensitive segment, but it cannot do so because the low-price customers can resell to the high-price customers and, ultimately, undermine the entire strategy. By forward integrating into the low-price segment, the supplier prevents reselling. There is evidence that the aluminum companies have forward integrated into fabrication segments with the most price-sensitive demands (such as can stock, cable, and automobile castings) and have resisted integration into segments where the threat of substitution is low.

RESPONDING TO INDUSTRY LIFE CYCLE

When an industry is young, companies sometimes forward integrate to develop a market. (This is a special case of vertical market failure.) During the early decades of the aluminum industry, producers were forced to forward integrate into fabricated products and even end-product manufacture to penetrate markets that traditionally used materials such as steel and copper. The early manufacturers of fiberglass and plastic, too, found that forward integration was essential to creating the perception that these products were superior to traditional materials.[5]

However, our experience suggests that this rationale for forward integration is overrated. It is successful only when the downstream business possesses proprietary technology or a strong brand image that prevents imitation by "free rider" competitors. There is no point in developing new markets if *you* cannot capture the economic surplus for at least several years. Also, market development will be successful only if the product has some real advantages over its current or potential substitutes.

When the industry is declining, companies sometimes integrate to fill the gaps left by independents who are pulling out. As an industry declines, weaker independents exit, leaving core players vulnerable to exploitation by increasingly concentrated suppliers or customers.

---

[5]See E. R. Corey, *The Development of Markets for New Materials* (Cambridge, Mass.: Harvard University Press, 1956).

For example, after the U.S. cigar industry began to decline in the mid-1960s, Culbro Corporation, a leading U.S. supplier, had to acquire distribution companies in key markets along the East Coast. Its major competitor, Consolidated Cigar, was already forward integrated, and Culbro's distributors had "lost interest" in cigars and were giving priority to numerous other product lines.[6]

WHEN NOT TO INTEGRATE

Do not vertically integrate unless absolutely necessary. This strategy is too expensive, risky, and difficult to reverse. Sometimes vertical integration is necessary, but more often than not, companies err on the side of excessive integration. This occurs for two reasons: (1) decisions to integrate are often based on spurious reasons and (2) managers fail to consider the rich array of quasi-integration strategies that can be superior to full integration in both benefits and costs.

SPURIOUS REASONS

The reasons used to justify vertical integration strategies are often shallow and invalid. Objectives like "reducing cyclicality," "assuring market access," "moving into the high value-added stage," or "getting closer to our customers" are sometimes valid but often not.

Reducing Cyclicality or Volatility in Earnings   This is a common but rarely valid reason for vertical integration—a variation on the old theme that internal portfolio diversification is valuable to shareholders. This argument is invalid for two reasons. First, returns in contiguous stages of an industry chain are often positively correlated and are subject to many of the same influences, such as changes in demand for the end product. Hence, combining them into one portfolio has little impact on total portfolio risk. This is the case in the zinc mining and zinc smelting businesses, for example. Second, even if returns are negatively correlated, the smoothing of corporate earnings is not all that valuable to shareholders, who can diversify their own portfolios to reduce unsystematic risk. Vertical integration in this case adds value for managers but not for shareholders.

Assuring Supply or Outlets   Owning captive supply sources or outlets, it is argued, eliminates the possibility of market foreclosure or unfair prices and insulates companies from short-run supply-and-demand imbalances in intermediate product markets.

Vertical integration can be justified where the possibility of market foreclosure or "unfair" prices is a symptom of VMF or of structural market power held by suppliers or customers. But where there is an efficient market, it is not necessary to own supply or outlets. A market participant will always be able to trade any volume at the market price, even though the price might seem "unfair" relative to costs. A firm that is integrated across such a market only deludes itself when it sets internal transfer prices that are different from market prices. It may even make suboptimal output and capacity decisions if integrated for this reason.

The subtle, although critical, factors that determine when to assure supply or outlets are the structures of the buying and selling sides of the market. If both sides are

---

[6]See K. R. Harrigan, *Strategies for Declining Businesses* (Lexington, Mass.: Lexington Books, 1980), ch. 8.

competitively structured, integration does not add value. But if the structural conditions give rise to VMF or a permanent power imbalance, integration may be justified.

Several times we have observed the interesting case where a group of oligopolists that supply a low-growth commodity product to a reasonably fragmented, low-power buying industry use forward integration to avoid price-based competition. The oligopolists understand that competing for market share on the basis of price is folly, except perhaps in the very short run, but they cannot resist the urge to steal market share. Hence, they forward integrate to secure all of their large purchases. Such behavior is rational so long as price competition is avoided—and so long as the oligopolists do not pay acquisition prices for downstream customers that are above their stand-alone net present values. This sort of forward integration makes sense only when it helps preserve oligopoly profits in the upstream stage of an industry chain in which a permanent power imbalance exists.

Capturing More Value   The popular prescription that firms should move into the high value-added stages of an industry chain is often combined with another sacred belief of the 1980s—that firms should move closer to their customers. Both prescriptions lead to increased vertical integration, usually forward integration toward final customers.

Although there probably is a positive correlation between the profitability of a stage in an industry chain and both its absolute value added and its proximity to final consumers, we believe the correlation is *weak and inconsistent*. Vertical integration strategies based on these assumptions usually destroy shareholder wealth.

It is *economic surplus*—not value added or closeness to the customer—that drives superior returns. Economic surplus is the return an enterprise receives in excess of its full costs of being in the business, including a fair return on capital. It is merely coincidental if the surplus arising in one stage of an industry chain is proportional to its value added (defined as the sum of full cost and surplus, less the cost of inputs sourced from the preceding stage in the industry chain). However, economic surplus is more likely to arise close to the customer because there, according to economists, you can get your hands directly on any available consumer surplus.

The general prescription should therefore be: *Integrate into those stages of the industry chain where the most economic surplus is available, irrespective of closeness to the customer or the absolute size of the value added.* Recall, though, that the consistently high-surplus stages must, by definition, be protected by barriers to entry, and the vertically integrating entrant must be able to scale those barriers at a cost less than the value of the surplus available. Usually the barriers to entry include the skills required to run the new business, and the entrant often does not possess those skills despite experience in an adjacent stage of the industry chain.

Consider the Australian cement and concrete industry chain (see Figure 7–3). Economic surplus is not proportional to the value added in the individual stages of production. In fact, the highest value-added stage, transport, does not even earn an adequate return on capital, whereas the smallest value-added stage, fly ash, earns a high economic surplus. Also, economic surplus is not concentrated at the customer end but, if anything, occurs upstream. In fact, our experience suggests that the pattern of economic surplus along industry chains is highly variable and needs examination on a case-by-case basis.

Quasi-Integration Strategies

Managers sometimes overintegrate because they fail to consider the rich array of quasi-integration strategies available. Long-term contracts, joint ventures, strategic

F I G U R E 7-3 | **Australian Cement and Concrete Industry: Value Added versus Economic Surplus**

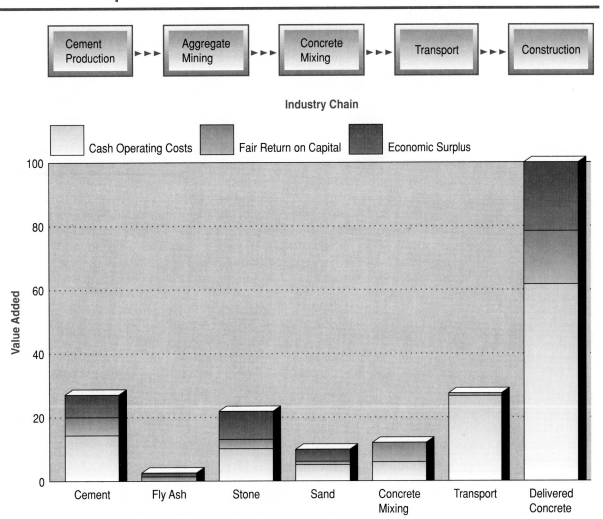

Index: Delivered price of concrete per ton = 100.

alliances, technology licenses, asset ownership, and franchising tend to involve lower capital costs and greater flexibility than vertical integration. Also, they often provide adequate protection from VMF and market power held by customers or suppliers.

Joint ventures and strategic alliances, for example, allow firms to exchange certain goods, services, information, or expertise while maintaining a formal trade relationship with others. Such mechanisms also allow the companies involved to retain their corporate identities and to avoid the risk of antitrust prosecution. The potential mutual advantages can be maximized, and the natural conflict in trade relationships can be minimized.

For these reasons, a majority of the upstream aluminum industry's plants are now joint ventures. These structures facilitate the exchanges of bauxite, alumina, technical know-how, and nation-specific knowledge; provide forums for oligopolistic coordination; and manage relations between global corporations and host-country governments.

Asset ownership is another quasi-integration arrangement. The host firm retains ownership of the critical assets in adjacent stages of the industry chain but contracts out all other aspects of ownership and control in these adjacent stages. For example, assemblers of products like motor vehicles and steam turbines own the specialized tools, dies, jigs, patterns, and molds that are unique to their key components. They contract with suppliers for the actual manufacture of components but protect themselves from opportunistic exploitation by owning the assets. Asset ownership is often all that is needed to thwart the opportunism associated with physical capital.

Similar arrangements are also possible on the downstream side. Franchises allow the host enterprise to control distribution without the drain on capital and management resources that full integration would require. Here, the host firm avoids ownership of the physical assets, as they are not especially specific or durable, but retains property rights on the intangible "brand" assets. By holding the right to cancel franchises, the host firm can control standards of quality, service, cleanliness, and value.

Licensing arrangements should always be considered as an alternative to vertical integration where buying and selling of technology is concerned. Markets for R&D and technology are prone to failure because it is difficult for innovators to protect their property rights. Often an innovation is valuable only when joined with specialized complementary assets, such as skilled marketing or service teams. Licensing may be the answer.

Figure 7–4 is a decision-making framework for the innovator of a new technology or product. It shows, for example, that when the innovator is protected from imitators by a patent or trade secret and specific complementary assets either are not critical or are available in competitive supply, the innovator should license to all comers and price for the long run. This strategy typically applies to industries like petrochemicals and cosmetics. As copying becomes easier and complementary assets more critical, vertical integration may be required, as illustrated earlier by the CAT scanner example.

CHANGING VERTICAL STRATEGIES

Companies should change their vertical integration strategies when market structures change. The structural factors most likely to change are the number of buyers and sellers and the importance of specialized assets. Of course, a company should also alter its strategy, even in the absence of structural change, when that strategy turns out to be wrong.

BUYERS AND SELLERS

The structural factor most likely to change is the number of buyers and sellers. In the mid-1960s, the crude oil market exhibited all the features of a vertically failed market (see Figure 7–5). The top four sellers accounted for 59 percent of industry sales and the top eight accounted for 84 percent. The buying side was equally concentrated. The number of relevant buyer-seller combinations was further reduced because refineries were geared to process specific types of crude. The assets were highly capital intensive and long lived, transactions were frequent, and the need for continuous plant optimization increased the level of uncertainty. Not surprisingly, there was almost no spot market, and most transactions were conducted in-house or through 10-year fixed contracts in order to avoid the transaction costs and risks of trading in an unreliable, vertically failed market.

F I G U R E 7-4 | **Vertical Strategy Framework for Innovators**

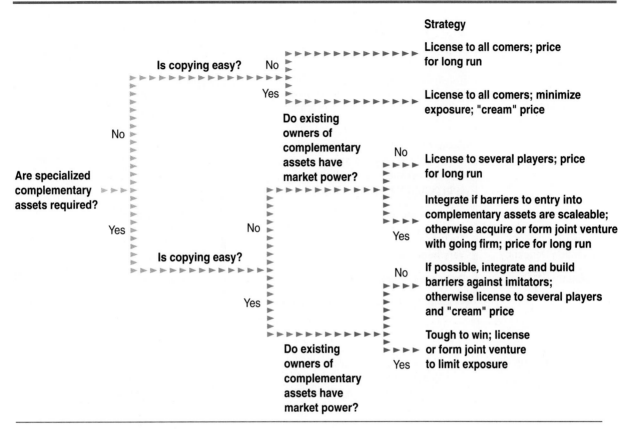

Source: For a detailed analysis of the thinking summarized here, see D. J. Teece, "Profiting from Technological Innovation," *Research Policy* 15 (1986), pp. 285–305.

However, over the past 20 years, there have been fundamental shifts in underlying market structure. The nationalization of oil reserves by OPEC producers (replacing the "Seven Sisters" with multiple national suppliers), combined with the huge growth of non-OPEC suppliers such as Mexico, has reduced seller concentration enormously. By 1985, the market share of the top four sellers had fallen to only 26 percent and the top eight to 42 percent. Concentration of refinery ownership had also fallen substantially. Furthermore, technological advances have reduced asset specificity by allowing modern refineries to process a much wider range of crudes with much lower switching costs.

The increase in the number of buyers and sellers and the decrease in switching costs have greatly reduced the need for vertical integration by allowing the development of an efficient market for crude oil. It is estimated that around 50 percent of transactions are now traded on the spot market (even by the large, integrated players), and there is a growing number of nonintegrated players.

DISINTEGRATION

Three forces seem to favor a general trend toward vertical disintegration during the late 1980s and early 1990s. First, many companies integrated in the past for spurious reasons and now, even in the absence of structural change, should disintegrate. Sec-

FIGURE 7-5 | **Changes in the Oil Industry's Vertical Market Structure**

Structural Element	1966	1985
• Number of sellers	Top 4 = 59% Top 8 = 84%	Top 4 = 26% Top 8 = 42%
• Number of buyers	Equally concentrated as selling side	Much less concentrated than before
• Asset characteristics –Specificity	Refineries geared to specific crude and unable to process the variety of crudes necessary to function as spot purchaser	Refineries much more flexible and able to process wide range of crudes
–Intensity –Durability	Highly capital intensive 20 years +	Highly capital intensive 20 years +
• Transaction frequency	Very frequent	Very frequent
• Uncertainty	Daily plant optimization changes	Daily plant optimization changes
Vertical coordination mechanism	• Virtually no spot market • Most transactions via vertical integration or 10-year fixed contracts	• Half of transactions on spot market • Independents growing • Vertical integration declining

ond, the emergence of a powerful market for corporate control is increasing pressure on overintegrated companies to restructure themselves—either voluntarily or at the hands of corporate raiders. And third, worldwide structural changes are occurring in many industries that increase the advantages and reduce the risks of trading. The first two reasons are self-explanatory, but the third reason needs elaboration.

In many industry chains, the costs and risks of trading have been reduced by increases in the number of buyers or sellers or both. Many industries, such as telecommunications and banking, are being deregulated to allow the entry of new players into national monopolies and oligopolies. Also, growth of the newly industrialized countries, including Korea, Taiwan, Hong Kong, and Mexico, has greatly increased the universe of potential suppliers in many industries, such as consumer electronics.

Similarly, the globalization of consumer markets and the pressures on individual firms to become "insiders" in each national market they serve are prompting many companies to build new manufacturing facilities in countries to which they previously exported. This, of course, increases the number of components buyers.

The growing need for manufacturing flexibility and corporate focus is another force that reduces the costs and increases the benefits of trading. For an auto manufacturer that assembles thousands of components, each of which may be characterized by increasing technological complexity and by shortening product life-cycles, it is difficult to maintain excellence in all areas. Purchasing from specialist suppliers and focusing on design and assembly can provide benefits.

In addition, managers have become more experienced and comfortable with quasi-integration techniques such as long-term preferred supplier relationships. In many industries, purchasing departments have transformed their adversarial stance toward suppliers into a cooperative one. The U.S. car industry, for example, is reducing its level of vertical integration and the number of suppliers to concentrate on establishing fewer, more cooperative independent supply agreements.

Working against these forces, however, is a trend toward consolidation. As conglomerates like Beatrice Foods are disaggregated, the pieces are finding their way into the hands of companies that use them to increase their own shares of particular markets. Our experiences suggest, however, that the forces promoting globally competitive industry structures are generally winning out.

In addition to the pressures to disintegrate industry chains, there are pressures on firms to disintegrate the business systems within their own stages. Low-cost foreign competitors are pressuring corporations to be more cost effective. Advances in information and communications technologies are reducing the costs of bilateral trading.

Although these forces tend to favor industry-chain and business-system disintegration, a word of warning is warranted. Our suspicion is that some managers, caught up with the zest to "downscale," "be like the Japanese," or "take a nonadversarial approach to suppliers," will end up throwing a few babies out with the bathwater. They will disintegrate some activities that are in fact critical because of VMF; they will form some strategic alliances that turn out to be institutionalized piracy; and they will find that "cooperative" sole suppliers have not forgotten how to flex their muscles after their competing suppliers have been thoroughly banished. In all cases, decisions to integrate or disintegrate should be analytical rather than fashionable or instinctual. To that end, we have developed a step-by-step vertical restructuring framework (see Figure 7–6). The key point, again, is this: *do not vertically integrate unless absolutely necessary.*

F I G U R E 7-6 | **Vertical Restructuring Framework**

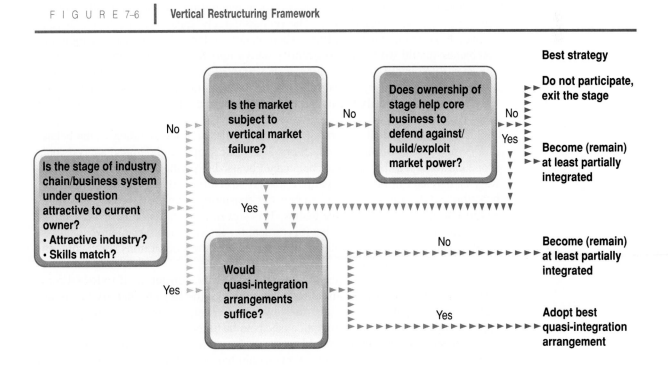

USING THE FRAMEWORK

We have successfully applied this framework in a number of situations where clients were trying to resolve make/buy decisions, such as the following:

- Should a steel plant retain all parts of its machine shop?
- Should a large exploration and mining company have its own legal department or use outside law firms?
- Should a bank produce its own checkbooks or contract the task to outside printers?
- Should a telecommunications company with 90,000 employees have its own in-house training unit or use outside trainers?

We have also used it to study strategic issues, such as the following:

- Which parts of a retail bank's business system (e.g., product development, branch network, ATM network, and central computer processing) should it own?
- What mechanisms should a government-owned research organization use to trade its services and knowledge with private industry customers?
- Should a miner and metals processor forward integrate into metals fabrication?
- What mechanisms should an agribusiness company use to penetrate the Japanese imported beef market?
- Should a brewer divest its network of tied pubs?
- Should a natural gas producer integrate downstream into pipelines and power generation?

PROCESS

In general, our consulting teams tackle vertical integration questions by following the process described in Figure 7–7. The process largely speaks for itself, but several points are worth emphasizing. First, where major strategic decisions are being made, companies should work hard to quantify the various factors. For example, it is usually critical to quantify the switching costs you would face if you became locked into a supply arrangement by investing in the assets specific to that arrangement. Similarly, you should quantify the transaction costs incurred when buying from or selling to third parties.

Second, most vertical integration analyses require an understanding of the behavior of small groups of buyers and sellers. Tools like supply and demand analysis help scope the set of feasible behavior but cannot be used to predict behavior deterministically as they can in more competitive market structures. To help predict competitor behavior and determine optimal strategy, our consulting teams use techniques such as payoff matrices and competitive games. This sort of problem solving is as much art as science, and we have found that it is critical for senior executives to have hands-on involvement in it so that they understand and believe the assumptions about competitor behavior that often must be made.

Third, the process is analytically demanding and time-consuming if followed comprehensively. We suggest an initial rapid pass through the steps to identify key issues and generate hypotheses and then a slower, more painstaking pass through. This approach allows subsequent in-depth analysis to be highly focused.

Fourth, prospective users should expect a lot of resistance. Vertical integration issues seem to be one of the last bastions within business strategy where gut feel and

F I G U R E 7-7 | **Applying the Framework**

	1	2	Static analysis		Dynamic analysis		5
			3		4		
Steps	Lay out stages of industry chain or business system	Identify participants at each stage; classify transactions across stages	Search for existing cases of vertical market failure (VMF)	Search for existing market power defense/ creation reasons to integrate	Predict changes in industry structure	Predict changes in market power issues due to changes in industry structure	Choose vertical integration strategy and supporting organization
Key tasks	• Disaggregate down to natural business (or work) units that could not reasonably be further disaggregated from an ownership perspective	• Measure number and sizes of participants on both sides of each "market" • Be careful to distinguish between pre- and post-investment phases when defining "markets" • Quantify current transactions by type (e.g., spot, contract, internal transfers) • Be careful to identify subtle ownership connections (e.g., joint ventures)	• Assess and, where possible, measure degrees of asset specificity (in both pre- and post-investment phases), durability, and intensity • Identify bilateral monopolies/oli-gopolies • Measure transaction frequency (e.g., number of deals per year) • Measure degree of uncertainty (e.g., variance over time in demand, output). Search carefully for cases of VMF due to information market failure (e.g., R&D, new products, infant industries)	• Measure economic surplus by stage of industry chain or business system • Identify cases of sustained market power asymmetry (i.e., monopoly/oligop-oly, monopsony/ oligopsony) • Test if vertical integration by weak participants would add more value to them than it would cost them • Test if vertical integration by powerful participants would strengthen their positions (e.g., raise barriers to entry, allow price discrimination)	• Predict future changes in industry structure. Focus on changes in: Power symmetry between stages Numbers/sizes of buyers and sellers Asset specificity (e.g., due to technological change) Transaction frequency • Infer changes in VMF and instances of market power asymmetry • Predict any changes in vertical behavior by other participants		• Quantify and weigh the criteria for choosing among vertical mechanisms (see Table 7–1) • Consider quasi-integration arrangements • Decide on optimal vertical strategy using normal criteria (e.g., net present value, risk, executability) • Develop recommenda-tions for changes required in structure, systems, etc., to support vertical strategy

tradition reign supreme. We have found no magic solutions to this problem, but one approach is to find examples of other companies in your industry, or in analogous industries, that illustrate your thesis. Another idea is to attack faulty logic head-on by decomposing it and revealing its weak links. Involving everyone in the problem solving itself is probably the most effective approach of all.

Vertical integration is a difficult strategy. It is usually costly and long lived, hence risky. It is not surprising, therefore, that some managers get it wrong—a problem for them but an opportunity for insightful and bold strategists adept at exploiting others' mistakes. We hope our framework helps produce more of the latter than the former.

WHY DIVERSIFY? FOUR DECADES OF MANAGEMENT THINKING

Michael Goold, Ashridge Strategic Management Centre
Kathleen Luchs, Ashridge Strategic Management Centre

Large, diversified corporations have been under critical scrutiny for many years. In 1951, the prevailing view in America was summarized in an article in the Harvard Business Review:

> The basic presumption is that a company turning from one type of activity to another is up to no good, especially if in the process it has become "big business."[1]

Such companies were accused of being too powerful, and, in particular, of cross-subsidizing their different businesses to force competitors from the field. They were therefore seen as anticompetitive.

Today, diversified companies are also regarded by many commentators as being "up to no good," but for just the opposite reason; they are now charged with being uncompetitive. The problem is not that they are overmighty competitors, but that they add no value to their businesses. In 1987, Michael Porter wrote of the failure of many corporate strategies:

> I studied the diversification records of 33 large, prestigious U.S. companies over the 1950–86 period and found that most of them had divested many more acquisitions than they had kept. The corporate strategies of most companies have dissipated instead of created shareholder value . . . By taking over companies and breaking them up, corporate raiders thrive on failed corporate strategies.[2]

How has thinking about the rationale for diversified companies evolved during this period of time? Why has fear of the power of diversified companies been replaced with skepticism about their results? What have we learned, both about diversification strategies that work and those that don't work? There have been rela-

---

Source: © *Academy of Management Executive* 7, no. 3 (1993), pp. 7–25. Reprinted with permission.

[1]Kenneth R. Andrews, "Product Diversification and the Public Interest," *Harvard Business Review,* July 1951, p. 94.
[2]M. E. Porter, "From Competitive Advantage to Corporate Strategy," *Harvard Business Review,* May–June 1987, p. 43.

tively few influential ideas about what constitutes a successful strategy for a diversified company. This article explores the development of these ideas, and examines current thinking about corporate level strategy.

DIVERSIFICATION AND CORPORATE STRATEGY IN THE 1950S AND 1960S

An important and enduring justification for the diversified company is the argument that the managers of these companies possess general management skills that contribute to the overall performance of a company. Kenneth Andrews argued that there had been a steady growth of executive talent in America, equal to the task of managing diversity. The establishment of business schools in the early 20th century created the basis for the education of professional managers, and the divisionalized structure of large corporations provided the opportunities for younger managers to gain the requisite experience.[3]

GENERAL MANAGEMENT SKILLS

The idea that professional managers possessed skills that could be put to good use across different businesses rested on the assumption that different businesses nevertheless required similar managerial skills. This assumption received support from management theory. During the 1950s and 1960s much scholarly attention focused on identifying basic principles of management, useful to all managers and applicable to all kinds of enterprises. Peter Drucker argued that "intuitive" management was no longer sufficient. He encouraged managers to study the principles of management and to acquire knowledge and analyze their performance systematically.[4]

The interest in investigating and analyzing underlying management principles continued into the 1960s. Harold Koontz wrote of the "deluge of research and writing from the academic halls." According to Koontz, it was the management process school, which aimed to identify universal principles of management, that held the greatest promise for advancing the practice of management.[5]

Theorists such as Koontz and Drucker naturally emphasized the issues and problems that were common across different types of businesses, since their aim was to help all managers improve their skills and the performance of their businesses. Though they did not explicitly claim that professional managers could manage any business, it was not a great leap to conclude that, if all managers face similar problems, professional managers might be able to use their skills in different businesses. Simple observation, as well as theory, supported this idea. Robert Katz noted that, "We are all familiar with those 'professional managers' who are becoming the prototypes of our modern executive world. These men shift with great ease, and with no apparent loss in effectiveness, from one industry to another. Their human and conceptual skills seem to make up for their unfamiliarity with the new job's technical aspects."[6] There was widespread respect for management skills, and businesspeople

---

[3]Andrews, "Product Diversification," pp. 91–107; "Toward Professionalism in Business Management," *Harvard Business Review,* March–April 1969, pp. 49–60.

[4]Peter Drucker, *The Practice of Management* (New York: Pan Books, 1968), p. 21.

[5]Harold Koontz, "The Management Theory Jungle," *Academy of Management Journal* 4, no. 3 (December 1961), p. 175.

[6]Robert L. Katz, "Skills of an Effective Administrator," *Harvard Business Review,* January–February 1955, p. 37.

were encouraged to apply their general management skills to improve the effectiveness of charities, universities, and government.[7]

In Europe, too, there was interest in general management skills. The founding of business schools in the U.K. and in France during the 1960s, and the growing interest in management training, was in part motivated by the perceived need to provide European managers with the same kind of general management skills as their U.S. competitors. Indeed, there was concern in Europe that the management skills of U.S. companies were so powerful that Americans would take over large chunks of European industry.[8]

RISE OF CONGLOMERATES

During the 1960s, the growth of conglomerates, with their numerous acquisitions of unrelated businesses across different industries, provided almost laboratory conditions in which to test out the idea that professional managers could apply their skills to many different businesses. Conglomerates such as Textron, ITT, and Litton not only grew rapidly, but also profitably, and top managers of these companies perceived themselves as breaking new ground. For example, David Judleson of Gulf & Western claimed, "Without the high degree of sophistication, skill, and effectiveness that management has developed only in the last two decades, the conglomerate could not exist. These management techniques provide the necessary unity and compatibility among a diversity of operations and acquisitions."[9] Harold Geneen used a system of detailed budgets, tight financial control, and face-to-face meetings among his general managers to build ITT into a highly diversified conglomerate.[10] In 1967, Royal Little, who masterminded Textron's broad diversification, explained that the company succeeded because, "we are adding that intangible called business judgment."[11] Textron had common financial controls, budgetary systems, and capital allocation procedures across its many businesses, but it provided few central services and had only a very small corporate office. The group vice presidents, who were responsible for a number of divisions, were appointed from outside the company. They acted as overseers and consultants to the divisions.

These new American conglomerates were admired abroad. In the U.K., one writer wrote glowingly of Litton Industries and its spectacular growth across high-tech industries, claiming that the company was " . . . a technological achievement of its own, an operation in the technology of management as much as the management of technology."[12] Several British companies, such as Slater Walker, embarked upon a strategy of conglomerate diversification during the 1960s and 1970s. The emphasis in Britain, however, was more on identifying and buying companies whose assets were

---

[7]Arthur B. Langlie, "Top Management's Responsibility for Good Government," and Thomas Roy Jones, "Top Management's Responsibility to the Community," both in H. B. Maynard, ed., *Top Management Handbook* (New York, N.Y.: McGraw-Hill, 1960); Andrews, "Product Diversification"; Y. K. Shetty and Newman S. Perry, Jr., "Are Top Executives Transferable Across Companies?" *Business Horizons,* June 1976, pp. 23–28.

[8]Richard Whitley, Alan Thomas, and Jane Marceau, *Masters of Business? Business Schools and Business Graduates in Britain and France* (London: Tavistock Publications, 1981); J. J. Servan-Schreiber, *The American Challenge,* translated by Ronald Steel (London: Hamish Hamilton, 1968).

[9]David N. Judelson, "The Conglomerate—Corporate Form of the Future," *Michigan Business Review,* July 1969, pp. 8–12, reprinted in John W. Bonge, and Bruce P. Coleman, *Concepts for Corporate Strategy* (New York, N.Y.: Macmillan, 1972), p. 458.

[10]Harold Geneen, with Alvin Moscow, *Managing* (New York: Doubleday, 1984).

[11]Norman A. Berg, "Textron, Inc.," HBS Case Study, 373-337, 1973, p. 16.

[12]R. Heller, "The Legend of Litton," *Management Today,* October 1967, reprinted in Igor Ansoff, ed., *Business Strategy* (Penguin Books, 1969), p. 378.

worth more than their stock market price and less on the application of sound, underlying general management principles by the top management group.[13]

Did the conglomerates add value to their numerous businesses across different industries? The practices of at least some conglomerates such as Textron held up well under academic scrutiny. Norman Berg argued that corporate executives in such companies were fulfilling new roles as "managers of managers." While he admitted that it was too early to draw firm conclusions about the long-term success of conglomerates, Berg suggested that corporate strategies based on improving the performance of a diverse collection of businesses would have important implications for the practice of management and also for public policy.[14]

For more than 20 years, faith in general management skills seemed to justify a kind of virtuous circle of corporate growth and diversification. Andrews summarized the basic premise, arguing that "successful diversification—because it always means successful surmounting of formidable administrative problems—develops know-how which further diversification will capitalize and extend."[15] The conglomerate movement of the 1960s, involving extensive diversification across a wide variety of industries, seemed to demonstrate that the specialized skills and practices of corporate general managers enabled them to manage ever greater complexity and diversity.

CONGLOMERATES AND PERFORMANCE PROBLEMS

There was little reason to question the belief that general management skills provided a sufficient rationale for diversified companies while such corporations were performing well and growing profitably. But by the late 1960s, conglomerates were encountering performance problems. In early 1969, the stock prices of conglomerates such as Litton, Gulf & Western, and Textron fell as much as 50 percent from their highs a year earlier, compared to a 9 percent decline in the Dow Jones industrial average over the period, and one observer foresaw a round of conglomerate divestitures if such companies were to survive. Even ITT's consistent record of increased quarterly earnings over 58 quarters during the 1960s and 1970s was broken in 1974.[16]

What became apparent was that sound principles of organization and financial control, coupled with a corporate objective of growth, were not, alone, sufficient to ensure satisfactory performance in highly diversified companies. Indeed, General Electric, a leader in the development of sophisticated techniques and principles for the management of a diverse portfolio of businesses, found by the early 1970s that its management approach had resulted in an extended period of what GE called "profitless growth." For example, the company's sales increased 40 percent from 1965 to 1970, while its profits actually fell.[17]

By the late 1960s, there was an increasing awareness that a new approach to the management of diversity was needed.

---

[13]Jim Slater, *Return to Go: My Autobiography* (London: Weidenfield and Nicolson, 1977), p. 91.

[14]Norman A. Berg, "What's Different about Conglomerate Management?" *Harvard Business Review,* November–December 1969, pp. 112–20.

[15]Kenneth R. Andrews, "Product Diversification and the Public Interest," *Harvard Business Review,* July 1951, p. 98.

[16]Robert S. Attiyeh, "Where Next for Conglomerates?" *Business Horizons,* December 1969, pp. 39–44, reprinted in Bonge and Coleman, *Concepts for Corporate Strategy;* Geneen, *Managing,* p. 43.

[17]Michael Goold and John Quinn, *Strategic Control* (London: Hutchinson and Economist Publications, 1990); Richard G. Hamermesh, *Making Strategy Work* (New York: John Wiley & Sons, 1986), p. 3; William K. Hall, "SBUs: Hot, New Topic in the Management of Diversification," *Business Horizons,* February 1978, p. 17.

DIVERSIFICATION AND CORPORATE STRATEGY IN THE 1970S

As a response to the increasing recognition that large and diversified companies present particular management problems, increasing attention was devoted to the question of the issues on which general managers should focus their efforts.

THE CONCEPT OF STRATEGY

One theme that emerged with increasing force during the 1960s and 1970s was the need for senior managers to focus their attention on the "strategies" of their companies. Strategy was more than long-range planning or objective setting; it was a way of deciding the basic direction of the company and preparing it to meet future challenges.[18]

C. Roland Christensen, one of the creators of the business policy course at Harvard during the 1960s, argued that the concept of strategy made it possible to simplify the complex tasks of top managers.[19] A focus on strategy prevented senior executives from meddling in operating details and day-to-day issues that should be left to more junior managers with direct responsibility for them. It allowed them to concentrate on the most important issues facing their companies—and it simplified management by providing a framework for decisions.

CEOs readily accepted that strategy should be their main and unique responsibility. During the late 1960s and 1970s many companies established formal planning systems, and the appropriate structure and uses of such systems received much attention from academics.[20] In the early 1970s, Louis Gerstner remarked on how quickly strategic planning had been adopted by companies, noting that, "Writer after writer has hailed this new discipline as the fountainhead of all corporate progress."[21]

The strategic frameworks, models, and tools being developed by academics and consultants focused mainly on strategic issues at the business-unit level, and they were, therefore, less relevant in helping to define an overall strategy for companies with many different businesses. Andrews, however, defined the main task of corporate-level strategy as identifying the businesses in which the firm would compete, and this became the accepted understanding of corporate strategy.[22] This general concept of corporate strategy, though, did not provide much practical guidance to some of the problems managers of diversified companies confronted. In particular, it did not help them decide how resources should be allocated among businesses, especially when investment proposals were being put forward by a large number of disparate

---

[18]Peter Drucker, "Long-Range Planning: Challenge to Management Science," *Management Science* 5, no. 3 (1959), pp. 238–49; Igor Ansoff, *Corporate Strategy* (New York: McGraw-Hill, 1965); Alfred P. Sloan, *My Years with General Motors* (New York: Doubleday, 1963); Alfred D. Chandler, Jr., *Strategy and Structure* (Cambridge, Mass.: MIT, 1962); Myles L. Mace, "The President and Corporate Planning," *Harvard Business Review,* January–February 1965, pp. 49–62.

[19]C. Roland Christensen et al., *Business Policy: Text and Cases* (Homewood, Ill.: Richard D. Irwin, 1965).

[20]R. F. Vancil and P. Lorange, "Strategic Planning in Diversified Companies," *Harvard Business Review,* January–February 1975, pp. 81–90; Peter Lorange and Richard F. Vancil, *Strategic Planning Systems* (Englewood Cliffs, New Jersey: Prentice Hall, 1977); K. A. Ringbakk, "Organized Planning in Major U.S. Companies," *Long Range Planning* 2, no. 2 (December 1969), pp. 46–57; Norman A. Berg, "Strategic Planning in Conglomerate Companies," *Harvard Business Review,* May–June 1965, pp. 79–92.

[21]Louis V. Gerstner, "Can Strategic Management Pay Off?" *Business Horizons* 15, no. 6 (December 1972), p. 5.

[22]Kenneth R. Andrews, *The Concept of Corporate Strategy,* rev. ed. (Homewood, Ill.: Richard D. Irwin, 1980), p. 35.

businesses, each with its own strategy. This problem was exacerbated when the aggregate demand for resources exceeded what was available.

PROBLEMS WITH RESOURCE ALLOCATION

Resource-allocation decisions in diversified companies are a key part of corporate strategy, but they present particular difficulties. Corporate management must grasp the relative merits of investment proposals coming from a range of businesses in different sectors, with different time horizons, competitive positions, and risk profiles, not to mention management teams with differing credibilities. This can be complex. In the early 1970s, for example, a company such as ITT had to allocate resources among businesses that included telecommunications, insurance, rental cars, bakeries, and construction. With many divisions competing for funds, how could a company be sure it was investing in the best projects for future growth?[23]

Joseph Bower explored in detail how a large, diversified firm allocated resources. His research highlighted the gulf between financial theory, which saw the manager's task as choosing projects with the highest returns, and corporate reality, where all proposed projects showed at least the return required by the corporate hurdle rate for investment. In practice, divisional managers only proposed projects with acceptable forecast returns, and corporate-level managers had little basis on which to choose among projects.

Bower argued that investment decisions should not be made on a project-by-project basis, but had to be integrally related to a business's strategic product and market decisions.[24] During the 1970s, the new techniques of portfolio planning that were introduced by the Boston Consulting Group and others gained wide acceptance because they helped corporate executives to resolve practical problems of capital allocation in the context of an overall corporate strategy.[25]

PORTFOLIO PLANNING

Portfolio planning provided corporate managers with a common framework to compare many different businesses. The industry attractiveness/business position matrix developed at GE, the Boston Consulting Group's growth/share matrix, and variations developed at other consultancies were used to classify businesses in terms of their strategic position and opportunities. These classifications helped managers both to set appropriate objectives and resource allocation strategies for different businesses, and to determine the overall cash requirements and cash generation of the corporate portfolio.[26]

The helicopter view provided by portfolio planning techniques was widely perceived as useful. For example, one CEO explained:

> Portfolio planning became relevant to me as soon as I became CEO. I was finding it very difficult to manage and understand so many different products and markets. I just grabbed at portfolio planning, because it provided me with a way to organize my thinking about our businesses, and the resource allocation issues facing the total company. I

[23]Berg, "Strategic Planning."

[24]Joseph L. Bower, *Managing the Resource Allocation Process* (Boston, Mass.: Harvard Business School Press, 1970), Harvard Business School Classics Edition, 1986.

[25]Ibid.; Hamermesh, *Making Strategy Work.*

[26]William K. Hall, "SBUs: Hot, New Topic in the Management of Diversification," *Business Horizons,* February 1978, pp. 17–25; George S. Day, "Diagnosing the Product Portfolio," *Journal of Marketing,* April 1977, pp. 29–38.

became and still am very enthusiastic. I guess you could say that I went for it hook, line, and sinker.[27]

During the 1970s, more and more corporations adopted portfolio planning, with the largest diversified companies being among the earliest adherents. One survey showed that by 1979, 45 percent of the Fortune 500 companies were using some form of portfolio planning.[28]

In many companies, portfolio-planning techniques became more than analytical tools to help chief executives direct corporate resources toward the most profitable opportunities: they became the basis of corporate strategy itself. The key concept here was the idea of a balanced portfolio made up of businesses whose profitability, growth, and cash flow characteristics would complement each other, and add up to a satisfactory overall corporate performance. Imbalance could be caused, for example, either by excessive cash generation with too few growth opportunities or by insufficient cash generation to fund the growth requirements elsewhere in the portfolio.[29] Often, the first step toward balancing the corporate portfolio was to identify businesses that were a drain on corporate resources. Monsanto, for example, used portfolio planning to restructure its portfolio, divesting low-growth commodity chemicals businesses and acquiring businesses in higher-growth industries such as biotechnology.[30]

Portfolio planning reinforced the virtuous circle of corporate growth and diversification that had been originally founded on general management skills. It helped corporate-level managers correct past diversification mistakes, leading to divestiture of weak businesses, and it encouraged them to invest in a mix of businesses, with different strategic (and cash) characteristics to balance their corporate portfolios and ensure future growth.

PROBLEMS WITH PORTFOLIO MANAGEMENT

Even as an increasing number of corporations turned to portfolio planning, problems emerged in managing balanced portfolios.[31] Companies discovered that while certain businesses appeared to meet all the economic requirements of the corporate portfolio, they did not fit easily into the corporate family. It turned out to be extremely difficult, for example, for corporate managers with long experience of managing mature businesses in a particular industry sector to manage effectively their acquired growth businesses in new, dynamic, and unfamiliar sectors.

Research on how companies actually used portfolio planning confirmed the difficulties of managing businesses with different strategic characteristics, missions, or mandates. Philippe Haspeslagh investigated whether companies adjusted their systems of financial planning, capital investment appraisal, incentive compensation, or strategic planning to fit the requirements of their different businesses. The focus of his study was on the role played by general management, rather than on specific busi-

---

[27]Hamermesh, *Making Strategy Work,* p. 30.

[28]Philippe Haspeslagh, "Portfolio Planning: Uses and Limits," *Harvard Business Review,* January–February 1982, pp. 58–73.

[29]Barry Hedley, "Strategy and the 'Business Portfolio,'" *Long Range Planning,* February 1977, pp. 9–15; Charles W. Hofer and Dan Schendel, *Strategy Formulation: Analytical Concepts* (New York: West Publishing, 1978).

[30]Hamermesh, *Making Strategy Work,* p. 71.

[31]Richard A. Bettis and William K. Hall, "The Business Portfolio Approach—Where It Falls Down in Practice," *Long Range Planning* 16, no. 2 (April 1983), pp. 95–104.

ness-level strategies. He found that companies made few changes in their formal corporate-level systems, but corporate-level managers in successful companies did make informal attempts to adapt these systems to their businesses.[32] In another study on the effectiveness of portfolio-planning techniques, the authors discovered that cash cows performed better in an organizational context of autonomy while fast-growing businesses benefitted from more control. They concluded that the administrative context was an important variable in explaining business performance, and that many companies were taking the wrong approach to some of their businesses.[33]

The recognition that different types of businesses had to be managed differently undermined the argument that general management skills, buttressed by the common frameworks of strategy and portfolio planning, provided the rationale for diversified companies. Many companies discovered that common systems and approaches, when applied to different kinds of businesses, could minimize value from those businesses. Portfolio planning helped corporate executives sort out the contribution of each of their businesses to the corporate portfolio, but it did not answer the other critical question confronting a diversified company: what contribution should the corporation make to each of its businesses?

DIVERSIFICATION AND CORPORATE STRATEGY IN THE 1980S

During the 1980s, there was widespread skepticism about the ability of companies to manage and add value to diverse, conglomerate portfolios. Raiders such as Carl Icahn and T. Boone Pickens demonstrated that they could acquire even the largest companies, break them up, and realize huge profits. The takeover activity of the 1980s prompted a rethinking of both the role of corporate management in large companies, and of the kinds of strategies that were appropriate for diversified companies.

COST CUTTING AT HEADQUARTERS

What seemed most obvious about the corporate level in many companies was not its contribution, but its cost. Thus, attention shifted to cutting headquarters costs. Some companies turned central services into profit centers, charged with selling their services to the business units, while other companies disbanded some central functions altogether. The pruning of corporate staffs often meant devolving more authority to line managers in decentralized units.[34]

Cost cutting and the downsizing of corporate staffs, however, were not alone sufficient to demonstrate that corporate management could add value to their businesses, and the overall performance of large, diversified corporations also came under increasing scrutiny. Michael Porter published a study showing the high rate of divestiture of acquisitions among American corporations, arguing that the diversification strategies of many companies had failed to create value.[35] Also, the wave of takeovers caused executives to pay increasing attention to their company's stock

---

[32]Haspeslagh, "Portfolio Planning."

[33]Richard G. Hamermesh and Roderick E. White, "Manage beyond Portfolio Analysis," *Harvard Business Review,* January–February 1984, pp. 103–109.

[34]Rosabeth Moss Kanter, *When Giants Learn to Dance* (London: Simon & Schuster, 1989), p. 94; Thomas More, "Goodbye, Corporate Staff," *Fortune,* December 21, 1987.

[35]Porter, "From Competitive Advantage."

price as analysts and raiders identified "value gaps," or the difference between the current stock market price of a company and its breakup value.[36]

VALUE-BASED PLANNING

Faced with the threat from raiders and the criticism of academics such as Porter, chief executives devoted themselves increasingly to the task of creating shareholder value. Managers were encouraged to evaluate corporate performance in the same terms as the stock market (and raiders), using economic rather than accounting measures, and to take whatever actions were necessary to improve their company's stock price. Value-based planning, using the financial tools of discounted cash flow, ROE spreads, and hurdle rates, provided corporate managers with a fresh perspective on the link between stock prices and competitive strategy.[37]

A company's stock price, according to proponents of value-based planning, is determined by the value of the strategies of its businesses. However, it can be very difficult for managers to assess the strategies of dissimilar businesses: " . . . corporate-level planners facing a portfolio of 4, 10, dozens, or dozens and dozens of units do not know—probably cannot know—enough about each unit's competitive position, industry, rivals, and customers to make this determination."[38] One of the appeals of value-based planning is that, like portfolio planning, it offers corporate-level executives a means of evaluating many different businesses using a common framework. The corporate level can require business units to make strategic choices on the basis of economic returns, and doing this systematically across all units, it is argued, provides corporate management with the basis for making decisions on capital allocation.

Value-based planning techniques gained many adherents, especially among American corporations. In 1987 an article in *Fortune* described how "managements have caught the religion. At first reluctant, they pound at the door of consultants who can teach them the way to a higher stock price—a price so high it would thwart even the most determined raider."[39]

But value-based planning also has limitations as a guide to corporate strategy. It can help corporate managers to focus on the goal of increasing shareholder wealth and to understand the criteria that must be met to do so. It does not, however, provide much insight into the kind of corporate strategies that should be pursued to meet these criteria. A higher stock price is a reward for creating value. But the key question remains: how can corporations add value to diverse business portfolios? Perhaps the most influential view on this vital topic to have emerged during the 1980s is that they should "stick to the knitting."

STICK TO THE KNITTING

The concept of corporate success based on core businesses, or stick to the knitting, gained popularity in 1982 with the publication of Peters's and Waterman's *In Search of Excellence*. Successful corporations, they observed, did not diversify widely. They

---

[36]David Young and Brigid Sutcliffe, "Value Gaps—The Raiders, the Market, or the Managers?" research paper, Ashridge Strategic Management Centre, January 1990.

[37]Alfred Rappaport, *Creating Shareholder Value: The New Standard for Business Performance* (New York: Free Press, 1986); Bernard C. Reimann, *Managing for Value* (Oxford: Basil Blackwell, 1987).

[38]William W. Alberts and James M. McTaggart, "Value-Based Strategic Investment Planning," *Interfaces,* January–February 1984, pp. 138–151; see also Enrique R. Arzac, "Do Your Business Units Create Shareholder Value?" *Harvard Business Review,* January–February 1986, pp. 121–126.

[39]John J. Curran, "Are Stocks Too High?" *Fortune,* September 28, 1987, p. 24.

tended to specialize in particular industries and focused intently on improving their knowledge and skills in the areas they knew best.[40]

Stick-to-the-knitting advice was also a reaction against the analytical techniques and impersonal approach of much of strategic and portfolio planning. Bob Hayes and Bill Abernathy voiced these concerns in their article "Managing Our Way to Economic Decline." In their view, too many American corporations were being run by "pseudo-professional" managers, skilled in finance and law, but lacking in technological expertise or in-depth experience in any particular industry. They warned that portfolios diversified across different industries and businesses were appropriate for stocks and bonds, but not for corporations.[41] The need for experience and deep knowledge of a business was also emphasized by Henry Mintzberg, who criticized the "thin and lifeless" strategies that result from treating businesses as mere positions on a portfolio matrix. He argued that instead of broad diversity, we need "focused organizations that understand their missions, 'know' the people they serve, and excite the ones they employ; we should be encouraging thick management, deep knowledge, healthy competition, and authentic social responsibility."[42]

The widespread conviction that companies should stick to the knitting increased skepticism about the ability of corporations to manage and add value to diverse portfolios. It reinforced the practical pressures created by the corporate raiders and contributed to a wave of retrenching. From the mid-1980s onward, a goal for many corporations has been to rationalize their portfolios to overcome the perceived disadvantages of broad diversification.

CORPORATE RESTRUCTURING

Restructuring (whether voluntary or not) has frequently led to the disposal of corporate assets. In 1985, for example, General Mills announced its intention to focus on its core businesses of consumer foods and restaurants, and the company sold off its toy and fashion businesses.[43] More recently, General Signal embarked on a strategy of "back to the basics," retreating from its earlier major investments in high-tech businesses to focus on its traditional "boring" products such as industrial mixers.[44]

Restructuring has been widely regarded as a salutary correction to the excesses of broad diversification. Michael Jensen has argued that corporate break-ups, divisional sell-offs, and LBOs are critical developments that can prevent the wasteful use of capital by managers of large public corporations, and other recent academic studies support the view that restructuring does help improve the performance of corporations.[45] But restructuring implies a sense of which businesses a company should retain and which it should divest. How should the core businesses be selected?

One answer is that companies should restructure to limit their businesses to one, or a few, closely related industries. In this way, managers stick to what they know

[40]Thomas J. Peters and Robert H. Waterman, *In Search of Excellence* (New York: Free Press, 1982).

[41]Bob Hayes and Bill Abernathy, "Managing Our Way to Economic Decline," *Harvard Business Review,* July–August 1980, pp. 67–77.

[42]Henry Mintzberg, *Mintzberg on Management* (New York: Free Press, 1989), p. 373.

[43]Michael E. Porter, "General Mills, Inc: Corporate Strategy," HBS Case Study 9-388-123, 1988.

[44]Seth Lubove, "Dog with Bone," *Fortune,* April 13, 1992, p. 106.

[45]Michael Jensen, "The Eclipse of the Public Corporation," *Harvard Business Review,* September–October 1989, pp. 61–74; S. Chatterjee, "Sources of Value in Takeovers: Synergy or Restructuring—Implications for Target and Bidder Firms," *Strategic Management Journal* 13, no. 4 (May 1992), pp. 267–286; S. Bhagat et al., "Hostile Takeovers in the 1980s: The Return to Corporate Specialization," Brookings Paper on Economic Activity: Microeconomics 1990.

well, and are best able to exploit corporate expertise. This approach is consistent with stick-to-the-knitting advice, but it is not a complete answer. Successful companies such as GE, Hanson, and Cooper Industries nevertheless have businesses in many different industries. Furthermore, sticking to a single industry does not necessarily limit complexity or ensure that companies expand into areas they "know." During the 1980s, companies such as Prudential and Merrill Lynch sought to combine different types of financial services businesses. They discovered that businesses such as insurance, stockbroking, and banking, though all in the financial services industry, nonetheless required very different approaches, resources, and skills.[46]

Another reservation about a stick-to-the-knitting strategy based on limiting diversification to closely related businesses is that, despite extensive research, empirical evidence on the performance of companies pursuing more and less related diversification strategies is ambiguous and contradictory. Many studies have compared the performance of single-product firms, companies that diversify into related products, markets, or technologies, and unrelated conglomerates, but no firm relationship between different diversification strategies and performance has been discovered.[47]

Some concept of what constitutes a "core portfolio"—or the corporate "knitting"—is required, though, if restructuring is to result in long-term improvement in corporate performance.

DIVERSIFICATION AND CORPORATE STRATEGY IN THE 1990S

The main issues for corporate strategy in the 1990s have therefore emerged as how to identify the businesses that should form a core portfolio for a corporation, and how to find ways of adding value to those businesses.

Three main alternative answers to these questions have received support in current management thinking:

1. Diversification should be limited to those businesses with synergy.
2. The corporate focus should be on exploiting core competencies across different businesses.
3. Successful diversification depends on building a portfolio of businesses that fit with the managerial "dominant logic" of top executives and their management style.

---

[46]Robert M. Grant, "On 'Dominant Logic,' Relatedness, and the Link Between Diversity and Performance," *Strategic Management Journal* 9, no. 6 (November–December 1988), pp. 639–42; Robert M. Grant, "Diversification in the Financial Services Industry," in Andrew Campbell and Kathleen Luchs, *Strategic Synergy* (London: Butterworth Heinemann, 1992).

[47]There is an extensive literature on this topic. See Richard P. Rumelt, *Strategy, Structure and Economic Performance* (Boston, Mass.: Harvard Business School Press, 1974); Richard P. Rumelt, "Diversification Strategy and Profitability," *Strategic Management Journal* 3 (1982), pp. 359–69; Richard A. Bettis, "Performance Differences in Related and Unrelated Diversified Firms," *Strategic Management Journal* 2 (1981), pp. 379–93; Kurt H. Christensen and Cynthia A. Montgomery, "Corporate Economic Performance: Diversification Strategy versus Market Structure," *Strategic Management Journal* 2 (1981), pp. 327–43; Gerry Johnson and Howard Thomas, "The Industry Context of Strategy, Structure and Performance: The U.K. Brewing Industry," *Strategic Management Journal* 8 (1987), pp. 343–61; Anju Seth, "Value Creation in Acquisitions: A Reexamination of Performance Issues," *Strategic Management Journal* 11 (1990), pp. 99–115.

SYNERGY

Synergy occurs when the performance of a portfolio of businesses adds up to more than the sum of its parts. The concept of synergy is based in part on economies of scale; two or more businesses can lower their costs if they can combine manufacturing facilities, use a common sales force, or advertise jointly, and in this way the combined businesses are worth more than they would be on a stand-alone basis.[48]

In much of the current management literature, synergy has become virtually synonymous with corporate-level strategy. Michael Porter views the management of interrelationships between businesses as the essence of corporate-level strategy, arguing that without synergy a diversified company is little more than a mutual fund.[49] Rosabeth Moss Kanter, too, argues that the achievement of synergy is the only justification for a multibusiness company.[50] In a review of the literature on mergers, Friedrich Trautwein, a German academic, found that managers almost always justified diversification moves in terms of the synergies available, and that most of the advice in the management literature on diversification was based on the concept of realizing synergies.[51]

In practice, however, many companies have found it very difficult to gain benefits from a corporate strategy based on synergy.[52] Acquisitions aimed at realizing synergies can be especially risky; for example, two academic commentators have noted that anticipated synergy benefits " . . . show an almost unshakeable resolve not to appear when it becomes time for their release."[53] Quantitative evidence appears to support the observation that synergies are hard to achieve; a recent study on takeovers concluded that most gains arise from asset disposals and restructuring rather than from synergy.[54]

Those who view synergy as the essence of corporate-level strategy, including Porter and Kanter, acknowledge that companies find it difficult to gain synergy benefits and that the failure rate is high. Much of the current literature, therefore, focuses on implementation—what companies have to do to gain benefits from sharing skills or activities across businesses. Porter, for instance, discusses the need for the evolution of a new organizational form, which he calls the "horizontal organization." These organizations facilitate interrelationships across different businesses by overlaying horizontal structures, systems, and managerial approaches onto the vertical relationships that currently characterize the ties between business units and corporate management.[55] Kanter describes the emergence of the "postentrepreneurial corporation," which aims to create the relationships and management processes required for cross-business cooperation.[56] Christopher Bartlett and Sumantra

---

[48]Igor Ansoff, *Corporate Strategy* (New York: McGraw-Hill, 1965).

[49]Michael E. Porter, *Competitive Advantage* (New York: Free Press, 1985).

[50]Kanter, *When Giants Learn*, p. 90.

[51]Friedrich Trautwein, "Merger Motives and Merger Prescriptions," *Strategic Management Journal* 11 (1990), pp. 283–95.

[52]Vasudevan Ramanujam and P. Varadarajan, "Research on Corporate Diversification: A Synthesis," *Strategic Management Journal* 10 (1989), pp. 523–51; Campbell and Luchs, *Strategic Synergy*.

[53]Richard Reed and George A. Luffman, "Diversification: The Growing Confusion," *Strategic Management Journal* 7 (1986), p. 34.

[54]S. Chatterjee, "Sources of Value in Takeovers: Synergy or Restructuring," *Strategic Management Journal* 13, no. 4 (May 1992), pp. 267–86.

[55]Porter, *Competitive Advantage*.

[56]Kanter, *When Giants Learn*.

Ghoshal argue a similar case for the complex problems facing multinationals attempting to make the most of their businesses in different countries. In their view, multinationals need to develop new organizational capabilities so that components, products, resources, people, and information can flow freely among interdependent units. Bartlett and Ghoshal describe such an integrated network as a "transnational organization."[57]

Transnational or horizontal or postentrepreneurial organizations, by definition, capture many synergy benefits because they have the organizational capabilities to manage complex interrelationships across businesses. There are, however, very few examples of companies that represent these new kinds of organizations, at least in full-fledged form. Consequently, much of the advice on synergy remains theoretical and prescriptive.

There is evidence, furthermore, that managing complex interrelationships to create synergies across businesses is not the only means of creating value. Michael Goold and Andrew Campbell, in their study of strategic management styles, found that companies such as Hanson and Courtaulds, which placed very little emphasis on synergy as a source of corporate value added, performed at least as well as companies that placed more emphasis on linkages across businesses.[58] These findings are reinforced by successful multibusiness companies such as KKR, the leveraged buyout specialists, and Berkshire Hathaway, managed by the renowned investor Warren Buffet, which are collections of independent businesses, and whose strategies are not based on exploiting synergies across their businesses. The assumption that synergy is the only rationale for a group of companies does not fit the available evidence, and this suggests that not all corporations need to focus their efforts on constructing and managing portfolios of interrelated businesses.

Synergy remains a powerful concept in our understanding of corporate strategy, but it is difficult to accept that it is the "one best way" to create value in a multibusiness company. For some companies, the advantages of managing stand-alone businesses may outweigh the long-term investment required to create linkages among those businesses, and the potential for synergy may simply not exist in some corporate portfolios. We need to discover more about when synergy is an appropriate corporate strategy, and we need to learn more about how companies successful at managing interrelationships across businesses go about it.

CORE COMPETENCIES

Another approach to corporate strategy stresses building on the core competencies of the corporation. This can be seen as a particular case of synergy, with corporate value creation dependent on exploiting unique skills and capabilities across a portfolio of businesses. Gary Hamel and C. K. Prahalad focus on technological competencies. They argue that the corporate portfolio should not be perceived simply as a group of businesses, but also as a collection of such competencies. In managing the corporate portfolio, managers must ensure that each part draws on and contributes to the core competencies the corporation is seeking to build and exploit. Even a poorly performing business may be contributing to an important core competence, and if managers divest such businesses they may also be discarding some of their competencies. If corporations are unable to transfer a core competence from one business to another,

---

[57]Christopher A. Bartlett and Sumantra Ghoshal, *Managing across Borders: The Transnational Solution* (Boston: Harvard Business School Press, 1989).

[58]Michael Goold and Andrew Campbell, *Strategies and Styles* (Oxford: Basil Blackwell, 1987).

then they are wasting their resources. According to Prahalad and Hamel, many of the current management approaches of Western corporations, including SBUs, decentralization, and resource-allocation practices, undermine the ability of corporations to build core competencies, since autonomous businesses seldom have the resources or vision to build world-class competencies.[59]

Hiroyuki Itami, a Japanese academic, focuses on building the corporation's "invisible assets," such as expertise in a particular technology, brand names, reputation, or customer information. Such assets, he argues, can be employed throughout the firm without being used up, and they are the only sustainable source of competitive advantage.[60] Philippe Haspeslagh and David Jemison, authors of a recent study on acquisitions, support a capabilities-based view of corporate value creation, defining core capabilities as managerial and technological skills gained mainly through experience. Such capabilities can be applied across the corporation's businesses and make an important contribution to customer benefits.[61] It can be difficult to define a corporation's capabilities objectively, but understanding what they are can provide important insights into its sources of competitive advantage and the strategic options of the firm.[62]

The work on core skills, capabilities, or resources has generated much interest. Walter Kiechel, in *Fortune* magazine, describes how some executives are perceiving their role, and that of the corporate management, as guardians and promoters of the company's core skills, and sums up the current understanding of these concepts: "To the extent that such skills can be exploited by each of the company's businesses, they represent a reason for having all those businesses under one corporate umbrella—a much better reason, the experts add, than the fabled synergies that multibusiness companies of yore were supposed to realize but seldom did."[63]

But corporations that do base their strategy on core competencies have to be careful that the overall competence-based strategy does not become an excuse for poor performance or poor judgment. IBM, for example, acquired Rolm to gain access to the smaller company's expertise in PBX systems. Five years later, however, following heavy losses, IBM sold a majority stake in Rolm to Siemens. Some commentators think that IBM was too optimistic about Rolm's competencies and potential and not sufficiently knowledgeable about changes under way in the PBX market or within Rolm.[64] It can be difficult to judge when an investment in a business is justified in terms of building a core competence, particularly if it means suspending normal profitability criteria and if the investment is in an unfamiliar business area.

Another danger with the competence approach to corporate strategy is that businesses may require similar core competencies, but demand different overall strategies and managerial approaches. Texas Instruments, for example, attempted to exploit the

[59]C. K. Prahalad and Gary Hamel, "The Core Competence of the Corporation," *Harvard Business Review,* May–June 1990, pp. 79–91; Gary Hamel and C. K. Prahalad, "Strategic Intent," *Harvard Business Review,* May–June 1989, pp. 63–76.

[60]Hiroyuki Itami, *Mobilizing Invisible Assets* (Cambridge, Mass.: Harvard University Press, 1987).

[61]Philippe Haspeslagh and David B. Jemison, *Managing Acquisitions* (New York: Free Press, 1991), p. 23.

[62]Robert M. Grant, "The Resource-Based Theory of Competitive Advantage: Implications for Strategy Formulation," *California Management Review,* Spring 1991, pp. 114–35; Andrew Campbell, "Building Core Skills," in Campbell and Luchs, *Strategic Synergy*; George Stalk, Philip Evans, Laurence E. Shulman, "Competing on Capabilities," *Harvard Business Review,* March–April 1992, pp. 57–69.

[63]Walter Kiechel, "Corporate Strategy for the 1990s," *Fortune,* February 29, 1988, p. 20.

[64]Robert D. Hof and John J. Keller, "Behind the Scenes at the Fall of Rolm," *Business Week,* July 10, 1989, pp. 82–84.

core competence it had developed in its semiconductors business in areas such as calculators, watches, and home computers. It failed in these new areas not because it lacked the core semiconductor competence, but because its top management had no experience in managing such consumer-oriented businesses.[65] Similarly, Procter & Gamble applied its skills in product innovation and consumer promotion to a soft-drinks business, Crush, but eventually divested the business because it ran into unfamiliar problems managing the local bottlers who largely control distribution of soft drinks.[66] Core competencies may add value in specific areas in a variety of different businesses, but this is no guarantee that, overall, a company will be able to manage those different businesses successfully.

The work on core competencies and capabilities broadens our understanding of a corporation's resources, and points out the important role of corporate management in building such resources and ensuring that they are used to best advantage. As with synergy, however, it is difficult to accept that this is the only way to add value to a corporate portfolio. Corporate executives are concerned not only with building skills and competencies in their businesses, but also with allocating resources to them, approving their plans and strategies, and monitoring and controlling their results. These important "shareholder" functions can also be a source of added value, if done well. Some companies such as Berkshire Hathaway and Hanson lay far more stress on these shareholder functions than on competence building; and, in all companies, the shareholder functions occupy a vital place, even where the management of core competencies is also a focus of attention.

DOMINANT LOGIC AND MANAGEMENT STYLE

A third approach to corporate success focuses on how corporate management adds value to a portfolio of businesses, in particular in its shareholder role. C. K. Prahalad and Richard Bettis argue that the more diverse a firm, the more complex the problems in managing it. Diversity, however, cannot be defined simply in terms of the number of products or markets in which a firm competes; the strategic variety of the firm's businesses is a more significant measure of its diversity. With firms in strategically similar businesses, executives can use common methods and approaches, using a single managerial dominant logic: "A dominant general management logic is defined as the way in which managers conceptualize the business and make critical resource allocation decisions—be it in technologies, product development, distribution, advertising, or in human resource management."[67]

When managerial dominant logic does not match the needs of the business, tensions and problems arise. Corporate management is liable to appoint the wrong managers to the business, to sanction inappropriate plans and investments, to control against the wrong targets and to interfere unproductively in the managing of the business.

Goold and Campbell's work on strategic management styles shows how dominant logic works in specific companies. In their research on large, diversified companies they identified different types of strategic management styles, with the main styles being financial control, strategic control, and strategic planning. The different styles each added value, but in different ways and to businesses with different characteris-

---

[65]C. K. Prahalad and R. A. Bettis, "The Dominant Logic: A New Linkage between Diversity and Performance," *Strategic Management Journal* 7 (1986), p. 495.

[66]Patricia Winters, "Crush Fails to Fit on P&G Shelf," *Advertising Age,* July 10, 1989.

[67]Prahalad and Bettis, "The Dominant Logic," p. 490.

tics and requirements. Financial-control companies, for example, have distinctive administrative and control systems, emphasizing the setting and meeting of annual budget targets. Although they may invest in a wide variety of industries, the portfolios of businesses of successful financial-control companies share common characteristics.[68] Hanson is a good example: "The company's strategy is to focus on mature, stable businesses: 'We avoid areas of very high technology. We do not want to be in businesses which are highly capital intensive, where decision making has to be centralized or which rely on huge and sometimes expensive research with a prospect of a return sometime or never.'"[69]

In this view, the dominant logic or management style of the corporate management group is central to the performance of a diversified firm, and a group of businesses is best managed when the dominant logic of top managers matches the strategic characteristics and requirements of the businesses. The importance of the "fit" between top managers and the businesses in the corporate portfolio has also been emphasized by executives. Orion Hoch of Litton, for example, has explained the reasons for Litton's extensive divestments and restructuring: "Our aim was to go back to businesses that we could be comfortable with . . . We want to get back to doing what we were good at doing."[70] Gary Roubos, CEO of Dover Corporation, argues that the company is a successful conglomerate because it invests only in businesses in which it has considerable management "feel," even though these businesses are highly diverse: "Automatic lifts and toggle clamps are different—but they have much more in common than, say, investment banking and selling soap."[71]

Dominant logic may help explain why conglomerate diversification can succeed, and also why diversification based on synergy or core competencies can fail. If conglomerate diversification, such as that of Hanson, is based on businesses with a similar strategic logic, then it is possible for corporate management to take a common approach and to add value to those businesses. On the other hand, businesses with opportunities for sharing activities or skills, or ones requiring the same core competence, may nonetheless have different strategic logics. This makes it difficult for corporate management to realize synergy or exploit a core competence across the businesses. Oil companies that diversified into other extractive, energy, or natural resource businesses in pursuit of synergies or core competencies tended to find that the benefits they sought were overwhelmed by the problems caused by dissimilarities in strategic logic between the new businesses and the core oil businesses.

The concepts of dominant logic and management style offer some promising insights into both successful and unsuccessful diversification efforts, but there are unanswered questions.[72] Should diversified corporations aim to build portfolios of strategically related businesses, to ensure that top management and corporate systems and approaches do add value? Or should corporations seek to differentiate their approaches—develop "multiple dominant logics"—to manage businesses with different strategic characteristics successfully?

Goold and Campbell discovered that companies tend to adopt a particular strategic-management style, even though the style was usually implicit, and that it was dif-

[68]Goold and Campbell, *Strategies and Styles.*

[69]Andrew Campbell et al., *A Sense of Mission* (London: Hutchinson, 1990), p. 242.

[70]*Barron's,* May 20, 1991.

[71]F. J. Aguilar, "Groen: A Dover Industries Company," HBS Case 9-388-055, 1988.

[72]Michael Goold and Andrew Campbell, "Brief Case: From Corporate Strategy to Parenting Advantage," *Long Range Planning* 24, no. 1 (February 1991), pp. 115–17.

ficult for managers to cope with a variety of approaches or styles. They argued that CEOs should aim to focus their portfolios on the kinds of businesses that would gain benefits from their strategic-management style.[73] On the other hand, authorities on multinationals argue that the increasing complexities of globally spread businesses and international competition require corporations to develop new capabilities to manage businesses facing different strategic issues. C. K. Prahalad and Yves Doz maintain that the winners in the struggle for global competitive advantage will be those companies that can develop differentiated structures, management processes and systems, appropriate to the wide variety of their businesses.[74] Bartlett and Ghoshal describe how the "administrative heritage" of companies emphasizes a particular approach to issues such as coordination across businesses, but they argue that the idealized transnational company should be able to combine different approaches and develop "a full arsenal of coordinating processes, practices, and tools, and to use those mechanisms in the most effective and efficient manner."[75]

The question of whether it is possible to differentiate your management approaches to add value to many different kinds of businesses remains open. Bartlett and Ghoshal found evidence that some companies were seeking ways to encompass much more variety, but none had yet become a true transnational. We need more research to establish when it is appropriate to differentiate your management approaches to encompass the needs of diverse kinds of businesses, and when it is reasonable to adjust the corporate portfolio to a particular management style, or to a single managerial dominant logic. Work is also needed to clarify how to operationalize the concepts of dominant logic and strategic relatedness. We do not yet know how the limits of a dominant logic should be defined, how managers and corporations develop a new strategic management style, or if this is even possible.

THE CHALLENGE OF DIVERSIFICATION

During the last four decades, managers and academics have sought both to understand the basis of successful diversification, and to address the problems created by it. Figure 8–1 summarizes the evolution of thinking and practice during this time.

From the 1950s onward, the development of management principles and the professional education of managers led to the belief that general management skills provided the justification for diversification. Diversified companies and conglomerates were seen to add value through the skills of their professional top managers, who applied modern management techniques and generalized approaches to a wide variety of businesses across different industries. During the late 1960s, however, the performance of many conglomerates weakened, and a new approach to corporate management of diversity was sought. The concepts of strategy and strategic management provided a new focus for senior management's attention during the 1970s, but soon proved unable to resolve many of the choices and trade-offs involved in resource allocation in the multibusiness firm. Portfolio-planning techniques helped many companies improve capital allocation across businesses with different strategic positions, and led to the idea of balanced portfolio management. But such analytical approaches

[73]Goold and Campbell, *Strategies and Styles.*
[74]C. K. Prahalad and Yves L. Doz, *The Multinational Mission* (London: Free Press, 1987), p. 261.
[75]Bartlett and Ghoshal, *Managing across Borders,* p. 166.

F I G U R E 8-1 | **Evolution of Thinking on Corporate Strategy and Diversification**

	Basis of Corporate Value Added		**Diversification Approaches and Issues**
1950s	General management skills	►►►►►►►►►►►►	Rise of conglomerates
1960s			▼▼
			Performance problems with conglomerates
			▼▼
1970s	Strategy concept	►►►►►►►►►►►►	Strategic management of diversity
			▼▼
	Portfolio planning techniques	◄◄◄◄◄◄◄◄◄◄◄	Resource allocation problems
		►►►►►►►►►►►	▼▼
			Balanced portfolio management
			▼▼
1980s			Manageability problems
	Value based planning concepts	►►►►►►►►►►►	▼▼
			Restructuring
1990s	Synergy Core competencies Dominant logic and management style	◄◄◄◄◄◄◄ ►►►►►►►►►►►	▼▼ "Core" portfolios

overlooked the problem of manageability. Many companies found it difficult to manage businesses facing different strategic issues, and during the 1980s poor corporate performance again became a critical issue. Raiders, executives, and academics realized that many diversified corporations were not creating shareholder value, and there was a wave of takeovers, corporate break-ups, and restructuring. The main themes of corporate strategy during the 1980s became restructuring back to core businesses and a resolve to stick to the knitting.

As we move into the 1990s, it has, however, become increasingly clear that there is no consensus on what sticking to the knitting in practice implies, or on how companies should be adding value to their remaining core businesses. Among the currently popular themes, the search for synergy and the building of core competencies each have significant followings. But both views need to be complemented with some account of how the corporation can discharge its shareholder functions well. Here the concept of understanding the dominant strategic logic of a portfolio, and its compatibility with the approaches of top management, seems promising.

In our view, it is probable that a full account of corporate strategy and of diversification will need to draw on several of the strands of thought we have reviewed. Ultimately, diversity can only be worthwhile if corporate management adds value in some way and the test of a corporate strategy must be that the businesses in the portfolio are worth more under the management of the company in question than they would be under any other ownership.[76] To achieve this goal with a diverse group of businesses, it may be necessary to restructure portfolios to allow more uniformity in dominant logic and management style, more effective means of realizing synergies, and more sharing of core competencies.

---

[76]Michael Goold and Andrew Campbell, "Corporate Strategy and Parenting Skills," research report, Ashridge Strategic Management Centre, 1991.

SUCCESS IN DIVERSIFICATION: BUILDING ON CORE COMPETENCIES

Philippe Very, Groupe ESC Lyon

Portfolio diversification is sometimes the only way to achieve growth for a company, or the only way to survive when sales and profitability of the core business are declining. Consequently, diversification is and will be a strategic option largely used by managers to reach the long-term objectives planned to ensure the future of the firm.

To diversify means to enter into a new strategic business domain. This strategic choice is risky: according to the study of 33 large U.S. companies made by Porter,[1] more than 50 percent of the diversification moves that occurred before 1975 were divested or sold by 1987. Pekar[2] also found high failure rates of diversifications through acquisitions, as did Kogut[3] in his study of diversifications through joint ventures.

These results explain why researchers have spent much time and effort in identifying the key success factors of diversification strategies. The results of these studies, however, are sometimes conflicting, especially when researchers have tried to evaluate the impact of synergy (between businesses) on the performance of the firm. The concept of synergy seems to highlight the relationship between diversification and success, but it is also very difficult to define and to measure. Research on synergy has greatly progressed during the 1980s, and new concepts have been introduced to replace the original blurred term: *relatedness,* and the *dominant logic of management.* These two concepts are at the origin of two different theoretical approaches to diversification. The purpose of our research is to test the validity of these theories and to assess the possible links between them.

Source: *Long Range Planning* 26, no. 5 (1993), pp. 80–92. Reprinted with permission.
[1]M. E. Porter, "From Competitive Advantage to Corporate Strategy," *Harvard Business Review* 63, no. 3, pp. 43–59.
[2]P. Pekar, "A Strategic Approach to Diversification," *Journal of Business Strategy* 5 (1985), pp. 99–104.
[3]B. Kogut, "Joint Ventures: Theoretical and Empirical Perspectives," *Strategic Management Journal* 9, no. 4 (1988), pp. 319–322.

DIVERSIFICATION AND PERFORMANCE

The pioneering work focusing on diversification and performance was carried out by Rumelt[4] who studied the evolution of the largest U.S. firms (according to "Fortune's 500") over the period 1949–69. He analyzed the impacts of the degree of diversification and the degree of synergy between businesses on the firms' economic performance. Rumelt showed that, among diversified firms, the best performers belong to the category named "related-constrained firms," that is, those having 70 percent of their total sales in businesses directly connected with the core business. In Rumelt's methodological frame, two activities are related when they are linked by markets or technologies. The first subsequent research in this field offered great support for Rumelt's findings. In particular, Montgomery,[5] Christensen and Montgomery,[6] and Bettis[7] found that *related-diversifiers outperform unrelated diversifiers*.

Yet some studies did not end up with the same results: Grinyer, Yasai-Ardekani, and Al-Bazzaz,[8] Hill,[9] Galbraith, Samuelson, Stiles, and Merrill,[10] Chang and Thomas,[11] and Grant and Jammine[12] did not find any significant difference in average performance between related and unrelated diversifiers. Moreover, according to Reed and Luffman,[13] *unrelated diversifiers proved to have a better return on capital than related ones*.

In order to understand such contradictory results, one should note that the measurement of performance, the type of company, and the period of investigation differed from one study to another. Researchers have offered supplementary explanations. Grant and Jammine considered that unrelated diversifiers can achieve good performance because of an increased efficiency in the management of unrelated businesses—which they link to the experience acquired by managers. Grant[14] suggested that the definition and the measurement of synergy are lacking in precision. In most of the studies, synergy is supposed to exist if there are potential links between business units in terms of markets and technologies. These links are either subjectively identified by the researcher or based on SIC-Code proximity. Using these methods, analysts can only note some of the possible interdependences between business units,

---

[4]R. P. Rumelt, *Strategy, Structure, and Economic Performance* (Cambridge, Mass.: Harvard University Press, 1974).

[5]C. A. Montgomery, "Diversification, Market Structure, and Firm Performance—An Extension of Rumelt's Work," doctoral dissertation, Purdue University (1979).

[6]H. K. Christensen and C. A. Montgomery, "Corporate Economic Performance: Diversification Strategy versus Market Structure," *Strategic Management Journal* 2 (1981), pp. 327–43.

[7]R. A. Bettis, "Performance Differences in Related and Unrelated Diversified Firms," *Strategic Management Journal* 7, no. 6 (1986), pp. 485–501.

[8]P. H. Grinyer, M. Yasai-Ardekani, and S. Al-Bazzaz, "Strategy, Structure, the Environment and Financial Performance in 48 United Kingdom Companies," *Academy of Management Journal* 23 (1980), pp. 193–220.

[9]C. W. L. Hill, "Conglomerate Performance over the Economic Cycle," *Journal of Industrial Economics* 32, no. 12 (1983), pp. 197–211.

[10]C. Galbraith, B. Samuelson, C. Stiles, and G. Merrill, "Diversification, Industry Research and Development, and Performance," *Academy of Management Proceedings*, 1986, pp. 17–20.

[11]Y. Chang and H. Thomas, "The Impact of Diversification Strategy on Risk-Return Performance," *Academy of Management Proceedings*, 1987, pp. 2–6.

[12]R. M. Grant and A. P. Jammine, "Performance Differences between the Wigley/Rumelt Strategic Categories," *Strategic Management Journal* 9, no. 4, (1988), pp. 333–46.

[13]R. Reed and G. A. Luffman, *The Strategy and Performance of British Industry, 1970–1980* (London: Macmillan, 1984).

[14]R. M. Grant, "On Dominant Logic, Relatedness, and the Link between Diversity and Performance," *Strategic Management Journal* 9, no. 6 (1988), pp. 639–42.

and they do not analyze whether synergy is *actually implemented* by the firm. For instance, an "unrelated" diversifier could be classified as a "related" one with regard to the similarity in managerial skills that are required and applied to manage diverse businesses.

CONGLOMERATES

What is an unrelated diversifier? Conglomerates—or unrelated diversified firms—result from past unrelated diversifications. A conglomerate is assumed to create value through diversification by reducing the variability of total cashflow in comparison to the sum of the variabilities inherent to the cashflows generated in each business. In a conglomerate, businesses generally differ in terms of growth rate, seasonality, levels of profitability, and capital investment. High performance comes from the process of financial resource allocation that is implemented between these structurally different businesses. This advantage of financial complementarity depends on the business portfolio of the firm. Not all conglomerates have succeeded in the creation of such advantages. As Gouillart[15] argues, financial heterogeneity between businesses may weaken the strategic position of the firm. For instance, the profitable businesses have to bear the financial burden imposed by other activities. If these attractive businesses were run alone, they could generate superior gains. On the other hand, the least profitable businesses are often overvalued because they only support a portion of their financial needs. Conglomerates consequently make attractive targets for raiders because they offer the greatest possibility of gains through their disruption and the selling of the company business by business.

It is one of the reasons why many big European companies have restructured their business portfolios during the 1970s and 1980s in order to concentrate their resources in related competitive areas. Nowadays managers systematically justify diversifications by potential synergy. So what is synergy?

WHAT IS SYNERGY?

Two recent theoretical approaches contribute to a better understanding of the concept of synergy: the first one shows how the implementation of synergy can increase the firm's overall performance; the second is built on the concept of "dominant logic of general management."

Synergy has been the main argument to justify the diversification trend that occurred in the 1960s and the 1970s, when firms looked for growth. As Porter[16] argued, synergy often seemed to be a good idea, but was rarely implemented. Porter used the concept of *relatedness* to explain how synergy is the cornerstone of value creation through diversification. He identified two types of relationships between the value chains of business units:

- The sharing of a resource (same manufacturing equipment, same distribution channels).
- The transfer of a skill (transfer of product or process technology, transfer of marketing techniques).

---

[15]F. J. Gouillart, *Strategie pour une Entreprise Competitive* (Paris, France: Economica, 1989).
[16]M. E. Porter, *Competitive Strategy: Techniques for Analyzing Industries and Competitors,* (New York: Free Press, 1980).

Implementing relatedness means that the firm shares a resource or transfers a skill in order to improve its competitive advantage in at least one of the linked businesses. The creation or the reinforcement of the advantage (lowering costs and/or increasing differentiation) leads to a better competitive position and consequently to higher profits. When the firm diversifies its portfolio according to this logic, managers can create a new set of businesses with a value superior to the sum of the intrinsic values of these businesses.

Managerial skills are also important in the context of diversification strategies. Ansoff[17] suggested that the management of a diversified company requires different managerial abilities in order to succeed in diverse businesses. The diversity or the strategic variety of business units can be assessed on several dimensions such as the required operational capabilities, the degree of turbulence of the environment, and the degree of maturity of the demand. Bettis and Pralahad[18] use the concept of *dominant logic of general management* to explain the success of diversified companies:

> Strategically similar businesses can be managed using a single dominant general management logic. A dominant general management logic is defined as the way in which managers conceptualize the business and make critical resource allocation decisions.

The capacity of the top management team to run a diversified company is limited by the dominant logics of management that were developed through the accumulated experiences in the company's core businesses. In other words, managers develop cognitive decision patterns that are appropriate in particular environmental and organizational contexts. Accordingly, there are two main ways of diversification. First, situations where the top managers want to manage the new business themselves, in which case they should choose businesses that can share the same dominant logic as the one developed in the core activity; and second, situations where the managers prefer to enter businesses that require different logics, in which case they should also recognize that they need to acquire new management skills. In the latter case, the managers must assess whether they can quickly learn a new logic of management or whether they have to recruit a skilled manager to run the new business.

In summary, researchers and practitioners should consider two levels of relatedness: the *operational level of relatedness* (sharing of resources or transfer of operational skills between the value chains) and the *managerial level of relatedness* (applying particular managerial skills to the new business). In both cases careful evaluations are needed to ensure that "synergies" are not merely "mirages."

ARMELPOF

The Armelpof (a pseudonym) Company is a leading French producer of heavy industrial equipment. At the end of the 1970s, the top management team of the company decided to diversify into a new business: the selling of entire factories furnished with the industrial machines that were built by the company. The objective of the diversification was to extend their existing electromechanical skills and technologies to a new area. The Armelpof Company decided to divest this new business in 1986, after nearly eight years of continual losses and inability to achieve a significant market share.

The main reasons for the failure were the mirages of managerial and operational synergy. At the managerial level, the new business required specific skills because

---

[17]H. I. Ansoff, *Implanting Strategic Management* (Englewood Cliffs, N.J.: Prentice Hall, 1984).
[18]R. A. Bettis and C. K. Pralahad, "The Dominant Logic—A New Linkage between Diversity and Performance," *Strategic Management Journal* 7 (1986), pp. 485–501.

the rules of the competitive game were quite different from those inherent to the core business. For instance, the main competitors in the market, the division of market shares among them, the competitive rivalry, and the bargaining power of suppliers were different. In terms of key success factors—the sources of competitive advantage—Armelpof had developed a technological advance in its core business that was not applicable in the new business. The main factors in the factory activity were the ability to manage complex projects, the capacity to find technical solutions to customers' problems, the reduction of delivery delays, and the mastery of the total cost of the project. So top managers of Armelpof had to deal with a different competitive structure and different key success factors in the new business. These characteristics required a different management approach. The top management team decided, however, to manage the new business itself, but the managerial gap between the businesses was greater than expected.

Moreover, at the operational level, the top management team decided to share resources between the core business and the new one using, as far as possible, the company's own equipment in each factory they sold, sharing the quality control for finished goods, and sharing the brand name. The operational links between the businesses had a positive impact on the key success factors for selling factories. However, the inclusion of the company's products in the package had a negative effect on the relationship with some customers.

This case illustrates the fact that sometimes expected synergies are actually mirages. The top managers of Armelpof did not realize that distinctive managerial skills were necessary to run the new business. They therefore implemented operational synergies that did not reinforce the competitive position of the firm in the new business.

It appears evident, then, that there is a need for researchers and practitioners to better understand what synergy really is.

THE RESEARCH

The field study was launched in 1988. Using the number of business codes as the selection criteria, we selected the *20 most diversified firms* from the 150 largest French industrial companies listed in the Kompass directory. Conglomerates with a pure financial logic were removed from the sample. Seven firms agreed to participate in the study. They represent a wide range of industries: energy, chemicals, telecommunications, electrical engineering, industrial gas, food and beverage, and sports equipment. In each firm, we interviewed a top manager who has been involved in the past diversifications of the company. The interviews lasted around three hours, divided between semistructured and structured phases. Each manager discussed three to five diversification moves that had been undertaken between 1965 and 1984. More recent diversification moves were not pursued because we wanted to be able to assess long-term success. The final sample includes 26 diversifications: 19 were classified as "successes" and 7 as "failures" (divested or sold between 1985 and 1988).

We built a conceptual framework to study the relationships between diversification, the two levels of synergy, and performance. For each diversification move, we gathered information on the following dimensions:

- The success or failure of the diversification; whether the new business still belonged to the firm or had been divested by 1989 (the use of this dichotomic measure is justified by the very high failure rates of diversification).

- The strategic similarity between the new business and the core business was used as a surrogate measure for managerial relatedness. It was measured first in terms of competitive structure (fifteen items describing the bargaining power of suppliers and of buyers, the rivalry between competitors, entry barriers and the threat of substitution; a dichotomic scale has been used for each item: "identical" or "different" between the new business and the core business) and second in terms of key success factors (the relevant sources of competitive advantage), using the percentage of key success factors of the new business that are identical to those of the core business.
- The degree of operational relatedness implemented between the new business and the core business [resource sharing and/or skill transfer between the value chains, measured on a five-point Lickert scale for each activity of the value chain: "no sharing (or transfer)" to "total sharing (or transfer)"].
- The impact of operational relatedness upon the competitive advantage of the firm in the new business and in the core business; we found that all in our sample tried to apply their existing capabilities to the new business. Consequently we could only analyze the impact of relatedness on the competitive advantage of the firm in the new business; for each shared resource and each transferred skill, managers answered on a five-point Lickert scale ranging from "no impact on the competitive advantage" to "very strong impact on the competitive advantage."

The core business of the firm was defined as the unit from which the decision of diversification had been taken. Sometimes it referred to a particular business; sometimes it referred to a whole set of businesses when the decision had been taken at the corporate level.

Our basic model was designed to compare the two theoretical approaches explaining performance: operational relatedness which improves competitive advantage versus managerial relatedness. We also analyzed the possible links between these two forms of relatedness. (For details of the statistical analysis see the Appendix.) Figure 9–1 summarizes the conceptual model.

BECLIN

All the firms in our sample have experienced successful and unsuccessful diversifications. For instance the Beclin company (a pseudonym), a leading French producer of electronic systems for telecommunications, diversified at the end of the 1970s into two areas: first into the manufacture of electronic systems integrated in customer products (business A), second into the development and manufacture of electronic systems for public transport (business B). In business A, the company produced electronic parts, bought the other components, made the assembly and sold the product through distribution channels for individual customers. In business B, the company found a technical solution to specific needs of local councils. The analysis of the key success factors shows great differences between those of the core business and those of business A. This difference is weaker between the core business and business B (see Figure 9–2).

Business A required heavy investments to reach a critical mass of production. This business was dominated by three bigger competitors. The Beclin company had to minimize the cost of its manufacturing operations and the purchasing cost which represented 70 percent of the total production cost. Unfortunately, the company was unable to compete with the bigger competitors on volume—scale economies were

F I G U R E 9–1 | **The Research Model**

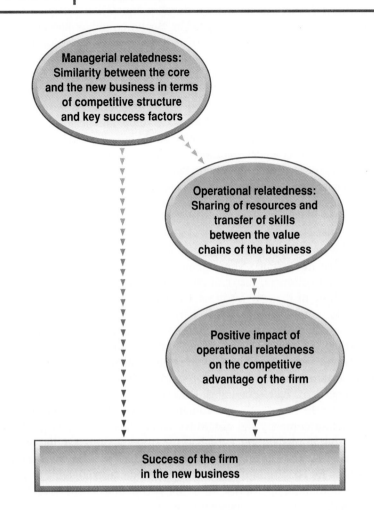

F I G U R E 9–2 | **Key Success Factors for the Businesses of the Beclin Company**

Core Business	Business A	Business B
• Minimize production costs	• Minimize purchasing costs	• Minimize production costs
• Master the management of complex projects	• Reach critical mass	• Master the management of complex projects
• Maintain good relationships with local councils	• Develop strong retail marketing	• Develop a niche strategy
• Master the technology of electronic systems	• Master the technology of electronic systems	• Maintain good relationships with local councils
		• Master the technology of electronic systems

very important—and consequently on the purchasing price. The third key success factor of business A was the capacity to develop aggressive customer marketing to create and sustain a strong brand image. The Beclin company had no experience of such actions, because the main clients of its core activity were local councils; top managers decided to develop a marketing plan specific to this business.

Most of the key success factors of business B were similar to those of the core business: control of production costs, ability to manage complex projects, technological know-how in electronic systems, and strong relationships with local councils. Only one factor was different: the necessity to develop a niche strategy, because each project had to be negotiated with a particular local council, which had specific needs that required different technical solutions. The Beclin company entered the business with its own technological system, relying upon its relationships with this kind of customer that had been developed in the core business to increase its market penetration.

Moreover, in terms of competitive structure, business A differed more from the core business than did business B (see Figure 9–3). In business A, products on the market were rather similar when Beclin decided to diversify; the potential competitive strategies were based on price (cost minimization) or differentiation by brand image (aggressive marketing). Three competitors shared most of the market on a worldwide basis. Customers, distribution channels, and most of the suppliers were different from those of the core business. Competitive rivalry was higher in business A and the Beclin company had a weak bargaining power with its main supplier: a Japanese firm who was also one of its competitors. Because of these differences, the competitive structure of business A required a specific management approach.

Business B and the core business were rather similar in terms of possibilities of technological differentiation, division of market shares, competitive rivalry, customers, and the size of scale economies. However, the main competitors and some of the suppliers were different and capital intensity was lower in business B. Top managers of the Beclin company did not worry about these differences, which did not prevent them from implementing a competitive strategy similar to the one developed in the core business. Their managerial skills seemed to be adequate for the management of business B. Therefore, it appeared that the managerial skills of the top management team were more appropriate to business B than to business A. Nevertheless, the team decided to manage both businesses itself.

In terms of operational relatedness, no resource had been shared between business A and the core business (see Figure 9–4). Methods of human resource management had

F I G U R E 9-3 | **Competitive Structures of the Businesses of the Beclin Company**

Structural Dimensions	Business A Compared to the Core Business	Business B Compared to the Core Business
Differentiation possibilities	Weaker	Similar
Concentration of competitors	More concentrated	Similar
Competitive rivalry	Higher	Similar
Customers	Different	Similar
Distribution channels	Different	Similar
Suppliers	Most of them are different	Some of them are different
Scale economies	Similar	Similar
Capital intensity	Similar	Lower
Degree of globalization of the market	Similar	Similar

FIGURE 9-4 | **Operational Relatedness between the Businesses of the Beclin Company**

Operational Relatedness between Business A and the Core Business	Impact on the Firm's Overall Performance
• Transfer of human resource management methods	None
• Transfer of production management methods	Strong

Operational Relatedness between Business B and the Core Business	Impact on the Firm's Overall Performance
• Same R&D department	Strong
• Sharing of the quality control for finished products	Average
• Same brand name	Strong
• Transfer of production management methods	Weak
• Transfer of human resource management methods	Average
• Transfer of technological skills	Strong
• Transfer of project management techniques	Strong

been transferred to business A without any impact on the firm's competitive advantage. Methods of production management were also transferred, which strongly decreased the cost of manufacturing operations. Unfortunately, no synergy was possible to reduce the cost of purchasing, which amounted to 70 percent of the total cost of the product. In fact, the Beclin company could not achieve a competitive position on costs.

Resources in technology development, in quality control of the finished products, and in marketing were shared between business B and the core business. The same brand name was used. Methods of production, implementation of technology, methods of human resource management, and techniques of project management were transferred to business B. These synergies had a strong positive impact on the technological differentiation of the Beclin company in business B (see Figure 9–4).

Business A was finally divested seven years later. The Beclin company never achieved profits in the business. The company reached the second position in terms of market share but only on the French market, whereas the competition occurred on a worldwide level. Top managers then realized that business A required specific managerial skills because the environment and the rules of the game greatly differed from those of the core business. They failed to compete either on cost or on marketing differentiation for individual customers.

In contrast, business B represented nearly 10 percent of the company's 1989 turnover. Today the Beclin company is the worldwide leader in this niche with a competitive advantage relying upon technological differentiation. The top managers' skills turned out to be appropriate for the management of business B and operational synergies strongly contributed to create an advantage over competitors. The top management team is aware today that it is not able to run just any business. So it has conceived a methodological process for the selection of any new business, taking into account the competitive structure and the possibility to differentiate through technology.

These contrasting examples show the importance of synergy—at the managerial level and at the operational level—to ensure the success of a diversification move driven by an industrial logic of development—as opposed to a purely financial logic.

IMPLICATIONS FOR MANAGEMENT

Our findings suggest a methodological approach of diversification to reduce the risks of failure linked to such strategic moves.

First, managers have to define a general logic of development for their firm. Do they want to build a conglomerate or a set of businesses founded on some kind of synergy?

More and more organizations are choosing the second way. Some have combined both logics. The French group Elf Aquitaine for instance is involved in two unrelated basic industries: petrochemicals and pharmaceuticals. But within each of the two industrial branches, the group has diversified into related businesses, in order to increase the intrinsic performance of each branch. The financial logic at corporate level is combined with a synergetic logic at branch level.

Defining a general logic of development raises the problem of defining the core competencies that will determine the path for future diversifications. But managers must be careful here! A competence is not necessarily a managerial skill. A French medium-sized firm was involved during the 1970s in the manufacture of metallic micromechanisms for watches. The firm's managers wanted to anticipate the definite evolution of technology in the watch industry: electronics were quickly replacing mechanical systems. They decided to diversify into new businesses where they could exploit their distinctive skills. The managers identified two basic skills:

- Their understanding of their customers' needs and their strong relationships with these customers (watch assemblers).
- Their know-how in the production of micromechanisms.

The firm's managers chose to assess their diversification of the first skill. They invested much time, money, and effort during one year, trying to conceptualize and to produce electronic display systems for watches. They never succeeded; they eventually realized that they were facing larger and better-armed competitors, and that most of their initial customers were disappearing from the watch industry.

They then totally reoriented their strategy. They looked for new businesses where their second skill, technological competence, was a potential source of competitive advantage. This medium-sized firm is now very profitable. Its managers have implemented a differentiation strategy with technologically innovative and custom-made products for the medical, military, home appliance (scales), and optic fiber industries.

This real-life example shows the difficulties encountered by managers in defining their core skills. We think that a *core competence:*

- Allows the firm to satisfy—better than its competitors—a key success factor of its business.
- Constitutes a barrier to the entry of new competitors into the business.

Consequently, a core competence must be a source of competitive advantage and must be inimitable by any firm.

A generic technology can be a core skill if it meets these conditions. According to Hamel and Pralahad,[19] a technology-based core competence gives a firm the advantage of being able to work in different business areas. Some service firms, like Societe Lyonnaise des eaux, have developed another competence: they are able to offer multiple services to a particular group of customers. The strong relationships between Societe Lyonnaise des eaux and local councils mean that the company has become the preferential supplier for most of these customers. The recent merger with the Dumez company, involved in building and public works, is consistent with this core competence and would reinforce the relationships with customers.

The managers of Salomon, the French producer of ski and golf equipment, changed the rules of the competitive game in a business where competition was originally fragmented. Their strategy, based on product innovation, aggressive marketing, and sales at a worldwide level, has allowed them to take the leadership with 20 percent to 30 percent of market share in most of their businesses. This capacity to turn fragmented markets around is a core competence.

A core competence then can be managerial skill or an operational competence. A long-term strategy based on the exploitation of core competencies reduces the scope of possible diversification. But it is not sufficient to ensure the success of the firm in new areas. Managers have to assess precisely how relatedness—at the managerial level and at the operational level—might guarantee future profits.

Assessing Managerial Relatedness   We have seen that the capacity of a corporate team to manage diverse businesses is limited by its dominant logic(s) of general management and by its ability to acquire new dominant logics. In other words, the decision process of a manager is linked to the organizational and environmental situations that he has experienced. This process may not be applicable and relevant in every other context. Consequently, when the managers of a firm want to keep the strategic control of their activities, they have to diversify into a business that fits their dominant logic of management. In this case, diversification criteria are based on the similarities in terms of competitive structure and key success factors between the new and the core business. The successive diversifications of Salomon, from ski bindings to ski boots and cross-country ski equipment, have been carried out keeping the managerial skills of the corporate team in mind. At the period of entry, these businesses had comparable characteristics in terms of market fragmentation, intensity of competition, geographical size of the market, and innovation as a key success factor. Salomon's managers wanted to diversify only in areas that presented such characteristics.

To assess the similarity in terms of competitive structure, Calori[20] used a tool that allows comparison between businesses on nine dimensions (see Figure 9–5). Key success factors can be compared using the table shown in Figure 9–6. When the diversification is characterized by key success factors that are new for the firm, members of the management team have to determine whether they possess the resources

---

[19]G. Hamel and C. K. Pralahad, "Strategic Intent," *Harvard Business Review,* May/June, 1989, pp. 63–76.
[20]R. Calori, "Strategie—Soyons Realistes," *Harvard l'Expansion,* Spring 1989, pp. 64–83.

F I G U R E 9-5 | **Worksheet to Assess the Similarity of Competitive Structures between Businesses**

	Comparison of Competitive Structures			
	Very Different	**Rather Different**	**Rather Similar**	**Very Similar**
• Differentiation possibilities				
• Scale economies				
• Concentration of competitors				
• Concentration of demand				
• Degree of globalization				
• Degree of maturity				
• Technological intensity				
• Marketing intensity				
• Labor intensity				

and skills required to master these factors. External experts in the diversification area (for instance, economists, researchers in the technology field, suppliers, customers) can help to fill in the tables.

Using these tools, a top management team is able to assess whether the way it manages the core business is transferable to the new business. The identification of a managerial gap may at least make managers aware that they will have to implement a new management approach for the new business. Either they decide to run this business themselves, which means that they are ready to learn and to acquire a new dominant logic of management, or they recruit a manager already involved in the new business or in a business with similar structural characteristics.

Assessing Operational Relatedness to Improve Competitive Advantages   The identification of the firm's core competencies allows managers to explore carefully how they may extend their business. The choice of a diversification area can be assessed in terms of managerial skills when managers want to run the new business themselves. But the achievement of performance through diversification is often more subtle: either the company can extend its capacities to a new attractive business (capacity extension), or the company can acquire a capacity transferable to the core business (capacity acquisition).

In the capacity extension strategy, managers are looking for a profitable business where they can create a competitive advantage. Selection criteria for a new business are the intrinsic value of the business (intrinsic perspectives of profitability) and the resources and skills that could be shared with or transferred to the new activity, in order that it could master the key success factors (i.e., the relevant sources of competitive advantage). Synergy in that case reinforces the competitive position of the firm in the new business, and then improves the expected profits. When the develop-

F I G U R E 9-6 | **Worksheet to Assess the Firm's Potential to Master Key Success Factors**

Key Success Factors (KSF) of the New Business	Comparison with the Key Success Factors of the Core Business	Capacities Required for New Key Success Factors	Potential Mastery of New Key Success Factors
List the KSF above.	Assess whether they are new or already mastered in the core business.	Identify the resource and skills required to master new KSF.	Assess whether the firm possesses the capacities required to master new KSF.
KSF 1	new or identical	if new • capacity 1 • capacity 2 •	• Yes or No • Yes or No • Yes or No
KSF 2	new or identical	if new • capacity 1 • capacity 2 •	• Yes or No • Yes or No • Yes or No

ment of the firm is based on core competencies, relatedness relies first of all on the transfer of these competencies. The entry of the Beclin company into the B business—described previously—illustrates this situation.

In the capacity acquisition strategy, the firm enters a new business (often by joint venture or merger) to acquire a distinctive skill. The transfer of this competence into the core business is supposed to reinforce the competitive position of the firm in that business, by a better mastery of the relevant key success factors. The French firm Maco-Meudon, producer of compressors for public works, entered a joint venture in 1988 with the U.S. firm Sullair in order to acquire the technology necessary to enter the market of industrial compressors. Moreover, the acquisition of this technology enabled Maco-Meudon to extend its product range in the core business to more powerful compressors. A wider range was essential to improve the market penetration of the firm's core business.

To assess the operational linkages that reinforce the competitive position of the firm, managers can fill in the table shown in Figure 9–7. The first column allows them to assess the impact of each potential linkage on the mastery of the key success factors of the new business and the core business. Each impact can be evaluated on a scale ranging from "nil" to "very strong." In the last column, managers can classify each linkage according to its overall importance. A scale ranging from "no impact on competitive position" to "essential impact on competitive position" can be used. Very[21] explains that this table permits identification of the linkages that most contribute to creating or increasing the competitive advantage of the firm.

---

[21]P. Very, *Strategies de Diversification—Nouvelles Perspective* (Paris, France: Liaisons, 1991).

F I G U R E 9–7 | **Worksheet for Assessing the Impact of Operational Relatedness on Competitive Position (Key Success Factors)**

		Impact on the Competitive Position of the Firm								Overall Importance of the Lnkage
		In the Core Business				In the New Business				
		KSF 1	KSF 2	KSF 3	KSF 4	KSF 1	KSF 2	KSF 3	KSF 4	
Possible Sharing of Resources	Res 1									
	Res 2									
	Res 3									
Possible Transfer of Skills from the Core Business to the New Business	Skill 1									
	Skill 2									
	Skill 3									
Possible Transfer of Skills from the New Business to the Core Business	Skill 1									
	Skill 2									
	Skill 3									

KSF = Key Success Factor

These important linkages must be analyzed in depth, because any synergy involves costs of implementation. Porter[22] found that the sharing of a resource adds costs of coordination between businesses, costs of compromise (linked to the differences in the exploitation of the resource), and costs of inflexibility (linked to the swiftness of reaction compared to that of the competitors). The transfer of a skill between the value chains involves costs linked to the transfer of the critical persons and the investment required to apply the competence in another business area. Consequently the most interesting linkages must be carefully analyzed from a cost/profit perspective. The results of this analysis influence the decision whether to exploit the operational linkages.

---

[22]M. E. Porter, *Competitive Advantages: Creating and Sustaining Superior Performance* (New York: Free Press, 1985).

CONCLUSION

Achieving superior performance through diversification is largely based on related-ness. According to the results of our study, relatedness is more easily implemented when the competitive structure and the rules of the competition are similar between businesses, in other words, when the top management team can extend its skills to the new business. These findings lead us to propose a methodological process for the choice of new businesses. This process does not guarantee success, but limits the risks of failure due to the selection of the "wrong" business (see Figure 9–8).

Diversification raises the problem of the managerial and operational skills that need to be developed and reinforced over the next years to guarantee the long-term prosperity of the firm. Managers of diversified firms must keep in mind that they not only manage a business portfolio, but that first of all they have to manage a portfolio of resources and skills.

F I G U R E 9-8 | **The Diversification Process**

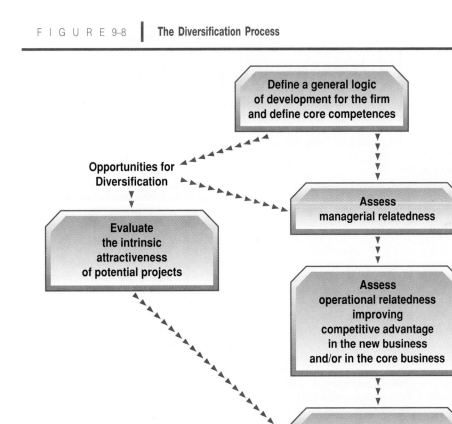

Factor analyses were done on the whole sample to reduce the number of variables in each dimension. We carried out a specific factor analysis for the similarities in the competitive structure which were measured on nominal scales. All these analyses were necessary, considering the small size of our sample. Then discriminant analyses between the group of successful diversifications and the group of unsuccessful ones uncovered determinants of success. Multiple linear regressions enabled us to test the link between the two forms of relatedness. We used the Fisher exact probability test to look for the statistical significance of the relationships. This nonparametric test is relevant for small samples.

Statistical Results

Four major factors describe similarities in terms of competitive structure, explaining 88 percent of the total variance of the answers to the items. These factors were independent variables in the discriminant analysis between successes and failures. Results proved to be highly significant under the 0.05 level (Wilks' lambda = 0.408; Fisher-Snedecor F test = 7.62): *the more similar the industry structures, the more likely the success of the diversification.*

The relationship between the similarity in key success factors and the success or failure of diversifications also proved to be significant (Fisher exact test between the successes and failures is significant under the 0.001 level): *when the sources of competitive advantage in the new business are similar to those in the core business, diversification is more likely to succeed.*

Then, using multiple linear regression, we found that the two measures—similarities in competitive structure and similarities in key success factors—were related. So we used a combined measure in further analyses.

The distance between strategic characteristics (similarities both in terms of competitive structure and in terms of key success factors) is linked to the success of a diversification move. When similarities between businesses are high, we assume that managerial relatedness is high, or in other words that the top managers of the company master the "dominant logic" required to manage the new business.

We factor analyzed the whole sample to reduce the number of variables describing resource sharing and skills transfer. Four main factors (eigenvalue superior to 1) explained 75 percent of the variance of resource sharing and four main factors (eigenvalue superior to 1) explained 81 percent of the variance of the transfer of skills. We found no significant correlation between these two sets of factors. These factors were independent variables in the discriminant analyses between successes and failures. Fisher-Snedecor F test was not significant under the 0.05 level: *synergy does not intrinsically explain the success of diversification.* Does this mean that synergy is not important?

The next step was to analyze whether the effects of operational relatedness on the firm's competitive advantage in the new business were linked to the success of diversification. These effects—for each activity of the value chain—were introduced as independent variables in the discriminant analysis between successes and failures. Relationships were highly significant under the 0.01 level (Wilks' lambda = 0.350; Fisher-Snedecor F test = 3.30): *when operational relatedness reinforces the competitive position of the firm in its new business, diversification is likely to succeed,* whatever the number of existing linkages between businesses. A glance at each successful diversification of the sample showed a case where only one resource is shared with a very strong impact on the firm's competitive advantage. So carefully chosen synergy is very important to assess the success of a diversification move.

Finally we looked for a link between the two forms of relatedness—similarities in competitive structure and operational relatedness. The results of multiple linear regression were significant under the 0.05 level (R2 = 0.563; Fisher-Snedecor F test = 2.74): *the more similar the competitive structure, the more relatedness is implemented between the value chains of the businesses.* Managerial relatedness is significantly related to operational relatedness. When competitive structures are similar, managers can apply their managerial skills to the new business; they can implement the same kind of competitive strategy as the one developed in the core business. As this strategy is built on the same broad sources of competitive advantage, operational relatedness can be exploited between the value chains and the firm can improve its position in the core business and/or in the new business.

The results, however, must be qualified by the limitations of our data and of our methodology. The small size of our sample reduced the range of statistical analysis methods we could use. This research was rather exploratory concerning the possible relationships between the two levels of relatedness.

THE HORIZONTAL CORPORATION

John A. Byrne

It's a job description that says nothing about your skills in manufacturing, finance, or any other business discipline. And as seismic changes continue to rumble across the corporate landscape, it's the kind of want ad the 21st century corporation might write.

Skeptical? No matter where you work, it's likely that your company has been, in today's vernacular, "downsized" and "delayered." It has chopped out layers of management and supposedly empowered employees with greater responsibility. But you're still bumping up against the same entrenched bureaucracy that has held you back before. The engineers still battle manufacturing. Marketing continues to slug it out with sales. And the financial naysayers fight everyone.

That's because, despite the cutbacks, you probably still work in the typical vertical organization, a company in which staffers look up to bosses instead of out to customers. You and your colleagues feel loyalty and commitment to the functional fiefdoms in which you work, not to the overall corporation and its goals. And even after all the cutting, too many layers of management still slow decision making and lead to high coordination costs.

Mere downsizing, in other words, does little to change the fundamental way that work gets done in a corporation. To do that takes a different organizational model, the horizontal corporation. Already, some of corporate America's biggest names, from American Telephone & Telegraph and DuPont to General Electric and Motorola, are moving toward the idea. In the quest for greater efficiency and productivity, they're beginning to redraw the hierarchical organization charts that have defined corporate life since the Industrial Revolution (see Figure 10–1).

F I G U R E 10-1 | **How to Create a Horizontal Corporation**

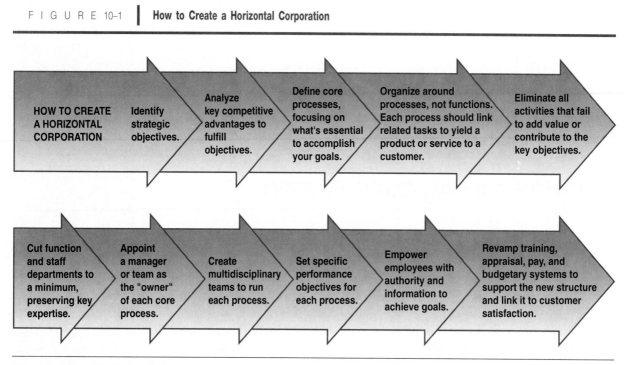

Source: Data McKinsey & Co., *Business Week.*

WAVE OF THE FUTURE

Some of these changes have been under way for several years under the guise of "total quality management" efforts, reengineering, or business-process redesign. But no matter which buzzword or phrase you choose, the trend is toward flatter organizations in which managing across has become more critical than managing up and down in a top-heavy hierarchy.

The horizontal corporation, though, goes much further than these previous efforts: It largely eliminates both hierarchy and functional or departmental boundaries. In its purest state, the horizontal corporation might boast a skeleton group of senior executives at the top in such traditional support functions as finance and human resources. But virtually everyone else in the organization would work together in multidisciplinary teams that perform core processes, such as product development or sales generation. The upshot: The organization might have only three or four layers of management between the chairman and the staffers in a given process.

If the concept takes hold, almost every aspect of corporate life will be profoundly altered. Companies would organize around process—developing new products, for example—instead of around narrow tasks, such as forecasting market demand for a given new product. Self-managing teams would become the building blocks of the new organization. Performance objectives would be linked to customer satisfaction rather than profitability or shareholder value. And staffers would be rewarded not just for individual performance but for the development of their skills and for team performance.

For most companies, the idea amounts to a major cultural transformation—but one whose time may be at hand. "It's a wave of the future," declares M. Anthony Burns, chairman of Ryder System Inc., the truck-leasing concern. "You just can't summarily lay off people. You've got to change the processes and *drive out the unnecessary work,* or it will be back tomorrow." Such radical changes hold the promise for dramatic gains in productivity, according to Lawrence A. Bossidy, chairman of AlliedSignal Inc. "There's an awful lot more productivity you're going to see in the next few years as we move to horizontally organized structures with a focus on the customer," says Bossidy.

How so? Just as a light bulb wastes electricity to produce unwanted heat, a *traditional corporation expends a tremendous amount of energy running its own internal machinery*—managing relations among departments or providing information up and down the hierarchy, for example.

A horizontal structure eliminates most of those tasks and focuses almost all of a company's resources on its customers. That's why proponents of the idea say it can deliver dramatic improvements in efficiency and speed. "It can get you from 100 horsepower to 500 horsepower," says Frank Ostroff, a McKinsey & Co. consultant. With colleague Douglas Smith, he coined the term "the horizontal organization" and developed a series of principles to define the new corporate model.

The idea is drawing attention in corporate and academic circles. In the past year, Ostroff has given talks on the horizontal organization before sizable gatherings of corporate strategic planners, quality experts, and entrepreneurs. He has also carried

---

SEVEN OF THE KEY ELEMENTS OF THE HORIZONTAL CORPORATION

Simple downsizing didn't produce the dramatic rises in productivity many companies hoped for. Gaining quantum leaps in performance requires rethinking the way work gets done. To do that, some companies are adopting a new organization model. Here's how it might work.

1. Organize around Process, Not Task

Instead of creating a structure around functions or departments, build the company around its three to five core processes, with specific performance goals. Assign an owner to each process.

2. Flatten Hierarchy

To reduce supervision, combine fragmented tasks, eliminate work that fails to add value, and cut the activities within each process to a minimum. Use as few teams as possible to perform an entire process.

3. Use Teams to Manage Everything

Make teams the main building blocks of the organization. Limit supervisory roles by making the team manage itself. Give the team a common purpose. Hold it accountable for measurable performance goals.

4. Let Customers Drive Performance

Make customer satisfaction—not stock appreciation or profitability—the primary driver and measure of performance. The profits will come and the stock will rise if the customers are satisfied.

5. Reward Team Performance

Change the appraisal and pay systems to reward team results, not just individual performance. Encourage staffer to develop multiple skills rather than specialized knowhow. Reward them for it.

6. Maximize Supplier and Customer Contact

Bring employees into direct, regular contact with suppliers or customers. Add supplier or customer representatives as full working members of in-house teams when they can be of service.

7. Inform and Train All Employees

Don't just spoon-feed sanitized information on a need-to-know basis. Trust staffers with raw data, but train them in how to use it to perform their own analyses and make their own decisions.

Companies Moving Toward the Horizontal Model

AT&T Network Systems Division reorganized its entire business around processes; now sets budgets by process and awards bonuses to employees based on customer evaluations

EASTMAN CHEMICAL Kodak unit has over 1,000 teams; ditched senior v-ps for administration, manufactoring, and R&D in favor of self-directed teams

GENERAL ELECTRIC Lighting business scrapped vertical structure, adopting horizontal design with more than 100 processes and programs

LEXMARK INTERNATIONAL Former IBM division axed 60% of managers in manufacturing and support in favor of cross-functional teams worldwide

MOTOROLA Government Electronics group redesigned its supply management organization as a process with external customers at the end; team members are now evaluating peers

XEROX Develops new products through multi-disciplinary teams that work in a single process, instead of vertical functions or departments

DATA: BUSINESS WEEK, McKINSEY & CO.

the message to MBAs and faculty at the University of Pennsylvania and Yale University, and he boasts invitations from Harvard University and several leading European business schools

Process and Pain   But this is much more than just another abstract theory making the B-school lecture rounds. Examples of horizontal management abound, though much of the movement is occurring at lower levels in organizations. Some AT&T units are now doing annual budgets based not on functions or departments but on processes such as the maintenance of a worldwide telecommunications network. They're even dishing out bonuses to employees based on customer evaluations of the teams performing those processes. DuPont Co. has set up a centralized group this year to nudge the chemical giant's business units into organizing along horizontal lines. Chrysler Corp. used a process approach to turn out its new Neon subcompact quickly for a fraction of the typical development costs. *Xerox Corp. is employing what it calls "microenterprise units" of employees that have beginning-to-end responsibility for the company's products.*

In early December, nearly two dozen companies—including such international giants as Boeing, British Telecommunications, Stockholm-based L.M. Ericsson, and Volvo Europe—convened in Boston under the auspices of Mercer Management Consulting, another consulting shop peddling the idea, to swap stories on their efforts to adopt horizontal management techniques. Indeed, nearly all of the most prominent consulting firms are now raking in tens of millions of dollars in revenues by advising companies to organize their operations horizontally.

What those consultants' clients are quickly discovering, however, is that *eliminating the neatly arranged boxes on an organization chart in favor of a more horizontal structure can often be a complex and painful ordeal.* Indeed, simply defining the processes of a given corporation may prove to be a mind-boggling and time consuming exercise. Consider AT&T. Initially, the company's Network Services Div., which has 16,000 employees, tallied up some 130 processes before it narrowed them down to 13 core ones.

After that comes *the challenge of persuading people to cast off their old marketing, finance, or manufacturing hats and think more broadly.* "This is the hardest damn thing to do," says Terry M. Ennis, who heads up a group to help DuPont's businesses organize along horizontal lines. "It's very unsettling and threatening for people. You find line and function managers who have been honored and rewarded for what they've done for decades. You're in a white-water zone when you change."

Some management gurus, noting the fervor with which corporate chieftains embrace fads, express caution. "The idea draws together a number of fashionable trends and packages them in an interesting way," says Henry Mintzberg, a management professor at McGill University. "But the danger is that an idea like this can generate too much enthusiasm. It's not for everyone." Mintzberg notes that *there is no one solution to every organization's problems. Indeed, streamlined vertical structures may suit some mass-production industries better than horizontal ones.*

Already, consultants say, some companies are rushing to organize around processes without linking them to the corporation's key goals. Before tinkering with its organization chart, Ostroff says, *a company must understand the markets and the customers it wants to reach and complete an analysis of what it will take to win them. Only then should the company begin to identify the most critical core processes to achieve its objectives*—whether they're lowering costs by 30 percent or developing new products in half the time it normally required.

Different Climate   In the days when business was more predictable and stable, companies organized themselves in vertical structures to take advantage of specialized exports. The benefits are obvious: Everyone has a place, and everyone understands his or her task. The critical decision-making power resides at the top. But while gaining clarity and stability, such organizations make it difficult for anyone to understand the task of the company as a whole and how to relate his or her work to it. The result: Collaboration among different departments was often a triumph over formal organization charts.

To solve such problems, some companies turned to so-called matrix organizations in the 1960s and 1970s. The model was built around specific projects that cut across departmental lines. But it still kept the hierarchy intact and left most of the power and responsibility in the upper reaches of the organization.

Heightened global competition and the ever increasing speed of technological change have since altered the rules of the game and have forced corporate planners to seek new solutions. "We were reluctant to leave *the command-and-control structure* because it had "worked so well," says Philip Engel, president of CNA Corp., the Chicago-based insurance company that is refashioning its organization. "But it no longer fit the realities."

Indeed, many companies are moving to this new form of corporate organization after failing to achieve needed productivity gains by simple streamlining and consolidation. "We didn't have another horse to ride," says Kenneth L. Garrett, a senior vice president at AT&T's Network Systems Division. "We weren't performing as well as we could, and we had already streamlined our operations."

In all cases, the objective of the horizontal corporation is to *change the narrow mind-sets of armies of corporate specialists who have spent their careers climbing a vertical hierarchy to the top of a given function.* As DuPont's Terry Ennis puts it: "Our goal is to get everyone focused on the business as a system in which the functions are seamless." DuPont executives are trying to do away with what Ennis calls *the "disconnects" and "handoffs" that are so common between functions and departments. "Every time you have an organizational boundary, you get the potential for a disconnect," Ennis says. "The bigger the organization, the bigger the functions, and the more disconnects you get."*

SPEEDIER CYCLES

The early proponents of the horizontal corporation are claiming significant gains. At General Electric Co., where Chairman John F. Welch Jr. speaks of building a "bound-aryless" company, the concept has reduced costs, shortened cycle times, and increased the company's responsiveness to its customers. GE's $3 billion lighting business scrambled a more traditional structure for its global technology organization in favor of one in which a senior team of 9 to 12 people oversees nearly 100 processes or programs worldwide, from new-product design to improving the yield on production machinery. In virtually all the cases, a multidisciplinary team works together to achieve the goals of the process.

The senior leadership group—composed of managers with "multiple competen-cies" rather than narrow specialists—exists to allocate resources and ensure coordi-nation of the processes and programs. "They stay away from the day-to-day activi-ties, which are managed by the teams themselves," explains Harold Giles, manager of human resources in GE's lighting business.

The change forced major upheavals in GE's training, appraisal, and compensation systems. To create greater allegiance to a process, rather than a boss, the company has begun to put in place so-called "360-degree appraisal routines," in which peers and others above and below the employee evaluate the performance of an individual in a process. In some cases, as many as 20 people are now involved in reviewing a single employee. Employees are paid on the basis of the skills they develop rather than merely the individual work they perform.

Ryder System is another convert. The company had been organized by division— each with its own functions—based on product. But it wanted an organization that would reduce overhead while being more responsive to customers. "We were reach-ing the end of the runway looking for cost efficiencies, as most companies have," says J. Ernie Riddle, senior vice president for marketing. "So we're looking at processes from front to back."

To purchase a vehicle for leasing, for instance, required some 14 to 17 handoffs as the documents wended their way from one functional department to another at a local, and then a national, level. "We passed the baton so many times that the chances of dropping it were great," says Riddle. By viewing this paperwork flow as a single process from purchasing the vehicle to providing it to a customer, Ryder has reduced the handoffs to two from five. By redesigning the work, weeding out unnecessary approvals, and pushing more authority down the organization, the company cut its purchasing cycle by a third, to four months.

A CLEAN SHEET

Some start-ups have opted to structure themselves as horizontal companies from the get-go. One such company is Astra/Merck Group, a new stand-alone company formed to market antiulcer and high-blood-pressure drugs licensed from Sweden's Astra. Instead of organizing around functional areas, Astra/Merck is structured around a half-dozen "market-driven business processes," from drug development to product sourcing and distribution. "We literally had a clean sheet of paper to build the new model company," says Robert C. Holmes, director of strategic planning. "A functional organization wasn't likely to support our strategic goals to be lean, fast, and focused on the customer."

Some fairly small companies are also finding the model appealing. Consider Modicon Inc., a North Andover (Mass.) maker of automation-control equipment with annual revenues of $300 million. Instead of viewing product development as a task of the engineering function, President Paul White defined it more broadly as a process that would involve a team of 15 managers from engineering, manufacturing, marketing, sales, and finance.

By working together, Modicon's team avoided costly delays from disagreements and misunderstandings. "In the past," says White, "an engineering team would have worked on this alone with some dialogue from marketing. Manufacturing wouldn't get involved until the design was brought into the factory. Now, all the business issues are right on the table from the beginning."

TEAM HATS

The change allowed Modicon to bring six software products to market in one-third the time it would normally take. The company, a subsidiary of Germany's Daimler Benz, still has a management structure organized by function. But many of the company's 900 employees are involved in up to 30 teams that span several functions and departments. Predicts White: "In five years, we'll still have some formal functional structure, but people will probably feel free enough to spend the majority of their time outside their functions."

So far, the vast majority of horizontal experimentation has been at the lower levels of organizations. Increasingly, however, corporations are overhauling their entire structures to bear a closer resemblance to the horizontal model defined by consultants Ostroff and others. Eastman Chemical Co., the $3.5 billion unit of Eastman Kodak Co. to be spun off as a stand-alone company on January 1, 1994, replaced several of its senior vice presidents in charge of the key functions with "self-directed work teams." Instead of having a head of manufacturing, for example, the company uses a team consisting of all its plant managers. "It was the most dramatic change in the company's 70-year history," maintains Ernest W. Deavenport, Jr., president of Eastman Chemical. "It makes people take off their organizational hats and put on their team hats. It gives people a much broader perspective and forces decision making down at least another level."

In creating the new organization, the 500 senior managers agreed that the primary role of the functions was to support Eastman's business in chemicals, plastics, fibers, and polymers. "A function does not and should not have a mission of its own," insists Deavenport. Common sense? Of course. But over the years, the functional departments had grown strong and powerful, as they have in many organizations, often at the expense of the overall company as they fought to protect and build turf. Now, virtually all of the company's managers work on at least one cross-functional team, and most work on two or more on a daily basis. For example, Tom O. Nethery, a group vice president, runs an industrial-business group. But he also serves on three other teams that deal with such diverse issues as human resources, cellulose technology, and product-support services.

These changes in the workplace are certain to dramatically alter titles, career paths, and the goals of individuals, too. At AT&T's Network Systems Division, each of 13 core processes boasts an "owner" and a "champion." While the owners focus on the day-to-day operations of a process, the champions ensure that the process remains linked with overall business strategies and goals. Through it all, collaboration is key. "An overriding challenge is how you get marketing people to talk to finance people when they've thrown rocks at each other for decades," says Gerald Ross, cofounder of ChangeLab International, a consulting firm that specializes in cultural transformation. "Your career will be dependent on your ability to work across boundaries with others very different from you."

Don't rush to write the obituary for functional management, however. No companies have completely eliminated functional specialization. And even advocates of the new model don't envision the end of managers who are experts in manufacturing, finance, and the like. "It's only the rarest of organizations that would choose to be purely vertical or horizontal," says consultant Douglas Smith. "Most organizations will be hybrids."

Still, the horizontal corporation is an idea that's gaining currency and one that will increasingly demand people who think more broadly and thrive on change, who manage process instead of people, and who cherish teamwork as never before.

CONGRATULATIONS, YOU'RE MOVING TO A NEW PEPPERONI

If the 21st century corporation goes horizontal, what will its organization chart look like? That's right, organization charts—those dull, lifeless templates that reduce power relationships to a confusing mass of boxes and arrows. As a growing number of planners try to turn a management abstraction into a pragmatic reality, organization charts are beginning to look stranger and stranger.

Consider Eastman Chemical Co., the Eastman Kodak Co. division to be spun off as a separate company in January. "Our organization chart is now called the pizza chart because it looks like a pizza with a lot of pepperoni sitting on it," says Ernest W. Deavenport Jr., who as president is the pepperoni at the center of the pie. "We did it in circular form to show that everyone is equal in the organization. No one dominates the other. The white space inside the circles is more important than the lines."

Each pepperoni typically represents a cross-functional team responsible for managing a business, a geographic area, a function, or a core competence in a specific technology or area such as innovation. The white space around them is where the collaborative interaction is supposed to occur.

Eastman Chemical's pizza isn't the only paper representation of the horizontally inclined corporation. PepsiCo flipped its pyramidal organization chart upside-down. To help focus on customers, Pepsi put its field reps at the top. Chief Executive Craig Weatherup now calls Pepsi-Cola, the huge beverage unit of PepsiCo, "the right-side-up company." Astra/Merck Group—nearly a pure horizontal company—boasts a chart with a stack of six elongated rectangles, each representing a core process of the pharmaceutical startup. Across the top are a series of functional boxes, or "skill centers," that drive down through the processes with arrows.

WILD SHAMROCKS

For its own conceptual model of what the horizontal organization should look like, McKinsey & Co., the consulting firm, came up with a fairly abstract rendering of three boxes floating above a trio of core processes. Each process is represented by a bar with three circles on the surface. The circles symbolize the multidisciplinary teams in charge of a specific process.

This is not the first time organizational theorists have tried to come up with a workable alternative to the vertical structure that has dominated business for a century or more. Some have been as wild as the shamrock image promoted by Charles Handy, a lecturer at the London Business School. Its three leaves symbolize the joining forces of core employees, external contractors, and part-time staffers. James Brian Quinn, a Dartmouth B-school prof, thought up the starburst to reflect the company that splits off units like shooting stars.

But these experimental designs are really just metaphors for the 21st century corporation, not pragmatic structures that any company has actually adopted. And for every upside-down pyramid, you'll still find thousands of conventional charts.

Just browse through the Conference Board's repository of organization charts, a collection that features the latest diagrams of 450 corporations, from Advance Bank Australia to Xerox. The New York-based organization has been selling charts, at $14 apiece, for nearly a decade. Over that time, the organizational diagrams have gotten flatter, with fewer reporting levels, and they've become more decentralized, too. More recently, in response to heightened concern over corporate governance, some companies such as Mobil Oil Corp. and Ford Motor Co. have put shareholders and the board of directors in boxes above the top dog. But they still favor the old vertical, command-and-control hierarchy.

All of the Conference Board's best-sellers—BankAmerica, Ford, General Electric, IBM, and Motorola—are pretty much what you would expect: plenty of boxes connected by lines in steep pyramids. Indeed, under Ford's office of the chief executive, there are a mind-boggling 59 boxes of divisions, departments, and functions.

Only a few of the charts reflect the trend toward horizontal organization. Why? For one thing, it's simply too early. "Organization charts lag what's happening," says Douglas Smith, a consultant who helped develop the horizontal idea. "And a lot of people can't figure out how to draw it any other way." For another, most of the more dramatic changes along horizontal lines are occurring at divisional or subsidiary levels. That's where—at PepsiCo and Eastman Kodak, at least—those pizzas and inverted pyramids are symbols that the business-as-usual days are long gone.

REENGINEERING: THE HOT NEW MANAGING TOOL

Thomas A. Stewart

Everybody's doin' it, doin' it, doin' it. Business process reengineering is the hottest trend in management. The mint should coin money as fast as the consulting firms that peddle reengineering, several of which publish glossy magazines about their work and charge up to $2,500 for admission to conferences that double as sales pitches, with fervent testimonials by client companies. "Reengineering is new, and it has to be done," asserts Peter F. Drucker, the most eminent of management experts. The telltales of faddishness are fluttering. Says a telephone company executive: "If you want to get something funded around here—anything, even a new chair for your office— call it reengineering on your request for expenditure."

Get ready for the backlash, right?

Wrong. Reengineering is for real. Done well, it delivers extraordinary gains in speed, productivity, and profitability. Union Carbide has used reengineering to scrape $400 million out of fixed costs in just three years. GTE expects reengineering to deliver huge benefits to its telephone operations—in some cases doubling revenues or halving costs.

But process redesign is strong medicine, not always needed or successful, and almost always accompanied by pain—or at least unpleasant side effects, such as causing executives' hair to fall out. By one estimate, between 50 percent and 70 percent of reengineering efforts fail to achieve the goals set for them. After a half decade of pioneering experience with reengineering, businesses have learned key lessons about what works and what doesn't, about the most common mistakes companies make, and about what executives can do to put their efforts in the win column.

Reengineering, a.k.a. process innovation and core process redesign, is the search for, and implementation of, radical change in business processes to achieve breakthrough results. Its chief tool is a clean sheet of paper. Most change efforts start with what exists and fix it up. Reengineering, adherents emphasize, is not tweaking old procedures and certainly not plain-vanilla downsizing. Nor is it a program for bottom-up continuous improvement. Reengineers start from the future and work backward, as if unconstrained by existing methods, people, or departments. In effect they ask, "If we were a new company, how would we run this place?" Then, with a meat ax and sandpaper, they conform the company to their vision.

That's how GTE looks at its telephone operations, which account for four-fifths of the company's $20 billion in annual revenues. Facing new competitive threats, GTE figured it had to offer dramatically better customer service. Rather than eke out steady gains in its repair, billing, and marketing departments, the company examined its operations from the outside in. Customers, it concluded, want one-step shopping—one number to fix an erratic dial tone, question a bill, sign up for call waiting, or all three, at any time of day.

GTE set up its first pilot "customer care center" in Garland, Texas, late last year and began to turn vision into fact. The company started with repair clerks, whose job had been to take down information from a customer, fill out a trouble ticket, and send it on to others who tested lines and switches until they found and fixed the problem. GTE wanted that done while the customer was still on the phone—something that happened just once in 200 calls. The first step was to move testing and switching equipment to the desks of the repair clerks—now called "front-end technicians"—and train them to use it. GTE stopped measuring how fast they handled calls and instead tracked how often they cleared up a problem without passing it on. Three times out of ten now, and GTE is shooting for upward of seven.

The next step was to link sales and billing with repair, which GTE is doing with a push-button phone menu that allows callers to connect directly to any service. It has given operators new software so their computers can get into databases that let the operators handle virtually any customer request. In the process, says GTE vice president Mark Feighner, "we eliminated a tremendous amount of work—in the pilots, we've seen a 20 percent or 30 percent increase in productivity so far."

GTE's rewired customer-contact process—one of eight similar efforts at the company—displays most of the salient traits of reengineering: It is occurring in a dramatically altered competitive landscape; it is a major change, with big results; it cuts across departmental lines; it requires hefty investment in training and information technology; and layoffs result. Says Michael Hammer, a former professor at MIT who runs a Cambridge, Massachusetts, business education firm that bears his name: "To succeed at reengineering, you have to be a visionary, a motivator, and a leg breaker."

Hammer is reengineering's John the Baptist, a tub-thumping preacher who doesn't perform miracles himself but, through speeches and writings, prepares the way for consultants and companies that do. *Reengineering the Corporation,* the book he wrote with James Champy, CEO of the CSC Index consulting firm, has 250,000 copies in print and has spent eight weeks on the New York Times bestseller list.

Most major consulting firms have added reengineering to their repertory, including such stalwarts as the Boston Consulting Group, Ernst & Young, Gemini Consulting, and McKinsey; firms with strong information technology backgrounds such as Andersen Consulting, CSC Index, and Symmetrix; and the new consulting arms of IBM and Digital Equipment. Business is booming: Index says its revenues have quintupled in five years.

The boldness of reengineering creates its perils and possibilities. Here is a partial list of what AT&T Global Business Communication Systems—which makes PBXs, private branch exchanges installed on the customer's premises, an operation with annual sales of $3.4 billion—had to do in two years as part of its reengineering effort: Rewrite job descriptions for hundreds of people, invent new recognition and reward systems, revamp the computer system, retrain massively, and make extensive changes in financial reporting, writing proposals and contracts, dealing with suppliers, manufacturing, shipping, installation, and billing.

It ain't cheap, and it ain't easy. At Blue Cross of Washington and Alaska, where redesigning claims processing raised labor productivity 20 percent in 15 months, CEO Betty Woods says the resource she drew on most was courage: "It was more difficult than we ever imagined, but it was worth it."

Therein lies the most important lesson from business's experience with reengineering: Don't do it if you don't have to. Says Thomas H. Davenport, head of research for Ernst & Young: "This hammer is incredibly powerful, but you can't use it on everything." Don't reengineer your buggy whip business; shut it. If you're in decent shape but struggling with cost or quality problems or weak brand recognition, by all means juice up your quality program and fire your ad agency, but don't waste money and energy on reengineering. Save reengineering for big processes that really matter, like new-product development or customer service, rather than test the technique someplace safe and insignificant.

The best corporate candidates for reengineering are companies facing big shifts in the nature of competition. It has spread as fast as gossip through financial services, for example, where deregulated banks, brokerage houses, and insurance companies now compete for the same investment dollar. Another hot spot is the vast, tumultuous field of telecommunications—local and long-distance phone companies, cable television providers, computer makers—where regulatory and technological barriers to entry have fallen precipitously.

In 1988, says Raymond W. Smith, CEO of Bell Atlantic, one of the seven regional Bell operating companies, "we looked at what happened to the airlines and the three blind mice [the broadcast networks] when new capacity came in. We had to reengineer." Five years later—and with 20,000 fewer employees in its traditional telephone business—Bell Atlantic seems decidedly more competitive. For example, the company cut the time needed to hook up customers to long-distance carriers from as much as 16 days to just hours—and began winning back market share from "alternate-access carriers," which had been moving in on its big corporate accounts.

There are two principal reasons to reengineer: fear and greed. If you can imagine—or worse, see—that an upstart rival, unburdened by your overhead, your loss leaders, or your history, could chew up your business, or if you can see how you could do unto him, reengineering may be the ticket. "It isn't fair," one insurance executive moaned to George B. Bennett, head of the Symmetrix consulting firm. "I've got mainframes to run and agents to pay, and I'm competing with little guys who just have PCs and telephones." Precisely.

All change is a struggle. Dramatic, across-the-company change is war. How can you increase the odds for success? Here are a few more lessons from the front.

GET THE STRATEGY STRAIGHT FIRST

"Don't fix stuff you shouldn't be doing in the first place," says Robert M. Tomasko, author of a new book, *Rethinking the Corporation*. Take a long look at what business you want to be in and how you intend to make money at it. Union Carbide made a fundamental decision to emphasize commodity chemicals rather than specialty products. That decision dictated the company's aim in reengineering: to seek its competitive advantage in the lowest possible manufacturing costs and provide added value in delivery and service.

Reengineering is about operations; only strategy can tell you what operations matter. An early hero of the reengineering movement was Mutual Benefit Life. The New Jersey insurer brilliantly redesigned the way it issued and underwrote policies—but that didn't keep disastrous real estate and mortgage investments from forcing it to seek shelter under the protection of the New Jersey State Department of Insurance in 1991.

Says John Hagel III, a reengineering specialist at McKinsey: "We did an audit of client experiences with process reengineering. We found lots of examples where there were truly dramatic impacts on processes—60 percent to 80 percent reductions in cost and cycle time—but only very modest effects at the business-unit level, because the changes didn't matter in terms of the customer." A computer company, convinced that customers needed more expertise from its sales force, poured tens of millions of dollars into reengineering its selling operations, training people in consultative sales techniques and outfitting them with costly electronic gear. It turned out that most customers didn't care. What mattered to them was price.

At Agway, the giant farm supply cooperative in the Northeast, two years of losses had convinced executives that the business was in trouble. Says Bruce Ruppert, senior vice president for planning and operations: "At the beginning, when we asked where Agway should go, all the top executives said different things."

Agway's 600 stores sold everything from cattle feed to garden trowels—basically a retail chain backed by 18 warehouses and feed mills. That setup was out of sync with the times. One out of eight farms in the Northeast disappeared in the 1980s. The survivors—often big, sophisticated outfits—wanted more expertise than store personnel could offer. Agway shipped directly from its mills and warehouses to many farmers, but they placed their orders at the stores, resulting in a costly tangle of bills and records.

Meanwhile, discount retailers like Wal-Mart had begun to siphon off general-merchandise sales from the stores, whose ability to respond was hampered by their need to serve commercial farmers. After a strategy review, Agway decided to split up its retailing and commercial farming businesses. Only then could reengineering begin.

Reengineering without strategy leads almost inexorably to market-blind cost cutting. It can maim the company. Says Thomas M. Hout of Boston Consulting Group: "If your only objective is cost reduction, not raising value, you will not engage the organization. People transfer out and seek shelter in a healthier division. It's like white flight."

LEAD FROM THE TOP

Reengineering is cross-functional. An insurance claim might pass through customer service, adjusting, and accounting before a check is cut. All three departments must be brought into any effort to reengineer the process—they all might end up being combined. Says William G. Stoddard, director of Andersen Consulting's reengineering practice: "Departments are stovepipes. We work in sewer pipes."

That means reengineering must be led by people with the authority to oversee a process from end to end or top to bottom. Says Hammer: "The guy at the top *must* have a lot of clout, because a lot of people are going to need to be clouted." The ideal reengineering czar, therefore, is not a department head, staff officer, or information officer but the CEO, COO, or her equivalent at the business-unit level. The leader should create a core team of first-rate people from all relevant departments—the very people their bosses are most loath to spare—as well as senior executives from human resources and information systems.

CREATE A SENSE OF URGENCY

Reengineering will break apart under political pressure or peter out after a few easy gains unless the case for doing it is compelling, urgent, and constantly refreshed. That is not hard for a major buyer of red ink. When the need is less clear, there is no better salesman than a customer.

Hallmark Cards shattered whatever complacency resulted from its cosseting culture and seemingly unassailable market position by making a series of videotapes to show to its top 40 executives. Chiefly at issue was the company's pokey process for bringing new products to market. First, small retailers talked about slowly falling store traffic. Then a senior vice president of Wal-Mart, a not-insignificant customer, delivered the not-subtle message that he hoped their companies could continue to do business. Says Steve Stanton, the CSC Index consultant who had the videos made: "By the time the lights went up, the temperature in the room had fallen 20 degrees."

Fear, resistance, and cynicism are inevitable as the reengineering team begins to unearth problems and toss around radical ideas for solutions. If not team members themselves, almost certainly their bosses and peers will defend their turf or be quick to show why a new idea can't possibly work.

To keep peace among the dukes and baronets, nothing is more critical than for the core team constantly to fill in the case for reengineering by talking to customers about their needs and learning where competitors are ahead. Says Joseph Ambrozy, Bell Atlantic's vice president for strategic planning: "Benchmarking is essential. You must know where you stand, function by function, process by process."

DESIGN FROM THE OUTSIDE IN

The point and power of reengineering is the clean sheet of paper with which it begins. Filling it in begins with customers: The right question is, How do they want to deal with us? not How do we want to deal with them? Says Steven Patterson, Gemini Consulting's chief reengineer: "To cross multiple boundaries in the company, you need a view of the organization that everyone agrees on but that doesn't depend on today's geography. So you start from the customer—then figure out how to execute the work."

That's easier said than done, particularly as reengineering moves from design to execution, and after the easy victories have been won. Glenn Hazard, the process reengineering vice president of AT&T's Global Business Communication Systems, says, "Designing from the outside in—all the way through—was *the* most critical success factor." To make the company wear its customers' shoes for the whole journey, Hazard's team enlisted several customers who served as a focus group, critiqued plans, participated in trial runs, and gave regular feedback.

Reengineering experts warn against spending too much time studying existing work flows—"the analysis tar pit," Hammer calls it. But don't throw out the old process map too fast. Especially if coupled with activity-based cost accounting, it can identify points of leverage where new thinking will provide the biggest benefit.

MANAGE YOUR CONSULTANT

You've used consultants before. They come in, interview people, run some numbers, present their findings, and leave you with a handsome black binder. (It's on the shelf to your right.) Reengineering consultants do that too, only they expect to stay around to help with implementation. Not just legions of bright young MBAs; behind them stand cadres of techies ready to help rebuild your information systems. You need them, because implementation is the tough part. Says J. Raymond Caron, chief information officer of insurance giant Cigna, who coaches the company's extensive reengineering effort: "When you start to implement, there will be nights when you go home and get sick." As reengineering is put into practice, old functional priorities (and their Praetorian guards) will reassert themselves: They'll insist that you can't eliminate the regional sales offices, for example. An outsider can help you contain such objections.

Trouble is, consultants bill by the hour. "Consultants are pushing the hell out of reengineering," says one of their brethren, "because it sells well and it's very labor-intensive." Bills of a quarter million dollars a month are common. Moreover, a clean-slate philosophy, says Davenport of Ernst & Young, "inevitably leads to multi-megabuck implementation projects." One giant office-products company lost sight of costs while designing a splendid order-management process, richly gewgawed with technology—then discovered that the price for hardware, software, and training would be $1 billion.

At Blue Cross of Washington and Alaska, Betty Woods instructed her consultant that each stage of reengineering had to generate enough savings to pay for the next. "It was a new experience for them," she says, laughing. An Andersen Consulting client announced up front: "I'll spend as much on information technology as you save me in inventory." Rules like these not only keep costs in line but also build enthusiasm and confidence as managers and employees nail coonskins to the wall. Most important, says Joseph Ambrozy of Bell Atlantic, ask your consultant for references, check them, and use him to train in-house experts who can carry the message deeper into the company.

COMBINE TOP-DOWN AND BOTTOM-UP INITIATIVES

At first blush, reengineering, with its emphasis on strong leadership, technology, and radical change, seems to be the antithesis of employee involvement, Total Quality Management, and other participative schemes your people have been beavering away at. It's true that reengineering cannot be led from the bottom of an organization, because it will be blocked by organizational boundaries, like a wave dashing against a sea wall. But top-down and bottom-up change needn't conflict. In fact, says Andersen's Bill Stoddard, "you can't do reengineering without an environment of continuous improvement or TQM."

When the consultants move on and the process map comes down from the wall, the painfully won gains will leak away unless the employees who have to live with the new work design had a hand in creating it and unless the human systems of the company—compensation, career paths, training—reinforce the changes.

Reengineering should not replace TQM or other initiatives. It should give them something to work on. In Union Carbide's industrial chemicals division, plant and equipment maintenance accounted for 30 percent of costs, making it an obvious target for reengineering. Top management took aim at it and made broad decisions about how the new process should look—notably that maintenance and operating staffs would work on the same teams and against the same set of ambitious goals. But the details—how to set up shifts, procedures for fixing a steam leak or cleaning a line—were developed on the floor of the pilot plant in Taft, Louisiana. Employees found savings of more than $20 million—50 percent more than management expected. In a nutshell, says vice president Vincent Villani, "top-down for targets, bottom-up for how to do it."

For all its macho rhetoric and technological content, reengineering in the end is like any other effort to change the way people work: Culture counts big. Change won't occur merely because management wills it. Says Agway's Bruce Ruppert: "You can survive the old way. You can survive the new way. It's the goddamn transition that'll kill you." When the once-clean sheet of paper is covered with boxes, lines, and arrows, the true test of leadership begins.

MAKING TOTAL QUALITY WORK: ALIGNING ORGANIZATIONAL PROCESSES, PERFORMANCE MEASURES, AND STAKEHOLDERS

Judy D. Olian, University of Maryland
Sara L. Rynes, University of Iowa

Total quality (TQ) is increasingly seen by corporate leaders as the most important strategic tool at their disposal. Reports[1] show that 93 percent of manufacturing companies and 69 percent of service companies have implemented some form of quality management, mostly in the last four years (The Conference Board, 1991). A majority (64 percent) of CEOs devote at least one-tenth of their time to quality improvement (KPMG Peat Marwick, 1991), and many commit a lot more. For example, James Houghton, Chairman and CEO of Corning, says that he spends more than half his time on quality (Houghton, 1990). Fifty-five percent of American executives and 70 percent of Japanese executives use quality improvement information at least monthly as part of their assessment of overall business performance (The American Quality Foundation and Ernst & Young, 1991). In short, quality improvement processes are part of the fabric of modern enterprises.

Penril Corporation, for instance, is a small manufacturer of data communications equipment located in Gaithersburg, Maryland. Every activity in the company is being reengineered to support quality (see Olian, 1991). From the president on down, all employees are involved in efforts to achieve improvements in quality. For example, the president heads the firm's quality council, works with vendors to redesign packaging that will simplify the unloading process, and actively leads the effort to identify and recognize individual employees for their quality improvements. The flow of the manufacturing process has changed to emphasize flexibility and speed. Before the

Source: *Human Resource Management* 30, no. 3 (Fall 1991), pp. 303–33. © 1992 by John Wiley & Sons, Inc.
The authors are grateful to Ramji Balakrishnan and Gary Gaeth for their useful comments and suggestions.

[1]Throughout this article, four survey sources are used repeatedly. They are KPMG Peat Marwick's (1991) survey of 62 major US-based companies classified as stage IV (very early) to stage I (advanced) in their TQM evolution. The Conference Board's (1989) survey of quality measurement practices in 149 firms. The Conference Board's (1991) survey of 158 of the Fortune 1000 regarding their approaches to achieve employee buy-in to TQM, and a joint survey by The American Quality Foundation and Ernst & Young (1991) of "more than 500" international corporations' strategic quality practices.

quality efforts, engineers designed products in a vacuum, then threw the product design "over the wall" to manufacturing, resulting in products that could not be manufactured. Today, goods are designed for manufacturability by deploying cross-functional design teams. Every employee receives extensive training in quality and functional cross-training that enables each of them to do several jobs. Movable carts replace stationary shelving. Information technology is used heavily in all parts of the design, manufacturing, and administrative operations of the company. The Penril "Hall of Fame" lists the names of employees who are champions of the TQ cause, and once a year the company's senior executives don aprons and cook lunch for all employees in the "Great Chefs of Penril" cookout. The company has gone from taking four to six weeks to process an order, to taking three days. Defects per unit have declined by 83 percent, and productivity is up 18 percent.

Although often mistaken as merely a tool or technique, TQ is an entire management system. When successfully implemented, TQ changes the way companies view and interact with each of their primary stakeholders—customers, employees, suppliers, and shareholders. Many organizational processes change, including factory and office layout, acquisition of raw materials, product development and manufacturing, interactions with customers and distributors, and measurement, feedback, and control systems. TQ processes refocus strategic priorities. The role and process of management also changes, from one based on authority and restricted access to one of mentoring, developing, and liberal sharing of information.

In this article, the organizational synergies that are critical in achieving a pervasive TQ culture are discussed. The following are considered:

1. *Organizational processes* that nudge people toward TQ-supportive behaviors.
2. *Outcome measures* that provide the information necessary to diagnose and continuously improve manufacturing and service processes.
3. Sources of *stakeholder support and opposition* to transition into a TQ culture.

Our premise is that TQ will become an organizational way of life only when all three aspects are "in sync" with one another: people (that is, stakeholders), processes, and outcomes all moving in the direction of market-driven quality and continuous improvement. Without creating such synergies, no single stakeholder, no matter how committed or charismatic, will be able to prevail in dragging the rest of the organization toward TQ since most will have a stake in the status quo and in the systems that support the old way of doing things. Figure 12–1 traces the synergies among processes, outcome measures, and stakeholder behaviors that are necessary in order to make the transformation into a market-driven quality organization. Each of these elements is discussed in a subsequent section.

THE ESSENTIALS OF TQ

Before discussing the organizational synergies that support TQ, the core components of a TQ approach are reviewed. Over the years, a number of quality experts such as Deming, Juran, Ishikawa, Crosby, Taguchi, and others, have developed and refined various TQ philosophies and systems. Although their approaches vary somewhat in terms of relative emphasis and techniques, in general, most TQ philosophies share the following characteristics (Saraph, Benson, & Schroeder, 1989; Tuttle, 1991):

- *Customer-driven quality as the main strategic priority* which is based on the presumption that other business goals (such as profit or market share) will follow if customers are fully satisfied or delighted.

F I G U R E 12-1 | **Getting to TQ: Organizational Processes, Outcome Measures, and Stakeholders**

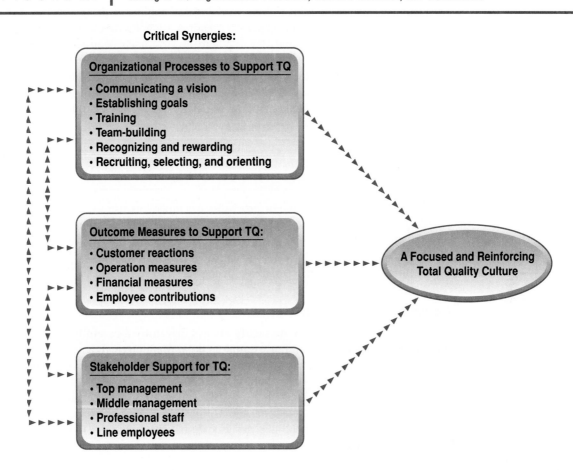

- *Visible, effective leadership,* where top management places quality ahead of other pressing demands and objectives—both symbolically and in day-to-day activities.
- *Data-driven processes,* where all decisions are made from verifiable data that track changes in performance trends over time.
- *Prevention rather* than inspection, in which building defect-free performance into product or service design is emphasized, rather than relying on subsequent inspection and rework.
- *Employee empowerment,* so that authority over delivering or improving products and services is in the hands of the "doers" rather than the overseers.
- *Vertical deployment* of quality initiatives so that everyone in the organization understands how their work affects key organizational objectives.
- *Emphasis on processes and cross-functional coordination* as the most likely source of problems and solutions. A process emphasis reduces buck passing and finger pointing, and encourages employees to think of themselves as internal customers and suppliers.
- *Continuous improvement philosophy,* which recognizes that performance can, and must, always be improved because the competition never rests.

Because TQ requires abandonment of some of our most cherished traditions and assumptions (managers think while workers do; engineers design while workers assemble), TQ implementation generally requires a wholesale change in the organizational culture. Organizational development experts have been saying for a long time that cultures change very laboriously and only when interdependent systems are simultaneously nudged in the same direction (Schein, 1985). For TQ to be successful, organizational processes must be altered, different forms of information must be attended to, and various stakeholder groups must be persuaded to buy into the process (see Figure 12–1).

ORGANIZATIONAL PROCESSES THAT SUPPORT TQ

In this section, some of the major processes organizations use to introduce and support TQ implementation are outlined. These include (a) communicating a quality vision; (b) translating that vision into quality goals; (c) training for quality; (d) team-building to enable quality processes; (e) recognizing and rewarding for quality; and (f) recruiting, selecting, and socializing quality-oriented employees.

COMMUNICATING A QUALITY VISION

Successful TQ organizations are nearly always driven by a carefully articulated and widely shared quality vision. For example, Globe Metallurgical, a small alloys company in Ohio, adopted the vision of being the highest-quality producer at the lowest price (Papay, 1990). Until very recently, this would have been dismissed as an impossible aspiration by most Western executives, academics, and consultants (Garvin, 1987). However, just four years into the TQ process, Globe has become an industry benchmark. Its CEO, Arden Sims, describes what was involved in communicating the quality message:

> When Globe Metallurgical first decided to pursue a quality program in 1985, there was no Baldrige Award and no prescribed quality criteria . . . Quality for Globe was a matter of economic survival, not part of a calculated effort to win an award. To compete in a global market, we had to provide our customers with the highest-quality products at the lowest possible cost.
>
> Once we established this vision, we communicated the values of quality to every employee at every level of the company . . . To demonstrate our commitment to our employees, we began a companywide profit-sharing program, eliminated time clocks at our main facility, and promised to respond to every quality-related question within 24 hours. In addition, I made a personal commitment to eliminate layoffs . . . and began to conduct small group meetings with every employee in the company to review our financial performance. (p. 126)

Another illustration is Motorola's former CEO, Bob Galvin, who focused on "six-sigma quality" (no more than 3.4 defects per million) in communicating Motorola's quality vision. Galvin spent significant amounts of time communicating this vision and ensuring that people in all areas of Motorola, even bakers and security guards, were able to translate it into personal work goals (Wiggenhorn, 1991).

In addition to communicating the quality vision downward, TQ organizations also increase upward and lateral communications. For example, the Conference Board (1991) notes that most TQ-practicing companies convene periodic employee meetings with top management (79 percent of manufacturing companies; 73 percent of service companies), face-to-face short-term teams (92 percent manufacturing, 97 percent service), focus groups (46 percent manufacturing, 71 percent service), and employee suggestion systems (60 percent manufacturing, 64 percent service). Another method used to enhance two-way communication and top management understanding of the business is for the top management team to adopt a regular schedule of working with line employees or service workers:

> It's not possible to analyze and control quality from behind a desk any more than a golf swing can be corrected by a teaching pro who isn't out on the course . . . it is for this reason that Honda managers go to the spot on the factory floor to have direct contact with an actual operation. (Shook, 1988, p. 158)

ESTABLISHING QUALITY GOALS

Not surprisingly, the specific goals that flow from overall quality visions such as six-sigma or "zero customer defections" (Reichheld & Sasser, 1990) are also extremely ambitious. In fact, many would argue that the "trick" to TQ goalsetting is to make the goals *so* ambitious that they cannot be achieved merely by incremental improvements to business-as-usual. For example, Motorola, which has already cut defects from 6,000 per million to only 40 per million in just five years, has a goal of further cutting defects by 90 percent every two years throughout the 1990s *(The Economist,* Jan. 4, 1992). Furthermore, Motorola is thinking ahead to the time (about 10 years from now) when its 68,040 microprocessor chips will contain 10 billion transistors (up from 1.2m at present), at which point even one-in-a-billion defects will mean a lot of "dud" chips. Thus, Motorola is already thinking about building "redundancy" into those products via such tactics as adding space capacity or alternative signal paths. Such thoughts are also triggering a search for structural ways in which Motorola can accelerate the dissemination of learning from already completed projects to new ones.

Similarly, as indicated by a Westinghouse official at their Quality Day (Jan. 23, 1992), the company has never set a cycle-time reduction goal of less than 50 percent the first time through the self-examination process. To date, Westinghouse (a Baldrige award–winner and two-time finalist) has not missed a single first-time target.

With goals such as these, it is clear that TQ is aimed at producing "quantum leaps" in performance. However, because most goal-setting research suggests that people will not embrace goals that they perceive to be impossible (Locke & Latham, 1990), achieving quantum leaps in performance through goal-setting often requires, as a first step, dramatic shifts in outlook regarding what *is* possible. Examination of industry practices suggests that this is being accomplished through two principal techniques: (a) benchmarking and (b) setting goals for the system rather than for individuals.

Benchmarking Traditionally, U.S. organizations have looked to past performance and to historically close competitors (e.g., GM, Ford, and Chrysler) to gauge how they are doing and to set performance objectives. However, in a global economy with continuously improving competitors, these insular and backward-looking practices are increasingly inadequate. Hence, the rapidly growing practice of benchmarking has arisen to provide more realistic and much higher standards (Camp, 1989).

Benchmarking turns the focus outward toward the "best in class" for a given function, regardless of industry. For example, many industries look to L.L. Bean for distribution benchmarks, to Honda for customer service, and to American Express for invoicing. Some companies engage in benchmarking to get a general feel for the best in class, regardless of the function or industry. Joseph Gorman, CEO of TRW and a major supplier to the American auto industry, was so impressed after driving a friend's Lexus that his company leased a top-of-the-line Lexus LS400 model to be driven by each of TRW's top executive team for two weeks (during the rest of the time they drive American cars). Says Gorman of the luxury Japanese car, "It's as good an example I know of what total quality and satisfaction to a customer mean" (Kretchmar, 1992, p. 121).

The motivational aspects of benchmarking were recently described by Jack Welch, CEO of General Electric:

> (We went to Wal-Mart) to observe the speed, the bias for action, the utter customer fixation that drives Wal-Mart and, despite our (own) progress, we came back feeling a bit plodding and ponderous, a little envious, but ultimately, fiercely determined that we're going to do whatever it takes to get that fast. (Jack Welch, quoted in Hyatt & Naj, 1992, p. B-6.)

System, Not Individual Goal Setting   A second aspect of TQ that seems to help people accept "stretch" goals is its insistence on looking at processes and systems, rather than individuals, as the most likely causes of and solutions to problems. To date, the focus of performance and reward systems for most U.S. employees has been individual performance. Thousands of individualized management-by-objectives plans and merit increases have often failed to produce world-class organizational performance. Indeed, according to Gabor (1990), W. Edwards Deming argues that individually based assessment and reward systems are fundamentally flawed in their basic assumptions:

> (Dr. Deming has argued that) performance appraisals, bonuses, and other reward systems that brand a few employees winners and encourage constant competition in the ranks are fundamentally unfair and ultimately harmful to the interests of both companies and employees. (He) believes that if the *system* in which people work is predictable—and if management has done its job well in selecting employees—then over time most employees will perform at about the same level, and that only a few will perform exceptionally well or poorly. Moreover, the influence of variation is such that it is impossible to accurately measure the overall performance of individuals within a variable *process* . . . it is impossible to separate the performance of the individual from that of the system. (pp. 26–27)

In contrast, TQ philosophies argue that if system outcomes are the ultimate determinants of success, then analysis and improvements must be focused primarily on the system rather than on the individual. People in TQ organizations make heavy use of process tools such as flow-charting, cause-and-effect diagrams, and plan–do–check–act cycles. Moreover, many of these efforts are conducted on a team basis across, rather than within, functional areas.

Looking at performance from a process or systems perspective appears to have a number of side benefits. Viewing one's role as a supplier of goods or services to other employees (internal customers) often brings a profound change in perspective. For example, while considering the role of accounting (staff) from a systems perspective, line managers may realize for the first time that when they do not deal promptly with accounting paperwork, they may be costing the company money in terms of late payment penalties, not to mention placing inordinate stress on those with accounts payable responsibilities. A second benefit is that people begin to speak the common language of quality, which facilitates further cross-functional process improvements.

A third benefit is that once people get used to the idea of looking at systems rather than people, the amount of finger pointing and turf protecting that goes on in functionally segregated systems decreases.

TRAINING FOR QUALITY

Another fundamental premise of TQ philosophies is that people who actually perform jobs are in the best position to understand them. Given this assumption, TQ advocates argue that more (and more radical) improvements occur when frontline employees are empowered to make them. For example, the most mature TQ cultures have factory workers who can stop the line over a quality issue or salespeople who are allowed to make very large deviations or adjustments for customers without supervisory approval (Garvin, 1991). However, a variety of support systems must be put in place before workers who are not accustomed to making decisions (or authorized to do so) become active problem solvers and decision makers.

Formal quality training appears to be the most common technique for initiating and sustaining employee involvement, at least during early stages of TQ implementation. According to the Conference Board (1991), 90 percent of manufacturing companies and 75 percent of service corporations report using some sort of training in their TQ efforts. However, KPMG Peat Marwick (1991) found that while training was the most important initiative in the early stages of TQ implementation, cross-functional quality teams and work process redesign became relatively more important in more mature implementations. Across TQ-practicing companies, the median number of hours devoted to quality training (per employee) was 20, with a larger commitment in corporations just launching their TQ efforts.

According to the General Accounting Office of the U.S. government (1990), TQ training is typically a two-stage process. The first stage consists of general awareness training to create a common frame of reference and a sense of the leadership commitment. The second stage focuses on concrete skill-based training designed to prepare individuals to become effective members of quality improvement teams. For example, in a small convenience sample of Fortune 100 firms, Olian and Rynes (1991) found the most common training content to be (in descending order of frequency): personal interaction skills, quality improvement processes and problem solving, team leading, team building, running meetings, statistical process control, supplier qualification training, and benchmarking.

Mature TQ organizations also frequently get involved in training people traditionally regarded as outsiders, for example, suppliers, customers, or public administrators. Indeed, one of the major contributions of TQ, and the analyses it fosters, is to blur entirely the lines between insider/outsider, and with that, to facilitate redesign and reengineering of a broader set of factors including those previously thought of as uncontrollable, because they were outside the system.

TEAM-BUILDING TO ENABLE QUALITY

The other major strategy to enable empowerment is the use of teams and team-building activities. A 1991 Conference Board survey found the formation of short-term problem-solving teams to be the single most commonly employed TQ implementation tactic.

As with training, the roles of teams and the issues for team facilitation change over time. Although most companies begin their team involvement with short-term single-issue teams, over time teams tend to become longer-standing, more cross-functional, multi-issue, and increasingly self-managed. For example, KPMG Peat Marwick (1991) found that only 15 percent of their total sample used completely self-managing work teams as a primary TQ tool. However, this figure rose to 50 percent in companies with the most developed TQ cultures.

RECOGNIZING AND REWARDING FOR QUALITY

Successful incorporation of TQ principles by all employees is also supported by a dramatically increased emphasis on employee recognition. TQ organizations have recognition-rich, even celebratory cultures. According to Schonberger (1990), world-class approaches to recognition are visible and public, have a strong next- and final-customer bias, focus on teams first and individuals second, are active and frequent, and ensure consistency (in the sense that self- and other-recognition are bestowed for the same things).

For example, Milliken, the Baldrige Award–winning textile manufacturer, has "Alcoves of Excellence," "Walls of Fame," and a company news magazine filled with recognition stories and photos of both individual and team accomplishments (Schonberger, 1990). Monsanto Agricultural Products has a "Big Meeting" day, in which more than 500 worldwide employees and team members come to corporate headquarters to be recognized for quality improvements. At Xerox, the Team Celebration Day turns into a "happening," with over 12,000 employees, customers, and suppliers attending a huge quality fair at one of four U.S. or international locations, all linked via satellite. As early as 1986, Honda of America's president began taking line workers (rather than other company executives) to Detroit's annual Automotive Hall of Fame Dinner, a meeting of approximately 600 of the industry's top-level executives.

In addition to verbal praise and visual recognition, many TQ organizations have also changed their financial reward systems to support employee involvement and quality achievements. For example, WTD Industries (sawmills) hands out $50 spot awards; Nucor steel has implemented profit sharing plus a variety of small group incentives; and PepsiCo, Inc. provides stock options for all of its roughly 100,000 permanent employees to involve everyone in the fate of the company (Kanter, 1989; Perry, 1988, Schonberger, 1990).

As is the case with most other aspects of TQ, reward systems tend to evolve in predictable ways as commitment to TQ grows. For example, both the Conference Board and KPMG Peat Marwick surveys showed that as companies mature along the TQ cycle, they increasingly shift their reward and recognition practices toward teams and broader units (see Table 12–1). In addition, the KPMG study showed an increasing linkage between incentive payouts and explicit quality improvement goals: 60 percent of the TQ "leaders" (those furthest along in TQ implementation) had incentive plans reflecting quality goals, as compared with none of those just beginning TQ.

Interestingly, the Peat Marwick study also revealed that companies are less willing to link quality to rewards for top executives than for middle managers. Indeed, contingent executive compensation awards are still driven almost exclusively by financials, a situation that Eccles (1991) argues undercuts TQ strategies.

Despite the lack of an explicit link between quality and executive compensation, highly evolved TQ firms in the United States tend to be more concerned about vertical pay equity than are less advanced companies. For example, companies such as Nike, Herman Miller, and Ben & Jerry's strictly limit the number of pay grades in the hierarchy, as well as the ratio of top executive to lowest-level employee pay. In addition, some have increased horizontal equity as well. For example, Mars, Inc.—a

T A B L E 12–1 | **Frequency of Distributing Awards**

Years TQ Process in Place:	To Individuals		To Teams		Unitwide	
	Cash	Noncash	Cash	Noncash	Cash	Noncash
8 years or more	10%	58%	10%	53%	10%	53%
1 year or less	15	23	8	31	4	11

N = 146

Source: The Conference Board (1991), p. 30.

highly successful multibillion-dollar enterprise—does not differentiate the pay of same-level managers in different functional areas (e.g., finance versus human resources) and has no individual merit or incentive system. Instead, all employees are held to very high work standards, paid at the 90th percentile against market competitors, and given equal annual increases (Cantoni, 1992). Indeed, the concept of simply paying higher-than-market wages to attract and retain high-involvement employees, rather than "incenting" every little action and outcome, has taken hold in many high-performance organizations, including Au Bon Pain, American Savings Bank, and the GE Answer Center (Sellers, 1990; Rice 1990).

Generally speaking, although TQ companies tend to treat employees well financially, most make a bigger issue out of employee recognition than of financial rewards. Although in part this may reflect the fact that praise and recognition are more predictable than payouts based on financial or productivity improvements, there is also some concern that tying formal pay systems too closely to short-term achievements focuses employees on the wrong things:

> We have never added up, and we never will, the cost savings that come out of employee involvement—on the simple basis that if that becomes the focus, some dumb cluck is going to decide that more is better, and then everybody's focus in going to be, "Gee, look at all the money I'm saving—I ought to get a piece." The thing we do is give 'em a belt buckle, a picnic once a year, all the beer they can drink (that's Harley beer, by the way) and we just say thanks. Their satisfaction is they made the product better, they had fun doing it, and they have some control over their environment—which is what it's all about. (Vaughn Beals, CEO of Harley-Davidson, quoted in Schonberger, 1990, pp. 200–201)

RECRUITING, SELECTING, AND SOCIALIZING QUALITY-ORIENTED EMPLOYEES

Consistent with recent evidence suggesting the critical importance of hiring the right people, TQ-practicing organizations tend to distinguish themselves in terms of the effort and expense devoted to recruitment, selection, and orientation at all organizational levels (Shook, 1988). For example, Hampton (1988) reports that Mazda and Diamond-Star Motors (a Chrysler-Mitsubishi joint venture) spend about $13,000 per production employee hire. Although specifics vary slightly across the two firms, each includes written tests, drug tests, medical exams, and several rounds of interviews, problem-solving exercises, and work sample tryouts.

In addition, TQ organizations often use realistic job previews and extensive orientation sessions to ensure appropriate applicant expectations and values. For example, Diamond-Star uses a realistic preview video that warns applicants they must learn several jobs, change shifts, work overtime, make and take constructive criticism, and submit a constant stream of suggestions for improving efficiency. The video concludes by saying, "It's not an easy decision; you've got to ask yourself if you're willing to dedicate yourself to the Diamond-Star team" (Hampton, 1988). In addition, many TQ firms (such as Honda and Wal-Mart) also involve family members in selection procedures in order to ensure familywide commitment to the new employer.

The importance of teams and teamwork is also reinforced in a number of ways. First, in many companies, ongoing teams play a large (or even solo) role in new employee recruitment and selection. Interpersonal skills and willingness to be a team player also form a large part of the interviewing and testing procedures. Finally, these characteristics are reinforced through general orientation and training which often lasts several months even for production workers. At Mazda, line workers receive several days of general philosophy training, followed by five to seven weeks of technical skills training, followed by three to four weeks of supervision when first placed on the assembly line. Thus, recruitment, selection, and orientation all work in concert to produce dedicated, team-oriented, and highly skilled employees.

Despite their screening rigor and demanding work requirements, employers such as Honda, Mazda, and Diamond-Star can afford to be very selective because they are widely regarded as good places to work. Selection ratios (number of hires relative to the size of the applicant pool) of 0.04 are reported at Diamond-Star; 0.13 at Mazda (Hampton, 1988); 0.095 at Honda, Marysville; and 0.025 at Honda Power Equipment (Shook, 1988).

OUTCOME MEASURES THAT SUPPORT TQ

> You cannot manage what you cannot measure . . . And what gets measured gets done.
> (Bill Hewlett, cofounder of Hewlett-Packard, quoted in House & Price, 1991, p. 93)

Given that implementation of TQ typically involves a multiplicity of changes, it is not surprising that many of the things that are measured and attended to in TQ organizations are quite different from those that drive traditional organizations. Also, consistent with recommendations from goal-setting research, employees in TQ organizations are given rich information and feedback to help them control and improve processes and outcomes. Fred Smith, chairman and CEO of Federal Express, explains the rationale for extensive, incessant measurement and feedback:

> We recognized long ago that when you get an operation that is as complex and as large as Federal Express, you must have very sophisticated measurement systems. That, in turn, requires extensive use of various technologies. We put a lot into mechanisms to feed information back to the people who are doing the job so if they have a quality problem or an error, they know it and can fix it. (Smith, quoted in Karabatsos, 1990, p. 25)

At least four groups of outcome measures are undergoing close scrutiny in TQM-driven organizations. These measures reflect (a) *customer* data, (b) *operations* data, (c) *financial* information, and (d) *employee* data and are all critical in supporting and directing the TQ efforts. Each is discussed in turn, followed by a brief discussion of the synergies across the various measurement categories.

MEASURING CUSTOMER REACTIONS

Interestingly, although such slogans as "The Customer is King" or "We're No. 1 on Service" have increased exponentially in recent years, these self-proclamations drive the day-to-day activities of only a fraction of companies. The survey conducted by the American Quality Foundation and Ernst & Young (1991) found that, at present, customer satisfaction is a primary criterion in the strategic planning process for only 37 percent of American, 42 percent of Japanese, and 22 percent of German companies. Similarly, evaluating and rewarding employees on the basis of customer service is rare at all levels, although the practice is growing (Rice, 1990; Sellers, 1990).

Still, even if customer satisfaction measures are not yet influencing many strategic plans or employee paychecks, firms are increasingly realizing that "zero defects" are of little ultimate value if products or services are not attuned to customer needs (*The Economist,* Jan. 4, 1992). Thus, consultants and firms increasingly talk about zero defects and market-driven quality to differentiate ultimate consumer-based objectives (first-time purchases, repeat buying, and service recovery) from narrower reliability or process improvements (e.g., Reichheld & Sasser, 1990; Hart, Heskett, & Sasser, 1990).

Businesses are responding to the growing "pickiness" of consumers and their increasing willingness to pay for quality in a variety of ways. In some cases, companies are merely paying more attention to the customer-satisfaction data they have always collected, but typically ignored. Even in these companies, however, just paying more attention typically leads to a desire for more, and more useful, information. Thus, more companies actively pursue customer feedback than in the past, and increasing numbers hire marketing research firms to conduct routine follow-ups with recent purchasers.

Other companies are more aggressively tracking both their products and their customers. Bar-code scanning techniques have made it possible to track not only what people are buying, but also who is buying it. Firms such as Nielson Marketing Research and Information Resources, Inc., recruit ordinary consumers to become part of "scanner panels" which provide detailed information about family demographics, income, and consumption patterns. Then, each time they shop, panel members pass a uniquely coded ID card to the cashier, whose register entries link everything purchased to the appropriate consumer. In this way, the success of new product launches, which have more than doubled over the past six years, can be tracked, particularly the all-important depth of repeat buying. In a world where approximately 80 percent of new products fail, such analyses can be critical determinants of success or failure (Caminiti, 1991). Some supermarket chains have instituted frequent buyer discount clubs that enable the creation of a database showing individual customer purchasing behavior against demographic information.

Similarly, toll-free complaint lines are no longer merely mechanisms for remedying customer problems, but rather information-gathering services to help identify recurring problems requiring correction. In the most sophisticated systems, producers systematically integrate customer feedback into the organizational-learning and product-design process. Honda of America has long posted engineers in centralized service positions to help licensed mechanics who call in with difficult service or repair problems. Each request for help is incorporated into a centrally maintained database so that what is learned from one repair job can be transmitted to future mechanics who encounter the same problem. The system is also used by design engineers to locate trouble spots in current designs so they can be eliminated from subsequent products. Similar systems now exist at Cadillac and at GE's 800-number answer center (Rice, 1990).

Increasingly, firms are using "groupware" (software designed to support the collective work of teams) to gather the insights of cross-functional teams with respect to customer needs. Marriott Hotels recently used a 25-minute, electronic brainstorming meeting to generate 139 ideas on how to improve customer satisfaction. Each idea was then rated on two criteria: likely size of impact on guests and likely cost. A major outcome of the meeting was the consensus that, among other things, hotel employees needed more thorough training (Kirkpatrick, 1992). Dell Computer used a similar session to generate 75 possible new product names, and then to whittle them down to five. Without the measurement technology, these processes would have taken several days.

Finally, consumer behavior has revealed that customers often are willing to pay hefty premiums for speed (Stalk & Hout, 1990). Consequently, retailers like Wal-Mart and J.C. Penney have put a great deal of effort into tracking inventories, working with suppliers, and improving distribution systems to make sure that shelves are stocked with in-fashion, fast-moving items. On the distribution end, transport firms such as Schneider have equipped their trucks with the necessary technology to provide just-in-time deliveries. On the production end, manufacturers such as Hewlett-Packard and IBM have used project mapping to cut design and production cycle times.

OPERATION MEASURES

Of the four measurement areas described in this paper, the most substantial changes have occurred in the documentation, reengineering, and measurement of operations and work processes. At the risk of oversimplifying, operational approaches to quality have, at least in one sense, come full circle. They have shifted from (a) the pre-mass-production assumption that quality is built into the product by a well-trained craftsman, to (b) the advent of inspection as a separate function, necessitated by the rise of mass production, unskilled labor, and the need for interchangeable parts, to (c) the development of statistical process controls and sampling procedures to meet the pragmatic goal of attaining adequate quality with less-than-100 percent inspection, to (d) the rise of broad quality-assurance programs, where a wide array of tools (psychological and social, as well as statistical) are employed to once again ensure that quality is built into the product. [The interested reader is encouraged to consult Garvin (1987) for further details.]

In the early phases of TQ implementation, the first challenge is to create an environment where improvements in quality take priority over the more usual short-term drivers such as scheduling, shipping, or cost reduction [for an excellent case description of this phenomenon, see Wiggenhorn (1990)]. Initially, attention tends to focus mainly on the elimination of defects. Once minimal quality standards are met, quality efforts branch out in a variety of additional directions.

One of those directions is in narrowing the acceptable tolerance zones by establishing higher standards that are met with increasing reliability. These ever-higher standards are imposed because of the danger in cumulative effects of minor quality deviations in products that may have hundreds, thousands, or even millions of component parts. Another more advanced application of TQ is design simplification, pursued so that there are fewer parts or processes where something can go wrong. A related approach is to break highly complex processes into a number of discrete, simpler subassemblies.

More recently, operation measures have shifted from defects and design for defect-reduction to factors such as cycle time or time-to-market (Stalk & Hout, 1990). This emphasis reflects the fact that for some products, speed and fashionability are of equal, and sometimes greater, importance to customers than freedom from defects. It also reflects the growing economic reality that industries typically have less time to bask in the returns from new products before they are imitated or even supplanted by competitors and newer designs. Financial issues posed by changing production processes are discussed in greater detail in the following section.

Financial Measures

Traditional management accounting systems provide virtually no information about value received by the customer, or about value added in the workplace . . . Lulled into complacency by traditional management accounting signals, American manufacturers were surprised by the high quality and low price of Japanese goods that began to flood our markets in the late 1970s.

Perhaps managerial accounting information should have allowed manufacturers to anticipate the changes occurring after 1970. Certainly it should have given manufacturers some indication of how to respond to these major developments once they had taken place. That management accounting information did neither evidences its inability to help companies compete in a global economy. (Johnson, 1990, pp. 8–9)

Ever since the publication of Robert Kaplan's (1984) widely read "Yesterday's Accounting Undermines Production," there has been a growing recognition that traditional financial and accounting measures do not adequately reflect, and may even obscure, actual operational effectiveness. To take just one example, Greene and Flentov (1992) describe a case in which the introduction of just-in-time production reduced manufacturing cycle time by a factor of seven, required floor space by 120 percent, defects per million from 2,500 to 50, material handling costs by a factor of 3, inspection costs by a factor of 5, and labor content per unit by more than half. Yet over the same period, traditional accounting reports showed unfavorable changes in labor utilization, labor absorption variance, and overhead absorption variance.

Several features of conventional accounting systems appear to limit their usefulness for managerial decision making. For example, conventional accounting systems are based on a decades-old, supplier-driven model of the firm which seeks to minimize *unit* costs by producing large batches of a standardized product. In addition, all indirect costs—including overhead—are generally (arbitrarily) allocated on the basis of direct labor hours.

Although these practices worked well in earlier times, they come with some potentially severe disadvantages in today's markets where labor costs are a much lower percentage of total costs, management and staff ranks have expanded dramatically, and products are custom tailored, sometimes into lot sizes of one. Under these circumstances, the practice of allocating overhead on the basis of direct labor diverts attention away from the need to understand, manage, and control indirect costs which often account for 70 percent to 80 percent of total product costs (Johnson, 1990; Kaplan, 1984). Thus, finding more informative ways of managing and allocating overhead is a major priority for TQ managers.

A contrast with Japanese accounting principles is quite telling. First, in order to maintain maximum flexibility across workers and products, Japanese manufacturers seek to minimize total (rather than unit) costs, to keep staff specialists to a minimum, and to calculate the value-added at each stage of the production process (including supplier-based stages). Second, whereas U.S. firms first develop a product and then price it at whatever level is necessary to turn a profit, Japanese companies turn this process upside-down through "target costing." With target costing, the firm first decides what the consumer will be willing to pay for the new product, and then works backward to drive design, production, distribution, marketing, and supplier costs down to the target figure (Sakurai, 1992; Worthy, 1991). Third, rather than using accountants to measure costs, the Japanese tend to use cost engineers who are experienced product developers. These individuals are instructed not only to measure costs, but also to reduce them. And finally, the Japanese are not so single-mindedly driven by anticipated profits in their capital investment decisions:

> In evaluating capital investments, [the Japanese] perform some of the quantitative analyses developed in the West, but it is hardly the crutch that it is for so many Western managers. Return on investment, such a focal point in the U.S., is merely a small implement found in the corner of a Japanese manager's toolbox . . . Their cost systems are designed not to take the place of human judgment, but to encourage managers and workers to exercise it. (Worthy, 1991, p. 75)

Although most U.S. firms have done little to overhaul their basic financial measurement systems, they have at least been making progress in the narrower area of tracking the costs of quality. The Conference Board (1989) reports that of the 111 firms surveyed that have a quality process in place, 75 percent attempt to measure quality costs in some form. Specifically, 72 percent measure internal failure costs (scrap, downtime, rework costs), 65 percent measure detection costs (inspecting and testing the finished product), 64 percent measure prevention costs (training, standards development, work process redesign), and 64 percent measure the costs of external failures (repairs, fulfilling warranties). In addition, a few cutting-edge firms have made substantial progress in improving the measurement of time-based costs. For the most part, however, internal U.S. business decisions are still driven by financial accounting systems designed for external reporting purposes rather than internal efficiency enhancement (Johnson, 1990).

MEASURING EMPLOYEE CONTRIBUTIONS

As in the financial area, despite increased concern about the need for new ways of measuring employee performance (e.g., Dobbins, Cardy, & Carson, 1991; Scholtes, 1987), actual performance measurement has changed very little with the advent of TQ. For example, KPMG Peat Marwick (1991) found that only 60 percent of companies with TQ processes already in place actually included quality goals in any employee appraisals. Quality goals were most prevalent in supervisory appraisals (strong or moderate link to quality in 29 percent of responding companies), less so for executives (23.5 percent) and middle managers (24.5 percent), and least prevalent for hourly nonunion employees (17 percent). The study authors suggest that the heavier emphasis on quality for supervisory employees relative to executive or managerial employees is probably due to the greater availability of quality measures for supervisory positions. Alternatively, these figures may give credibility to supervisory and employee complaints that top managers do not actively involve themselves in the quality process. After all, even if quality measures are established primarily at the operational level, that does not mean that top managers should be relieved of accountability for quality-related achievements.

Comparable figures emerged in the Conference Board (1991) survey, where quality achievements were linked to performance measurement for only 32 percent of managers in manufacturing industries (versus 21 percent in services), and to promotions for only 28 percent in manufacturing and 24 percent in service organizations. Similarly, Olian and Rynes (1991) found that although most firms conduct consumer surveys to a considerable extent, far fewer use the results to reward employees for improvements in customer satisfaction, improved cycle time, increased reliability, or speeded innovation. These findings are not very encouraging, given that these are the most obvious places for linking quality to employee measurement and reward.

TQ proponents also argue that *who* does the measuring needs to change right along with *what* is being measured (e.g., Scholtes, 1987; Schonberger, 1990). Specifically, they advocate that a variety of evaluators be involved in performance measurement including customers, suppliers, team members, and subordinates. Again, however, actual practices appear to diverge considerably from prescriptive advice. For example, KPMG Peat Marwick's (1991) study showed that even in companies with three to five years of TQ experience, internal customers contributed to performance appraisals in only 22 percent of the cases, external customers in 17 percent, and co-workers and subordinates in 0 percent!

SYNERGIES ACROSS THE QUALITY MEASURES

Although TQ organizations typically measure more (and different) processes and outcomes, there is no assurance that the various measures will work in concert to produce higher product quality, greater customer satisfaction, lower cost, greater speed, or higher profitability. Indeed, without conscious integration it is likely that each set of measures will remain the property of isolated functional areas and may contribute little to overall TQ objectives.

By way of contrast, in well-established TQ systems, measures are integrated both vertically (across levels) and horizontally (across functions):

> What really blows us away (in later-stage TQ firms) is the integration and deployment. You can't go anywhere in the company that isn't affected by quality management; the right hand and the left hand know what they're doing, and cycles are fast. (Baldrige examiner, quoted in Garvin, 1991, p. 88)

Each type of integration is discussed below.

Vertical Integration "Vertical deployment" (sometimes called "Hoshin planning" or "catchball") is a central concept in TQ implementation. Garvin (1991) defines deployment as "the cascading of senior management's vision down through the organization so that at each succeeding level (as activities become more operational and detailed) they are still aligned with and derived from higher goals" (p. 86). Simply put, when vertical integration has been accomplished, everyone (including the receptionist and the delivery person) understands how his or her behavior ultimately affects key organizational objectives.

Nearly all descriptions of deployment suggest that the first step is to identify a small number of critical success factors, outcomes so important that without any one of them, the company would fail (Beischel & Smith, 1991). For example, Westinghouse has three such factors and corresponding measures: one reflecting customer satisfaction (value-to-price ratio), another for financial performance (value-to-cost), and a third for operational effectiveness (error-free performance).

Once overarching success factors and measures have been determined, the next step is to create aligned objectives and measures for organizational subunits. Again, Westinghouse establishes linked, but individualized, divisional objectives, called divisional "pulse points." The concept of pulse points is based on the medical analogy, wherein continuous monitoring is the only way to detect problems before they become visible and increasingly difficult and expensive to remedy. The creation of specific processes, such as training and planning, to facilitate vertical goal alignment is critical because insufficient linkages between organizational objectives and operational priorities are one of the main causes of TQ failure [*Harvard Business Review* Debate (Piper), Jan.–Feb. 1992].

Horizontal Integration   In addition to vertical deployment, it is critical to link various targets of TQ measurement together, for example, operational process improvements and customer satisfaction. So far, most companies have launched TQ implementations on faith, hoping that operational improvements or increased attention to the customer will eventually translate into the bottom line. Although data from Baldrige award–winners (Garvin, 1991) and the General Accounting Office (1990) suggest that this has generally been the case for *successful* TQ implementations, there nevertheless appear to be a substantial number of TQ stall-outs and failures. Not surprisingly, along with the failures have come criticisms (for example, see the *Harvard Business Review* Debate, Jan.–Feb. 1992, or Sharman, 1992).

One of the most frequently leveled criticisms is that the TQ concept itself is flawed, particularly in its emphasis on process rather than outcomes. However, the fact that it has succeeded dramatically in so many organizations, including some in the United States (see Schonberger, 1986, or Umble & Srikanth, 1990) suggests that failures probably are due, not to the concept itself, but to the quality or effectiveness of its implementation. Seasoned observers have already supplied a long list of implementational stumbling blocks that can cause TQ programs to fail: top managers espousing quality but rewarding short-term performance; middle managers subverting employee empowerment, doing the *wrong* things right the first time (e.g., reducing defects in obsolete designs), and failing to translate strategic objectives into operational guidelines. As TQ spreads, it will be increasingly important to analyze successes and failures against the *precise nature* and *extent* of TQ implementation, not just its nominal presence or absence.

Regarding linkage with market outcomes, it is certainly true that in the intermediate and longer terms, empirical linkages between process improvements (e.g., cycle time reduction) and bottom-line results (market share and profitability) must be established to prevent TQ efforts from emphasizing irrelevant processes (Kaplan & Norton, 1992). In establishing these linkages, however, it is important to find a way to keep short-term financial results from completely dominating the analyses and, where unfavorable, from short-circuiting the implementation process before it can succeed (Eccles, 1991). Goldratt and Cox (1986) and others have shown how a dominant emphasis on traditional accounting procedures can cause organizations to pursue dysfunctional operational policies. Although it is clear that TQ processes must produce financial results in the longer term, it is unrealistic and self-defeating to expect them to do so in the typical quarterly or annual financial time frames:

> This shortsightedness [to expect immediate increases in sales and earnings growth] is typical of some U.S. companies. Any investment with big payoffs requires a longer-term investment—at least five or more years . . . We can't possibly expect to gather all our chips in such a short time. [*Harvard Business Review* Debate (Hockman), 1992, p. 137]

GETTING TO TQ: STAKEHOLDER SUPPORT AND OPPOSITION

Given that successful implementation of TQ requires an extensive cultural change, a wide variety of stakeholders need to be won over for them to risk change and buy into an entirely new set of values and behaviors. In addition to the obvious candidates (current managers and employees), a number of outsiders (suppliers, shareholders) also affect the success of TQ. In the next section, however, the discussion is limited to organizational insiders, particularly top managers, middle managers, professional staff, and line employees.

Top Management

It is difficult to find a TQ consultant, book, or article that does not cite top-management support as the preeminent, indispensable requirement for successful TQ implementation (Crosby, 1979; Garvin, 1991; Juran, 1989; Walton, 1986). To date, however, only the most advanced TQ companies appear to have firmly entrenched TQ visionaries and mentors among their top leadership (KPMG Peat Marwick, 1991; Yates, 1992).

According to Garvin, successful TQ leadership requires both *symbolic leadership* and *active involvement*. Symbolic acts are those which help to elevate in employees' minds the importance of quality above the more traditional decision drivers such as cost or efficiency. For example, Wiggenhorn (1990) describes how Bob Galvin reinforced his preference for quality in the earliest days of Motorola's quality implementation:

> Bob Galvin believed quality training was useless unless top managers gave quality even more attention than they gave quarterly results. He dramatized the point at operations review meetings. He insisted that quality reports come first, not last, on the agenda, and then he left before the financial results were discussed. (p. 76)

Similarly, the president of SAS airlines, Jan Carlzon, described how he reinforced the primacy of quality service for business customers by flying coach (instead of first class) and by giving up his own seat to wait-listed customers (Carlzon, 1987).

Taken by themselves, however, sporadic shows of commitment to quality are ineffective. Indeed, one of the most frequently mentioned sources of TQ failure involves top management's failure to back up their quality talk through daily, personal actions such as by rewarding quality over production, by maintaining a physical presence in quality training programs, by personally conducting quality systems reviews, by involving themselves in customer and employee quality efforts, and by empowering their *own* subordinates (middle managers) in the same way they exhort these middle managers to empower first-level employees.

Managerial day-to-day commitment to quality over all other objectives is represented by this Honda manager in Marysville, Ohio:

> When it comes to quality, we never compromise. *Never.* There is only one standard that is acceptable and it never varies. It's so easy to let people off the hook in the heat of the day when you're being pushed. So you always must remember that no product, under any circumstance, ever goes out the door if quality is compromised. You can't say, "Okay, shipping must go on today. Just this one time we'll slacken our standards and let the car go out the door, and hope and pray that it goes unnoticed." Once you do, you've taught your people that a double standard exists, one that's dependent upon how management feels at a particular time. Once you do that, you've violated your rules on what your real objective is, and you've lost it. And once it's lost, you can never get it back. (Shook, 1988, p. 116)

Middle Management

Another characteristic of successful TQ implementation is that the support of middle managers is gained. Because of their critical role as channelers of information both to and from work teams and as those who can choose to share or, alternatively, to jealously guard power, middle managers can make or break a TQ effort.

Despite their importance to successful TQ implementation, however, middle managers often become obstacles to bringing about a TQ improvement. Upon close inspection, it is hardly surprising that this should be the case. Middle managers stand to lose much of their unilateral decision-making authority under a TQ system. In addition, however, they often receive inadequate informational and resource support to enable their roles as change agents. For example, middle managers often complain that they are expected to empower employees while they themselves are kept in the dark about strategies and plans affecting their units.

Additionally, middle managers' sense of personal security has been affected dramatically by changes of the last decade. Such strategic actions as "de-layering," "flattening the pyramid," and "removing hierarchy" have all been aimed at eliminating middle-management jobs. Although middle managers make up only 5 to 8 percent of the labor force, they accounted for 17 percent of all dismissals between 1989 and 1991 (Fisher, 1991).

Under these conditions, it is hardly surprising that middle managers have often contributed less-than-enthusiastic support to wholesale change efforts. Again, the critical role of top management comes into play, as only top management can provide the information, security, and support necessary to allay middle-management apprehension:

> The best companies concentrate on managers' concerns *first,* says Peter Gelfond, who directs research at the Hay Group. Otherwise you get what I call supervisory scapegoating. The manager conveys, either in words or attitude, to the people under her or him, "Top management doesn't give a damn about me, so they probably don't care what happens to you, either." (Fisher, 1991, p. 76)

PROFESSIONAL STAFF

One of the most striking things about TQ organizations is the range of functions that line workers are empowered to perform. For example, in a production situation, line workers may help select vendors, answer customer service lines, conduct consumer surveys, reengineer work processes to solve manufacturing or service problems, plan daily production schedules, and hire replacement personnel. In short, in well-developed TQ organizations, line workers do a large part of what has traditionally been regarded as the work of staff professionals.

This simple fact, combined with the increase in cross-functional decision making, has created both status and job security issues for staff specialists. Status is threatened because work that was formerly regarded as thinking or expert work, often requiring college or even graduate training, is now increasingly performed by "doers," typically, with high school diplomas. Status is also eroded (at least in some people's minds) by being increasingly required to conduct work outside the private office, in consultation with line workers on or near the shop floor. Although this has long been common practice in Japanese firms, it is still quite a shock to many U.S. professionals (Shook, 1988).

Although the advent of TQ poses a challenge to virtually all staff functions (including product designers, engineers, basic researchers, marketers, accountants, lawyers, MIS specialists, and operations researchers), several that are particularly germane to the human resource (HR) function are elaborated on here. One of the most important of these concerns is the overwhelming predominance of an individualistic orientation to all major HR functions (Dobbins et al., 1991). At present, the vast majority of employees are still selected for their individual accomplishments, evaluated on the basis of their individual (that is, independent) contributions, and rewarded with individualized pay increases. Moreover, HR textbooks continue to emphasize individualistically based techniques, thus shaping the assumptions and tool kits of future generations of HR professionals.

A second shortcoming concerns the failure of HR professionals to routinely collect and evaluate data for improved future decision making (Fitz-Enz, 1990). This runs counter to the core TQ principle of collecting information on all important processes and outcomes for the purpose of reducing variability, improving processes, and developing a better understanding of covariances among activities and outcomes. Although progress certainly has been made in this regard (Cascio, 1987), lack of adequate experimentation, design, and evaluation continues to be cited in most areas of HR.

A third issue for HR departments concerns the substantial proportion of practitioners who remain functionally isolated from mainstream business operations. Functional isolation not only prevents practitioners from understanding business issues, but may also yield an overly optimistic assessment of the adequacy of HR services provided (Bellman, 1986; Fitz-Enz, 1990). As TQ gets under way, line managers typically are inundated with people-management issues that include the need for training, teambuilding, goal setting, problem solving, ways of reducing absenteeism, incentives for skill building, and the independent initiation of process improvements (Bell & Burnham, 1991; Ciampa, 1992). Unfortunately, it is not clear how many HR practitioners are equipped to provide such a wide range of services.

The final issue concerns the legalistic, inflexible bent of such long-standing HR practices as job analysis, job description, job evaluation, performance appraisal, and merit increase grids. Although one can certainly sympathize with the fact that HR practitioners have been charged with keeping things legal—and new legal requirements continue to be churned out with a distressing imperviousness to the business utility of some of the practices called for—the simple truth is that keeping legal is not the main strategic priority of any organization. Given that the influence of any department is contingent upon the extent to which it supports the strategic objectives of the firm, most HR departments will have to realign their priorities dramatically if they wish to play a central role in TQ organizations (see also Fitz-Enz, 1990; Schuler, 1990).

Moreover, emerging evidence suggests that HR departments do not have long to make these modifications. Because of perceived unwillingness or inability to change, some organizations already are bypassing HR departments in their quality efforts (Olian & Rynes, 1991). In these situations, HR is being left with its legal control function, while the strategically more important change agent role is being carried out by newly created functions, such as the Quality Office.

LINE EMPLOYEES

In contrast to middle managers and staff professionals, line employees in service and manufacturing operations are seen as major beneficiaries of TQ systems. For example, TQ management is touted as a method for giving workers more control over their immediate work lives, in stark contrast to Mintzberg's (1989) description of what typically occurs when the thinkers impose strategies onto the doers:

> Then, once (top management) has the final answer, (they) let others lower down in the hierarchy work it all out. It's called "implementation." Implementation means dropping a solution into the laps of people informed enough to know it won't work, but restricted from telling anyone with power what can. So while administrators in the executive suites are smiling about how "Quality is Job 1" or whatever, the implementers are running around the factories trying to plug the holes. (p. 358)

In addition, TQ offers the promise of greater job security, first by increasing workers' personal knowledge and skills, and second by improving the chances that their companies will survive intense worldwide competition.

Despite these optimistic promises of what TQ can do for workers, line workers have sometimes resisted TQ programs. Although resistance generally has been strongest in ongoing units with union representation, it has also occurred in other organizational settings. From experience, it appears that at least two major factors have to be addressed before line employees become TQ champions.

The first of these is the fear of job loss. Although anxieties exist in any major change situation, fears are typically magnified when the changes involve improved efficiency. This is especially true when, as has often been the case, TQ processes are adopted after several rounds of efficiency improvements and downsizing. In such situations, additional attempts to increase efficiency may be seen simply as hastening the workers' demise. For example, a subset of the UAW (*Business Week,* July 10, 1989) has gone on record as arguing that "the team concept pits worker against worker and eliminates jobs, all in the name of 'competitiveness'" (p. 61).

Clearly, the most compelling way to overcome such fears is through explicit assurances of job security. For example, Globe Metallurgical's CEO personally committed to a no-layoff policy when the TQ program was first launched. Although this approach is admirable, some companies cannot afford to offer such guarantees. Consider, for example, the position of Robert Haas, chairman and CEO of Levi-Strauss & Co.:

> You can't promise employment security and be honest. The best you can do is not play games with people. You can't make any guarantees . . . We're now in a real-world situation where market forces are less favorable, external competitive pressures are more intense, and change is more rapid. Sometimes the only solution is to close a plant, and if we don't have the guts to face that decision, then we risk hurting a lot of people—not just those in one plant. We need to be honest about that. We tie it to our (corporate aspirations and values) by asking, "How are we going to treat the people who are displaced?" (*Harvard Business Review,* Sept.–Oct. 1990, pp. 142–143)

Haas goes on to say that while Levi-Strauss does not guarantee against layoffs, it does everything it can to prevent them and to soften the blow when they do occur. For example, Levi's gives more advance notice than required by law; provides higher-than-industry-average severance packages; extends health care benefits after severance; supports local job-training and job-finding initiatives; continues philanthropic support in communities where closings occur; and has changed the criteria for plant closing decisions to give more weight to community impact.

A second issue that often must be addressed concerns the increased level of commitment expected from a TQ workforce. Organizations committed to quality, customer service, and on-time delivery must be able to depend on a workforce that does more than go through the motions from 9 to 5. For example, requirements for improved capacity utilization increasingly require worker commitment to more flexible work rules, schedules, and sometimes third-shift employment. Although this is sometimes attained rather painlessly through selection in start-up organizations, it is a major sticking point in ongoing concerns. For example, GM recently announced the closing of a Michigan plant that, despite more than 10 years of downsizing at GM, refused to budge on work rules, schedules, and third-shift employment (Ingrassia & White, 1992).

More generally, Kanter (1987) and others have argued that attempts to make workers more committed, involved, and entrepreneurial buck up against a number of counterpressures. These include not only the traditional bureaucratic control and reward systems, but also the long working days already put in by two-earner families where both work and family obligations tend to clash (O'Reilly, 1990; Schor, 1992).

For these reasons, management must show that there are tangible organizational benefits to TQ. Sometimes, the main selling point is that without dramatic improvements in results, employees will be left without jobs. In other cases, the message revolves around the immediate intrinsic benefits of more interesting work and greater control over work decisions, and the potential for elimination of fruitless paperwork and procedures. In still others, the focus is on longer-term benefits that come from being part of a successful quality-driven company. GM has stressed how joint UAW-GM quality initiatives have saved thousands of jobs in its component parts operations (*Business Week,* 1989). In the longer term, however, there are going to be increasing numbers of workers who, like marathon runners, "hit the wall" after extended periods of continuous effort or, like the Japanese, complain about "karoshi" or death by overwork. For these individuals, support for TQ will come only after they truly share in organizational TQ successes.

CONCLUDING REMARKS

Our premise is that getting to TQ is dependent upon fundamental changes in organizational processes and measurement strategies, which will drive and reinforce changes in the behaviors of key stakeholders. It is understandable that the label is total quality, since isolated changes are likely to be doomed in the face of forces favoring the status quo. Recent media attention to failures of TQ efforts (*The Economist,* April 18, 1992) reinforce the point that TQ cannot succeed if it is only a program, a bag of tools, or a bureaucracy created to manage microprocesses. Instead, TQ must reflect a systemwide commitment to the goal of serving the strategic needs of the organization's customer bases, through internal and external measurement systems, information and authority sharing, and committed leadership.

This is where we come full circle, back to the imparative for strong leadership among the top management team. These team members are the ones who set the tone for everyone else in the organization including the managers and professional staff who perceive that they have a lot to lose from adoption of TQ. The top leadership can affect managerial behaviors by holding middle managers accountable for TQ behaviors and implementation. Much more importantly, resistance to TQ will slowly dissipate when middle managers perceive the senior executives as exemplars of TQ in every aspect of their behavior, day-in and day-out. Corning's CEO, James Houghton (1991), describes what it takes:

> One of the leader's key roles is to inspire, and inspiration only comes from setting an example. That is why a leader's commitment to quality must be a very personal one. For example, I regularly visit every Corning unit—about 50 locations—every year. On these visits, about the only thing I talk about is quality: I want to know what they are doing and how they are doing it . . . I also deal with the other issues, but, since I believe so much in quality, I apply its principles to every issue. The message is simple: The first person who must be involved in quality is the leader; it is the leader's responsibility. (p. 22)

REFERENCES

American Quality Foundation and Ernst & Young, *International Quality Study: Top-Line Findings* (Cleveland: Ernst & Young, 1991).

Beischel, M. E., and K. R. Smith, "Linking the Shop Floor to the Top Floor," *Management Accounting,* October 1991, pp. 25–34.

Bell, R. R., and J. M. Burnham, *Managing Productivity and Change* (Cincinnati: South-Western Publishing, 1991).

Bellman, G. M., *The Quest for Staff Leadership* (Glenview, Ill.: Scott, Foresman, 1986).

Business Week, July 10, 1989, "The Payoff from Teamwork," pp. 56–62.

Caminiti, S., "What the Scanner Knows about You," *Fortune,* December 3, 1991, pp. 51–52.

Camp, R. C., *Benchmarking* (White Plains, N.Y.: Quality Resources Publishers, 1989).

Cantoni, C. J., "Quality Control from Mars," *The Wall Street Journal,* January 28, 1992, p. A-14.

Carlzon, J., *Moments of Truth,* (New York: Harper & Row, 1987).

Cascio, W. F., *Costing Human Resources,* 2nd ed. (Boston: PWS-Kent, 1987).

Ciampa, D., *Total Quality* (Reading, Mass.: Addison-Wesley, 1992).

Crosby, P. B., *Quality Is Free* (New York: Mentor Books, 1979).

Dobbins, G.; Cardy, R. L.; and Carson, K. "Examining Fundamental Assumptions: A Contrast of Person and System Approaches to Human Resource Management," in G. Ferris and K. Rowlands, eds., *Research in Personnel and Human Resources Management,* vol. 9 (1991), pp. 1–38.

Eccles, R. G., "The Performance Measurement Manifesto," *Harvard Business Review* 69, (Jan./Feb. 1991), pp. 131–37.

Fisher, A. B., "Morale Crisis," *Fortune,* November 18, 1991, pp. 71–76.

Fitz-Enz, J., *Human Value Management* (San Francisco: Jossey-Bass, 1990).

Gabor, A., *The Man Who Discovered Quality* (New York: Random House, 1990).

Garvin, D. A., "How the Baldrige Really Works," *Harvard Business Review* 69 (Nov.–Dec. 1991), pp. 80–93.

Garvin, D. A., *Managing Quality* (New York: Free Press, 1987).

General Accounting Office, *Management Practices—U.S. Companies Improve Performance through Quality Efforts* (Washington, D.C.: U.S. General Accounting Office, 1990).

Greene, A. H., and P. Flentov, "Managing Performance: Maximizing the Benefits of Activity-Based Costing," in B. J. Brinker, ed., *Emerging Practices in Cost Management* (Boston: Warren, Gorham & Lamont, 1992), chap. J-5.

Goldratt, E. M., and J. Cox, *The Goal: A Process of Ongoing Improvement* (Croton-on-Hudson, N.Y.: North River Press, 1986).

Hampton, W. J., "How Does Japan Inc. Pick Its American Workers?" *Business Week,* October 3, 1988, pp. 84–88.

Hart, C. W. L.; J. L. Heskett; and W. E. Sasser, "The Profitable Art of Service Recovery," *Harvard Business Review* 68 (Sept.–Oct. 1990), pp. 105–14.

Harvard Business Review Debate: "Does the Baldrige Award Really Work?" *Harvard Business Review* 70 (Jan.–Feb. 1992), pp. 126–47.

Houghton, J. R. "Leadership and Total Quality," in F. Caropreso, ed., *Making Total Quality Happen* (New York: The Conference Board, Report No. 937, 1990), pp. 21–23.

House, C. H., and R. L. Price, "The Return Map: Tracking Product Teams," *Harvard Business Review* 69 (Jan.–Feb. 1991), pp. 92–101.

Hyatt, J. C., and A. K. Naj, "GE Is No Place for Autocrats, Welch Decrees," *The Wall Street Journal,* March 3, 1992, pp. B-1, B-6.

Ingrassia, P., and J. B. White, "GM Posts Record '91 Loss of $4.45 Billion and Identifies a Dozen Plants for Closing," *The Wall Street Journal,* February 26, 1992, pp. A-1, A-6.

Johnson, H. T., "Professors, Customers and Value: Bringing a Global Perspective to Management Accounting Education," in P. Turney, ed., *Performance Excellence in Manufacturing and Service Organizations* (Sarasota: American Accounting Association, 1990).

Juran, J. M., *Juran on Leadership for Quality* (New York: Free Press, 1989).

Kanter, R. M., "The New Workforce Meets the Changing Workplace: Strains, Dilemmas, and Contradictions in Attempts to Implement Participative and Entrepreneurial Management," *Human Resource Management* 25 (1987), pp. 515–37.

Kanter, R. M., *When Giants Learn to Dance* (New York: Touchstone, 1989).

Kaplan, R. S., "Yesterday's Accounting Undermines Production," *Harvard Business Review* 62 (July–August 1984), pp. 95–101.

Kaplan, R. S., and D. P. Norton "The Balanced Scorecard—Measures that Drive Performance," *Harvard Business Review* 70 (Jan.–Feb. 1992), pp. 71–79.

Karabatsos, N., "Absolutely, Positively Quality," *Quality Progress,* 1990, pp. 24–28.

Kirkpatrick, D., "Here Comes the Payoff from PCs," *Fortune,* March 23, 1992, pp. 93–102.

KPMG Peat Marwick, *Quality Improvement Initiatives through the Management of Human Resources* (Short Hills, N.J.: KPMG Peat Marwick, 1991).

Kretchmar, "CEO to Execs: "'Drive a Lexus,'" *Fortune,* March 23, 1992, p. 121.

Locke, E. A., and G. Latham, *A Theory of Goal Setting and Task Performance* (Englewood Cliffs, N.J.: Prentice Hall, 1990).

Mintzberg, H., *Mintzberg on Management* (New York: Free Press, 1989).

Olian, J. D., "Penril DataComm Networks, Inc., Wins U.S. Senate Productivity Award for Manufacturing," *The Maryland Workplace* 13, no. 4 (1991), p. 4.

Olian, J. D., and S. L. Rynes, "Survey of Quality Practices," unpublished, 1991.

O'Reilly, B., "Is Your Company Asking Too Much?" *Fortune* (March 12, 1990), pp. 38–46.

Papay, L. J., "Process Quality Is the Driver of Corporate Competitiveness," in F. Caropreso, ed., *Making Total Quality Happen* (New York: The Conference Board, Research Report No. 937, 1990), pp. 30–34.

Perry, N., "Here Come Richer, Riskier Pay Plans," *Fortune,* December 19, 1988, pp. 50–58.

Reichheld, F. F., and W. E. Sasser, Jr., "Zero Defections: Quality Comes to Services," *Harvard Business Review* 68 (Sept.–Oct. 1990), pp. 105–11.

Rice, F., "How to Deal with Tougher Customers," *Fortune,* December 3, 1990, pp. 38–48.

Sakurai, M., "Target Costing and How to Use It," in B. J. Brinker, ed., *Emerging Practices in Cost Management* (Boston: Warren, Gorham & Lamont, 1992), chap. 5-2.

Saraph, J. V.; P. G. Benson; and R. G. Schroeder, "An Instrument for Measuring the Critical Factors of Quality Management," *Decision Sciences* 20 (1989), pp. 810–29.

Schein, E. H., *Organizational Culture and Leadership: A Dynamic View* (San Francisco: Jossey-Bass, 1985).

Scholtes, P. R., *A New View of Performance Appraisal* (Madison, Wisc.: Joiner Consultants, 1987).

Schonberger, R. J., *Building a Chain of Customers* (New York: Free Press, 1990).

Schonberger, R. J., *World Class Manufacturing: Lessons in Simplicity Applied* (New York: Free Press, 1986).

Schor, J. B., *The Overworked American: The Unexpected Decline of Leisure* (New York: Basic Books, 1992).

Schuler, R. S., "Repositioning the Human Resource Function: Transformation or Demise?" *Academy of Management Executive* 4 (1990), pp. 49–60.

Sellers, P., "What Customers Really Want," *Fortune,* June 4, 1990, pp. 58–68.

Sharman, G., "When Quality Control Gets in the Way of Quality," *The Wall Street Journal,* February 24, 1992, p. A-14.

Shook, R. L., *Honda: An American Success Story* (Englewood Cliffs, N.J.: Prentice Hall, 1988).

Stalk, G., Jr., and T. M. Hout, *Competing against Time: How Time-Based Competition Is Reshaping Global Markets* (New York: Free Press, 1990).

The Conference Board, *Current Practices in Measuring Quality* (New York: The Conference Board, Report No. 234, 1989).

The Conference Board, *Employee Buy-In to Total Quality* (New York: The Conference Board, Report No. 974, 1991).

The Economist, "Future Perfect," January 4, 1992, p. 61.

The Economist, "The Cracks in Quality," April 18, 1992, pp. 67–68.

Tuttle, T. C., "Implementing Total Quality," *The Maryland Workplace* 12, no. 1 (1991), pp. 1, 4–5.

Umble, M., and M. L. Srikanth, *Synchronous Manufacturing* (Cincinnati: South-Western Publishing, 1990).

Walton, M., *The Deming Management Method* (New York: Perigee Books, 1986).

Wiggenhorn, W., "Motorola U: When Training Becomes an Education," *Harvard Business Review* 68, July–August, 1990, pp. 71–83.

Worthy, F. S., "Japan's Smart Secret Weapon," *Fortune,* August 12, 1991, pp. 72–75.

Yates, R., "Deming's Game Plan," *Chicago Tribune Magazine,* February 1992, pp. 16–22.

INCENTIVE PLAN PUSHES PRODUCTION

Carolyn Wiley, University of Tennessee at Chattanooga

In 1984, an article printed in the *New York Times* praised Control Data, IBM, Hewlett-Packard, Motorola, Digital Equipment, Nissan USA, DuPont, Procter & Gamble, Exxon, Lincoln Electric, Bank of America, 3M, Upjohn, and R. J. Reynolds Tobacco for maintaining extensive no-layoff policies. Today, at least one of these firms still can boast the survival of its no-layoff policy. That company is the Lincoln Electric Co., which hasn't had a layoff in 45 years.

Although the Cleveland-based manufacturer of welding machines and motors suffered a 40 percent decline in sales during the 1981 to 1983 recession, it didn't lay off one employee. Instead, because of an incentive plan that rewards workers based on their productivity, workers had brought Lincoln's sales back to normal by 1984—and had earned shared profits of about $15,000 each.

During the current recession, the firm lost money in its foreign operations—its first loss since it began filing consolidated annual reports. Still, it didn't lay off any U.S. employees, and even rewarded them with a total of $48 million in year-end bonuses. In 1992, production workers received bonuses averaging between $18,000 and $22,000, which equalled approximately 75 percent of their salaries. Their total annual pay, including wages, profit sharing, and bonuses, averaged $45,000.

These high wages are the result of a reward-and-recognition system that successfully connects the company's and the employees' goals. The comprehensive, organizationwide Lincoln Electric Incentive Plan, which combines pay for output, bonuses, and job security, has enabled Lincoln to gain a competitive advantage in its industry. It has helped the organization increase production efficiency and lower the cost of its products.

According to Paul Beddia, vice president of human resources for Lincoln, the company's productivity rate is double to triple the productivity rate of any other manufacturing operation that uses steel as its raw material and that employs 1,000 or more people.

Source: *Personnel Journal,* August 1993, pp. 86–90.

Carolyn Wiley an associate professor of management at the University of Tennessee at Chattanooga.

(He measures the productivity rate by dividing the total sales, which are approximately $500 million for Lincoln, by the total number of employees, which at Lincoln is 2,700.)

On top of maintaining a high rate of productivity, Lincoln has been able to maintain a stable price structure as a result of increased employee output. For several decades, Lincoln maintained 1933 prices on most of its products. These pricing policies held until the 1970s, when inflation caused a shift in pricing philosophy.

THE LINCOLN INCENTIVE PLAN LINKS EMPLOYEE SUCCESS TO COMPANY SUCCESS

The Lincoln family always has been interested in the well-being of its employees as well as the productivity of its business. When John C. Lincoln established Lincoln Electric Co. in 1895, he developed a win-win philosophy. The prime tenet of this philosophy is simply that all stakeholders in a business venture can win. The Lincoln Electric Incentive Plan satisfies the bottom line for:

- The stockholder, through enhanced stock values and regular dividends.
- The customer, through lower-priced, quality products.
- The manufacturer, through efficient operations, minimal customer problems, no strikes, increased market share, and increased sales.
- The employee, through job security, empowerment, and good wages.

Many experts argue that, given the pressures in today's economy, compensation plans and policies quickly lose their punch. Therefore, most managers continually tinker with their pay systems. This isn't the case with the Lincoln Electric Incentive Plan. It has been in its present form since 1959. Indeed, it has been enhanced, in spite of two World Wars, the Great Depression, and two recessions. Although the company's biggest customers have been in highly cyclical markets, such as oil, steel, and construction, Lincoln has remained solvent because of its approach to managing and rewarding people.

Lincoln Electric isn't an easy place in which to work, however. The turnover rate for employees within their probationary first two months is 20 percent. There's no room for the nonchalant, disengaged worker. The success of the entire enterprise depends on a high level of employee input and output, dependability, and cooperation. There are no paid holidays or sick days. Workers must accept job reassignments, and overtime is mandatory. There are no reserved parking spaces, no special seats in the cafeteria, and no definite or restrictive lines of promotion. The firm posts all promotional opportunities (including many senior positions), and bases promotions on merit only. There's no seniority. Workers also must compete with co-workers for bonuses based on merit. Despite all these policies, Lincoln is a desirable place in which to work. It receives nearly 1,000 unsolicited job applications a month, and the post-probationary turnover rate at Lincoln is less than 3 percent per year, including deaths and retirements.

THE LINCOLN ELECTRIC INCENTIVE PLAN COMBINES COMPENSATION WITH SECURITY

Lincoln's multifaceted incentive system comprises:

- Piecework pay.
- Shared profits.

- Suggestion systems.
- Year-end bonuses.
- Stock-ownership opportunities.
- Job security.

Performance-based or gainsharing programs like Lincoln's are designed to improve overall performance by allowing contributing workers to share in the proceeds. Gene Epstein, former editor and publisher of *The Managers' Consultant,* called the Lincoln Electric plan the most successful gainsharing or productivity-sharing plan at a single company. It has become a classic, focusing on employee efficiency and productivity.

The plan rewards workers for turning out high-quality products efficiently while controlling costs. Consumers throughout the industry recognize these products for their reliability. Few customers return products for repairs or replacements, so the firm makes a higher profit, and workers who produce the products enjoy larger bonuses.

The focus of the incentive program is its compensation plan. All employees receive a base annual wage. Production-support workers receive hourly wages, and production workers receive piecework pay. The piecework method encourages not only productivity but quality results as well, because the organization only pays workers for defectless products. If a customer sends a defective part back to the company, the employee who produced it must repair it on his or her own time.

The company's methods-engineering department uses past performance standards, work measurements, and time studies to determine piece rates. So far, Lincoln's engineering group has established 70,000 piece rates for various production jobs. The rates don't change, except for adjustments in the cost of living or for substantial changes in manufacturing procedures. Some rates, for example, have been in effect for more than 30 years.

Because Lincoln pays its production employees on a piece-rate basis, management allows them to challenge the results of any time study or periodic piece-rate review. Workers challenge fewer than one-fifth of 1 percent of all rate changes. Also, if a time study results in a lower rate, the worker may request a transfer to a job that pays an equal or a higher rate.

The piece-rate concept at Lincoln Electric is a fundamental part of the capitalistic process underlying its incentive-compensation system, which allows workers to earn more for more output. The firm doesn't review the piece rate periodically to limit earnings. It also isn't a speed-up tool, but rather a tool to facilitate reward distributions that match employee output.

To reward workers further for their output, Lincoln has established a year-end bonus system that enables workers to increase their base wages to nearly double. It began in 1934 when chairman James Lincoln denied a request by employees for a 10 percent wage increase because Lincoln's profit picture didn't warrant such an increase. The workers responded with a request for a year-end bonus if, through increased productivity and lower costs, the annual profits increased. Lincoln agreed to their proposal, which he established as a bonus plan the same year. "We haven't missed a year since," says Beddia. This success has resulted in a distribution to employees of more than $500 million. Each year, the company allocates a percentage of U.S. sales for dividends, seed money, and year-end bonuses, based on a 10-year average. Last year, 12.1 percent of the company's income went into bonuses and annuities.

A MERIT-RATING
SYSTEM DETERMINES BONUSES

Workers receive merit ratings or merit report cards twice a year as the basis of their reviews. These ratings determine the amount of bonus that they will receive at the end of the year. The company rates employees on four merit criteria:

- Output.
- Quality.
- Dependability.
- Personal characteristics.

Output is the most measurable criterion. The production department determines this rating for each employee based on the amount of work that he or she produces.

The quality measurement involves a more complex system. "When a product comes back in from a customer as defective, the quality-assurance department traces who made each component," says Beddia. Employees in quality assurance identify which components are faulty. They identify who produced the defective product parts. This department rates each employee for the quality criteria.

An employee's department head determines his or her ratings for both the dependability and personal characteristics categories. The dependability rating is based on the number of absences, late arrivals, availability for overtime, and so on. Department heads take into account how individuals work together as a team for the cooperation rating. They also evaluate such factors as:

- Attitude toward supervision, co-workers, and the firm.
- Efforts to share expert knowledge with others.
- Cooperation in installing new methods.

To determine the rating for the ideas portion of the criteria, department heads look at their employees' participation in the organization's suggestion program. An advisory board, comprising several executives and approximately 26 to 30 employees whom the employee base elects, reviews suggestions with methods engineers for implementation feasibility. The organization implements approximately 50 suggestions monthly. Implemented suggestions have saved the company from $2,000 to more than $200,000. This, in turn, affects the suggesting workers' merit ratings, which affects their year-end bonuses.

Here's how the rating system works. The firm allocates each department 100 points per employee (25 points for each criterion). If a worker performs at a superior level, he or she can receive more than the allocated 25 points for any category. That means that another worker will have to receive fewer than 100 total points because there are only so many points available. Most workers in a group typically receive between 80 and 120 points.

An employee may have points deducted as well as added. A defective product shipped to a customer can reduce the merit points of its producer by as much as eight points. This could amount to as much as $1,600 in bonus money. In addition, an employee can lose points for absenteeism. "Each day of absenteeism is worth four-tenths of a point," says Beddia. "That gets deducted from the output rating." The president of the company reviews all ratings and meets with disgruntled employees to discuss perceived discrepancies.

HOW LINCOLN ELECTRIC CALCULATES EMPLOYEES' BONUSES

Under the Lincoln Electric Incentive Plan, employees at Cleveland-based Lincoln Electric Co. receive bonuses based on their productivity. The bonus is determined by a simple bonus-factor formula.

First, the board of directors sets the amount of the year's bonus pool, based on a recommendation by the chairman. The chairman looks at such factors as how much money the company has made, how much seed money is needed, and how much money is needed for taxes and dividends. The average bonus pool during a recent 10-year period was 10.6% of sales revenue.

The company then divides this bonus pool amount by the total wages paid. This quotient is the bonus factor. A bonus factor of 1.00 means that the bonus pool is the same as the total companywide wages. This past year, the bonus pool was approximately 75% of wages paid.

Once the bonus factor has been determined, the company calculates bonuses by multiplying the bonus factor by individual earnings and merit ratings. Here's an example. A production worker earned $35,000. His merit rating was 100%, or 1.00. The bonus factor is .75. The formula for determining his bonus would be as follows:

$$
\begin{array}{r}
\$35{,}000 \text{ (earnings)} \\
\times\, 1.00 \text{ (merit rating)} \\
\hline
\$35{,}000 \\
\end{array}
$$

$$
\begin{array}{r}
\$35{,}000 \\
\times\, .75 \text{ (bonus factor)} \\
\hline
\$26{,}250 \text{ (bonus)} \\
\end{array}
$$

This employee's full bonus would be $26,250. However, according to Paul Beddia, VP of HR at Lincoln, employees must pay for their own hospitalization insurance, which costs approximately $3,000. The company deducts this money from employees' year-end bonuses. Thus, this production worker would receive a bonus of $23,250 (before taxes), bringing his annual salary to $58,250.

The organization then plugs the final merit rating that an employee receives into a formula to determine that employee's bonus (see the box "How Lincoln Electric Calculates Employees' Bonuses"). Most bonuses nearly equal employees' base wages, almost doubling their annual salaries. Figure 13–1 provides more details on how the incentive plan works.

STOCK OWNERSHIP OPPORTUNITIES AND JOB SECURITY PROVIDE EMPLOYEES FURTHER INCENTIVE AND SECURITY

As part of its incentive program, Lincoln also has an employee stock-ownership plan (ESOP) and an employee stock-purchase plan (ESPP). The ESPP allows only employees to buy stock, and the ESOP allows them to receive stock shares annually out of profits. Approximately 80 percent of the employees participate in these plans and own more than 40 percent of the total company stock. The firm trades the stock privately. However, it does trade the stock over the counter. Employee-shareholder dividends and voting rights are the same as for stock that's owned outside the plan. Workers may buy, at book value, a certain number of shares each year, based on their base wages. Employees must pay for the shares within a 12-month period. The company has first option to repurchase shares that employees sell.

The stock opportunities provide employees not only with the incentive to produce so that they can share in the profits, but also with security for their futures. The company's guaranteed-employment plan provides employees additional security. Workers

T A B L E 13–1 | **Components of Lincoln Electric's Incentive Plan**

Lincoln's incentive plan combines job security with a lucrative compensation program. Below is a summary of the plan's elements.

Features	Description	Criteria
Job security	Guaranteed 30-hour workweek.	Employees are eligible after three years of service. • Pay rates aren't guaranteed. • Job transfers may be necessary. • Overtime is required during peak demand. • Guaranteed hours may be terminated by the company with a six-month notice.
Base wage	Standard job evaluation procedures are used to set the base wage. However, job evaluation and market requirements determine the actual dollar value of jobs.	Job evaluation compensable factors include skill, responsibility, mental aptitude, physical application, and working conditions.
Piecework	For every job that can be standard-ized, normal time-study procedures are employed to establish piece rates.	Piece rates are based on the following calculation for consistency and to eliminate constant revisions: 1934 wage rates times cost of living, which fluctuates with the Index (Bureau of Labor Statistics). This product is then compared with the area-average skilled hourly rate to determine the adjustments to the piece rate.
Advisory board	Employees elect representatives to an Advisory Board. All employees, except department heads and members of the engineering and time-study departments, are eligible.	The Advisory Board analyzes suggestions that lead to organizational progress. Implemented suggestions have ranged from a savings of $2,400 to over $200,000.
Merit ratings	Twice a year, managers appraise employee performance through a merit-rating program.	This program uses four report cards. Each card rates work performance on one of the following: output, quality, dependability, and personal characteristics, such as the ability to come up with ideas and cooperation.
Profit sharing	All business profits are split three ways: among the company, the shareholders, and the employees.	The company receives seed money; the shareholders receive a dividend; and the employees receive a year-end, profit-sharing bonus.
Year-end bonus	The annual cash bonus closely approximates the employee's annual earnings.	An employee's bonus is a function of his total annual earnings, biannual merit ratings, and company profits.
Employee stock-ownership plan	Each employee has the opportunity to purchase a limited number of shares of company stock per year.	Employees are eligible after one year of service. On retirement or termination of employment, the company has the option to repurchase the stock.

who have been at the firm for at least three years receive a guarantee of at least 30 hours of work a week. That work doesn't have to be in the job for which the company hired that employee, however. For example, Beddia says that during a slow period, a worker who was hired as an accountant may be assigned to paint fences or resurface the parking lot. That worker would receive the pay rate for the job that he or she performs, rather than the pay rate for the job for which he or she was hired.

In 1982, the company put this policy into practice and received an unexpected result. When sales fell behind production, management asked its factory workers for help in the sales department. More than 100 workers volunteered, out of which management chose 54. After a quick sales-training course, the production workers started calling on body shops across the country. Their efforts ended up bringing in $10 million in new sales and established the small arc welder as one of Lincoln's best-selling items. Lincoln took a risk on its people, and the risk paid off.

This faith in and recognition of its workers continues to pay off for the firm. "We're not only surviving, we're prospering," says Beddia. "I think that this is unusual in the current business climate. We see companies downsizing, merging, consolidating, and leaving the country. We're doing just the opposite. We're still growing. Within the past five years, we've gone from 5 plants in four countries to something like 23 plants in 17 countries."

For people who are willing to accept the idea of individual responsibility and who are willing to commit themselves to the success of the enterprise, instituting a plan similar to the Lincoln Electric Incentive Plan can be a win-win situation. Having gone more than 54 years without losing any money in its domestic business, and more than 40 years without a layoff, Lincoln has proven that its plan survives the test of time.

TRANSPLANTING CORPORATE CULTURES GLOBALLY

Charlene Marmer Solomon

It's midday in Kuwait, but it's unnaturally dark. As far as the eye can see, blazing oil-field fires spew up tornadoes of black smoke. A blanket of sooty, acid clouds seal in hundreds of miles of desert. On the ground, an army of workers toil amid the heat, providing support activities to the actual fire fighters. They construct roads for the trucks, create pipelines for pumping water, build hospital facilities for the workers, and cook and serve meals to the cadre of smoke-coated personnel.

More than 7,000 miles away from the flames and wreckage of the Gulf War, in a 14th-floor office in San Francisco's financial district, men and women of Bechtel Corp. sweat over 30,000 employee files and résumés. Culling through 105,000 phone inquiries, the HR staff works frantically to supply the necessary manpower to the Middle East operation. The debris here isn't burned rubber and charred metal; it's fax paper and plastic coffee cups used by the HR staff as it dispatches calls from San Francisco to London to Manila to Bangkok, so that it can hire and assign foreign-contract personnel. Gathering and transferring employee information from headquarters to the ground operations in Kuwait, human resources managers mobilize more than 16,000 Americans, Britons, Filipinos, Australians—people from 37 countries in all—to rectify the Kuwaiti disaster.

"We're almost nationality-blind," says Patrick Morgan, human resources manager for special projects at Bechtel, an engineering-construction firm that has offices in more than 70 countries throughout the world. The company has projects that range from restoring postwar Kuwait's oil-production facilities to building the Channel Tunnel between France and England. The company builds airports, power plants, petroleum pipelines, and chemical-waste treatment centers. "A person's passport is about as meaningful to us as the name of the bank on their savings-account passbooks," says Morgan.

Source: *Personnel Journal,* October 1993.

Charlene Marmer Solomon is a freelance writer based in Los Angeles.

Call it what you like—global, transnational, international—but when business looks to the entire world for capital and supplies, when there's an official company language, when human resources professionals become interested in work hours in Seoul and Stockholm, and when fluctuation in exchange rates for yen and deutsche marks becomes meaningful, you've entered a global frame of mind.

As noted author and globalist Kenichi Ohmae puts it, free access to information has made this a "borderless world." Political boundaries between countries may remain, but when it comes to finance, industry, and even tourism, geographic borders are blurring continually. Information, music, and fashion reach Europeans, Asians, and Americans simultaneously. There's no lag time; we're all global citizens.

But a borderless world doesn't mean that corporations are without personality. Indeed, corporate culture is the framework of an effective corporation. It's the language that communicates the company's mission and its ways of doing business. It provides guidelines for people to follow and communicates the company's unique identity. The ability to transplant the corporate culture from one country to another—in some form—is critical to the success of most international businesses. Ultimately, it shows up on the bottom line. No matter what the type of corporate culture, when business goes global, the culture is translated overseas. It mixes with the host-country culture and changes, just as translated language undergoes changes from its origins.

HR managers are the translators. They're faced with an array of issues:

- Is it helpful to have a strong corporate culture abroad?
- How can HR executives determine and communicate the important elements of the culture in the international arena?
- How do you know if the communication process is working?
- How does the corporate culture change as a result of globalization?

A STRONG CORPORATE CULTURE IS AN ADVANTAGE IN THE GLOBAL UNIVERSE

"It's vitally important that the [transnational] company have a strong company culture," says Calvin Reynolds, senior fellow at the Wharton School of the University of Pennsylvania and senior counselor for New York City-based Organization Resources Counselors. "If you don't have a strong set of cultural principles from which to function, when people get overseas, they're so lacking in clarity that no one knows where they're going."

Asea Brown Boveri, Inc. (ABB), the electrical-engineering giant, is the quintessential global company. It has a clearly defined mission statement and a culture that supports the mission. Owned jointly by ASEA AB in Sweden and BBC Brown Boveri Ltd. in Switzerland, the enterprise purchased U.S.-based Combustion Engineering and a large division of U.S.-based Westinghouse in 1989, which raised its worldwide employee population to 213,000 and its revenues to about $30 billion a year.

"We think about ABB as a company without any regard to national boundaries," says Richard P. Randazzo, who, as ABB's vice president of HR, works out of the company's Stamford, Connecticut, base and oversees the company's HR operations in the United States "We just operate on a global basis. A lot of other companies see boundaries and barriers, but from a business standpoint, this company is intent on transcending those boundaries." Indeed, more than 50 percent of its sales are in

Europe, 20 percent are in North America, 20 percent in Asia, and the rest are in South America and Africa. The official language is English; the official currency is the dollar.

It's easiest to think of the ABB Group as a federation of national companies—1,300 in all. ABB uses a matrix structure with worldwide business activities grouped into seven business segments that comprise 65 business areas. Some of these business segments include environmental control, transmission and distribution, and financial services. Each business area is responsible for global strategies, business plans, allocation of manufacturing responsibilities, and product development. Then, there are geographic subgroups or companies. In other words, employees are likely to have two supervisors: the local-country supervisor, who's responsible for employees and customers; and the business area supervisor (of which there are 65), who's responsible for regional profits, research and development, capacity, product design, and more.

It's a highly decentralized business (the United States alone has 50 companies, each with its own president). Divisions treat each other as vendors and customers, invoicing one another and maintaining accounts payable and receivable from other divisions.

Characterized by *Forbes* as a company that has no discernible national identity, ABB's corporate culture is one of its strong defining features. The company embodies the phrase *think globally, act locally.*

According to Randazzo, ABB's culture is focused tightly on making money. Its personality profile is a hands-on, action-oriented, travel-to-the-opportunity kind of business. Each division acts locally in response to customers and employees. But managers are required to think globally about sourcing. For example, if the dollar is strong relative to the Swedish krona, then the company sources more from Sweden because goods and services are cheaper there. When that changes, sourcing also changes.

Corporate culture mixes with the culture of the country in which ABB operates. "There's no attempt by the corporation to tell us in the United States how we should behave relative to our customers or to our employees," says Randazzo. (Other HR executives oversee ABB's HR operations in its different business segments and the different countries in which the company operates.) The senior management team is composed largely of Europeans, so at times they give Randazzo quizzical looks when he says that they can't ask a person's age or marital status when recruiting. "They don't understand some of the affirmative-action targets we have, but they don't attempt to influence any of that. The motivation is that we know more about the U.S. marketplace than the Germans, the Swedes, or the Swiss will ever know, and therefore, we're better able to deal with it."

Although the United States business culture emphasizes such concepts as individual empowerment and the appropriate way to hire and terminate people, the Swedish, Swiss, and German HR professionals have their own issues to deal with. For example, Germany and Switzerland have particular HR issues regarding women.

There have been laws passed recently in Sweden and Switzerland that require some dedication and affirmative action with respect to employment of women. Therefore, companies in those countries must dedicate resources to see that they're complying. American firms can help them understand the new laws.

But cultures aren't static. They influence each other. For one, HR management plays a much more significant role in the United States than it does in Europe. According to Randazzo, this is the arena in which Americans have had significant influence on ABB's Europeans, addressing such issues as employee involvement, empowerment, and total quality. In fact, the United States HR staff developed materials for conducting management training, some of which were translated into German.

Likewise, the Europeans have influenced the Americans. They've brought a sense of business urgency to the company. They helped with downsizing, lowering the break-even point, and getting the organization focused.

UNDERSTANDING LOCAL ATTITUDES HELPS CORPORATE CULTURES TAKE ROOT

Not all corporate cultures transplant well overseas. Companies that try to graft the Stars and Stripes forever in a foreign location will likely encounter resistance. Those that are sensitive to local attitudes and customs are bound to be more successful.

"The HR executives I find most effective do a good job of listening," says Reynolds. "They take the time to understand local problems and learn why something may or may not work. Having listened, they come up with a fairly clear statement of where they're going."

Just ask Shirley Gaufin, vice president of human resources at San Francisco-based Bechtel Corp. She oversaw a massive companywide employee-satisfaction survey, administered to 22,000 people worldwide.

In April 1992, Chairman Riley P. Bechtel issued the company's new strategic plan called *Toward 2001*. In it, he articulated his global vision and core values, making a commitment to analyze and change the corporate culture within a global context. To be most effective, it was essential to learn about employees' beliefs and attitudes. Gaufin's HR staff issued a 102-question survey to 22,000 employees. Questions asked employees about communication, training-and-advancement opportunities, the work environment, and the importance of international and domestic field experience to professional development. The staff followed up with more than 200 focus groups at the firm's domestic and international locations.

In response to the results, each large office developed specific action plans to address employee concerns, which included communication between management and employees and the availability of training programs for people at field locations. Corporatewide priorities address the areas of reward and recognition, training and development, and employee participation, among others.

For example, the company is developing a communication plan to disseminate information more effectively throughout all locations, including field operations. It's reinstating a companywide newsletter that will go to all employees worldwide to help improve communication between the company and its employees. Performance appraisals are being revised to reflect the kind of culture that Bechtel wants to become. Rather than have a reportcard-like performance-review form, it will be a tool to increase communication between supervisors and employees, and also help each employee reach his or her objectives. The review promotes better communication because it requires employees to take the initiative to communicate with their managers. It addresses on-the-job and outside training needs.

"The survey is a way of listening to employees. It gives us ways to implement the corporate culture more effectively," says Gaufin. The 1992 survey is the baseline. Periodic surveys will provide means of measuring progress.

There are a lot of challenges when it comes to implementing some of the changes, says Gaufin. For example, different cultures perceive performance reviews in different ways. "We have to be sure that we're not going against accepted practices in other parts of the world," she says. Furthermore, part of the new strategic plan focuses on empowered teams. Gaufin says that that will be a challenge, too.

The 1992 survey wasn't translated into other languages, but Gaufin says they'll consider translating the next ones into Spanish and other major languages. There are just too many instances when English doesn't communicate adequately.

The survey and the desire to translate it into other languages attest to a change in corporate culture at Bechtel. "We're trying to be more open and communicative—internally as well as externally," says Morgan. "We need to understand the environment in which we operate."

In the 20 years since Morgan joined Bechtel, he's seen dramatic changes. It used to be that the company operated almost as if it were two entities—one group of employees in the United States, another who worked internationally. Today, that's totally different. It's much more integrated. Many more U.S. employees have taken overseas assignments, and foreign nationals frequent the U.S. offices.

"The barrier has come down, and an international assignment is part of the career progression," he says. People are trying to get overseas as part of their career development. In general, they're more exposed to the global workplace.

Of course, state-of-the-art telecommunications facilitate the cultural exchange. Many employees have considerable international phone contact with each other. Video conferencing and in-person meetings with foreign colleagues build social relationships. The company also televises major company meetings to Europe.

These are key ways to convey corporate culture. In Bechtel's case, this is particularly important. As the speedy mobilization to help fight the Kuwaiti fires attests, employees sometimes are called on to move to another location on a few days' notice. A highly decentralized, flexible structure makes this rapid response possible. Work often is done with project teams. They form to accomplish specific tasks. U.S. expatriates, other expatriates, and local nationals do the job and then demobilize. This type of work arrangement, the speed at which the company can respond, and the company's flexibility also make it imperative that employees fully comprehend the company's mission.

"Obviously, you have to communicate the company's purpose and its objectives," says Morgan. "The culture provides guidance for the employee on how the company wants to achieve those objectives. When you're given the responsibility to do these kinds of jobs, you have to mobilize very, very quickly and operate quite independently."

In addition, the HR staff (which includes 45 people in Bechtel's corporate offices in San Francisco and 340 people in regional and area offices, and many field locations) uses pre-employment interviews to communicate some of the company's culture, particularly when hiring managers. The issue of *fit* not only involves technical skills and qualifications, but also in knowing that the employee will be comfortable with Bechtel's way of doing things. For example, all new employees sign a standard of conduct agreement.

Training and development are other areas in which Bechtel communicates its goals and values. Morgan, who is Australian and has lived in a variety of offshore settings, says that international training is heightened when you teach mixed groups of U.S. expatriates and local nationals. The training goes both ways. U.S. expatriates communicate the company's ideals and personality to local nationals, and the nationals transmit the host culture to the Americans.

COMMUNICATION HELPS USAIR AND BRITISH AIRWAYS INTEGRATE CORPORATE CULTURES

You don't have to speak different languages to need an interpreter. The USAir–British Airways partnership is an example of that. What happens when two English-speaking groups get together and have to learn each other's way of doing business? Culture shock.

In January 1993, London-based British Airways and Arlington, Virginia-based USAir formed an alliance designed to benefit both companies financially and operationally. USAir wanted an international presence over the long term, but lacked the resources to purchase international routes. The airline was looking for a strategic partner. The alliance allows USAir access to the strong international presence and markets of the British company while giving British Airways entry to the U.S. domestic market, so that it can continue its expansion throughout the world.

Now, the Britons and Americans have to transmit their values and blend their corporate cultures as well as their work forces. "The mission we have essentially is winning the hearts and minds of our employees—at both companies—with respect to the benefit of the alliance," says Ollie Lawrence, Jr., vice president of employee communications at USAir (and previously assistant vice president of employee relations). "We need to develop an understanding of each other's cultures."

GLOBAL BUSINESS STRATEGIES NEED HR's INPUT

No matter what the corporate culture, for it to be advantageous to the company, the culture must be an outgrowth of a well-conceived global plan. "From a human resources point of view, it's critical that the company have a clearly articulated business strategy that spells out why it wants to become more international, what it's trying to achieve, and how it plans to harness senior-level commitment," says Dale E. Smith, an independent HR consultant located in Wilmington, North Carolina, who specializes in helping organizations develop global strategic plans.

First, you must have a clear mission and vision statement. Then, you need to understand the global environment or the specific region in which you're attempting to do business—its history, economies, political situations, and cultures. Smith suggests that you accomplish this complex task by interviewing key managers and customers, trying to distinguish if it is indeed best for the company to become international. Identify specific product lines and specific countries in which the business will begin to venture out.

"Define what globalization means and how you're going to approach it," he says.

Next, HR professionals must identify the key human resources concerns that will support those strategies. Interview managers and customers, analyze data on the work force, relate external changes in the areas of the world into which you're planning to move specifically to the business plan.

For example, if the business strategy is growth, the company needs sufficient management talent to support international growth. If there are enough managers for this, the next question is, do they have a global perspective? Do they have the competencies required to perform on a global basis?

The same goes for compensation and recognition. The first question asks whether the compensation and recognition system supports the business strategy. Does the bonus system, for example, recognize the appropriate elements for increasing international market share? If so, then HR professionals move to the next level and ask how different reward-and-recognition programs abroad will send the message to employees that the company wants to grow its market share.

Based on a thorough analysis of the business strategy, which is confirmed with management, HR can then develop specific action plans. These plans form the foundation for all other HR supports, including communication strategies, compensation, and professional development.

In *Organizational Dynamics,* David Lei, John Slocum, Jr., and Robert Slater suggest that the best way for a company to instill its corporate culture is to ensure that its values are simple and clear, driven from the top, and consistent over time. A carefully defined strategic plan will facilitate these objectives.

The companies are in the process of doing that. First, there's an exchange program in which management personnel from one company *shadow* a counterpart at the other company to learn how they do business, make decisions, and manage employees. For example, an individual from British Airways will work side by side in Washington, D.C., with USAir's director of employee relations, learning how the company makes key personnel decisions. In turn, the USAir individual will then go to London to spend several weeks at British Airways' headquarters. It's one way for people to begin to understand and be sensitive to the internal workings of the other company.

Second, there will be corporate training programs so that key individuals will be able to recognize cultural differences and deal with them. And, third, they're developing working committees within major departments of both companies, such as operations, marketing, and sales, to hammer out programs and procedures by which both carriers can work as partners.

"We recognize there are some cultural differences between the two companies in the way they operate and manage," says Lawrence. "By recognizing those differences, we'll be more successful as we work together."

One of the more surprising differences is language. Although both groups speak English, vocabulary and style can cause problems. Cautions Lawrence, these can be very subtle but can contribute to creating stubborn barriers. For example, he says, the British tend to be more conservative and straightforward than the Americans. They're deliberate in the way in which they communicate and do business.

"We want to identify those significant cultural differences so they don't get in the way of our being able to manage this alliance effectively," he says. "With respect to this partnership, each company has to appreciate that the other has its own culture. We're not a merger. But we also want to recognize the shared vision that created the alliance and identify mutual values so both groups of employees will rally behind that vision."

How does the HR staff plan to go about that? Once management establishes a clear vision statement, the staff will create a focused message to communicate with employees. Already, both companies use the weekly employee newsletters and E-mail to tackle corporate-culture issues head-on. Internal company handouts detail the benefits of the USAir–British Airways alliance to passengers, to local communities, and to USAir and British Airways workers. A handout of *Interesting Facts* underscores the independence and interdependence of each carrier in the alliance.

The way in which each enterprise communicates the alliance to its work force is different. "At USAir, we believe this alliance is going to help the long-term future of the airline. Ultimately, by entering into a strategic alliance to be part of a global airline network, it will help with the job security of our employees," says Lawrence.

British Airways will have to communicate its rationale a little differently since it already is an international carrier. It wants to be a predominant international carrier through the development of partnerships around the world.

In addition to the more-formal communications, the companies are developing a line of apparel for employees that will heighten awareness of the alliance. They're also cohosting special events, such as fish-and-chips parties.

How does the HR staff know if the cultural communications are working? It measures employee reaction. USAir conducts random telephone interviews and leads focus groups. An outside consultant meets with a cross section of employees to learn about their understanding of the alliance. The feedback provides management with information about where to put more emphasis or provide more explanation.

Equally important, simply by concentrating on these questions, it reinforces the message that management is trying to convey to the workers. In other words, employees know that the company doesn't measure something that isn't important.

"I think human resources professionals need to recognize that messages are sent not only through formal communications. They're sent through management action or inaction—how an organization rewards its employees, what's rewarded, and what isn't. It's reinforced through what's measured," says Lawrence. "If the company measures productivity, that tells employees that the company is concerned about how many units get out. If it measures service, that tells employees service is important."

What the HR staff communicates and how it communicates the message builds an understanding of the company mission. That's one reason these business partners stress personal communication along with the more-formalized ways. Executives have *adopted* cities that they must visit three or four times a year. They reinforce the alliance, answer questions, and explain some of the specifics of the partnership in employee meetings.

COMMUNICATION AND INFORMATION-SHARING CAN EMPOWER EMPLOYEES

It's high levels of communications and information-sharing that make the difference. The executives at Pepsi-Cola International know this firsthand.

Pepsi-Cola International is another company in a period of rapid growth and international expansion. It's becoming involved in more joint-venture positions with businesses around the world. Primarily, though, it operates as a franchise system.

According to John Fulkerson, vice president of organization and management development, the company is trying to ensure that it has plenty of skilled and empowered people in the organization as it expands. It's emphasizing customer service, innovation, and marketing even more than before. Most important, though, is the ability to maintain a consistently high-quality product. This is challenging in an environment in which franchise bottling facilities are as diverse as their locations in Uruguay, Hong Kong, and Pakistan.

"How do you go about building a business and a superior organization on the inside that's customer-focused as opposed to internally focused?" asks Fulkerson. "It's more complicated when you're working in the international arena because of cross-cultural differences."

What do you have to do to make this an effective working arrangement for all? You create HR systems that allow flexibility on a local basis but maintain consistency with the headquarters. Like USAir and British Airways, Pepsi-Cola uses such communication tools as newsletters, video conferencing, and internal publications to convey these messages.

"Number one, you have to talk about what it is you're trying to communicate," says Fulkerson. "We're trying to convey how we provide value and the best product in the marketplace. So, we try to transfer knowledge through lots of discussions and personal conversation."

In addition, every few years, there's a management conference in which senior employees gather for two to four days. The Pepsi-Cola International Management Institute is another way to disseminate ideas. It's a place in which employees learn skills and absorb cultural information. The Institute delivers skilled training programs throughout the world.

Every year, there's a formal meeting for the human resources planning process. At the meeting, the HR staff determines the human resources activities that will support the business plan. Then staff members discuss it with their employees.

"Building trust across borders is very critical to getting things done," says Fulkerson. "We might have a person spend six months to one-and-a-half years in the United States before they ever go back to their native country and start running their operation. Although they might know something about the beverage business, we want to help them understand how we function. We want them to build a network of people they can talk to when they call from Moscow, for example."

This network is important when there are operational changes. If you want empowered people, then you can't make all the decisions from headquarters. You have to teach foreign nationals who work in the United States the best operational practices and help them understand the Pepsi-Cola way of doing things. You can do this most effectively if the business plan is clear.

"What are you really trying to accomplish?" asks Fulkerson. "What does it take to be successful? You have to be very clear about the strategic advances for the business, and once everyone understands the strategic plan, everybody is pulling in the same direction."

However, with such a decentralized operating structure, flexibility is crucial. Take a concept like innovation. Being innovative in Argentina is very different from what it is in Norway. "I think we learn a lot from folks who don't do it the American way," says Fulkerson. "I don't care where good ideas come from. In the long run, we all get credit when those things work well."

Non-U.S. ways of doing things can bring a lot to the home company. For example, the plastic returnable bottle is being used in Europe. Developed outside the United States, it first hit the market in Europe, and then the company moved it to Latin America. Operational practices can vary widely, too. Not only do they reflect the host culture's personality, but they offer other alternatives to the parent company.

"Corporate culture isn't an export," sums up Bechtel's Morgan. "It isn't one-way. Companies don't realize it, but they're also importing from overseas." It penetrates through returning expatriates and senior management from abroad.

Morgan offers an example. When he first came from Australia to the United States approximately 20 years ago, he used the English form of spelling—*labour* instead of labor, *cheque* instead of check, *advertizement* instead of advertisement. It was frowned upon then, and often corrected. "No one notices anymore," he says. "It's just an alternative way of spelling, and now it doesn't even get retyped."

ETHICS: ARE STANDARDS LOWER OVERSEAS?

Andrew W. Singer

When American businesspeople venture abroad, a common view is that they're wandering into an ethical no-man's-land, where each encounter holds forth a fresh demand for a "gratuity," or baksheesh.

William C. Norris, who founded and for many years headed Control Data Corporation, says, "No question about it. We were constantly in the position of saying how much we were willing to pay" to have a routine service performed overseas. Norris recalls frequently facing situations such as: "The computer is on the dock, it's raining, and you have to pay $100 to get it picked up . . ."

In South America, firms often face a "closed bidding system" when dealing with that region's large, nationalized companies, says John Swanson, a senior consultant of communications and business conduct at Dow Corning Corporation. He says that his company has been locked out of the South American market at times because it refused to pay the bribes necessary to get that business.

In Japan, bids for government construction jobs are routinely rigged, according to one former U.S. government official who asked to remain anonymous—a result of Japanese firms purchasing "influence" from politicians.

Donald E. Petersen, former chairman and chief executive officer of the Ford Motor Company, cites ethical challenges in much of the developing world. "Give me a military dictator with absolute power, and it doesn't matter if he's South American or African or Asian—you've got problems."

IS THE UNITED STATES MORE ETHICAL?

Is this common perception borne out by reality? Are business standards overseas in fact lower than those at home? In 1987, Touche Ross, the accounting firm (now

Source: *Across the Board,* September 1991.

Andrew W. Singer is editor and publisher of *Ethikos,* a New York-based publication that examines ethical issues in business.

Deloitte & Touche), surveyed a range of U.S. business executives, members of Congress, and business school deans. Asked to rank the top five countries in terms of ethical standards, respondents placed the United States first, followed by the United Kingdom, Canada, Switzerland, and West Germany.

Some differences were found among respondent groups. Business school deans, for instance, put Japan at the top of their list—while business executives did not rank Japan among their top five at all.

When asked about the survey, William Norris says, "I agree with the second group. Control Data tried unsuccessfully for 15 years to get into the Japanese market. They kept us out with laws and subterfuges until they could catch up [to the U.S. computer industry]. Then they opened up to U.S. firms. I think that is very unethical."

Referring to the *keiretsu,* the famed Japanese business groups, Norris says, "In our country, we call that collusion."

Many U.S. executives agree that from a business ethics standpoint, the Japanese are a special case. Take gift giving. "It is an important part of how they conduct themselves," says Donald Petersen. Often, there is little thought given to the idea: "Give me the business and I'll give you a gift."

When dealing with the Japanese, Petersen found that it was futile to try to convince them of the superiority of the American approach to business, in which, for instance, the receipt of gifts of any value in the course of a business transaction is frowned upon as a potential conflict of interest. His solution when dealing with the Japanese was simply to present the policy of accepting no gifts of any value as an American idiosyncrasy.

Bruce Smart, former U.S. Undersecretary of Commerce for International Trade, says that the Japanese are very consistent in sticking to their standards. However, those standards—which accept practices such as companies buying influence from politicians—may sometimes be looked at askance by U.S. eyes. Still, if by business ethics one means consistency with standards, "then the Japanese are probably very ethical," says Smart. Probably fewer Japanese executives cheat on their business expense sheets than Americans, Smart opines.

UNDERDEVELOPED NATIONS: "YOU'LL BE TESTED CONSTANTLY"

In general, U.S. executives see only minor differences in business ethics as practiced in the United States, Canada, and Northern Europe. But most agree that there are some departures in the practice of business ethics when it comes to Southern Europe—Italy and Spain, for instance—and a tremendous difference in the underdeveloped nations.

"Based on my 40 years at Ford, there were no more difficult problems with ethical standards in Europe than here," says Petersen. But among the underdeveloped nations—particularly those countries with autocratic governments in which power is absolute and concentrated—it is often ordinary practice to hold out a hand for a bribe, or to take a company official for a slow walk through customs, until he gets the message that a "grease" payment is required.

Petersen maintains that a company can adhere to high standards—prohibiting bribery or even grease payments—and still function. "It's difficult. You'll be tested constantly, and at times you'll think you've lost business. But if you have a service that they want, they'll come around."

A "HOLIER-THAN-THOU" ATTITUDE

Not all agree that the United States is justified in taking such a superior position. "We ment professor at Bentley College in Waltham, Massachusetts. He maintains that U.S. standards are artificial and naive rather than too high.

"We are often prepared to pay bribes because we hear that's expected—but that's because we hear from people who want bribes," says Seeger, explaining that managers don't often speak with the people who don't pay or receive bribes. "We expect to be held up, and so we get held up. It is the classic self-fulfilling prophecy."

When discussing overseas ethical standards, there is a danger of stereotyping people. Seeger, in fact, recently wrote a prize-winning management case based on a real incident in which the owner of a Persian Gulf company, Sameer Mustafa, an Arab, refused to bribe the engineer in charge of a Gulf construction project—and suffered economically as a result. Not *only* Americans have an abhorrence of bribery, Seeger suggests.

Kent Druyvesteyn, staff vice president of ethics at General Dynamics Corporation, agrees that we should put away ideas of American superiority when discussing ethics. Too often, says Druyvesteyn, ethical discussions take the form of: "We really do things well here. But when we go abroad, they do things so badly."

William S. Lipsman, associate general counsel of the Sara Lee Corporation, recently returned from a two-year assignment in the Netherlands. He says that he found litigation ethics standards in Europe to be higher than those in the United States. Business there is conducted on a more personal basis, Lipsman explains. "The concept that you, as a business leader, would sue another business without first sitting down at a meeting, face-to-face, is unheard of."

Bruce Smart doesn't even place the United States in the top echelon when it comes to national business standards. The Canadians, British, Australians, and perhaps even the Germans rate higher, in his view. His thinking: A kind of noblesse oblige still exists among the business classes in those countries. Conversely, in the United States, where there is a less entrenched business group, the prevailing attitude is that you make it whatever way you can. This attitude reached its apotheosis in the 1980s with the insider trading scandals on Wall Street, which Smart describes as "the biggest ethical blot on U.S. business" in recent memory.

Whether U.S. standards are in fact higher than those abroad is likely to remain a moot point. But in one respect the United States stands alone: It is the only nation that has sought to legislate moral business conduct overseas.

CAN WE LEGISLATE MORALITY?

Passed in the late 70s in the wake of Watergate and the overseas bribery scandals, the Foreign Corrupt Practices Act (FCPA) made it a felony for U.S. companies to obtain business by paying off foreign government officials. From its inception, the FCPA has been controversial. "Managers in other countries often chuckle at the United States' hoping to export its morality in the form of the Foreign Corrupt Practices Act," says Gene Laczniak, management professor at Marquette University in Milwaukee.

"It's anachronistic in today's world," says William Norris, the former Control Data chief. "It's like the antitrust laws in many ways. The world has passed it by." (The antitrust laws, enacted at the turn of the century, originally embodied a strong ethical element: The government didn't want the nation's enormous "trusts" to run roughshod over the "little guy." That worked fine as long as the U.S. economy was an isolated system, say critics. But now antitrust laws may be inhibiting large U.S. firms from competing in the international arena.) In any case, says Norris, most U.S. companies don't want to become involved in activities such as bribing foreign officials.

R. John Cooper, executive vice president and general counsel of Young & Rubicam Inc., the New York-based advertising agency, makes a similar argument. The FCPA was enacted at a time when the competitive position of U.S. companies in the world was stronger—or at least perceived to be stronger—than it is today, Cooper points out. In 1970, the United States was the source of 60 percent of the world's direct foreign investment. By 1984, according to the United Nations, that figure had dropped to 12 percent. Japanese, European, and East Asian firms have picked up much of the slack, launching economic forays even into America's own backyard.

The United States risks becoming economically hamstrung by statutes such as the Foreign Corrupt Practices Act, suggests Cooper. "We have to reexamine some of these high-toned notions."

In the late 1980s, Young & Rubicam and three of its executives were indicted on a conspiracy charge under the FCPA. The government asserted that the company had "reason to know" that one of its Jamaican agents was paying off that country's minister of tourism to obtain advertising business. In order to avoid a lengthy trial, the company paid a $500,000 penalty, says Cooper.

One outcome of that experience is that Young & Rubicam now has a policy that forbids even facilitating payments. Facilitating (or grease) payments are considerations to secure some ordinary service in a country, such as getting a ship unloaded in a harbor, or having a telephone installed. These are permitted under the FCPA.

SHOULDERING AN ETHICAL BURDEN

According to Cooper, Young & Rubicam's recent experience "puts us in a position in which we're very reluctant to engage in a very common practice in some foreign countries: hiring people with relationships, who have the ability to generate business from official sources." The company can't go near such people, Cooper says. With increasingly heated international competition, the act is out of date, he says. It puts too much of a burden on U.S. corporations to know everything about their foreign agents—a burden not shouldered by foreign competitors.

The FCPA might have been an "overreaction" on the part of Congress to events such as Watergate and the overseas bribery scandals, suggests John Swanson of Dow Corning. (See box, "The Murky Land of the FCPA.") "We're competing out there with strong and vibrant economies—Japan, the Common Market. We're a player but not a dominant player. We can't have this legislation that is clearly not understood [but which] has such an effect on the viability of trade."

The FCPA brings back bitter memories for William Norris. Some years ago, Control Data Corporation was prosecuted by the U.S. government under the Foreign Corrupt Practices Act for making payments in Iran.

"I never felt we did anything wrong," says Norris, explaining that the company was conforming to the laws of Iran. (In 1978, Control Data Corporation pleaded guilty to three criminal charges that it made improper payments to unnamed foreign officials. It was fined $1,381,000 by the U.S. Customs Service.) Looking back on his long tenure as Control Data's chief executive, Norris says that settling—and not fighting—that case was one of the few things that he ever regretted.

But the FCPA also has its defenders. "It's a tough trade-off," admits Marquette's Laczniak, but the bottom line is that the "U.S. public doesn't want its companies to secure business by paying huge sums of money to foreign officials." The FCPA, in other words, is really just a reflection of the prevailing values of American society.

"I have sort of a hard time arguing that it should be repealed," says Bruce Smart. Bribing foreign officials tends "to run counter to the idea of democratic representa-

THE MURKY LAND OF THE FCPA

The Foreign Corrupt Practices Act (FCPA) became law in 1977, in the wake of foreign bribery scandals involving U.S. companies that shook the governments of Belgium, the Netherlands, Honduras, Italy, and Japan. One of the most notorious incidents involved an estimated $25 million in concealed payments made overseas by Lockheed Corporation in connection with sales of its Tristar L-1011 aircraft in Japan. This culminated in the resignation and subsequent criminal conviction of Japanese Prime Minister Kankuie Tanaka.

The FCPA, which makes it a crime for a U.S. corporation to bribe officials of foreign governments to obtain or increase business, is controversial, in part, because it seeks to forge a distinction between "bribes" (which it deems illegal) and "gratuities" (which the FCPA permits). The difference is murky, according to the FCPA's critics.

"The law marked the difference between gratuities paid to low-level officials and payments made to authorities," writes Duane Windsor in his book, *The Foreign Corrupt Practices Act: Anatomy of a Statute.* "In many countries a payment to a customs official is a matter of course and a matter of economic necessity. A customs official may backlog an order or hinder a shipment by elaborately checking each imported item. The detrimental effect to the shipment is obvious. In response, lawmakers sought to delineate gratuities and bribes very clearly. But in reality the definition of gratuities was so vague that some people felt it had a chilling effect [on business]."

tive government. If we countenance bribery, we make it more difficult for those people to find a better way to do business."

As for the idea that U.S. standards have to be adjusted to reflect the new economic realities: "That's an ancient argument, morally," says General Dynamic's Druyvesteyn. "It's one that goes back to Deuteronomy, in the Bible. 'Sure, things are rough. We've had a drought, and the sheep aren't fat. We may have to add a little to the weight.'"

THE SLIPPERY SLOPE OF GREASE PAYMENTS

What about facilitating, or grease, payments, which are permitted under the FCPA as long as they are documented? Such payments are the norm for doing business in some parts of the world. Indeed, government employees are often intentionally underpaid in the expectation that they will receive such gratuities.

The issue of facilitating payments is addressed in Dow Corning's ethics code. "The company felt in the early 1980s that if it didn't put it in the code, it would be like the ostrich with its head in the ground," explains John Swanson. Because grease payments are going on in many parts of the world, they should be recognized.

If the company sends a person to Mexico, and his household possessions are locked up on the dock, and he can't get them delivered to his house without a facilitating payment, then Dow Corning will pay it, says Swanson. "We don't like it. But to get that person to work a few weeks early, we will do it."

What did William Norris do when a big computer was stuck on the dock for want of a $100 payment? "I told them to pay the $100." To fail to make the grease payment in that instance would be "carrying it too far," says Norris. In many other cases, though, Control Data refused to yield to such extortion, and the company lost sales as a result.

"It depends upon what amount of money is involved," says Gene Laczniak. "If you are paying small amounts of money to individuals just to do their jobs [and that is part of the country's culture], then that is just the cost of doing business in that part of the world. But if the money is paid to sway people to make decisions that they would not otherwise make, then that is subverting the nature of the free market system," says Laczniak. "I don't think anyone wants the system to work that way."

Joanne Ciulla, a professor at the University of Pennsylvania's Wharton School, acknowledges that facilitating payments can be somewhat problematic. In many developing countries, bureaucracies are hopelessly inefficient, she says. One is, in effect, paying for an efficient service within an inefficient system.

This presents some moral problems. If everyone uncomplainingly pays facilitating payments, a government has no incentive to be efficient. On the other hand, there is not a whole lot one company can do to change the system. Ciulla is reluctant to recommend that companies "fight windmills" by banning such payments in toto. What companies can do, she suggests, is put pressure on governments to clean up their act. Airing such concerns might have an impact in the long run.

The argument that U.S. global standards are too high, however, is "totally absurd," in Ciulla's view. People sometimes overlook the deleterious effects that bribery has on developing countries, where the widespread practice impedes the development of a free market, she says. "How do you develop if you can't open a fruit stand without paying a bribe?"

She notes that even where bribery and corruption is widely practiced, it's not condoned—at least officially. Even in the Dominican Republic—considered by many to be one of the most corrupt places on earth—no one says bribery is okay, Ciulla points out. No one bribes publicly, it's done privately.

Barbara Burns, a public relations consultant and a member of the board of directors of the International Public Relations Association, says that in some South American countries, notably Brazil, it is not unusual for public relations professionals to pay to have favorable stories for corporate clients placed in publications, often by remunerating a journalist. "But everyone knows which publications these are—so placement is not so valuable to the client," says Burns. "And if you start paying off, it undermines your credibility, and finally your business." She adds that there are also many high-quality publications in Brazil that can't be "bought."

From a company's point of view, the practice of giving grease payments can be economically hazardous—apart from possible legal sanctions. "It's very hard to figure out the expenses. How do you anticipate costs?" asks Ciulla. Governments change, and a "contact" may fall from favor. How much additional extortion might one face down the road?

INTEGRITY HAS ITS REWARDS

Adhering to higher standards doesn't have to have negative economic consequences, suggests Dow Corning's Swanson. Some years ago, Dow Corning surveyed its top customers. These customers found the company wanting in certain areas, namely response time and certain quality issues. On the positive side, the customers said: "We know you're a company of integrity, and that you stand behind your products, people, and service." Because of the company's integrity, says Swanson, "they gave us a three-year period of grace to improve our response times and quality. Otherwise, they might have taken their business to a foreign competitor."

U.S. standards are too high, then? "I don't carry that feeling with me," says Donald Petersen. "In general, I wouldn't want to see us say it's okay to reduce our standards to those of others."

And while William Norris is opposed to legislation like the FCPA—which was badly drawn and arbitrarily enforced, in his view—he doesn't recommend that U.S. companies compromise their high standards when operating abroad, either. "I don't think it's necessary to reassess those standards," says Norris. "It's better to lose a deal now and then than to lower standards, which will demoralize the workforce." In the long run, he sees high ethical standards simply as part of a quality management approach toward business.

PART THREE

APPENDIX: CASES IN STRATEGIC MANAGEMENT

A GUIDE TO CASE ANALYSIS

In most courses in strategic management, students practice at being strategy managers via case analysis. A case sets forth, in a factual manner, the events and organizational circumstances surrounding a particular managerial situation. It puts readers at the scene of the action and familiarizes them with all the relevant circumstances. A case on strategic management can concern a whole industry, a single organization, or some part of an organization; the organization involved can be either profit seeking or not-for-profit. The essence of the student's role in case analysis is to *diagnose* and *size up* the situation described in the case and then to recommend appropriate action steps.

WHY USE CASES TO PRACTICE STRATEGIC MANAGEMENT

The foregoing limerick was used some years ago by Professor Charles Gragg to characterize the plight of business students who had no exposure to cases.[1] Gragg observed that the mere act of listening to lectures and sound advice about managing does little for anyone's management skills and that the accumulated managerial wisdom cannot effectively be passed on by lectures and assigned readings alone. Gragg suggested that if anything had been learned about the practice of management, it is that a storehouse of ready-made textbook answers does not exist. Each managerial situation has unique aspects, requiring its own diagnosis, judgement, and tailor-made actions. Cases provide would-be managers with a valuable way to practice wrestling with the actual problems of actual managers in actual companies.

The case approach to strategic analysis is, first and foremost, an exercise in learning by doing. Because cases provide you with detailed information about conditions and problems of different industries and companies, your task of analyzing company after company and situation after situation has the twin benefit of boosting your analytical skills and exposing you to the ways companies and managers actually do things. Most college students have limited managerial backgrounds and only fragmented knowledge about different companies and real-life strategic situations. Cases help substitute for actual on-the-job experience by (1) giving you broader exposure to a variety of industries, organizations, and strategic problems; (2) forcing you to assume a managerial role (as opposed to that of just an onlooker); (3) providing a test of how to apply the tools and techniques of strategic management; and (4) asking you to come up with pragmatic managerial action plans to deal with the issues at hand.

OBJECTIVES OF CASE ANALYSIS

Using cases to learn about the practice of strategic management is a powerful way for you to accomplish five things:[2]

1. Increase your understanding of what managers should and should not do in guiding a business to success.
2. Build your skills in conducting strategic analysis in a variety of industries, competitive situations, and company circumstances.
3. Get valuable practice in diagnosing strategic issues, evaluating strategic alternatives, and formulating workable plans of action.
4. Enhance your sense of business judgment, as opposed to uncritically accepting the authoritative crutch of the professor or "back-of-the-book" answers.
5. Gaining in-depth exposure to different industries and companies, thereby gaining something close to actual business experience.

If you understand that these are the objectives of case analysis, you are less likely to be consumed with curiosity about "the answer to the case." Students who have grown comfortable with and accustomed to textbook statements of fact and definitive lecture notes are often frustrated when discussions about a case do not produce concrete answers. Usually, case discussions produce good arguments for more than one

---

[1]Charles I. Gragg, "Because Wisdom Can't Be Told," in *The Case Method at the Harvard Business School,* ed. M. P. McNair (New York: McGraw-Hill, 1954), p. 11.
[2]Ibid., pp. 12–14; and D. R. Schoen and Philip A. Sprague, "What Is the Case Method?" in *The Case Method at the Harvard Business School,* ed. M. P. McNair, pp. 78–79.

course of action. Differences of opinion nearly always exist. Thus, should a class discussion conclude without a strong, unambiguous consensus on what do to, don't grumble too much when you are *not* told what the answer is or what the company actually did. Just remember that in the business world answers don't come in conclusive black-and-white terms. There are nearly always several feasible courses of action and approaches, each of which may work out satisfactorily. Moreover, in the business world, when one elects a particular course of action, there is no peeking at the back of a book to see if you have chosen the best thing to do and no one to turn to for a provably correct answer. The only valid test of management action is *results*. If the results of an action turn out to be "good," the decision to take it may be presumed "right." If not, then the action chosen was "wrong" in the sense that it didn't work out.

Hence, the important thing for a student to understand in case analysis is that the managerial exercise of identifying, diagnosing, and recommending builds your skills; discovering the right answer or finding out what actually happened is no more than frosting on the cake. Even if you learn what the company did, you can't conclude that it was necessarily right or best. All that can be said is "here is what they did. . . ."

The point is this: *The purpose of giving you a case assignment is not to cause you to run to the library to look up what the company actually did but, rather, to enhance your skills in sizing up situations and developing your managerial judgment about what needs to be done and how to do it.* The aim of case analysis is for *you* to bear the strains of thinking actively, of offering your analysis, of proposing action plans, and of explaining and defending your assessments—this is how cases provide you with meaningful practice at being a manager.

PREPARING A CASE FOR CLASS DISCUSSION

If this is your first experience with the case method, you may have to reorient your study habits. Unlike lecture courses where you can get by without preparing intensively for each class and where you have latitude to work assigned readings and reviews of lecture notes into your schedule, a case assignment requires conscientious preparation before class. You will not get much out of hearing the class discuss a case you haven't read, and you certainly won't be able to contribute anything yourself to the discussion. What you have got to do to get ready for class discussion of a case is to study the case, reflect carefully on the situation presented, and develop some reasoned thoughts. Your goal in preparing the case should be to end up with what you think is a sound, well-supported analysis of the situation and a sound, defensible set of recommendations about which managerial actions need to be taken.

To prepare a case for class discussion, we suggest the following approach:

1. *Read the case through rather quickly for familiarity.* The initial reading should give you the general flavor of the situation and indicate which issue or issues are involved. If your instructor has provided you with study questions for the case, now is the time to read them carefully.

2. *Read the case a second time.* On this reading, try to gain full command of the facts. Begin to develop some tentative answers to the study questions your instructor has provided. If your instructor has elected not to give you assignment questions, then start forming your own picture of the overall situation being described.

3. *Study all the exhibits carefully.* Often, the real story is in the numbers contained in the exhibits. Expect the information in the case exhibits to be crucial enough to materially affect your diagnosis of the situation.

4. *Decide what the strategic issues are.* Until you have identified the strategic issues and problems in the case, you don't know what to analyze, which tools and analytical techniques are called for, or otherwise how to proceed. At times the strategic issues are clear—either being stated in the case or else obvious from reading the case. At other times you will have to dig them out from all the information given.

5. *Start your analysis of the issues with some number crunching.* A big majority of strategy cases call for some kind of number crunching on your part. This means calculating assorted financial ratios to check out the company's financial
condition and recent performance, calculating growth rates of sales or profits or unit volume, checking out profit margins and the makeup of the cost structure, and understanding whatever revenue-cost-profit relationships are present. See Table 1 for a summary of key financial ratios, how they are calculated, and what they show.

6. *Use whichever tools and techniques of strategic analysis are called for.* Strategic analysis is not just a collection of opinions; rather, it entails application of a growing number of powerful tools and techniques that cut beneath the surface and produce important insight and understanding of strategic situations. Every case assigned is strategy related and contains an opportunity to usefully apply the weapons of strategic analysis. Your instructor is looking for you to demonstrate that you know *how* and *when* to use the strategic management concepts presented earlier in the course. Furthermore, expect to have to draw regularly on what you have learned in your finance, economics, production, marketing, and human resources management courses.

7. *Check out conflicting opinions and make some judgments about the validity of all the data and information provided.* Many times cases report views and contradictory opinions (after all, people don't always agree on things, and different people see the same things in different ways). Forcing you to evaluate the data and information presented in the case helps you develop your powers of inference and judgment. Asking you to resolve conflicting information "comes with the territory" because a great many managerial situations entail opposing points of view, conflicting trends, and sketchy information.

8. *Support your diagnosis and opinions with reasons and evidence.* The most important things to prepare for are your answers to the question "Why?" For instance, if after studying the case you are of the opinion that the company's managers are doing a poor job, then it is your answer to "Why?" that establishes just how good your analysis of the situation is. If your instructor has provided you with specific study questions for the case, by all means prepare answers that include all the reasons and number-crunching evidence you can muster to support your diagnosis. *Generate at least two pages of notes!*

9. *Develop an appropriate action plan and set of recommendations.* Diagnosis divorced from corrective action is sterile. The test of a manager is always to convert sound analysis into sound actions—actions that will produce the desired results. Hence, the final and most telling step in preparing a case is to

TABLE 1 | A Summary of Key Financial Ratios, How They Are Calculated, and What They Show

Ratio	How Calculated	What It Shows
Profitability Ratios		
1. Gross profit margin	$\dfrac{\text{Sales} - \text{Cost of goods sold}}{\text{Sales}}$	An indication of the total margin available to cover operating expenses and yield a profit.
2. Operating profit margin (or return on sales)	$\dfrac{\text{Profits before taxes and before interest}}{\text{Sales}}$	An indication of the firm's profitability from current operations without regard to the interest charges accruing from the capital structure.
3. Net profit margin (or net return on sales)	$\dfrac{\text{Profits after taxes}}{\text{Sales}}$	Shows after tax profits per dollar of sales. Subpar profit margins indicate that the firm's sales prices are relatively low or that costs are relatively high, or both.
4. Return on total assets	$\dfrac{\text{Profits after taxes}}{\text{Total assets}}$ or $\dfrac{\text{Profits after taxes} + \text{interest}}{\text{Total assets}}$	A measure of the return on total investment in the enterprise. It is sometimes desirable to add interest to aftertax profits to form the numerator of the ratio since total assets are financed by creditors as well as by stockholders; hence, it is accurate to measure the productivity of assets by the returns provided to both classes of investors.
5. Return on stockholder's equity (or return on net worth)	$\dfrac{\text{Profits after taxes}}{\text{Total stockholders' equity}}$	A measure of the rate of return on stockholders' investment in the enterprise.
6. Return on common equity	$\dfrac{\text{Profits after taxes} - \text{Preferred stock dividends}}{\text{Total stockholders' equity} - \text{Par value of preferred stock}}$	A measure of the rate of return on the investment which the owners of the common stock have made in the enterprise.
7. Earnings per share	$\dfrac{\text{Profits after taxes} - \text{Preferred stock dividends}}{\text{Number of shares of common stock outstanding}}$	Shows the earnings available to the owners of each share of common stock.
Liquidity Ratios		
1. Current ratio	$\dfrac{\text{Current assets}}{\text{Current liabilities}}$	Indicates the extent to which the claims of short-term creditors are covered by assets that are expected to be converted to cash in a period roughly corresponding to the maturity of the liabilities.
2. Quick ratio (or acid-test ratio)	$\dfrac{\text{Current assets} - \text{Inventory}}{\text{Current liabilities}}$	A measure of the firm's ability to pay off short-term obligations without relying on the sale of its inventories
3. Inventory to net working capital	$\dfrac{\text{Inventory}}{\text{Current assets} - \text{Current liabilities}}$	A measure of the extent to which the firm's working capital is tied up in inventory.
Leverage Ratios		
1. Debt-to-assets ratio	$\dfrac{\text{Total debt}}{\text{Total assets}}$	Measures the extent to which borrowed funds have been used to finance the firm's operations.
2. Debt-to-equity ratio	$\dfrac{\text{Total debt}}{\text{Total stockholders' equity}}$	Provides another measure of the funds provided by creditors versus the funds provided by owners.

T A B L E 1 | **A Summary of Key Financial Ratios, How They Are Calculated, and What They Show (*cont.*)**

Ratio	How Calculated	What It Shows
Leverage Ratios (*cont.*)		
3. Long-term debt-to equity ratio	$\dfrac{\text{Long-term debt}}{\text{Total shareholders' equity}}$	A widely used measure of the balance between debt and equity in the firm's long-term capital structure.
4. Times-interest-earned (or coverage) ratio	$\dfrac{\text{Profits before interest and taxes}}{\text{Total interest charges}}$	Measures the extent to which earnings can decline without the firm becoming unable to meet its annual interest costs.
5. Fixed-charge coverage	$\dfrac{\text{Profits before taxes and interest} + \text{Lease obligations}}{\text{Total interest charges} + \text{Lease obligations}}$	A more inclusive indication of the firm's ability to meet all of its fixed-charge obligations.
Activity Ratios		
1. Inventory turnover	$\dfrac{\text{Sales}}{\text{Inventory of finished goods}}$	When compared to industry averages, it provides an indication of whether a company has excessive or perhaps inadequate finished goods inventory.
2. Fixed assets turnover	$\dfrac{\text{Sales}}{\text{Fixed Assets}}$	A measure of the sales productivity and utilization of plant and equipment.
3. Total assets turnover	$\dfrac{\text{Sales}}{\text{Total Assets}}$	A measure of the utilization of all the firm's assets; a ratio below the industry average indicates the company is not generating a sufficient volume of business, given the size of its asset investment.
4. Accounts receivable turnover	$\dfrac{\text{Annual credit sales}}{\text{Accounts receivable}}$	A measure of the average length of time it takes the firm to collect the sales made on credit.
5. Average collection period	$\dfrac{\text{Accounts receivable}}{\text{Total sales} \div 365}$ or $\dfrac{\text{Accounts receivable}}{\text{Average daily sales}}$	Indicates the average length of time the firm must wait after making a sale before it receives payment.
Other Ratios		
1. Dividend yield on common stock	$\dfrac{\text{Annual dividends per share}}{\text{Current market price per share}}$	A measure of the return to owners received in the form of dividends.
2. Price-earnings ratio	$\dfrac{\text{Current market price per share}}{\text{After tax earnings per share}}$	Faster-growing or less-risky firms tend to have higher price-earnings ratios than slower-growing or more-risky firms.
3. Dividend payout ratio	$\dfrac{\text{Annual dividends per share}}{\text{After tax earnings per share}}$	Indicates the percentage of profits paid out as dividends.
4. Cash flow per share	$\dfrac{\text{After tax profits} + \text{Depreciation}}{\text{Number of common shares outstanding}}$	A measure of the discretionary funds over and above expenses that are available for use by the firm.

Note: Industry-average ratios against which a particular company's ratios may be judged are available in *Modern Industry* and *Dun's Reviews*

published by Dun & Bradstreet (14 ratios for 125 lines of business activities), Robert Morris Associates' *Annual Statement Studies* (11 ratios for

develop an action agenda for management that lays out a set of specific recommendations on what to do. Bear in mind that proposing realistic, workable solutions is far preferable to casually tossing out off-the-top-of-your-head suggestions. Be prepared to argue why your recommendations are more attractive than other courses of action that are open.

As long as you are conscientious in preparing your analysis and recommendations, and as long as you have ample reasons, evidence, and arguments to support your views, you shouldn't fret unduly about whether what you've prepared is the right answer to the case. In case analysis there is rarely just one right approach or one right set of recommendations. Managing companies and devising and implementing strategies are not such exact sciences that there exists a single provably correct analysis and action plan for each strategic situation. Of course, some analyses and action plans are better than others; but, in truth, there's nearly always more than one good way to analyze a situation and more than one good plan of action. So, if you have done a careful and thoughtful job of preparing the case, don't lose confidence in the correctness of your work and judgement.

PARTICIPATING IN CLASS DISCUSSION OF A CASE

Classroom discussions of cases are sharply different from attending a lecture class. In a case class students do most of the talking. The instructor's role is to solicit student participation, keep the discussion on track, ask "Why?" often, offer alternative views, play the devil's advocate (if no students jump in to offer opposing views), and otherwise lead the discussion. The students in the class carry the burden for analyzing the situation and for being prepared to present and defend their diagnoses and recommendations. Expect a classroom environment, therefore, that calls for *your* size-up of the situation, *your* analysis, what actions *you* would take, and why *you* would take them. Do not be dismayed if, as the class discussion unfolds, some insightful things are said by your fellow classmates that you did not think of. It is normal for views and analyses to differ and for the comments of others in the class to expand your own thinking about the case. As the old adage goes, "Two heads are better than one." So it is to be expected that the class as a whole will do a more penetrating and searching job of case analysis than will any one person working alone. This is the power of group effort, and its virtues are that it will help you see more analytical applications, let you test your analyses and judgments against those of your peers, and force you to wrestle with differences of opinion and approaches.

To orient you to the classroom environment on the days a case discussion is scheduled, we compiled the following list of things to expect:

1. Expect students to dominate the discussion and do most of the talking. The case method enlists a maximum of individual participation in class discussion. It is not enough to be present as a silent observer; if every student took this approach, there would be no discussion. (Thus, expect a portion of your grade to be based on your participation in case discussions.)

2. Expect the instructor to assume the role of extensive questioner and listener.

3. Be prepared for the instructor to probe for reasons and supporting analysis.

4. Expect and tolerate challenges to the views expressed. All students have to be willing to submit their conclusions for scrutiny and rebuttal. Each student needs to learn to state his or her views without fear of disapproval and to overcome the hesitation of speaking out. Learning respect for the views and approaches of others is an integral part of case analysis exercises. But there are times when it is OK to swim against the tide of majority opinion. In the practice of management, there is always room for originality and unorthodox

approaches. So while discussion of a case is a group process, there is no compulsion for you or anyone else to cave in and conform to group opinions and group consensus.

5. Don't be surprised if you change your mind about some things as the discussion unfolds. Be alert to how these changes affect your analysis and recommendations (in the event you get called on).

6. Expect to learn a lot from each case discussion; use what you learned to be better prepared for the next case discussion.

There are several things you can do on your own to be good and look good as a participant in class discussions:

- Although you should do your own independent work and independent thinking, don't hesitate before (and after) class to discuss the case with other students. In real life, managers often discuss the company's problems and situation with other people to refine their own thinking.

- In participating in the discussion, make a conscious effort to contribute, rather than just talk. There is a big difference between saying something that builds the discussion and offering a long-winded, off-the-cuff remark that leaves the class wondering what the point was.

- Avoid the use of "I think," "I believe," and "I feel"; instead, say, "My analysis shows . . ." and "The company should do . . . because . . ." Always give supporting reasons and evidence for your views; then your instructor won't have to ask you "Why?" every time you make a comment.

- In making your points, assume that everyone has read the case and knows what it says; avoid reciting and rehashing information in the case—instead, use the data and information to explain your assessment of the situation and to support your position.

- Always prepare good notes (usually two or three pages' worth) for each case and use them extensively when you speak. There's no way you can remember everything off the top of your head—especially the results of your number crunching. To reel off the numbers or to present all five reasons why, instead of one, you will need good notes. When you have prepared good notes to the study questions and use them as the basis for your comments, *everybody* in the room will know you are well prepared, and your contribution to the case discussion will stand out.

PREPARING A WRITTEN CASE ANALYSIS

Preparing a written case analysis is much like preparing a case for class discussion, except that your analysis must be more complete and reduced to writing. Unfortunately, though, there is no ironclad procedure for doing a written case analysis. All we can offer are some general guidelines and words of wisdom—this is because company situations and management problems are so diverse that no one mechanical way to approach a written case assignment always works.

Your instructor may assign you a specific topic around which to prepare your written report. Or, alternatively, you may be asked to do a comprehensive written case analysis, where the expectation is that you will (1) *identify* all the pertinent issues that management needs to address, (2) perform whatever *analysis* and *evaluation* is appropriate, and (3) propose an *action plan* and *set of recommendations* addressing the issues you have identified. In going through the exercise of identify, evaluate, and recommend, keep the following pointers in mind.[3]

Identification It is essential early on in your paper that you provide a sharply focused diagnosis of strategic issues and key problems and that you demonstrate a good grasp of the company's present situation. Make sure you can identify the firm's strategy (use the concepts and tools in Chapters 1–8 as diagnostic aids) and that you can pinpoint whatever strategy implementation issues may exist (again, consult the material in Chapters 9 and 10 for diagnostic help). Consult the key points we have provided at the end of each chapter for further diagnostic suggestions. Consider beginning your paper by sizing up the company's situation, its strategy, and the significant problems and issues that confront management. State problems/issues as clearly and precisely as you can. Unless it is necessary to do so for emphasis, avoid recounting facts and history about the company (assume your professor has read the case and is familiar with the organization).

Analysis and Evaluation This is usually the hardest part of the report. Analysis is hard work! Check out the firm's financial ratios, its profit margins and rates of return, and its capital structure, and decide how strong the firm is financially. Table 1 contains a summary of various financial ratios and how they are calculated. Use it to assist in your financial diagnosis. Similarly, look at marketing, production, managerial competence, and other factors underlying the organization's strategic successes and failures. Decide whether the firm has core skills and competencies and, if so, whether it is capitalizing on them.

Check to see if the firm's strategy is producing satisfactory results and determine the reasons why or why not. Probe the nature and strength of the competitive forces confronting the company. Decide whether and why the firm's competitive position is getting stronger or weaker. Use the tools and concepts you have learned about to perform whatever analysis and evaluation is appropriate.

In writing your analysis and evaluation, bear in mind four things:

1. You are obliged to offer analysis and evidence to back up your conclusions. Do not rely on unsupported opinions, over-generalizations, and platitudes as a substitute for tight, logical argument backed up with facts and figures.

2. If your analysis involves some important quantitative calculations, use tables and charts to present the calculations clearly and efficiently. Don't just tack the exhibits on at the end of your report and let the reader figure out what they mean and why they were included. Instead, in the body of your report cite some of the key numbers, highlight the conclusions to be drawn from the exhibits, and refer the reader to your charts and exhibits for more details.

3. Demonstrate that you have command of the strategic concepts and analytical tools to which you have been exposed. Use them in your report.

4. Your interpretation of the evidence should be reasonable and objective. Be wary of preparing a one-sided argument that omits all aspects not favorable to your conclusions. Likewise, try not to exaggerate or overdramatize. Endeavor

---

[3]For some additional ideas and viewpoints, you may wish to consult Thomas J. Raymond, "Written Analysis of Cases," in *The Case Method at the Harvard Business School,* ed. M. P. McNair, pp. 139–63. Raymond's article includes an actual case, a sample analysis of the case, and a sample of a student's written report on the case.

to inject balance into your analysis and to avoid emotional rhetoric. Strike phrases such as "I think," "I feel," and "I believe" when you edit your first draft and write in "My analysis shows," instead.

Recommendations The final section of the written case analysis should consist of a set of definite recommendations and a plan of action. Your set of recommendations should address all of the problems/issues you identified and analyzed. If the recommendations come as a surprise or do not follow logically from the analysis, the effect is to weaken greatly your suggestions of what to do. Obviously, your recommendations for actions should offer a reasonable prospect of success. High-risk, bet-the-company recommendations should be made with caution. State how your recommendations will solve the problems you identified. Be sure the company is financially able to carry out what you recommend; also check to see if your recommendations are workable in terms of acceptance by the persons involved, the organization's competence to implement them, and prevailing market and environmental constraints. Try not to hedge or weasel on the actions you believe should be taken.

By all means state your recommendations in sufficient detail to be meaningful— get down to some definite nitty-gritty specifics. Avoid such unhelpful statements as "the organization should do more planning" or "the company should be more aggressive in marketing its product." For instance, do not simply say "the firm should improve its market position" but state exactly how you think this should be done. Offer a definite agenda for action, stipulating a timetable and sequence for initiating actions, indicating priorities, and suggesting who should be responsible for doing what.

In proposing an action plan, remember there is a great deal of difference between, on the one hand, being responsible, for a decision that may be costly if it proves in error and, on the other hand, casually suggesting courses of action that might be taken when you do not have to bear the responsibility for any of the consequences. A good rule to follow in making your recommendations is: *Avoid recommending anything you would not yourself be willing to do if you were in management's shoes*. The importance of learning to develop good judgment in a managerial situation is indicated by the fact that, even though the same information and operating data may be available to every manager or executive in an organization, the quality of the judgments about what the information means and which actions need to be taken does vary from person to person.[4]

It goes without saying that your report should be well organized and well written. Great ideas amount to little unless others can be convinced of their merit—this takes tight logic, the presentation of convincing evidence, and persuasively written arguments.

THE TEN COMMANDMENTS OF CASE ANALYSIS

As a way of summarizing our suggestions about how to approach the task of case analysis, we have compiled what we like to call "The Ten Commandments of Case Analysis." They are shown in Table 2. If you observe all or even most of these commandments faithfully as you prepare a case either for class discussion or for a written report, your chances of doing a good job on the assigned cases will be much improved. Hang in there, give it your best shot, and have some fun exploring what

---

[4]Gragg, "Because Wisdom Can't Be Told," p. 10.

T A B L E 2 | **The Ten Commandments of Case Analysis**

To be observed in written reports and oral presentations, and while participating in class discussions.

1. Read the case twice, once for an overview and once to gain full command of the facts; then take care to explore every one of the exhibits.
2. Make a list of the problems and issues that have to be confronted.
3. Do enough number crunching to discover the story told by the data presented in the case. (To help you comply with this commandment, consult Table 1 to guide your probing of a company's financial condition and financial performance.)
4. Look for opportunities to use the concepts and analytical tools you have learned earlier.
5. Be thorough in your diagnosis of the situation and make at least a one- or two-page outline of your assessment.
6. Support any and all opinions with well-reasoned arguments and numerical evidence; don't stop until you can purge "I think" and "I feel" from your assessment and, instead, are able to rely completely on "My analysis shows."
7. Develop charts, tables, and graphs to expose more clearly the main points of your analysis.
8. Prioritize your recommendations and make sure they can be carried out in an acceptable time frame with the available skills and financial resources.
9. Review your recommended action plan to see if it addresses all of the problems and issues you identified.
10. Avoid recommending any course of action that could have disastrous consequences if it doesn't work out as planned; therefore, be as alert to the downside risks of your recommendations as you are to their upside potential and appeal.

SUBJECT INDEX